WORLD WAR II

4,139 STRANGE AND FASCINATING FACTS

WORLD WAR II

4,139 STRANGE AND FASCINATING FACTS

DON McCOMBS AND FRED L. WORTH

Wings Books
New York

This 1996 edition is published by Wings Books,
a division of Random House Value Publishing, Inc.,
201 East 50th Street, New York, New York 10022,
by arrangement with Warner Books.

Random House
New York • Toronto • London • Sydney • Auckland
http://www.randomhouse.com/

Printed and bound in the United States of America

Library of Congress Cataloging-in-Publication Data
The Library of Congress has catalogued this book under the Greenwich House edition.

McCombs, Don.
4139 fascinating facts about World War II.
1. World War, 1939-1945—Miscellanea. I. Worth, Fred L.
II. Title.
D744.M37 1983 940.53 83-15341

ISBN 0-517-42286-7

25 24 23 22 21 20 19 18 17 16

Dedication

To my wife Mavis,
whose patience and understanding were at times tested to the limit, yet who persevered. Without her help this book could not have been written

D.M.

To my father-in-law Carl Beckwell

F.L.W.

Acknowledgments

We wish to thank the following gentlemen for their kind assistance and sharing of knowledge: Richard Trewitt, David Strauss, John Carr, and our editor, Brian M. Thomsen.

A special thanks goes to Mavis McCombs for an excellent job of typing this manuscript.

There is no substitute for victory.
—General Douglas MacArthur

To my mind, to kill in war is not a whit better than to commit ordinary murder.
—Albert Einstein

War is delightful to those who have had no experience of it.
—Desiderius Erasmus

Worse than war is the fear of war.
—Seneca (The Younger)

My first wish is to see this plague of mankind, war, banished from the earth.
—George Washington

O war thou son of Hell!
—William Shakespeare

I have never advocated war except as a means of peace.
—Ulysses S. Grant

There never was a good war or a bad peace.
—Benjamin Franklin

War is as much a punishment to the punisher as to the sufferer.
—Thomas Jefferson

That mad game the world so loves to play.
—Jonathan Swift

I am insulted by the persistent assertion that I want war. Am I a fool? War! It would settle nothing.
—Adolf Hitler (November 10, 1933)

Introduction

We have not attempted to write an all-inclusive encyclopedia of World War II, since there are numerous such volumes already available. Rather, we have tried to present facts that are not generally covered by the standard historical approaches to World War II. In doing so we wished to convey the human element of history in what we feel are the more interesting aspects of world events. Therefore, the main criterion for inclusion of information in the book was that the material should be *interesting*.

It is hoped that this work will be expanded and revised at a later date. With this in mind, we ask you, the reader, to let us know about any interesting facts that you are aware of. We are also interested in the World War II careers of noted personalities, whether they be actors, politicians, singers, or athletes. If you know anyone who is mentioned here or can help us with additions or corrections, please drop us a line in care of the publisher.

Don McCombs

Fred L. Worth

A

A-4

Allied designator of the German V-2 rocket. It was first successfully launched on October 3, 1943, at Peenemunde and was pioneered by Dr. Wernher von Braun (see V-2).

AAA

Morse code emergency signal sent by ships in distress to indicate the vessel was under attack by aircraft. AAA was the equivalent of an SOS signal.

AAA-O

Slogan devised by Colonel Harry A. (Paddy) Flint for the 39th Regiment of the 9th Infantry Division in Sicily in 1943. The abbreviation stood for "Anything, Anytime, Anywhere—Bar Nothing." Colonel Flint ordered the letters painted on all equipment as a means of instilling pride in his unit. (Flint was rated as one of the best American commanders in World War II and was killed at Normandy by a sniper.)

A-A Line

Designated objective of Hitler's invasion of Russia, Operation Barbarossa, June 22, 1941. It consisted of a 1,250-mile line stretching from Archangel on the Arctic Ocean to Astrakhan on the Caspian Sea. Hitler believed that the Russians could be contained east of this line in Asiatic Russia with armed patrols.

Aaron Ward, U.S.S.

U.S. Navy destroyer (DM-34) that was hit by five kamikaze aircraft in May 1945, and survived. It was stationed off Okinawa as Radar Picket Ship #10 and was commanded by W. H. Sanders.

ABC-1

Designator of the most important conference in World War II. The meeting was held in Washington, D.C., from January to March, 1941, between American and British staff officers. It was decided that if the United States and Britain were involved in World War II as allies, their main effort should first be directed toward defeating Germany.

ABCD

Acronym applied to the Australian, British, Chinese, and Dutch Allies in the beginning stages of World War II in the Southwest Pacific.

ABC Express

Nickname given to an Allied supply route that stretched from Antwerp, Belgium, to the northern battle lines of Europe. This supply line was patterned after the more famous Red Ball Express that transported material inland from the Normandy beachhead.

ABC Ferry Command

Designator given to the Assam, Burma, and China logistics force that was set up by Colonel Caleb V. Haynes and Colonel Robert L. Scott. The organization flew supplies to the retreating Allied armies in Burma and later over the Himalayas to beleaguered China. Colonel Scott is most well known for his 1943 book, *God Is My Co-Pilot,* about his experiences with the Flying Tigers (see Flying Tigers).

ABDA

Designator for the combined commands of the American, British, Dutch, and Australian forces in the Far East. The ABDA was established on December 28, 1941, and encompassed all the territory from Australia to India. The first Supreme Commander was General Sir Archibald Wavell. It was dissolved on February 25, 1942.

Abel, Rudolph

Soviet spy captured by the FBI and exchanged for U-2 pilot Francis Gary Powers. He was a spy behind German lines during World War II for the Russians.

Abetz, Otto (1903–　　)

German ambassador to France before and during World War II. Abetz was primarily responsible for intelligence material useful to the German military before the invasion of France in May 1940.

Abraham Lincoln Battalion

Name of the American volunteers that fought in the International

Brigades of the Spanish Civil War against fascism. These people were recruited by the Communist International, a fact most of them were not aware of. The official designator was the 17th Battalion, XV Brigade. (There are still a few survivors in the United States who proudly wear their uniforms and insignia on special occasions to commemorate their early commitment to oppose fascism before the world realized the dangers of the movement.)

Abrams, Creighton, Jr. (1914–1974)

U.S. Army officer who commanded the 37th Tank Battalion during World War II. Abrams spearheaded the tank column that broke through the German encirclement of the 101st Airborne Division at Bastogne during the Battle of the Bulge. General George S. Patton said that he was one of the best tank commanders in the Army. Abrams later became a four-star general and commanded all U.S. forces in Vietnam.

Abucay Line

Name given to the first line of defense set up by General Douglas MacArthur's forces across the Bataan peninsula in 1941.

Abwehr

German name for the secret service branch of the German navy. Headed by Admiral Wilhelm Canaris, it was divided into three subsections: espionage, sabotage, and counterespionage. Hitler and the German High Command depended on the Abwehr for world-wide intelligence and counterintelligence support. The insignia for the organization consisted of three brass monkeys—hear no evil, speak no evil, see no evil.

Acasta, H.M.S.

British destroyer under Commander C. E. Glasford. While attempting to protect the British carrier H.M.S. *Glorious* in June 1943, the *Acasta* fired a torpedo at and struck the German cruiser *Scharnhorst*, severely damaging it. The *Scharnhorst* then sank the *Acasta* with shell fire, leaving only one survivor of the ship's crew.

A Card

U.S. gas ration card. It indicated the lowest priority of gas rationing and entitled the holder to three gallons of gas per week.

Accolade Certificate

Document sent to the next-of-kin of a serviceman who was killed in action or who died in the performance of his duties.

Ace

Title given to a fighter pilot who had shot down five enemy

aircraft. Less than one percent of all pilots ever achieved acedom, yet over forty percent of the aircraft destroyed in World War II were at the hands of aces.

George Welch	first U.S. pilot to shoot down four aircraft in a single day, December 7, 1941
Edward O'Hare	first U.S. pilot to shoot down five aircraft in a single day, February 20, 1942*
Neel Kearby	first U.S. pilot to shoot down six aircraft in a single day, October 11, 1943
William Levarette	first U.S. pilot to shoot down seven aircraft in a single day, October 9, 1943
David McCampbell	first U.S. pilot to shoot down nine aircraft in a single day, October 24, 1944

Achilles

Royal New Zealand cruiser that participated along with H.M.S. *Exeter* and H.M.S. *Ajax* in the Battle of the River Plate. This engagement took place on December 13, 1939 and resulted in the scuttling of the German pocket battleship *Graf Spee* in Montevideo, Uruguay. It was the first German naval loss of World War II.

Ack-Ack

British designator for antiaircraft fire. It originated from the British phonetic alphabet of World War I that used Ack to designate the letter *A* (see: Flak).

Acosta, Bert

American who commanded the Yankee Squadron, a group of U.S. fliers who fought for the Loyalists in the Spanish Civil War. He was also the pilot for Admiral Richard E. Byrd's trans-Atlantic flight in 1927.

Acoustic mine

Mine set off by the sound vibrations given off by a ship's propeller or engine.

Acuff, Roy (1903–   )

Country-and-western singer voted the most popular singer by G.I.'s overseas during World War II. (Frank Sinatra was second.)

Adam and Eve

Nickname of the 1st Pursuit Squadron of General Claire Chennault's American Volunteer Group in China, more commonly known as

---

*The American Volunteer Group, which was not a part of official U.S. forces, had a fighter pilot who equalled O'Hare's record—Robert Hedman, on December 23, 1941. He was therefore the first *American* pilot to down five enemy aircraft in a single day.

the Flying Tigers. The Adam and Eve were primarily former U.S. Army pilots, although former Marine Gregory (Pappy) Boyington was also a member.

Adam, Ken (1921–　　)

Art director for such films as *Dr. Strangelove* (1963) and the James Bond movie *Goldfinger* (1964). He served in World War II as a Royal Air Force pilot.

Adam, Ronald (1896–1979)

British actor who appeared in such films as *The Lavender Hill Mob* (1951) and *Zeppelin* (1971). He was a prisoner of war during World War I and served as a Royal Air Force Wing Commander in World War II.

A-Day

Designator for General Douglas MacArthur's invasion of the Philippines, October 20, 1944.

Adler Tag, Der (Eagle Day)

Name given to August 13, 1940, the day the German Luftwaffe launched an all-out offensive against the Royal Air Force and the British aircraft industry in southern England. The initial phase was a series of attacks against radar sites followed by a concentrated effort against fighter bases. Hitler hoped to knock out any aerial opposition to a cross-channel invasion of the British Isles (Operation Sea Lion).

Admiral Graf Spee (see **Graf Spee**)

Admiral Q

Code name used to designate President Franklin D. Roosevelt while he was en route to the Casablanca Conference in 1943.

Admiral Scheer

12,100-ton German pocket battleship commanded by Captain Theodor Kranke. It had a range of 19,000 miles and broke through the British blockade in November 1940 to travel to the Indian Ocean and sink British shipping supplying the Middle East. While en route, it sank H.M.S. *Jervis Bay* and did not return to Germany until April 1941, having sunk sixteen more ships. It was damaged beyond repair during an R.A.F. attack in April of 1945.

AF

Code group used by Japanese Admiral Isoruku Yamamoto to designate the island of Midway as the target for his carrier attack in June 1942. U.S. codebreakers knew of the impending Japanese attack but did not know the specific location. They contrived to have Midway broadcast a message stating that the island's freshwater distilling plant had broken down and that they were short of water. Yamamoto then sent a message to his aircraft carriers that AF was short of water, thus confirming U.S. suspicions and allowing the U.S. forces to concentrate and deal the Japanese a decisive defeat.

Afrika Korps

Name given to the German forces under Field Marshall Erwin Rommel. The Afrika Korps was originally sent to North Africa in 1941 to aid the Italians, who were repeatedly defeated by the British forces. From a strictly secondary role, Rommel succeeded in taking on the brunt of the fighting in the desert.

Agnew, Spiro T. (1917–)

U.S. Vice-President under Richard Nixon. During World War II Agnew was a company commander in the 10th Armored Division in Europe, winning a Bronze Star.

Ain't It Gruesome

One of several B-17 bombers in which Clark Gable flew missions. *Ain't It Gruesome* was the leader of a bomber attack on Gelsenkirchen, Germany, in August 1943 and Gable flew along to take pictures for a training film he was producing for the U.S. Army Air Force.

Aioi Bridge

Hiroshima bridge in the center of the city. It was the targeting point for the *Enola Gay* to drop the atomic bomb on August 6, 1945.

Air America

Name of the 885th Bombardment Squadron (Special) stationed at Brindisi. The unit was organized and commanded by Brigadier General Monro MaCloskey to support guerrilla operations behind enemy lines. The squadron primarily supplied OSS and SOE forces in Italy. (The OSS was the forerunner of the CIA and Air America is still the name of the official CIA support air forces.)

Airborne Divisions (American)

11th Abn. Div.	Fought at Leyte, Cavite, and Manila
13th Abn. Div.	Only airborne division not to see action in World War II
17th Abn. Div.	Fought at the Rhine Crossing and in Germany
82nd Abn. Div.	Fought in Sicily, Italy, Normandy, Ardennes, and Nijmegen.

101st Abn. Div.	Fought in Normandy and the Battle of the Bulge

U.S. airborne troops were the only parachute troops in the world who had a reserve parachute in case the main chute failed.

Aircraft carrier designators (American)

CV	aircraft carrier
CVA	attack aircraft carrier
CVB	large aircraft carrier (battle carrier)
CVL	small aircraft carrier
CVE	escort aircraft carrier
CVS	seaplane aircraft carrier

Airedale

Name given to World War II U.S. Marine Corps aviators by their ground crews.

Air Medal

U.S. military decoration awarded to anyone for meritorious achievement while in flight. The medal could be given for single acts or for cumulative performance over a period of time. The first woman to win the air medal was Second Lieutenant Elsie Ott on March 26, 1943, for a medical evacuation flight from India to Washington, D.C.

Air Mica

Code words used in U.S. Navy radio messages when referring to Rear Admiral Marc Mitscher.

Airplane Names

Person	*Name*	*Type*
General Harold Alexander	*Patches*	C-47
General Omar Bradley	*Mary Q*	C-47
General George H. Brett	*Swoose*	B-17
Winston Churchill	*Commando*	LB-30
Charles de Gaulle	*France*	C-56
General Ira C. Eaker	*Yankee Doodle*	B-17
General Roy S. Geiger	*Blue Goose*	PBY
General George C. Kenney	*Sally*	B-17
General Douglas MacArthur	*Bataan*	B-17
Field Marshall Bernard Montgomery	*#19082*	B-17
Elliott Roosevelt	*Jingle Jangle*	B-17
President Franklin D. Roosevelt	*Sacred Cow*	C-87
President Harry S Truman	*Independence*	C-87
Wendell Willkie	*Gulliver*	C-87

"Air Raid Pearl Harbor This Is No Drill"

Message sent out at the height of the Japanese attack on Pearl Harbor on December 7, 1941. It has been attributed to both Rear Admiral Patrick Bellinger and Captain Logan C. Ramsey.

Aitken, John

Son of Lord Beaverbrook, the head of British aircraft production at the beginning of World War II. John was a fighter pilot with No. 601 Squadron and is officially credited with having shot down sixteen enemy aircraft. While his father helped build British aircraft, the son helped destroy German aircraft.

Ajax, H.M.S.

British Navy cruiser that fought the German pocket battleship *Graf Spee* in the Battle of the River Plate on December 13, 1939, resulting in the first German Navy loss of World War II when the *Graf Spee* was scuttled in Montevideo, Uruguay. The *Ajax* later served the remainder of the war in the Mediterranean.

AK

Designator for the Polish Home Army. It was sponsored and built up by the Polish government in exile in London during World War II. Its policy was to wait until the Russians and the Germans had exhausted themselves, and then to rise up en masse against both.

Akagi

Japanese aircraft carrier weighing 36,500 tons. The keel was laid for a battle cruiser, but the ship was later converted to a carrier that could accommodate ninety-one aircraft. On December 6, 1941, in preparation for the attack on Pearl Harbor the next day, it flew the same flag that had flown over Admiral Togo's flagship in the 1905 defeat of the Russians at the Battle of Tsushima Strait. The *Akagi* was later a participant in the Battle of Midway, where it was damaged so severely by aircraft from the carrier U.S.S. *Enterprise* that Japanese forces had to sink it. It was the first ship in Japanese history to be scuttled.

AL-504

British Prime Minister Winston Churchill's private airplane. It was an LB-30 (B-24) and was named *Commando*.

AL-523

Designator of the B-24 *Liberator*, in which Polish General Wladyslaw Sikorski was killed on July 4, 1943. The only survivor was the pilot, a Czech named Edward Prchal. There was a question of whether the aircraft had been sabotaged by the British to get rid of

Sikorski because he was against Polish cooperation with the Russians.

Alameda, California

U.S. Navy base on San Francisco Bay from which the aircraft carrier U.S.S. *Hornet* departed with Doolittle's Raiders aboard in April 1942 to attack Tokyo. The Alameda Estuary almost became the site of Admiral Chester Nimitz's demise when the aircraft he was aboard crashed on June 30, 1942. Luckily, Admiral Nimitz escaped unhurt to lead the U.S. forces to victory in the Pacific.

Alamo

Code name for General Walter Kruger's Sixth U.S. Army which fought against the Japanese under the overall command of General Douglas MacArthur.

Almagordo, New Mexico

Site of the first successful atomic bomb test on July 16, 1945. It was called the Day of Trinity.

Alaska Highway

Joint Canadian–United States venture to build a road linking the continental U.S. to Alaska via British Columbia and the Yukon Territory. It was known as America's Burma Road and was built to reinforce Allied forces in the Pacific as well as Russia and China. Ten thousand soldiers and six thousand civilians progressed at a rate of eight miles a day, completing it on March 18, 1942.

Albacore, U.S.S.

U.S. Navy submarine under Commander James W. Blanchard that sank the Japanese carrier *Taiho* on June 19, 1944. It was later lost with all hands when it struck a mine on November 7, 1944.

Albert, Eddie (1908–   )

Hollywood actor who served as a civilian informant for U.S. Army Intelligence in Mexico. In July 1942 he enlisted in the U.S. Navy and earned a commission. He was assigned to the amphibious transport U.S.S. *Sheridan* as a lieutenant (j.g.) and was in charge of a casualty evacuation boat at the invasion of Tarawa on November 20, 1943. He was discharged on the anniversary of Pearl Harbor on December 7, 1945.

Albert, Marcel

Leading French ace of World War II. He is officially credited with downing twenty-three enemy aircraft during the war.

Aldebaran

Yacht purchased by future actor Sterling Hayden on November 21,

1939 in Panama. It was originally built in 1902 for the German Kaiser, Wilhelm II, and was launched by Alice Roosevelt. Unfortunately, a storm battered the *Aldebaran* while Hayden attempted to sail from Panama to Boston in December 1939, and he barely made port in Florida. After this, Hayden turned to acting.

Alexander, Sir Harold (1891–1969)

British field marshall during World War II. He commanded British and Allied troops in Burma, North Africa, Sicily, and Italy. He was the Supreme Allied Commander in the Mediterranean in 1944. He had been part of the British Expeditionary Force in France in 1940 and was the last man to leave the beaches at Dunkirk.

MOVIE PORTRAYAL:
Patton (1970), by Jack Gwillim
Churchill and the Generals (1981 TV movie), by Terence Alexander

Alexander, Stewart F.

U.S. Army medical corps lieutenant-colonel. He was the first to discover that mustard gas was the cause of many of the casualties at Bari, Italy, when a German Luftwaffe bombing raid blew up a Liberty ship loaded with mustard gas. The disaster was the worst involving chemical agents of World War II.

All American

Name of a B-17 of the 97th Bomb Group of the Eighth Army Air Force in England. It became famous as the result of one of the most famous events of the war that epitomized the durability of the B-17. While on a bombing mission over Europe, a crippled German fighter collided with the *All American* just forward of the tail section and nearly sliced through the entire fuselage. The aircraft held together for the long flight back with a major section of the fuselage destroyed. It landed and rolled to a stop, then immediately broke in two when a crew member opened one of the exit hatches. The pilot was Kenneth Bragg.

Allegro, John

British actor. During World War II he enlisted in the Royal Navy and held the rank of sub-lieutenant.

Allen, Steve (1921–)

Composer, musician, and comedian. He was drafted into the U.S. Army in 1943 and served only five months. He received a medical discharge for asthma.

Allen, Terry (1888–1969)

U.S. major general. He commanded the 1st Infantry Division in North Africa and during the invasion of Sicily. General Omar Bradley relieved Allen of command because he was too individualistic and disclaimed military bearing and discipline for his men. Allen finally returned to Europe in command of the 104th Infantry Division, leading it to the Elbe River and the collapse of Germany. Allen was one of the best infantry generals the U.S. Army had, yet he had flunked out of West Point. He died in 1969 shortly after his son, Terry Jr., was killed in Vietnam.

Alles für Deutschland

German phrase that meant "Everything for Germany." It was the inscription on the blade of Storm Trooper daggers and was used in Allied propaganda to symbolize German fanaticism. However, the same sentiment was inscribed above Chequers, Churchill's manor in England: *Pro Patria Omnia*, Latin for "Everything for the Fatherland."

Alliance of Animals

Clandestine organization in France that gathered intelligence information about German forces prior to the D-Day landings on June 6, 1944. The members of the unit adopted names of animals to mask their true identities and communicated with London via carrier pigeon and radio. Paul Gallico's novel *The Zoo Gang*, which was made into a 1975 NBC mini-series, dealt with the reunion of such a group thirty years later.

Allied Intelligence Bureau

U.S. Army organization that worked out of Australia for General Douglas MacArthur. The Bureau's purpose was to plan and support intelligence missions behind Japanese lines throughout the Southwest Pacific during World War II. MacArthur would not let the OSS, the forerunner of the CIA, into his territory, so he relied on his own organization to harass the Japanese.

Allied V-2

Nickname given by the press to U.S.O. singer Dinah Shore during World War II.

Alligator

Nickname of an amphibious tracked landing craft used in the Pacific island assaults in World War II. It was designed in the 1930's by Donald Roebling to rescue people in the Florida Everglades and found wide application in the Pacific because it could climb over reefs without being stranded like conventional landing craft. The official designator was LVT—Landing, Vehicle, Tractor.

Allotment Annie

Nickname given to girls who attempted to defraud the U.S. government by marrying a number of servicemen and receiving allotments from the government to which a serviceman's wife was entitled. They specialized in GI's who were about to be shipped overseas.

Alsop, Stewart (1914–1974)

American newspaper columnist. He was classified 4F—unfit for duty—by the U.S. Army because of asthma and high blood pressure, so instead enlisted in the British Army, with which he fought in North Africa and Italy. He was later transferred to the OSS and made a night parachute jump into occupied France to aid the Resistance against the Germans.

Alsos Mission

Name given to the U.S. Army unit formed to study the German progress toward development of the atomic bomb. In the final days of World War II, members of this unit combed Germany and the occupied territories in search of Axis scientists. The scientists were then either persuaded to work for the Western powers or forcibly kidnapped to prevent them from falling into the hands of the Russians. The commander was Colonel Boris Pash.

Altman, Robert (1921–   )

Hollywood director and producer of the 1970 movie *M*A*S*H*. He enlisted in the U.S. Army Air Force in 1943 and flew forty-six missions as a bomber pilot in Borneo and the Dutch East Indies. He was discharged in 1947.

Altmark

A 12,000-ton German auxiliary warship. The *Altmark*, which was disguised as a tanker, had three six-inch guns and was capable of cruising at twenty-five knots. It was the supply ship for the pocket battleship *Graf Spee* and was used as a prisoner-of-war transport for British sailors captured when the *Graf Spee* sank their ships. On February 16, 1940, the *Altmark* was hiding from British Naval forces in a Norwegian fiord when it was attacked and boarded by the crew of the British destroyer H.M.S. *Cossack* under command of Captain Philip Vian. Two hundred ninety-nine British seamen were rescued from internment in Germany, precipitating Hitler's invasion of Norway, at a time when the British public needed any victory no matter how insignificant. Vian became a national hero and the *Cossack* a household word.

Aluminum Trail

Nickname of the air route over the Himalayas from India to China. It was so named due to the high number of crashed aircraft along the route.

Amagiri

Japanese destroyer that rammed and sank Lt. John F. Kennedy's PT-109 on August 3, 1943, in Blackett Strait, Solomon Islands. The *Amagiri* sank in April 1944 off Balikpapan in Makassar Strait after striking a mine planted by the submarine U.S.S. *Tautog*. After Kennedy was elected President of the United States, the captain of the *Amagiri* sent him a note of apology!

Amann, Max (1891–   )

Business manager of the Nazi party newspaper. He had been a regimental clerk with Hitler in the 16th Bavarian Infantry during World War I. Amann became an S.S. general during World War II.

Amazon Corps

Name given to a British women's organization formed at the height of the threat of German invasion of Britain in 1940. The women wished to do their part for the defense of their country and drilled with umbrellas and canes. The name was later changed to Women's Volunteer Defense Corps.

Ambler, Eric (1909–   )

Author of popular spy stories. During World War II he enlisted in the Royal Artillery and was assigned to the anti-aircraft battery guarding Chequers, Winston Churchill's country estate.

Ambrosia, Vittorio (1879–1958)

Italian general. He was chief of the general staff and attempted to convince Mussolini to break off his agreement with Hitler.

America First

Isolationist organization that listed itself as a "patriotic society." It was started by Robert Douglas, Jr., a Yale law student, and General Robert E. Wood, head of Sears, Roebuck and Co. The goal of the group was to prevent the entry of the U.S. into the war. What was not known at the time, even among some of the key people, was that it was financed primarily by German backers. Many people were duped into affiliation with America First without knowing the real source of funding.

Americal Division

U.S. Army Infantry Division formed in 1942 by Major General Alexander Patch. The name came from *America* and *New Caledonia* and the division fought at Guadalcanal, Bougainville, the Philippines, and participated in the occupation of Japan. It was the only U.S. Army division that did not have a numeric designator.

America's Top Twenty Aces of World War II

Richard Bong—40
Thomas B. McGuire—38
David S. McCampbell—34
Francis S. Gabreski—28
Gregory Boyington—28
Robert S. Johnson—28
Charles H. MacDonald—27
Joseph J. Foss—26
George E. Preddy—25.83
Robert M. Hanson—25
John C. Meyer—24
Cecil E. Harris—24
Eugene A. Valencia—23
Raymond S. Wetmore—22.6
David C. Schilling—22.5
Gerald R. Johnson—22
Neel E. Kearby—22
Jay T. Robbins—22
Don S. Gentile—21.84
Frederick J. Christiansen—21.5

Amerika

Name of one of Hitler's personal armored trains. The other was named *Brandenburg*.

Amery, John

British-born propaganda broadcaster for the Nazis during World War II. His father was the Secretary of India, Leopold Amery.

AMGOT

Abbreviation for the Allied Military Government of Occupied Territory.

Amphibious Eighth

Name given to the U.S. Eighth Army under General Robert Eichelberger, Jr., which participated in fifty-eight amphibious assaults in the Pacific and fought on every occupied island in the Philippines. It was selected to spearhead the planned invasion of the Japanese home islands in November 1945.

Anchors

The U.S. Navy puts out a length of anchor chain that is four-and-one-half times the depth of the water. Most people believe that it is the anchor that holds the ship in place in the water, but it is actually the weight of the chain.

Anders, Wladyslaw (1892–1970)

Polish General who was captured by the Russians in 1939 and imprisoned. He was released after the German invasion of Russia in June 1941 to resurrect the Polish army to fight the Germans.

Anders and his army were allowed to leave Russia via Iran and travel to the Allied forces in the Mediterranean theater. The Polish Army units under Anders fought well in Italy in World War II. After the war, Anders and all except 14,000 of his 112,000 men decided not to return to Poland. From that time Anders took up residence in exile in Great Britain, where he remained an outspoken critic of Communism.

Andersen, Lala (1913–1972)

Swedish-born Berlin cabaret singer in World War II. She was known throughout Europe as the voice of "Lili Marlene" over German radio. The song by the same name was the theme song of the German Army radio station and was listened to nightly by Axis *and* Allied forces in Europe and North Africa. Lala made no attempts to propagandize her audiences but merely sang. She was portrayed in the movie *Lili Marlene* (1981) by Hanna Schygulla.

Anderson, Jack (1922–)

Syndicated newspaper columnist who succeeded Drew Pearson in writing the column "Washington Merry-Go-Round." He was drafted into the U.S. Army in late 1945 and served with the Quartermaster Corps until his discharge in 1947.

Anderson, Jane (1893–)

American-born Axis propaganda broadcaster at the beginning of World War II. She was known as "Lady Haw Haw." During the Spanish Civil War, she was sentenced to death by the Loyalist government as a spy but intervention by the U.S. State Department resulted in her release. Her last broadcast was in April 1942, when she told American audiences of the luxurious living available in Berlin and of the exotic foods and champagne that could be purchased in the night clubs. The U.S. Office of War Information taped her story and rebroadcast it to the German people, after which she was not heard from again.

Anderson, Sir Kenneth A.N. (1891–1959)

British lieutenant general who commanded forces at Dunkirk and North Africa. Anderson, a Scot, was born on Christmas day.

Anderson Shelter

British air raid shelter named after Sir John Anderson, who was in charge of British home security. The shelter consisted of corrugated steel walls that were bolted to steel rails and buried three feet in the ground. The exposed roof was then covered with a foot and a half of dirt. The project of supplying these to the poor in the likeliest target areas was started in 1938 and officially completed by June 12, 1940. This simple idea was credited with saving numerous lives during the German bombings of Britain.

Anderson, William R. (1921–)

U.S. Navy officer who was the commander of the world's first nuclear submarine, the U.S.S. *Nautilus*. He commanded the submarine on its record-setting cruise under the North Pole in 1954. During World War II, he made eleven war patrols, first as communications officer of the U.S.S. *Tarpon*, then as gunnery officer on board the U.S.S. *Narwhal*. Anderson finished the war on the U.S.S. *Trutta* as engineering and diving officer.

Andrade, Edward

British professor who conceived the idea for the metallic crickets that were used by Allied airborne troops as recognition signals during the D-Day jump on June 6, 1944. Confusion reigned when the sound of the German Mauser's bolt resembled that of the crickets.

Andrews, Adolphus (1879–1948)

U.S. Navy admiral who commanded the eastern sea frontier during World War II. He was one of three officers selected to serve on the Board of Inquiry concerning the Pearl Harbor attack.

Andrews, Frank M. (1884–1943)

U.S. Army lieutenant general. He had been designated as the commander of all U.S. forces in Europe but was killed in an aircraft crash in Iceland. General Dwight Eisenhower was then selected.

Andrus, Burton C.

U.S. Army colonel who was the chief security officer for the German prisoners during the Nuremberg trials in 1946. As such, he was able to become closely acquainted with the top Nazis.

Anfa Camp

Name given to the area around the Anfa Hotel in Casablanca, which was selected as the site for the Casablanca Conference in 1943. President Franklin D. Roosevelt's villa was named *Dar-es-Saada* and Prime Minister Winston Churchill's was *Mirador*.

Angel of Stalingrad

Name given to a German doctor, Ottmar Kohler, for his efforts to care for the wounded during the Battle of Stalingrad. He was captured by the Russians and remained in a Soviet prison camp in Siberia until 1955.

"Angels of Mercy"

Song written in 1942 by Irving Berlin to commemorate the Red Cross in World War II.

Ankara Committee

Joint British–American intelligence agency that was responsible for the Balkans, the eastern Mediterranean, and the Middle East during World War II.

Anschluss

German name for the Nazi annexation of Austria on March 13, 1938. From 1938 until 1945, the country of Austria ceased to exist and was merely a part of greater Germany. The Anschluss was also known as the Battle of Flowers, due to the tremendous welcome the German forces received.

Antarctica

Germany claimed 230,000 square miles of the South Pole on April 12, 1939, after an expedition under Captain Alfred Ritscher returned to Germany. Nothing came of this claim since the world soon erupted into war and Antarctica was too far from Germany to be of any use.

Antares, U.S.S.

U.S. Navy repair ship that a Japanese midget submarine attempted to follow through the antisubmarine nets at the entrance to Pearl Harbor on December 7, 1941. The submarine was sighted and sunk by the U.S.S. *Ward* at 6:45 A.M.

Anthropoid

Code name of the commando team dropped into Czechoslovakia to assassinate Reinhard Heydrich. The team departed Tangmere on December 28, 1941, and consisted of Josef Gabcik and Jan Kubis.

Anton

Name of the front gun turret of the German battle cruiser *Scharnhorst*. The other two were called *Bruno* and *Caesar.*

Antonescu, Ion (1882–1946)

Rumanian marshall and dictator who joined the Axis forces during World War II. He was motivated more by his hate for Russia than by his love for Germany. Antonescu attempted to conclude an armistice with the Western Allies in 1944 but failed. He was tried and sentenced to death in 1946. The firing squad members were selected from Communist shock troops because it was feared that Rumanians would not have shot him. The firing squad failed to kill him on the first volley. As Antonescu slowly sank to his knees, he said, "You can't even shoot straight!" He survived a second bungled attempt and was finally killed by a pistol shot to the head.

Antwerp

Belgian port desperately needed by the advancing Allied armies in Europe. It was the greatest freight port in Europe, capable of handling over twenty-three million pounds of cargo. It was virtually useless after its capture because Field Marshall Bernard Montgomery failed to clear the Scheldt estuary of German troops. Antwerp was also the Allied target most struck by V-1's and V-2's during World War II, receiving 2,448 V-1's and 1,265 V-2's. By comparison, London only had 2,419 V-1's and 517 V-2's.

Antwerp X

Name given to the antiaircraft defenses surrounding Antwerp. The Allies positioned more than five hundred antiaircraft guns and over eighteen thousand personnel to protect the port facilities after they were finally opened.

"Any Bonds Today?"

Song composed in 1941 by Irving Berlin for the U.S. War Bond drive during World War II.

Anzio

Site of an Allied invasion of Italy that was intended to cut off German forces in the lower part of the Italian peninsula. The initial objectives of the assault were not accomplished because of a lack of aggressive drive on the part of the American commander, Lieutenant General John P. Lucas, who was subsequently relieved of command. The struggle in the area developed into a stalemate between the German and American forces that prompted Axis Sally to call it "The largest self-supporting prisoner-of-war camp in the world."

Anzio Express

Nickname given by the GI's at Anzio to a German railway gun that bombarded the beachhead with 562-pound shells, then withdrew into a tunnel for protection. There were actually two guns, the other being called *Anzio Annie*.

Appendectomies on U.S. Submarines during World War II

Darrell Rector	by Wheeler B. Lipes	on U.S.S. *Seadragon*
W. R. Jones	by Harry B. Roby	on U.S.S. *Grayback*
George Platter	by Thomas Moore	on U.S.S. *Silversides*

Apple

Designator of the beach west of Algiers assaulted in Operation Torch, November 8, 1942.

Arandora Star

British 15,501-ton passenger ship that was sunk on July 2, 1940, by the German submarine *U-47*, commanded by Gunther Prien. The ship was transporting 1,500 Italian and German prisoners of war to Canada, most of whom were killed.

Arbeit Adelt

German slogan meaning "Work ennobles." It was found on the daggers of the RAD, the Nazi Labor Service in World War II.

Arbeit Macht Frei

German motto meaning "Work will make you free." It was conspicuously displayed over the gates of the concentration camps, giving those who entered at least transitory hope for the future.

Arcadia Conference

Meeting held in Washington, D.C., from December 1941 to January 1942 between British Prime Minister Winston Churchill and the American President Franklin D. Roosevelt. It was decided to defeat Germany first, then to direct all effort against Japan.

Archerfish, U.S.S.

U.S. Navy submarine under Commander Joseph F. Enright. It sank the 71,000-ton Japanese carrier *Shinano* on November 29, 1944. The Japanese spent four years constructing the aircraft carrier, which was sunk outside Tokyo Bay two hours after launching.

Arden, Elizabeth (1882–1966)

American cosmetic manufacturer who produced black face cream for GI's to use as camouflage on night missions.

Ardennes Offensive

Advance of German forces in December 1944 through the Ardennes Mountains of Belgium, also known as the Battle of the Bulge. The German success was due to the fact that the Allies had no prior knowledge of the attack. Even before the war started, the Western powers were able to read the most secret German codes. They called these intercepts *Ultra*. In the planning for the Ardennes offensive, the Germans sent all orders through other means. Allied intelligence was not aware of the German buildup in which Hitler concentrated twenty-four divisions, ten of which were armored, opposite a seventy-mile Allied line held by only six divisions.

Areopagus

Name of a conference called by Reichsmarschall Hermann Goering, head of the German Luftwaffe. It was held at the Air Force School at Gatow, Berlin, in October 1944. Goering met with thirty top Luftwaffe officers to discuss changes that could be introduced to make the Luftwaffe more efficient at fighting the war. Goering withdrew from the conference rather than listen to criticism; thus nothing came of the meeting.

Arfons, Art (1926–   )

Automobile racer. He served in the U.S. Navy during World War II and participated in several Pacific assaults in 1945. He also manned a landing craft on the Yangtze River in China.

Arethusa

Name of the British royal yacht used by King George VI.

Argonaut

Code name for a series of conferences held between January and February 1945. They were actually two separate conferences, the first between President Franklin D. Roosevelt and Prime Minister Winston Churchill at Malta, called *Cricket*. The second, known as *Magneto*, was held at Yalta and included Russian Premier Joseph Stalin. Roosevelt traveled under the code word *Sawbuck*.

Argonaut, U.S.S.

U.S. Navy submarine designated *V-4*. It was designed experimentally as a minelayer, and was equipped with four torpedo tubes forward, two minelaying tubes aft, and two six-inch deck guns. The *Argonaut*, which was 381 feet long, displaced 2,700 tons of water, making it one of the largest submarines in the U.S. fleet. It was so large, in fact, that it was not practical, since it was difficult to maneuver and presented a huge target to the enemy. It was used to deliver Edson's Raiders for the Makin Island raids and as a supply transport to guerrillas in the Philippines. For this type of mission, her size was an asset, since she could carry tons of material. The *Argonaut* was sunk on January 10, 1943, by Japanese destroyers, while attempting to attack a convoy freighter.

Argonauta

Italian submarine that was the first submarine sunk by aircraft during World War II, when a Sunderland flying boat coming out of Egypt bombed her on June 28, 1940.

Argus, H.M.S.

British aircraft carrier weighing 14,000 tons. Originally the keel of the *Argus* was laid to be an Italian passenger liner, but the ship was converted at the end of World War I into a carrier. It aided in both the reinforcement of Malta and in the support of the North African landings.

Arisan Maru

Japanese transport with 1,790 Filipino and American prisoners-of-war on board that was sunk off the coast of China on October 29, 1944. Only five POW's survived.

Arizona, U.S.S.

U.S. Navy battleship sunk at Pearl Harbor on December 7, 1941. Out of a crew of 1,400 there were 1,103 casualties, including Rear Admiral Isaac C. Kidd and Captain Franklin von Falkenburgh. In the 1934 movie *Here Comes the Navy,* James Cagney and Pat O'Brien played sailors assigned to the U.S.S. *Arizona.*

Ark Royal, H.M.S.

British aircraft carrier weighing 23,000 tons. German propaganda claimed that it was sunk on September 26, 1939, by a JU-88 bomber flown by Corporal Karl Francke, a boast that the Germans regretted when aircraft from the *Ark Royal* crippled the pocket battleship *Bismarck* in May 1941. The carrier finally was sunk in the Mediterranean on November 14, 1941, by the German submarine U-81. Remarkably only one life was lost.

Armed Services Edition

Special paperback books published for U.S. servicemen overseas beginning in 1943. The first title (A-1) was *The Education of Hyman Kaplan* by L. Q. Ross.

Armegruppe Patton

German intelligence name for the Allied forces under General George S. Patton that were thought to be in readiness for an invasion of the Pas de Calais in conjunction with the Normandy landings on June 6, 1944. In actuality, this force never existed and was only a camouflage unit to deceive the Germans into holding their reserves in the Pas de Calais area rather than committing them to the critical Normandy area.

Armies of the United States

Army	*Commander*	*Site of Action*
First Army	General Omar Bradley	fought in France and Germany
Second Army		remained stateside
Third Army	General George S. Patton	fought in France and Germany
Fourth Army		remained stateside

Fifth Army	General Mark Clark	fought in Italy
Sixth Army	General Walter Krueger	fought in Leyte
Seventh Army	General Alexander Patch	fought in southern France and Germany
Eighth Army	General Robert Eichelberger	fought in the Philippines
Ninth Army	General William H. Simpson	fought in France and Germany
Tenth Army	General Simon Buckner	fought at Okinawa

Armistice of Cassibile

Armistice signed on September 3, 1943, that ended the war between Italy and the Allies. It was also known as the "Short Armistice" and was signed by Giuseppe Castellano, who was chief of staff to General Vittorio Ambrosio.

Armour, Richard (1906–   )

Author of humorous books such as *It All Started With Columbus* (1953) and *Twisted Tales From Shakespeare* (1957). During World War II, he rose from the rank of second lieutenant to lieutenant colonel, serving on General Eisenhower's General Staff. Armour received the Legion of Merit medal for his contributions to the war effort and wrote his first books while in the service.

Armstrong, George Thomas (–1941)

British sailor who sold military information to the German consul in New York in the early days of World War II. He was the first British traitor to be tracked down by the FBI. He was caught in a U.S. port and placed on a ship returning to England, where he was arrested by Scotland Yard. Armstrong was hanged in Wandsworth Jail on July 9, 1941, becoming the first Briton executed for treason in the war.

Army Air Corps

Name of the aviation branch of the U.S. Army until June 20, 1941, when the name was officially changed to *Army Air Forces.*

"Army Air Corps Song"

Song written in 1939 by Robert M. Crawford, who was then a student at Princeton University. During World War II, Crawford flew for the Air Transport Command as a major.

Army Air Forces of the United States

First Air Force	Northeast Air District continental U.S.
Second Air Force	Northwest Air District continental U.S.

Third Air Force	Southeast Air District continental U.S.
Fourth Air Force	Southwest Air District continental U.S.
Fifth Air Force	Southwest Pacific
Sixth Air Force	Panama Canal Zone and Caribbean
Seventh Air Force	Central Pacific
Eighth Air Force	England
Ninth Air Force	North Africa and England
Tenth Air Force	India, Burma
Eleventh Air Force	Aleutian Islands and Northern Pacific
Twelfth Air Force	North Africa
Thirteenth Air Force	Southwest Pacific
Fourteenth Air Force (formerly American Volunteer Group)	China
Fifteenth Air Force	Italy
Twentieth Air Force (B-29's)	Japan

Army Group A

German designator for the forces under General Karl von Runstedt that held the central part of the line opposing France in 1940. These forces were based in the Ardennes and were the key assault group in the invasion of France in May and June 1940.

Army Group B

German designator for the forces under General Fedor von Bock that were aimed at the Low Countries in the assault on the West in May and June 1940.

Army Group C

German designator for the forces under General Wilhelm von Leeb that attacked the Maginot Line during the assault on the West in May and June 1940.

Army Group Center

German designator for the assault forces under Field Marshall Fedor von Bock during the Russian offensive (Operation Barbarossa) in June 1941. The objectives of Army Group Center were Smolensk and Moscow.

Army Group North

German designator for the assault forces under Field Marshall Wilhelm von Leeb during Operation Barbarossa. The objective was the capture of Leningrad.

Army Group South

German designator for the assault forces under Field Marshall

Karl von Rundstedt in Operation Barbarossa. The objectives included Kiev and the Ukraine.

Army Organization

Unit	*Composition*	*in charge*
squad	8 to 12 men	sergeant
platoon	3 or more squads	lieutenant
company	3 or more platoons	captain
battalion	3 or more companies	lieutenant colonel
regiment	3 or more battalions	colonel
brigade	3 or more regiments	brigadier general
division	3 or more brigades	major general
corps	3 or more divisions	lieutenant general
army	3 or more corps	general
army group	3 or more armies	general or fleld marshall

Arness, James (1923–)

Hollywood actor who is six feet, seven inches in height. He served in the U.S. Army during World War II and was wounded in the leg during the landings at Anzio, Italy, in January 1944. Arness is the brother of actor Peter Graves.

Arnaz, Desi (1917–)

Hollywood entertainer. At the outbreak of World War II, Arnaz was offered a commission in the Cuban Army, which he turned down to enlist in the U.S. Navy. He was refused by the Navy because of a regulation that stated that noncitizens could not join, although they could be drafted. While trying to join the Navy he was making a movie for RKO entitled *The Navy Comes Through*. Arnaz played Private Felix Ramirez in the 1942 movie *Bataan*, shortly after which he received his draft notice. He attempted to join the Army Air Forces but failed the physical and ended up in the infantry. After straining the torn cartilage in his knees—the reason for his failing the physical—he was given limited duty with the Medical Corps as an entertainer. Arnaz, whose serial number was 392-956-43, was discharged on November 16, 1945, as a staff sergeant.

von Arnim, Jurgen (1889–1971)

German general who was captured in North Africa on May 12, 1943, with the defeat of the Afrika Korps, but only after he had severed communications with his units so that he could not call for the surrender of all his troops. He was imprisoned at first in England and was later moved to Camp Clinton, Mississippi.

Arnold, Henry H. (Hap) (1886–1950)

U.S. general and Chief of the Army Air Forces. He was taught to fly by the Wright Brothers, becoming one of the Army's first four aviators. During the 1920's he wrote a number of books for young people, known as the Bill Bruce Series, that dealt with aviation. Arnold was an advocate of a separate Air Force and of heavy bombers. He became the first five-star general of the U.S. Army Air Forces.

MOVIE PORTRAYALS:
The Glenn Miller Story (1954), by Barton MacLane
The Court Martial of Billy Mitchell (1955), by Robert Brubaker
The Amazing Mr. Howard Hughes (1977 TV movie), by Walter O. Miles

Arnold, Richard (1909–1943)

U.S. Army major in World War II. He was the fiancé of Kay Summersby, driver for General Dwight Eisenhower. Arnold graduated from West Point in 1932 as an engineer. He was killed by a land mine on June 6, 1943, after hostilities had ended in North Africa.

MOVIE PORTRAYAL:
Ike (1979 TV movie), by Laurence Luckinbill

ARP

British organization of air defense. The initials stood for Air Raid Precaution.

Arsenal of Democracy

Name given by President Franklin D. Roosevelt to the United States in his fireside chat of December 29, 1940, to gain public sympathy for sending military supplies to the Allies.

Arsenic and Old Lace

Broadway play and later a movie (1944) starring Cary Grant, who donated his salary of $100,000 to the U.S. War Relief. The play was the first foreign play to open in Paris after its liberation from the Germans in August 1944.

Artificial limbs of famous World War II figures

Artur Axmann, chief of Hitler Youth	right arm
Douglas Bader, British fighter pilot	both legs
Alexander de Seversky, aviation proponent	leg
John Hoskins, U.S. Navy admiral	leg
Sam Logan, U.S. fighter pilot	leg

Ted Lawson, U.S. bomber pilot	leg
Erich Marcks, German general	leg
Hans Rudel, German Stuka pilot	leg
Mamoru Shigemitsu, Japanese foreign minister	leg
Claus von Stauffenberg, German colonel	arm
Edward Teller, physicist	foot

ASBD

Advanced Base Sectional Dock. This was a ten-section dry dock of the U.S. Navy capable of raising the largest battleship. It could accommodate 56,000 to 100,000 tons and was so large it had to be tipped on its side to pass through the Panama Canal.

ASDIC

Acronym for Antisubmarine Detection Investigation Committee. An ASDIC was a shipboard detection device that picked up submerged submarines by emitting a sound wave into the water that would bounce back to a receiver. It had numerous limitations but helped the British finally achieve dominance in the Battle of the Atlantic. The American version was called SONAR.

Ashcan

Code name for the American detention center established to hold high-ranking Germans. It was located at Mondorf-les-Bains, Luxembourg, and held such people as Seyss-Inquart, Hans Frank, von Ribbentrop, Goering, Doenitz, Robert Ley, Kesselring, Streicher, Funk, Keitel, Horthy, and von Papen. The British equivalent was called Dustbin.

Ash Wednesday

Nickname given by the residents of Cairo to June 17, 1942. As Field Marshall Erwin Rommel advanced across the desert toward the city, the British burned all their secret documents and the ashes filled the sky.

Ashworth, Frederick L.

U.S. Navy commander who armed the B-29 *Bock's Car* with the atomic bomb while en route to Nagasaki, on August 9, 1945.

Asia

Name of Reichsmarschall Hermann Goering's personal armored train.

Asiatic Fleet

Name of the U.S. Navy fleet stationed in Asian waters prior to World War II. It was commanded by Admiral Thomas C. Hart, who ordered it removed from China to Manila as a safeguard against a Japanese attack. The fleet consisted of two cruisers, thirteen destroyers, twenty-seven submarines, and some auxiliary ships. The surface ships were antiquated and outdated, and the only bright spot was the potential of the relatively modern submarines. After hostilities began on December 8, 1941, even this factor was a disappointment, because most of the submarine commanders lacked aggressiveness and looked for any excuse to return from a patrol without engaging the enemy.

Asimov, Isaac (1920–)

American science fiction writer. During World War II, he was a chemical analyst at the Philadelphia Navy Yard. He served in the U.S. Army in Hawaii and Virginia.

Assault Detachment Koch

Name of the German parachute unit that captured the Belgian forts at Eben Emael on May 10, 1940. Commanded by Captain Koch, there were four detachments:

Code name	*Detachment leader*	*Objective*
Granite	First Lieutenant Witzig	Eben Emael
Concrete	Lieutenant Schacht	bridge at Vroenhoven
Steel	First Lieutenant Altmann	bridge at Veldwezelt
Iron	Lieutenant Schachter	bridge at Kanne

Asterion, U.S.S.

U.S. Navy Q-ship. It was converted from the S.S. *Evelyn,* an interisland cargo ship, to be a special antisubmarine decoy ship and was commanded by Lieutenant Commander G. W. Legwen (see U.S.S. *Atik* and U.S.S. *Eagle*).

ASV

"Air to surface vessel." This was the acronym given to radar carried on airplanes in order to detect ships on the surface.

Atabrine

Antimalarial drug administered to U.S. military personnel daily during World War II. It caused the skin to turn yellow and tasted bitter, neither side effect of which appealed to the men who had to use it. Ironically, atabrine was originally invented in the 1920's by I. G. Farben, the chemical company that became one of the largest manufacturers in Nazi Germany.

ATA Girls

Nickname given to the women of the British Air Transport Auxiliary. The women were not part of the Royal Air Force, yet they flew every type of aircraft on all but combat missions. The auxiliary was commanded by Pauline Gower.

Athenia

British Cunard passenger liner. It was the first ship to be sunk in World War II. The *Athenia* was bound from Belfast to Montreal on September 3, 1939, with 1,400 passengers, 292 of whom were U.S. citizens, when it was torpedoed by the German submarine *U-30* under Fritz Julius Lemp. This event occurred shortly after the British declaration of war on Germany took effect at eleven in the morning, and killed 112 people. Because of the high number of Americans on board, Joseph Goebbels broadcast the propaganda story that a British submarine had sunk the *Athenia* to gain American public support for the war effort.

The *Athenia* was used as the setting for the 1940 movie *Arise My Love* with Ray Milland.

Atik, U.S.S.

U.S. Navy Q-ship, or decoy ship, used to lure submarines within range and equipped to attack and sink them. The *Atik* was formerly the S.S. *Carolyn*, an interisland cargo ship that was converted to a Q-ship and armed with four four-inch deck guns, four 50-caliber machine guns, numerous small arms, and depth charges. It was under Lieutenant Commander Harry L. Hicks that she was torpedoed and sunk by a German U-boat on her maiden voyage on March 27, 1942, three hundred miles east of Norfolk, Virginia. All 141 crewmembers were lost without a trace but Hicks was awarded a posthumous Navy Cross. The U.S. Navy took no further interest in Q-ships after this dismal start (see U.S.S. *Asterion* and U.S.S. *Eagle*).

Atlantic Charter

Agreement between President Franklin D. Roosevelt and Prime Minister Winston Churchill. It was signed on board the U.S.S. *Augusta* in Placentia Bay, Newfoundland, on August 12, 1941, before the U.S. entry into World War II; it became the cornerstone of the United Nations. The name was coined by the *London Daily Herald*.

Atlantico

Name of Italian dictator Benito Mussolini's white stallion.

Atlantic Wall

Defensive barrier built by the Germans that ran along the coast of the continent of Europe. It was designed personally by Hitler and was constructed by the Todt Organization with over eighteen million tons of concrete. Nazi propaganda touted it as impregnable but the D-Day invasion of June 6, 1944, proved that there were weak spots.

Atlantis

German auxiliary cruiser. It was a former merchant ship converted to a commerce raider with six 5.9-inch guns and ninety-three mines as well as two aircraft for spotting victims. Her job was to catch and sink Allied merchant ships; to do this, the ship was equipped with disguises enabling it to appear as nearly any other ship in the world inventory of shipping. The *Atlantis* was under Captain Bernhard Rogge and operated from March 31, 1940, until November 22, 1941, in the Indian and Atlantic Oceans. During this time she sank twice as much tonnage as the more infamous *Graf Spee*. She terrorized the British Navy for nearly two years and sank twenty-two ships for a total of more than 145,000 tons. The *Atlantis* was finally sunk by the H.M.S. *Devonshire* on November 22, 1941. The Germans designated her HSK II, or simply Ship 16.

ATS

Auxiliary Territorial Service. This was the women's branch of the British Army and primarily was responsible for antiaircraft duty. The first female killed in action was Nora Caveney, who was hit by a bomb fragment in April 1941. Other famous members of the ATS were Mary Churchill, daughter of Winston Churchill, and Elizabeth Windsor, now Queen Elizabeth.

Atsugi

Japanese airfield on Honshu where the first Allied occupation forces officially landed on August 28, 1945. Actually, the first landing took place the day before when a PBY, supposedly with mechanical problems, landed at Atsugi for repairs.

Attenborough, Richard (1923–)

British actor. He debuted in Noel Coward's 1942 movie *In Which We Serve* and joined the Royal Air Force the following year. He served three years with the R.A.F. In the 1963 movie *The Great Escape*, he portrayed R.A.F. squadron leader Roger Bushell.

Attlee, Clement (1883–1967)

British Prime Minister who succeeded Winston Churchill. Attlee had been Deputy Prime Minister under Churchill from 1942 to 1945 and was at the Potsdam Conference with U.S. President Harry S Truman and Russian dictator Joseph Stalin. Attlee was a Labor Party candidate, reforming Britain along socialist lines, including the dissolution of the British Empire.

MOVIE PORTRAYAL:
Churchill and the Generals (1981 TV movie), by Barry Jackson

Auchinleck, Sir Claude (1884–1981)
British general. He commanded British forces in Northern Norway in 1940. After the retreat from Norway, he was placed in command of British forces in India. As the situation deteriorated in North Africa, Auchinleck was moved once more to take over command from Sir Archibald Wavell. He began a war of maneuver against the Axis forces by constantly attacking and eliminating Italian units. This forced German Field Marshall Erwin Rommel to utilize German forces to plug the gaps, thus further weakening his own position. In spite of this, Churchill relieved Auchinleck from duty because Churchill felt he was not making enough headway and sent him back as Commander in Chief in India, a post he held until Indian independence in 1947.

MOVIE PORTRAYAL:
Churchill and the Generals (1981 TV movie), by Patrick Allen

Audacity, H.M.S.
British escort carrier that could carry six aircraft and was used to protect convoys crossing the Atlantic. It was formerly a German merchant ship, the *Hannover,* that had been captured by the British in the Caribbean and converted in September 1940 to an escort carrier. H.M.S. *Audacity* was the first of many escort carriers built in World War II and was sunk by a German U-boat on December 21, 1941.

Audisio, Walter (1909–1973)
Italian communist partisan who killed dictator Benito Mussolini and his mistress Clara Petacci. Audisio was pardoned from a jail term in 1934 after he wrote a letter to Mussolini. He then fought in the Spanish Civil War with the Loyalists. On April 28, 1945, under the pseudonym Colonel Valerio, he took custody of Mussolini and Petacci after they were captured while fleeing to Switzerland. He attempted to shoot the pair with an Italian submachine gun, but it would not fire. He then pulled his Italian pistol from the holster, but it also failed to fire. In desperation he grabbed a French weapon, an MAS 7.65, from a guerilla and killed both of them.

Auer, Grace
U.S. Women's Army Corps captain who was in charge of guarding female prisoners at Nuremberg in 1945 and 1946.

Auer, Theodor

German representative to the French Vichy government in Casablanca. Under the guise of chief of the German military mission, he headed German espionage activities in French territory.

Augusta, U.S.S.

U.S. Navy cruiser and flagship of the Asiatic Fleet prior to Pearl Harbor attack. On August 14, 1937, while at anchor in Shanghai, the glass throughout the *Augusta* shattered when Chinese aircraft attempted to bomb the Japanese cruiser *Idzumo*, but missed. In 1941, she took President Franklin D. Roosevelt to Newfoundland for the drafting of the Atlantic Charter with British Prime Minister Winston Churchill. The *Augusta* was selected to be the flagship for the invasion of North Africa in November 1942 and also on D-Day, June 6, 1944. In 1945 it transported President Harry S Truman to Antwerp for the Potsdam Conference.

Aunt Jemima

Nickname given to an explosive developed by the OSS during World War II that looked like flour. It could be mixed with water into dough, baked into bread, and was even edible. This camouflage was devised to enable agents to cross enemy lines successfully and was used primarily against the Japanese in Southeast Asia.

Auschwitz

German extermination camp in Upper Silesia. It covered eighteen square miles and was set up shortly after the defeat of Poland in 1939 under Commandant Rudolph Hoess. It was the worst death camp established by the Germans, followed closely by Buchenwald, Dachau, and Treblinka. The Poles have left it intact as a memorial to all those who died there. (Other camps in Poland were Chelmno, Treblinka, Sobibor, and Belzec.)

Australia, H.M.A.S.

Royal Australian heavy cruiser that was struck by five kamikazes off Okinawa in April 1945 without being put out of action.

Autry, Gene (1908–   )

Hollywood actor known as the "Singing Cowboy." He was a pilot for the U.S. Army Air Force during World War II and was the copilot on a New York-to-Los Angeles flight when two GIs were bumped from the passenger list so that Elliott Roosevelt's dog Blaze could ride. Elliott was President Franklin D. Roosevelt's son and the incident created such a public outcry that Elliot nearly lost a promotion to Brigadier General. Autry enlisted in July 1942 as a staff sergeant and learned to fly on his own time. He spent most of the war flying C-47's in the China-Burma-India theater for the Air Transport Command. He was discharged in September 1945.

Auxiliary Cruisers

Armed merchant ships of World War II. The German versions served as raiders, preying on unsuspecting Allied shipping; the British versions were used for convoy protection.

British auxiliary cruisers

Alcantara (22,209 tons)	damaged by German raider *Thor*
Carnarvon Castle (20,122 tons)	damaged by German raider *Thor*
Jervis Bay (14,000 tons)	sunk by German cruiser *Admiral Scheer*
Voltaire (13,301 tons)	sunk by German raider *Thor*

German auxiliary cruisers

Atlantis	sank 22 ships for 145,697 tons
Coronel	unable to escape British blockade
Komet	sank 6 ships for 31,005 tons
Kormoran	sank 11 ships for 68,274 tons
Michel	sank 3 ships for 27,632 tons
Orion	sank 10 ships for 62,915 tons
Pinguin	sank 32 ships for 154,619 tons
Stier	sank 4 ships for 29,409 tons
Thor	sank 12 ships for 96,602 tons
Widder	sank 10 ships for 58,644 tons

AVG

American Volunteer Group, more widely known as the Flying Tigers, who fought for China against the Japanese. They were commanded by General Claire Chennault and officially existed from December 18, 1941, to July 4, 1942, when they became the Fourteenth Army Air Force. During this period the AVG is credited with shooting down 286 Japanese planes confirmed, with another 300 possibles. They reported eight pilots killed in action, four pilots missing in action, two pilots and one crew chief killed from bombs, and nine others killed in accidents.

Avis

British method of communicating with Resistance forces in western Europe. Every evening from 7:30 until 9 P.M., the BBC broadcast phrases that meant specific things. These messages consisted of an "A" part that alerted a particular resistance group and a "B" part that ordered them to carry out a specific action.

Awa Maru

Japanese merchant ship that was promised safe passage in February 1945 while conducting Red Cross business. The Japanese took the opportunity to transport much-needed aviation parts to the south and had planned on shipping, by return voyage to Japan, critically needed supplies for the home islands. The U.S. Navy broadcast instructions to allow the ship to proceed safely, but one U.S. submarine, the U.S.S. *Queenfish*, did not receive the message. When the *Awa Maru* crossed her sights on March 28, 1945, she sank the ship. This created a diplomatic problem for both countries. The Japanese were carrying war material, a fact that they did not want known, and the U.S. had apparently reneged on their promise of safe conduct. Both sides chose to ignore the incident, which has continued to raise questions to this day.

Axis Countries

Name coined by Benito Mussolini in a speech given on November 1, 1936, in Milan, when he referred to an "axis" that other European countries could work around. The countries were Germany (including Austria), Italy, Bulgaria, Hungary, Rumania, Finland, and finally Japan.

Axis Sally

Nickname given to Mildred E. Gillars, who broadcast propaganda for the Nazis during World War II. The Japanese equivalent was called Tokyo Rose.

Axmann, Artur (1913–)

Head of the Hitler Youth from 1940 until 1945. He is reputed to have been one of the witnesses of Martin Bormann's death in Berlin.

Ayres, Lew (1908–)

Hollywood actor and husband of actress Ginger Rogers (1934–1941). He was a conscientious objector during World War II and served in the Medical Corps under fire. His status during the war almost destroyed his acting career.

Azon Bomb

U.S. guided bombs. The bomb could be guided by the bombardier, who could only make corrections left or right of the designated course—thus the name *Az*imuth *On*ly. It was designated VB-1 or Vertical Bomb and was first used on December 27, 1944, on a railway bridge in Burma.

B

B-17

U.S. four-engine heavy bomber, also called the *Flying Fortress*. It was developed privately in 1935 by Boeing Aircraft Company because the government procurement officials did not see the need to spend the money. It was originally designed for coastal protection of the United States, Hawaii, and Alaska.

B-23

U.S. bomber built by Douglas. It was considered by General James Doolittle as a possibility for the Tokyo Raid in April 1942. Because the wing span was ninety-three feet, it was not chosen. (The B-25, which was used instead, had only a sixty-seven-foot wing span and aircraft carrier decks that were seventy-five feet wide.) The B-23 was named *Dragon* and was relegated primarily to training roles during World War II.

B-24

U.S. four-engine heavy bomber built by Consolidated. It was called the *Liberator* and had a longer range than the B-17, and so was used primarily in the Pacific.

B-25

U.S. twin-engine bomber built by North American. It was named *Mitchell*, after General Billy Mitchell.

B-26

U.S. twin-engine bomber built by Martin. The official name was the *Marauder*, but it was unofficially called the "Incredible Prostitute" because the early models had wings so short that it was said that the aircraft had no visible means of support.

B-29

U.S. four-engine heavy bomber built by Boeing. By World War II standards, the B-29 was an incredible aircraft. It could carry a load of nine tons, a capacity almost equal to its own weight, and could operate at between 30,000 and 40,000 feet. When it was first designed it flew higher, faster, and farther than any fighter in use anywhere in the world. There were separate pilot consoles in the rear of the aircraft from which it could be flown if the front cockpit was knocked out. General Hap Arnold conceived the idea for the B-29 in 1939 to counter the possibility of a total Nazi victory in Europe, which would prevent the U.S. from attaining bases on the European side of the Atlantic to strike back.

FACTS ABOUT THE B-29:

The first B-29 to be shot at was piloted by Charles Hanson, April 26, 1944.

The first B-29 mission was flown June 5, 1944, against railway shops in Bangkok, Thailand.

The first B-29 mission over Japan was an attack on Yawata, June 15, 1944, and was flown from bases in China.

B-32

American four-engine bomber built in the last days of World War II. It was named *Dominator* and only 118 were built, fifteen of which actually saw combat. It is believed to be the last U.S. aircraft to have been involved in combat in World War II, when two B-32's on photo-reconnaissance missions over Tokyo on August 18, 1945, were attacked by fourteen Japanese fighters. One crew member was killed and two wounded. The aircraft was named *Hobo Queen II*.

B-3211

General Douglas MacArthur's office telephone number in Brisbane, Australia. The operator answered each call with "Hello, this is Bataan."

B2H2

Acronym given by the Washington press corps to a bipartisan group of U.S. Senators who in 1943 advocated U.S. involvement in a United Nations after World War II. They were Joseph H. Ball and Harold Burton, Republicans, and Lister Hill and Carl A. Hatch, Democrats.

Babington-Smith, Constance

British Women's Air Force photo-reconnaissance expert. Her

specialty was German aircraft and she worked with the U.S. Eighth Army Air Force to pinpoint aircraft factories as bombing targets. She is officially credited with being the first to recognize the ME-163 rocket plane and the first to spot the V-1 buzz bombs at Peenemunde in May 1943.

MOVIE PORTRAYAL:
Operation Crossbow (1965), by Sylvia Sims

Baby Blitz

Name given by the British to the period from January to March 1944, when German bombers attacked England in retaliation for the heavy strikes on Germany. It was directed by Dietrich Peltz.

Baby Flattops

Nickname given to U.S. Navy escort carriers. The first U.S. carrier was the U.S.S. *Long Island,* which was built by converting the cargo vessel S.S. *Mormacmail.*

Bachstelze

Name given to a kite devised by the Germans during World War II. It was towed behind a surfaced submarine and had a small platform from which a man could watch for potential targets. It was used only on rare occasions in the South Atlantic.

von dem Bach-Zelewski, Erich (1898–1972)

German S.S. Lieutenant General. He commanded the S.S. forces that suppressed the Warsaw uprising in 1944. He was used as a witness at the Nuremberg trials against other Nazis. When he himself was finally tried in 1951 for his war crimes, he was given a ten-year suspended sentence.

Bader, Douglas (1910–1982)

British Royal Air Force ace during World War II. Bader lost both legs in an aircraft crash in 1931 and was invalided out of the service. With the advent of war and the shortage of qualified pilots, he was able to talk his way back into the R.A.F. flying Spitfires. He commanded the 242nd Squadron at Tangmere and had his initials "DB" on the side of his aircraft as an identifying mark. His call sign was "Dogsbody" and he is officially credited with 22.5 aircraft destroyed, becoming the third person to be awarded the bars of the Distinguished Service Order and the Distinguished Flying Cross. On August 9, 1941, an ME109 collided with him in the air over the continent, and he spent the rest of the war as a guest of the Germans. After several escape attempts (one of which was from Stalag Luft III, "The Great

Escape'' camp), he was imprisoned in Colditz Castle, a special prisoner-of-war camp for exceptionally difficult prisoners.

He wrote the introduction for Hans Ulrich Rudel's 1958 book *Stuka Pilot* and is the subject of the 1954 biography *Reach For the Sky,* by Paul Brickhill.

MOVIE PORTRAYAL:
Reach For the Sky (1956), by Kenneth More

Badoglio, Pietro (1871–1956)

Italian Field Marshall. Badoglio took over command of Italian forces in Ethiopia in November 1935 and immediately ordered the use of mustard and other poisonous gases against the Ethiopians. After his victory in Ethiopia, he was made Chief of Staff to Italian dictator Benito Mussolini but resigned in 1940 in protest against Italy's entry into World War II. Badoglio arranged the 1943 surrender of Italy to the Allied armies and became Italy's first post-Fascism premier.

Baedeker Raids

Name given to renewed Luftwaffe bombing of England from April to June 1942. The raids were named after a German publishing house that printed tourist guide books to European points of interest, which were graded with one, two, or three stars. The Luftwaffe announced that it would bomb every building in Britain to which Baedeker had awarded three stars. The first raid took place April 24, 1942, on Exeter. The Baedeker guide book was also used by Hitler's panzer forces in the March 12, 1938, occupation of Austria, since they had no military maps of the roads.

Baependy

Brazilian passenger liner that, after being converted to a troop transport, was attacked and sunk by a German submarine on August 15, 1942, out of Rio de Janeiro. Over three hundred people died; as a result, the Brazilian government declared war on the Axis a week later.

Bailey Bridge

Portable bridge used throughout Europe during World War II by the Allied armies. Invented by Sir Donald Bailey, it was lightweight and easily transported and assembled. The bridge was constructed of interchangeable parts and could be easily repaired if damaged.

Baillie-Stewart, Norman (1909–1966)

Former British Army officer who broadcast propaganda for the Germans during World War II. He had been a lieutenant in the Seaforth Highlanders but was caught giving military secrets to the Germans in 1933. He was convicted of betraying secrets and imprisoned until 1938 in the Tower of London, where he was known as the "Officer in the Tower." After his release, he became a German citizen and began broadcasting for the Nazis. Baillie-Stewart was captured in 1945 in Austria and received another five-year prison sentence for treason.

Baker, George (1915–)

American cartoonist and creator of the Sad Sack character. He worked for Walt Disney until he was drafted into the U.S. Army in 1941, drawing for the animated movies *Dumbo* (1941), *Pinocchio* (1940), and *Bambi* (1942). He joined the staff of *Yank* magazine and used the *Sad Sack* to represent the GI's and their conflicts with the Army.

Baker, Howard (1925–)

U.S. politician and Senator from Tennessee. He served during World War II on PT boats in the Pacific. Baker was discharged in 1946 as a lieutenant (j.g.).

Baker, Jimmy (1931–)

U.S. Marine Corps private who enlisted in 1943 but was honorably discharged after seven months when it was revealed that he was only twelve years old.

Baker Street Irregulars

Nickname given to a group of British intellectuals who were responsible for breaking the German codes that were sent via the Enigma enciphering machine.

Balbo, Italo (1896–1940)

Italian air marshall. He was an advocate of massive formations of aircraft and was instrumental in building up and reorganizing the Italian Air Force, the Regia Aeronautica. Ironically, Balbo was shot down and killed by his own antiaircraft units over Tobruk on June 28, 1940.

Balikpapan, Borneo

Site of the last D-Day invasion of World War II. On Sunday, July 12, 1945, Australian troops of the 77th Division under the personal command of General Douglas MacArthur assaulted the beaches, with MacArthur coming ashore four hours later.

Balkan Entente

Agreement signed in 1934 by Turkey, Greece, Rumania, and Yugoslavia, calling for mutual aid to protect themselves against Bulgaria.

Bambi

Animated Walt Disney movie released in 1942. It was the last movie Disney made before turning his studios over to the war effort.

Bamboo Fleet

Nickname given to what remained of the Philippine Army Air Force after the initial Japanese attacks in December 1941. The Bamboo fleet consisted of four old commercial aircraft that attempted to fly supplies to besieged Bataan. The first flight was made by Lieutenant David L. Obert.

Bamboo Telegraph

Nickname given to native forms of communication in underdeveloped countries. Information was passed by word of mouth, by drums, or by any number of other methods and could travel great distances in a very short time.

BAMS

Nickname given to women in the U.S. Marine Corps. While the other services had names for the women in their organization—WAC for Women's Army Corps, WAF for Women's Air Force—the Marine Corps preferred to call them Women Marines. *BAMS* was soon coined as a slang term and stood for Broad-Assed Marines. (see Hams)

Bandera Gangs

Soviet name for supporters of the Germans in World War II.

Bandera, Stephan (1909–1959)

Ukrainian nationalist whose followers fought both the Germans and the Russians for an independent Ukraine from June 1941 until 1948, well after World War II. Bandera was first imprisoned by the Germans but was released in 1944 to oppose the advancing Red Army. He fled to Germany in 1947 and died in 1959 from poisoning.

Bandit

U.S. Navy code name for an enemy aircraft.

Banner, John (1910–1973)

Hollywood actor known for his role as Sergeant Hans Schultz in the television series "Hogan's Heroes." He was a Jew who fled from Austria after the German Anschluss of 1938. During World War II, he posed for U.S. Army recruiting posters. Banner portrayed Rudolph Hoess in the 1961 movie *Operation Eichmann* and Gregor Strasser in the 1962 movie *Hitler.*

Baptist Cemetery

Cemetery in Creeds, Virginia, where British sailors who died on the east coast of the United States were buried.

BAR

Browning Automatic Rifle. It was developed by John Browning during World War I and was the U.S. Army's principal light automatic weapon in World War II.

Bar, Heinz (1913–1957)

Luftwaffe lieutenant colonel and history's first jet ace. He was Germany's ninth-ranked ace, with a total of 220 aircraft destroyed, sixteen of which were downed while he flew the German jet, the ME-262. Bar, who was awarded the Knight Cross with oak leaves and swords, was shot down himself on eighteen occasions.

Barbed Wire

Name given by German air crews to the antennae on the nose of night fighter aircraft, used by the onboard radar to locate enemy aircraft.

Barb, U.S.S.

U.S. Navy submarine that is credited with being the third highest-scoring submarine of the U.S. Navy during World War II. It sank 96,628 tons of enemy shipping. First ranked was the U.S.S. *Flasher* and second was the U.S.S. *Rasher.*

Bari

Italian port site of the only major accident involving poison gas during World War II. The port was attacked by Luftwaffe bombers on December 2, 1943; they sank seventeen ships and damaged eight others, killing over a thousand people. Part of the cargo on board the S.S. *John Harvey* was mustard gas, which inflicted numerous casualties as it spread in the immediate area. At first it was thought that the Germans had employed the gas, but the truth was soon learned from the cargo manifests. This was the worst seaport disaster since Pearl Harbor.

General Jimmy Doolittle was there at the time (see Doolittle, James H.).

Barkhorn, Gerhard (1919–)

Luftwaffe major and second-highest-scoring ace of all time with 302 victories. He flew over 1,100 combat missions and was shot down nine times. Barkhorn was the recipient of the Knight's Cross with oak leaves and swords. In 1955 he joined the new West German Luftwaffe and became a general.

Barre, George (1886–1970)

French general and commander of the Army of Tunisia. He actively opposed the Germans and joined the Allies in the fighting. His counterpart in command of the French Naval forces in Tunisia was Admiral Louise Derrien, who elected to join the Axis.

Bartlett, Sy S. (1909–)

Hollywood writer. During World War II he was a major in the U.S. Army Air Force and served as an aide to General Carl Spaatz in England. He flew as an observer on an R.A.F. bombing mission over Berlin in March 1943. Bartlett coauthored the book *Twelve O'Clock High* with Beirne Lay, Jr. In 1950, he helped produce the movie of the same name and in 1963 produced *A Gathering of Eagles*.

Baruch, André

Former CBS radio announcer. During World War II, as a major in the U.S. Army, he headed the Armed Forces Radio Network operated in the Mediterranean area by and for the GI's.

Baruch, Bernard M. (1870–1965)

President Franklin D. Roosevelt's personal representative in England during World War II. He was head of the War Industries Board during World War I but refused any such post in World War II after Henry Ford accused him of participating in a Jewish conspiracy to take over control of the economy of the world.

Baseball World Series Games

1941	New York Yankees defeated the Brooklyn Dodgers
1942	St. Louis Cardinals defeated the New York Yankees
1943	New York Yankees defeated the St. Louis Cardinals
1944	St. Louis Cardinals defeated the St. Louis Browns
1945	Detroit Tigers defeated the Chicago Cubs

Base T

Secret British naval base at Addu Atoll in the southern Maldive Islands in the Indian Ocean. Security was so tight that the Japanese never discovered its location throughout World War II. It was also designated *Port T.*

Basilone, John (1916–1945)

Sergeant, U.S. Marine Corps. He was the first enlisted man to win the Congressional Medal of Honor in World War II. Basilone was awarded the medal for action on Guadalcanal in October 1942. He returned to the United States to participate in War Bond Drives but tired of the routine and requested transfer back to the Pacific. He returned in time for the Iwo Jima invasion, where he was killed in action in 1945.

Bass, Raymond Henry ("Benny")

U.S. Navy officer and commander of the submarine U.S.S. *Plunger* during World War II. Bass had been an Olympic Gold Medal winner in the 1932 Olympics at Los Angeles, California.

Bastion 32

Designator of the French headquarters at Dunkirk during the evacuation of the British Expeditionary Force in May and June 1940. It was commanded by Admiral Jean Abrial.

Bastogne

Belgian town and road junction that achieved prominence when the Germans failed to capture it during the Ardennes Offensive in December 1944. It was defended by the U.S. 101st Airborne Division under the temporary command of Brigadier General Anthony C. McAuliffe, who answered a German ultimatum to surrender with one word, "Nuts." (The surrender note had been typed on a captured American typewriter.) Bastogne was relieved by elements of the 37th Tank Battalion commanded by Creighton Abrams, Jr.

Bataan

Peninsula guarding the entrance to Manila Bay. It was defended by General Jonathan Wainwright and the I Corps in the west and by General George Parker and the II Corps in the east. On April 9, 1942, 75,000 defenders surrendered to the Japanese, becoming the largest U.S. military force in history to surrender.

Bataan

Name of General Douglas MacArthur's personal aircraft. For most of the war he used a B-17 but later changed to a C-54.

Bataan

Aircraft recognition signal of the Japanese peace delegation headed by Lieutenant General Kawabe. The aircraft were painted white with large green crosses and flew to Manila on August 19, 1945, to meet with General Douglas MacArthur to establish operational plans for the initial Allied entry into the main islands of Japan.

Bataan Death March

Infamous forced march of prisoners of war captured by the

Japanese on Bataan. The march was under the command of General Masaharu Homma who was sentenced to death by the U.S. War Crimes Tribunal after the war. Nearly 25,000 prisoners died along the sixty-five miles of the trek to Camp O'Donnell, with another 22,000 dying in the first two months at the camp.

Bataan, U.S.S. (CVL-29)

U.S. Navy light aircraft carrier. It was the first ship to bear the name of a World War II battle when it was launched on August 1, 1943.

Batfish, U.S.S.

U.S. Navy submarine commanded by Jake Fyfe. It holds the distinction of sinking three Japanese submarines in four days after the U.S. Navy codebreakers alerted Fyfe to the fact that the Japanese were evacuating pilots from Luzon to Formosa. He picked up the enemy submarines, *RO-115*, *RO-112*, and *RO-113*, on radar and sank all three.

Batter Up

Code phrase used to indicate that the French were resisting the American landings in North Africa during Operation Torch on November 8, 1942. It was followed by the code phrase "Play Ball," which was the order for Allied forces to attack.

Battle Bowler

Nickname given to the helmets used during the Battle of Britain for protection against falling shrapnel.

Battle of Britain

Official name given to the period from July 10 to October 31, 1940, when the German Luftwaffe attempted to knock out the British Royal Air Force in preparation for a German invasion of the British Isles. The R.A.F. lost a total of 415 pilots out of a force of 1,500. The life expectancy of a fighter pilot was eighty-seven flying hours or about two weeks.

Battle of the Bulge

Last major offensive of the Germans in World War II. It is also known as the Ardennes Offensive and took place in December 1944. One of the U.S. divisions defending the area was the green 106th Infantry Division, which surrendered over 8,000 men to the Germans for the second largest surrender of American troops ever made. It was exceeded only by the surrender of Bataan.

Battle of the Coral Sea

First modern naval engagement in history, i.e., the first aircraft carrier battle. The opponents in the battle (which was not fought in the Coral Sea but rather in the Solomon Sea) neither sighted each other nor exchanged a single shot. It was the first Japanese naval defeat of World War II and the first success for the United States in the Pacific. The battle took place May 7 and 8, 1942, when the Japanese attempted to send an invasion force to Port Moresby. The Japanese lost the carrier *Shoho* and the carrier *Shokaku* was severely damaged. The U.S. had to sink the carrier *Lexington* because of damage and the *Yorktown* was damaged. It was the first time the Japanese were stopped short of their objective.

Battle of Leyte Gulf

The largest naval battle in history, which took place in October 1944 and ended Japanese sea power for the duration of World War II. The Japanese lost three battleships, four aircraft carriers, ten cruisers, and nearly a dozen other ships; the U.S. lost six ships. Of the U.S. ships in the battle five were survivors of Pearl Harbor—the U.S.S. *West Virginia*, U.S.S. *Maryland*, U.S.S. *Tennessee*, U.S.S. *California* and the U.S.S. *Pennsylvania*.

Battle of Midway

Documentary film produced by Navy Commander John Ford in 1942. Ford was present during the Battle of Midway, was wounded, but continued to film the action.

Battle of Samar

Only time in the Pacific war that battleships engaged aircraft carriers. It was part of the larger Battle of Leyte Gulf in October 1944, and the Japanese succeeded in sinking the escort carriers U.S.S. *Gambier Bay*, and U.S.S. *St. Lo*, as well as the destroyers U.S.S. *Johnston*, U.S.S. *Roberts*, and U.S.S. *Hoel*.

Battle of San Pietro

Documentary film produced by U.S. Army Major John Huston about a battle for a small Italian village in 1943 and 1944. The film was not released until after the end of the fighting in Europe because of the horror of war depicted by Huston.

Battle of Savo Island

First surface battle fought by the U.S. Navy since 1898 and one of its worst defeats. It took place on August 9, 1942, off Guadalcanal, with the U.S. losing the cruisers U.S.S. *Quincy*, U.S.S. *Vincennes*, and U.S.S. *Astoria* and the Australians losing the cruiser H.M.A.S. *Canberra*. The Japanese did not lose a single ship during the battle.

Battleship Row

Nickname given to the area of Pearl Harbor where deep-draft ships—primarily battleships—were moored and the principal target of the Japanese surprise attack of December 7, 1941.

Battle Stations

Short film made during World War II telling of the activities of women in the U.S. Coast Guard. The film was narrated by Spencer Tracy and Ginger Rogers.

Batz, Wilhelm (1916–)

Luftwaffe major and sixth-ranked ace of all time with 237 aerial victories. He flew with JG52 and was awarded the Knight's Cross with oak leaves and swords. Batz is credited with shooting down an astounding fifteen aircraft in a single day.

Bauer, Hank (1922–)

Major league baseball manager. During World War II he was a platoon sergeant in the U.S. Marine Corps and was wounded by shrapnel on Guam. He was awarded two Bronze Stars, two Purple Hearts, and eleven campaign ribbons.

Bauer, Harold William (1908–1942)

U.S. Marine Corps lieutenant colonel. Bauer commanded VMF 212 at Guadalcanal. On October 16, 1942, while approaching Henderson Field and nearly out of gas, he attacked a flight of Japanese dive bombers who were attacking a ship and shot down four of the aircraft. He barely made it to the field and was awarded the Congressional Medal of Honor for his feat. However, he was shot down and lost at sea before he could receive the medal.

Baumbach, Werner (1916–1953)

Luftwaffe colonel. As a bomber pilot, he flew missions in every part of Europe throughout the war. He was the recipient of the Knight's Cross with oak leaves and swords. Baumbach was designated "General of the Bombers," although he was never promoted to the rank of general. Possibly this was because he was highly critical of Hitler and the leadership of the Luftwaffe. He was captured by the British at the end of the war and, after his release, immigrated to Argentina, where he was killed in an air crash.

Baumler, A. J. "Ajax" (–1973)

U.S. Army Air Force major. He was the first American to become an ace in two wars. He is credited with shooting down eight aircraft during the Spanish Civil War and five Japanese aircraft during World War II as a pilot with the Fourteenth Army Air Force in the China-Burma-India Theater.

Baur, Hans

Adolf Hitler's personal pilot. He became a lieutenant general in the Luftwaffe and was present during the last days of the Third Reich in the bunker in Berlin. Baur lost a leg in an escape attempt from the Russian encirclement, and was captured and tortured by them in an effort to gain information about the fate of Hitler.

MOVIE PORTRAYAL:
The Bunker (1980 TV movie), by Karl Held

Baur, Harry (1881–1943)

French actor who played the lead in the pre–World War II movies *Les Miserables* (1934), *The Life And Loves of Beethoven* (1935), and *Rasputin* (1937). He was arrested by the Nazis for carrying forged identity papers in May 1942, and died in captivity shortly thereafter.

Bauxite

Principal source of aluminum, which was desperately needed by Germany for aircraft, electrical equipment, and motors for the war effort. Twenty-two percent of the world's supply came from Hungary and Yugoslavia, a factor that figured into Hitler's plans for European domination.

Bayerlein, Fritz (1888–1970)

German lieutenant general who served in Africa as chief of staff to Field Marshall Erwin Rommel and commanded the Afrika Korps in his absence. Bayerlein, who fought at Normandy, the Battle of the Bulge, and the Rhine, was captured by the Americans in April 1945.

Bayeux

First important town to be liberated in Normandy. It was also the only large Normandy town not damaged by the fighting. It was captured on June 7, 1944, by the British 50th Infantry Division. Bayeux was also the site of the first postinvasion speech given by General Charles de Gaulle on June 14, 1944.

Bayfield, U.S.S.

U.S. Navy rocket ship that saw action at Omaha Beach during the D-Day invasion on June 6, 1944. Future baseball catcher Lawrence "Yogi" Berra was stationed aboard the vessel during the invasion.

Bayler, Walter

GI credited with being the last American off Wake Island in 1941 and the first American to return in September 1945.

Bayonet

Code name given to General Dwight Eisenhower's personal railway car used for traveling around England during World War II.

Bazna, Elyesa (1904–1971)

Valet of the British ambassador to Turkey during World War II, Sir Hughe Knatchbull-Hugessen. As such, he copied secret documents and sold the information to the Germans under the alias *Cicero*. This included facts about the Casablanca and Moscow Conferences, as well as plans for Operation Overlord, the D-Day landings. His prices were high but the Germans did not hesitate, probably because they paid him in counterfeit British money, a fact he pestered the West German government about until his death. Apparently he also worked for the British secret service and gave out only the information the British wanted the Germans to know in an attempt to deceive them about the D-Day landings.

Bazooka

U.S. Army antitank rocket launcher. It was designed so that the individual infantryman would have an adequate defense against armored vehicles. It could penetrate three inches of steel. The name was derived from a musical instrument used by radio comedian Bob Burns, the "Arkansas Traveler." It was named in 1943 by Major Zeb Hastings.

B Card

U.S. gas-rationing card that categorized the holder as essential to the war effort and therefore entitled him to more gas than the A card holder. War workers were placed in this group.

BCRA

Bureau Central de Renseignements et d'Action. This was General Charles de Gaulle's personal intelligence organization and was headed by André Dewavrin. It used any means possible to entrench de Gaulle in French politics and had its headquarters on Duke Street in London.

Beach, Edward L. (1918–   )

U.S. Navy officer and author. He graduated from the U.S. Naval Academy in 1938, choosing submarine duty. During World War II, Beach served as the executive officer of the U.S.S. *Trigger* and the U.S.S. *Tirante*, where he was awarded the Navy Cross. He became the commanding officer of the U.S.S. *Piper*, which was the last U.S. submarine to return from patrol duties at the end of World War II. Beach has written such excellent books as *Run Silent Run Deep, Dust on the Sea,* and *Submarine.*

Beach Code Names

Algiers	Apple, Beer, Charlie
Attu	Red
Dieppe	Blue, Green, Orange, Red, White, Yellow
Dulag	Violet, Yellow
Guadalcanal	Red
Normandy	Gold, Juno, Omaha, Sword, Utah
Okinawa	Blue, Purple
Saipan	Blue, Green, Red, Yellow
Salerno	Amber, Blue, Green, Red, Uncle, Yellow
Sicily	Cent, Dime, Joss
Tacloban	Red, White
Tarawa	Green, Red
Tripoli	X, Yorker, Zebra
Tulagi	Blue

Beaufort

British twin-engine aircraft. It was used as a torpedo plane, a minelayer, and a medium bomber, carrying a crew of four. It could fly 265 miles per hour.

Beaverbrook, Lord (1879–1964)

British minister of aircraft production. His real name was Max Aitken and he was a Canadian-born newspaper publisher asked by Prime Minister Winston Churchill to increase lagging British production of aircraft. He used unorthodox methods of stimulating production and, by cutting red tape and utilizing methods he had learned from publishing, he was able to increase production to the point that by June 1940 the British factories were turning out nearly five hundred fighters a month. His son, Max Aitken, was a fighter pilot, and it was said that while Beaverbrook made British aircraft, his son destroyed German ones. They were, therefore, the perfect combination.

Beaver bugs

Nickname given to special British armored cars used to defend the 250 aircraft factories in the early days of World War II. The name was derived from the Minister of Aircraft Production, Lord Beaverbrook.

Beavers

Name given to German Navy two-man submarines. They displaced six and a quarter tons of water and the first one built was appropriately named *Adam*. The 324 vessels manufactured between December 1944 and April 1945 sank over 90,000 tons of shipping in the Scheldt Estuary in the approaches to the port of Antwerp. The attrition rate, however, was between sixty and seventy percent.

Beck, Josef (1894–1944)

Foreign Minister of Poland at the outbreak of World War II. He fled before the advancing Germans into Rumania. It was Beck who had signed the Ten-Year Nonaggression Pact with Germany on January 26, 1934. He died in exile in Rumania on June 6, 1944, the very day that the Allies returned to the continent of Europe.

Beck, Ludwig (1880–1944)

German general. He was the last peacetime Chief of Staff of the German army and was forced into retirement by the Nazis. Beck was one of the leaders of the attempted assassination of Hitler on July 20, 1944; as a result of its failure, he committed suicide. Berlin radio announced that he "was no longer among the living."

Beer

Designator of the beach to the west of Algiers assaulted in Operation Torch, November 8, 1942.

Beetle

Miniature remote-controlled tank invented by the Germans. It was loaded with explosives and sent against Allied positions with a timing device set to detonate at a certain distance. Beetles were first used at Anzio in January 1944, but Allied riflemen were able to explode them at a safe distance.

Beethoven

Name given to a German tandem aircraft. It consisted of a crewless bomber, loaded with four tons of explosives, that was attached to the bottom of a fighter aircraft. The fighter pilot flew to a target, began a shallow dive to aim the bomber, and released it about 3,000 feet above the ground. The Germans claimed eighty percent accuracy against fixed targets. It was also known as "Father and Son." A similar Allied effort was called Operation Aphrodite.

Beethoven's Fifth Symphony

Favorite record of the U.S. ambassador to England, Joseph P.

Kennedy. The opening notes—three shorts and a long—were used during World War II as a code signal for *V* for "victory."

Belafonte, Harry (1927–)

Popular singer of calypso music, who later appeared as a dramatic actor. He was the first black to win an Emmy on television and his *Calypso* LP, recorded in 1956, was the first popular nonsoundtrack album to sell over one million copies. During World War II, he dropped out of high school to enlist in the U.S. Navy. He was sent to the Navy's storekeeper school and served two years and four months before being discharged.

Belden, Jack

War correspondent for the International News Service. He was present at the Marco Polo Bridge Incident, in July 1937, that began the war between China and Japan, as well as at the siege of Malta and the attack on the Mareth Line in North Africa. Belden was with General Joseph Stilwell in Burma and was the only reporter to march out of Burma with Stilwell during the retreat in 1942. He roomed with Brigadier General Theodore Roosevelt, Jr. on the U.S.S. *Barnett* enroute to the invasion of Sicily in 1943.

Belinda

Code name for the German Navy's intelligence service headquarters. The branch of the navy that was called the Abwehr was headed by Admiral Wilhelm Canaris.

Bell, Laurence D. (1894–)

U.S. aircraft manufacturer who built the P-39 *Aircobra*.

Bella Russa

Soviet ship that was accidentally sunk by the submarine U.S.S. *Sundlance* in May 1943. The submarine commander Makolm Garrison mistakenly believed that it was the Japanese ship, the *Florida Maru*.

Bellinger, Patrick N. L. (1885–1962)

U.S. Navy Vice Admiral. He commanded U.S. Navy aviation in the Atlantic during World War II. Bellinger was taught to fly in 1913 by Jack Towers who commanded Navy aviation in the Pacific. Bellinger was the eighth naval aviator and commanded the NC-1 on the trans-Atlantic crossing of May 1919. He was present at Pearl Harbor on December 7, 1941, and is credited by some with sending the message "Air Raid Pearl Harbor This Is No Drill."

Bellow, Saul (1915–)

Pulitzer Prize–winning author who served during World War II in the merchant marine, where he worked on his first published novel *Dangling Man* (1944).

Bellows Field

One of the three U.S. Army Air Force fields on Oahu attacked by the Japanese on December 7, 1941. The other two were Wheeler and Hickam Fields.

Bells

Code name for messages sent from U.S. Navy headquarters in Canberra, Australia, to all ships in the Navy in the southwest Pacific. Every ship monitored the broadcasts and deciphered only those messages addressed to them.

von Below, Nikolaus (1908–　　)

Hitler's personal Luftwaffe adjutant and one of the witnesses at the wedding of Hitler and his mistress Eva Braun. Von Below was reported to have been the last person to leave the bunker during the fall of Berlin.

Belsen

Nazi concentration camp. Originally established as a detention camp for Jews who were to be exchanged for German nationals held abroad, it was later converted into an extermination camp until it was liberated by Allied forces on April 13, 1945.

Belvedere Palace

Seventeenth-century palace built in Vienna for Prince Eugene of Savoy. It was the home of Kurt von Schuschnigg, chancellor of Austria at the time of the German Anschluss.

Bendetsen, Karl Robin

U.S. Army colonel. He was in charge of evacuating the Japanese from the West Coast of the United States in 1942 for which he was awarded the Distinguished Service Medal.

Beneš, Edward (1884–1948)

President of Czechoslovakia until 1938. After the outbreak of World War II, he set up a Czech government-in-exile in Paris, then moved to London with the fall of France in June 1940. He returned to Prague in 1945, where he served as President until 1948.

Benjamin Warner, S.S.

Last Liberty ship built during World War II. It was constructed in 1944 at the Henry J. Kaiser Company shipyard on the West Coast.

Bennett, Donald (1910–　　)

Royal Air Force officer who developed the use of pathfinders to guide bombers to their targets. As a civilian, he flew Polish General Wladyslaw Sikorski from France to Britain in 1940.

Bennett, Paul G.

U.S. Army private slapped by General George S. Patton on August 10, 1943, in the 93rd Evacuation Hospital on Sicily. Patton felt that battle fatigue was simply an excuse for cowardice and that slapping Private Bennett would shame him into fighting again. Omar Bradley felt that Bennett did more than any other private to win the war in Europe, because the trouble that Patton incurred from General Dwight Eisenhower made him a more stable field commander and subsequently one of the greatest tacticians of the war. Bennett's serial number was ASN 70000001.

(The *first* GI to be slapped by General Patton was Private C. H. Kuhl, on August 3, 1943.)

Bennett, Tony (1926–)

Singer who served with the U.S. Army as an infantryman in Europe. It was while in the Army that he got his first opportunity to sing with a band—a military band.

Berbera

Capital of British Somaliland. The battle here ended in the first victory of the Italians over the British in World War II and was one more example of the maneuver called "strategic withdrawal."

Berchtesgaden

Town in the Bavarian Alps. It was the site of the Haus Wachenfeld purchased for Hitler by Martin Bormann. Hitler changed the name of the house to Berghof.

Berg, Moe (1902–1972)

Former major league catcher, for the Washington Senators and the Boston Red Sox. He was a graduate of Princeton and spoke sixteen languages. In 1934 Berg traveled to Tokyo, where he took pictures that were used for the Doolittle Raid on Tokyo on April 18, 1942. He became an OSS agent and traveled to Switzerland to gain information from Werner Heissenberger, the head of the German atomic project.

Berghall, U.S.S.

U.S. Navy submarine associated with the number thirteen. On May 13, 1942, her keel was laid. Thirteen months later to the day, John Hyde assumed command. The submarine was launched on February 13, 1944, and arrived in Pearl Harbor after a shakedown cruise on August 13, 1944. She sank her first Japanese ship on October 13, 1944. Hyde torpedoed the Japanese cruiser *Myoko* on

December 13, 1944, and received battle damage from a destroyer that rendered the submarine unable to dive. He then proceeded to travel across 1,300 miles of enemy-infested waters to Australia and arrived unscathed. After repairs, while patrolling close to Hainan Island, Hyde fired at and hit a Japanese ship on February 13, 1945, which he had located at 12:30. Throughout the war the *Berghall* was a lucky ship. In the middle of 1945, she struck a mine, which usually sank submarines, but she survived with only minor damage.

Berger, Gottlob (1896–1975)

German S.S. lieutenant general. He set up the S.S. Sonderkommandos, who were responsible for the deaths of millions on the eastern front. For his crimes Berger was sentenced at Nuremberg to twenty-five years imprisonment.

Berlin

Capital of Germany. In the third week of April 1945, before the fall of Berlin, U.S. Army First Lieutenant Arthur Hadley of the 2nd Armored Division led a jeep with two newspapermen across the Elbe toward Berlin. They soon came upon some Russian soldiers. Hadley's orders would not allow him to go further, but the newspapermen drove on to Berlin and entered and left unmolested by the Germans. They were Ernest Leiser of *Stars and Stripes* and Mack Morris of *Yank* Magazine.

The first U.S. flag flown over Berlin on July 20, 1945, was the same flag that was flying over the Capitol in Washington, D.C., on December 8, 1941, when war was declared (see Flags).

Before the war, the terrain around Berlin was flat. After VE Day, all the rubble was bulldozed into seven hills that transformed the appearance of the city. One of these is named Junk Hill.

Berlin Betty

Nickname given to one of the female propaganda broadcasters who broadcast in English to the Americans in North Africa.

Berlin Diary

Book written by William L. Shirer chronicling his days as a correspondent in Berlin and warning of the Nazis' aggression. It was number one on the bestseller lists of December 7, 1941.

Berlin, Irving (1888–)

Popular American composer who wrote a number of patriotic songs for the war effort. He was given the Medal of Merit by General George C. Marshall for his contributions.

Berlitz, Charles F. (1913–)

Author of *The Bermuda Triangle* and other books. During World War II, he enlisted in the U.S. Army as a private and rose to the rank of captain. He was in the counterintelligence corps and served in Europe and Latin America.

Bernadotte, Folke (1895–1948)

Swedish Red Cross representative in Germany during World War II. He saved many Swedes and Jews by serving as an intermediary with the German authorities. Toward the end of the war, he was approached several times by the S.S. head Heinrich Himmler to act as a courier for an armistice with the West, but nothing came of this. Ironically the man who helped so many Jews to leave Germany was assassinated in 1948 by a Jewish extremist group in Palestine while he was serving as a United Nations mediator.

Berne Report

Name given to a package of documents given to OSS chief Allen Dulles in Switzerland by Fritz Kolbe on August 23, 1943. These contained German diplomatic messages of the highest secrecy.

Bernhardt, Berndt

German submarine commander who surrendered his U-boat in 1941 to a Hudson aircraft while on his maiden voyage. Apparently this occurred because of both his and the crew members' inexperience. Bernhardt was interned in Canada, where the other prisoners-of-war made things so unbearable for him that he escaped. He was recaptured and, when informed that he would be returned to the same camp, broke away and ran, only to be shot and killed.

Berra, Lawrence "Yogi" (1925–)

Baseball player for the New York Yankees. He enlisted in the U.S. Navy in 1943 and was a gunner on the rocket ship U.S.S. *Bayfield* at Normandy. He was discharged in May 1946.

Berrigan, Philip (1923–)

Former Jesuit priest who protested against the U.S. Government's policies in the 1960's. During World War II, he was drafted into the U.S. Army and sent to Europe with the infantry. During one fierce battle in France, he was given a battlefield commission of second lieutenant.

MOVIE PORTRAYAL:

The Trial of the Catonsville Nine (1972), by Douglas Watson

Beser, Jacob

U.S. Army Air Force radar officer. He was the only person to be on board both the *Enola Gay* and *Bock's Car* when they dropped the atomic bombs on Hiroshima and Nagasaki respectively.

MOVIE PORTRAYAL:
Enola Gay (1980 TV movie), by Billy Crystal

Best, Robert H. (1896–)

United Press correspondent. He was born in Sumter, South Carolina, and during World War I served as a lieutenant in the Coast Artillery. Best was a close friend of William L. Shirer and became a propaganda broadcaster for the Nazis, making over three hundred broadcasts, on which he called himself "Guess Who." At one point Best announced his candidacy for President of the United States in the 1944 elections. He was indicted by a Federal Grand Jury in July 1942 and, after the war, was sentenced to life imprisonment and fined $10,000 by Federal Judge Francis J. W. Ford in Boston's Federal District Court.

Best, S. Payne

British Army captain. He was a member of the British Intelligence Service and was captured at Venlo, Holland, by the S.S. under Walter Schellenberg, who accused him of an assassination attempt on Hitler in Munich in 1939. He and R. Henry Stevens, who was captured with him, were the two senior MI-6 officers in Europe who reported directly to Sir Stewart Menzies, the head of MI-6. They spent the rest of the war in a concentration camp.

Best, Dr. Werner

Ranking Nazi in Denmark. He was the former legal adviser to Reinhard Heydrich and later worked for the military government in Paris. In Denmark he protected the people in whatever ways he could from the Nazis. After the war, he testified at the Nuremberg trials and was extradited to Denmark, where he was condemned to death. Best appealed his sentence with new evidence and it was changed to five years' imprisonment.

Bettencourt, Amaro Soares

Brazilian general and military attaché in Washington, D.C. He was the first foreigner to receive the Legion of Merit Commander Order, on October 22, 1942.

Betty

Allied code name for the Japanese OB-01 heavy torpedo bomber. It was also a land-based medium bomber and was the aircraft that Admiral Isoruku Yamamoto was flying when he was shot down and killed on April 18, 1943, by U.S. Army P-38's over Bougainville.

Beurling, George F. (1922–1948)
Canadian flight lieutenant credited with 31.33 enemy aircraft shot down in World War II, making him the leading ace of Canada for the war. In fourteen days over Malta, he destroyed twenty-seven aircraft and was nicknamed "Screwball" by his fellow pilots for his unorthodox flying ability. Before the Royal Air Force would let him join, he had to return to Canada, get his birth certificate and take it back to England. (Canada's top-scoring ace is William A. Bishop who shot down seventy-two aircraft in World War I.)

Bhagat, Premindra Singh
Second lieutenant in the Royal Bombay Sappers. He was the first Indian to receive the Victoria Cross during World War II. He cleared a road of Italian mines and dug up fourteen separate mine fields, containing three hundred mines each, over a ninety-six-hour period. He was ambushed twice, blown up once, and had his eardrum shattered.

Bianchi Torpedo
Name of the first automobile purchased by Benito Mussolini (1920).

Biddle, Francis (1886–1968)
U.S. Attorney General during World War II. He was selected as a judge for the Nuremberg trials in 1946.

Big Apple
GI nickname for a section of Okinawa where the Japanese continued to hold out for a full week in June 1945.

Big B
Nickname given by Allied bomber crews to Berlin, one of the most respected targets of World War II.

Big Bill
Nickname given to William Donovan, the head of the OSS during World War II, to differentiate him from William Stevenson, the head of the British secret services in New York. Stevenson's nickname was "Little Bill."

Big Blue Blanket
Nickname of the air cover over Luzon provided by Admiral William F. "Bull" Halsey's carrier-based aircraft, December 14–16, 1944. The U.S. Navy aviation mission was to prevent Japanese reinforcements from reaching Mindoro during the Allied invasion of the Philippines. A total of 270 Japanese aircraft were destroyed.

Big Ditch
Nickname given to the English Channel by U.S. airmen stationed in England during World War II.

Big E
Nickname of the U.S. Navy aircraft carrier U.S.S. *Enterprise*.

Big Four
Term used to refer to the four major Allied countries. They were the United States, Britain, Russia, and China. The term was coined at the Arcadia Conference in January 1942.

Big Friends
Name given to U.S. bombers by the fighter pilots that escorted them in World War II. The fighter aircraft were known as "Little Friends."

Big Inch
Nickname given to what was the world's largest pipeline at the time. It was constructed to send oil from Longview, Texas, to Phoenixville, Pennsylvania, to help the war effort and dedicated on July 19, 1943. The pipeline was two feet in diameter, 1,381 miles long, and could move 300,000 barrels of oil a day.

Big Mamie
Nickname given to the U.S. Navy battleship U.S.S. *Massachusetts*. It participated in thirty-five sea battles and never lost a man.

BIGOT
Code word for the highest priority of top-secret classification used in conjunction with the invasion of Normandy, June 6, 1944. It originated from a reversal of the stamp "To Gib," which was put on orders for those going to Gibraltar for the North African invasion, November 8, 1942. It also included those people who were in on the plans for D-Day. They were known as "bigots."

Big Three
Nickname given to the top three leaders of World War II, President Franklin D. Roosevelt, Prime Minister Winston Churchill, and Marshall Joseph Stalin.

Big Week
Name given to the week of February 19–26, 1944, when massive Allied bombing attacks were launched against German aircraft production in preparation for the invasion of Europe. Approximately 3,300 bombers of the Eighth Army Air Force from England and 500 bombers of the Fifteenth Army Air Force in Italy, dropped nearly ten thousand tons of bombs. In the air

battles, the Luftwaffe lost 355 fighters and 360 personnel were killed or wounded. Despite the tremendous tonnage dropped, German production actually increased, due to the efforts of Albert Speer, the production minister.

Birch, John (1918–1945)

Baptist missionary who had gone to China prior to World War II. He became a field intelligence officer for General Claire Chennault's Fourteenth Army Air Force and was the first American to meet then Lieutenant Colonel James Doolittle after he crashed in China from the Tokyo Raid in April 1942. Birch was shot by the Chinese communists and was the first American killed in The Cold War, the ostensible basis for the John Birch Society.

(An interesting coincidence is that the survivors of the U.S. gunboat *Panay,* after it was attacked by Japanese aircraft in December 1937, were met by an American missionary, Dr. C. A. Birch. Therefore, the first Americans attacked by the Japanese (1937) and the first Americans to attack the Japanese (1942) were met by missionaries named Birch in China. The two were not related.)

Bird Island (Otori Shima)

Name that the Japanese gave Wake Island after its surrender by U.S. forces on December 1941.

Bir Hacheim

Battle in North Africa June 2–10, 1942. The Germans attacked a position held by the Free French under the command of General Pierre Koenig of the French Foreign Legion. This was the first time that the French and Germans had opposed each other since the fall of France in 1940.

Biscay Cross

Name given to a cumbersome antenna affixed to the conning towers of German submarines. It was part of the Metox early radar warning system.

Bishop, Joey (1919–)

Comedian and writer. He was drafted into the U.S. Army in 1942 and spent the next three years in special services. Bishop was discharged in 1945 with the rank of sergeant.

Bismarck

Germany's largest battleship of World War II, which displaced 42,000 tons of water. It was launched on February 14, 1939, and attempted to break out of the British blockade in May 1941 to prey on convoys in the Atlantic. It was commanded by Admiral Gunther Lutjens and Captain Ernst Lindemann and was the first ship ever to use radar to fire at other ships at night. The *Bismarck* sank the pride of the British fleet, H.M.S. *Hood;* this began the longest-running sea battle in naval history. The *Bismarck* disappeared for a time and was officially located by a Catalina flying boat flown by U.S. Navy Ensign Leonard Smith. In reality, it was located by Ultra intercepts that were decoded. The *Bismarck* was finally sunk on May 27, 1941, by the British cruiser H.M.S. *Dorsetshire*.

Biuro Szyfrow

Name of the Polish cypher bureau prior to World War II.

Black Buffaloes

Nickname of the blacks in the 92nd Infantry Division, the only U.S. black division to fight in World War II.

Black Cats

Nickname that the U.S. Navy gave the night-patrolling Catalina flying boats in World War II.

Black Caviar

Name given to a new smokeless powder invented by Western Cartridge Company in 1944. It was manufactured under water, creating less danger of explosion, and could be made five times faster than conventional powder.

Black Code

U.S. State Department cipher code thought to be foolproof. The Italians broke into the U.S. embassy in Rome in September 1941, stole the code books, photographed them, and returned them to the safe. They gave the photos to Field Marshall Erwin Rommel, who was able to decode top-secret messages sent from Cairo to Washington, D.C. by Colonel Bonner Fellers, the U.S. military attaché in Cairo, about British strengths and weaknesses. This was the real reason for Rommel's amazing early successes in the desert war. In June 1942, the British succeeded in breaking the code and persuaded the U.S. to change it under the assumption that if they could break it so could the Germans.

Black Crows

Name given by Russian civilians to the S.S. Einsatzgruppen that traveled in the rear of the advancing German Army in Russia, killing all Jews and communist commissars.

Black Day

Name given by the Japanese to August 17, 1943, when U.S.

aircraft from Port Moresby virtually destroyed all Japanese aviation on Wewak, New Guinea.

Black Napoleon

Nickname given to the Ethiopian emperor Haile Selassie.

Black Orchestra

Nickname given to the anti-Hitler conspirators within Germany during World War II. It was named "black" because the organization had connections with the Vatican and "black" to a German denoted a Catholic priest.

Black Saturday

June 13, 1942. British General Neil Ritchie ordered over 300 tanks to attack the Germans under Field Marshall Erwin Rommel whose 88mm field guns knocked out 230 tanks. Rommel was able to use information from the Black Code and turned the attack into a rout for the British. He captured Tobruk, including 33,000 men, after which he moved toward the Egyptian border.

Black Sheep

Nickname of the members of the VMF-214 under command of U.S. Marine Corps Major Gregory (Pappy) Boyington in the Pacific.

Black Shirts

Name given to Italian dictator Benito Mussolini's organization by which he strongarmed his way into Italian politics. They wore black shirts and were the equivalent of Hitler's Brown Shirts.

Black Thursday

Nickname given to the third day of the Battle of Britain, August 15, 1940, when a sudden improvement in the weather over England allowed the Luftwaffe to launch over 2,000 aircraft of all types against the British.

Black Thursday

Name given to the October 14, 1943, daylight bombing mission of the Eighth Army Air Force against Schweinfurt, Germany. Of 220 bombers in the attack, sixty were shot down and sixteen others were so severely damaged, they were beyond repair. It was the largest percentage of aircraft lost on a single mission by the U.S. in World War II.

Black Wednesday

Name given to September 28, 1938, which marked the height of the feeling of impending doom that permeated all the capitals of Europe as a result of Hitler's apparent determination to go to war over Czechoslovakia.

Black Widow

Name of the U.S. P61 nightfighter, which was the largest and most powerful fighter aircraft of World War II. It was designed and built by John K. Northrop.

Blair, Clay, Jr. (1925–)

American author. He served in the U.S. Navy during World War II on the submarine U.S.S. *Guardfish*.

Blakeslee, Donald (1915–)

American ace who served with the 4th Fighter Group of the Eighth Army Air Force. He had been a member of the 133rd Eagle Squadron of the British Royal Air Force prior to U.S. entry into the war. Blakeslee is credited with shooting down fifteen enemy aircraft but would not paint kill marks on his aircraft (P47) like other aces. He wouldn't even give his airplane a name, apparently believing this would bring him bad luck.

Blamey, Sir Thomas (1884–1951)

Australian general who commanded all Australian forces under General Douglas MacArthur during World War II.

Blanchfield, Florence A. (1884–)

U.S. Army colonel and head of the Army Nurse Corps. She was one of the only two female colonels in the U.S. Army during World War II. The other was Oveta Culp Hobby, the head of the Women's Army Corps.

Blaschke, Hugo Johannes

Hitler's personal dentist. He attended dental school at the University of Pennsylvania and the Royal Dental Hospital in London. Blaschke also treated Reichsmarschall Hermann Goering.

Blaskowitz, Johannes (1883–1948)

German general and commander of Holland. During the Polish campaign, he was relieved of command by Hitler because he opposed the exterminations of the S.S. In the last weeks of the war, he agreed to a truce and the freezing of the battle lines with the Allies, who were reluctant to launch an all-out offensive against Holland. This did not appreciably change the overall Allied or German position vis-à-vis the impending collapse of Germany. Blaskowitz committed suicide at Nuremberg prison while awaiting trial.

Blaze

Elliott Roosevelt's dog. It made news in 1945 when the 130-pound bull mastiff was given priority on a military flight from New York to Los Angeles, causing two servicemen to be bumped from the flight. One of them was Seaman First Class Leon Leroy who was en route home for his father's funeral. Elliott, the son of President Roosevelt, was up for promotion to Brigadier General and was nearly passed over due to this incident. Gene Autry was the copilot of the plane.

Bleiburg Incident

On May 14, 1945, at Bleiburg on the Austro-Yugoslavian border, nearly 50,000 Croatians attempted to surrender to the British rather than fall into the hands of Yugoslav partisans. The British turned them over to the Titoists who conducted a forced march that very few of the Croatians survived.

Blenheim

British twin-engine fighter. It was used primarily at night during the Battle of Britain, because it was slow and lacked maneuverability against German fighter aircraft. It was the plane used in the first British aerial mission of the war, when #6215, a Mark IV, took off for a photo reconnaissance of Wilhelmshaven. Piloted by Flight Officer A. McPherson, it took off forty-eight minutes after the British declaration of war, on September 3, 1939. (The civilian prototype of the Blenheim was called "Britain First.")

Blesse, Frederick

U.S. Brigadier General. He was General Dwight Eisenhower's Surgeon General who investigated the slapping of Privates C. H. Kuhl and Paul Bennett in Sicily by General George S. Patton.

Bletchley

English country town where a team of British intellectuals set up their team to decipher intercepted German secret messages. The messages were called *Enigma*, after the machine used by the Germans; the British unit was called *Ultra*.

Bligh, H.M.S.

British destroyer that was named after Vice-Admiral William Bligh of *Mutiny on the Bounty* fame.

Blitz

Name given to the part of the Battle of Britain between September 7 and November 2, 1940, when the German Luftwaffe bombed London nightly in an attempt to terrorize the British.

Blitz Bomber

Name given to the German jet, the ME-262, after it was modified to carry bombs at Hitler's express order. This greatly hindered the aircraft and made it vulnerable to Allied fighters. Hitler hoped to retaliate against England for the massive bombing campaign being conducted against Germany.

Blitzkrieg

German word meaning "lightning war" that became synonymous with the German military operations in the early days of World War II. They pioneered the use of massed armored formations to spearhead attacks, followed by infantry and other support troops to consolidate territory.

Blitzmas Cards

Name given to the Christmas cards sent out by King George VI of England in 1940. The cards showed a picture of the King and Queen posing in front of a part of Buckingham Palace that had been bombed by the Germans.

Blivet

One of General Dwight Eisenhower's favorite words. It referred to "a one-pound bag filled with two pounds of horse manure."

Blizhny

Name of Russian dictator Joseph Stalin's *dacha*, or country house, located at Kuntsevo near Moscow. It was the Russian word for "near."

Blockade Mutton

Nickname that the Germans gave to dog meat, a part of the German diet during every major crisis since the seventeenth century. As of January 1, 1940, it was legal to purchase dog meat from a butcher shop. Dachshunds were supposedly the tastiest.

von Blomberg, Werner (1878–1946)

German Army officer and first field marshall of Nazi Germany, a rank to which he was promoted in 1936. He was the Minister of Defense in Hitler's cabinet from 1933 until 1938, when he married his secretary, Erika Gruhn. Hitler had been a witness at the wedding. Shortly afterwards, a police dossier was found indicating that Erika had been a prostitute; this so infuriated Hitler that he fired Blomberg, who then retired to the Isle of Capri in the Bay of Naples. Ironically, it was Blomberg who had the Reichswehr swear allegiance to Hitler on the day that President Paul von Hindenberg died, August 2, 1934. Also it was Blomberg's son-in-law who was first given the dossier and who turned it over to Hermann Goering, thus initiating the sequence of events. The son-in-law was General Wilhelm Keitel. After the Nuremberg trials of 1946, Erika Blomberg spoke up and said that she was never a prostitute and that the file was a forgery, a fact that would have been in keeping with past Nazi practices.

Blondi

Name of Hitler's German shepherd dog. It was given to Hitler by his party secretary, Martin Bormann, after the defeat at Stalingrad in an attempt to get Hitler's mind off his troubles and make him feel better. Albert Speer, the armaments minister, said that Blondi meant more to Hitler than any human being. Just before Hitler committed suicide, Blondi was killed by Professor Werner Haase (substitute physician to Hitler) who crushed a capsule of potassium cyanide in the dog's mouth with a pair of pliers to test the effect of the cyanide.

Bloody Bucket

Nickname given to the U.S. 28th Infantry Division after it was decimated in the Battle of the Hurtgen Forest at the end of 1944.

Bloody Ridge

Nickname given to the site of a major Japanese attack on Guadalcanal on September 12, 1942. The Japanese Kawaguchi 35th Brigade assaulted positions held by Lieutenant Colonel Merritt Edson and his U.S. Marine Corps Raider Battalion. The Marines were outnumbered five to one, yet they repulsed the Japanese. Edson and Major Kenneth Bailey were both awarded the Congressional Medal of Honor.

Blucher

German Navy cruiser. *Blucher*'s first and only action in World War II was an attempt to penetrate the defenses of the Oslo fiord in Norway on April 9, 1940. It was damaged initially and later sunk by the defense fortress of Kaholm.

Blue Division

Name given to a Spanish Infantry division that was sent by dictator Francisco Franco to the Russian front in the fall of 1941 to carry on the struggle against world Communism. Franco intended this as a means of repaying Hitler for the aid Germany gave him during the Spanish Civil War. This unit fought primarily in the Leningrad area and was recalled to Spain at the end of 1943. Franco had tried to save the Jews of Germany (he was part Jewish); rebuffed by Hitler, he ordered his troops home.

Blue Ghost

Nickname of the Essex-class aircraft carrier U.S.S. *Lexington* because it was the only carrier in the U.S. Navy not painted camouflage.

Blue Goose

U.S. Marine Corps Major General Roy S. Geiger's personal aircraft. It was a PBY flown by Major Jack Crum at Guadalcanal. At one point, Crum used the aircraft to successfully attack a Japanese transport with torpedoes and was nearly shot down on the way back to Henderson Field by a Japanese Zero. Geiger nearly court-martialed Crum for destroying government property but reconsidered and awarded him the Navy Cross instead.

Blue Line

Name given to the secondary defense line of Tobruk that consisted of a continuous mine field. The outer line was called the Red Line.

Blue Monday

Nickname given to March 6, 1944, after an Allied bomber attack on Berlin. Of 660 bombers, sixty-nine were lost, along with eleven fighters. However, the Germans did not do well either, having lost half of their defending force of 160 fighters.

Blue Peter

Code signal sent out by the British Admiralty to notify all boats participating in the Dunkirk evacuation of 1940 to halt evacuation attempts and return to England.

Blue Police

Nickname given to German city policemen because of their blue uniforms.

Blue Shirts

Name of China's fascist organization, the Kuomintang, under Chiang Kai-shek.

Blum, Léon (1872–1950)

French premier before World War II. He was tried by the Vichy government at Riom in 1942 for the defeat of France, but no verdict was given. Blum was turned over to the Germans who put him in Buchenwald concentration camp. He was liberated by U.S. forces at the end of the war.

Blut und Ehre

"Blood and honor." This was the motto of the Hitler Youth and was engraved on their scout knives.

Bob Hopes

British nickname for the German V-2 rockets that struck England in the latter part of World War II. The name referred to the only response possible for civilians—to "bob down and hope for the best."

von Bock, Fedor (1885–1945)

German Field Marshall. He commanded Army Group B in the assault on the Low Countries in 1940 and Army Group Center in the invasion of Russia in 1941. While in command of the German drive into the Caucasus in July 1942, he was dismissed following a dispute with Hitler. He was killed by a strafing aircraft north of Hamburg in May 1945.

Bock's Car

Name of the B-29 that dropped the atomic bomb (designated "Fat Boy") on Nagasaki on August 9, 1945. It was flown by Major Charles Sweeney and the bombardier was Captain Kermin K. Beahan. U.S. Navy Commander Frederick L. Ashworth assembled and armed the bomb en route to Japan.

Boeing Aircraft Company

Major American aircraft manufacturer. The family originally came to the United States from a village near Hagen, Hohenlimburg, Germany. The name then was Boing.

Boeing 218

First American aircraft shot down by the Japanese. It was a demonstration fighter flown by an American, Robert Short, to show the Chinese its capabilities. He attacked a Japanese torpedo bomber from the aircraft carrier *Kaga* anchored at Shanghai on February 22, 1932. Short killed the gunner and was then attacked by three other Japanese aircraft, shot down, and killed.

von Boetticher, Friedrich

German general. He was the military and air attaché in Washington, D.C., prior to the U.S. entry into the war. He endeared himself temporarily to the German high command when he reported that a pro-German military establishment actually dominated the United States. Of all the reports he turned in, this was one he wished had been misplaced.

Bogarde, Dirk (1921–   )

British actor. He enlisted in the British Army in 1940 and served at Normandy and in battles across France and Germany. He made sketches of the D-Day landings that are now in the British War Museum in London. During the battle for the Arnhem Bridge in September 1944, Bogarde served under General Frederick Browning, whom he portrayed in the 1977 movie *A Bridge Too Far.* He was discharged in 1946 as a major.

Bogey

Navy code name for an unknown aircraft that might or might not be friendly.

Bohemian Corporal

Nickname for Hitler coined by Field Marshall Gerd von Rundstedt, who held Hitler in such contempt that he would never telephone Hitler directly, although he possessed that right by rank.

Bohlen, Charles Eustis (1904–1974)

Interpreter for Presidents Franklin D. Roosevelt and Harry S. Truman. He was in Tokyo during the Japanese attack on Pearl Harbor and was interned there for six months. After his exchange for other diplomatic prisoners, he was posted to Moscow as part of the U.S. embassy. Because of his knowledge of Russia and the Russian language, Bohlen was the official U.S. interpreter at the conferences of Teheran, Yalta, and Potsdam.

Bohr, Niels (1885–1962)

Danish physicist and Nobel Prize winner in 1922. He was allowed to continue his atomic research after the Germans invaded Denmark because the Nazis needed his expertise. The British rescued him from the Germans in 1943 and spirited him out of the country. When he was rescued, he quickly grabbed out of his refrigerator a beer bottle in which he stored his heavy water used for atomic experiments. As he went out the back door, the Germans were entering through the front door. The British flew him back to England in a Mosquito; en route, his oxygen mask fell off and he nearly died. When he arrived in England, clutching the only possession he had chosen to take, it was discovered that he had actually grabbed a bottle of beer! He worked the remainder of the war on the U.S. atomic bomb project at Los Alamos, New Mexico.

MOVIE PORTRAYAL:

A Man Called Intrepid (1979 TV miniseries), by Larry Reynolds

Boldt, Gerhardt (1918–　　)

German General Staff Officer. He was General Heinz Guderian's adjutant and won the Knight's Cross in Russia. He helped destroy the Soviet General Andrei Vlasov's unit on the Volkov front in 1941.

MOVIE PORTRAYAL:

Hitler: The Last Ten Days (1973), by Kenneth Colley

Bolero Plan
Code name for the invasion of the continent of Europe projected in 1942. It was later changed to "Operation Overlord."

Bomb Alley
Nickname given to the highway between London and Dover during the Blitz of 1940. It was so named because German bombers jettisoned their bombs along this route on their return flights to France. The name was also applied in 1944 to the flight route of the V-1s aimed at London. They often went down and exploded before reaching their target.

Bomber Offensive
Name given to the Allied aerial assault on Germany that lasted throughout the war. It has been a controversial subject since the results often did not justify the cost. In the first year of mass bombing there were more Allied airmen lost than there were German casualties.

Bonesteel, Charles H. (1909–)
U.S. Army colonel. While stationed at the Pentagon during the closing days of World War II, he arbitrarily selected the 38th parallel as the dividing line between U.S. occupation forces and Soviet occupation forces in Korea to facilitate the surrender of the Japanese forces. This decision was probably one of the most important made in terms of its consequences for the Cold War. Bonesteel was a former Rhodes scholar and his father was a major general during World War II.

Bong, Richard I. (1920–1945)
U.S. Army Air Force major. He was the top-scoring American ace of all time, with forty Japanese aircraft to his credit. Bong flew a P-38 named *Marge* and was awarded the Congressional Medal of Honor by General Douglas MacArthur. He was killed while test flying a P-80 jet fighter for Lockheed Aviation Company on August 6, 1945, the same day that the atomic bomb was dropped on Hiroshima.

Bonhoeffer, Dietrich (1907–1945)
German evangelical theologian. He was one of the few German clerics who actively opposed the Nazis and their ruthless disregard of morality. For his anti-Hitler stance, he was arrested by the Gestapo and imprisoned in Flossenburg concentration camp in Bavaria, where he was executed just prior to its capture by the Americans in 1945.

Bon Homme Richard, U.S.S. (CV-31)

U.S. Navy aircraft carrier. It was commissioned in November 1944, in time for the invasion of Okinawa and the occupation of Japan. Two of the men who served aboard her were later known for quite different talents, comedians Shecky Greene and Jonathan Winters.

Bonnier de la Chappille, Fernand (1922–1942)

Twenty-year-old Frenchman who assassinated Admiral Jean Darlan on Christmas Eve, 1942. Darlan agreed to join the Allies after the invasion of North Africa on November 8, 1942, although he had been actively pro-Axis. The Allied high command was highly criticized for accepting Darlan, who became an embarrassment to General Dwight Eisenhower and to top-level British government officials. Bonnier had been in training with the British SOE school of Massingham at Ain Taya, Algiers, to become a secret agent. He solved an embarrassing dilemma for the Allies and it was not known if he acted on other than French patriotic motives, since he was captured, tried, and executed within a brief forty hours after the assassination.

Bonzano, Mario

Italian colonel and fighter pilot. He was the most successful Italian pilot of the Spanish Civil War, with fifteen enemy aircraft to his credit.

Booker T. Washington, S.S.

10,500-ton Liberty ship launched on September 29, 1940, at Wilmington, Delaware. It was the first U.S. merchant ship to bear the name of a black, the first ship to be christened by a black (Marian Anderson), and the first ship to be commanded by a black, Captain Hugh Mulzac.

Books presaging World War II

Claire Chennault	*The Role of Pursuit Aviation* (1935)
Charles de Gaulle	*The Army of the Future* (1932)
Giulio Douhet	*Command of the Air* (1921)
John F. C. Fuller	*Field Service Regulations* (1933)
Heinz Guderian	*Achtung Panzer* (1936)
Adolf Hitler	*Mein Kampf* (1925)
Basil Liddell-Hart	*Infantry Training Manual* (1920)
Erwin Rommel	*Infantry Attacks* (1937)

Boone, Richard (1917–1981)

Hollywood actor. He served for three and a half years during

World War II as a tail gunner on U.S. Navy torpedo planes and was stationed aboard the ships U.S.S. *Intrepid,* U.S.S. *Enterprise,* and the U.S.S. *Hancock* in the Pacific.

Borghese, Junio Valerio (1906–1974)

Italian prince. He commanded the 10th Light Flotilla, a special Italian navy unit that conducted frogmen and midget submarine attacks on British shipping. He planned several missions against ships at anchor in Gibraltar and Alexandria harbors. In one attack, his men damaged the H.M.S. *Queen Elizabeth* and H.M.S. *Valiant*. He later collaborated with the Germans against Italian partisans and, because of his ruthlessness, was known as the Black Prince. He was planning an attack on New York harbor when Italy surrendered.

Borgnine, Ernest (1917–)

Academy Award–winning actor (Best Actor for the 1955 movie *Marty*). After high school in 1935, he enlisted in the U.S. Navy and served initially on board the U.S.S. *Lamberton* as an apprentice seaman. With the outbreak of World War II, he became a gunner's mate aboard a destroyer. After the war, he attended drama school on his GI Bill.

Boris III, King (1894–1943)

Bulgarian ruler who was pro-German. He apparently attempted to protect the Jews in Bulgaria, which did not ingratiate him to his Axis partners. He died in 1943 under mysterious circumstances. It is fairly widely believed that German intelligence agents killed him.

Bor-Komorowski, Tadeusz (1895–1966)

Polish commander of the underground army opposing the Germans during World War II. He led the ill-fated Warsaw uprising in August 1944 and was imprisoned in Colditz Castle after the suppression of that revolt. He was released by the Americans and moved to London, where he remained in exile until his death rather than live in Communist Poland.

Bormann, Albrecht

Brother of Hitler's party secretary Martin Bormann. Albrecht was one of Hitler's personal adjutants and today lives in Munich, Germany, where he is a businessman.

Bormann, Martin (1900–1945)

Nazi party secretary, 1940–1945. He joined the Nazi party in 1927 and became Rudolph Hess's assistant. After Hess flew to England in 1941, he took over the office of party secretary and increased his power throughout the war by determining who got to see Hitler. Bormann supposedly was killed May 1, 1945, while escaping from Hitler's command bunker in Berlin. However, he was tried at Nuremberg and sentenced to death *in absentia*. The West German government declared him officially dead in April 1973.

MOVIE PORTRAYALS:
Hitler (1962), by G. Stanley Jones
Hitler: The Last Ten Days (1973), by Mark Kingston
The Bunker (1981 TV movie), by Michael Lonsdale
Inside the Third Reich (1982 ABC-TV miniseries), by Derek Newark

Bosch Fontein

Name of the Dutch ship that transported the third contingent of the American Volunteer Group, more commonly known as the Flying Tigers, from San Francisco to Burma in 1941. Gregory "Pappy" Boyington was one of those on board.

Bose, Subhas Chandra (1897–1945)

Indian nationalist leader. During World War II, he volunteered to aid the Nazis in establishing the Free Indian Legion, consisting of Indian military personnel who had fought with the British Army and who were taken prisoner by the Germans. Their objective was to overthrow British rule of India and establish an independent country. After the Japanese entered the war, he joined them again to organize prisoners of war for a free India. He was killed in 1945 in an airplane crash on Formosa.

Bosnia

Name of the first British merchant ship sunk in World War II. It was torpedoed on September 5, 1939, near Scotland.

Bostrom, Frank P.

U.S. Army Air Force lieutenant who, as a B-17 pilot, flew General Douglas MacArthur from the Philippines to Australia in 1942. He was piloting an unarmed B-17 and about to land in Hawaii, when the Japanese attacked Pearl Harbor on December 7, 1941. Bostrom set the plane down in a golf course since all the airfields were under attack.

Bouncing Betty

Nickname given to a German antipersonnel mine. It was filled with steel pellets and had three prongs that protruded above ground level. When the prongs were disturbed, either directly or by a trip wire, it was shot about four feet into the air where it exploded and hurled the pellets for a radius of fifty feet. The theory behind it was that a wounded soldier required four other people to carry him off the battlefield, whereas a larger charge would have killed him and the rest would continue to attack.

Bourke-White, Margaret (1904–1971)

Photographer for *Life* magazine. She did the cover photographs for the first covers of *Life* and *Fortune* magazines and was the first woman accredited to the U.S. Army Air Force. Miss Bourke-White was on board the S.S. *Strathallan*, along with General Dwight Eisenhower's secretary Kay Summersby, when it was torpedoed off North Africa in 1942. She also photographed Buchenwald concentration camp while attached to General George S. Patton's Third Army in the closing days of the war.

MOVIE PORTRAYAL:
Gandhi (1981), by Candice Bergen

Bowlly, Al (1898–1941)

Popular singer of the 1930's. He recorded with a number of bands, including Ray Noble. On April 17, 1941, he was killed by a German bomb while in London.

Boyce, Westray Battle (1901–   )

U.S. Women's Army Corps lieutenant colonel. She was the first woman to receive the Legion of Merit medal. Miss Boyce received the award on September 22, 1944, for service in North Africa, August 12, 1943 to August 8, 1944. She became the head of the Women's Army Corps in 1945, replacing Colonel Oveta Culp Hobby.

Boyer, Charles (1899–1978)

French actor. At the outbreak of World War II, he enlisted in the French army in the 37th Artillery. He was released from duty in 1940 and was sent to the United States as a goodwill ambassador. Boyer was an ardent supporter of General Charles de Gaulle.

Boyes, H.

British rear admiral. He was the naval attaché at the British embassy in Norway. Boyes was assigned the code *MA-2* as an operative for British intelligence and sent important data about German rocket testing conducted at Peenemunde prior to World War II.

Boyington, Gregory "Pappy" (1912–   )

U.S. Marine Corps major. He was a member of the original

Flying Tigers, the American Volunteer Group under General Claire Chennault. As a fighter pilot with the First Pursuit Squadron, he shot down six Japanese aircraft and, due to differences of opinion, was given a "dishonorable discharge" from the AVG. He traveled back to the United States, rejoined the Marine Corps, and was sent to the Pacific where he commanded VMF214, known as the *Black Sheep*. Boyington is officially credited with downing twenty-eight Japanese aircraft, winning the Congressional Medal of Honor before he too was shot down. It was assumed at the time that he was dead and a number of newspapers printed obituaries on him. Instead he was a prisoner of war at Ofuna POW Camp for twenty months until the end of the war. He narrated the 1960 TV series "Danger Zone."

TV PORTRAYAL:
"Baa Baa Black Sheep"—later retitled "Black Sheep Squadron" (TV series), by Robert Conrad

Boy Scouts

British Boy Scouts were included on a special extermination list of the S.S. to be implemented after the German conquest of England. Hitler believed the Boy Scouts to be an arm of British intelligence. He probably arrived at this conclusion because the founder of the Boy Scouts, Lieutenant General R.S.S. Baden-Powell, was an inspector general of British cavalry units prior to World War I. He traveled throughout Germany, Algeria, and Tunisia disguised as a butterfly collector, carefully sketching all fortifications he encountered for British intelligence.

Bradbury, Ray (1920–)

American science fiction writer. During World War II, he wrote radio commercials for the war effort.

Bradley, Omar Nelson (1893–1981)

U.S. Army general. He graduated from West Point in 1915 and was a classmate of General Dwight D. Eisenhower. Bradley began World War II as a division commander and ended by commanding four armies. His command gave the final knockout to the Afrika Korps in three weeks, went through Sicily in record time, pushed the Germans out of France in less than a month, fought at the Battle of the Bulge, captured the Remagen bridge, and met the Russians on the Elbe River. He was rated as the best Allied general of World War II by both Ernie Pyle and Richard Tregaskis.

Movie portrayals:
The Longest Day (1962), by Nicholas Stuart
Is Paris Burning? (1966), by Glenn Ford
Patton (1970), by Karl Malden*
MacArthur (1977), by Fred Stuthman
Ike (1979 TV miniseries), by Richard T. Herd

Brady, Pat (1914–1972)
Hollywood actor and sidekick of Roy Rogers. He was awarded two Purple Hearts for wounds received in France.

Braemer, Fred
U.S. Army Air Force Bombardier. He was on board Lieutenant Colonel Jimmy Doolittle's B-25 during the April 18, 1942, Tokyo raid. Braemer released the first bomb ever to be dropped on Japan.

Brain of the Army
Nickname given to General Mark Clark's Chief of Staff in World War II, Alfred M. Gruenther, due to his extraordinary staff abilities.

Brain Trust
Nickname given to a group of personal advisors to President Franklin D. Roosevelt in World War II. Some of the members were Adolph Besle, Francis Biddle, Tom Corcoran, Ernst Cuneo, Morris Ernst, Harry Hopkins, Lowell Mellet, David Niles, and Robert Sherwood.

Brand, Joel (1906–1964)
Hungarian Jew. He was selected as an emissary for Adolf Eichmann to arrange a trade with the Allies of a million Jews for ten thousand trucks. Brand was received with skepticism by the Allies and imprisoned by the British in the Middle East. Nothing came of the scheme.

Brand, Max
(see Frederick Faust)

Brand, Neville (1920–   )
Hollywood actor. He was in the U.S. Army during World War II and is listed as the fourth most decorated U.S. soldier of the war.

Brandenburg
Name of one of Hitler's personal armored trains. The other was *Amerika*.

---

*Bradley received ten percent of the gross of the movie *Patton* for permitting Karl Malden to portray him.

Brandenburg Unit

Secret group of Admiral Wilhelm Canaris's Abwehr, the German intelligence service in World War II. The members were both paratroopers and language experts who specialized in infiltrating enemy lines, usually wearing enemy uniforms and carrying enemy equipment. They were employed to capture bridges in the opening days of the invasion of Russia in June 1941. The Brandenburgers were also parachuted well behind Russian lines to sabotage transportation networks and serve as undercover agents.

Brandt, Willy (1913–)

German chancellor and Nobel Peace Prize winner. He was a Social Democrat prior to the Nazi seizure of power and was forced to flee to Norway to escape the Gestapo. Brandt changed his name from Karl Frahan to Willy Brandt and worked as a reporter until the Germans invaded Norway. He then fled to Sweden where he spent the remainder of the war.

von Brauchitsch, Heinrich (1881–1948)

German field marshall. He was the Commander in Chief of the German Army from 1938 to 1941 and commanded the invasion of the Sudetenland, as well as the invasion of Poland. He attempted to talk Hitler out of invading the West because he felt that the British would be too tenacious a foe. Brauchitsch also advocated the immediate capture of Moscow rather than Hitler's favored assault against the Ukraine. Due to his differences of opinion with Hitler, he resigned his post in late 1941 and Hitler took over as Commander in Chief. (Another theory attributes his resignation to a serious heart attack he suffered just prior to his December 1941 resignation.) He spent the remainder of the war in forced retirement, dying in 1948 while awaiting trial as a war criminal.

Braun, Eva (1912–1945)

Hitler's mistress and wife in the last days of the Third Reich. She met Hitler when she was an assistant to the Nazi Party photographer, Heinrich Hoffman. Miss Braun spent the years in the shadow of Hitler in an obscure position, known only to the closest associates of Hitler and only coming to the public eye when she married Hitler on April 29, 1945. The next day she and Hitler committed suicide rather than fall into Russian hands.

MOVIE PORTRAYALS:
The Magic Face (1951), by Patricia Knight
Hitler (1962), by Maria Emo

Hitler: The Last Ten Days (1973), by Doris Kunstman
The Bunker (1981 TV movie), by Susan Blakely
Inside the Third Reich (1982 ABC-TV miniseries), by Renee Soutendijk

von Braun, Wernher (1912–1977)

German rocket scientist. He was employed by the German Army in 1932 to develop a liquid fuel rocket. In 1937, he began work at the test site of Peenemunde that led to the development of the V-2 rocket, which was launched from Holland and Germany against London and other European cities. He even envisioned a rocket that would reach New York.

MOVIE PORTRAYAL:
I Aim at the Stars (1960), by Curt Jurgens

Brazil

Only Latin American country to send troops to the European theater. Brazil declared war on the Axis powers in July 1942 and sent a 25,000-man expeditionary force to Italy. It was one of only two Latin American countries to actually fight in World War II, the other being Mexico.

Brazzi, Rossano (1916–)

Italian actor. He and his father worked for the Italian underground during World War II.

Bren Gun

British 303 machine gun widely used in World War II. It was originally developed in Czechoslovakia at Brno. The British manufactured it at Enfield; the name was a combination of *Br*no and *En*field.

Brereton, Lewis H. (1890–1967)

U.S. Army Air Force lieutenant general. He graduated from the U.S. Naval Academy in 1911, not from West Point like the majority of his contemporaries. In the 1920's, he attempted, with General Billy Mitchell, to prove that aircraft could destroy ships, and became one of the pioneers in military aviation. In 1942, he commanded a bomber force in India that struck the first blows against the Japanese in the Far East on Burma Road. In 1944, he was selected to command the First Allied Airborne Army in "Operation Market-Garden."

Bricker, John W. (1893–)

U.S. Vice-Presidential candidate in the 1944 elections with running mate Thomas Dewey for President. They were defeated.

Brinkley, David (1920–)
Television newsman. He enlisted in the U.S. Army in 1940 and spent two years as a supply sergeant at Fort Jackson, South Carolina.

Brinkmann, Helmuth
German Naval officer. He was captain of the *Prinz Eugen* when the *Bismarck* sank the British cruiser H.M.S. *Hood* in May 1941.

Brissex
Code name given to special British intelligence teams who were parachuted into occupied France prior to the D-Day landings in June 1944 to organize the French Resistance.

Brissie, Lou (1924–)
Major league baseball pitcher. In World War II, he lost part of his leg in combat. After twenty-three operations, he was fitted with an aluminum plate that allowed him to play baseball until 1953.

Britain First
Name given to the civilian prototype aircraft that became the *Blenheim*, an aircraft widely used in World War II. It was financed by Lord Rothermere of the *Daily Mail* newspaper.

British aces
Squadron Leader M. T. St. John Pattle—40
Wing Commander James (Johnny) Johnson—38
Group Captain Adolph G. Malan—35
Wing Commander Brendan E. Finucane—32
Flight Lieutenant George Beurling—31
Wing Commander Robert Tuck—29
Squadron Leader John R. D. Braham—29
Squadron Leader Neville R. Duke—28.83
Wing Commander Clive R. Caldwell—28.5
Group Captain Frank R. Carey—28.33

British aircraft privately developed and built
Blenheim
Mosquito
Spitfire
Wellington
(See individual entries)

Britt, Maurice L. (1919–)
U.S. Army captain. He was the first soldier to receive the three highest decorations that the United States awards. He was given the Silver Star in September 1943, the Congressional Medal of Honor in November 1943, and the Distinguished Service Cross in

January 1944. All medals were earned as a result of his fighting in Italy.

Broadcasters' famous opening lines

Douglas Chandler: "Misinformed, misgoverned friends and compatriots."

William Joyce: "This is Jairmany (Germany) calling."

Edward R. Murrow: "This is London."

Walter Winchell: "Good evening, Mr. and Mrs. America and all the ships at sea, let's go to press!"

Broadcasters of propaganda for the Axis

Jane Anderson (Lady Haw Haw)
Norman Baille-Stewart
Douglas Chandler (American Lord Haw Haw)
Edward L. Delaney
Constance Drexel
Charles Flicksteger
William Joyce (Lord Haw Haw)
Frederick W. Kaltenbach
Max Otto Koischwitz
George Nelson Page
Ezra Pound

The Nazis paid each a standard one thousand marks per month (about four hundred dollars).

Bronson, Charles (1921–)

Hollywood actor. Publicity information has stated that Bronson flew as a gunner in bombers during World War II. Actually, his war experiences are far from that glorious, since he drove a delivery truck in Kingman, Arizona, for the 760th Mess Squadron.

Brooke, Sir Alan F. (1883–1963)

British field marshall. He was the Chief of the Imperial General Staff throughout World War II and was the British counterpart to U.S. General George C. Marshall.

MOVIE PORTRAYALS:
Churchill and the Generals (1981 TV Movie), by Eric Porter

Brooke, Edward (1919–)

U.S. Senator from Massachusetts. During World War II, he served as an officer with the all-black 366th Combat Infantry Regiment and rose to the rank of Captain. He was awarded the Bronze Star medal and the Combat Infantry Badge.

MOVIE PORTRAYALS:
The Boston Strangler (1968), by William Marshall

Brooks, Mel (1926–)
Hollywood producer, director, actor. During World War II, he served in the U.S. Army as a combat engineer and took part in the Battle of the Bulge in December 1944, where his job was to deactivate land mines. After the battle, the Germans broadcast propaganda to U.S. troops via loudspeakers and Brooks answered by doing an Al Jolson imitation of "Toot Toot Tootsie."

Brooks, Richard
American author who served during World War II with the U.S. Marine Corps as a combat cameraman.

Brooks, Robert
U.S. Army private. He was the first black to be killed by the Japanese in land combat in World War II. Brooks was killed in March 1943 at Portlock Harbor, New Guinea, and was awarded posthumously the second highest decoration of the United States, the Distinguished Service Cross.

Brown, Francis
U.S. Navy officer. He was the only U.S. submarine commander to lose two submarines during World War II. The *S-39* was sunk in Australia early in the war when it ran aground. He was the commander of the *S-44*, which was sunk by a Japanese destroyer in the Aleutians, October 7, 1943. Only two men survived the sinking and both spent the rest of the war in a Japanese prisoner-of-war camp.

Brown, Joe E. (1892–1973)
Hollywood comedian. He was the first entertainer to travel to both the South Pacific and Alaska to visit U.S. troops during World War II. Brown was one of only two civilians to be awarded the Bronze Star medal. (The other was correspondent Ernie Pyle.) He traveled over 200,000 miles at his own expense to entertain troops and General Douglas MacArthur once told newspaper reporters "there isn't a man in uniform or out who has done more for our boys than Joe E. Brown." His son Captain Don E. Brown was killed in a plane crash in World War II.

Browning, Sir Frederick Arthur (1896–1965)
British lieutenant general. He was the creator and chief of all British airborne forces. He was a graduate of Sandhurst and participated in the 1920 Olympic games where he ran the 120-yard hurdles, rode in the horse-jumping competition, and broke his leg

bobsledding. On May 10, 1940, he was in Arras, France, and was awakened by the opening barrage of the German offensive against the West. In 1918, he was asleep on the same street when the Germans began their last great offensive of World War I and was awakened by the first artillery salvos. He was the originator of the phrase "a bridge too far" to characterize the overambitious plan of the Arnhem offensive in 1944. His wife was Daphne du Maurier, author of *Rebecca* and many other novels.

MOVIE PORTRAYAL:
A Bridge Too Far (1977), by Dirk Bogarde

Browning, Miles (1898–1954)
U.S. Navy admiral. He was chief of staff to both Admiral William F. "Bull" Halsey and Admiral Raymond Spruance and was described by naval historian Samuel Eliot Morrison as having a "slide-rule brain."

Brown Shirts
Official designator of Hitler's Nazi party members who were in the S.A. Brown shirts were selected as the uniform of the S.A. because a large number were available through German government surplus at minimal cost. They had been intended for shipment to the German army in East Africa, but with her defeat in World War I, Germany lost all her colonies.

Brubeck, Dave (1920–   )
U.S. jazz musician. He served as a member of a U.S. Army jazz band during World War II.

Bruce, David
U.S. London chief of the OSS during World War II. Later, he was a delegate to the Paris peace talks between the U.S. and North Vietnam after having been U.S. ambassador to France, Germany, Britain, and China.

Bruno
Name of the number two forward gun turret on the German battle cruiser *Scharnhorst*.

Brutus
Code name of Captain Roman Garby-Czerniawaski, who before World War II was a member of the Polish General Staff. He was recruited by the Germans as an intelligence agent to be used in England, but when he arrived there, he immediately turned himself over to British intelligence and became a double agent as part of the XX Committee which fed fictitious information back to

the Germans. During the Normandy invasion of June 1944, he was credited with duping the Germans into keeping their main forces in the Pas de Calais area by passing information to them that the Allied main thrust would be aimed at the Pas de Calais. He had been an Olympic skier before the war.

Bryant, Ben (1905–)

British Navy officer. In World War II, he commanded the submarines H.M.S. *Sealion* and H.M.S. *Safari*. Bryant developed the then unorthodox tactic of surface attack when doctrine advocated submerged approaches. He survived more patrols than any other British submarine commander and was the tallest man in the Royal Navy.

Brylcreem Boys

Nickname given to Royal Air Force personnel during World War II by the other British services because of the belief that the R.A.F. were better educated, and that those that were not pretended to be.

Brynner, Yul (1917–)

Hollywood actor and director. During World War II he worked as a French announcer and commentator for the Office of War Information broadcasting propaganda to occupied France.

BSC

British Security Coordination. It was the name of the headquarters in New York City of the British intelligence service in North America headed by Sir William Stephensen. The BSC trained American and Canadian agents to be dropped behind enemy lines and also carried on espionage against Axis agents in the Americas. Stephensen had his offices in Rockefeller Center and worked closely with William Donovan's OSS, the forerunner of the CIA.

B Service

German Navy intelligence section. It monitored the British naval radio transmissions and located the positions of the British ships. B Service was headed by Lieutenant Commander Heinz Bonatz.

Bucket Brigade

Nickname given to the system of defense along the eastern coast of the United States to protect shipping against German submarines in the early days of World War II. Basically it consisted of anything that would float, equipped with a radio to communicate the positions of German submarines.

Buccaneer

Nickname given by General Douglas MacArthur to his aviation

commander in the Southwest Pacific, General George C. Kenney. One of Kenney's units, the Fifth Army Air Force, was called the "Flying Buccaneers."

Buchenwald

Nazi extermination camp. It is categorized as the second worst camp, exceeded only by Auschwitz. Buchenwald was located near Weimar and was liberated by the American Third Army on April 11, 1945, the day before President Franklin D. Roosevelt's death. Until 1951, the Russians used it as a concentration camp for enemies of East Germany.

Buckley, William F. (1925–)

American author and lecturer. He spent from 1944 until 1946 in the U.S. Army, rising from private to second lieutenant before his discharge.

Buckmaster, Elliott

U.S. Navy officer. During World II, he was captain of the U.S.S. *Yorktown* during the Battle of the Coral Sea in 1942 and the Battle of Midway in June 1942, where the *Yorktown* was sunk.

Buckner, Simon Bolivar, Jr. (1886–1945)

U.S. Army lieutenant general. His father had been a lieutenant general in the Confederate Army and surrendered to General Ulysses S. Grant in 1865. Buckner commanded the U.S. Tenth Army on Okinawa in April 1945, where he was killed during the final phase of the battle by a Japanese artillery barrage.

Buchwald, Art (1925–)

American columnist and author. He served in the U.S. Marine Corps between 1942 and 1945, stationed at Eniwetok Island as an enlisted man with the Fourth Marine Air Wing. Buchwald joined the Marines when he was sixteen years old.

Budanova, Katya

Soviet pilot. She was the second-highest-scoring female fighter pilot in history, credited with shooting down eleven German aircraft during World War II. She flew sixty-six combat missions during the Battle of Stalingrad in 1942, becoming a Hero of the Soviet Union, for which she was awarded the Order of the Red Banner and the Order of the Patriotic War. The top-scoring female ace was Lilya Litvak.

Budenny, Semyon Mikhailovich (1883–1973)

Marshall of the Soviet Union. He was the Commander in Chief of the Southwestern Front in June 1941 who failed to halt the German offensives around Kiev. As a result, he was relieved of command, but because he was a personal friend of Joseph Stalin, was not shot but instead posted as an adviser in the Kremlin. In January 1943, he was made Commander of the Cavalry of the Soviet Army. He was awarded the Order of Lenin eight times.

Bug

Name given to a radar warning device issued to German submarines. It could detect the low-range-frequency radar pulses of the later airborne radar systems and replaced Metox, which could only receive the obsolete high ranges.

Bug

Polish river that formed the boundary between the German and Russian forces during the occupation of Poland in 1939. The Russians felt secure with the river as an obstacle protecting them, but the Germans devised a tank that could go under water. The tank was specially adapted with a schnorkel device so that it could be used in the planned invasion of England, Operation Sea Lion; it was utilized instead in the opening assault against the Russians on June 22, 1941. It could operate up to thirty feet under water, drawing air through the snorkel to feed the engines. Eighty of these tanks were used to secure bridgeheads across the Bug River and were an awesome sight to the Russians as they emerged from the river in the predawn hours.

Bulkeley, John Duncan (1911–)

U.S. Navy officer. He commanded *PT41*, which evacuated General Douglas MacArthur and his family from Corregidor to Mindanao in 1942. At the time, Bulkeley was commander of Torpedo Boat Squadron 3, which was the first U.S. Navy unit to actively engage the Japanese in the Philippines. During the D-Day landings at Normandy, June 6, 1944, he commanded Torpedo Boat Squadron 2, which worked with the OSS in infiltrating and gathering information about the Normandy area. Later, he commanded the destroyer U.S.S. *Endicott* in the Mediterranean. For his services in World War II, Bulkeley was awarded the Congressional Medal of Honor, the Navy Cross, the Army Distinguished Service Cross, the Silver Star, the Legion of Merit, and the Purple Heart.

MOVIE PORTRAYALS:

They Were Expendable (1945), by Robert Montgomery (as Lt. John Brickley)

MacArthur (1977), by William Wellman, Jr.

Bullet Decree

July 1944 order issued by Hitler calling for all saboteurs to be executed as soon as captured and suspects turned over to the security branch of the S.S.

Bullfight Brandy

Nickname given to a drink concocted by members of Merrill's Marauders after they were withdrawn from jungle fighting in Burma in 1944. Anyone who drank it became virtually uncontrollable, probably due to one of the major ingredients—marijuana.

Bullitt, William (1891–1967)

U.S. ambassador to France, 1936–1941. In 1914, he witnessed the first air raid on Paris by the Germans of World War I. In 1940, he again witnessed the first German air attack against Paris, this time of World War II. He served as the first U.S. ambassador to the USSR from 1933 to 1936.

Bulovka Hospital

Medical facility in Prague, Czechoslovakia, where Reinhard Heydrich was taken after a British-sponsored assassination attempt in 1942. He later died from the wounds he received.

Buna

New Guinea site of a major Japanese landing on July 22, 1942, in an attempt to march overland and capture Port Moresby. General Douglas MacArthur's headquarters had been warned by codebreakers of the Japanese plans, but he did not believe the warnings. Later, the U.S. 32nd Infantry Division and the 7th Australian Division launched a counterattack on Buna, only to find the Japanese extremely well dug in. By the end of the campaign, three thousand American and Australian troops were dead and over 5,400 wounded—one of the highest casualty rates of any campaign in the Pacific in World War II. The Battles of Buna and Guadalcanal caused planners to recognize the tenacity of the Japanese and what would be the cost of head-on attacks. After this, MacArthur developed his strategy of by-passing strongly fortified areas.

Bundles for Britain

Organization set up to send supplies of a nonmilitary nature to the British populace during the first years of the war. These included blankets, clothing, and medicines.

Bundy, William P. (1917–   )

American statesman. He enlisted in 1941 in the U.S. Army and served in the Signal Corps, rising from private to the rank of major before his discharge in 1946. He was awarded the Legion of Merit medal and several British decorations.

Bunker Hill, U.S.S. (CV-17)

27,000-ton U.S. aircraft carrier. It was launched on December 7, 1942, a year to the day after the Japanese attack on Pearl Harbor. It was nicknamed the "Holiday Express" because all of the major air strikes were launched on holidays. During the battle for Okinawa in May 1945, the *Bunker Hill* was struck by two Kamikaze aircraft that nearly sank the ship. Captain George A. Seitz ordered the vessel to make a seventy-degree turn, which caused water that had been used to fight fires in the hangar deck to be dumped into the sea. This action saved the ship.

Bunyachenko, Sergei

Russian general who fought with the Germans in the German-sponsored Russian Army of Liberation (POA). This unit was made up of Russians taken as prisoners of war who decided to fight with the Germans against Communism. They wore German uniforms and were classified as traitors by the Russians and renegades by the Americans. Toward the end of the war, Bunyachenko commanded one division of the POA that came to the aid of the Czech Resistance, who were fighting the S.S. in Prague. The POA helped liberate the city on May 5, 1945. It was ironic that Prague was liberated by foreign troops, no matter how disconcerting the uniforms. At the end of the war Bunyachenko was handed over to the Soviets, who hanged him.

Burbridge, Bransome

Royal Air Force night fighter pilot. He was the highest-scoring night fighter of the British during World War II, with twenty-one aircraft shot down, in spite of the fact that he had been a conscientious objector at the beginning of the war. His radar operator was F. S. Skelton.

Burger Brau Keller

Name of the beer hall in Munich where Hitler attempted his 1923 Putsch. It was also the site of an assassination attempt on him in 1939 that killed and injured a number of his old guard. The hall is still in existence on the edge of Munich, having escaped the extensive bomb damage inflicted on the city throughout World War II.

Burger, Ernst Peter (1906–)

German spy who was landed on Long Island, New York, on June 13, 1942, on the German submarine *U202* as part of Operation Pastorius. He had been with the Nazis during the Munich beer hall Putsch of 1923, lived in America from 1927 until 1933, and was an American citizen. After returning to Germany upon Hitler's accession to power, Burger became an aide to Ernst Roehm, head of the S.A.

When Roehm was killed under Hitler's orders, Burger was imprisoned by the Gestapo for seventeen months. In 1940 he joined German Naval intelligence, the Abwehr, and was trained as an agent to infiltrate the U.S. and conduct espionage missions. After arrival in the U.S., he and one other spy, George Dasch, surrendered to the FBI and stated that they had been tortured by the Gestapo and swore to betray Hitler. Burger was tried by a military court martial and condemned to death, but the sentence was commuted to life imprisonment by President Franklin D. Roosevelt since he had voluntarily turned himself in. He was released in 1948 and deported to Germany.

Burke, Arleigh A. (1901–)

U.S. Navy captain. He commanded a destroyer flotilla in the Solomons and New Guinea through twenty-two battles of the South Pacific. Burke was nicknamed "thirty-one-knot Burke" because at one time during a night operation he ordered his destroyers at full speed through the treacherous waters of the Slot near Guadalcanal to cut off Japanese reinforcements. When asked what he thought he was doing he answered, "Thirty-one knots!" He later became Chief of Staff to Admiral Marc Mitscher.

Burnett, Chester Arthur (1910–1976)

Blues singer who sang under the name of "Howlin' Wolf." He served in the U.S. Army between 1941 and 1945, when he also entertained troops with his singing and guitar playing.

Burr, Raymond (1917–)

Hollywood actor. He served in the U.S. Navy during World War II and was discharged in 1946.

Burroughs, Edgar Rice (1875–1950)

American author and creator of "Tarzan." He was present at Pearl Harbor during the Japanese attack on December 7, 1941, and, as a civilian, helped dig slit trenches on the beaches in preparation for repelling a Japanese assault. Burroughs and his family were staying at the Niumalu Hotel. During World War II, he traveled throughout the Pacific as a war correspondent.

Burton, Richard (1925–)

British actor who served in the Royal Air Force from 1944 to 1947 as a navigator. He was sent to Canada for training just prior to V-E Day and finished on V-J Day, so he never made it to an operational combat unit.

Busch, Ernst (1885–1945)

German Field Marshall. He commanded the northern armies against Russia toward the end of World War II. Busch attempted to surrender his forces to the British but was refused. Instead, he and one army gave up to the British and the remainder had to surrender to the Russians. Busch died in a British prisoner-of-war hospital in England.

Bush, George (1924–)

U.S. Vice President. He was the youngest commissioned pilot in the U.S. Navy, having received his wings in 1942 at age eighteen. Bush served in the Pacific and flew Avengers from the aircraft carrier U.S.S. *San Jacinto*. In 1944, while attacking a Japanese radio site in Iwo Jima, he was shot down, landed in the ocean, and was rescued by the submarine U.S.S. *Finback,* a feat photographed by an amateur cameraman on board. Bush was awarded the Distinguished Flying Cross for continuing his attack on the radio site and later three air medals for other missions.

Bush, Vannevar (1890–1974)

American scientist. During World War II, he was the chief scientific coordinator for the U.S. and an adviser to President Franklin D. Roosevelt.

Busko

Name of the first German ship captured by the U.S. in World War II. It was captured by the Coast Guard cutter *Northland* under Commander Edward Smith off the coast of Greenland on September 12, 1941. The *Busko* was a weather-reporting picket ship for the German Navy with a crew of twenty men and a woman on board.

Butcher, Harry C. (1902–)

U.S. Navy lieutenant commander. Prior to World War II, he had been a vice-president of CBS Radio. During the war Butcher was personal aide to General Dwight Eisenhower.

Byrd, Charlie (1925–)

Jazz guitarist. He served in the U.S. Army Special Services as a member of a GI orchestra during World War II.

Byrd, Richard E. (1888–)

U.S. Navy Admiral and arctic explorer. He surveyed the South Pacific after the Pearl Harbor attack on December 7, 1941, in search of prospective naval bases.

Byrnes, James Francis (1879–1972)

U.S. Supreme Court Justice. In 1941, he helped gain passage of the Lend-Lease Bill allowing shipment of war supplies to England. Byrnes headed the Office of Economic Stabilization until May 1943, then took over the Office of War Mobilization until April 1945. After President Franklin D. Roosevent died, Byrnes was appointed Secretary of State by President Harry S Truman.

C

C

Code identifier for the head of the British Secret Intelligence Service MI-6. During World War II, C was Major General Sir Stewart Menzies. Traditionally the code use of the letter "C" dates back to its application to the first Director of MI-6, Sir Mansfield Cumming (see Menzies, Stewart).

C-46

U.S. Army Air Force cargo aircraft which was originally designed for rapid deployment of paratroopers. It had a door on each side for the exit of parachute troops but had one major drawback. Due to its large fuel tanks, it was quick to catch fire. General "Hap" Arnold had gambled on the aircraft and pushed production ahead of testing. The C-46 was named the *Commando*.

C-47

U.S. Army Air Force cargo aircraft built by Donald Douglas. Over ten thousand C-47's were built. The civilian version was known as the DC-3. The Japanese copied the design and their C-47 was known to U.S. Army intelligence as *Tess*. The U.S. designated the aircraft the *Skytrain* while the British called it the *Dakota*.

Cabot, Bruce (1903–1972)

Hollywood actor who played the leading male role in the 1933 movie *King Kong*. During World War II he was an intelligence officer with the Army Air Force and served in North Africa, Sicily, and Italy.

Cactus

Code name used by the Allies for Guadalcanal.

Cactus Airforce

Name given to the U.S. fighter aircraft stationed on Henderson Field, Guadalcanal. U.S. Marine Corps Captain John L. Smith shot down the first Japanese aircraft on August 21, 1942.

Caen

French city in Normandy that was scheduled to be captured by Field Marshall Bernard Montgomery by June 7, 1944—i.e., within twenty-four hours after the D-Day landings of June 6, 1944. Montgomery took more than a month to cross the eight miles to the city with British casualties exceeding the total number of troops estimated by the British General Staff as necessary for the entire drive to Berlin.

Caen, Herb

Author and columnist for the *San Francisco Chronicle* who coined the word "beatnik." He was a pilot during World War II in Europe.

Caesar

Name of the rear turret of the German battle cruiser *Scharnhorst*. The forward turrets were *Anton* and *Bruno*.

Caesar

Name of Reichsmarschall Hermann Goering's pet lion cub.

Caesar, Sid (1922–   )

Hollywood comedian. He enlisted in the U.S. Coast Guard November 5, 1942 and was assigned guard duty at the Brooklyn Pier. He was discharged on December 10, 1945.

Caldwell, C. R.

Royal Australian Air Force wing commander who shot down 28.5 aircraft during World War II. He was the leading ace of Australia.

California, U.S.S.

U.S. Navy battleship sunk at Pearl Harbor on December 7, 1941, salvaged to fight the Japanese at the Battle of Leyte Gulf on October 20, 1944.

Callaghan, Daniel I. (1890–1942)

U.S. Navy Rear Admiral. He was naval aide to President Franklin D. Roosevelt from 1938 to 1941 and was a personal friend of FDR. Callaghan, who was on the cruiser U.S.S. *San Francisco* during the Battle of Guadalcanal November 12–17, 1942, was killed on the bridge. He was awarded the Congressional Medal of Honor posthumously.

CAMCO

Central Aircraft Manufacturing Corporation. It was the parent company that served as liaison between the Flying Tigers and the Chinese government during World War II. CAMCO's vice-president was Richard T. Aldworth, a former World War I pilot.

Camm, Sydney (1893–1966)

British aircraft designer. He was responsible for the development of the Hurricane fighter, which first flew on November 6, 1935, and the Typhoon fighter.

Campbell, Kenneth (–1941)

Royal Air Force flight officer. He made the first successful R.A.F. torpedo attack on a major target of World War II, when on April 6, 1941, he torpedoed the German cruiser *Gneisenau* at Brest, France. Campbell was posthumously awarded Britain's highest decoration for valor, the Victoria Cross, for this attack.

Campbeltown, H.M.S.

Former U.S. Navy destroyer, the U.S.S. *Buchanan*, and one of the fifty destroyers given to Britain in 1941. The British loaded it with five tons of explosives, strengthened the bow, and rammed it at full speed into the docks at St. Nazaire on March 28, 1942. The ship struck with such impact that she penetrated the dry dock as far as her bridge before she blew up and put the docks out of action for the remainder of World War II.

Camp Upton

U.S. Army camp where composer Irving Berlin was stationed during both World War I and World War II in order to produce his musicals.

CAM Ship

Catapult Aircraft Merchant. Merchant ship fitted with a catapult to launch a Hurricane fighter to attack German reconnaissance aircraft seeking the Murmansk convoys.

Canaris, Wilhelm (1887–1945)

German Navy Admiral and head of the German secret service, the Abwehr, from 1935 to 1943. He began his career in World War I on the cruiser *Dresden*, which was scuttled off Chile. He made his way back to Germany and joined the intelligence service until 1917, when he became a submarine commander credited with sinking seventeen ships in the Mediterranean. Canaris was a monarchist and was opposed to Hitler and the Nazis. He was horrified with Nazi excesses and began to use his position to plot against Hitler. He helped terror victims escape, falsified reports to dissuade Hitler from invading Spain, and saved the lives of French generals Henri Giraud and Maxim Weygand after Hitler ordered them killed. Canaris kept a card file of all Nazi crimes since 1933 and on all Nazi leaders. He was involved in the attempted assassination of Hitler on July 20, 1944, was arrested by the Gestapo, and imprisoned in Flossenburg concentration camp where he was executed on April 9, 1945. (At one time during World War I, Canaris was an intelligence operative in Spain. The British sent Stewart Menzies to either kill or capture Canaris but Menzies failed. Ironically, they each became the heads of their respective intelligence services during World War II.)

Movie portrayals:
Voyage of the Damned (1976), by Denholm Elliot
The Eagle Has Landed (1977), by Anthony Quayle

Canberra, U.S.S. (CL-81)
U.S. Navy cruiser. Only ship of the U.S. Navy to be named after a foreign city. It was commissioned on October 14, 1943, and was christened in memory to H.M.A.S. *Canberra*, an Australian cruiser lost at the Battle of Savo Island in 1942.

Can Do
Motto of the construction battalions, the Seabees, of the U.S. Navy.

Canned Goods
Code name for the people employed by Reinhard Heydrich to dress up in Polish uniforms and attack the German radio station at Gleiwitz on August 31, 1939. These people were then killed so that there would be no witnesses. This was intended by the S.S. to be the excuse for the invasion of Poland and the start of World War II on September 1, 1940.

Cannon, George H. (1915–1941)
U.S. Marine Corps lieutenant. He was the first Marine to win the Congressional Medal of Honor for action in World War II. It was awarded to him for his bravery on December 7, 1941, at Sand Island, Midway. He was battery commander of coastal guns on the island, where he was mortally wounded by a Japanese bombardment but refused evacuation until his men were cared for. Cannon died from loss of blood.

Can Openers
Nickname given by Royal Air Force personnel to a specially armed Hurricane fighter used to attack and knock out enemy tanks in North Africa.

Cantacuzene, Prince Constantine
Rumanian fighter pilot who shot down sixty aircraft during World War II. He was the leading ace of Rumania.

Captain Carlo
Code name used by future U.S. Senator Edward Brooke, who parachuted behind enemy lines in Italy as a liaison officer to meet with Italian partisans.

Cardboard Division
Nickname given to the section of Field Marshall Erwin Rommel's Afrika Korps that had taken Italian Fiats and put canvas and dummy guns on them to make them resemble tanks. This was done to deceive British forces at El Agheila.

Carell, Paul
German historian of World War II. His real name was Schmitt and during the war, he was the head of Joachim von Ribbentrop's intelligence service in the German Foreign Ministry.

Cargo Ship Designators (U.S. Navy)

AK	cargo ship
AKA	attack cargo ship
AKD	deep-hold cargo ship
AKS	general stores issue ship
AKV	cargo ship and aircraft ferry

Carlson, Evans F. (1896–1947)
U.S. Marine Corps officer and leader of Carlson's Raiders. He was the assistant naval attaché to China in 1937 and served as a private informant to President Franklin D. Roosevelt on conditions in China. Carlson campaigned with the Communist Chinese prior to the war and traveled with the Communist Eighth Route Army. When he formed Carlson's Raiders, he took the motto *Gung Ho* ("work together") from the Chinese Communists. The executive officer of the Raiders was Major James Roosevelt, son of the President. Carlson retired as a brigadier general.

MOVIE PORTRAYAL:
The Gallant Hours (1960), by Carleton Young

Carney, Art (1918–)
Hollywood Academy Award–winning actor. He was drafted into the U.S. Army on March 15, 1944, after being the voice of General Dwight D. Eisenhower on the radio program "Report to the Nation" the evening before. Carney was hit by shrapnel on Omaha beach during the D-Day landings. Wounded in the leg on

his first day of combat, he never got to fire a shot. As a result of the wound his right leg is now three-quarters of an inch shorter than his left leg, causing him to limp.

Carol II (1893–1953)

King of Rumania who abdicated the throne in 1940. He and his mistress, Magda Lupescu, were exiled to Spain at the request of Hitler.

Carole Lombard, S.S.

U.S. Liberty ship named after actress Carole Lombard, who was killed in an airplane crash while on a war bonds tour during World War II. Launched by actress Irene Dunne, the vessel's crew later included TV host Mike Douglas.

Carre, Mathilde (1910–)

Secret agent during World War II known as "the Cat." She worked for the French underground until captured by the Germans in 1941, who recruited her to work for them. Carre later got a chance to go back to England, where she confessed to the British what had happened. Being suspicious of her the British did not use her as an agent. After the war, Carre was returned to France for trial and sentenced to life imprisonment, but was released in 1954. (She was originally captured by Sergeant Bleicher [Colonel Henri], one of the best counteragents the Germans had in France.)

Carrier Division One (Japanese)

Designator for the two Japanese aircraft carriers *Akagi* and *Kaga*, Both took part in the Pearl Harbor attack on December 7, 1941, and both were sunk during the Battle of Midway on June 6, 1942.

Carrier Division One (Japanese)

Reconstituted aircraft carrier unit made up of the Japanese carriers *Zuikaku* and *Zuiho*. It was commanded by Vice Admiral Jisaburo Ozawa.

Carrier Division One (U.S.)

Designator of the U.S. Navy aircraft carriers U.S.S. *Lexington* (CV-2) and U.S.S. *Saratoga* (CV-3) in the early days of World War II.

Carrier Division Two (Japanese)

Unit made up of the Japanese aircraft carriers *Soryu* and *Hiryu*. Both were involved in the Pearl Harbor attack on December 7, 1941 and both were sunk during the Battle of Midway June 6, 1942.

Carrier Division Two (Japanese)

Unit composed of two merchant ships converted into aircraft

carriers, the *Hiyo* and *Junyo*. During the Battle of the Philippine Sea in June 1944, *Hiyo* was sunk and the *Junyo* was seriously damaged.

Carrier Division Two (U.S.)

Designator for the U.S. Navy aircraft carriers U.S.S. *Enterprise* (CV-6) and U.S.S. *Yorktown* (CV-5) at the outbreak of World War II.

Carrier Division Three (U.S.)

Unit made up of the aircraft carriers U.S.S. *Wasp* (CV-7) and U.S.S. *Hornet* (CV-8) during the early days of World War II.

Carrier Division Four (Japanese)

Unit made up of the aircraft carriers *Ryujo* and *Junyo*. Both were sent to Alaskan waters as part of a diversion while the remainder of the Japanese forces attacked Midway in June 1942. The *Ryujo* was sunk by aircraft from the U.S.S. *Saratoga* during the Battle of the Eastern Solomons, August 24, 1942. The *Junyo* was damaged in June 1944 during the Battle of the Philippine Sea.

Carrier Division Five (Japanese)

Unit made up of the aircraft carriers *Shokaku* and *Zuikaku*.

Pearl Harbor attack	December 1941
Battle of Coral Sea	May 1942
Battle of Eastern Solomons	August 1942
Battle of Santa Cruz	October 1942
Battle of Philippine Sea (*Skokaku* sunk)	June 1944
Battle of Leyte Gulf (*Zuikaku* sunk)	October, 1944

Carriers in the U.S. Fleet at outbreak of World War II

Langley (CV-1)*
Lexington (CV-2)
Saratoga (CV-3)
Ranger (CV-4)
Yorktown (CV-5)
Enterprise (CV-6)
Wasp (CV-7)
Hornet (CV-8)

The U.S. ended the war with over 100 aircraft carriers.

---

*Technically not a carrier, the *Langley* had most of her flight deck removed and served as an aircraft tender. She was sunk by the Japanese on February 27, 1942, off Java.

Carroll, John (1905–1979)
Hollywood actor. During World War II, he served as an Army Air Force pilot in North Africa and survived a plane crash in which he broke his back.

Carroll, Madeleine (1909–   )
British actress who gave up a Hollywood career in 1943 to join the American Red Cross as a hospital worker. She served in hospitals in Naples and Foggia, Italy. After the war, she helped concentration camp victims and was a member of the United Nations Appeal for Children to help orphans around the world. In 1942, Madeleine Carroll was voted by U.S. servicemen as the girl with whom they would most like to be marooned on an island.

Cars of wartime figures

Jeep	U.S. General Omar Bradley
Packard	U.S. General Dwight Eisenhower
Mercedes	Dr. Joseph Goebbels, German propaganda minister
Bentley	R.A.F. Air Marshall Arthur T. Harris
Mercedes	Hirohito, Emperor of Japan
Mercedes 770-K	Adolf Hitler
Mercedes	Robert Ley, German labor leader
Rolls Royce	U.S. General Douglas MacArthur
Jeep	Bill Mauldin, U.S. Army cartoonist
Rolls Royce	British Field Marshall Bernard Montgomery
Ford	Lord Louis Mountbatten
Jeep	U.S. Admiral Chester Nimitz
BMW	Albert Speer, German armaments minister

Carter, Jimmy C. (1924–   )
Thirty-ninth President of the United States. He entered Annapolis Naval Academy in 1943 and graduated fifty-ninth out of a class of 820 in 1946.

Cartland, Ronald (–1940)
First member of the British Parliament to be killed in World War II. He was the brother of romance author Barbara Cartland. Their other brother, Captain Anthony Cartland, was killed on May 21, 1940, one day before Major Ronald Cartland.

Casablanca Conference
Conference held in January 1943 between President Franklin D. Roosevelt and Prime Minister Winston Churchill to decide where the next attack was to be after the fall of North Africa. They decided on Sicily. The conference marked the first time an

American president flew in an airplane and it was where the phrase "unconditional surrender" originated. Casablanca means "white house," which caused the Germans to believe that the conference was actually held in Washington, D.C.

Casablanca Directive

Agreement reached by the British and American planners at the Casablanca Conference in January 1943. It called for round-the-clock bombing of Germany, with the British bombing by night and the Americans by day. The priority targets were

1. German submarine construction yards
2. sites of aircraft industry
3. transportation
4. oil production
5. sites of war industry

Casamento, Anthony J.

U.S. Marine Corps private who fought on Guadalcanal. He was wounded fourteen times in a Japanese assault and singlehandedly held off an entire battalion, for which he was finally awarded the Congressional Medal of Honor on September 1, 1980, by President Jimmy Carter. This is the last Medal of Honor to have been awarded for World War II.

Case Blue

Code name for Hitler's 1942 campaign to capture the Caucasus and join with Field Marshall Erwin Rommel in Persia. The offensive was concentrated against the Russian strong points of Sevastopol and Stalingrad.

Case Green

Code name of Hitler's occupation of Czechoslovakia in 1938.

Case Margarethe I

Plan by Hitler to invade Hungary if it appeared that Hungary would defect from the Axis to the Allies. It was put into effect March 19, 1944.

Case Margarethe II

Planned invasion of Rumania by German forces if she appeared to be ready to drop out of the Axis.

Case Red

Code for the German offensive across the Somme and Seine Rivers in France, June 5, 1940.

Case White

Code name for Hitler's plan to invade Poland on September 1, 1939.

Case Yellow

Code name of Hitler's planned offensive against the West on May 10, 1940.

Casiana

Philippine President Manuel Quezon's personal yacht.

Cassedy, Hiram

U.S. Navy submarine officer selected to command a Japanese submarine that had surrendered at sea at the end of World War II. He gave several swords found on board to members of his American crew in violation of specific orders against removing anything in the way of souvenirs. Admiral William F. Halsey relieved Cassedy of command, making him the only American Naval officer to be relieved of command of a Japanese submarine.

CAST

Name given to the U.S. military codebreaker unit in the Philippines in the early days of World War II. It was one of only three teams that could decipher the Japanese Purple Code and the Japanese Naval code JN-25. It was commanded by Rudolph Fabian and was based at Cavite and later Corregidor. On February 5, 1942, the first contingent was evacuated by the submarine U.S.S. *Seadragon* to Melbourne, Australia. There it continued to decode messages that informed General Douglas MacArthur of Japanese strengths and weaknesses and enabled him to take action against them. After the unit was established in Australia, the name was changed from CAST to FRUMEL. The other two decoding units were HYPO and NEGAT.

Casualty Abbreviations

AI	accidental injuries
DAI	death from accidental injuries
DD	death from disease
DOW	died of wounds received in action
KIA	killed in action
M	missing
MIA	missing in action
PWOP	pregnant without permission
SIW	self-inflicted wounds
SK	sickness
WIA	wounded in action

Cats

Figaro	Admiral Sir James F. Somerville
Jack	Prime Minister Winston S. Churchill

Cavalla, U.S.S.

U.S. submarine under Commander Herman J. Kossler that sank the Japanese aircraft carrier *Shokaku* on June 18, 1944, in the Battle of the Philippine Sea.

C Card

U.S. gas rationing card that categorized the holder as very essential to the war effort. Doctors were included in this category.

Cecil J. Doyle

Name of the first vessel to reach the survivors of the cruiser U.S.S. *Indianapolis* after it was sunk by the Japanese submarine *I-58* on July 30, 1945. The commander of the *Cecil J. Doyle* was William Graham Clayton, Jr., who became Secretary of the Navy in 1976.

Celestes

Allied code name for Chiang Kai-shek at the Cairo Conference in November, 1943.

Cellastic

Code name of a German espionage agency located in Paris. Its mission was to spy on French scientists and their discoveries in order to determine if the scientists were working on anything that was either detrimental to Germany or of possible use to their war effort.

CH

Designator of the twenty-one operational British *C*hain *H*ome radar stations. They could detect aircraft up to 120 miles away but could not pick up low-flying aircraft. These radar sites contributed greatly to the winning of the Battle of Britain by the Royal Air Force.

Chamberlain, Sir Neville (1869–1940)

British Prime Minister from 1937 to 1940. He is known for his appeasement of Hitler, which is judged to have contributed to the outbreak of World War II. In Chamberlain's defense, it has been said that he realized the sorry state of affairs in the British military and was buying time so that it could be strengthened. He resigned his post on May 10, 1940, the day Hitler invaded western Europe, and was replaced by Winston Churchill.

MOVIE PORTRAYAL:

Churchill and the Generals (1981 TV Movie), by Edward Jewesbury

Champion

Code name of the U.S. 82nd Airborne Division's message center in Normandy immediately after D-Day on June 6, 1944.

Chancellor, John (1927–)
Journalist and NBC newscaster. He joined the U.S. Army as a private in 1945 and served as a public relations specialist until his discharge in 1947.

Chandler, Douglas (1889–)
Chicago-born Nazi propaganda broadcaster during World War II. He was known as the American Lord Haw Haw and used the radio name Paul Revere. Chandler had served in the U.S. Navy during World War I and married a descendant of financier John Jay in 1924. He began each broadcast with "Misinformed, misgoverned friends and compatriots" and was sentenced by a Federal Court to life imprisonment after the war.

Chaney, James Eugene (1885–1967)
U.S. Army brigadier general. He was the first commander of the U.S. Defense Command which was created on February 26, 1940. Later, he commanded the captured island of Iwo Jima.

Channel Islands
Guernsey, Jersey, Sark, and Alderney. They were the only part of Britain occupied by the Germans during World War II. Guernsey was captured in 1940 by the crews of four transport aircraft. The occupation came to an end on May 9, 1945, when the German garrison surrendered.

Chaplin, Charlie (1889–1977)
Hollywood actor and producer. He was born on April 16, 1889, four days before Adolf Hitler, whom he satirized in the 1940 movie *The Great Dictator.* Chaplin was knighted January 1, 1975, by Queen Elizabeth II.

Chapman, Eddie (1906–1972)
British safecracker and convict who was imprisoned on the Isle of Jersey when the Germans occupied it in 1940. He immediately offered his services as a spy and was accepted and trained by the Abwehr. After training, Chapman was parachuted into England where he surrendered, agreeing to become a double agent by radioing false information back to the Germans. He was credited by the Germans for sabotaging an aircraft factory, which in fact the British camouflaged to appear destroyed. Chapman was awarded the Iron Cross for this. He also sent back false strike reports that caused the Germans to incorrectly aim their V-2 rockets. He was pardoned after the war by the British government and given the Order of the British Empire. Chapman was portrayed in the 1967 movie *Triple Cross* by Christopher Plummer.

Charlemagne Division

Name of a German Army division made up of French volunteers who joined to fight world communism. The unit was formed in the spring of 1941 as part of the Army but was transferred to the Waffen S.S. in August 1943. During Hitler's last days in the Chancellery bunker in Berlin, it was this division that guarded the outside approaches, a fact that Hitler was not pleased about. During the Battle of Berlin, they fought against the Germans of the von Seydlitz division, who were fighting under the Russian flag. Thus Frenchmen once again opposed Germans, except this time not under their respective national colors. There were few survivors.

Charlie

Designator of the beach east of Algiers assaulted in Operation Torch on November 8, 1942.

Charlie

GI term for Japanese soldiers during World War II. It was later applied to the Viet Cong in Vietnam.

Chayefsky, Sidney (Paddy) (1923–1981)

American playwright. During World War II, he served as a machine gunner with the 104th Infantry Division in Europe. Near Aachen, Germany, he stepped on a land mine and was sent to a hospital in England to recuperate. It was while hospitalized that he wrote his first musical comedy, *No Time Out For Love*.

Chenfalls, Alfred (–1943)

British look-alike of Prime Minister Winston Churchill who was aboard BOAC Flight 777, flying from Algiers to London in June 1943. The aircraft, also carrying actor Leslie Howard, was shot down over the Bay of Biscay, killing everyone on board. The British were aware that the Germans intended to shoot down the plane but did not warn anyone for fear the secret of their ability to read the German codes would be revealed.

Chennault, Claire L. (1890–1958)

U.S. Army officer. He was a pioneer of Army aviation but was medically disqualified and retired. He became an adviser to Chiang Kai-shek, for whom he set up the American Volunteer Group more commonly known as the Flying Tigers. Chennault taught his fighter pilots what were radical tactics at the time but later became common practice in World War II. It is rumored but not substantiated that Chennault shot down over forty Japanese aircraft prior to the U.S. entry into the war. If true, this would make him the top-scoring ace of the United States. When the Fourteenth Army Air Force was activated from the Flying Tigers, he was made a major general in command.

MOVIE PORTRAYAL:
God Is My Co-Pilot (1945), by Raymond Massey

Chequers

Name of Prime Minister Winston Churchill's personal residence outside London. Over the gate was the motto *Pro Patria Omnia* or "Everything for the Fatherland."

Cherbourg

French port captured on June 27, 1944. It was the first large city of France to be captured as well as the first deep-water port. It was defended by German Lieutenant General Karl von Schlieben and Admiral Walter Hennecke, who surrendered to U.S. Major General J. Lawton Collins. Cherbourg had the same problem as Singapore; its defenses all faced seaward and no contingency plan had been made for an assault from land.

Chernova, Tania

Soviet female sniper. During the Battle of Stalingrad, she killed over eighty Germans, whom she called "sticks." Miss Chernova was seriously wounded by a land mine and evacuated; otherwise her score would have been much higher.

Cherchell Beach

Rendezvous site between U.S. General Mark Clark and French General Mast to prepare for the surrender of French forces in North Africa. They went ashore on October 22, 1942, seventy-five miles east of Algiers.

Cherry stone

German code name for the V-1 rocket.

Cherry, William T., Jr.

U.S. Army Air Force captain. He was the pilot of the aircraft that went down in the Pacific on October 2, 1942, with Eddie Rickenbacker aboard. They were on an inspection tour from Hawaii and were finally rescued on November 11, 1942, six hundred miles north of Samoa.

MOVIE PORTRAYAL:
Captain Eddie (1945), by Richard Crane

Cherwell, Lord (1886–1957)

Principal scientific adviser to Prime Minister Winston Churchill. His name was Frederick Alexander Lindemann and he was credited with conceiving barrage balloons for London, airborne radar, and antimine devices for ships.

MOVIE PORTRAYAL:
Operation Crossbow (1965), by Trevor Howard

Cheshire, Leonard (1917–)

British Royal Air Force group captain. He was the British observer on board the camera plane over Nagasaki when the second atomic bomb was dropped on August 9, 1945. Cheshire had been commander of a pathfinder unit in Europe.

Chetniks

Name given to the Yugoslavian partisans led by Draga Mihailovitch. The name meant "men of the companies." Chetniks were proroyalist and therefore opposed to the Communists under Tito. The Chetniks began the war by actively fighting the Germans, but as the war progressed an unofficial truce developed, whereby the Germans left them alone and in return they did not attack the Germans.

Chevalier, Maurice (1902–1972)

French entertainer. He served in the French Army at the outbreak of World War I and was wounded and captured by the Germans. While he was in a prisoner of war camp, he forged a stamp on his military record to indicate that he was a medical corpsman, and the Germans repatriated him in 1916. Chevalier entertained U.S. troops toward the end of the war. During World War II, he entertained French prisoners of war held by the Germans in the same camp where he had been a prisoner, Alten Grabow. He lived in Vichy territory with a Jewish girlfriend, and the Germans used threats against her to get him to perform in German-occupied territory and to entertain German troops, which they then used for propaganda purposes. At the same time, Chevalier was acting as an intermediary for the Resistance, a fact that was not well known. The Germans were so successful in propagandizing his performances that Radio London announced his name on a list of collaborators. After D-Day, June 6, 1944, a group of Maquis tried to capture and kill him. German radio even announced his death at their hands, but he was able to prove his affiliation with the Resistance and was not harmed. His first performance after the liberation of Paris was with Noel Coward and Marlene Dietrich.

Chiang Kai-shek (1887–1975)

Ruler of China. He was a Methodist and had studied four years at the Military College in Tokyo, Japan. Chiang was the Supreme

Allied Commander of China. General Joseph Stilwell, his Chief of Staff, called him "the Peanut" out of contempt for his ability. His government was highly corrupt and never was a viable force in opposing the Japanese.

Chicago pianos

Nickname given to the antiaircraft pom-pom guns on board U.S. Navy ships in World War II.

Chicago, U.S.S.

U.S. Navy cruiser that was severely damaged at the Battle of Savo Island, August 9, 1942. It was commanded by Captain Howard Bode, who later committed suicide because of his inadequate performance during the battle. The *Chicago* was sunk in January 1943 in the Battle of Rennell Island.

Chicken farmer

Occupation of Heinrich Himmler before he became a member of the Nazi party. It was also the occupation taken up by Adolf Eichmann after World War II to hide from Allied search teams prior to his escape to Argentina.

Chidson, Montague Reaney (–1957)

British lieutenant colonel. He was the assistant military attaché at Ankara, Turkey, at the same time that Cicero was selling top secret military information to the Germans. As the MI-6 executive, Chidson may have been feeding Cicero material that the British really wanted the Germans to have. In 1940, he stole all of Holland's industrial diamonds to prevent them from falling into the hands of the Germans. In fact, he was going out the rear of the building as the Germans entered at the front to confiscate them. He also personally organized the escape of Queen Wilhelmina and the Dutch royal family (see Cicero).

Child, Julia (1912–)

Famous cook and television personality. During World War II, she served as a file clerk with the OSS in Washington, D.C.

Childers, Ernest

U.S. Army lieutenant. He was the first American Indian to win the Congressional Medal of Honor during World War II, receiving it as a result of action in Italy in 1943.

Chimara

Greek passenger liner. It was formerly a German hospital ship of 1,800 tons and was sunk on January 19, 1947, off Greece, by a mine left over from World War II. Three hundred ninety-three people were killed including forty Greek communist guerrillas who had been chained together in the hold of the ship and who were left to drown (see Kiangya).

Chindits

Name given to a unit organized by British General Orde Wingate. The name came from a mythical Hindu figure—the Chinthe—which was a dragonlike image carved in stone to guard the entrances to Burmese temples. The Chindits were long-range groups that penetrated deep into the Japanese interior of Burma to harass the enemy.

Chips

German shepherd dog and the only animal to win the Silver Star and Purple Heart medals for bravery during World War II. He was a mongrel member of the K-9 Korps and his handler was Private John R. Powell. Chips landed on Sicily with the 3rd Infantry Division on July 10, 1943, and singlepawedly silenced an Italian machine-gun position. Both medals were subsequently revoked due to adverse public reaction to a dog's receiving medals. Another version of the story stated that he was awarded a Distinguished Service Cross by General Lucian Truscott, which was rescinded February 3, 1944.

Chiswick

Target of the first V-2 rocket launched against Britain. It landed at 6:34 P.M. on September 8, 1944, killing a number of Britons.

Chiyoda

Japanese light aircraft carrier, which was sunk in the Battle of Leyte Gulf in October 1944. It was commanded by Captain Ellchiro Jyo who was an early advocate of Kamikaze attacks. Ironically, he went down with his ship on the very same day that the first U.S. ship was sunk by Kamikazes.

CHL

Chain Home Low radar stations. These supplemented the British Chain Home (CH) radar stations by detecting low-flying aircraft up to fifty miles away. There were thirty CHL stations operational for the Battle of Britain.

von Choltitz, Dietrich (1894–1966)

German general who surrendered Paris to the Allies without destroying the city as Hitler had ordered. He was the German officer who persuaded the Dutch commander of Rotterdam to surrender in 1940, after which the Luftwaffe erroneously bombed and destroyed a major portion of the city. He was the first German officer to invade the Low Countries, arriving on May 10, 1940, in the first JU-52 transport to land at Rotterdam, and was the commander who laid siege to and captured the Russian fortress of Sebastopol in 1942. As the Paris commander, von Choltitz was responsible to Hitler for the destruction of the city, but rather than destroy the beauty and tradition of Paris, he carefully stalled the demolition teams while negotiating with the French. He surrendered the city on August 24, 1944, to General Leclerc of the 2nd Free French Armored Division. Von Choltitz, who was portrayed in the 1966 movie *Is Paris Burning?* by Gert Frobe, died the same year that the movie premiered.

Chop Line

Name given to the 130° latitude line that was used as the divider between General Douglas MacArthur's Southwest Pacific Command and Admiral Chester Nimitz's Pacific Command.

Chou En-lai (1898–1976)

Chinese Communist leader. Chou was the official liaison officer between the Chinese Communist party and Chiang Kai-shek's Kuomintang party during World War II. He had served under Chiang at the Whampoa Military Academy in the 1920's and had saved Chiang's life when he was kidnapped in 1936 during the revolt of a local war lord known as the Sian Mutiny.

Christian X (1870–1947)

King of Denmark. He was very courageous in facing the Germans, who occupied Denmark in 1940. King Christian tried to protect his subjects from the Nazis. When the Germans ordered the Jews to wear the Star of David, he was the first to put one on himself, followed by the entire population of Denmark. He then secretly began sending the Danish Jews to Sweden, thus saving most of them. One day while riding through Copenhagen, King Christian noticed a swastika flag flying from a public building in violation of the Danish-German agreement. When ordered to take it down, a German officer said it was there on orders from Berlin and would remain. Christian replied that if the flag were not down by noon, a soldier would be sent to remove it. The German haughtily stated that the soldier would be shot if he came. King Christian then told him that he, the King of Denmark, would be that soldier. The flag came down.

Christie, Ralph Waldo (1893–)

U.S. Navy Admiral. He graduated from the Naval Academy of Annapolis in 1915 and was one of the first graduates of the newly created submarine school at New London, Connecticut. Between the wars, he was involved in torpedo research and was instrumental in the development of a magnetic torpedo. He commanded U.S. submarines in Australia during World War II and was the first Admiral to make a war patrol on a submarine, the U.S.S. *Bowfin*, on January 29, 1944.

Christman, Allen Bert (Crix) (–1942)

Artist who helped draw Milton Caniff's comic strip *Terry and the Pirates*. As a pilot with General Claire Chennault's Flying Tigers in China, Christman painted the world-famous shark mouths on the P-40 fighters. He was shot down by a Japanese fighter in January 1942 and was machine-gunned to death while hanging in his parachute after he had bailed out.

Christmas Tree

Nickname given to a board with a series of red and green lights on U.S. submarines used to indicate that all was well with the pressure hull as the sub dived.

Christmas Trees

Nickname given to marker flares used by Pathfinder units to locate bombing targets over Europe. The flares cascaded down in a shower of red and green.

Chrysler

U.S. automobile manufacturer that converted to war production and became the largest tank factory in the U.S. Chrysler was able to produce 25,507 tanks in the course of World War II.

Chuikov, Vassili I. (1900–   )

Russian general known for his defense of Stalingrad. He had been chief advisor to Chiang Kai-shek in the 1930's and had participated in the Russo-Finnish War of 1940. Chuikov took over command of the encircled Red Army at Stalingrad and turned the battle into a Russian victory. In 1945, he commanded the Soviet forces that advanced on Berlin. After the war he wrote an account of the Battle of Stalingrad entitled *The Beginning of the Road*.

Churakov, Ivan

Russian soldier who discovered Hitler's and Eva Braun's bodies outside the Chancellery building in Berlin in May 1945. He was a member of the 79th Rifle Corps of the Soviet Counter Intelligence Section which was known as *Smersh*. Smersh later was immortalized by Ian Fleming in his James Bond thrillers as 007's arch enemy.

Churchill, H.M.S.

Former U.S. destroyer rechristened the H.M.S. *Churchill* when it became part of the British Navy in August 1941. Prime Minister Winston Churchill paid his namesake a visit and promised the crew to return if it ever sank a German submarine.

Churchill, John S.

Brother to Winston Churchill. John successfully remained out of the limelight during World War II.

Churchill, Mary

Daughter of Winston Churchill. She was a member of the ATS (Auxiliary Territorial Service), the women's branch of the British Army during World War II.

Churchill, Peter Morland (1909–1972)

British Army captain and no relation to Winston Churchill. As part of SOE, he helped to organize the Resistance movement in France during the German occupation and parachuted behind enemy lines several times. He was finally captured by the Germans in 1943 and spent the rest of the war in a concentration camp. The Germans did not kill him as they normally would have because they thought he was related to Winston Churchill.

Churchill, Randolph (1911–1968)

British Army major and only son of Winston Churchill. Randolph served in North Africa as an intelligence officer and was later parachuted into Yugoslavia to act as a liaison officer with Tito's guerrillas. In 1958, he appeared on the American TV quiz show "Twenty-One." He missed the first question on British history when he not could identify the origin of the word "boycott."

Churchill, Sarah Oliver (1914–)

Daughter and aide to Winston Churchill. She served as a photo reconnaissance interpreter with the Women's Auxiliary Air Force and worked on the planning for the North African invasion with Constance Babington-Smith. Sarah was present at the Cairo, Teheran, and Yalta Conferences as an aide to her father. After the war, she became an actress, playing opposite Fred Astaire in the 1951 film *Royal Wedding*.

Churchill, Winston S. (1874–1965)

British Prime Minister. He began his career as a correspondent in the Boer War, where he was captured by Louis Botha, who later became the first prime minister of the Union of South Africa. He held nearly every post in the British government at one time or another. He was:

Undersecretary to the Colonies	(1906)
Privy Councillor	(1907)

President of the Board of Trade	(1908–10)
Home Secretary	(1910–11)
First Lord of the Admiralty	(1911)
Chancellor of the Duchy of Lancaster	(1915)
Minister of Munitions	(1917)
Secretary of State for War and Air	(1919)
Undersecretary of the Colonies	(1921)
Chancellor of the Exchequer	(1924–29)
First Lord of the Admiralty	(1939)
Chairman of the Armed Services Committee	(1940)
Prime Minister	(1940–45)
Minister of Defense	(1940)
First Lord of the Treasury	(1940)
Prime Minister	(1951–55)

Churchill was famous for his cigar smoking; he consumed three cigars per hour for eighteen of every twenty-four hours. When he didn't smoke, he ate. Wherever he traveled, he carried a number of different military uniforms so that when he met anyone, he could do so in the same uniform as his host.

MOVIE PORTRAYALS:
Mission to Moscow (1943), by Dudley Field Malone
The Finest Hours (1964), by Patrick Wymark (voice only)
A King's Story (1965), by Patrick Wymark (voice only)
Operation Crossbow (1965), by Patrick Wymark
The Man Who Never Was (1965), by Peter Sellers (voice only)
Young Winston (1972), by Simon Ward
"Hallmark Hall of Fame" (1974 TV movie), by Richard Burton
Truman at Potsdam (1976 TV movie), by John Houseman
Eleanor and Franklin (1977 TV movie), by Arthur Gould-Porter
A Man Called Intrepid (1979 TV miniseries), by Nigel Stock
Ike (1979 TV miniseries), by Wensley Pithey
FDR: The Last Year (1980 TV movie), by Wensley Pithey
The Wilderness Years (1981 TV movie), by Robert Hardy
Churchill and the Generals (1981 TV movie), by Timothy West

His imitator on the BBC during World War II was Norman Shelley.

Chu Teh (1886–1976)
Chinese Commander in Chief of the Communist Army. He was the only Chinese Communist general that Chaing Kai-shek was

unable to defeat in the long civil war between the Nationalists and the Communists.

Chuyo

Japanese aircraft carrier of 20,000 tons. It was sunk on December 4, 1943, by the submarine U.S.S. *Sailfish* (formerly U.S.S. *Squalus*) and was the first Japanese carrier sunk by a U.S. submarine.

Ciano, Count Galeazzo (1903–1944)

Italian Foreign Minister and son-in-law of Benito Mussolini. He was a bomber pilot during the Ethiopian war and is said both to have dropped the first bombs of the war and to have been the first Italian to enter Addis Ababa. As Foreign Minister, Ciano was mistrustful of the Germans, preferring that Italy not get involved with them. The OSS in Bern, Switzerland, transmitted information via a U.S. State Department code about the Italian political situation that included names of Fascists who were disenchanted; Ciano was one of the names on this list. The Germans had previously broken the code and gave this information to Mussolini, along with tapes of indiscretions made by Ciano in the S.S.-run Kitty Salon, a brothel in Berlin. Ciano was shot by the Fascists under German pressure on January 11, 1944.

Cicero

Code name of Elyesa Bazna, personal valet to the British ambassador to Turkey, Sir Hughe Knatchbull-Hugessen. Cicero copied important dispatches from the embassy safe and sold them to the Germans. Some of this information was used by the German ambassador Franz von Papen to convince the Turks not to enter the war on the side of the Allies (see Elyesa Bazna).

MOVIE PORTRAYAL:
*Five Fingers** (1952), by James Mason

Cigar Smokers of World War II Era

Jack Benny	comedian
George Burns	comedian
Harry Butcher	naval aide to Eisenhower
Dietrich von Choltitz	German general who surrendered Paris
Winston Churchill	Prime Minister of Britain
Charles de Gaulle	French General, Commander of Free France

*In the film, the combination to the German safe was 1-30-33, the date that Hitler came to power.

Ira C. Eaker	U.S. Army Air Force General
Joe Foss	U.S. Marine Corps fighter ace
Adolf Galland	Luftwaffe fighter ace
Heinrich Himmler	Head of German S.S.
Edmund Ironsides	British Field Marshall
Wilhelm Keitel	German Field Marshall
Curtis Lemay	U.S. Army Air Force General
Robert Ley	Nazi labor leader
George S. Patton	U.S. Army General
Babe Ruth	U.S. baseball player
David Shoup	U.S. Marine Corps Colonel
Holland Smith	U.S. Marine Corps General

Ciliax, Otto (1891–1964)

German admiral. He was in charge of the break-out from Brest of the cruisers *Scharnhorst, Gneisenau,* and *Prinz Eugen* in 1941. In 1942, Ciliax was Commander in Chief of battleships (the *Tirpitz*) at Trondheim in Norway.

CINCUS

Pronounced "sink-us." It was the abbreviation for the Commander in Chief of the U.S. fleet. When Ernest J. King was appointed to the post at the end of 1941 his first official action was to change the abbreviation to COMINCH.

Circus

Name given to the attempts by Royal Air Force crews to get the Luftwaffe aircraft into air battles over the continent. The technique called for a small force of bombers to attack German installations while a large force of fighters protected the bombers. The idea was for the bombers to lure German fighter aircraft in close so that the R.A.F. fighters could attack. The first such mission was conducted on January 10, 1941, when six Blenheim bombers attacked the Pas de Calais with a covering force of six squadrons of Spitfires and Hurricanes. Only two ME109's were shot down.

Clan MacAlister

6,900-ton cargo ship from Glasgow, Scotland. It was the largest merchant vessel used during the evacuation of Dunkirk in May 1940. It was sunk off the beach on May 29, 1940, and settled evenly to the bottom in shallow water with the decks above water. It served thereafter as an unintentional decoy target for the German Stukas. The British Admiralty later estimated the *Clan MacAlister* saved over a million pounds (sterling) worth of shipping.

Clark, Bradley

Older brother of TV and music producer Dick Clark who was killed in action during World War II.

Clark Field

U.S. Army Air Force base near Manila where the Japanese destroyed a majority of General Douglas MacArthur's aircraft on December 8, 1941.

Clark, Golland L., Jr.

U.S. Marine Corps captain. He was ordered to serve as the instrument for the surrender of Corregidor to Japanese Lieutenant General Masaharu Homma. Clark later died on board a Japanese prisoner-of-war ship, the *Enoura Maru* at Formosa, January 9, 1945.

Clark, Mark (1896–   )

U.S. Army lieutenant general. He was born in Madison Barracks, New York, and graduated from West Point in 1917. In October 1942, Clark slipped ashore in French North Africa to negotiate terms with the French prior to the invasion of North Africa in Operation Torch, for which he was awarded the Distinguished Service Medal. He later commanded the U.S. Fifth Army in the Italian campaign. Clark was very publicity-conscious and had his own personal photographer. Anyone else taking pictures of him could only do so of his left side (his best side). Prime Minister Winston Churchill dubbed him the American Eagle because of his prominent nose.

MOVIE PORTRAYALS:
The Devil's Brigade (1968), by Michael Rennie
Ike (1979 TV movie), by William Schallert

Clark, Arthur C. (1917–   )

Author of science and science fiction. He served in the Royal Air Force from 1941 to 1946 as a radar instructor. After receiving a commission, Clark was in charge of the first GCA (ground control approach) radar unit.

Clary, Robert

Actor who played a French prisoner of war in the TV series "Hogan's Heroes." He actually spent three years in a German concentration camp during World War II. He still has his camp number, A5714, tatooed on his left forearm.

Class 26

U.S. Army Air Force classification for aircraft that were so badly damaged on a mission that they were relegated to the scrap pile.

Clavell, James (1924–)

Author who during World War II served as a captain with the British Royal Artillery. He was captured by the Japanese and spent half the war in Changi prison camp. In 1963, he wrote the screenplay for the movie *The Great Escape*, and in 1967, directed *To Sir With Love*. Clavell is best known for writing the novels *King Rat*, *Tai Pan*, *Shogun*, and *Noble House*.

Clement

British freighter weighing 5,051 tons. It was the first ship sunk by the *Graf Spee* on September 30, 1939.

Clifton-James, E. (1897–)

British actor who served in the British Army Pay Corps as a lieutenant during World War II. In 1944, he was contacted and asked by Colonel David Niven to serve as a double for Field Marshall Bernard Montgomery. This was part of Operation Hambone, an attempt to deceive the Germans into believing that the D-Day assault would occur elsewhere than at Normandy. Clifton-James flew to Gibraltar and North Africa, where, it was rumored, he was spotted smoking and drinking, neither of which the authentic Montgomery did. Clifton-James was then secretly sent back to England and given back his old boring job. He portrayed himself in the 1958 movie *I Was Monty's Double*.

Climb Mt. Niitaka

Japanese code signal sent by Admiral Isoruku Yamamoto on December 2, 1941, to notify the Japanese Naval task force en route to Pearl Harbor to commence its attack, which was planned for December 7, 1941. Mt. Niitaka, on Formosa, was the highest peak of the Japanese empire and Yamamoto was encouraging the Japanese to "reach for heaven."

Clostermann, Pierre (1922–)

French Air Force captain and top-scoring French ace of World War II, with thirty-three aircraft to his credit. He flew with the Royal Air Force and was the only Frenchman to command an R.A.F. squadron.

Clyde, H.M.S.

British submarine under Lieutenant Commander D. C. Ingram that torpedoed and severely damaged the German cruiser *Gneisenau* off the coast of Norway on June 20, 1940.

Cobb, Lee J. (1911–1976)

Hollywood actor who served as a Civil Air Patrol pilot during World War II.

Cobham, Sir Alan John (1894–1973)

British pioneer aviator. He developed an air-to-air refueling system that was first used off the coast of Ireland in 1939.

Coca-Cola

Popular American soft drink. It was the drink given to Richard Bong by General Douglas MacArthur when the two met to celebrate Bong's surpassing ace Eddie Rickenbacker's World War I score of twenty-six enemy aircraft. Bong was a teetotaler. U.S. General Clarence Huebner, after being notified that American forces had just linked up with Russian forces at the Elbe in 1945, celebrated by drinking a Coke. Coke bottles were used on December 7, 1941 at Pearl Harbor to store blood from donors since the usual containers were in short supply. They were also used on December 23, 1941, in defense of the Philippines, when a Private Soria made Molotov cocktails from Coke bottles and hurled them at Japanese tanks. Jimmy Carter, future President of the United States, rolled his feet on Coke bottles before his admission to the Naval Academy at Annapolis in 1943 to cure what he believed to be flat feet.

Cochran, Jaquelin (1910–1980)

American female aviation pioneer. She was the first woman to make an instrument landing (1937), winner of the Bendix Trophy (1938), first woman to fly a bomber across the Atlantic (1941), and the head of the WASP's (Woman's Air Force Service Pilots) during World War II. Cochran was present at the surrender of Japanese General Tomoyuki Yamashita in the Philippines in 1945 and was the first American woman to enter Japan after World War II. She was the first woman elected to the Aviation Hall of Fame and also the first woman to fly faster than the speed of sound, in an F104 in 1953.

Code names

Alamo	U.S. Sixth Army
Conquer	U.S. Ninth Army
Eagle	U.S. Twelfth Army Group
Lion	British Twenty-first Army Group
Lucky	U.S. Third Army
Master	U.S. First Army
Shellburst	SHAEF Headquarters
Speedy	U.S. II Corps

Codrington, H.M.S.

British destroyer that took Major General Bernard Montgomery from Dunkirk to England in June 1940.

Coffee

Rationed item in the U.S., beginning November 29, 1942. All those over fifteen years old were allowed one pound of coffee every five weeks. Rationing was necessary because of the merchant ship losses to German submarines, and ended in July 1943.

Coffin Corner

Nickname given to the most vulnerable position in a bomber formation. This was the bottom rear position, usually the first to be attacked by enemy fighters.

Coghlan, Frank, Jr. (1917–)

Hollywood actor from 1921 to 1941. He enlisted in the U.S. Navy during World War II and eventually was promoted to the rank of lieutenant commander.

Cohen, Morris (1889–)

Englishman who is said to be the only person raised in the East End of London to become a General in the Chinese Army. He first became interested in the Chinese when he was hired as a bodyguard for Sun Yat-sen on a Canadian trip in 1922. Cohen then went to China as an arms merchant, selling supplies to the Kuomintang Army and eventually being given the rank of General. Nicknamed Two Gun Cohen, he was captured by the Japanese in Hong Kong in 1941 and spent the rest of the war as a prisoner in Stanley Prison.

COI

Coordinator of Information. U.S. governmental department set up by President Franklin D. Roosevelt in July 1941 to deal with the war situation. William (Wild Bill) Donovan was head of the COI, which became the OSS in June 1942.

Coinage

U.S. Lincoln pennies in 1943 were made of steel due to the shortage of copper. In 1944, they were made of reclaimed shell casings and usually had a deep reddish tone. The 1943 steel one-cent piece will today bring several times the original value of the coin.

Colby, William E. (1920–)

CIA head. During World War II, he was a major in the OSS and parachuted behind the German lines into Brittany as head of Team Frederick in support of the D-Day landings. Colby was part of a Jedburgh Team that worked with French Resistance groups. In 1945, he commanded a Norwegian-American paratroop unit that performed sabotage missions against German railway operations in Northern Norway.

Cold Douche

British code name for the effort to use all available aircraft against German bombers attacking Coventry, England, November 14, 1940.

Colditz Castle

German prisoner-of-war camp officially designated Oflag IV C. It was located in Saxony thirty miles south of Leipzig and was supposedly escape-proof. Colditz was a castle on top of a rocky hill used to imprison the most difficult Allied prisoners of war. Ironically twenty people successfully escaped during the war—the highest number of any camp in Germany. In addition to such conventional methods of escape as "over-the-wall" and tunneling, one group of prisoners also succeeded in constructing a glider for an aerial escape attempt but were liberated before it could be utilized. The glider is still entombed within the walls. This was fictionalized in a 1971 TV movie entitled *The Birdmen* (also called *The Escape of the Birdmen*).

Colman, Ronald (1891–1958)

Hollywood actor who, along with his wife, actress Benita Hume, headed the Hollywood division of the British War Relief Fund.

Collaborators with the Nazis

Croatia	Ante Pavelic
Denmark	Clausen
France	Pierre Laval
Holland	Anton Mussert
Hungary	Szalassy
Norway	Vidkun Quisling
Rumania	Sim

Collingwood, Charles C. (1917–)

CBS newscaster throughout World War II. He was hired by Edward R. Murrow and made broadcasts from London, North Africa, Sicily, and Italy while covering the Allied armies.

Collins, J. Lawton (1896–1963)

U.S. Army general. He commanded the U.S. Army forces on Guadalcanal in 1942 and the U.S. VII Corps in the D-Day assault on Utah Beach, June 6, 1944. Collins was nicknamed "Lightning Joe."

Cologne

German city that was the target of the first thousand-plane bomber strike of World War II by the Royal Air Force in May 1942.

Colonel Blimp

British political cartoon figure created by David Low, political cartoonist for the *Evening Standard.* Colonel Blimp was an overweight reactionary recognized throughout England as one of the many barbs Low devised to ridicule the establishment.

Colonel Bogey March

Name of a British Army song used around the world wherever the British military served. It became world famous as "The Bridge on the River Kwai March," the song defiantly whistled by prisoners of war in the 1956 movie *Bridge on the River Kwai.*

Colonel Britton

BBC broadcasting name known throughout Europe during World War II as an advocate of using the first notes of Beethoven's Fifth Symphony as Morse code for "V" for victory. Colonel Britton's identity was a secret until after the war, when he was identified as Douglas Ritchie, the BBC Director of the European News Department.

Colonel Henri

Code name of Hugo Bleicher, a German counterintelligence sergeant with the Abwehr in France. Bleicher was one of the most efficient agents working against the French Resistance and the one who personally captured Mathilde Carre, alias "the Cat," Captain Peter Churchill, and Odette Sansom. He was arrested by the Dutch police in 1945 and imprisoned.

Colonel Passy

Code name of André de Wavrin, the head of General Charles de Gaulle's Central Bureau of Intelligence and Action (BCRA), which dealt in espionage and resistance throughout occupied France.

Colonel Valerio

Pseudonym of Walter Audisio, the Italian partisan leader who shot and killed Benito Mussolini and his mistress Clara Petacci in April 1945 (see Audisio, Walter).

Colonel Warden

Code name used by Winston Churchill for many of his conferences in connection with the war.

Colonial Life Insurance Building

Location of the headquarters of the U.S. submarine force stationed in Perth, Australia, after the Asiatic Fleet withdrew from Manila in 1942.

Colorado
British code name for the island of Crete.

Colossus
First modern computer which was assembled to help decipher the Enigma code intercepts of the Germans by the British codebreaking team. This was part of Ultra (see Ultra).

Columbus
Third largest ocean liner and one of the most luxurious of the German merchant fleet. It was owned by the North German Lloyd Line and was scuttled by her crew on December 19, 1939, off the coast of Virginia after being intercepted by a British warship.

Comando Supremo
Name of the headquarters of the Italian Armed Forces in Rome.

Combattante
Name of the French destroyer that returned General Charles de Gaulle to France from England in June 1944, shortly after the D-Day landings.

Combined Chiefs of Staff
Title given to the amalgamation of the American Joint Chiefs of Staff and the British Chiefs of Staff. They met at the conferences of Washington, London, Casablanca, Quebec, and Malta to discuss global strategy.

Combined Operations
British military organization set up to test landing techniques and to conduct small raids on German occupied territory.

Comic strip characters who served in World War II
Sad Sack
Willy and Joe
Terry and the Pirates
Buz Sawyer
Joe Palooka
Flying Jenny
Mandrake the Magician

"Comin' in on a Wing and a Prayer"
Song composed in 1943 by Harold Adamson with lyrics by Jimmy McHugh. The tune was popular with American pilots.

Comiso Airfield
First airfield captured by the Allies on Sicily. It was taken on July 11, 1943, by the U.S. 45th Infantry Division. The first plane to land was a JU88 that U.S. flak units shot at as it approached. The

pilot landed, climbed out, shook his fist at the flak battery, and was promptly taken prisoner. He was followed shortly afterwards by two ME109's that also landed, believing that the field was still in German hands; these pilots were also taken prisoner.

Commando Order

Order issued by Hitler in 1942 that called for all Allied commandos to be executed even if they had surrendered.

Commerce Raiders

Another name given to German merchant ships that were converted into armed raiders to prey on Allied shipping (see Auxiliary Cruisers).

Commissar Order

Order issued by Hitler on June 6, 1941, that called for the immediate execution of all Russian political commissars as soon as they were captured. This was loosely interpreted by the S.S. to justify shooting many captives who were not Communists.

Compiegne

Site of the German surrender to the Allies in France at the end of World War I. It was chosen by Hitler for the French surrender to the Germans on June 22, 1940.

Concentration Camps (major camps of World War II)

- Auschwitz
- Belzec
- Belsen
- Buchenwald
- Chelmno
- Dachau
- Flossenburg
- Mauthausen
- Oranienburg
- Ravensbrück
- Sachsenhausen
- Sobibor
- Theresienstadt
- Treblinka

Concrete ships

Experimental idea of U.S. industrialists—primarily Henry Kaiser—to build ships out of concrete. This was an effort to save steel and at the same time allow manufacturers who did not have the facilities for steel ships to build ships. One of these is permanently beached south of Santa Cruz, California, and has a boardwalk built out to it. It has withstood the heaviest storms of the Pacific and survives as a permanent reminder of the creativity of U.S. industry.

Condor Legion

Name of the German Luftwaffe contingent sent to help General Francisco Franco during the Spanish Civil War 1936–1939. Spain was the testing area for ground support tactics as well as of fighter aircraft and equipment in Germany's preparation for World War II. The Condor Legion was commanded by Hugo Sperrle and the chief of staff was Wolfram von Richtofen.

Condoms

Versatile piece of U.S. military equipment. They were used by U.S. soldiers who placed them over their rifle barrels to keep out moisture when they waded ashore at Normandy on June 6, 1944.

Conferences

Arcadia	December 1941–January 1942	Washington, D.C.
Argonaut	January–February, 1945	Malta and Yalta
Eureka	November–December, 1943	Teheran
Octagon	September 1944	Quebec
Quadrant	August 1943	Quebec
Sextant	November–December, 1943	Cairo
Terminal	July–August, 1945	Potsdam
Trident	May 1943	Washington, D.C.

Confessions of a Nazi Spy

Movie (1939) starring Edward G. Robinson. Word got back from the Swiss consulate to the U.S. that the Nazi government intended to severely punish everyone involved in the production of the film once the Germans won the war.

Congressional Medal of Honor

The highest award for valor in the United States. It was instituted during the American Civil War and is the oldest continuous U.S. decoration. During World War II, fewer than five hundred were issued. Some notable winners were

Anthony J. Casamento—September 1, 1980—the last for World War II

Ernest Childers—first American Indian to win the CMH during World War II

George H. Cannon—first U.S. Marine to win the CMH during World War II

Desmond T. Doss—first conscientious objector to receive the CMH

Jake Lindsey—the 100th infantryman to win the CMH during World War II

Robert M. McTurcous—listed as the last U.S. Marine to win the CMH during World War II

Sadao Munemori—only Nisei Japanese-American to win the CMH

Joseph T. O'Callaghan—only Chaplain to win the CMH since the Civil War

Coningham, Sir Arthur (1895–1948)

British air vice-marshall of the Royal Air Force. He was nicknamed Maori while commanding New Zealand troops during World War I. He served under General Dwight Eisenhower and was lost at sea in an aircraft crash.

MOVIE PORTRAYAL:
Patton (1970), by John Barrie

Connaught, Arthur W. (1850–1942)

British Field Marshall who was the last of four sons of Queen Victoria.

Connally, John (1917–)

U.S. congressman and governor of Texas. During World War II, he enlisted in the U.S. Navy, where he helped plan the invasion of Italy in 1943 as part of General Dwight Eisenhower's staff. Connally also served in the Pacific as fighter aircraft director (CIC) on board the aircraft carriers U.S.S. *Essex* and U.S.S. *Bennington*. He was awarded a Bronze Star for controlling fighters from the *Essex*, which shot down sixty-nine Japanese planes, on April 6, 1945. Connally was discharged in 1946 with the rank of lieutenant commander and a Legion of Merit medal.

Control

Special OSS document classification indicating that the information could be hostile to an ally. Therefore, the information was to be kept from the ally at all costs.

Convoy designations

HX—Halifax to England (fast convoys)
KN—Northbound convoys traveling along east coast of the U.S.
KS—Southbound convoys traveling along east coast of the U.S.
ON—England to Canada (fast convoys)
ONS—England to Canada (slow convoys)
PQ—England to Russia (changed to "JW" in December 1942)
QP—Russia to England
SC—Sydney or New York to England

Coogan, Jackie (1914–)

Well-known child actor of the 1930's and first husband of actress Betty Grable. He was a glider pilot with the U.S. Army during World War II. Coogan piloted the first glider to land at Myitkyina in March 1944 during the first Allied airborne operation of the Asiatic war. Coincidentally, the code name for the landing zone was "Broadway."

Cook, Cordelia E.

U.S. Army Nurse Corps first lieutenant. She was the first woman to receive the Bronze Star. She was also awarded the Purple Heart and was the first woman to receive two decorations during World War II. Both were given for the period from November 1943 to January 1944 in North Africa.

Cooper, Alfred Duff (1890–1954)

British politician. At the time of the Munich Agreement between Sir Neville Chamberlain and Hitler, he was the First Lord of the Admiralty and resigned in protest against the policy of appeasement. He became the Minister of Information under Prime Minister Winston Churchill and later served as the British representative to General Charles de Gaulle. In November 1944, Cooper was appointed British ambassador to Paris.

Cooper, Merian C. (1893–1973)

Hollywood movie producer and director who was a fighter pilot during World War I. He co-wrote and co-directed the 1933 movie *King Kong* and during World War II served as General Claire Chennault's chief of staff in China. Cooper retired from the U.S. Air Force as a brigadier general.

MOVIE PORTRAYAL:

God Is My Co-Pilot (1945), by Stanley Ridges

COPP

Combined Operations Pilotage Party. This was the name of a special British unit that surveyed potential landing beaches using small boats launched from submarines.

Corncob

Name given to the merchant ships used to form a breakwater for the beaches at Normandy in June 1944.

Corncob pipe

Symbol of General Douglas MacArthur during World War II. General John P. Lucas, commander of the Anzio landings in January 1944, also used a corncob pipe, as did George Lincoln Rockwell, the head of the American Nazi Party in the 1960's.

Coronel

Name of a German auxiliary cruiser. It was formerly the 5,600-ton merchantman *Togo* and was converted to an armed commerce raider by the addition of six six-inch guns and six four-centimeter antiaircraft guns. It had a speed of seventeen knots but, after being bombed in Dunkirk by the Royal Air Force, failed to make an escape into the Atlantic due to the damage it sustained.

Corporal
Rank held by both Hitler and Mussolini during World War I. Actually, Hitler never made full corporal but was one grade lower—what in the British military and U.S. Marines would be a lance corporal. (Peter Sellers, the British actor who portrayed Hitler in the 1975 movie *Undercover Heroes*, was a corporal in the Royal Air Force during World War II.)

Corps
Designator of a U.S. Army fighting unit that contains from two to five divisions. It contains artillery, tank, mortar and antitank units and, therefore, is self-supporting.

Corregidor
Island at the mouth of Manila Bay that guarded the seaward approach to the capital of the Philippines. The name of the base there was Fort Mills; Corregidor was commonly referred to as "The Rock." The main guns covered the entrance to Manila Bay but could not fire back at Bataan. As a result, when the Japanese captured Bataan, Corregidor was doomed. It finally surrendered on May 6, 1942 (see Bataan).

Corrigan, Douglas Gorce (1907–   )
U.S. pioneer aviator known as "Wrong Way" Corrigan. He flew from New York to Dublin on July 18, 1938, while maintaining that he was headed for San Diego, California. He had originally helped build Charles Lindbergh's *Spirit of St. Louis* and was the one who pulled the wheel chocks for the first test flight of the aircraft.

Corsair
U.S. fighter designated the F4U. The Americans nicknamed it "Bent-winged bird" and the Japanese called it "Whispering Death." The first ace of the Corsair was Kenneth Walsh, U.S. Marine Corps pilot with *VMF214*.

Corvina, U.S.S.
U.S. Navy submarine. It was commanded by Roderick S. Rooney and was sent to sink the Japanese submarine *I-176*. Ironically *I-176* succeeded in sinking the *Corvina*, making it the only U.S. submarine known to have been sunk by a Japanese submarine during World War II. The *Corvina* was sponsored by the wife of Ralph Christie, head of U.S. submarines in Australia, when it was launched.

Cosell, Howard (1920–   )
Lawyer and sportscaster. He served throughout World War II in

the U.S. Army at the New York Port of Embarkation and rose from the rank of private to major. At the time he was one of the youngest majors in the U.S. Army.

Cossack, H.M.S.

British destroyer under the command of Captain Vian. It captured the German auxiliary cruiser *Altmark* in Norwegian waters on February 16, 1940, freeing a number of British prisoners. Later, the *Cossack* fought at the Battle of Narvik and participated in the sinking of the *Bismarck*.

COSSACK

Abbreviation for Chief of Staff Supreme Allied Command. It was headed by Lieutenant General Sir Frederick E. Morgan, under whom they did the initial planning for Overlord, the D-Day invasions of June 6, 1944. Headquarters was located at Norfolk House in St. James Square, London, but was later moved to St. Paul's School in Hammersmith.

Cota, Norman D. (1893–1971)

U.S. Army major general. As the assistant commander of the U.S. 29th Infantry Division, he was the first American general ashore on D-Day, June 6, 1944, in Normandy. Cota later commanded the U.S. 28th Infantry Division and led it down the Champs Elysées in the Paris liberation parade in August 1944.

Cotton, Frederick Sidney

Australian who, with the help of F. Winterbotham, developed high altitude aerial photography for the Royal Air Force by using a stripped-down Spitfire. He was awarded the Order of the British Empire.

Country houses

Berghof	Adolf Hitler
Blizhny	Joseph Stalin
Bridges Court	Sir Stewart Menzies
Checquers	Winston Churchill
Haus am Bodensee	Dr. Joseph Goebbels
Karinhall	Hermann Goering
Telegraph Cottage	General Dwight Eisenhower
Warm Springs	Franklin D. Roosevelt

Courageous, H.M.S.

British Navy aircraft carrier weighing 22,500 tons. It was the second ship to be sunk in World War II (the first was the *Athenia*) and the first major loss of the war. It was torpedoed on September 17, 1939, west of Ireland by the German submarine *U-29* under

Lieutenant Schuhart. Five hundred fifteen crew members were killed or drowned, including the commander, Captain W. W. Makeig-Jones, who went down with the ship while saluting the flag from the bridge.

Cousteau, Jacques (1911–)

French oceanographer. He was the gunnery officer aboard the French cruiser *Dupleix* in the early days of World War II. Cousteau then became a gunnery officer at a coastal fort overlooking Toulon harbor, where he was stationed during the German occupation of France in 1940. He did research for the Navy and in 1943 developed the aqualung for skindiving. At the same time he worked for the Resistance movement. After the war, he helped clear the French coast along the Mediterranean of mines.

Coventry

British Midlands manufacturing city and site of Lady Godiva's famous ride. It was bombed by the German Luftwaffe on November 14, 1940. The raid, which was led by Colonel General Alexander Lohr, dropped five hundred tons of high explosives and thirty tons of incendiaries, which all but destroyed the main part of the city. Coventry was bombed by the express orders of Hitler in retaliation for the British bombing of Munich on November 8, 1940, the seventeenth anniversary of the Beer Hall Putsch. Hitler hoped to terrorize the British and only succeeded in galvanizing their resolve to hold out. Prime Minister Winston Churchill knew of the impending raid via Ultra intercepts but chose not to tip off the Germans that the British were reading their codes.

Coward, Charles

British sergeant major. He was captured by the Germans shortly before the fall of France in 1940. In an escape attempt, Coward hid in a hospital ward with German wounded and was awarded the Iron Cross in error. He ended up in a prisoner-of-war camp near Auschwitz, where he set up an intelligence network that sent back information about Auschwitz as well as the German V-1's and V-2's.

MOVIE PORTRAYAL:
The Password Is Courage (1963), by Dirk Bogarde

Coward, Noel (1899–1973)

British actor who performed clandestine work for British intelligence in South America during World War II. He also entertained British Commonwealth troops around the world.

MOVIE PORTRAYALS:
Star! (1968), by Daniel Massey
Ike (1979 TV movie), by Francis Mathews

Cox, Wally (1924–1973)

Hollywood comedian. He was drafted into the U.S. Army during World War II and sent to Fort Walters, Texas, where the intense heat put him in the hospital several times with heat stroke. He was later given an honorable discharge for medical reasons.

Crab

Allied tank that was fitted with a rotary drum on the front and various lengths of chain attached to detonate mines. It was invented by the British for the D-Day landings on June 6, 1944, and could travel one and a half miles per hour while flailing the ground. The Crab was an improvement over an earlier attempt called Scorpion.

Cracker Jacks

Molasses-coated popcorn created by F. W. Rueckheim in 1873. During World War II, the prizes in each box were all military-oriented.

Cranston, Alan (1914–   )

U.S. Senator from California. Prior to U.S. entry into World War II, he printed copies of Hitler's *Mein Kampf* along with his own views about the methods used by Hitler in fulfilling his aims. Cranston sold these for ten cents each and succeeded in selling over half a million in ten days. Since Hitler owned the copyright to *Mein Kampf* and Cranston had not obtained permission for the printing, lawyers for the Germans were able to get a court order to stop further publication.

C Ration

Name of an individual ration for one day in the field, developed by the U.S. Army during World War II. The C Ration consisted of three cans of meat and vegetables, three cans of crackers, sugar, coffee, and a confection.

Crerar, Henry D. G. (1888–1965)

Canadian lieutenant general. He commanded the Canadian First Army, which was the first Canadian force in history large enough to be designated an army. It fought at Normandy in 1944.

Crete

Greek island captured by the Germans in May 1941 using airborne forces exclusively. The cost of the victory was high, however; one out of every four paratroopers was killed and the attack, though successful, broke the back of the German parachute corps for the remainder of the war. Hitler relegated them to an infantry role after Crete because he felt their day of surprise was over. Ironically, it was the Crete attack that convinced Winston Churchill to expand the British paratroop forces from 500 to 5,000 and two years later to 20,000 men.

Cricket

Code name for the military conference between British and American planners prior to the Yalta conference. It was held for four days beginning January 30, 1945, on the island of Malta.

Crocodiles

Name given to the Allied tanks used during the D-Day invasion of June 6, 1944; they were equipped with flame-throwers to help subdue German strong points.

Cromwell

Code signal to be sent by the British high command if they felt a German invasion was imminent. The signal was sent out inadvertently on September 7, 1940, causing some confusion among the Home Guard and local authorities.

Cromwell, John P. (1901–1943)

U.S. Navy captain. He was the commander of the submarines of Division 43 and went out on patrol with the U.S.S. *Sculpin* in November 1943. On November 18, the submarine was forced to the surface by Japanese destroyers north of Truk, causing the crew to abandon ship. Cromwell was privy to top secret information about future submarine operations as well as tactics and equipment and, rather than be captured and possibly forced to reveal his knowledge under torture, elected to go down with the *Sculpin*. He was awarded the Congressional Medal of Honor posthumously after the war when the full story was related by the survivors.

Cronkite, Walter, (1916–)

CBS newscaster. During World War II he flew on several bomber missions over Europe including the first B-17 raid over Germany in 1943. Cronkite also parachuted into the Netherlands with the 101st Airborne Division during Operation Market-Garden in September 1944.

Crosby, Bing (1904–1977)

Popular American singer. While serving with a USO tour in Europe, he and his jeep driver found themselves behind enemy lines and in a German town far from where they were supposed to be.

Cross of Lorraine
Symbol of the Free French Forces under General Charles de Gaulle during World War II.

Crossword
Winston Churchill's name for Operation Sunrise, the secret surrender of German forces in Italy in May 1945.

Cruiser designations (U.S. Navy)
CA—Heavy cruiser of 10–15,000 tons, named for U.S. cities
CB—Large cruiser over 25,000 tons, named for U.S. territories
CC—Battle cruisers
CF—Flying deck cruisers
CL—Light cruisers of 6–10,000 tons
CLK—Antisubmarine cruisers

Cruwell, Ludwig (1892–1958)
German general who commanded the Afrika Korps under Field Marshall Erwin Rommel from September 1941 to May 1942. Cruwell was captured by the Allies and imprisoned at Camp Clinton, Mississippi.

Cryptographic sections
British—MI-6
French—2bis
German—Forschungsamt
Polish—BS-4

Culin, Curtis G., Jr.
U.S. Army tank sergeant. He invented the Rhino attachment for tanks, which could dig through the hedgerows of Normandy. Culin was awarded the Legion of Merit for this weapon, which is considered one of the great contributions to the Allied breakout of Normandy. He later lost a leg in the Battle of the Huertgen Forest and was sent home to New York City.

Cummings, Robert (1910–   )
Hollywood actor and godson of aviation pioneer Orville Wright. During World War II, he served in the U.S. Army Air Force as a flight instructor. Cummings also appeared in a number of savings bond drives for the war effort.

Cummings, William (1902–1945)
American Catholic priest who said "there are no atheists in foxholes." He was captured by the Japanese at Bataan as a civilian and died in 1945 aboard a Japanese prison ship.

Cunningham, Sir Alan G. (1887–   )
British Army general. He was the younger brother of Admiral

Andrew Cunningham and commanded the British forces that captured Ethiopia. He also served in the western desert and later was the commanding officer of Northern Ireland.

Cunningham, Sir Andrew B. (1883–1963)

British admiral. He was Commander in Chief in the Mediterranean from 1939 to 1943 and as such commanded the forces that attacked the Italian Navy base at Taranto in 1940 and the Italian fleet at Cape Matapan. These two actions eliminated the Italians as a viable naval threat in the Mediterranean. Cunningham also was responsible for the bloodless immobilization of the French fleet at Alexandria. Between 1943 and 1946 he served as First Sea Lord and Chief of the Naval Staff. He is buried at St. Paul's Cathedral, London.

Cunningham, John (1917–)

British Royal Air Force wing commander. He was a pilot in No. 604 Squadron, flying a Beaufighter equipped with Mark IV radar as a nightfighter. Cunningham is the second-highest-scoring British nightfighter pilot in World War II, with twenty aircraft shot down. His radar operator was Flight Lieutenant C. F. Rawnsley.

Curie, Eve (1904–)

Daughter of Marie Curie, the discoverer of radium. Eve escaped from France aboard the British cargo ship *Madura* after the French surrendered in 1940. She wrote and traveled extensively in support of the Allied war effort and the Free French. Her brother-in-law, Frederick Joliot-Curie, was an active member of the Paris Resistance and assembled Molotov cocktails from chemicals in Marie Curie's laboratory for the Paris uprising of August 1944.

Currahee

Battle cry and official motto of the U.S. 506th Infantry Regiment of the 101st Airborne Division. It was an Indian word meaning "stand alone."

Curtis, Henry Osbourne

British major general and commander of Iceland until May 1942. He received the Distinguished Service Medal, the first U.S. decoration given to a Briton in World War II.

Curtis, Tony (1925–)

Hollywood actor, born Bernard Schwartz, who was inspired to drop out of high school and join the U.S. Navy submarine force after watching Tyrone Power in the 1943 movie *Crash Dive*. He was assigned to the U.S.S. *Dragonette* which ran aground on an uncharted coral reef on December 15, 1944, flooding the entire forward torpedo room. It was the only submarine to survive such an accident. Curtis was injured on Guam while loading torpedoes when a chain broke and struck him across the back. The incident paralyzed him for awhile, and he spent seven weeks in the hospital where a nurse read to him from Shakespeare. This rekindled his interest in acting. After he returned to the submarine, he developed an impersonation of Cary Grant from the many times he saw *Gunga Din* (1939), which was the only movie aboard. After his discharge, he studied acting on the GI Bill and he and Cary Grant later acted together in a submarine movie *Operation Petticoat* (1959). Curtis also did his Cary Grant imitation in another 1959 movie *Some Like It Hot,* starring Marilyn Monroe. In 1964, Tony Curtis took actress Christine Kaufmann as his second wife. During World War II, Christine's father had served as a Luftwaffe pilot.

Cushing, James (1910–1963)

U.S. Army lieutenant colonel who commanded Philippine guerrilla forces on Cebu Island during World War II. His unit captured Japanese Admiral Fukudome after Admiral Kaga's plane crashed off the coast of Cebu. Cushing subsequently released Fukudome to halt reprisals against the Filipino civilians, an act for which General Douglas MacArthur demoted him to private. Later Cushing's rank was given back.

Cushing, Robert E.

U.S. Marine Corps officer. During the Pearl Harbor attack on December 7, 1941, he commanded the marine detachment on board the U.S.S. *Pennsylvania,* losing one third of his personnel. Cushing later fought as a lieutenant colonel at Bougainville, Iwo Jima, and Guam, where he was awarded the Navy Cross.

Cutie

Acoustical torpedo developed by the U.S. It could home in on noise from a ship and was to be fired by submarines. Cutie was copied from a German acoustic torpedo. It was believed that the torpedo had to be fired from at least 150 feet deep so that it would not return to the noise of the submarine. It was first used by Captain Carter Bennett on the U.S.S. *Sea Owl* to sink a small Japanese patrol craft in the Yellow Sea. A disadvantage to its use was that it could only be fired at a target traveling eight and a half knots or less.

Cynthia

Code name of Elizabeth Thorpe, a spy for the BSC (see Thorpe, Elizabeth).

Cynthia Olson

2,140-ton American merchant ship. It was the first ship to be sunk by a Japanese submarine in World War II when it was torpedoed by the I-26 750 miles northwest of Seattle, on December 7, 1941.

D

D

Coded identifier for the chief of the British SOE during World War II. Until September 1943, D referred to Sir Charles Hambro and afterwards, to General Colin Gubbins.

Dachau

First Nazi concentration camp. It was established in March 1933 outside Munich, the birthplace of the Nazi party. By the end of World War II, it was the third worst extermination camp, ranking only behind Auschwitz and Buchenwald.

Dachshund

Name given by German Luftwaffe personnel to auxiliary fuel tanks used on the ME110 fighters. These tanks held an extra 220 gallons and were attached beneath the fuselage.

Da de da

Code name used by General Dwight Eisenhower's staff in referring to his retreat on the outskirts of London, Telegraph Cottage.

Dahl, Harold "Whitey"

An American flying with the Loyalist Air Force in the Spanish Civil War. He holds the distinction of being the first American shot down by an ME109. He was downed in July 1937 and taken prisoner. His unit was made up primarily of Russian pilots.

Daily Telegraph

London daily newspaper in which a number of top secret names associated with D-Day appeared in its crossword puzzles. What appeared to be a major security leak was on closer investigation found to be pure coincidence.

#5775, "One of the US"—Utah
#5792: "Red Indian on the Missouri"—Omaha
#5797: "But some bigwig like this has stolen some of it at times"—Overlord
#5799: "This bush is a center of nursery revolutions"—Mulberry
"Britannia and he hold the same thing"—Neptune

Dakota Queen

Name of the B-24 Liberator bomber piloted by George S. McGovern, a future U.S. presidential candidate. He flew fifty-five missions in Europe and was awarded the Distinguished Flying Cross for bringing the *Dakota Queen* back to the base after it was severely damaged.

Daly, James (1918–1978)

Hollywood actor who served in the U.S. Army Air Corps and the U.S. Navy during World War II.

Daly, John (1914–)

CBS newscaster. A pen of his was one of the three used in the signing of the German surrender at Rheims, May 7, 1945.

Daniels, Bebe (1901–1971)

Hollywood actress who was given the Presidential Medal of Freedom in 1946 for entertaining U.S. troops overseas during World War II. She was also the first female civilian to enter Normandy after the D-Day invasion of June 6, 1944.

d'Aquino, Iva Toguri

Japanese-American who was caught in Japan when war broke out. She took a job as a broadcaster with a radio station transmitting English programming to U.S. forces in the Pacific. Although she was only one of many broadcasters, and according to her testimony did not broadcast propaganda, at the end of World War II, she was arrested by U.S. authorities and branded the "Tokyo Rose" known throughout the Pacific by GI's. D'Aquino was tried, found guilty of treason, and sentenced to ten years' imprisonment and a ten-thousand-dollar fine. She was finally granted a full pardon by President Gerald Ford on his last day as President on January 19, 1977.

Darby, William Orlando (1911–1945)

U.S. Army colonel who organized and commanded the Rangers in World War II. He established the First American Ranger Battalion in Northern Ireland in the summer of 1942. The Rangers fought in North Africa, Sicily, and Italy; by the summer of 1944, there were only 199 still alive out of the original 1,500 members. Darby turned down several promotions of the rank of general because he would have to leave his Rangers for another unit. He was killed on April 16, 1945, in the Po Valley in Italy by a German 88mm shell and was promoted to brigadier general posthumously.

MOVIE PORTRAYALS:
Darby's Rangers (1958), by James Garner

Dargue, Herbert Arthur (1886–1941)

U.S. major general and the first American major general killed in World War II, when his aircraft crashed on December 12, 1941. He was a graduate of West Point in 1911.

Darlan, Jean François (1881–1942)

French Admiral and Commander in Chief of the French Navy. He was the Vichy commander in Africa who passed military information to the Germans that the U.S. received from the French embassy in Washington, D.C. He held several high British military decorations, including Knight Grand Cross of the Royal Victorian Order. Darlan changed allegiance upon the Allied invasion of North Africa on November 8, 1942, and proved a great embarrassment to General Dwight Eisenhower. The problem was solved Christmas Eve, 1942, when Darlan was assassinated by Bonnier de la Chappille, a Frenchman who was in training to become a British agent (see *Chappille, Bonier de la*).

Darnand, Joseph (1897–1945)

French head of the Fascist Milice (police), whom he caused to be even more feared than the S.S. Before the war, he had owned a brothel in Nice. He took command of a French S.S. unit on the Russian front in 1943. After returning to France, Darnand became Secretary General for the Maintenance of Order, forcing his followers to take an oath to oppose "democracy, Gaullist dissidence, and the leprosy of Jewry." He was executed for treason after the war.

Darre, R. Walther (1895–)

Argentina-born racial theorist for Hitler's Nazi party. He was an S.S. General during World War II.

D'Artagnan

French ocean liner weighing 15,100 tons. It was captured by the Japanese at the beginning of World War II and renamed the *Teiku Maru*. It was sunk by the submarine U.S.S *Puffer* under Gordon Selby on February 22, 1944. (Her sister ship *Porthos* remained in Allied hands.)

Darter, U.S.S.

U.S. submarine that fired the first shots in the Battle of Leyte Gulf by torpedoing and sinking the Japanese cruiser *Atago* and damaging another cruiser, the *Takao*, on October 23, 1944, as they steamed to do battle with the U.S. Fleet off the Philippines.

Dasch, Georg Johann (1903–   )

German spy who landed on Long Island on June 13, 1942, from the submarine *U202*. He was part of Operation Pastorius and was the leader of three other saboteurs who planned to disrupt U.S. production. Dasch had lived in the U.S. from 1922 until 1941. When he returned to Germany he was recruited by the Abwehr, the German intelligence service. When he reached the U.S. on his spy mission, he turned himself in to the FBI and told everything he knew about the other members and their plans. Dasch was tried by a military court-martial and sentenced to death, but this was commuted by President Franklin D. Roosevelt to thirty years' imprisonment. He was released in 1948 and deported to Germany where he wrote a book entitled *Eight Spies Against America* (1958).

Dastagir, Sabu (1924–1963)

Actor known as Sabu the Elephant Boy. During World War II, he flew forty-two missions in the South Pacific and was awarded the Distinguished Flying Cross and the Air Medal with four clusters, in addition to the Presidential Unit Citation.

Dauntless Dotty

Name of the B-29 that led the first U.S. bomber raid on Tokyo (November 24, 1944) since the Doolittle Raid of April 18, 1942. It was flown by Brigadier General Emmett O'Donnell.

Dauser, Sue Sophie

U.S. Navy captain and superintendent of the Nurse Corps during World War II. She was the first woman in U.S. Navy history to hold the rank of captain, being promoted on February 26, 1944.

Davenport, Roy M.

U.S. Navy officer. He was the third-ranked U.S. submarine skipper of World War II, having sunk 151,900 tons of enemy shipping. Davenport was awarded five Navy Crosses and was credited with being the most decorated submariner of the war. He commanded the U.S.S. *Haddock* and the U.S.S *Trepang*.

David, Albert L. (1902–   )

U.S. Navy lieutenant (j.g.) who commanded the boarding party that captured the German submarine *U505* on June 4, 1944, off the coast of French West Africa. He was awarded the Congressional Medal of Honor for disregarding his own safety and going into the submarine to disarm explosive charges and close sea-cocks to keep it from sinking. It was the first enemy vessel captured by the U.S. Navy on the high seas since 1815.

Davies, Joseph E. (1876–1958)

U.S. ambassador to Russia from 1936 to 1938 and afterwards ambassador to Belgium until 1940.

MOVIE PORTRAYAL:

Mission to Moscow (1943), by Walter Huston

Davis, Benjamin O. (1877–1970)

U.S. Army officer and the only black general in the Army during World War II. He was the grandson of a slave who had purchased his freedom in 1800.

Davis, Benjamin O., Jr. (1912–)

U.S. Army Air Force officer. He was the son of the only black general of the Army and would become, in 1954, the first black general of the U.S. Air Force. Davis, Jr. was the fourth black to graduate from West Point since 1802. During World War II, he founded the 99th Pursuit Squadron of black fighter pilots at Tuskegee Institute, Alabama, and commanded it in combat in Tunisia, Sicily, and Italy. He later commanded the all-black 332nd Fighter Group and flew over sixty missions, winning the Distinguished Flying Cross, Silver Star, three Legion of Merit medals, and an Air Medal with four oak-leaf clusters.

Davis, Elmer H. (1890–1958)

Radio news broadcaster who was appointed Director of the Office of War Information by President Franklin D. Roosevelt in 1942. His job was to coordinate all government news and propaganda.

Davis, Thomas Jefferson

U.S. Army officer. As a colonel, he was adjutant general to General Dwight Eisenhower. Davis had been a former aide to General Douglas MacArthur.

Dawley, Ernest J. (1886–)

U.S. Army major general who as a corps commander at Salerno was relieved of command by Major General John Lucas, who was himself later relieved of command at Anzio.

Dayan, Moshe (1915–1981)

Israeli Defense Minister. Prior to World War II, he was second-in-command to Orde Wingate over Jewish commandos. Dayan was arrested and sentenced to five years' imprisonment by the British for Hagganah terrorist activities in 1939. He was released in 1941 to join the British Army and fight against the Vichy French in Syria and Lebanon. It was while in Lebanon that Dayan put a telescope to his left eye and the telescope was hit by a bullet, causing the loss of the eye.

MOVIE PORTRAYAL:

A Woman Called Golda (1982 TV miniseries), by Yossi Graber

"Day that will live in infamy"

Phrase coined by President Franklin D. Roosevelt in referring to the December 7, 1941, sneak attack by the Japanese on Pearl Harbor. He used it in his speech to Congress calling for a declaration of war.

D-Day

June 6, 1944, a Tuesday, marked the greatest invasion in history when the Allies assaulted Normandy. Involved in the initial assault were 185,000 troops, 18,000 paratroopers, 13,175 aircraft, 4,066 landing ships, 745 large ships, 20,000 vehicles, and 347 minesweepers. The British landed at Gold, Juno, and Sword beaches, which were defended by Russians in German uniform. They broke and ran leaving only their German officers and NCO's to fight. This allowed the British to break out of confines of the beach into the interior fairly rapidly. The Americans, who landed at Utah and Omaha beaches in the midst of a German division well dug in on practice maneuvers, were nearly pushed back into the sea. In the naval support forces was an American battleship, the U.S.S. *Nevada*, which had been at Pearl Harbor on December 7, 1941. The British battleship H.M.S. *Warspite* was the only battleship present both at the Battle of Jutland in 1916 and the D-Day assault. The 6th of June, 1944 was also:

Birthday of German Field Marshall Erwin Rommel's wife
Birthday of General Marcks (b. 1891), German commander at Normandy
Birthday of Italian Air Marshall Italo Balbo (b. 1896)
Birthday of author Thomas Mann (b.1875)
Graduation day of John Eisenhower (Dwight's son) from West Point
Anniversary of U.S. Admiral Ernest King's commissioning in 1903
Date of death of Polish Foreign Minister Josef Beck

Date of death twenty-five years later to the day (1968) of British General Sir Miles Dempsey, who was in command of the British Second Army at Normandy

DD Tank

Dual-drive amphibious tank devised by the British in 1943. It was a conventional tank with an auxiliary propeller and was surrounded by a canvas float that acted like water wings to keep the tank afloat. A small charge blew off the canvas and its frame when the tank hit the beach. A total of sixty-four DD tanks were used by the Americans at D-Day, but most were swamped and sunk by the high seas.

Dealey, Samuel D. (1906–1944)

U.S. Navy officer and commander of the submarine U.S.S. *Harder.* He was called the ''Destroyer Killer'' because of the number of Japanese destroyers he sank (five in one patrol). In the course of five patrols, he sank sixteen ships totaling 54,000 tons, before he was sunk on August 24, 1944, by a Japanese minesweeper off the Philippine coast. Dealey, who was awarded the Congressional Medal of Honor posthumously, was the fourth submariner to win the medal.

Dean, Jimmy (1928–)

Country-and-western singer who served in the Merchant Marine toward the end of World War II.

Decoy, H.M.S.

British ship that evacuated the Greek King George II from Crete to Egypt on May 23, 1941.

de Gaulle, Charles (1890–1970)

French General and head of the Free French Forces during World War II. In World War I, he was wounded three times before being captured by the Germans at Verdun in 1916. He escaped from German prisoner-of-war camps on five occasions but was recaptured each time because of his conspicuous height (6′4″). He began World War II as a colonel and was promoted to brigadier general on May 15, 1940. De Gaulle went to England in June 1940 rather than fall into the hands of the Germans again; there he set up the French French forces. He was tried *in absentia* on August 1, 1940, by a French court-martial and condemned to death.

MOVIE PORTRAYALS:

Francis Gary Powers: The True Story of the U-2 Spy Incident (1976 TV movie), by Marcel Hillaire

Ike (1979 TV miniseries), by Vernon Dobtcheff
Churchill and The Generals (1981 TV movie), by Jacques Boudet

De Grelle, Leon (1906–)

Belgian Rexist leader who allied himself with the Nazis during World War II. He became an S.S. officer and fought on the Russian front, earning the Knight's Cross for bravery. After the war he fled to Spain where he lives today. He feels that Hitler was the greatest statesman of the modern era.

de Guingand, Francis (1900–1979)

British Army major general. He was Director of Military Intelligence under General Sir Claude Anchinleck in North Africa and, as such, was one of only three recipients of Ultra information on German coded messages. De Guingand became Chief of Staff under Field Marshall Bernard Montgomery and was largely responsible for acting as an intermediary between General Dwight Eisenhower and Montgomery, thus preserving Anglo-American unity. He was also the escort of German General Alfred Jodl to the surrender of Rheims on May 7, 1945.

MOVIE PORTRAYAL:
Patton (1970), by Douglas Wilmer

de Havilland, Sir Geoffrey (1882–1965)

British aircraft manufacturer. He designed and flew fighters in World War I. Toward the end of 1940, he believed that constant-speed propellers would greatly improve the Spitfire but could not obtain either British government approval or money to test his theory. De Havilland privately talked No. 609 Squadron into converting a Spitfire; the remarkable improvement of performance proved him correct. He began converting Spitfires throughout England. This is considered one of the technical innovations that won the Battle of Britain.

Delaney, Edward Leo

American who broadcast propaganda for the Nazis during World War II. Prior to World War I, he traveled throughout the U.S. as an actor in a road show and wrote several books. As a propagandist, Delaney used the alias E. D. Ward.

de Laveleye, Victor

Belgian refugee exiled to England who is credited with introducing the "V" as the sign of victory during World War II. It was adopted and used by Prime Minister Winston Churchill.

Delhi Maru

First Japanese Q-ship commissioned in World War II. Built from a converted merchant ship especially armed for antisubmarine duty, it went to sea in January 1944. The 2,182-ton ship was equipped with sonar, depth charges, and hidden guns. On her maiden voyage, the *Delhi Maru* was torpedoed and sunk by the U.S. submarine U.S.S. *Swordfish* under Karl Hensel.

Demara, Ferdinand Waldo, Jr. (1921–1982)

Adventurer who became known as The Great Imposter. At the time of the Japanese attack on Pearl Harbor, he was in the U.S. Army, but he went AWOL to enlist in the U.S. Navy. He served eight weeks aboard the destroyer U.S.S. *Ellis* then went AWOL from the Navy in search of other adventures.

MOVIE PORTRAYAL:

The Great Imposter (1960), by Tony Curtis

du Maurier, Daphne (1907–)

British author. Her husband was Major General Frederick Browning, the father of the British parachute forces in World War II. While they were stationed in Alexandria, Egypt, in 1937, du Maurier began writing *Rebecca*. It was destined to become a bestseller and also the cipher base for coded intelligence messages from the German Kondor spy team in Cairo during the North African campaign. The Kondor mission transmitted valuable intelligence back to Field Marshall Erwin Rommel that greatly aided in his continuous good fortune against the British army. It was ironic that a novel written by a British general's wife should have been used with such effect against the British.

Demon

American code for the U.S. Navy.

Dempsey, Jack (1895–)

U.S. heavyweight boxing champion. He attempted to enlist in the U.S. Army immediately after Pearl Harbor but was rejected for being overage and because he had no prior military training. Dempsey then enlisted in the U.S. Coast Guard, where he became the physical fitness director and morale officer at Sheepshead, New York. In 1945, Dempsey went to the Pacific, landing with the assault forces on Okinawa. During the battle, he pursued, caught, and after a struggle subdued a fleeing Japanese, only to find out that he had caught what appeared to be a ninety-year-old man.

Dempsey, Sir Miles (1896–1969)

British Army lieutenant general. He commanded a rear-guard action during the evacuation of Dunkirk in June 1940. He led the British Eighth Army in Sicily and Italy but his most important position was at the head of the British Second Army at the D-Day landings in Normandy on June 6, 1944. He died exactly twenty-five years later, on June 6, 1969.

Demyansk

Site of a major battle on the Eastern Front in 1942. The Russians broke through German lines and encircled six German divisions, a total of 100,000 men, in January 1942. It was the first major encirclement of World War II in which the Germans were the surrounded forces. The Luftwaffe began to supply the cut-off forces by airlift, which succeeded over a period of three months. It was the first time in history that an entire army was supplied by air and set the precedent that was followed when the Sixth Army was surrounded at Stalingrad at the end of the year.

Denning, Richard (1914–)

Hollywood actor. He enlisted in the U.S. Navy during World War II and served on a submarine.

Denver, U.S.S.

U.S. Navy cruiser that fired the first shots during the invasion of Leyte Gulf on October 17, 1944 at 0802. It therefore fired the first shots for the liberation of the Philippines.

Der Adler

"The Eagle." It was the official German propaganda magazine of the Luftwaffe during World War II.

Derby House

Hotel in Liverpool, England. It was the headquarters of Admiral Horton, Commander in Chief of the Atlantic convoy systems.

Derek, John (1926–)

Hollywood actor and husband of actresses Ursula Andress, Linda Evans, and Bo Derek. He enlisted in the U.S. Army in 1944 and volunteered for paratrooper training. Derek made sixteen jumps before being discharged in 1946.

"Der Fuehrer's Face"

Popular World War II novelty song written by Oliver Wallace and recorded by Spike Jones and His City Slickers in 1942. The song was written for the 1943 Academy Award–winning animated cartoon *Donald Duck in Nutzy Land* and sold over a million and a half copies.

Dern, George H. (–1936)
Former governor of Utah. He was selected by President Franklin D. Roosevelt as the U.S. Secretary of War in 1933. He was the grandfather of actor Bruce Dern.

Derrien, Louis
French admiral. As the commander of naval forces in Tunisia, he consented to surrender his weapons to the Germans in a December 7, 1942, ultimatum. As a result, Tunisia became part of a secured rear protecting Field Marshall Erwin Rommel from the Americans in Algeria, who had landed November 8, 1942.

Derry, Sam
British Army major. Rather than become a prisoner of war in Italy, he sought asylum in the Vatican where he headed the British Organization in Rome for assisting Allied escaped POW's. Derry was responsible for the successful evacuation and escape of hundreds of Allied airmen.

de Sainte Exupery, Antoine (1900–1944)
French aviator and writer who flew P-38's in World War II on reconnaissance missions. These unarmed aircraft flew behind enemy lines depending on their speed alone for protection. De Sainte had over 3,000 hours total flight time and disappeared on a reconnaissance mission somewhere over the Mediterranean in 1944.

Desert Fox
Nickname given by the British to German Field Marshall Erwin Rommel.

Desert Rats
Nickname given to the British Seventh Armored Division, which fought in North Africa.

de Seversky, Alexander (1894–1974)
Russian-born U.S. aircraft designer and manufacturer. In World War I, he was a pilot with the Czarist Air Force and lost a leg when his aircraft was shot down. De Seversky flew again using an artificial leg and subsequently shot down thirteen German aircraft. He came to the U.S. in 1918 after the Russian Revolution and designed a bomb sight for General Billy Mitchell. He joined the U.S. Army Air Corps reserve, rising to the rank of major in addition to founding Seversky Aircraft Corporation, which later became Republic Aviation Corporation.

Destroyer designators (U.S. Navy)
DD—Destroyer

DDE—Destroyers converted to destroyer escorts
DE—Destroyer escort (antisubmarine)
DER—Destroyer escort picket
DL—Destroyer leader (large)

U.S. Navy destroyers were named after dead Navy, Marine Corps, and Coast Guard personnel.

Detroit, U.S.S.

U.S. Navy heavy cruiser. It was the only ship present at Pearl Harbor on December 7, 1941, at the opening of World War II and also at Tokyo Bay on September 2, 1945, at the Japanese surrender ceremonies. U.S.S. *Detroit* was tied up behind the U.S.S. *Missouri*.

Deutschland

German cruiser that was renamed the *Lutzow* on November 15, 1939, because Hitler felt it would be bad for morale if a ship bearing the name *Deutschland* should ever be sunk. The *Deutschland* had already made an Atlantic sortie.

Deuxieme Bureau

Free French intelligence service in World War II. It was founded by André Dewavrin; the name was later changed to BCRA.

de Valera, Eamon (1882–1975)

Prime Minister of Ireland, which was one of only five European countries to remain neutral in World War II. He made the only condolences on the death of Hitler when he called on the German foreign minister to Ireland on May 3, 1945. De Valera defended himself by saying it was part of normal diplomatic protocol.

Devereaux, James P. S. (1903–)

U.S. Marine Corps brigadier general (retired). He was a major in command of the defenses on Wake Island at the outbreak of World War II. Although outgunned, outnumbered, and poorly equipped, the defenders held out for sixteen days against the Japanese at a time when the situation in the Pacific was nearly hopeless for the U.S. The Wake Island shore batteries consisted of five-inch guns, and Devereaux ordered them to hold their fire until Japanese warships were well within range. This led the Japanese to assume that Wake was undefended and they moved in close to the island. When Devereaux opened fire, his batteries sank two destroyers and damaged three cruisers. The Japanese later captured Wake and imprisoned everyone there for the remainder of the war.

Movie portrayal:
Wake Island (1942), by Brian Donlevy

Devil's Brigade

Name given by a German officer to the First Special Service Force. The unit was composed of Canadians and Americans who trained at Helena, Montana, under Colonel Robert T. Frederick. The training program included airborne and amphibious operations. The unit participated in the Kiska, Alaska, invasion and were then sent to Italy, fighting throughout the Italian campaign. The Devil's Brigade were rated man-for-man as one of the best military units of the war.

Devildog

Slang term for a U.S. Marine.

Devonshire, H.M.S.

British Navy cruiser that evacuated King Haakon of Norway, the rest of its government, and the country's gold reserves out of the path of the advancing Germans. H.M.S. *Devonshire* also sank the German auxiliary cruiser *Atlantis* on November 22, 1941.

Dewavrin, André

French Army captain. He escaped across the English Channel when France collapsed, after which he was ordered by General Charles de Gaulle to establish a Free French intelligence service, the Deuxieme Bureau. Dewavrin set up a network of agents in France to gather information on the Germans aimed at the liberation of France. His code name was Colonel Passy, after a subway station in Paris.

Dewey, Thomas E. (1902–1971)

U.S. politician. He ran against President Franklin D. Roosevelt in the 1944 presidential election and also against President Harry S Truman in 1948.

DeWitt, John L. (1880–1962)

U.S. Army lieutenant general. He was the commander of the Western Theater of Operations, which was headquartered at the Presidio in San Francisco; as such, he was responsible for the incarceration of Japanese-Americans. DeWitt moved all Japanese-Americans from the West Coast inland to camps without the benefit of due process of law and in violation of their constitutional rights.

DeWohl, Louis (1903–1961)

Hungarian astrologer. He was given information by the British Security Coordinator about upcoming events in the war that he included in his astrology columns. His accuracy rate was naturally extraordinarily high, creating quite a following. DeWohl's mission was to undermine the confidence of smaller countries in Hitler and German superiority. He also was employed by the British military to keep them advised of what German astrologers were reading in the stars for Hitler and the Nazi hierarchy.

DeWolfe, Billy (1916–1974)

Hollywood actor. He enlisted in the U.S. Navy on January 20, 1942, as Seaman First Class William A. Jones (his real name). He was discharged in 1945.

DIABI

International registration code of the first ME109 German fighter.

Diablo

Spanish word meaning "devil" and the war cry of the 508th Parachute Infantry Regiment of the U.S. 82nd Airborne Division.

Diablo

Name of Rex Barber's P-38 fighter that was involved in the April 18, 1943, downing of Admiral Isoruku Yamamoto's aircraft. One hundred bullet holes were found in *Diablo* after the mission.

Dickey, James (1923–)

American poet who, during World War II, flew in over 100 combat missions in the Pacific while assigned to the 418th Night Fighter Squadron.

Dickman, Otto (–1944)

German S.S. major who commanded the detachment of the *Das Reich* S.S. Division that executed the inhabitants of the French town of Oradour-sur-Glane in 1944. He was killed a week later in the fighting in Normandy.

Dieppe

Allied raid of August 19, 1942, ostensibly to test invasion techniques and the strength of German defenses. It was planned by then General Bernard Montgomery, but after it failed he washed his hands of the event.

Dietl, Edward (1890–1944)

German general who headed the mountain and ski troops of the army. He was the victor in the Battle of Narvik in 1940 and as a result was awarded the oak leaves of the Knight's Cross, the first person to be so honored. Dietl was killed in an aircraft accident, after which his eulogy was personally delivered by Hitler.

Dietrich, Marlene (1901–)

German-born Hollywood actress. Her father was a German cavalry officer in the Franco-Prussian War of 1870 who was awarded the Iron Cross. Dietrich entertained Allied troops around the world throughout World War II and also performed for German prisoners of war in the U.S. She was awarded the French Legion of Honor, the U.S. Medal of Freedom, and a Russian medal for her contributions to the war effort.

Dietrich, Otto (1892–1954)

Hitler's press chief. He was sentenced to seven years' imprisonment at the Nuremberg trials. While in prison he wrote the book *The Hitler I Knew.*

Dietrich, Sepp (1892–1976)

German S.S. general who commanded Hitler's personal bodyguard. He commanded the execution squad for Ernst Roehm in 1934 and later headed the *Adolf Hitler* S.S. Division. Dietrich was arrested in 1946 for the Malmedy Massacre of U.S. prisoners during the Battle of the Bulge in December 1944. He was sentenced to twenty-five years in prison but was released in 1955, only to be arrested again in 1957 for killing S.A. men during the Night of the Long Knives back in 1934. Dietrich received an eighteen-month sentence from a German court for his crime.

Dill, Sir John G. (1881–1944)

British Chief of the Imperial General Staff at the outbreak of World War II. He was replaced by Sir Alan Brooke and sent to Washington, D.C., as the British representative to the U.S. Dill, who died in 1944, was the only foreigner to be buried at Arlington National Cemetery. (A memorial was dedicated by President Harry S Truman on November 1, 1950, an hour after an assassination attempt had been made against Truman.)

MOVIE PORTRAYAL:

Churchill and the Generals (1981 TV movie), by Peter Copley

Dilley, Bruno

German Luftwaffe first lieutenant. He led the first Stuka attack of World War II, which actually occurred eleven minutes before the official start of hostilities. Dilley bombed the approaches to a bridge over the Vistula at Dirschau to prevent the Poles from blowing up the bridge. They were able to repair the wiring and blow up one of the spans of the bridge anyway.

Dilworth, Richardson C.

Mayor of Philadelphia. As a U.S. Marine Corps major in World War II, he was wounded in the fighting for Guadalcanal in 1942.

Dilworth was later a passenger on board the *Andrea Doria* when it was rammed and sunk by the liner *Stockholm* in 1956.

Di Maggio, Joseph Paul (1914–)

Major league baseball player. He enlisted in the U.S. Army Air Force in 1943 and was part of the physical training program in the U.S. and Hawaii. Di Maggio, who was promoted to staff sergeant, spent most of his service time hospitalized due to stomach ulcers.

Dimbleby, F. Richard (1913–1965)

British broadcaster. In 1936 he became the BBC's first news observer and in 1939 their first war correspondent. Dimbleby traveled to all the theaters of World War II.

Dimitrov, Georgi (1882–1949)

Bulgarian communist who was arrested by the Germans for setting the Reichstag Fire on February 27, 1933. He was tried by the German Supreme Court and was cross-examined so amateurishly by Hermann Goering that all the defendants except Marinus Vanderlubbe were acquitted. Dimitrov became the admiration of the world. He later became a Russian citizen and was Premier of Bulgaria in 1946.

Dimples 82

Call sign of the B-29, *Enola Gay,* on the August 6, 1945, mission to drop the first atomic bomb on Hiroshima.

Directives

Numbered orders personally issued by Hitler controlling the war effort:

No. 1 (August 31, 1939)—ordered German attack on Poland
No. 6 (October 9, 1939)—ordered invasion of the West
No. 9 (November 29, 1939)—ordered concerted effort against British supply lines
No. 16 (July 16, 1940)—ordered preparations for the invasion of England.
No. 17 (August 1, 1940)—ordered unrestricted air and sea operations against England.
No. 19 (December 10, 1940)—ordered plans for occupation of Vichy, France
No. 20 (December 13, 1940)—ordered invasion of Greece
No. 21 (December 18, 1940)—ordered invasion of Russia
No. 25 (April 6, 1941)—ordered invasion of Yugoslavia
No. 28 (April 25, 1941)—ordered occupation of Crete

No. 40 (March 23, 1942)—ordered construction of the Atlantic Wall

No. 41 (April 5, 1942)—ordered attack on the Caucusus oil fields that led to Stalingrad

No. 51 (November 3, 1942)—made provisions for the Allied invasion of Europe

von Diringshofen, Hein (–1967)

Luftwaffe's chief medical officer in World War II. He was the first to study the effects of high gravity forces and weightlessness in the 1930's. Von Diringshofen used himself as a guinea pig in diving Stukas and free-fall parachute jumps.

Dirschau

Polish town on the Vistula river. It was the first town to be attacked in World War II when at 4:34 A.M., Stukas of Geschwader One, led by Bruno Dilley, attacked approaches to the bridges over the river. This was eleven minutes before the war was scheduled to officially begin by the German high command.

Disasters of the U.S. Navy

U.S.S. *Indianapolis* torpedoed by *I-58* on July 30, 1945—883 died

U.S.S. *Franklin* attacked by Japanese bomber on March 19, 1945—772 deaths

U.S.S. *Juneau* torpedoed by *I-26* on September 15, 1942—676 died

U.S.S. *Liscombe Bay* torpedoed by *I-175* November 24, 1943—644 died

Distinguished Flying Cross

U.S. medal awarded for gallantry in flight. The first medal to be issued went to Charles Lindbergh for his 1927 trans-Atlantic flight. The first U.S. Navy man to receive the Distinguished Flying Cross was Commander Richard E. Byrd and the only woman civilian so honored was Amelia Earhart.

Distinguished Service Medal

U.S. medal awarded for meritorious service, usually in the Army. The first Englishman to receive the medal in World War II was Major General Henry Osborne Curtis, who commanded forces in Iceland. The first soldier to receive four DSM's was Lieutenant General Daniel Isom Sultan, who commanded U.S. forces in the China-Burma-India Theater.

Ditmar, Karl

German lieutenant general. He broadcast radio commentaries on the German Army radio and became known as the "Voice of the Wehrmacht." Ditmar surrendered to the U.S. Ninth Army in 1945 after crossing the Elbe river in a small boat.

Dixon, Jean Butler

Washington socialite. Her husband was killed while in the Royal Air Force and her ship was torpedoed off North Africa in November 1942. Mrs. Dixon also helped Harry Butcher, General Dwight Eisenhower's naval aide, to write the book *My Three Years With Eisenhower* in 1946.

Dobson, Sir Roy H. (1891–1968)

British aircraft designer who designed the Lancaster bomber.

Doctors

Physician	*Patient*
Lord Bertrand Dawson-Dawson	King George VI
Brigadier General Wallace H. Graham	President Harry S Truman
Dr. Felix Kersten	Heinrich Himmler
Admiral Ross T. McIntyre	President Franklin D. Roosevelt
Dr. Theodor Morell	Adolf Hitler
V. N. Vinogradov	Joseph Stalin
Sir Charles Wilson	Winston Churchill

Doenitz, Karl (1891–1980)

German admiral and commander of German submarines in World War II. Doenitz, who commanded *U-68* in World War I, spent that war as a prisoner of war when his submarine malfunctioned and surfaced in the middle of a British convoy. He masterminded the "wolf pack" tactics of World War II, having succeeded Admiral Eric Raeder as Commander in Chief of the German Navy in 1943. Hitler selected him to be his successor as Fuehrer of the Third Reich. Doenitz did not know of the Nazi atrocities and continued protecting Jewish Navy personnel and their families. He assumed the leadership of the Third Reich on April 30, 1945 and negotiated the surrender of the German forces in the West. He was sentenced to ten years in prison by the Nuremburg Tribunal in 1946.

Doenitz Volunteer Corps

Name that German submarine personnel adopted to emphasize their special status in the German Navy (Kriegsmarine).

Dogpatch

Nickname of the city that grew up surrounding the Oak Ridge,

Tennessee, atomic research facility in World War II. The name was borrowed from Al Capp's comic strip *Li'l Abner.*

Dogs

Blackie	Cocker Spaniel	Douglas MacArthur
Blaze	Bull Mastiff	Elliott Roosevelt
Blondie	German Shepherd	Adolf Hitler
Charlie		Benito Mussolini
Fala	Scottie	Franklin D. Roosevelt
Fella	Mongrel	Gregory "Pappy" Boyington
Hitler		Bernard Montgomery
Joe		Claire Chennault
Makalepa	Schnauzer	Chester Nimitz
Negus	Terrier	Eva Braun
Pitini		Benito Mussolini
Rommel		Bernard Montgomery
Sambo		Guy Gibson (R.A.F. pilot)
Seppl	Dachshund	Wilhelm Canaris
Stasi	Terrier	Eva Braun
Telek	Scottie	Dwight Eisenhower
Tigar	Dalmatian	Josef Tito
Wags	Cocker Spaniel	Forrest P. Sherman
Willie	Bull Terrier	George S. Patton

Dogsbody

Call sign of Royal Air Force ace Douglas Bader. It was also British slang for an aide or someone always under foot and therefore easy to kick.

Doihara, Kenji (1883–1948)

Japanese lieutenant general and commander of the 14th Division, who was called "the most hated man in China." He engineered the fall of Manchuria in 1931 and became known as the "Lawrence of Manchuria" because of his ability to gain the cooperation of native leaders. In 1941, Doihara was promoted to Commander in Chief of the Japanese air force. He was found guilty of war crimes and hanged on December 22, 1948.

Donahue, Arthur

Royal Air Force flight lieutenant. Born in Minnesota, he was the first American to fly with the R.A.F. in Britain and later flew Hurricanes at Singapore. Donahue was awarded the Distinguished Flying Cross for the Malayan campaign and later successfully escaped to Java. He wrote *Last Flight From Singapore* before being killed in the war.

Donlevy, Brian (1899–1972)

Hollywood actor. He was bugler for General Pershing in the 1916 Mexican campaign against Pancho Villa. In World War I he flew as a fighter pilot with the Lafayette Escadrille before the U.S. entered the war.

Donovan, William "Wild Bill" (1883–1959)

U.S. government figure and head of the OSS in World War II. Donovan won the Congressional Medal of Honor for fighting with the 42nd Infantry Division in World War I and was President Franklin D. Roosevelt's roving ambassador prior to the U.S. entry into World War II. He witnessed the takeover of Ethopia in 1935, the Spanish Civil War in 1936, and was in the Balkans just prior to the Nazi invasion in 1941. He went ashore with the invading forces at Sicily, Salerno, and Normandy where he was wounded in the throat. Donovan was the first person to receive all four of the highest U.S. decorations—the Medal of Honor, the Distinguished Service Cross, the Distinguished Service Medal, and the National Security Medal.

MOVIE PORTRAYALS:

The Fighting 69th (1940), by George Brent

A Man Called Intrepid (1979 TV movie), by Dick O'Neill

Doolittle, James H. (1896–   )

U.S. Army Air Force officer and aviation pioneer. He was the first to fly across the continent in a single day, the first army pilot to do an outside loop, and the first to try instrument flying. On April 18, 1942, he led a bomber attack of sixteen B-25's called the Tokyo Raid. The aircraft were launched from the aircraft carrier U.S.S. *Hornet* and made the first bombing strike on Japan, then flew on to China. Doolittle was awarded the Congressional Medal of Honor and promoted from lieutenant colonel to brigadier general, by-passing colonel. He later commanded U.S. Army Air Force units in North Africa and Europe.

MOVIE PORTRAYAL:

Thirty Seconds Over Tokyo (1944), by Spencer Tracy

Doolittle Raid

Sixteen twin-engine B-25 bombers flew off the carrier U.S.S. *Hornet* and attacked the Japanese home islands on April 18, 1942. It was the first strategic bombing attack on Japan of the war and was led by Lieutenant Colonel Jimmy Doolittle. The bombers dropped sixteen tons of bombs on Tokyo, Yokohama, Kobe,

Nagoya, and Yokosuka, causing little damage but lifting the spirits of the peoples opposing the Japanese. The attack took place on the 167th Anniversary of Paul Revere's ride.

MOVIES:
The Purple Heart (1943)
Thirty Seconds Over Tokyo (1944)
Midway (1974) in which some scenes were borrowed from the 1944 movie *Thirty Seconds Over Tokyo*

Dora

Name of a siege cannon used by the Germans at Sevastopol. The shell was 31.5 inches across, weighed five tons, and had a range of twenty-nine miles. A special seven-ton shell could travel twenty-four miles. The barrel was 107 feet long and the gun could fire three shells per hour. Sixty railway cars were required to move it. The crew for *Dora* was commanded by a major general and consisted of 4,120 men. It was sometimes called "Heavy Gustav" and one round is known to have destroyed an ammunition dump one hundred feet below the ground.

Doran, K. C.

Royal Air Force Squadron Leader, who on September 4, 1939, led the first British bomber attack of the war against the Germans. Five Blenheims of No. 110 Squadron and five from No. 107 Squadron attacked the pocket battleship *Admiral Scheer* anchored at Wilhelmshaven on a low-level mission. Unfortunately the bombs were set with eleven-second fuses and, although three hit the ship, they did not explode.

Dorchester, S.S.

Ship on which beatnik author Jack Kerouac sailed to Greenland in 1942. The ship was torpedoed and sank on its next voyage.

Dorn, Frank (1901–)

U.S. Army officer. As a lieutenant colonel, he was an aide to General Joseph Stilwell, following him out of Burma to Imphal, Assam, traveling from May 1 to May 20, 1942. Dorn later commanded the training of Chinese troops and the U.S. 11th Airborne Division artillery in the Philippines.

Dornberger, Walter (1896–1980)

German general who was in charge of the German rocket program. He was the head of the Peenemunde research center and later supervised the bombardment of London with V-1's and V-2's. At the end of the war, Dornberger was captured by the

British, who kept him prisoner for two years. He later became a U.S. citizen.

Dornier, Claude (1884–1969)

German aeronautical engineer. In 1911 he designed the first all-metal aircraft. In World War II, he built bombers and flying boats for the Luftwaffe.

Dorsetshire, H.M.S.

British cruiser which finally sank the German pocket battleship *Bismarck* on May 27, 1941, after the longest naval engagement in history. The *Dorsetshire* was sunk by Japanese carrier planes in the Indian Ocean later in 1941.

Doss, Desmond T. (1919–)

U.S. Army private first class. He was the first conscientious objector to receive the Congressional Medal of Honor on October 12, 1945, for action on Okinawa. Doss was a medical corpsman who also saw combat at Guam and Leyte with the 77th Infantry Division.

Dostler, Anton (–1945)

German general. He was the first member of the General Staff to be tried on war crimes charges by an American tribunal. In March 1944, Dostler ordered fifteen American OSS agents to be executed when they were caught behind German lines. For this he was found guilty and executed December 1, 1945, in Aversa, Italy.

Double-Cross System

Name given to a special British counterintelligence unit that caught German spies in England and forced them to work for the Allies. They were given controlled information to send back to the Germans. The unit was also called the XX Committee with the *X*'s standing for "double-cross." From this was derived yet another name—the Twenty Committee.

Doubles

Impersonators hired by prominent people to confuse their enemies and safeguard themselves. Hitler had three doubles; one stayed at Berchtesgaden, one in Berlin, and one in Munich. The Russians found the double in Berlin dead near the Chancellery bunker. At first, they thought it was actually Hitler but realized the truth when it was discovered that the corpse wore darned socks.

Winston Churchill's double—Alfred Chenfelts
Dwight Eisenhower's double—Baldwin B. Smith
Bernard Montgomery's double—E. Clifton-James

Douglas, Donald W. (1892–1981)
American aircraft designer and manufacturer. He was a witness to the first flight of the Wright Brothers in 1909, which sparked his interest in aviation. He designed the DC series (Douglas Commercial) and over ten thousand C-47's (known in peacetime as DC-3's) were built during World War II for the military.

Douglas, Kirk (1916–)
Hollywood actor. He enlisted in the U.S. Navy as a communications officer and served in Anti-Submarine Unit 1139 in the Pacific. Douglas received internal injuries when a depth charge exploded close to the patrol vessel he was aboard and was hospitalized for five months in San Diego. While in the hospital, he married Diana Dill on November 2, 1943, receiving a medical discharge in 1944.

Douglas, Melvyn (1901–)
Hollywood actor. He was the first actor to become a delegate to a national political convention when, in 1940, he was the California representative to the Democratic National Convention. To do his part for the war, Douglas enlisted in the U.S. Army as a private in December 1942 and made it through the rigors of basic training in spite of his age—forty-two. He served in the China-Burma-India Theater entertaining troops and was discharged in 1945.

Douglas, Paul H. (1892–1976)
U.S. politician who was a pacifist in World War I. In the spring of 1942, at 50 years old, he enlisted as a private in the U.S. Marine Corps and joined the 1st Marine Division in the Pacific. Douglas rose through the ranks to become a lieutenant colonel and fought at Pelilieu and Okinawa, being wounded in both battles. After spending eighteen months in hospitals, he was discharged in November 1946.

Douhet, Giulio (1869–1930)
Italian Air Force officer. He was Benito Mussolini's first Undersecretary of Air and was well known as an air tactician. Douhet wrote the book *Air Power,* which advocated the theory of using air attacks to overpower an enemy. The Luftwaffe adapted his ideas to their needs.

Dowding, Hugh (1882–1970)
British Royal Air Force airchief marshall. He was responsible for the development of radar and the monoplane fighter and was Commander in Chief of the R.A.F. fighter command. Dowding had been the chief of research and development in the 1930's;

helping to build up the British defensive system that warded off the German Luftwaffe. He talked Churchill into not sending more fighters to what he thought was a lost cause in France in 1940. Dowding received top secret Ultra intercepts and skillfully placed his fighters to do the most damage to the Luftwaffe during the Battle of Britain. He was replaced November 25, 1940, by Sholto Douglas and never really received the recognition he deserved for saving England. His nickname was Stuffy.

Movie portrayal:
Reach For the Sky (1956), by Charles Carson

Dowding's Chicks
Nickname given to the Royal Air Force fighter pilots commanded by Hugh Dowding in the Battle of Britain in 1940. It was coined by Prime Minister Winston Churchill.

Dowell, Saxie (1904–)
U.S. bandleader and composer who wrote the 1919 popular song "Three Little Fishies." He served on the U.S. aircraft carrier U.S.S. *Franklin* as the ship's bandleader and was aboard on March 19, 1945, when it was hit by two bombs, which caused the deaths of 772 crewmembers, in the U.S. Navy's second worst disaster.

Downfall
Code word for the Allied invasion of Japan. It was to consist of Operation Olympic and Operation Coronet.

Downs, Hugh (1921–)
Television talk show host and game show M.C. He was drafted into the U.S. Army during World War II after unsuccessfully attempting to join the Navy, Air Force, and Coast Guard. As an experiment his group's basic training was condensed from thirteen weeks to four weeks; as a result Downs collapsed from exhaustion. He was medically discharged after spending several weeks in the hospital.

Drabik, Alex
First U.S. soldier to cross the Remagen Bridge across the Rhine River into Germany, in March 1945.

Draecker, Edmund F.
Fictitious German diplomat conceived in 1936 by Hasso von Etzdorf, vice-consul in Rome. Draecker came to be a minor weapon against Teutonic bureaucracy and stupidity and was rumored to be involved in many historic events. The press continually

referred to him although no one could find him. The American equivalent was Kilroy, and the British had J. Hamilton Forby.

Draft of 1940

The first number drawn was 158. Henry L. Stimson drew it from the same bowl that was used in the 1917 draft for World War I. It took a total of seventeen and one-half hours to draw all the numbers and Lewis B. Hershey drew the last number, which was 2,114.

Draft Classifications

1A—fit for general military service
1B—fit for limited military service
1C—member of the armed forces
1D—students fit for general military service
1E—students fit for limited military service
IIA—deferred for critical civilian work
IIIA—deferred due to dependents
IVA—already served in the armed forces
IVB—deferred by law, i.e., draft officials
IVC—alien
IVD—ministers
IVE—conscientious objector
IVF—physically, mentally or morally unfit for service

Dragon Wagon

Name given to a U.S. Army truck trailer especially designed to carry the thirty-ton Sherman tank to save it from unnecessary wear and tear.

D Ration

U.S. emergency ration for field use when no other rations were available. It was a specially fortified chocolate bar that was the equivalent of a single meal.

Dreamboat

Code word for the B-29 superfortress.

Dresden

German city. It was the target of the last major attack of the strategic air offensive in Europe on February 14, 1945. Between 30,000 and 135,000 people were killed in what was a pointless tactical exercise. The city was thought to be a communications center for the German military against the Russians, but in fact it was a refugee collection point.

Dronne, Richard

Free French captain in General Jacques Leclerc's 2nd French

Armored Division. Dronne, who was from the French Territory of Chad, was the first French soldier to enter Paris.

Duchez, Rene

French housepainter who in 1941 stole a German plan for fortifications of the Atlantic Wall in the Normandy area. He accomplished this while on a wallpapering job for the Todt Organization, first hiding the map behind a picture, then recovering it later. Duchez was awarded the U.S. Bronze Star for an act General Omar Bradley called an "incredible and brilliant feat—so valuable that the landing operation succeeded with a minimum loss of men and material."

Duchin, Eddy (1909–1951)

Pianist who enlisted in the U.S. Navy in 1942. He was trained in antisubmarine detection gear because he had perfect pitch and his hearing allowed him to differentiate sounds readily. Duchin took part in the D-Day invasion on a destroyer escort and was later involved in the invasions of Iwo Jima and Okinawa. He was discharged in 1945 as a lieutenant commander.

MOVIE PORTRAYAL:

The Eddy Duchin Story (1956), by Tyrone Power

Duckwitz, Georg Ferdinand (1904–1973)

German shipping attaché to the German legation in Copenhagen, Denmark, during World War II. In September 1943, he warned the Danish Resistance about the prospective deportation of Danish Jews, which allowed the Danes to evacuate over 6,000 Jews to safety in Sweden.

Dugout Doug

Nickname given to General Douglas MacArthur by the men of Bataan and Corregidor because they felt he spent all his time hiding in dugouts.

Dugout Sunday

Name given to October 25, 1942, because bad weather on Guadalcanal and mud on Henderson Field prevented U.S. aircraft from taking off. Japanese aircraft from Rabaul attacked and heavily damaged the field while Japanese warships shelled the island with no opposition.

Duke of Hamilton (see Douglas Douglas Hamilton)

Duke of Kent (1902–1942)

Youngest brother of King George VI. He was a member of the Royal Air Force, serving as a group captain in Training Command. The Duke was killed when his aircraft crashed during an inspection tour to Iceland. He hit a mountain in Scotland on August 25, 1942. President Franklin Roosevelt was the godfather of his youngest child, Prince Michael George Charles Franklin, born July 4, 1942.

Duke of York, H.M.S.

British 35,000-ton battleship which sank the German cruiser *Scharnhorst* in the Battle of North Cape, December 26, 1943. It was commanded by Captain G.H.E. Russell and Admiral Sir Bruce Fraser. The *Duke of York* was also present in Tokyo Bay on September 2, 1945, for the Japanese surrender.

DUKW

Acronym for a U.S. Army six-wheel-drive, two-and-a-half-ton amphibious truck used in World War II. The name came from the model number of the manufacturer, General Motors. D=year of origin (1942); U=utility; K=all-wheel drive; W=six-wheeled. It was first used at Sicily and could carry twenty-five men on land or fifty in the water.

Dulles, Allen W. (1893–1969)

OSS chief in Switzerland during World War II. He was responsible for the negotiated surrender of German troops in Italy that saved thousands of American lives. Dulles's sources told him about the plot against Hitler and the V-2 rocket experiments at Peenemunde as early as 1943. He later became the head of the CIA. Ian Fleming dedicated his 1962 James Bond novel, *The Spy Who Loved Me*, to Dulles.

MOVIE PORTRAYAL:

Francis Gary Powers: The True Story of the U-2 Spy Incident (1976 TV movie), by Lew Ayres.

Dumbarton Oaks

Meeting held in Washington, D.C., August 21–29, 1944, in which the United Nations organization was agreed upon.

Dumbo

Nickname of U.S. aircraft used for the air-sea rescue of downed air crews. B-29s, due to their size, were called "super Dumbo."

Duncan, Donald W.

U.S. Navy captain. He was an air officer on Admiral Ernest J. King's staff who helped transform the idea of a carrier strike on Japan into the Doolittle Raid of April 18, 1942.

Dunedin, H.M.S.

British cruiser of the Dragon class. It was torpedoed and sunk on November 24, 1941, by the German submarine *U-124* under Johann Mohr. The magazine was struck, sending the *Dunedin* down in minutes.

Dunkern, Anton

S.S. general and commander of Lorraine. He was the first S.S. general to be captured by the U.S. Third Army and was personally interrogated by General George S. Patton, who used a Jewish lieutenant as interpreter.

Dunkirk

Greatest evacuation in history, made possible by British Ultra intercepts of German messages. It was called Operation Dynamo and 1,200 Allied naval and civilian craft succeeded in removing 338,226 military personnel, of which 112,000 were French, from the beaches between May 27 and June 4, 1940. British officers who escaped the Germans to contribute to the German defeat later included Lord Gort, Bernard Montgomery, Brian Horrocks, Sir Oliver Lesse, Sir Harold Alexander, Sir Miles Dempsey, Sir Kenneth Anderson, and Sir Alan Brooke.

Dunn, William Robert

First American to become an ace in World War II. He had joined the U.S. Army in 1934 and was assigned to the 4th Infantry Regiment. With the outbreak of the war, Dunn joined a Canadian army unit and fought in France. He then transferred to the Royal Air Force and flew with No. 71 Eagle Squadron, becoming an ace on August 27, 1941. He later transferred to the U.S. Army Air Force and served in Europe, Burma, and China, ending the war with a total of fifteen and one-half enemy aircraft shot down and twelve destroyed on the ground. After the war, Dunn was an adviser to Chiang Kai-shek for two years.

Duppel

German code name for radar. It was taken from the name of the estate near Berlin where experimentation on radar took place.

Dustbin

Code name for the British detention center for high-ranking Nazis at the end of World War II. The American equivalent was Ashcan.

Dutch collaborators

Only one Dutch general collaborated with the Germans during World War II. He was Hendrik Seyffardt and was assassinated on February 5, 1943, by the Dutch Resistance in the Hague.

E

Eighth Army Air Force

U.S. Army Air Force unit that was stationed in England during World War II. The mission of the 8th AAF was the bombing of Axis targets. It was established on January 28, 1942, and flew its first mission on August 17, 1942.

8-Ball

Name of a B-17 in which Clark Gable flew a mission over Europe. The aircraft was from the Eighth Army Air Force and Gable flew as a tail gunner.

84.3 pounds

Weight carried by the average American infantryman during World War II. This gave GI's the heaviest load of any foot soldier in the history of world warfare.

88mm

High velocity German artillery piece used throughout World War II. It was called the triple-threat artillery because it could be used as an antiaircraft, antipersonnel, or antitank cannon. A disadvantage was that it had a high profile and was difficult to camouflage. The 88mm was tested in the Spanish Civil War and observed by a British officer with the Loyalists. He filled out an intelligence report describing the capabilities, but when the report was sent back to England, it was thrown away because the British said the officer had exaggerated.

11

Number of Japanese delegates present on the battleship U.S.S. *Missouri* in Tokyo Bay on September 2, 1945, at the Japanese surrender that ended World War II.

Eleventh Army Air Force

U.S. Army Air Force unit established February 15, 1942, to protect the North Pacific from the Aleutian Islands to the Kurile Islands.

E 234

Registration number of the first Mosquito aircraft to be built. The number was later changed to W 4050 and the aircraft is now preserved at Hatfield, England.

Eadie, William F.

U.S. Navy lieutenant and PBY pilot who rescued Eddie Rickenbacker and his men on November 11, 1942, after they had been adrift in the South Pacific for twenty-seven days.

Eagle Day

(see Adler Tag, Der)

Eagle, H.M.S.

British aircraft carrier originally built as a battleship for the Chilean Navy. It was converted to a carrier and was the oldest and slowest ship of its class in the British Navy. On one mission the *Eagle* sent aircraft to attack the Italian fleet at anchor at Taranto on November 11, 1940. It was also involved in transporting Spitfires to besieged Malta; while on one of these missions, it was sunk by the *U-73*, on August 11, 1942.

Eagles' Nest

Name of Hitler's private tea room that sat atop the 5,500-foot Kehlstein peak at Berchtesgaden. It was built by Martin Bormann to win Hitler's favor, but Hitler never cared for it. Today it is a restaurant.

Eagle Squadrons

Name given to special Royal Air Force units that were made up of Americans who volunteered to fly and fight for the British before the U.S. entry into World War II. The first unit established was No. 71 Squadron. Organized by Colonel Charles Sweeney, a soldier of fortune, it had thirty-four U.S. citizens as the original contingent. No. 71 was commanded by Chesley Gordon Peterson of Salmon City, Idaho. Later, two other squadrons were formed, No. 121 Squadron and No. 133 Squadron. The Eagle Squadrons were officially credited with shooting down seventy enemy aircraft in their short time. These Americans were incorporated into the U.S. Army Air Force 4th Fighter Group when the U.S. entered the war; by then, of the original thirty-four members, only four were left.

Eagle, U.S.S.

U.S. Navy Q ship. Formerly the S.S. *Wave* and a Boston trawler, the *Eagle* was given a single four-inch gun to attack German submarines. She was commanded by Lieutenant Commander L. F. Rogers and had a short-lived career due to the loss of her sister ship, the U.S.S. *Atik* (see *Atik*, U.S.S. and *Asterion*, U.S.S.).

Eaker, Ira C. (1898–)

U.S. Army Air Force major general. An early advocate of air power and strategic bombing, he led the first American daylight raid of the war in Europe; twelve B-17's escorted by seventy-five Spitfires attacked a locomotive repair depot at Rouen, France, on August 17, 1942. Eaker piloted a B-17 named *Yankee Doodle*. He later planned the bombing mission on the Italian monastery of Monte Cassino in March 1944.

EAM

Name of the Greek Communist Resistance movement. The letters stood for National Liberation Front, although the members were not actively involved in fighting the Germans; they were conserving their forces and supplies until the end of the war when they could make a bid for power. Their army was called ELAS.

Early, Steven T. (1889–1950)

Press secretary to President Franklin D. Roosevelt. Prior to this he had worked for Paramount Newsreel.

Eastman Kodak Company

U.S. photographic company. A branch of the company was located at Oak Ridge, Tennessee, where it was the first to produce Uranium 235 for the atomic bomb. Kodak also developed a camera without a lens to photograph the atomic explosions.

Eatherly, Claude (–1978)

U.S. Army Air Force officer. He was the pilot of the B-29 *Straight Flush* which flew over Hiroshima on August 6, 1945, reporting on the weather and visibility. His information caused Hiroshima to be selected as the target for the first atomic bomb. Eatherly had trouble adjusting to civilian life after the war and was in trouble with the law several times. He became known as "the Hiroshima Pilot" and was identified in many people's minds, erroneously, as the one who dropped the bomb. This may have been a cause of his entering mental institutions on several occasions.

MOVIE PORTRAYAL:

Enola Gay (1981 TV movie), by Michael Tucci

Earthquake Bomb

British bomb designed by Barnes Wallis that weighed ten tons. It was large enough to set up shock waves in the ground strong enough to destroy a target without the necessity for pinpoint accuracy.

Eben-Emael

Belgian fort commanding the confluence of the Meuse River and the Albert Canal. It was touted as the strongest fort in the world and was captured by German paratroopers on May 11, 1940. It was the first large-scale airborne assault in history and the Germans of Assault Detachment Kock captured 1,200 Belgians with a loss to themselves of six dead and twenty wounded.

Eberhardt, Aubrey

U.S. Army private, who originated the "Geronimo" yell used by American paratroopers.

Eberly, Bob (1916–)

American singer and brother of singer Ray Eberle. He was drafted into the U.S. Army in December 1943 and served in a Special Service unit that entertained servicemen. He later became a singer with the Wayne King Orchestra.

Ebsen, Buddy (1908–)

Hollywood actor. In 1942, he joined the U.S. Coast Guard and was assigned to the subchaser U.S.S. *Pocatello*. As a lieutenant junior grade, Ebsen served in the Aleutian Islands before being discharged in January 1946.

Eden, Anthony (1897–1977)

British Foreign Secretary from 1935 to 1938 and again from 1940 to 1945 under Prime Minister Winston Churchill. He resigned in 1938 in protest to Chamberlain's attitude toward Mussolini and the appeasement of Hitler.

MOVIE PORTRAYAL:

Churchill and The Generals (1981 TV movie), by Richard Easton

Edinburgh, Philip, Third Duke of (1921–)

Husband of Queen Elizabeth II. He was born on Corfu, a Greek island, and in World War II served with the Royal Navy. Philip fought on the H.M.S. *Valiant* in the Battle of Matapan against the Italian fleet. In 1944, he was transferred to destroyer duty in the Pacific and was present for the official Japanese surrender ceremonies in Tokyo Bay on September 2, 1945.

Edison, Charles (1890–)
Son of American inventor Thomas A. Edison. He served as U.S. Secretary of the Navy under President Franklin D. Roosevelt until his resignation in June 1940 to run for governor of New Jersey.

Edson, Merritt A. (1897–1955)
U.S. Marine Corps general. During World War II, as a colonel, he commanded the 1st Raider Battalion which was known as Edson's Raiders. Edson, who was nicknamed "Red Mike," won the Congressional Medal of Honor for the Battle of Bloody Ridge, September 12, 1942, on Guadalcanal.

Edward Livingston, S.S.
Name of the 1,000th Liberty Ship built.

Edwards, Blake (1922–)
Hollywood writer and producer. He was hospitalized during World War II with a broken neck and back.

Egan, Richard (1923–)
Hollywood actor. During World War II, Egan served as a judo instructor at a basic training camp.

Ehrler, Heinrich (–1945)
German Air Force major. He was the tenth top scoring ace of the Luftwaffe with a total of 209 enemy aircraft shot down. Ehrler was awarded the Knight's Cross with oak leaves and swords. He was killed April 6, 1945.

Eichelberger, Robert L. (1886–1961)
U.S. Army lieutenant general. He graduated from West Point in 1909 and was the second highest ranking officer to General Douglas MacArthur in the Pacific. Eichelberger held three Japanese decorations for his part in the Siberian intervention of 1918 to 1919, the Imperial Order of Meiji, Order of the Sacred Treasure, and the Order of the Rising Sun. He commanded the 32nd Infantry Division and the US 8th Army in the Pacific. Eichelberger authored the book *Our Jungle Road to Tokyo*.

MOVIE PORTRAYAL:
MacArthur (1977) G. D. Spiradlin

Eichmann, Adolf (1906–1962)
S.S. officer and administrator of the Nazi Final Solution during World War II. He was overseer of the transport of Jews to the concentration camps, at which point his responsibility ended. Eichmann escaped the dragnet for important Nazis at the end of

the war and lived in hiding in Argentina, until he was kidnapped by Israeli agents in 1960 and brought to trial. The most chilling revelation of the trial was that Eichmann had no violent anti-Semitic feelings but was rather an exceptionally efficient bureaucrat interested only in doing a good job. For him morality was separate from work.

MOVIE PORTRAYALS:
Operation Eichmann (1961), by Werner Klemperer
Holocaust (1978 TV mini-series), by Tom Bell
The House on Garibaldi Street (1979 TV movie), by Alfred Burke

Einsatzgruppen

Special German killing squads that were set up by Reinhard Heydrich in March 1941 to travel behind the advancing German Army to the east. Four special units were established, composed of between 500 and 800 men. Most of the members were either criminals or soldiers drafted for punitive duty. These fewer than three thousand men accounted for over a million people killed in just two years. The largest single operation was the killing of 33,000 Jews in two days at Kiev in a ravine named Babi Yar.

Group A—Baltic Area (Leningrad); commanded by Franz Stahlecker, who was killed by Estonian guerrillas

Group B—White Russia (Moscow); commanded by Arthur Nebe, who was shot by Gestapo after July 20, 1944, attempt to kill Hitler

Group C—Ukraine; commanded by Otto Rasch, who survived the war but was unfit to stand trial at Nuremberg due to Parkinson's disease

Group D—South Russia; commanded by Otto Ohlendorf, who was tried at Nuremberg

Einstein, Albert (1879–1955)

Jewish physicist who won the Nobel Prize in 1921. He fled Germany when Hitler took over the government, traveling to the U.S., where he convinced President Franklin D. Roosevelt to go ahead with atomic bomb research.

MOVIE PORTRAYALS:
The Beginning of the End (1946), by Ludwig Stossel
A Man Called Intrepid (1979 TV miniseries), by Joseph Golland

Eisenhower Cup

Nickname given by Allied correspondents to the race among

themselves to leave a military briefing, rush to their typewriters, do a story, then get it on the wire service before any other newsman. It was also called "The Camel Corps Stakes" or "The Poor Man's Futurity."

Eisenhower, Dwight D. (1890–1969)

U.S. Army general who was Allied Supreme Commander of the Sicily, Italy, and later Normandy invasions. He maintained the broad front assault across Europe rather than a single thrust. Eisenhower was offered the Congressional Medal of Honor at the same time that General Douglas MacArthur received his, but turned it down because he said it was given for valor and that he had not done anything in that category.

MOVIE PORTRAYALS:

The Long Gray Line (1956), by Harry Corey, Jr.
The Longest Day (1962), by Henry Grace
Francis Gary Powers: The True Story of the U-2 Spy Incident (1976 TV movie), by James Flavin
Tail Gunner Joe (1977 TV movie), by Andrew Duggan
Backstairs at the White House (1979 TV miniseries), by Andrew Duggan
Ike (1979 TV miniseries), by Robert Duvall
Churchill and the Generals (1981 TV movie), by Richard Dysart

Eisenhower, John S. D. (1922–   )

Son of Dwight Eisenhower. He graduated from West Point June 6, 1944, the day his father was carrying through the D-Day Invasion of Normandy. He fought in Europe as an infantry officer in the last months of the war.

Eisenstaedt, Alfred (1898–   )

German-born photographer. He was one of the first four photographers hired by *Life* magazine in 1935. Eisenstaedt was drafted into the German army in 1916 and nearly lost his legs due to shrapnel from a British artillery shell. He was the only survivor of his artillery battery. He couldn't walk for over a year because of his injuries. Because he was Jewish, he fled Nazi Germany in 1935. Eisenstaedt took the picture on V-J Day of a sailor kissing a nurse in Times Square that became world-famous.* He also has

---

*ABC-TV's "20/20" news program in 1980 attempted to identify the names of the sailor and the girl but were unsuccessful when a number of people who claimed to be the pair came forward, all believing they were the people in the photograph.

photographed most of the notables of history in the twentieth century, including Joseph Goebbels, Marlene Dietrich, John F. Kennedy, Laurence Olivier, Sophia Loren, Dwight Eisenhower, Shirley Temple, George Bernard Shaw, and Ernest Hemingway.

El Agheila

Site of Field Marshall Erwin Rommel's corps first victory over the British in North Africa on March 23, 1941. Oddly enough, Rommel was in Berlin at the time.

El Alamein

Site of several famous battles in the North African desert fighting in World War II. It was only seventy miles from the main British Naval base of Alexandria.

Eldridge, U.S.S.

U.S. Navy destroyer (DE176) alleged to have been rendered invisible and tele-transported from the Philadelphia Naval Yard to Norfolk Virginia and back again in 1943. It was part of a Navy experiment in magnetic fields referred to as "The Philadelphia Experiment."

Electric Boat Company

American shipbuilding company located in New London, Connecticut. During World War II, it was the largest builder of submarines for the U.S. Navy, producing seventy-four. It also built 398 patrol torpedo boats.

Elliott, Denham (1922–　)

British actor. During World War II, he spent three years in a German prisoner-of-war camp.

Elliott, George, Jr.

U.S. Army private. He was training Joseph Lochard on radar operations on December 7, 1941, when they detected incoming planes that turned out to be the Japanese flying in to attack Pearl Harbor. They were on the north shore of Oahu as part of the 515th Signal Aircraft Warning Service.

Elser, George

German carpenter arrested by the Gestapo for a bomb that exploded in the Burgerbrau keller in Munich, November 8, 1939, in an assassination attempt against Hitler. As it turned out, he was in Dachau concentration camp where he was promised his freedom if he did as the Gestapo said. They took him to the beer hall where he assembled a bomb in one of the wooden pillars. An alarm clock was installed but not hooked up and a fuse was wired instead to an outside electrical source. Elser was captured while trying to cross the Swiss border and served with S. Payne Best in a concentration camp.

Emden

German light cruiser. It was the first medium-sized ship built after World War I for the German Navy. On January 23, 1945, the *Emden* removed the bodies of Field Marshall Paul von Hindenburg and his wife Gertrude from Königsberg so that the Russians would not get them.

Empire State Building

During World War II it was the world's tallest building (102 stories high). On July 28, 1945, a B-25 named *Old Feather Merchant* struck the building between the seventy-eighth and seventy-ninth floors, killing fourteen people and injuring twenty-five. The pilot of the aircraft was Lieutenant Colonel William F. Smith, Jr., a graduate of West Point in 1942, who had flown two years' combat in Europe and been awarded two Distinguished Flying Crosses and four Air Medals.

England

The British said there were three things wrong with U.S. troops in England; they were "overpaid, oversexed, and over here."

England, U.S.S.

U.S. destroyer escort under Lieutenant Commander Walton B. Pendleton that sank six Japanese submarines in twelve days. On May 19, 1944, it sank *I-16*, commanded by Lieutenant Commander Yoshitaka Takeuchi; on May 22, 1944, the *RO-116*, of Lieutenant Eyasu Uda was sunk; on May 23, 1944, the *RO-104* of Lieutenant Hisashi Izubuchi went down, followed by *RO-116*, *RO-104*, and *RO-108*. All the submarines were part of a picket line from Truk to New Guinea and their locations were discovered by U.S. Navy codebreakers who alerted hunter-killer groups. On May 9, 1945, the U.S.S. *England* was severely damaged by a kamikaze attack off Okinawa but survived, prompting Admiral Ernest King to say "There'll always be an *England* in the U.S. Navy."

Enigma

German coding machine invented by a Dutchman, Hugo Koch, in 1919. It looked like a typewriter and encoded and decoded messages via a series of drums that could be selected for a prescribed pattern. Enigma was originally designed for business use but was adopted by the German armed forces, who believed it was foolproof. However, the British were able to obtain a working model before Poland fell and were able to decipher nearly all Enigma messages for the rest of the war. The British intercepts were called Ultra.

Enola Gay

Name of the B-29 that dropped the atomic bomb on Hiroshima on August 6, 1945. It was piloted by Colonel Paul Tibbets, Jr., who named it after his mother. Other crewmembers were Captain Robert A. Lewis, copilot; Second Lieutenant Maurice Jeppson, electronics officer; Wyatt E. Duzenberry, flight engineer; Major Thomas W. Ferebee, bombardier; PFC Richard H. Nelson, radar operator; Staff Sergeant George R. Ceron, gunner; Sergeant Robert R. Shumard, assistant gunner; Captain Theodore Z. Van Kirk, navigator; and U.S. Navy Captain William S. Parsons, who assembled and armed the bomb. Accompanying aircraft were *Great Artiste*, piloted by Major Charles Sweeney, and #44-27291, flown by Captain George W. Marquardt. The *Enola** *Gay* had its name and the number *82* on the nose and is now in storage at the Smithsonian Institution.

Enright, Joseph

U.S. Navy commander of the submarine U.S.S. *Archerfish* who, while on his first patrol of the war, sank the largest ship ever sunk by a submarine and the largest warship ever built when he torpedoed the Japanese aircraft carrier *Shinano*, November 29, 1944, outside Tokyo Bay. Enright was awarded the Navy Cross.

Enterprise, U.S.S. (CV-6)

U.S. aircraft carrier that fought in every major sea battle in the Pacific war. It is responsible for shooting down over one thousand enemy aircraft and sinking more than seventy ships. The Japanese reported sinking the *Enterprise* six times and it was known by various nicknames such as the "Big E," "The Old Lady," and "The Galloping Ghost of the Oahu Coast." A kamikaze aircraft flown by Tomi Zai struck the *Enterprise* on May 14, 1945, and although severely damaged, it survived the war. It was finally cut up for scrap in 1958.

Erickson, Leif (1921–   )

Hollywood actor. During the Japanese attack on Pearl Harbor on December 7, 1941, he was blown overboard while on the U.S.S. *Nevada*. Erickson also was shot down several times by Japanese pilots during World War II.

---

*Enola is "alone" spelled backwards.

Ericson, Eric

OSS agent who worked in Stockholm during World War II gathering information on the German oil industry. He had many German acquaintances and was even given a tour of the German synthetic oil industry in October 1944. Ericson was known as Agent Red. He was portrayed by William Holden in the 1962 movie *The Counterfeit Traitor.*

Erk

Nickname given to Royal Air Force enlisted men who were part of the ground personnel.

Erlanger, Alene Stern (1894–1969)

Civilian consultant (1942–1945) to the Quartermaster General. He was the organizer of the K-9 Corps, which were the infantry scout dog platoons of the U.S. Army during World War II.

Ervine-Andrews, Harold

British Army captain. He won the first Victoria Cross issued to an officer in World War II for leading a counterattack of the East Lancastershire Regiment during the evacuation of Dunkirk in June 1940.

Escort carriers

U.S. Navy aircraft carriers that were converted merchant ships. They were designed to carry a maximum of thirty aircraft, which would fly reconnaissance for convoys in an effort to thwart German submarines in the mid-Atlantic. They were also known as "Baby Flattops."

Esmond, Eugene (1909–1942)

British captain. He was the pilot of the torpedo plane that hit and crippled the German pocket battleship *Bismarck*. He was later shot down and killed while leading a torpedo attack on the cruisers *Scharnhorst, Gneisenau*, and *Prinz Eugen* in 1942. Esmond was awarded the Victoria Cross posthumously for this attack. Although he did not hit his target, the *Scharnhorst*, he caused it to swerve out of a cleared channel, after which it struck a mine and was damaged on February 12, 1942.

Essex, U.S.S. (CV-9)

U.S. aircraft carrier which was commissioned December 31, 1942. It fought in every major Pacific battle from Tarawa to Tokyo Bay.

Eta Jima

Island in Hiroshima Bay. It was the site of the Japanese Naval Academy, the equivalent of Annapolis, the U.S. Navy Academy.

Eureka
Code name for the Teheran Conference held between President Franklin D. Roosevelt, Prime Minister Winston Churchill, and Russian Premier Joseph Stalin from November 26 to December 2, 1943.

Evil I
Nickname given to the U.S. aircraft carrier *Intrepid* because it had survived numerous bomb and torpedo strikes during World War II.

Ewell, Tom (1909–)
Hollywood actor. He served in the U.S. Navy during World War II as a member of a gunnery unit in the Atlantic before he was discharged in 1945 with the rank of lieutenant senior grade. Ewell played the Bill Mauldin character Willie in both the 1951 movie *Up Front* and in the 1952 sequel *Back to the Front*.

Excelsior
Code name for the Philippine Islands.

Execute Pontiac
Code message sent out by General Jonathan Wainwright to notify his commands of the surrender of Corregidor, May 6, 1942.

Executive Order No. 9066
Controversial order signed by President Franklin D. Roosevelt on February 19, 1942, that resulted in all Japanese-Americans on the West Coast being rounded up and incarcerated in camps throughout the United States. Over 112,000 people were sent to relocation centers for most of the war.

Exercise Hornpipe Plus Six
Message sent out by General Dwight D. Eisenhower to alert all commanders in chief that D-Day would be June 5, 1944, weather permitting.

Exercise Weser
Code name of the German invasion of Norway, April 9, 1940.

Exeter, H.M.S.
British cruiser under the command of Admiral Sir Henry Harwood that battled the *Graf Spee* in 1939, causing Captain Hans Langsdorff to scuttle the German ship. The *Exeter* was later sunk by Japanese forces in March 1942.

Extractor, U.S.S.
U.S. Navy salvage vessel. It was the only U.S. ship to be

accidentally* sunk in World War II by a U.S. submarine. *Extractor* was torpedoed on January 23, 1945, by the U.S.S. *Guardfish* under Douglas Hammond, who mistakenly identified it as a Japanese I-class submarine in the difficult light before sunrise. The attack killed six men and the rest (seventy-three) were picked up by the *Guardfish*. *Extractor*'s commander H. M. Babcock shared the blame with Hammond before a Board of Inquiry because he had received a garbled message ordering him to return to Guam, and he did not request a repeat even though he could not decipher the signal.

*Several U.S. ships were scuttled by U.S. submarines during the war.

F

First Army

U.S. Army unit that was the

first to break a hole at St. Lo for the Third Army to pour through
first to reach Paris
first to enter Belgium and Luxembourg
first to crack the Siegfried Line
first into Germany and across the Rhine
first to meet the Russians at the Elbe
it also captured more prisoners and buried more Americans than any other U.S. Army

First Motion Picture Unit

U.S. Army Air Force training film unit that was commanded by Colonel Jack Warner. A few members were Captain Ronald Reagan, First Lieutenant William Holden, Lloyd Bridges, and Leslie Nielsen.

4th Fighter Group

Part of the Eighth Army Air Force stationed in England. It was made up primarily of veterans of the Royal Air Force Eagle Squadrons. The 4th was the highest-scoring group of the European war, having destroyed 1,016 enemy aircraft. It was commanded during most of its existence by Donald Blakeslee.

Four Chaplains

Clergymen who were immortalized on a U.S. postage stamp for giving their life vests to others on the torpedoed U.S. Army transport *Dorchester* in the North Atlantic in February 1943. They were George L. Fox and Clark V. Poling, Protestants; John P.

Washington, a Catholic priest; and Alexander D. Goode, a Jewish rabbi. Each chaplain was posthumously awarded the Distinguished Service Cross by the U.S. Army.

Four Duties

The duties or responsibilities required of a people in order to protect and preserve The Four Freedoms, as outlined in U.S. President Franklin D. Roosevelt's State of the Union Speech of January 6, 1941:

to produce to the maximum capacity
to transport supplies to the field of battle as quickly as possible
to fight in an all-out effort
to work in building a peace that was just, charitable, and lasting (see Four Freedoms)

4 F (unfit for military service)

Stewart Alsop—asthma and high blood pressure
Dana Andrews—back trouble
William Bendix—asthma
Marlon Brando—injured knee received in high school football
Jack Carson—heart murmur
Montgomery Clift—chronic diarrhea
Steve Cochran—heart murmur
Gary Cooper—displaced hip
Jack Dempsey—overage
Dan Duryea—prior heart attack
George Fenniman—unknown
Red Foxx—unknown
Errol Flynn—heart condition
John Garfield—heart condition
Jackie Gleason—overweight (100 pounds)
Dick Haymes—hypertension
Van Johnson—head injuries received in an auto accident
Danny Kaye—bad back
Lee Liberace—spine injury
Dean Martin—hernia
Ray Milland—impaired left hand
Gregory Peck—ruptured vertebrae from college athletics
Cliff Robertson—impaired left eye
Joe Rosenthal—poor eyesight
Paul Scofield—unknown
Phil Silvers—poor eyesight

Frank Sinatra—punctured eardrum
James Stewart—underweight
Superman—faulty vision
Sonny Tufts—football trick knee
David Wayne—defective vision
John Wayne—perforated eardrum and overage
Richard Widmark—perforated eardrum

Four Freedoms

Goals set up by President Franklin D. Roosevelt for the United States and the world. He listed them in his "State of the Union" speech on January 6, 1941. They were

freedom of speech and expression
freedom of religion
freedom from want
freedom from fear

Four Jills in a Jeep

Movie of 1944 about female stars entertaining servicemen during World War II, based on a book by actress Carole Landis. The four Jills were Carole Landis, Martha Raye, Mitzi Mayfair, and Kay Francis. The name of the jeep was *Jessica*.

4 Y

Comedian Bob Hope's suggested classification for the draft during World War II. He said the *Y* stood for "yellow."

Fourteenth Army Air Force

U.S. Army Air Force unit created in China from the veterans of the Flying Tigers. It was commanded by Major General Claire Chennault.

46

Number of nations that made up the Allies in World War II.

40–2370

Serial number of the B-24 destroyed by the Japanese at Hickam Field on December 7, 1941. It was the first American bomber lost in World War II.

442nd Regimental Combat Team

Most highly decorated unit in U.S. Army history. It was composed of Japanese-Americans who had volunteered to fight for the U.S. Their unit did not have a single case of desertion during all of World War II, a record unequaled by any other American unit. The unit's motto was "Go for Broke" and in the course of the Italian campaign the members of the 442nd were awarded:

1	Congressional Medal of Honor
52	Distinguished Service Crosses
1	Distinguished Service Medal
560	Silver Stars (28 with oak-leaf clusters)
22	Legions of Merit
4,000	Bronze Stars (1,200 oak-leaf clusters)
15	Soldier's Medals
12	French Croix de Guerre
2	Italian Crosses for Military Merit
2	Italian Medals for Military Valor

450th Anti-Aircraft Artillery Battalion

An all-black U.S. Army unit. It was the first black unit in North Africa and the first black unit to enter combat in Europe. General Mark Clark cited it for "outstanding performance of duty."

5:5:3

Battleship and aircraft carrier ratio that was determined by the Washington Naval Agreement of February 6, 1922. For every five battleships built by America and Britain, the Japanese could only build three.

5 Japanese medals

Decorations attached to the bombs carried by Doolittle's Raiders on the Tokyo bombing mission of April 18, 1942. The medals had been given to U.S. Navy personnel prior to World War II, who decided to return them to the rightful owners.

Fifth Army Air Force

U.S. Army Air Force unit that was set up February 5, 1942, in the Southwest Pacific. It was commanded by Lieutenant General George C. Kenney and was called "the Flying Buccaneers."

Fifth Column

Term used to describe secret sympathizers behind enemy lines that engaged in espionage, sabotage, and other types of subversive activity. The term was coined by General Emilio Mola, second-in-command of the Spanish Nationalists, who said that four columns of troops were converging on Madrid from the outside while a fifth column was waiting to strike from within.

Fifth Panzer Army

Second German army to surrender to the Allies in World War II. The first to surrender was Field Marshall von Paulus's Sixth Army at Stalingrad. The Fifth Panzer Army under General Gustav von Vaerst surrendered to U.S. General Omar Bradley on May 9, 1945.

Five-Star Rank

Special rank created by the U.S. to recognize the top military leaders:

Generals of the Army	*Fleet Admirals*
George C. Marshall	Ernest J. King
Dwight D. Eisenhower	William D. Leahy
Douglas MacArthur	Chester Nimitz
Henry H. "Hap" Arnold	

Only five men have ever held the rank of General of the Army, the fifth being Omar Bradley, who held it after the war.

Fifteenth Army Air Force

U.S. Army Air Force unit created on November 1, 1943, to strike at the Axis countries from the south. After the capture of southern Italy, the Fifteenth Air Force moved into former enemy air bases and began their attacks. The first mission was on November 2, 1943, against the Messerschmitt factory of Wiener Neustadt, Austria.* The men of the unit called themselves "the Forgotten Air Force" because the Eighth Army Air Force in England received all the publicity. But the Fifteenth developed on a large scale techniques of bombing through cloud covers and conducted many shuttle bombing missions.

52-20 Club

Nickname given to GI's returning to the states after World War II. They collected twenty dollars a week for a maximum fifty-two weeks while unemployed.

$500

Bonus given to the pilots of the American Volunteer Group in China for every Japanese plane that they shot down, if confirmed.

509th Composite Group

Secret B-29 unit set up to drop the atomic bombs on Japan. It consisted of fifteen B-29's commanded by Colonel Paul Tibbets, Jr., with specially trained crews. A pilot after the release of the bomb would dive and turn 158 degrees, a move which allowed the aircraft to be eight miles from the point of release within forty-three seconds. The 509th was based at North Field, Tinian.

F

Code designator for Colonel Maurice Buckmaster, Chief of the

---

*The coauthor's father, Arlie "Bud" McCombs, served with the Fifteenth at Foggia, Italy.

French section of the British SOE. He had formerly been the head of the Ford Motor Company in France.

F-7

Number of the berth on battleship row where the U.S.S. *Arizona* was tied on December 7, 1941, at Pearl Harbor.

F-13

Designator of the reconnaissance version of the B-29. Only a few were built.

Fabien, Pierre

French communist and colonel of the Resistance. Before French occupation, he was wounded twice during the Spanish Civil War and once as a volunteer in Czechoslovakia. Fabien was also arrested twice by the Gestapo in France but escaped both times. One escape was only minutes before he was to be executed. In 1942, he shot the first German soldier to be killed in Paris during World War II and in August 1944, he led the attack on the first German strongpoint in Paris to be assaulted during the liberation of the city.

Fabius

Code name for a practice landing of four Allied divisions in England in preparation for the D-Day assault on Normandy.

Fahneneid

Oath of allegiance to Hitler sworn by every member of the German armed forces.

Fairbanks, Douglas, Jr. (1909–   )

Hollywood actor, son of silent screen star Douglas Fairbanks, Sr. He joined the U.S. Navy in 1928 and served for several years as a lieutenant aboard the U.S.S. *Mississippi*, U.S.S. *Washington*, and the cruiser U.S.S. *Wichita* before his discharge in order to go into acting. With the outbreak of World War II, Fairbanks enlisted again in the Navy and was posted to Lord Louis Mountbatten's Combined Operations staff, where he devised gadgetry intended to confuse the Germans and was involved in several planned commando raids. Not content with staff work, he commanded and led a commando assault on the Casquet lighthouse on the coast of France in September 1942. Two months later, Fairbanks conducted a desert raid on Sened Station in North Africa. In September 1943, he and four others conducted a commando raid on Ventotene, an Italian island off Sicily, to capture a German radar station. As a lieutenant commander, Fairbanks was in command of a detachment of PT boats that sailed toward the coast of France to deceive the Germans into believing an invasion was imminent. He was awarded a Silver Star medal (the first actor so honored), the British Distinguished Service Cross, and the French *Croix de Guerre*.

Fairfield

Code name of General Dwight Eisenhower's advance command post in Algiers for the invasion of Italy.

Faith, Hope, and Charity

Names given to the only three Gladiator aircraft on Malta at the outbreak of World War II. They continually took on the collected might of the Italian air force until wear and tear took their toll and they could not fly anymore.

Falaise Gap

Site of an attempted Allied encirclement of most of the German forces in western France. The failure of the Allies to close up the circle resulted in the escape of half the German troops, allowing them to fight again. At the time Field Marshall Bernard Montgomery was still giving orders to U.S. ground forces, although General Omar Bradley should have been, and would not allow General George Patton to advance and complete the encirclement.

Falk, Peter (1927–)

Hollywood actor. He lost his right eye as a child due to a tumor. In 1945, he enlisted in the U.S. Marine Corps and memorized the eye chart so that he could pass the physical, but the examiner became suspicious since his right eye did not move. The Marines would not let him join, so he became a cook in the Merchant Marine for a year.

von Falkenhausen, Alexander (1878–1966)

German general and winner of Germany's highest decoration in World War I, the *Pour le Mérite*. In World War II, he was the military governor of Belgium and northern France until his arrest by the Gestapo in connection with the July 20, 1944, assassination attempt against Hitler. Von Falkenhausen was put in Niederhausen concentration camp in the south Tirol, from which he was freed by the Americans on May 4, 1945. After the war, he was tried and convicted for complicity to kill 240 Belgian hostages, but he was released because he had already served four years while awaiting trial.

von Falkenhorst, Nikolaus (1885–1968)

German general who commanded the invasion and occupation of

Norway. He commanded German forces until 1944, when he was relieved of command because of opposition to the Nazis. Von Falkenhorst was tried by the British in 1946 for the shooting of British commandos who had been landed in Norway and was sentenced to twenty years' imprisonment. He was given a reprieve and freed in 1953 due to ill health.

Falley, Wilhelm (–1944)

German general and commander of the 91st Infantry Division at Normandy on June 6, 1944. He was the first general killed on D-Day when he was shot by paratroopers of the U.S. 508th Parachute Infantry Regiment. Falley was killed by Lieutenant Malcomb D. Brennan when, after being wounded, he tried to grab his pistol.

Fall River

Code name of Milne Bay, New Guinea. At the height of the fighting in New Guinea, desperately needed supplies were accidentally routed to Fall River, Massachusetts, where they sat on the docks rusting away.

Farago, Ladislas (1906–1980)

Hungarian-born U.S. author. He had been a newspaperman in Hungary at the outbreak of World War II and escaped to the United States. Farago, although an alien, became the chief researcher for the U.S. Navy Special Warfare Activities, a part of U.S. intelligence; his job was to mastermind new subversive attacks against the enemy.

Farrow, John (1904–1963)

Movie producer and father of actress Mia Farrow by Maureen O'Sullivan. As a lieutenant commander in the Royal Navy, he was wounded in action.

Farrow, William

U.S. Army Air Force officer. He was the pilot of the sixteenth and last B-25 to depart the U.S.S. *Hornet* to bomb Japan as part of the Doolittle Raid on April 18, 1942. The propeller of his aircraft gashed a deck hand's arm, which had to be amputated. Farrow and crew were captured by the Japanese. He and two others were executed because they had signed blank papers on which confessions of war crimes were later filled in. The other two were Lieutenant Dean Hallmark and Harold Spatz.

Far Shore

Nickname used in Allied military conferences in referring to the beaches at Normandy.

Fascist organizations

Argentina	Gov	Juan Perón
Austria	National Socialists	Arthur Seyss-Inquart
Belgium	Rexists	Leon Degrelle
Brazil	Integralistas	Plinio Salgado
Bulgaria	Ratnizi	
Chile	Nacista	Jorge Gonzalez von Maree
China	Kuomintang	Chiang Kai-shek
Czechoslovakia	Sudeten deutsch	Konrad Henlein
England	Union of Fascists	Leonard Mosbey
France	Croix de Feu	Charles Maurras
Germany	NSDAP	Adolf Hitler
Holland	NSB	Anton Mussert
Hungary	Arrow and Cross	Ferenc Szalasi
Italy	Fasci di Combattimento	Benito Mussolini
Japan		Hideki Tojo
Norway	Nasjonal Samling	Vidkun Quisling
Portugal	Mocidade	Antonio Salazar
Rumania	Iron Guard	Ian Antonescu
Spain	Falangists	Francisco Franco
Union of South Africa	Ossewa Brandweg	Daniel F. Malan
United States	German American Bund	Fritz Kuhn

Fascist slogan (Mussolini's Italy)

''Believe, Obey, Fight''

Fast Carrier Force

Name of the U.S. Navy forces involved in the invasion of the Marianas under command of Admiral Marc Mitscher. It was composed of fifteen aircraft carriers and was part of Task Force 38 (when Admiral William Halsey commanded) or Task Force 58 (when Admiral Raymond Spruance commanded).

Fat Boy

Code name of the atomic bomb, made from plutonium, that destroyed Nagasaki on August 9, 1945. It was 128 inches long and 60 inches in diameter and was dropped from the B-29, *Bock's Car*. Fat Boy was named for Prime Minister Winston Churchill.

Faurot, Robert

U.S. Army Air Force captain. He is credited with the first

Japanese Zero to fall to a P-38, although it did not occur in any usual way. While carrying two 500-pound bombs over the Japanese airbase at Lae in December 1942, Faurot saw a Zero begin its takeoff roll and dove down to attack it. He descended to an altitude of 2,000 feet before he remembered the bombs and their hindrance to aerial combat, so he released them and pulled up to escape the blast. The bombs landed in the water at the end of the strip and the resulting water column knocked the Zero down. General George C. Kenney had promised an Air Medal to the first P-38 pilot to get a Zero and razzed Faurot about not having actually shot the aircraft down. Nevertheless, Kenney awarded Faurot the medal. Faurot was killed during the Battle of the Bismarck Sea while trying to prevent a Japanese aircraft from strafing a bomber crew in parachutes.

Faust, Frederick Schiller (1892–1944)

American writer of western novels and creator of Dr. Kildare under the pen name of Max Brand. He was killed in Italy while serving as a war correspondent.

Favorite reading

Dwight Eisenhower—any western
Adolf Hitler—Karl May westerns
Bernard Montgomery—*Pilgrim's Progress* and the *Bible*
Benito Mussolini—Dante and Virgil
Erwin Rommel—*Generals and Generalship* by Archibald Wavell

Fegelein, Herman (1906–1945)

German S.S. general. He was Heinrich Himmler's liaison officer to Hitler's staff and was married to Eva Braun's sister. Fegelein participated in the equestrian events in the 1936 Olympics and had a good combat record on the Eastern Front early in the war. In the last days before the fall of Berlin, Fegelein attempted to hide but was caught and taken to the Bunker. There he was denounced as a defeatist and a traitor, for which he was executed on April 29, 1945. The accepted interpretation of this event is that Himmler was negotiating with the Allies; Hitler heard of this and had Fegelein shot in place of Himmler.

MOVIE PORTRAYAL:

The Bunker (1980 TV movie), by Terrence Hardiman

Fegen, Edward F. (1895–1940)

British captain in command of the auxiliary cruiser *Jervis Bay*. He was killed in action protecting a convoy from the German pocket battleship *Admiral Scheer* in November 1940. Fegen was awarded a posthumous Victoria Cross, the highest decoration the British have.

Feldt, Eric

Australian lieutenant commander who developed the coast-watcher organization that contributed significantly to the Solomon Islands battles.

Feller, Robert W. (1918–)

U.S. baseball pitcher. He was a gunner on the battleship U.S.S. *Alabama* and won eight battle stars.

Fellers, Bonner (1896–1974)

U.S. Army officer. As a colonel, he was the U.S. military attaché in Cairo and sent information back to the U.S. about the British forces in North Africa via the Black Code. What he did not know was that the Germans could read the Black Code and Field Marshall Erwin Rommel could anticipate every move the British made, as well as their strengths and weaknesses. This went on from September 1941 to August 1942, when the British realized the source of the leak and had the U.S. change its code. Fellers thus inadvertently contributed to the German victories in North Africa. When he was brought back to the U.S. he was awarded a Distinguished Service Medal for his concise and factual reporting—a fact the Germans probably also appreciated.

Fellgiebel, Erich (1888–1944)

German general and head of German Army communications. He was the person who recommended the adoption of the Enigma coding machine by the German military. It is believed that Fellgiebel passed secrets about Enigma to the British throughout the war, until he was arrested by the Gestapo for taking part in the July 20, 1944, conspiracy against Hitler. He was tried before the People's Court by Dr. Roland Feisler and executed on September 4, 1944.

Ferdinand

Code name for the system of Australian coast watchers who lived behind Japanese lines in the Solomon Islands and radioed military intelligence to the Allies. They were largely responsible for the victory at Guadalcanal.

Ferdinand

Name of a German self-propelled gun. It was protected by 200mm armor that was thicker than a navy battle cruiser's armor plate.

Ferdinand, Louis

Second eldest son of the Crown Prince of the House of Hohenzollern and grandson of Kaiser Wilhelm II. Ferdinand headed the foreign department of Lufthansa airlines and was involved in the anti-Hitler conspiracy that resulted in the July 20, 1944, assassination attempt against Hitler. He was selected by the conspirators as the new head of the German government after the overthrow of the Nazis and, in spite of this, survived the war.

Ferdinand Magellan

Name given to President Franklin D. Roosevelt's private railroad car. It weighed 285,000 pounds and was sold to him for one dollar by the Association of American Railroads. Roosevelt used it for many top-level meetings. It also transported his body from Warm Springs, Georgia, back to Washington, D. C., after his death in April 1945.

Ferdinand Tank

German tank built in the latter half of World War II. It weighed seventy-three tons and had 120mm armor on the front with 82mm armor on the sides. As awesome as it was, it had a slight design error, in that there were no machine guns for protection. Russian infantry could approach the tank and drop incendiaries into the engine air intakes that would set it on fire.

Ferebee, Thomas (1918–   )

U.S. Army Air Force officer. He was the bombardier on the *Enola Gay* who dropped the atomic bomb on Hiroshima on August 6, 1945.

Movie portrayals:
Above and Beyond (1953), by Jeff Richards
Enola Gay (1981 TV movie), by Gary Frank

Fermi, Enrico (1901–1954)

Italian-born nuclear physicist. He won the Nobel Prize for physics in 1938 but became a fugitive from Hitler because he was Jewish. Fermi was instrumental in research in the U.S. Manhattan Project that resulted in the atomic bomb.

Movie portrayal:
The Beginning of the End (1946), by Joseph Calleia

Fermor, Patrick Leigh (1915–   )

Irish author. During World War II, he enlisted in the Irish Guard and fought in Greece and Crete. After the German capture of Crete in 1941, he went underground and hid out, disguised as a shepherd. He and Major W. Stanley Moss captured German General Karl Kreipe, commander of the German forces on Crete, and used the General's car to escape. They eventually got him back to Cairo, in what was one of the war's most unusual episodes.

Fest, Joachim (1927–   )

German historian and author. He was drafted into the German Army at fifteen years of age and was captured by the Americans at Remagen Bridge in March 1945. He is known for his biography of Adolf Hitler entitled *Hitler.*

FFI

French Forces of the Interior. It was part of the French Resistance opposing the Germans.

FHO

Fremde Heere Ost. It was the principal Germany Army intelligence agency for the Eastern Front and specifically aimed at the Russians. It was commanded by Reinhard Gehlen, who later became head of the West German intelligence service.

Fictitious people of World War II

Edmund F. Draeker—German
J. Hamilton-Forby—British
Kilroy—American

FIDO

Fog Investigation and Dispersal Operation. FIDO was the code word for the Allied effort at fog dispersal in England during World War II. England was sometimes covered with such intense fog that it was impossible for aircraft to land, and a method was needed for temporarily removing it. The system that was devised consisted of laying horizontal pipes parallel to the edge of the landing strip. Gas was then forced out of perforations in the pipes and ignited. The flames burned off the thickest fog, and this kept fifteen British airfields operational at all times.

Fielding, Temple

Writer who enlisted in the U.S. Army as an artillery officer during World War II and transferred to the OSS in early 1944. He was sent to Italy, Algeria, and Yugoslavia for propaganda work and is credited with more than 30,000 enemy capitulators. In civilian life, he became a roving reporter and eventually wrote *Fielding's Guide to Europe*.

Field Marshalls (British)

Sir Harold Alexander
Sir Claude Auchinleck
Sir Alan Brooke
Arthur W. Connaught
Sir John Dill
John Gort
Sir Edmund Ironsides
Bernard Montgomery
Jan Christian Smuts
Sir Archibald Wavell
Sir Henry Maitland Wilson

Field Marshall (Finland)

Karl von Mannerheim

Field Marshalls (Germany)

Werner von Blomberg (also Germany's first Field Marshall, commissioned in 1936)
Fedor von Bock
Walther von Brauchitsch
Ernst Busch
Johann Friessner
Ritter von Greim (also Germany's last Field Marshall, commissioned in 1945)
Wilhelm Keitel
Albert Kesselring
Paul von Kleist
Hans von Kluge
Georg von Kuchler
Ritter von Leeb
Siegmund List
Erich von Manstein
Erhard Milch
Walther Model
Friedrich von Paulus
Walther von Reichenau
Wolfram von Richtofen
Erwin Rommel
Gerd von Rundstedt

Ferdinand Schorner
Hugo Sperrle
Maxmilian von Weichs
Erwin von Witzleben

Field Marshalls (Italian)

Pietro Badoglio
Ettore Bastico
Ugo Cavallero

Field Marshalls (Japanese)

Shunroku Hata
Kotohito Kanin
Hajime Sugiyama
Hisaichi Terauchi

Field Marshall (Philippines)

Douglas MacArthur

Fighting Lady

Name of a 1944 film about the U.S. aircraft carrier U.S.S. *Yorktown*, produced by Louis de Rochemont. In the movie, an island is under attack by a carrier aircraft. Next to Truk's airfield, hiding in a slit trench, is the newly captured Gregory "Pappy" Boyington, U.S. Marine Corps ace. According to Boyington, one of the camera shots clearly shows him in the trench. The name *Fighting Lady* was subsequently given to the *Yorktown* because of the movie.

Finacune, Brendon (1921–1942)

Royal Air Force wing commander. He was the fourth-highest-scoring ace of the R.A.F. in World War II, credited with shooting down thirty-two aircraft. He was an Irishman whose emblem was a three-leaf clover. His one hatred was of the English Channel, which all pilots referred to as "the ditch." Finacune's aircraft was hit by a machine-gun nest while on a low-level mission along the coast of France in 1942, preventing him from making it back to England. His plane belly landed in the Channel but unfortunately he did not make it out.

Finback, U.S.S.

U.S. Navy submarine that rescued future Vice-President George Bush after he was shot down while attacking Iwo Jima in 1944.

Finch, Barbara

Female war correspondent for Reuters News Agency. She was the first woman to set foot on Iwo Jima during the battle. Finch arrived on a Navy C-47 hospital plane, *Peg O' My Heart*, and stayed only thirty minutes because of the intensity of the battle.

Finch, Peter (1916–1977)

British actor. He served with the Australian Army as a gunner in the Middle East during World War II.

Finland

Only country to repay its World War I debt. It was the only country to continue to repay the loans made to it after World War I, during the Depression. Finland was the only member of the Axis countries not to declare war on the United States during World War II.

Fire Cards

British invention that was dropped on German wheat fields and forests at the beginning of World War II to set them on fire. Fire cards consisted of a disc of paper with phosphorus impregnated and moistened with water. When the water evaporated, the phosphorus burst into flame. The Japanese attempted a similar result by launching balloons from Japan to cross the Pacific in jetstreams, fall on the forests in the Northwest of the U.S., and destroy timber.

Firefly

Name of a gadget invented by the OSS to be placed in the gas tanks of enemy vehicles. The device would detonate anytime from an hour and a half to ten hours later, thus setting the vehicle on fire.

Fireside Chats

Name of the speeches that were given by President Franklin D. Roosevelt and broadcast over nationwide radio. He attempted to explain his policies to gain support for them from the American people. The first broadcast was made from the Oval Room in the basement of the White House shortly after Roosevelt took office in 1933.

Firth of Forth

Name of the bay at Edinburgh, Scotland. It was the site of the first German bombings of Britain during World War II. On October 16, 1939, JU-88 bombers attacked British warships at anchor. The Germans attempted to bomb the H.M.S. *Hood*, but because it was close to civilians, they went on to bomb other targets. The Royal Air Force shot down two JU-88's, claiming the first victories of the war for British land-based fighters.

Fisher, Harold

U.S. Army Air Force first lieutenant. On June 4, 1943, while piloting a B-17 named *Bonnie Sue* on his twentieth mission, Fisher lost two engines on a bombing run over Pantelleria. As he was returning to his base in North Africa, he was attacked and shot down by a P-38 that had been captured by the Italians and used to down unsuspecting U.S. bombers. Most bomber crews relaxed their vigilance when they spotted the unmistakable silhouette of the P-38, because they believed that they then had protection from enemy fighters. The P-38 was flown by Italian pilot Guido Rossi who had a number of bombers to his credit. Fisher was the only survivor of the crash. In retaliation, he acquired a specially armed B-17, had painted on the fuselage the name and a picture of Rossi's wife, (who was behind Allied lines in an overrun village), and began flying the decoy ship. After several weeks, while flying a mission, Rossi encountered Fisher in his B-17. Via the radio Rossi asked the name of the aircraft, to which Fisher replied that he had been living with her. This so incensed Rossi that he attempted a head-on attack. But he was shot down by Fisher, only to survive to be picked up by an Allied rescue boat and made a prisoner of war. Fisher was awarded a Distinguished Flying Cross for the feat and every member of the crew was given an Air Medal. Fisher was killed in 1948 while flying a transport into Berlin as part of the Berlin air lift.

Fiske, William M. III (–1940)

Royal Air Force fighter pilot and the first American to join the R.A.F. He had been an Olympic bobsled winner in 1928 and 1932 and flew with No. 601 Squadron at Tangmere. Fiske was killed on August 16, 1940, while attempting to make a belly landing at Tangmere after his plane was attacked by Stukas. He is the only American buried at St. Paul's Cathedral in London and is honored by a plaque that says "An American citizen who died that England might live."

Fitch, Aubrey (1883–1978)

U.S. Navy admiral. He commanded the aircraft carrier U.S.S. *Lexington* during the Battle of the Coral Sea in 1942, the first battle in which Japanese forces were halted.

Flags

The Japanese flag on board the aircraft carrier *Akagi*, flagship of the Pearl Harbor attack force, was the flag originally flown on

Admiral Togo's flagship during the Battle of Tsushima Strait in the 1905 defeat of the Russians. It was called the Z flag and the attack on Pearl Harbor became known as Operation Z.

The first American flag to fly over Rome on June 4, 1944; Berlin July 20, 1945; and over Tokyo September 7, 1945; was the same flag that had flown over the nation's Capitol Building on December 7, 1941. It also was flown over Guam, Iwo Jima, Okinawa, and on the U.S.S. *Missouri* on September 2, 1945, during the Japanese surrender ceremonies.

The same flag that was carried ashore by U.S. Marines at Tarawa, November 20, 1943, was given to the U.S. aircraft carrier U.S.S. *Tarawa* (CV-40) when it was launched on December 8, 1945.

Flaherty, Pat (1903–1970)

Hollywood character actor. He served in the U.S. military during the Mexican Border Campaign of 1916, in World War I, World War II, and the Korean Conflict.

Flak

Name given to antiaircraft fire during World War II. It came from the German Flieger Abweher Kanone, or antiaircraft cannon.

Flandin, Pierre Etienne (1889–1958)

French premier, 1934–1935. In 1936, as the foreign minister of France, he urged the British and French to expel the Germans from the newly occupied Rhineland. Flandin was a minister in the Vichy government and was convicted at the end of the war for collaboration. He was pardoned when Winston Churchill came to his defense.

Flasher, U.S.S.

U.S. Navy submarine credited with sinking the most Japanese tonnage (100,231 tons) of any U.S. submarine in World War II. It was first commanded by Reuben Whitaker, who sank 56,513 tons, then by George Grider who accounted for 43,718 tons. Number two was the U.S.S. *Rasher* and three was the U.S.S. *Barb*.)

Flash—Thunder

Sign and countersign used by the U.S. 82nd Airborne Division during the D-Day invasion June 6, 1944.

Flattop

U.S. Navy slang term used to refer to an aircraft carrier.

Fleet Problem 9

U.S. Navy exercise in 1929 to test the preparedness of the

military. It was a simulated attack on the Panama Canal by the aircraft carrier U.S.S. *Saratoga*, which represented a Japanese attack force.

Fleet Problem 14

U.S. Navy exercise eight years prior to Pearl Harbor (1933). The Navy conducted elaborate maneuvers in the Pacific under the assumption that an enemy would attack a U.S. naval base using carrier-based planes.

Fleet Problem 19

U.S. Navy exercise in 1939 conducted by Admiral H. E. Yarnell, who led a surprise attack on Pearl Harbor from the aircraft carrier U.S.S. *Saratoga* on a Sunday morning. Aggressor aircraft attacked and supposedly sank many of the ships at anchor in Pearl Harbor; they also strafed Ford Island, as well as Hickam and Wheeler Fields. They returned safely to the carrier.

Fleming, Ian (1908–1964)

British author and creator of super-spy James Bond. His father, Valentine Fleming, was the eleventh minister of Parliament to be killed in World War I. Winston Churchill wrote the obituary about him for the *London Times* and signed it simply W.S.C. During World War II, Fleming was Aide to the Chief of British Naval Intelligence, Sir John Godfrey, and used the code "17F." Early during the war, Fleming and Godfrey were in Lisbon en route to the United States, and Fleming recognized several German agents playing cards. He decided to disable them by winning all their money; instead he lost all of his own. In the 1942 Dieppe Raid, Fleming was on a destroyer with orders to go ashore if the raid was successful, and to collect any German code books on intelligence material he could locate. During D-Day on June 6, 1944, he commanded the No. 30 Assault Unit with the mission of capturing enemy codes. Fleming is thought to have modeled "M" after Sir Stewart Menzies, the head of MI-6 in World War II, and James Bond after Dusko Popov, a double agent.

Fleming, Peter (1907–1968)

Brother of Ian Fleming. He was a colonel in the British Army and the LCS (London Controlling Section) representative in India and Southeast Asia during World War II.

Fleming, Richard E. (1917–1942)

U.S. Marine Corps captain. He was awarded the Congressional Medal of Honor posthumously for the Battle of Midway in June 1942. Fleming flew from Midway in pursuit of the retreating

Japanese fleet and attacked the cruiser *Mikuma*. Although his engine was hit, he continued to hold his course to release his bomb and crashed into the rear turret of the cruiser.

Fletcher, Frank J. (1885–1973)

U.S. Navy admiral. He had won a Congressional Medal of Honor during the Battle of Vera Cruz in 1914 and commanded the aircraft carrier U.S.S. *Yorktown* in the Battle of the Coral Sea and Midway. Fletcher had both the U.S.S. *Yorktown* and the U.S.S. *Lexington* sunk from under him.

MOVIE PORTRAYAL:
Midway (1974), by Robert Webber

Flicksteger, Charles

American who broadcast propaganda for the Nazis during World War II. He was a friend of journalist William Shirer and at one time was the manager of German-owned XGRS radio, which broadcast anti-American propaganda from Shanghai. Flicksteger became a German citizen and was a lieutenant in the Wehrmacht.

Friedman, Elizabeth S. (1892–1980)

Wife of William Friedman. Together, they constituted one of the best U.S. cryptoanalyst teams. She worked in the 1920's for the U.S. Navy and later for the Justice Department, breaking codes used by smugglers.

Friedman, William F. (–1969)

Head of the U.S. Army Cryptoanalysis Bureau during World War II that broke the Japanese Purple Code.

Flossenburg

Nazi concentration camp located in the Upper Palatinate. It was primarily used for special categories of people such as Peter Churchill, General Hans Oster, General Franz Halder, Dr. Hjalmar Schacht, and Fabian von Schlabrendorff. Flossenburg was the place where Admiral Wilhelm Canaris and Dietrich Bonhoffer were executed just before the camp was liberated.

Flounder, U.S.S.

U.S. submarine that collided with another U.S. submarine, U.S.S. *Hoe*, while both were submerged off the coast of Indochina, February 23, 1945. It was the only known instance in which two submarines collided while underwater during World War II. Although both were damaged, they survived.

Fluckey, Eugene B. (1913–   )

U.S. Navy submarine officer. He was the second-highest-scoring submarine commander of World War II and was awarded four

Navy Crosses in addition to the Congressional Medal of Honor. Fluckey commanded the U.S.S. *Barb,* which sank the Japanese escort carrier *Unyo* in November 1944. He later became an aide to Admiral Chester Nimitz.

Fly

Name of a German submarine warning device that detected the lowest ranges of radar pulses and also gave the direction to the source of the emissions. Fly was an unsuccessful attempt to protect the submarines from aircraft using special radar sets to attack.

Flying Admiral

Nickname of Admiral Marc Mitscher, who earned his U.S. Navy wings in October 1915.

Flying Barn Door

Nickname given by the British Royal Air Force personnel to the Whitley bomber.

Flying Boxcar

Nickname given to both the C-82 and the C-87, both of which were U.S. Army Air Force cargo aircraft.

Flying Castles

Self-imposed nickname of the Army Air Force engineers who built runways in the Pacific islands during World War II. The castle was the symbol for the U.S. Army Corps of Engineers.

Flying Cigar

Nickname that Japanese aircrews gave to the Betty bomber because the designers had sacrificed armor to achieve a farther range. This made the Betty highly vulnerable to U.S. fighters.

Flying Coffin

Nickname given by German fighter pilots to early models of the B-17E. Given to the British in 1941, it was poorly protected and therefore easy prey for German fighters.

Flying Fireworks

Nickname given to the HE177, a German four-engine bomber that was never fully operational.

Flying Fortress

Nickname given to the U.S. B-17 bomber because of the heavy armament it carried.

Flying Knights

Name given to top-scoring U.S. ace Richard Bong's P-38 squadron in the Pacific during World War II. It was part of the Fifth Army Air Force.

Flying Pencil

Nickname of the German bomber DO-17 because of its long, thin fuselage.

Flying Panhandle

Nickname given to the British medium bomber, the Hampden, because of its distinctive shape.

Flying Porcupine

German nickname given to the Sunderland, a British flying boat flown during World War II. It was used in antisubmarine patrols because of its eight machine guns.

Flying Special Tribunal West

Name given to German military court-martial team set up by Hitler on March 8, 1945, in response to the loss of the Lundendorff Bridge at Remagen. The team, commanded by S.S. Major General Rudolf Hubner, was empowered to try on the spot deserters and defeatists, and to execute them immediately if found guilty.

Flying Target

British nickname for the B-17E they received in 1941 for experimental daylight bombing. Because the B-17E lacked adequate machine-gun protection the British lost many of them to German fighters.

Flying Tigers

Name given to the American Volunteer Group (AVG) in China, led by Major General Claire Chennault. It was the only mercenary air force in World War II; the pilots were civilians who were hired to fight the Japanese. Their first aircraft were P-40's that had been built for Sweden, then rejected by the Royal Air Force as obsolete. The aircraft were world-famous for a shark's mouth, devised by Erikson E. Schilling, which was painted on the front. A common misconception is that the Flying Tigers were fighting the Japanese before U.S. entry into the war, but they actually began operations thirteen days after the Pearl Harbor attack of December 7, 1941.

Flynn, Errol (1909–1959)

Hollywood actor. During World War II, he was classified "4F" due to a heart condition. A controversy surrounds him today due to the belief that he was an agent of the Nazis, although this has not been established beyond question.

Foggia

Italian city and site of a major Axis airfield complex. It was captured by the Allies on September 28, 1943, and became a heavy bomber base for the Fifteenth Army Air Force.

Foley, Francis

British Army major. He was the passport control officer in Berlin from 1920 to 1939 and was, in reality, the MI-6 representative. German Admiral Wilhelm Canaris fed information through him to the British about Hitler's intended war.

Follmer, Willard

U.S. Army captain in the 82nd Airborne Division. He was the first person whom General Matthew Ridgway met when the General moved inland on Sicily after the Allied parachute assault in 1943. On that occasion, Ridgway found him propped up against a tree with a broken ankle. Again Follmer was the first person Ridgway encountered after the Normandy parachute jump of June 6, 1944, and again Ridgway found him out of action, this time due to a sprained back.

Fonda, Henry (1905–1982)

Hollywood actor. He enlisted in the U.S. Navy in August 1942, and was stationed on board the destroyer U.S.S. *Satterlee* as a quartermaster third class. At the recommendation of the ship's executive officer, Fonda was commissioned a lieutenant (j.g.) and was put into Air Combat Intelligence in the Central Pacific. He was awarded a Bronze Star medal and discharged in October 1945.

Foo-Fighter

Name given to unexplained fireballs and lights that followed Allied aircraft beginning early in 1945. The theory at the time was that they were remote controlled via radio signals. Since 1948 they have been called *flying saucers*.

Forby, J. Hamilton

British colonel. He was a fictitious character dreamed up by the Allied press corps, who made him into a Paul Bunyan of the Mediterranean theater. People reported seeing him everywhere and he was credited with many daring feats that supposedly shortened the war, including behind-the-lines reconnaissance of Sicily. The American counterpart was Kilroy and that of the Germans, Edmund R. Draecker.

Force 141

Name given staff at General Dwight Eisenhower's headquarters for planning the invasion of Sicily. The name came from the number of the room of the St. George Hotel in Algiers where they first met.

Force C

British Royal Navy unit commanded by Rear Admiral E.L.S. King. The unit was involved in preventing German reinforcements from reaching Crete from the sea.

Force D

British Royal Navy unit commanded by Rear Admiral I. G. Glennie, and which stopped the German seaborne assault on Crete in 1941.

Force H

British Royal Navy unit commanded by Admiral Sir James Somerville. It was responsible for sinking the French fleet at Oran in 1940 and the destruction of the *Bismarck* in 1941.

Force K

British Royal Navy unit commanded by Captain W. G. Agnew and based at Malta. It was set up as part of an attempt to stop supplies from reaching Field Marshall Rommel in North Africa.

Forces Sweetheart

Nickname given to British radio singer Vera Lynn, who performed every evening on a radio show called "Sincerely Yours" and transmitted to British troops overseas. She was identified with the song, "We'll Meet Again," which had the same nostalgic appeal for British forces as "Lili Marlene" had for German forces. "We'll Meet Again" was used at the end of the 1964 Peter Sellers movie *Dr. Strangelove;* Vera Lynn sings it as the world is annihilated by H-bomb explosions.

Force Z

British Royal Navy unit consisting of the *Prince of Wales* and the *Repulse* plus escort destroyers. They were sent to Singapore, but both battleships were sunk on December 10, 1941, by Japanese aircraft.

Ford

U.S. automobile manufacturer that made the last civilian car of World War II on February 10, 1942, before converting to full wartime production. The serial number was 30-337509. Ford made 277,896 jeeps during World War II.

Ford, Gerald (1913–)

Thirty-eighth President of the United States. During World War II, he enlisted in the U.S. Navy in April 1942 and served on the aircraft carrier U.S.S. *Monterey* as the director of physical education and assistant navigation officer. Ford won ten battle stars before being discharged as a lieutenant commander in 1946.

Ford, Glenn (1916–   )

Hollywood actor. During World War II, he directed a camera crew that landed at Normandy on D-Day, June 6, 1944. Ford also filmed the German atrocities at Dachau concentration camp in April 1945. Commander Ford later saw limited action in the Vietnam war.

Ford Island

Island in Pearl Harbor where U.S. battleships were moored at the time of the December 7, 1941, attack by Japan.

Ford, John (1895–1973)

Hollywood movie director. He enlisted in the U.S. Navy in the fall of 1941 and became head of a photographic unit with the rank of commander. Ford was present on the U.S.S. *Hornet* and filmed the departure of Doolittle's Raiders to attack Tokyo on April 18, 1942. He was wounded while filming the Battle of Midway in May 1942 and was awarded two Oscars for his World War II documentaries *The Battle of Midway* and *December Seventh*. Ford was loosely portrayed by Ward Bond as the character John Dodge, in the 1957 movie *Wings of Eagles*.

Ford, "Tennessee" Ernie (1919–   )

Country singer and comedian. During World War II, he served in the U.S. Army Air Force as a bombardier and navigator. Ford also became an instructor before his discharge in 1945.

Forester, C. S. (Cecil Scott) (1899–1966)

British author and creator of Horatio Hornblower. During World War II, he was a propagandist for the Allies.

Forgy, Howell

U.S. Navy chaplain. He was stationed on board the U.S.S. *New Orleans* at Pearl Harbor on December 7, 1941. He apologized to the gun crews for not providing church services on that Sunday morning but exhorted them to "praise the Lord and pass the ammunition."

Forrestal, James Vincent (1892–1949)

U.S. Secretary of the Navy (1944–1947). He had been a navy pilot during World War I and was Undersecretary of the Navy for Frank Knox, who died in 1944. Forrestal was also the first Secretary of Defense. He committed suicide by jumping from a sixteenth-floor window at Bethesda Maryland Naval Hospital in May 1949.

Forrest, Steve (1925–   )

Hollywood actor, brother of actor Dana Andrews, who served in the U.S. Army during World War II and was wounded by shrapnel during the Battle of the Bulge in December 1944.

Fort Canning

Name of the British military headquarters for Malaya, which was located in Singapore.

Fort Drum

Name of the U.S. installation on the island of El Fraile five and a half miles from Corregidor in Manila Bay. It was also called the "Concrete Battleship."

Fort Frank

U.S. Army fort on the island of Carabao off Corregidor in Manila Bay.

Fort Hughes

U.S. Army fort located on the island of Caballo a quarter of a mile from Corregidor.

Fort Mills

Name of the U.S. Army fort located on the island of Corregidor in Manila Bay.

Fort Oskarsbarg

Name of a Norwegian fort that guarded the Drobak Narrows of Oslo Fjord. It put up a spirited defense against the German invasion of 1940 and contributed to the sinking of the German cruiser *Blucher.*

Fort Shafter

Name of the U.S. Army headquarters in Hawaii. It was the oldest army post in the islands.

Fort Wacky

Nickname of the Hal Roach production studios in Hollywood during World War II.

Foss, Joseph T. (1915–)

U.S. Marine Corps officer. He was a fighter pilot with VMF121 at Guadalcanal and was the first person to match Eddie Rickenbacker's World War I record of shooting down twenty-six enemy planes. Foss was awarded the Congressional Medal of Honor for combat in defense of Guadalcanal.

MOVIE PORTRAYAL:

The Gallant Hours (1960), by Harry Landers

Foulois, Benjamin D. (–1967)

American aviation pioneer and major general in the U.S. Army Air Corps. He was the first to fly combat against Pancho Villa in

1916; the first to fly more than one hundred miles nonstop; the first to operate a radio in flight; first to command the U.S. Air Service in the First Army in World War I. In 1935, he selected the B-17 to fill U.S. needs for a long-range bomber.

Fox

Identifier for messages sent in code from Pearl Harbor to U.S. Navy ships. All vessels monitored the broadcasts and only deciphered those messages addressed to them.

Fox, Annie G.

U.S. Army nurse. She was the first woman to receive a Purple Heart when she was awarded the medal for wounds sustained on December 7, 1941, during the Japanese attack on Hickam Field.

Foxer

Name of a device towed behind a merchant ship that generated more noise than the ship's propellors and thus attracted German acoustic torpedoes.

Foxhole

Name given to a deep hole dug by one or two infantrymen for protection in the field.

Francke, Karl

German Air Force pilot. As a corporal, he flew one of the four JU-88's that made the first operational strike of World War II. The bombers attacked the British aircraft carrier H.M.S. *Ark Royal* on September 26, 1939. Goering credited Francke with hitting the carrier though he didn't, promoted him to lieutenant, and gave him the First and Second Class Iron Cross. He later became the Director of Testing at the Luftwaffe Testing Ground at Rechlin. Francke was the German equivalent of Colin Kelly.

Franco, Francisco (1892–1975)

Spanish dictator. Franco accepted aid from Hitler and Mussolini during the Spanish Civil War. However, when it came time to repay them, Franco consistently side-stepped giving help. At one point, Hitler asked to allow German troops through Spain to attack Gibraltar; Franco let it be known that Spain would defend herself from attacks by either side. Franco made many attempts to save the Jews of Europe but was rebuffed by Hitler. He was not willing to join Hitler in declaring war because he himself was part Jewish—a fact hidden from Hitler by his advisers.

Frank, Anne (1929–1945)

German-born Jewish girl known for her *Diary of a Young Girl,* which was written during two years of hiding above a Dutch warehouse. She always addressed her entries "Dear Kitty." She and her family were discovered by the Gestapo in August of 1944 and shipped to concentration camps. Anne died at Bergen-Belsen of typhus at fifteen years of age, only two months before the camp was liberated.

MOVIE PORTRAYALS:
The Diary of Anne Frank (1959), by Millie Perkins
The Diary of Anne Frank (1980 TV movie), by Melissa Gilbert

Frank, Clinton E.

Heisman trophy winner in 1937 for his performance as a quarterback for Yale University. He served as an aide to General James Doolittle during World War II.

Frank, Hans (1900–1946)

Nazi governor of Poland. He was largely responsible for the atrocities committed in Poland and was tried at Nuremberg and hanged on October 16, 1946.

MOVIE PORTRAYAL:
Holocaust (1978 TV miniseries), by John Bailey

Frank, Karl Hermann (1898–1946)

Sudeten German leader of the prewar Czechoslovakian Parliament. He later became the Nazi protector and ordered the destruction of Lidice and Levzaky in retaliation for the assassination of Reinhard Heydrich in May 1942. After the war, Frank was charged with treason, the murder of over 300,000 Czechs, propagation of Nazism, and coresponsibility for the destruction of Lidice. He was hanged in Prague's Pankrac Prison in May 1946.

Frank, Otto (1889–1980)

Father of Anne Frank and the sole survivor of his family. He had been a German officer in World War I and was decorated for bravery. He and his family fled to Holland before the outbreak of World War II but were trapped by the invading Germans in 1940. They went into hiding in June 1942 and were discovered in August 1944. Frank was liberated from Auschwitz by the advancing Russians.

MOVIE PORTRAYALS:
The Diary of Anne Frank (1959), by Joseph Schildkraut
The Diary of Anne Frank (1980 TV movie), by Maximilian Schell

Franklin, U.S.S. (CV-13)

27,000-ton U.S. aircraft carrier known as "the ship that wouldn't die." On March 19, 1945, while sixty miles from Japan, the *Franklin* was struck by two bombs that reduced her to a burning hulk. Eight hundred thirty-two crewmembers were killed in what was the U.S. Navy's second worst disaster in history. Commanded by Captain Leslie E. Gehres, the crew sailed her 12,000 miles back to the Brooklyn Navy yard for repairs. The *Franklin* was the most decorated ship of U.S. Navy history and had the most decorated crew. Two Congressional Medals of Honor, nineteen Navy Crosses, and twenty-two Silver Star Medals were awarded for this one incident (see Wolf, Samuel).

Fraser, Sir Bruce (1888–1981)

British Royal Navy admiral. He was the son of an Army general and was Commander in Chief of the British Home Fleet. Fraser commanded H.M.S. *Duke of York* in the Battle of North Cape in December 1943, which resulted in the sinking of the German cruiser *Scharnhorst*. He was also the British representative at the Japanese surrender on the U.S.S. *Missouri* in Tokyo Bay September 2, 1945.

Fräulein Anna

Nickname given by associates to Rudolph Hess, Hitler's party secretary, because of his homosexuality.

Freddie

Name given to a bomb-defusing device invented by Royal Air Force Squadron Leader E. L. Moxey to render bombs harmless from a safe distance. Moxey was killed while trying to disarm a bomb, and was the first R.A.F. member to win the George Cross, an honor second only to receiving the Victoria Cross.

Fredendall, Lloyd R. (1884–)

U.S. Army major general who was relieved of command of II Corps after his defeat at Kasserine Pass in February 1943. He believed he was sacrificed due to the whim of British General Harold Alexander. Fredendall wanted American units to be employed intact, but he had to shuttle battalions from one location to another to satisfy Alexander's apprehensions, which were often based on faulty intelligence. When the Germans attacked, they easily broke through the lines, which gave them freedom of action. Probably the reason Fredendall was relieved was that his subordinate commanders had lost confidence in him, resulting in low morale.

Frederick, Robert T. (1907–1970)

U.S. Army major general. He established and commanded the First Special Service Force made up of Canadians and U.S. forces. It was known as the "Devil's Brigade" because of the unorthodox methods used in fighting the Germans in Italy. Frederick was awarded two Distinguished Service Crosses and eight Purple Hearts.

MOVIE PORTRAYAL:
The Devil's Brigade (1967), by William Holden

Freedom

Code name of General Dwight Eisenhower's Allied Force Headquarters located in Algiers for the North African and Sicily campaigns.

Free Indian Legion

German unit recruited from Indian prisoners of war, who fought with the Nazis in the hope of freeing India from British rule. It was designated Infantry Regiment 950 and served antiaircraft duty in southern France.

Freeman, Orville L. (1918–   )

U.S. Secretary of Agriculture under President John F. Kennedy. During World War II, Freeman served as a U.S. Marine Corps officer and had part of his jaw shot off by a Japanese bullet in Bougainville in 1943.

Freeman's Folly

Nickname given to the Mosquito, a British aircraft made of wood that was sponsored by Sir Wilfrid Freeman. His son, Flight Officer Keith Freeman, later was assigned to a Mosquito squadron and named his aircraft *Folly*.

Freeman, Sir Wilfrid (1888–1953)

Royal Air Force airchief marshall. He is a little-known architect of R.A.F. growth from 1936 to 1940 as head of Research and Development. Freeman was responsible for the development and production of the Hurricane, Spitfire, and Mosquito. He also advocated building large four-engine bombers.

Free Officers Movement

Anti-British organization of Egyptian nationalists who aided a German intelligence group, Kondor Mission, in sending military information to Field Marshall Erwin Rommel. Two of the leaders of the Free Officers Movement were Gamal Abdel Nasser and

Anwar el-Sadat. Nasser was finally caught and imprisoned by the British after they had broken up the Kondor Mission.

Freiburg

German city bombed by an unidentified high-flying aircraft at noon on May 10, 1940, the day Hitler began his offensive against the West. Freiburg was an open city and the Nazi press immediately began a propaganda campaign against the Allies, who they claimed had indiscriminately bombed the undefended city. Hitler then rescinded his own promise not to bomb the open cities. After the war, it was revealed that the city was actually bombed by Luftwaffe aircraft, HE111's, as a pretext for a heightened offensive.

Freisler, Dr. Roland (1893–1945)

Nazi judge who presided over the People's Court trials of the conspirators against Hitler after the July 20, 1944, attempted assassination. He had been a prisoner of war during World War I and a Communist until the Nazis came to power. Freisler was killed February 3, 1945, when a beam in his courtroom fell on him during an American air raid.

Freya

Name of a German mobile radar unit used to plot the path of aircraft and ships along the coast of Europe. It had a range of up to one hundred miles. Its first success occurred on September 4, 1939, when British Blenheims attacked Wilhelmshaven and Luftwaffe fighters intercepted them with the help of early detection by a Freya unit.

Freyberg, Bernard C. (1889–1963)

British general. He won the Victoria Cross and was wounded three times during World War I. Freyberg commanded a New Zealand infantry division during the evacuation from Greece. He then took over command of the defense of Crete but had to be evacuated when the island fell to German airborne forces in 1941. Freyberg commanded a New Zealand Corps during the Battle of Cassino in Italy in 1944 and was the person who made the controversial decision to bomb the monastery of Cassino.

Frick, Wilhelm (1877–1946)

Nazi Minister of the Interior under Hitler. He had been a former Munich policeman and, as Premier of Thuringia, conferred German citizenship on Austrian-born Hitler. Frick was later the protector of Bohemia and Moravia. He was found guilty of war crimes by the Nuremberg tribunal and hanged on October 16, 1946.

von Friedeberg, Hans Georg (1895–1945)

German admiral and last Commander in Chief of the German Navy during World War II. He signed the armistices at Luneburg Heath on May 4, 1945; at Rheims on May 7, 1945; and at Berlin on May 8, 1945. Friedeberg then committed suicide by taking poison.

Friedenthal Division

Name of an S.S. unit headed by Otto Skorzeny that trained for special operations behind enemy lines. They were a type of commando unit and took their name from their headquarters, the Friedenthal Castle.

Friendly, Fred (1915–)

Television producer. As a correspondent, he flew on two B-29 missions and also on night missions with the first P-61 Black Widow fighters. Friendly won four battle stars, the Soldier's Medal, and the Legion of Merit for service in World War II. After he was awarded the Legion of Merit, he was reprimanded for being out of uniform.

Frost, John

British Army colonel. He led the 500 men of the First British Airborne Division who attempted to seize the north end of the Nijmegen Bridge at Arnhem in 1944.

FRUMEL

Code name for the Fleet Radio Unit located at Melbourne, Australia. It was the U.S. Navy codebreaking unit formerly known as *CAST* that had been on Corregidor.

F Section

French part of the British SOE that armed and directed the Resistance in occupied France during World War II.

Fubar

Allied superlative that stood for "fouled (used in place of an expletive deleted) up beyond all recognition."

Fuchida, Mitsuo (1902–1976)

Japanese Navy pilot who commanded the air strike on Pearl Harbor on December 7, 1941. He had been inspired to take up flying after seeing the U.S. battleship *Maryland* in San Francisco Bay with three scout planes on board. The object of his inspiration became one of his targets at Pearl Harbor. Fuchida flew from the carrier *Akagi*. He landed at Hiroshima on August 6, 1945, shortly after the atomic bomb blast, in order to assess the damage. Fuchida survived the war and became a Protestant Minister, often visiting the United States.

Movie portrayal:
Tora! Tora! Tora! (1970), by Takahiro Tamura

Fuchikami, Tadao

RCA messenger boy in Pearl Harbor who delivered a cable from General George C. Marshall to General Walter Short on December 7, 1941. The message was an alert telling Short of a Japanese ultimatum to the U.S. and advising him to be prepared for any eventuality. The telegram arrived during the middle of the Japanese attack on Pearl Harbor.

Fuehrer

German word for leader that became synonymous with Hitler. Other countries had their equivalents:

Chinese: Ling Siu (Chiang Kai-shek)
German (WWI): Kaiser (Wilhelm II)
Italian: Duce (Benito Mussolini)
Russian (WWI): Czar (Nicolas II)
Spanish: Caudillo (Francisco Franco)

Fuehrer Paket

Name of a package given by Hitler to visitors of his headquarters at Rastenburg East Prussia. It contained items not available to German society, that is, chocolate, jam, candy, etc. One of the recipients was General Dietrich von Choltitz when he was given command of Paris in 1944.

Fugitives from Hitler

Well-known people who fled Nazi Germany during World War II.

Hannah Arendt—author
Sig Arno—actor
John Banner—actor
Hans Bethe—physicist
Bruno Bettelheim—psychologist
Werner Michael Blumenthal—U.S. Secretary of Treasury
Niels Bohr—physicist
Max Born—physicist
Bertholt Brecht—poet and dramatist

Alfred Eisenstaedt—photographer
Albert Einstein—physicist
Enrico Fermi—physicist
James Frank—physicist
Sigmund Freud—psychologist
Sir Bernard Katz—biophysicist
Henry Kissinger—U.S. Secretary of State
Martin Kosleck—actor
Willy Ley—rocket scientist
Thomas Mann—author
Herbert Marcuse—philosopher
Lise Meitner—physicist
John von Neumann—physicist
Erich Maria Remarque—author
Ludwig Stossel—actor (best known as the Little Old Wine Maker of American TV commercials)
Leo Szilard—physicist
Edward Teller—physicist
Paul Tillich—theologian
Walter Ulbricht—German politician

Fugo

Japanese code name for the bombing of America by high-altitude balloons launched from Japan. The balloons were released into the jet streams and crossed the Pacific in sixty-eight hours to release incendiary bombs over the forests of the Pacific Northwest in an attempt to start forest fires. The name stood for "windship weapon" and the project was commanded by Major General Sueki Kusaba. Throughout the war, over six thousand balloons were launched, carrying 30,000 bombs, but very few reached their target. They depended on Seiko timing devices and Toshiba electronics.

Fujita, Nobuo (1911–)

Only person ever to bomb the United States. He flew from the Japanese submarine *I-25* on September 9, 1942, and bombed Mount Emily in Oregon, returning again on September 29, 1942. Fujita was eventually transferred to a pilot instructor's job and spent the rest of the war training navy pilots.

Fukudome, Shigeru (1891–1971)

Japanese admiral. He was Chief of Staff to Admiral Isoruku Yamamoto and later to Admiral Mineichi Koga. After the war, Fukudome was convicted of war crimes and imprisoned.

Fuller, John F. C. (1878–1966)

British military tactician known as the father of modern war because of his writings in the 1920's identifying the trends of future wars. He was ignored in Britain but studied diligently in Germany, Russia, and France. In 1933 he wrote *Field Service Regulations III*, a manual on armored warfare.

Fuller, Sam (1911–)

Hollywood producer who served as an infantryman with the First Infantry Division in World War II. His 1980 movie *The Big Red One* is based on his experiences. Fuller was awarded the Silver Star, Bronze Star, and Purple Heart for service in North Africa and Europe.

Fulton, U.S.S.

U.S. Navy submarine tender that was dispatched from Pearl Harbor to bring back the survivors of the stricken aircraft carrier U.S.S. *Yorktown*. The *Fulton* arrived at Pearl Harbor on June 8, 1942, with 2,025 survivors.

Fumtu

Allied superlative used during World War II. It stood for "fouled up more than usual."

Funk, Leonard A.

U.S. Army sergeant with Company C, 508th Parachute Infantry Regiment of the 82nd Airborne Division. He is the most decorated American paratrooper of World War II, winning the Congressional Medal of Honor, the Distinguished Service Cross, the Silver Star, and the Purple Heart, among others.

Funk, Walter (1890–1960)

Nazi president of the German Reichsbank. He was planted in the Nazi party by German industrialists in 1931 to tone down the radicalism of the party, but became one of Hitler's most ardent followers. Funk was captured along with Japanese embassy personnel by the Russians in May 1945, and was sentenced to life imprisonment at Nuremberg. He was released in 1958.

Funt, Allen (1914–)

Television producer and host of the TV series "Candid Camera." During World War II, Funt served in the U.S. Army, where he trained Nisei soldiers. He was later transferred to the Signal Corps, where he came up with the idea that developed first into "Candid Mike" for radio and then "Candid Camera" for television.

Furious, H.M.S.

British aircraft carrier built as a cruiser in 1917 but converted to a carrier during World War II. It was the only British carrier to survive the entire war.

FUSAG

Abbreviation for the First U.S. Army Group, supposedly set up for the D-Day landings and commanded by General George S. Patton. In reality, the force was totally fictitious and was established to deceive the Germans into fortifying the Pas de Calais instead of Normandy. This was part of the overall plan of deception in Operation Fortitude.

Fustian

Code name of the fourth and final parachute drop on the east coast of Sicily by the British First Parachute Brigade. The mission was to capture the Primasole bridge north of Lentini.

FW 200

German four-engine aircraft designed as an airliner but converted to the needs of the Luftwaffe. It was the heaviest aircraft in the arsenal of the Luftwaffe and was called *Condor.* The *Condor* first flew in July 1937 and set several records: Berlin to New York in twenty-five hours; New York to Berlin in twenty hours; Berlin to Tokyo in forty-eight hours and sixteen minutes. It had a radius of one thousand miles, which with auxiliary fuel tanks could be extended to one thousand four hundred miles. During World War II the FW 200 was used primarily for reconnassiance over the Atlantic to spot convoys for German submarines.

FX1400

Designator of a German remote-controlled, rocket-powered, armor-piercing bomb. It was first used at Salerno in 1943.

Fyfe, Jake

U.S. Navy officer. As the commander of the submarine U.S.S. *Batfish,* he sank an unprecedented three Japanese submarines in four days.

G

G

Letter painted on all vehicles under command of German General Heinz Guderian. It was a tactical identification used by him in Poland, France and Russia.

G-1

U.S. Army staff position in charge of personnel. The Air Force equivalent was A-1; the joint staff equivalent was J-1; and the special staff equivalent was S-1.

G-2

U.S. Army staff position in charge of intelligence and censorship. The Air Force equivalent was A-2; the joint staff equivalent was J-2; and the special staff equivalent was S-2.

G-3

U.S. Army staff position in charge of operations. The Air Force equivalent was A-3; the joint staff equivalent was J-3; and the special staff equivalent was S-3.

G-4

U.S Army staff position in charge of logistics. The Air Force equivalent was A-4; the joint staff equivalent was J-4; and the special staff equivalent was S-4.

G-5

U.S. Army staff position in charge of civil affairs.

G-6

U.S. Army staff position in charge of psychological warfare and public relations.

Gabaldan, Guy

U.S. Marine Corps private. He was the Japanese language interpreter for the 2nd Marine Division that assaulted Saipan and repeatedly risked his life to talk Japanese civilians and military into surrendering rather than committing suicide. Gabaldan is personally credited with capturing more than half of the two thousand Japanese taken between June 15 and August 1, 1944.

MOVIE PORTRAYAL:
Hell to Eternity (1960), by Jeffrey Hunter

Gable, Clark (1901–1960)

Hollywood actor. When his wife Carole Lombard was killed in a TWA plane crash in 1942, he retired from movies and joined the Army Air Force as a private. His enlisted serial number was 19125047 but he was soon commissioned and put in charge of making training films. Gable flew with B-17's on missions over Germany to film footage for an aerial gunner film. Goering heard of this and put a bounty on his head of $5,000 to any Luftwaffe pilot who could shoot him down. The lucky pilot would also receive an automatic promotion and a leave of absence. Gable's serial number as an officer was 056-5390. He was discharged as a Major by Captain Ronald Reagan having won the Distinguished Flying Cross and the Air Medal.

MOVIE PORTRAYALS:
Gable and Lombard (1976), by James Brolin
Rainbow (1978 TV movie), by Jolan Murat
Moviola (1980 TV miniseries), by Ed Winter

Gabreski, Francis S. (1919–)

U.S. Army Air Force colonel. He had been at Wheeler Army Air Field in Hawaii on December 7, 1941, during the Japanese attack. As a member of the 56th Fighter Group of the Eighth Army Air Force in England, Gabreski shot down twenty-eight enemy aircraft to become the third-top-scoring ace of the Army Air Force. He was finally downed on July 20, 1944, and served the rest of war as a prisoner.

G-AFTL

International registration number of a Lockheed aircraft flown by Frederick Winterbotham prior to World War II. He painted it light green and equipped it with hidden cameras so that he could photograph German military installations on his many trips to the Reich. Wintherbotham depended on high altitude and speed for protection, but the aircraft was finally destroyed when the Luftwaffe bombed the hangars at Wembley in September 1940.

Galahad

Code name given to Merrill's Marauders that operated behind Japanese lines in Burma from March until August 1944.

Galbani, Luigi (1918–)

Italian barber of Benito Mussolini. Today he is the barber at the Excelsior Hotel in Rome and was used as a consultant for the 1981 movie about Mussolini, *Lion of the Desert,* starring Rod Steiger.

Gale, Richard (1896–)

British Army major general. He commanded the British 6th Airborne Division in the assault on Normandy of June 6, 1944, to secure the left flank of the beachhead. Gale was the first British general to land on French soil; his glider touched down at 3:30 A.M.

Galic, Critan

Yugoslavian pilot who shot down thirty-six aircraft during World War II to become the leading ace of Yugoslavia.

Galileo Galilei

Italian submarine that was captured on June 22, 1940, by a British trawler, the *Moonstone*. It forced the submarine to the surface with a couple of depth charges, then persuaded it to surrender with four shells from her deck gun. *Moonstone* towed the submarine into Aden Harbor.

Galland, Adolf (1912–)

Luftwaffe officer who is credited with shooting down 103 enemy aircraft. He eventually became a lieutenant general and was the first person to receive the oak leaves and swords of his Knight's Cross, which he was awarded for his 70th victory. Galland's emblem on his aircraft was Mickey Mouse.

Gallery, Daniel V (1901–1977)

U.S. Navy officer. He commanded the escort carrier U.S.S. *Guadalcanal* when it captured the German submarine *U505* off the coast of French West Africa in 1944. It was the first enemy warship captured by the U.S. Navy on the high seas since 1815. He was also the author of such books as *Cap'n Fatso, Clear the Decks,* and *Stand By-y-y to Start Engines*.

Galley yarn

U.S. navy slang for a rumor. It was also known as "scuttlebut."

Galloping Ghost of the Java Coast

Nickname given to the U.S.S. *Houston* which the Japanese

erroneously reported sunk twice. It was finally sunk on February 28, 1942, in the Battle of the Java Sea.

Galloping Ghost of the Oahu Coast

Nickname given to the aircraft carrier U.S.S. *Enterprise* in the days just prior to World War II.

Gambier Bay, U.S.S.

U.S. Navy escort carrier (CVE) which was a converted merchantman weighing 10,000 tons. It was sunk in the Battle of Samar, part of the larger Battle of Leyte Gulf in 1944.

Gamelin, Maurice (1872–1958)

French general and Supreme Commander of French forces from 1939 to 1940. He was relieved of command ten days after the German invasion and replaced by General Maxime Weygand. Gamelin was arrested by Vichy France and tried at Riom in 1942 for his part in the defeat of France. He was later imprisoned in Buchenwald concentration camp.

MOVIE PORTRAYAL:
Churchill and the Generals (1981 TV movie), by Andre Maranne

Gamma Mortar

Name of a German siege mortar used at Sebastopol. It had a twenty-two foot barrel that fired a one-ton shell a distance of up to nine miles. The crew was made up of 235 men.

Gann, Ernest

American author. During Worla War II, he flew for the Air Transport command. After Victory in Europe (V-E) Day, he was selected to fly General Mark Clark from Paris to Chicago for a hero's welcome.

GAPSALS

Organization founded by radio broadcaster Arthur Godfrey during World War II in his effort to recruit blood donors. It stood for "Give a Pint . . . Save a Life Society."

Garand, John C. (1888–1974)

Ordnance engineer for the U.S. Armory in Springfield, Massachusetts. He invented the M-1 Garand rifle that became the standard infantry weapon of the U.S. in World War II.

Garbo, Greta (1905–)

Hollywood actress. She was the favorite actress of Hitler and supposedly was recruited by the British in 1939 as a spy. It has been alleged that Garbo helped Niels Bohr escape from Denmark before the Germans could pick him up.

Garcia-Morato, Joaquin

Spanish Nationalist fighter pilot. He was the top-scoring ace of the Spanish Civil War, with forty victories.

Garfield, John (1913–1952)

Hollywood actor. He was the first major star to entertain U.S. troops during World War II. Garfield attempted to join the U.S. Army but was rejected because of heart problems (he had a heart attack in June 1944). His son David Patton Garfield, born in July 1943, was named in honor of General George S. Patton.

Garner, Erroll (1921–1977)

Jazz pianist. He served one year in the U.S. Army before receiving a medical discharge for an asthmatic condition.

Garroway, Dave (1913–1982)

Radio and TV broadcaster. He enlisted in the U.S. Navy in 1942 and served on minesweepers as an ensign until his discharge in 1945.

Gas (Poison)

Use of poison gas was outlawed by the Geneva convention. However, it was used by the Italians in Ethopia in 1936 to subdue the Ethiopians. The Japanese also used gas at the Battle of Ichang, China, on October 20, 1941, as reported by Jack Belden, correspondent for the International News Service. He saw Chinese soldiers with gas blisters as large as tennis balls. Winston Churchill had every intention of using poison gas if the Germans invaded England in 1940.

Gasoline

An infantry division required six times as much gasoline as food, and an armored division needed eight times as much.

Gavin, James (1907–   )

U.S. Army officer. He commanded the 82nd Airborne Division and fought at Sicily, Salerno, Anzio, Normandy, the Battle of the Bulge, and Nijmegen. Gavin made plans for a parachute drop on Berlin in the last days of the war and believed the city could have been captured.

MOVIE PORTRAYALS:

The Longest Day (1962), by Robert Ryan

A Bridge Too Far (1973), by Ryan O'Neal

Gavutu

Island twenty miles north of Guadalcanal in the Solomons. It was the site where the first American paratroopers entered combat in World War II. The U.S. Marine Corps First Parachute Battalion did not jump, though; they assaulted the island from barges, because Gavutu was beyond the operational range of any aircraft flying out of New Zealand. The unit was led by Lieutenant Colonel Robert Hugh Williams.

Gay, George

U.S. Navy ensign. He was the sole survivor of Torpedo Squadron 8 (thirty men) at the Battle of Midway in June 1942. After being shot down, he watched the rest of the battle from his liferaft. Gay was present at the launching of the aircraft carrier U.S.S. *Midway* (CV-41) on March 20, 1945.

MOVIE PORTRAYAL:

Midway (1974), by Kevin Dobson

Gearhart Mountain

Site, located near Bly, Oregon, of the only Japanese bomb on continental North America that is known to have killed anyone. The bomb, dropped from a balloon, killed six people on a picnic (five were children). It was known as the Bly Bombing.

Gehlen, Reinhard (1902–1979)

German Army officer and chief of intelligence for the Eastern Front during World War II. He predicted Russian capabilities very accurately but angered Hitler with constant news that Hitler did not care to hear, so Hitler ordered him incarcerated in an insane asylum. Instead, Gehlen fled to the Bavarian Alps with fifty cases of intelligence data on the Red Army and gave these to the U.S. in exchange for its support. After the war, Gehlen became the head of the West German intelligence service, retiring in 1968. (The Russians had a $250,000 price on his head.)

Gehres, Leslie E.

U.S. Navy captain. He commanded the aircraft carrier U.S.S. *Franklin* when it was attacked off Japan on March 19, 1945, and severely damaged by bombs. Gehres was the first enlisted man carrier captain to have worked his way up through the ranks. He received the Navy Cross for saving the *Franklin* in what was the Navy's third worst disaster in history.

Geiger, Roy S. (1885–1947)

U.S. Marine Corps major general. He commanded Marine Corps aviation on Guadalcanal and succeeded General Alexander Vandegrift as commander of the Marines in the South Pacific. Geiger died on January 23, 1947, two days before his birthday and seven days before he would have retired from the U.S. Marine Corps.

MOVIE PORTRAYAL:
The Gallant Hours (1960), by Robert Burton

Genda, Minouru (1904–)

Japanese Navy officer. In 1937, he devised the innovative tactics of forward airbases in China so that fighter aircraft did not have so far to fly to escort bombers. Genda also drew up the specifications needed by the Navy for a fighter aircraft that became the Zero in 1940. That same year he was air attaché in London and reported on the British torpedo attack on the Italian fleet at Taranto, in which torpedoes were launched successfully from aircraft into relatively shallow water. Genda planned the attack on Pearl Harbor for Admiral Isoruku Yamamoto based on what he learned in London.

MOVIE PORTRAYAL:
Tora! Tora! Tora! (1970), by Tatsuya Mihashi

General Lyon

Code name given to King George VI during World War II to maintain secrecy when he visited the theaters of operation.

General Mud, General Snow, and General Distance

The three great Russian generals that Benito Mussolini felt would defeat Hitler after he invaded Russia in June 1941.

Generals

At the end of World War II, the U.S. had 1,500 generals, the Germans had almost 2,500, and the Russians had over 10,000.

General Tojo

Name of the cook's monkey on the *PT-41* that took General Douglas MacArthur and his family from Corregidor to Cagayon on the first leg of their trip to Australia from the doomed Philippines in 1942.

Genn, Leo (1905–1978)

British actor. He served with the Royal Artillery as a lieutenant colonel in World War II and was awarded the French Croix de Guerre.

Gentile, Donald (1920–1951)

U.S. Army Air Force officer. As a member of the 4th Fighter Group of the Eighth Army Air Force in England, he is officially credited with shooting down 19.84 enemy aircraft during World War II. Gentile had been rejected by the U.S. Army Air Corps, although he had over three hundred flying hours as a civilian. He then joined the Royal Air Force as a member of the Eagle Squadrons, until he was transferred to the 4th Fighter Group. Gentile flew a P-51 named *Shangri-La* and returned to the U.S. prior to D-Day. He was killed in 1951 in a jet aircraft accident.

George

Nickname of the automatic pilot in U.S. Army Air Force bombers in World War II.

George

Name of a dog that landed with U.S. Marines on Iwo Jima. It was his third landing.

George VI (1895–1952)

King of England throughout World War II. He became king after his older brother Edward VIII abdicated the throne in 1936 to marry American divorcée Wallis Simpson.

Movie portrayals:
Ike (1979 TV movie), by Martin Jarvis
Churchill and the Generals, (1981 TV movie), by Lyndon Brook

George F. Elliott, S.S.

U.S. transport that was sunk off Guadalcanal on August 8, 1942, when a Japanese Betty bomber crashed into it. The *George F. Elliott* was the first U.S. ship to go down in Iron Bottom Sound.

German-American Bund

Name of a pro-German organization in the United States led by Fritz Kuhn. It had seventy-one units with over 25,000 members located in industrial centers and near munitions works.

German Command Structure in 1939

Hitler—Commander in Chief
Wilhelm Keitel—Chief of Staff of the military (OKW)
Alfred Jodl—Chief of Operations Staff of the military (OKW)
Walter von Brauchitsch—Army Commander in Chief
Franz von Halder—Army Chief of Staff
Hermann Goering—Air Force Commander in Chief
Hans Jeschonnek—Air Force Chief of Staff
Erich Raeder—Navy Commander in Chief
Otto Schniewind—Navy Chief of Staff

German Generals

There were approximately 2,500 generals in the German military, 786 of whom died in World War II. Of these

- 253 were killed in action

- 44 died of wounds
- 81 committed suicide
- 23 were executed by Hitler
- 41 were executed by the Allies
- 326 died of other causes

Germania

New name to have been given to Berlin after it was modernized. Hitler had many plans for the new city; it was to have been designed by Albert Speer.

Gestapo

Acronym for Geheime Staats Polizei (Secret State Police). It was created by Hermann Goering to be used against political enemies and was headed by Heinrich Muller.

G for George

Name of the Lancaster bomber flown by Guy Gibson on the Ruhr Dams bombing mission on May 16, 1943.

Ghormley, Robert L. (1883–1958)

U.S. Navy admiral. He graduated from the U.S. Naval Academy at Annapolis in 1906 and was U.S. Naval attaché in London in the spring of 1941. Ghormley commanded the U.S. naval forces during the initial phases of the Battle of Guadalcanal in 1942 and was replaced by Admiral William F. "Bull" Halsey. After the war, he was in charge of the demobilization of the German Navy.

MOVIE PORTRAYAL:

The Gallant Hours (1960), by Carl Benton Reid

Ghost Corps

Nickname given to the U.S. XX Corps commanded by General Walton H. Walker. Part of General George S. Patton's Third Army, the XX Corps captured Metz, liberated Buchenwald, and penetrated into Austria to Linz.

GI

Term used throughout World War II in referring to nearly anything related to the U.S. Army. It was generally understood to stand for Government Issue, but actually began when supply clerks listed garbage cans as GI for galvanized iron.

Gibraltar

British military base guarding the entrance to the Mediterranean Sea. It was attacked by French planes on July 5, 1940, in retaliation for the British attack at Oran on the French fleet. Gibraltar was attacked again by French aircraft on September 24, 1940, in response to the British attacks on Dakar the day before.

Gibson Girl

Name given to an emergency radio transmitter carried by Allied aircrews in World War II. The radio was designed to float, and when downed, the crew simply turned a crank to broadcast an S.O.S. message.

Gibson, Guy P. (1918–1944)

Royal Air Force wing commander. He led the May 16, 1943, attack on the Ruhr Dams, for which he was awarded the Victoria Cross. Gibson was then pulled off operations to travel to the U.S. with Winston Churchill, but he was able to talk his way back into combat. He was killed in 1944 while flying a Mosquito as a pathfinder for bombers attacking the Ruhr.

MOVIE PORTRAYAL:

The Dam Buster (1955), by Richard Todd

GI Jill

Name given to females in the Women's Army Corps in World War II. The term inspired the title of actress Carole Landis's book, *Four Jills and a Jeep,* about her USO tours during the war. It was made into a movie in 1944.

GI Joe

Name given to the American soldier during World War II. It was derived from the initials GI (government issue) and was first used in print by Lieutenant Dave Berger's comic strip in *Yank* magazine on June 17, 1942.

GI Joe

Name of a carrier pigeon that was credited with saving over a thousand British soldiers by taking a message across the lines in Italy on October 18, 1943.

GI Joe Diners

Nickname given to rest stops for the truck drivers that drove constantly to supply the U.S. Seventh Army across the Rhine river. The driver could bring in his cold rations and exchange them for hot food.

Gilbert, Henry (1920–1941)

First Flying Tiger pilot killed in combat, December 23, 1941, over Rangoon. Gilbert was also the youngest member of the Flying Tigers and was in the third squadron, known as *Hell's Angels*.

Gillars, Mildred (1909–)

American-born propaganda broadcaster mistakenly known as Axis Sally. At the outbreak of World War II, she was teaching English in Berlin and began broadcasting for the Nazis using the name Midge (Axis Sally was actually used by Rita Louise Zucca broadcasting from Rome.) Her partner was named George. Gillars was put on trial for treason in Washington, D.C., in February 1949, found guilty, and imprisoned. She was paroled in 1961 and went to Columbus, Ohio, where she became a teacher of French and German in a convent.

Gillespie, Norvell (1914–1973)

American horticulturist who designed the camouflage patterned uniforms used by U.S. GI's in the Pacific throughout World War II. He was the garden editor of *Sunset* magazine as well as *Better Homes and Gardens*.

Gilmore, Howard (1902–1943)

U.S. Navy officer and commander of the submarine U.S.S. *Growler.* He was the first submariner to win the Congressional Medal of Honor. His submarine rammed a Japanese ship while attempting to torpedo it, and the Japanese fired on the conning tower with machine guns, killing several of the crew. Gilmore ordered the rest to go below and then ordered the submarine to dive, leaving himself topside to die.

GI Quiz

In December 1944 during the Battle of the Bulge, Germans dressed in American uniforms infiltrated U.S. lines to confuse relief forces moving forward. Overcautious military police began asking unknown soldiers trivia questions that supposedly any red-blooded American would know. General Omar Bradley was stopped on three occasions by cautious GI's. In order to check his identity as an American, he was asked: 1) What is the capital of Illinois? 2) Where is a guard placed on a scrimmage line? 3) Who was the present husband of Betty Grable? General Bradley answered the first two (Springfield and "between the center and tackle") but was stumped on the third (Harry James). He was released anyway.

Giraud, Henri Honoré (1879–1949)

French general. He had been captured by the Germans in World War I and escaped from a prisoner-of-war-camp. He was captured by them at Sedan in May 1940 and escaped in 1942 to join the Free French Forces under General Charles de Gaulle. Giraud helped to rebuild the French army.

MOVIE PORTRAYAL:
Ike (1979 TV movie), by Maurice Marsac

Gisevius, Hans Bernd (1903–1974)

German Vice-Consul and head of the Abwehr network in Switzerland during World War II. He was one of the conspirators against Hitler and was involved in the July 20, 1944, attempt to assassinate him. Gisevius had met frequently with Allen Dulles, head of the OSS in Switzerland, to keep the U.S. informed on the progress of the anti-Hitler factions in Germany. After the failure of the plot, Gisevius hid in Berlin for six months and finally escaped to Switzerland, using Gestapo papers forged by the OSS.

GI Sinatra

Nickname given to Sergeant Johnny Desmond, singer with the Glenn Miller Air Force Band during World War II.

Gleiwitz

German town on the Polish border. It was the site of a contrived incident in which Polish troops were supposed to have attacked a German radio station August 31, 1939. This was used as a pretext for Hitler to attack Poland the next day. The incident was staged by S.S. men of Reinhard Heydrich's S.D., who used condemned inmates of a concentration camp dressed in Polish uniforms. It was called Operation Canned Goods.

Glenn, John (1921–   )

U.S. astronaut and senator from Ohio. (In 1963 he was the first American to orbit the Earth.) During World War II, he was a Marine F4U fighter pilot who logged fity-nine missions in the Marshall Islands. Glenn was awarded two Distinguished Flying Crosses and ten Air Medals. He again fought in the Korean War where he won two more Distinguished Flying Crosses and eight Air Medals and flew ninety combat missions.

Gliders

Aircraft used throughout World War II by nearly all participants to deliver airborne forces behind enemy lines. By the end of the war, the U.S. had more than 13,000 gliders and 10,000 trained glider pilots. There were three glider centers: Sedalia, Missouri; Alliance, Nebraska; and Laurinburg—Maxton Army Air Base, North Carolina.

Glorious, H.M.S.

British aircraft carrier. It was built in 1917 as a battle cruiser but was later converted into a carrier. The *Glorious* was sunk by the German cruiser *Scharnhorst* on June 8, 1940, in the retreat from Narvik, Norway.

Gluckstein
British code word used in referring to the German cruiser *Gneisenau.*

Gneisenau
German battle cruiser of 31,000 tons. As the sister ship of the *Scharnhorst,* they had nine eleven-inch guns and could travel at thirty-one knots. They were faster than any British ship that could sink them and outgunned all ships that could catch them. The *Gneisenau* was hit and damaged by an R.A.F. raid on Kiel in February 1942 and saw no further action. It was scuttled at the end of the war.

Gnys, Wladyslaw
Polish fighter pilot who shot down the first German aircraft (JU87 Stuka) of World War II. This occurred during the German invasion of Poland in September 1939. Gnys later escaped to England and served with the R.A.F.'s No. 302 Squadron (Polish) in the Battle of Britain.

Gobbledygook
World War II slang term coined by Maury Maverick in 1944 to refer to anything verbose.

Gobel, George (1920–   )
Hollywood comedian who served as an instructor pilot on B-26's throughout World War II in Oklahoma. He enlisted in 1943 and was discharged in 1945 as a first lieutenant. Gobel often claims, "Not one Japanese plane got past Tulsa!"

Goddard, Paulette (1911–   )
Hollywood actress and wife of Charles Chaplin. She was the first female civilian to fly over the Himalayas during World War II.

MOVIE PORTRAYAL:
Moviola (1980 TV miniseries), by Gwen Humble

Goddard, Robert H. (1882–1945)
U.S. father of rocketry. During World War II, he was the head of the U.S. Navy research on jet-propelled aircraft.

Godfrey, Arthur (1903–   )
Radio broadcaster. He served in the U.S. Navy from 1920 to 1924 and the U.S. Coast Guard from 1927 to 1930. He remained in the U.S. Navy Reserve and was a lieutenant commander at the outbreak of World War II. Godfrey was not allowed to go on active duty because of injuries received in an auto accident in 1931. He conducted recruiting drives and went to the South Pacific as a war correspondent.

Godfrey, John H. (1888–1971
British Rear Admiral and head of British Naval Intelligence from 1939 to 1942. Ian Fleming was his assistant.

Goebbels, Joseph P. (1897–1945)
Nazi propaganda minister. He was one of the few intellectuals at the top of the Nazi hierarchy and stood by Hitler to the end, committing suicide with his wife in Berlin. Goebbels had been a Marxist before he joined the Nazi party. His wartime address was Berlin W. 8, Wilhelmplatz 8–9.

MOVIE PORTRAYALS:
Confessions of a Nazi Spy (1939), by Martin Kosleck*
That Nazty Nuisance (1943), by Charles Rogers
The Hitler Gang (1944), by Martin Kosleck
Hitler (1962), by Martin Kosleck
Hitler: The Last Ten Days (1973), by John Bennett
The Hindenburg (1975) by David Mauro
The Bunker (1980 TV movie), by Cliff Gorman
Inside the Third Reich (1982 TV miniseries), by Ian Holm

Goering, Hermann (1893–1946)
Nazi head of the German Luftwaffe. He had been a fighter pilot in World War I and was credited with shooting down twenty-two aircraft. Goering took over command of Manfred von Richtofen's squadron when von Richtofen (the Red Baron) was shot down and killed by Canadian Roy Brown in 1918. He was an early member of the Nazi party and was wounded in the abortive 1923 Beer Hall Putsch in Munich. He became a drug addict as a result of the treatment for the wound. After Hitler took power, Goering held numerous offices:

- Prime Minister of Prussia
- Commandant of the Prussian Police
- Head of the State Secret Police (Gestapo)
- President of the Reichstag
- Air Minister
- Commander in Chief of the Luftwaffe
- Chief Forester of the Reich
- Reich Commissioner of the Four-Year Plan
- Supreme Head of the National Weather Bureau

---

*Kosleck was a Jew who had fled Nazi Germany.

- Chief Liquidator of Sequestered Estates
- Chief Huntsman and Game Warden
- Minister of the Interior of Prussia
- Chief of the SA Feldherrnhalle
- Field Marshall
- Reichsmarschall of the Greater German Reich

Goering's address during World War II was Berlin W. 8, Leipziger Strasse 3. He was known as the flying tailor due to the great variety of uniforms he had made. At one point he took an interest in raccoon coats and imported four raccoons from the United States to breed, so that he could start his own fur coat business. It failed and he turned the raccoons loose in the German forests, where they have proliferated ever since. (Europe today has a plague of raccoons!) Goering surrendered to the U.S. 36th Infantry Division assistant commander Brigadier General Robert Stack in Bavaria in May 1945. He had with him over 20,000 pills of paracodin, a synthetic drug similar to morphine, and had rouged his cheeks and painted his toenails. He was tried at Nuremberg, where his serial number was 31G350013. Goering was found guilty and sentenced to be hanged but committed suicide just before he was to be executed.

MOVIE PORTRAYALS:
The Great Dictator (1940), by Billy Gilbert (as Herring)
That Nazty Nuisance (1943), by Rex Evans
The Hitler Gang (1944), by Alexander Pope
The Magic Face (1951), by Hermann Ehrhardt
Hitler (1962), by John Mitchum
Battle of Britain (1969), by Hein Riess
von Richtofen and Brown (1970), by Barry Primus
The Bunker (1980 TV movie), by David King
Inside the Third Reich (1982 TV miniseries), by George Murcell

Go For Broke

Motto of the Nisei-American unit of the U.S. Army, the 442nd Regimental Combat Team that fought in Italy. It was also the title of a 1951 movie starring Van Johnson as the lieutenant in charge of a squad of Japanese-Americans in World War II.

Gold Beach

Name of the D-Day beach assaulted by the British 50th Division and the 8th Armored Brigade June 6, 1944. The objective was

Bayeux and the overall command belonged to Lieutenant General Bucknall and the XXX Corps.

Goldberg, Arthur (1908–)

U.S. Supreme Court Justice. He was an OSS officer in Washington, D. C., during World War II.

Goldfish Club

Name of an organization begun by the British in World War II. It was made up exclusively of Allied airmen who had to be rescued from British coastal waters after having been shot down or ditching their aircraft due to mechanical problems. The only requirement was that the individual had to be fished out of salt water. The club had an unofficial insignia of a winged goldfish flying over waves on a cloth patch.

Golding, William (1911–)

British author whose most famous work is *Lord of the Flies* (1954). During World War II, he served as a British naval officer and was present at the sinking of the *Bismarck* in May 1941. Golding commanded a rocket-launching ship in support of the D-Day landings on June, 6, 1944.

Goldwater, Barry (1909–)

U.S. government official and one-time presidential candidate. During World War II, he was an instructor pilot in the Air Transport Command; he was discharged in 1945 as a lieutenant colonel.

Golf, Cheese, and Chess Society

Name given to the initials for the British *G*overnment *C*ode and *C*ypher *S*chool, which listened to German radio signals and deciphered them throughout World War II.

Goliath

Name given to a miniature tank built by the Germans during World War II. They filled it with explosives and guided it to a target, where it was detonated by remote control. The Goliath was first used in the Battle of Cassino in 1944 and was also used on the Russian front to detonate mines.

Goliath

Name of Grand Admiral Karl Doenitz's giant transmitter at Frankfurt an der Oder (Eng. Frankfurt on the Oder) used to communicate with his submarines at sea during World War II.

Gonzalez, Manuel (–1941)

U.S. Navy ensign. He was the first American to officially be killed by Japanese forces during World War II when his aircraft was shot down while en route from the U.S.S. *Enterprise* to Pearl Harbor on December 7, 1941.

"Goodbye Mama, I'm off to Yokohama"

Name of a popular juke box song composed by Fred J. Coats early in 1942.

Gooseberry

Name given to artificial harbors along the Normandy coast for support of the D-Day landings. There were a total of five: Varreville, Saint Laurent, Arromanches, Courseulles, and Ouistreham. (Ouistreham was later abandoned because of its vulnerability to German artillery.)

Gort, Viscount (1886–1946)

British Field Marshall. His real name was John Standish Surtees Prendergust Vereker and he was Chief of the Imperial General Staff. He won the Victoria Cross in World War I and commanded the British Expeditionary Force in France and Belgium in 1940. Lord Gort also led the retreat of Dunkirk and in 1942 was put in command of the Allied defense of Malta, where he traveled around the island on a bicycle.

Gorton, John (1911–   )

Prime Minister of Australia. He enlisted in the Royal Australian Air Force in November 1940 and flew as a fighter pilot in England, Singapore, New Guinea, and Australia in World War II. In 1942 he was shot down by a Japanese fighter twenty miles south of Singapore. In 1944, Gorton was shot down a second time near Australia and was medically discharged in December 1944 with the rank of flight lieutenant.

Goto, Inichi

Japanese Navy pilot who released the first torpedo during the Pearl Harbor attack of December 7, 1941. It hit the battleship U.S.S. *Oklahoma*.

Gott, William H. (1897–1942)

British lieutenant general. He was made Commander of the British Eighth Army in North Africa but was killed before he could accomplish anything. His aircraft was attacked by a German fighter; the pilot succeeded in landing, but the fighter fired into the fuselage and a bullet struck Gott. He was replaced by Bernard Montgomery.

Gowdy, Curt (1919–   )

Sportscaster who enlisted in the U.S. Army Air Force to become a pilot in World War II. He ruptured a disc in his back during calisthenics just prior to beginning flight training; after being hospitalized, he received a medical discharge in 1943.

Gowdy, Hank (1889–1966)

Professional baseball player. He was the only pro baseball player to serve in both World War I and World War II.

Gower, Pauline (1910–1947)

Commander of the British female Air Transport Auxiliary (ATA Girls) during World War II. They served as auxiliaries to the Royal Air Force and flew every type of aircraft the British had in every role except combat. Gower had over 20,000 hours of flying time prior to World War II.

Go West

Marx Brothers movie (1940) that Prime Minister Winston Churchill was watching when he was notified that Rudolph Hess had parachuted into Britain in May 1941. Hess could have passed for one of the Marx Brothers with his disheveled hair and wild eyes; he too, went west!

Grable, Betty (1916–1973)

Hollywood actress. She was the favorite pin-up girl of U.S. troops during World War II. Grable was said to be the girl with the million dollar legs, but they were only insured for $250,000.

Graf Spee

German pocket battleship that was scuttled outside Montevideo Harbor in December 1939, as a result of the first major naval engagement of World War II. She was engaged in the Battle of the Plate River by the cruiser H.M.S. *Exeter,* light cruiser H.M.S. *Ajax,* and the Royal New Zealand cruiser *Achilles,* all under Commodore Henry Harwood, and forced into sanctuary in Montevideo. Captain Hans Langsdorff of the *Graf Spee* believed he was opposed by a larger force and scuttled the ship, after which he committed suicide.

Graf Zeppelin

Name of Germany's only aircraft carrier. The keel was launched in 1938, but the ship was still under construction at the end of the war and was captured unfinished by the Russians. It was pictured in the *National Geographic* magazine for July 1942.

Graf Zeppelin

German airship. It had been decommissioned, but Luftwaffe General Wolfgang Martin, head of the signals unit, talked Goering into using it as a floating laboratory to study British radar. On August 2, 1939, it sailed on a friendship mission to England but was really packed with electronic gear and technicians to monitor British radar. However, the British turned off all radar while the *Graf Zeppelin* cruised up and down the coast, and the mission failed, forcing the ship back into retirement.

Graham, Calvin (1929–)

Known as the "Baby Vet." He enlisted in the U.S. Navy shortly after the outbreak of World War II when he was only twelve years old. He served on the battleship U.S.S. *South Dakota* and earned a Bronze Star and a Purple Heart in the South Pacific. When the Navy discovered he was underage, they took away his medals and locked him in the brig. Graham was released but did not get his honorable discharge until May 1978.

Graham, Virginia (1913–)

Radio and television commentator. During World War II, she joined the American Red Cross Volunteer Services and served as a master sergeant in the motor corps.

Grand Alliance

Term used by Winston Churchill to refer to the United States, the United Kingdom, and Russia. He took the term from a name given to England's Allies in the War of the Spanish Succession (1701–1714) in which the Duke of Marlborough, an ancestor of Churchill, became famous.

Grand Slam

Name of a ten-ton bomb invented by Barnes Wallis. It was designed to set up vibrations similar to an earthquake that would destroy any target close to the point of impact. The Grand Slam was first dropped by No. 617 Squadron on Bielefeld Viaduct near Bremen toward the end of the war.

Gran Sasso

Highest peak in the Italian Appeninnes. It was the site of the hotel where Mussolini was held after Italy surrendered to the Allies in 1943. He was subsequently rescued in an airborne assault led by Otto Skorzeny.

Grant, David (1891–1964)

U.S. Army Air Force major general. He was the first surgeon general of the Army Air Force (1941–1946) and as such was the first to use helicopters equipped with litters to evacuate wounded from the front. Grant was also the first to use transport aircraft for medical evacuations. By the end of the war, he was responsible for evacuating over four thousand casualties a month across the Atlantic.

Grant, Ulysses Simpson III (1881–1968)

U.S. Army major general. Grant, who was the grandson of Civil War hero and President of the United States Ulysses S. Grant, fought in both World War I and World War II.

Gray, Augustine H. (1888–   )

U.S. Navy commodore. He was in charge of logistics in the Pacific and was known as the "Oil King of the Pacific" because of his ability at supply.

Graye

Name of a French beach at the western end of Juno beach. It was the site where Winston Churchill landed along with Field Marshall Bernard Montgomery, Jan Christian Smuts, Sir Alan Brooke, and Admiral Philip Vian on June 12, 1944, to inspect the Normandy beachhead area. On June 16, 1944, King George VI landed there also.

Grayling, U.S.S.

U.S. submarine that was attacked on June 7, 1942, by twelve B-17's based on Midway, even though the submarine had given the proper recognition signal. The *Grayling* submerged and survived. When the bomber crews returned to Midway, they claimed sinking a Japanese cruiser.

Graziani, Rodolfo (1882–1955)

Italian marshal. He was the commander in Italian Somalia who invaded Ethiopia. As the governor of Ethiopia after its capture, he ruled with an iron hand, exterminated the intelligentsia, and indiscriminately killed the hierarchy of the Coptic Church in savage reprisals to suppress the Ethiopians. Graziani was made Commander in Chief in Africa until the fall of Benghazi on February 7, 1941, after which he was replaced by General Garibaldi. In September 1943, he became Minister for War. At the end of the war, he was captured by Italian partisans but rescued by Donald Jones and Emilio Daddario, two OSS agents. Graziani was put on trial by the Italian government and sentenced to nineteen years in prison. He was released in 1950.

MOVIE PORTRAYAL:

Lion of the Desert (1981), by Oliver Reed

Great Artiste

Name of the B-29 observation aircraft flown by Major Charles W. Sweeney over Hiroshima after the atomic bombing of August 6, 1945. The *Great Artiste* was also flown over Nagasaki on August 9, 1945, after the second atomic bomb.

Great East Asia Co-Prosperity Sphere

Title used by the Japanese to refer to their intended sphere of influence throughout Asia after the expulsion of Caucasian rule. It was coined by Yosuke Matsuoka, the Japanese Foreign Minister from 1940 to 1941.

Great Escape

Name given to the escape of 76 prisoners of war from Stalag Luft III sixty miles northeast of Berlin on March 25, 1944. The prisoners dug a huge tunnel, planning to get two hundred men out before being discovered. One of the greatest manhunts in history ensued, when over five million Germans were used to track down the escapers. All but three were recaptured and fifty of these were executed by the Gestapo. (For a list of the fifty executed, see *Free as a Running Fox,* by T. D. Calnan.)

Great Marianas Turkey Shoot

Name given to the air battle portion of the Battle of the Philippine Sea on June 19, 1944. The Japanese lost 346 planes; only thirty U.S. aircraft were lost. The name was coined by Commander Paul Buie of the carrier U.S.S. *Lexington*.

Great Pacific War

Novel written in 1925 by Hector C. Bywater, who was the naval correspondent for the London Daily Telegraph. In the book, Bywater imagined a surprise attack by the Japanese to knock out the U.S. Pacific Fleet at anchor in Pearl Harbor with simultaneous attacks on Guam and the Philippines. The book was adopted as a textbook of the Japanese Naval War College.

Great Patriotic War

Russian name for the conflict between Germany and Russia from June 1941 to May 1945, to differentiate it from the larger global conflict of World War II.

Great Plan

German idea advocated by Admiral Eric Raeder that called for a thrust through the Middle East to link up with the Japanese and encircle the British Empire in Asia.

Greenberg, Hank (1911–   )

Pittsburgh Pirates baseball player. He was the first star baseball player to enlist in World War II. Greenberg joined the U.S. Army Air Force several days after the Pearl Harbor attack and became an administrative officer for a B-29 unit in China. He was discharged as a captain in June 1945.

Green Diamond

Name of the Allied supply route from the port of Cherbourg to Dol. It was copied from the more famous Red Ball Express.

Green Dragons

Nickname that the Japanese gave to American PT boats in World War II.

Greene, Lorne (1915–)

Canadian-born Hollywood actor. He served with the Canadian Army during World War II.

Greene, Graham (1904–

British author who served on a secret mission for the British Foreign Office in West Africa during World War II.

Green Frogs

Nickname that Dutch Resistance personnel gave to Gestapo agents who specialized in tracking down clandestine radio transmitters. The name came from the green uniforms used by this branch of the German secret police.

Green Hats

Name Russians gave to the N.K.V.D. secret police that shot supposed deserters as an example to the citizenry.

Green Plan

Name the French Resistance gave to the operation to cut railroad tracks in over a thousand places to prevent the Germans from bringing reinforcements to Normandy after the June 6, 1944, D-Day landings. The Allies named it Operation Vert.

Green Police

Name given to German state police because of their green uniforms.

Green Shirts

Symbol of the Hungarian fascists prior to World War II. It was also adopted by the Brazilian fascists known as the Integralists. The Nazis used brown shirts, while the Italians used black shirts.

Greenwood, Edith

First woman to receive the Soldier's Medal. She was awarded the medal on January 27, 1943, for risking her life to save the lives of patients under her care in a fire in Arizona.

Greer, Jane (1924–)

Hollywood actress who modeled the first Women's Army Corps uniform in *Life* Magazine in 1942. The photo led to her discovery by a Hollywood producer, which in turn led to her acting career.

Greer, U.S.S.

U.S. destroyer. It was the first U.S. ship to be fired on in World War II when, on September 4, 1940, a British patrol bomber spotted the German submarine *U-652* commanded by Lieutenant Georg W. Fraatz. The *Greer* answered a call by the bomber and proceeded to the area 175 miles from Iceland to help track the submarine. As it arrived, another aircraft dropped depth charges. Fraatz thought the destroyer was attacking, so he retaliated by firing torpedoes, which luckily missed. This took place while the U.S. was still officially neutral.

Greif

Name of Field Marshall Erwin Rommel's personal command vehicle used in the North African campaign.

von Greim, Ritter (1892–1945)

Luftwaffe officer and last head of the Luftwaffe. He was the pilot of the aircraft that took Hitler on his first airplane ride from Munich to Berlin in the early 1920's. Von Greim was promoted to Field Marshall on April 27, 1945, and was to be the last Field Marshall of World War II. He flew with Hanna Reitsch into encircled Berlin to be appointed head of the Luftwaffe by Hitler after Goering's "ultimatum," in which he attempted to take over the German government. Von Greim committed suicide with the fall of Berlin rather than be taken prisoner by the Russians.

MOVIE PORTRAYAL:
Hitler: The Last Ten Days (1973), by Eric Porter

Gremlins

Mythical creatures that were first reported by the Royal Air Force early in World War II. They were described as being about a foot tall and wearing little pointed shoes. Gremlins were credited with countless malfunctions of aircraft and aircraft systems that otherwise were inexplicable. Female gremlins were called *finella* and the children were *widgets*.

Grew, Joseph C. (1877–1965)

U.S. ambassador to Japan from 1931 until the attack on Pearl Harbor. He had been a member of the U.S. Embassy staff in Germany until 1916 and the Austro-Hungarian Empire in Vienna until 1917. Grew's wife was the granddaughter of Commodore Matthew C. Perry who had originally opened Japan to outsiders. As ambassador, Grew heard numerous rumors, which he passed to the U.S. State Department, that the Japanese intended to attack

Pearl Harbor. After he was repatriated from Japan in 1942 he became Undersecretary of State.

Griffin, John Howard (1920–1980)

Author of *Black Like Me*. He was blinded for ten years as a result of injuries suffered in World War II and diabetes, but regained his sight in 1957.

Grille

Name of Hitler's personal yacht.

Gripsholm

Swedish ship used in World War II to exchange civilians and diplomatic prisoners between the belligerents. It was first used in an exchange with the Japanese in the spring of 1942. In 1943, the *Gripsholm* returned axis nationals to Europe and picked up Americans to be repatriated. In March 1944, it returned 663 Americans to the United States.

Groves, Leslie R. (1896–1970)

U.S. Army major general. He was the engineering officer who built the Pentagon and who headed the Manhattan Project, in which the U.S. developed the atomic bomb. He died on July 13, 1970, three days short of the twenty-fifth anniversary of the first atomic bomb test in Alamogordo, New Mexico.

Gruenther, Al (1899–)

U.S. Army major general. He was chief of staff for the U.S. Fifth Army and was known as the "Brain of the Army," because of his exceptional staff work.

Grynszpan, Herschel

German Jew who, on November 7, 1938, assassinated Ernst von Rath, a member of the German Embassy in Paris, in protest against German persecution of the Jews. Grynszpan mistook von Rath for the German ambassador. Hitler used this as the pretext to unleash the Night of the Broken Glass, in which Nazi mobs ran rampant throughout Germany attacking Jews and destroying their property. This was the first use of collective punishment to gain the obedience of the entire Jewish community. Ironically, von Rath was the only member of the German embassy who was pro-Jewish and was actually under investigation by the Gestapo.

Guadalcanal

Island in the Solomon chain. The first U.S. offensive of World War II occurred when U.S. Marines stormed ashore on August 7, 1942, in an attempt to halt the steady Japanese advance toward Australia. The last Japanese soldier, except for isolated stragglers, was evacuated February 7, 1943, six months to the day after the U.S. landing.

Guadalcanal veterans

James Jones
Robert Leckie
William Manchester
James Michener
Leon Uris

Guam

The first U.S. territory to be captured by the enemy in World War II. It fell to the Japanese on December 10, 1941, and was not retaken until July 21, 1944 (see Tweed, George).

Gubbins, Colin McVeigh (1896–1976)

Scotsman who held the rank of colonel in the Royal Artillery. He was a member of the British Intelligence Directorate and was the head of a British military mission to Poland prior to World War II. Gubbins was responsible for stealing a complete Enigma cipher machine from the Germans, which allowed the British to break the German military codes and read them throughout the war. Toward the end of the war, Gubbins became head of the SOE as a major general; his identifier was "D."

MOVIE PORTRAYAL:
A Man Called Intrepid (1979 TV movie), by Peter Gilmore

Guderian, Heinz (1888–1954)

German general and tank expert. He borrowed his ideas for Blitzkrieg warfare from de Gaulle, J.F.C. Fuller, and Liddell-Hart. He was relieved of command by Hitler in 1941 because he had conducted a strategic withdrawal. Hitler used him as the scapegoat for the failure of the Moscow campaign and he was not called back to duty until February 1943. July 1944, the day after the attempt on Hitler's life, he replaced Zeitzler as Chief of General Staff. Guderian, as a member of the military court, expelled hundreds of his colleagues from the army so that they could be tried as civilians for the assassination attempt. Guderian was one of the few people who dared to contradict Hitler and in the final days, he was relieved again and sent on sick leave. He was captured by the U.S. Army at Berchtesgaden.

MOVIE PORTRAYAL:
Hitler (1962), by Martin Brandt
The Bunker (1980 TV movie), by Yves Brainville

Gudgeon, U.S.S.

U.S. submarine that was the first to conduct offensive operations in Japanese waters in World War II. It was commanded by Lieutenant Commander Joseph Grenfell and, on the return from enemy waters, on January 27, 1942, sank the Japanese submarine *I-173*, the first Japanese submarine sunk by an American submarine in the war.

Guernica

Spanish town attacked on April 26, 1937, by German aircraft of the Condor Legion during the Spanish Civil War. It was the first case of terror bombing in history. The Germans bombed the town on market day (Monday) at noon, so they would have a large portion of the population outdoors and could evaluate their bombing techniques. They used high explosives followed by incendiaries and strafing. Out of a population of 7,000, 1,654 people were killed and 889 wounded. A well-known painting by Picasso depicts the incident.

Guess Where II

First U.S. aircraft specifically built for Presidential use. It was a C87 (a converted B-24) and had the advantages of long range and a ramp for Franklin D. Roosevelt to board by wheelchair. The serial number was 41-24159. The aircraft was never used.

Guinness, Sir Alec (1914–   )

British actor. He enlisted in the Royal Naval Volunteer Reserve in 1941 as an ordinary seaman. In 1942, Guinness was commissioned as a lieutenant and was discharged in 1945.

Guisan, Henri (1874–1960)

Swiss general who was elected by the Federal Assembly on August 30, 1939. Switzerland has no general in peacetime and only elects one when her neutrality is threatened. Guisan was only the fourth in history. The others were General Guillance Dufour during the 1859 war between Italy and Austria; General Herzog during the 1870 Franco-Prussian War; and General Ulrich Will during World War I.

Gun Club

Nickname given to the U.S. Navy's battleship admirals who were opposed to the aircraft carrier-minded admirals before World War II.

Gung Ho

Chinese for "work together." It was the motto of the U.S. Marine Corps unit known as Carlson's Raiders in World War II. Carlson had been the assistant U.S. naval attaché in China prior to the war and fought with the Chinese Communists.

Gunsche, Otto

Personal S.S. adjutant to Hitler in the latter part of World War II. He poured the gasoline over the bodies of Hitler and Eva Braun and lit it after their suicides on April 30, 1945. Gunsche was captured by the Soviets on May 2, 1945, and released in 1955.

Gunther, John (1901–1970)

American journalist. Hitler marked him to be executed because Gunther referred to Hitler's sex life in his book *Inside Europe*. President Harry S Truman had a copy of his book *Inside Asia* on his desk on V-J Day.

MOVIE PORTRAYAL:
Death Be Not Proud (1975 TV movie), by Arthur Hill

King Gustav (1858–1957)

King of Sweden. He became King in 1907 and was the oldest living monarch in Europe during World War II. He accepted the Danish Jews into Sweden to prevent them from falling into the hands of the Germans.

Gustav Line

Name of a German defensive line across central Italy. It was based on the Rapido, Garigliano, and Sangro Rivers. The Gustav Line was followed by the Hitler Line and a third one called the Caesar Line, which was never completed.

Guthrie, Woodrow Wilson "Woody" (1912–1967)

American folk singer. In 1943, he joined the Merchant Marine; over the next eleven months he was torpedoed twice and took part in three invasions. On May 8, 1945 (V-E Day), Guthrie was drafted into the U.S. Army, where he served for eight months until he was given a dependency discharge.

MOVIE PORTRAYAL:
Bound For Glory (1978), by David Carradine

Gyrene

Slang term for a U.S. Marine.

H

H2S

Designator of a British radar set designed to be carried on board aircraft. It gave a radar picture of the terrain below and allowed bombers to attack targets through cloud cover and at night. H2S was used for the first time at Hamburg in July 1943. It was nicknamed "Home Sweet Home," was not accurate, and was later replaced by H2X. H2S is the chemical formula for hydrogen sulfide, which smells like rotten eggs—a reminder of the initial response of a British scientist to the radar idea; he said, "It stinks."

H2X

American-manufactured version of the H2S nicknamed "Mickey." It was a much better set for bombing because it presented a more accurate picture of the terrain below.

Haakon VII (1872–1957)

King of Norway. He was the nephew of King Christian X of Denmark and grandson of King Edward VII of England. Haakon was the first of the European kings to be pushed out of his country by the Germans (1940) and he was also the first to return (1945). He was head of the Norwegian government in exile in England throughout the war.

Habakkuk

Code name of a British scheme to make a floating airfield from ice and place it in the English Channel to provide protection for fighter aircraft during the D-Day landings.

Hacha, Emil (1872–1945)

President of Bohemia and Moravia after the Nazi occupation and dissolution of Czechoslovakia. Hacha died while awaiting trial for war crimes.

Hahn, Otto (1879–1968)

German physicist. He worked on the German atomic bomb throughout World War II and was awarded the Nobel Prize in 1944 for work done in 1938 on nuclear fission. Germany's first nuclear-powered freighter, which was launched in 1968, was named after him.

Haigerloch

German town that was the site of the German uranium stockpile. A small group of scientists, in the spring of 1945, made one last attempt to start a chain reaction. They were not aware that Enrico Fermi had done this two years previously in the United States, and were determined to have Germany be the first country to conduct a nuclear chain reaction. The experiment failed. It is interesting to note that the Germans had not provided for their own protection from radiation; if the experiment had been successful, most would have died from lethal doses of radiation poisoning.

Hailey, Arthur (1920–)

British-born author. He served in the Royal Air Force as a pilot in World War II. Hailey was originally sent to Americus, Georgia, for pilot training but failed due to a susceptibility to airsickness. He then went to Canada where he underwent pilot training again; this time he successfully passed the course, finishing in 1943. He spent the rest of the war flying reconnaissance missions in the Mediterranean. It was while in the service that Hailey wrote his first published short story, entitled "Rip Cord."

Halberd

Code word sent out by British intelligence, MI-6, in August 1939, to warn its operatives that war was inevitable.

Halcyon

Code name for the projected day when all preparations would be completed for the invasion of Normandy. It was also called "Y-Day."

Halcyon Plus Four

Message sent by General Dwight Eisenhower to General George C. Marshall to advise him that D-Day was scheduled for June 5, 1944.

Halder, Franz (1884–1972)

German general. He was Chief of the General Staff during the 1938 Sudeten Crisis, commanded the Polish campaign, and planned the invasion of England. Halder was suspected of being one of the conspirators against Hitler in the assassination attempt of July 20, 1944, and was sentenced to death by the People's Court. He was imprisoned in Dachau concentration camp, only to be freed by the Americans in 1945.

Haley, Alex (1921–   )

American author whose study of his family became the bestselling novel *Roots*. During World War II, he enlisted in the U.S. Coast Guard, serving as a messboy and later as ship's cook in the Southwest Pacific. It was in the Coast Guard that he developed his writing skills.

MOVIE PORTRAYAL:

Roots: The Next Generations (1979 ABC-TV), by Damon Evans and James Earl Jones

Half-Americans

Winston Churchill—British Prime Minister
Ernest Hanfstaengl—early friend and adviser of Hitler
William Joyce (Lord Haw Haw)—Nazi propagandist
Sir Dudley Pound—British First Sea Lord
Baldur von Schirach—head of the Hitler Youth

Halifax, Lord (1881–1959)

British ambassador to the United States (1941–1946). Born Edward Frederick Lindley Wood, he succeeded Lord Lothian after his death.

MOVIE PORTRAYAL:

Churchill and the Generals (1981 TV movie), by Bernard Archard

Hall, Charles B.

U.S. Army Air Force officer. He was the first black to shoot down an Axis aircraft (FW190) in World War II. Hall was a member of the all-black 99th Fighter Squadron and shot the enemy aircraft down on the first mission of the squadron. He was awarded the Distinguished Flying Cross.

Halsey, William F. "Bull" (1882–1959)

U.S. Navy admiral. He commanded the U.S. Navy in the Pacific during World War II, becoming one of the most aggressive commanders of the war. Halsey graduated from the U.S. Naval Academy at Annapolis in 1904, the same year his adversary Admiral Isoruku Yamamoto graduated from the Japanese Naval Academy. The first ship Halsey was assigned to was the U.S.S. *Missouri*, the ship that culminated his career on September 2, 1945, with the signing of the Japanese surrender. Halsey personally signed the citation awarding the Navy and Marine Corps Medal to John F. Kennedy for heroism in saving his crew of the *PT109* after it was rammed and sunk in 1943.

MOVIE PORTRAYALS:
Thirty Seconds Over Tokyo (1944), by Morris Ankrum
The Eternal Sea (1955), by John Maxwell
The Gallant Hours (1960), by James Cagney
Tora! Tora! Tora! (1970), by James Whitmore
Midway (1974), by Robert Mitchum
MacArthur (1977), by Kenneth Tobey

Halsey was mentioned in Paul and Linda McCartney's 1971 Number One hit record "Uncle Albert/Admiral Halsey."

Halverson, Harry A.
U.S. Army Air Force colonel. He was head of Project No. 63, a B-24 unit scheduled to fly to China but diverted to North Africa in 1942. Halverson led the first American attack on a European target when twelve B-24's bombed the Ploesti oil field on June 11, 1942.

Hamburg
Second largest city of Germany and the busiest port of Europe. Forty-five percent of all German submarines were produced in Hamburg. It was bombed by the Allies on July 27, 1943. The attack started a fire storm that developed winds of 150 m.p.h. and temperatures in excess of 1,000° C. that seared or suffocated anyone within range. The bombing was part of *Operation Gomorrah,* which killed over fifty thousand people. Thirteen percent of all German deaths due to bombing during World War II occurred during this attack.

Hamilton, Douglas Douglas-Hamilton (1903–1973)
Lord Stewart of the British Royal Household. He was the first person to fly over Mount Everest. Rudolph Hess parachuted into Scotland in May 1941, in the hopes of using Hamilton as a go-between for peace negotiations between Germany and England.

Hamilton, John
Name used by actor Sterling Hayden when he served as an officer with the OSS during World War II.

Hammann, U.S.S.
U.S. destroyer sunk by the Japanese submarine *I-168* on June 6, 1942, as it was tied to the damaged aircraft carrier U.S.S. *Yorktown*. The *Hammann* was supplying electrical power to the

carrier in an attempt to save her after the Battle of Midway. Minutes after the *Hammann* sank, the *Yorktown* also went down.

Hammelburg

Site of a German prisoner-of-war camp for U.S. troops. General George S. Patton sent a task force of the 4th Armored Division led by Captain Abraham Baum behind German lines in an attempt to free the prisoners in March 1945. The force, which consisted of nineteen tanks and assault guns and thirty-one other vehicles, penetrated fifty miles of German resistance to reach the camp. They arrived with only a third of their original complement and liberated the prisoners, who escaped to the countryside, but had to surrender while returning to Allied Lines because they ran out of gas and ammunition. Patton learned nine days later that his son-in-law, Lieutenant Colonel John Waters, who had been captured in North Africa in 1943, was in the camp. Patton believed his only real failure in the European war was not sending a larger force to Hammelburg.

Hamp

Allied code name for the Japanese fighter aircraft A6M3, which was an updated version of the Zero. The plane was originally called "the Hap," but U.S. Army Air Force General Henry H. "Hap" Arnold objected to the name and it was changed to Hamp.

Hams

Nickname given to U.S. Marine men by the female Marines. It stood for "hairy-assed marines." (see BAMS).

Hanabusa, Hiroshi

Japanese Navy lieutenant commander. He was in charge of the submarine *I-24*, which dropped off the midget submarine at Pearl Harbor on December 7, 1941 that carried Kazuo Sakamaki. Sakamaki became the first prisoner of war of the U.S. in World War II. Hanabusa was lost when *I-24* failed to report in June 1943, during the evacuation of Kiska in the Aleutian Islands.

Hancock, Joy Bright (1898–)

U.S. Navy commander. As a member of the WAVES, she was a representative to the Bureau of Aeronautics. Mrs. Hancock was first married to Lieutenant Charles Little, a Navy aviator who had won the Navy Cross during World War I. He was killed in the 1921 crash of the dirigible *ZR-2* at Humber River, England. In 1924, she met and married Lieutenant Commander Lewis Hancock, Jr., another U.S. Navy aviator who had also won a

Navy Cross in World War I, and who was also killed in the crash of a dirigible, the *Shenandoah*, on September 3, 1925.

Handrick, Gotthardt

German Luftwaffe major. He was the gold medalist in the 1936 Olympics, winning the Pentathlon. Handrick commanded a fighter wing in the Battle of Britain.

Hanemann, Walter

German Luftwaffe interrogation officer who questioned prisoners of war from the U.S. Twelfth Army Air Force and the Fifteenth Army Air Force from North Africa and Italy.

Hanfstaengl, Ernst

Half-American, half-German graduate of Harvard. One of his ancestors on his mother's side had been a general in the Union Army during the Civil War and was a pallbearer at Abraham Lincoln's funeral. Hanfstaengl returned to Germany and was sent to observe Hitler by the U.S. military attaché in Berlin in 1922. He became a close personal friend of Hitler and an adviser and friend of a great many of the top Nazis as the party struggled for power. Hanfstaengl escaped from Germany in 1937 because he thought he was to be assassinated. After internment in England and Canada, he worked for U.S. intelligence services.

Hansen, Charles H.

U.S. Army Air Force major. He was the pilot of the first B-29 to be attacked by the enemy. On April 26, 1944, while flying supplies over the Hump at 16,000 feet, he was attacked by six Japanese Oscar fighters near the India-Burma border. The aircraft sustained only light damage; the first casualty on board the B-29 was Sergeant Walter W. Gilonske, a waist gunner, who was wounded.

Hansen, Larry

U.S. Army Air Force captain. He was the personal B-17 pilot of General Dwight Eisenhower. The copilot was Captain Dick Underwood.

Hanson, Robert Murray (1920–1944)

U.S. Marine Corps officer and third-highest-scoring Marine Corps ace of World War II, with twenty-five enemy aircraft to his credit. He was a pilot with VMF-215 and won a Congressional Medal of Honor for action near Bougainville. In a single seventeen-day period, Hanson shot down twenty Japanese aircraft. He was killed on February 3, 1944, while on a strafing mission near Rabaul.

Happy Valley

Nickname given by Allied bomber crews to the Ruhr Valley because of the flak concentrations positioned there to protect Germany's industrial center. The Germans used barges anchored in the Rhine river to support the flak guns.

Harbin, Michael (–1942)

U.S. Navy enlisted man assigned to the submarine U.S.S. *Silversides*. During a battle in May 1942, *Silversides* and a Japanese trawler engaged in a surface battle. Harbin was killed, becoming the first American to die in a submarine surface engagement of the war.

Harmon, Tom (1919–)

1940's Michigan football star. He joined the U.S. Army Air Force, where he became a fighter pilot, initially flying P-38's in North Africa. In April 1943, his aircraft crashed in the jungle of French Guiana, and he was the sole survivor. Harman then was assigned to General Claire Chennault's Fourteenth Army Air Force in China and shot down two Japanese aircraft, winning a Silver Star. On November 30, 1943, he was shot down by a Japanese fighter and was reported missing in action. After thirty days, he was smuggled back to the base by Chinese guerillas. Harmon married the daughter of the U.S. Secretary of War, Frank Knox; her wedding dress was made from the parachute he used in one of his bailouts. Their daughter, Kristin was married for a time to singer Rick Nelson.

Harmon, U.S.S.

U.S. destroyer that became the first warship to be named after a black. The *Harmon* was launched July 25, 1943, and named for mess attendant Leonard Roy Harmon, who gave his life saving a friend from enemy gunfire during the Battle of Guadalcanal while on the U.S.S. *San Francisco*. He was awarded the Navy Cross posthumously.

Harriman, W. Averell (1891–)

American government figure. He was in charge of the U.S. Lend-Lease program with England in 1941. Harriman served President Franklin D. Roosevelt as a roving adviser and was appointed U.S. ambassador to Russia in October 1943.

MOVIE PORTRAYAL:
MacArthur (1977), by Art Fleming

Harris, Arthur (1892–)

Royal Air Force commander in chief of the bomber command.

He advocated area bombing and initiated the policy of night bombing in 1943. Harris was nicknamed "Bomber Harris" because of his total involvement in bombing and bomber tactics.

MOVIE PORTRAYAL:
The Dam Buster (1955), by Basil Sydney

Harris' Juke Box

Nickname given to a stereopticon used by Air Marshall Arthur Harris to show guests at his home the devastation to which the German cities were being subjected by bomber command.

Harrison, Rex (1908–)

British actor. He enlisted in the Royal Air Force in 1941 to become a pilot; but because of poor eyesight (he has a glass eye) he became a radar operator instead. Harrison served for two years with the Eleventh Group Headquarters, guiding bombers on the return leg of raids over Germany by providing them with fixes on their positions. In 1943, Harrison's home was partially destroyed while he and his wife, actress Lilli Palmer, were in it, when a bomb fell only fifteen feet away. He received only a cut forehead. In 1945, a V-2 struck in the front yard of their new house with only minor damage.

Hart, Thomas C. (1877–1971)

U.S. Navy admiral. He commanded the U.S. Asiatic Fleet at the outbreak of World War II. In February 1942, Hart was relieved of command at his own request and went back to Washington, D.C., where he became part of the Pearl Harbor investigation.

Hartmann, Eric (1922–)

German Luftwaffe fighter pilot and the top-scoring ace of all time, credited with having shot down an incredible 352 enemy aircraft. Hartmann flew an ME109 on over 1,425 missions and fought in over 800 air combats. He was shot down sixteen times himself and surrendered at the end of the war to the Americans, who turned him over to the Russians. Hartmann was sentenced to ten years in prison and returned to Germany in 1955. He was known as the Blond Knight of Germany and was awarded the Knight's Cross with oak leaves, swords, and diamonds, Germany's highest decoration.

Haruna

Japanese battleship erroneously reported sunk by Colin Kelly only days after the outbreak of World War II. In fact, the *Haruna* was the last surviving Japanese battleship. It was finally sunk at the dock in Kure harbor on July 28, 1945, by a U.S. Navy carrier aircraft.

Harvard

American university that contributed (unwillingly) its "Fight Fight Fight" song to the Nazi party when Hitler had it adapted as the "Sieg Heil Sieg Heil" marching song. This probably came about because Ernst Hanfstaengl, one of Hitler's close friends and advisers in the early days of the Nazi Party, was a Harvard graduate.

Harvester, H.M.S.

British destroyer that rammed and sank the German submarine *U-444* in March 1943. The *Harvester* was disabled and, while dead in the water, was sunk by *U-432*.

Harvey, Laurence (1928–1973)

British actor born in Lithuania, later emigrating with his family to South Africa. At the age of fourteen, Harvey ran away from home and enlisted in the Royal South African Navy but was discharged when his mother reported his real age. In 1943, he enlisted in the South African Army, again lying about his age, and took part in the North African and Italian campaigns. He was discharged in 1946.

Harwood, Sir Henry (1880–1950)

British Naval commodore. He was responsible for driving the German pocket battleship *Graf Spee* into Montevideo harbor, Uruguay, in 1939, which resulted in the scuttling of the vessel. This was the first major naval victory for the British in World War II. Harwood was knighted and promoted to rear admiral for his skillful use of the ships under his command, the *Ajax*, *Achilles*, and *Exeter.* He died in 1950 in an unusually named English town, Goring-on-Thames.

Hasbrouck, Robert (1896–   )

U.S. Army general. He commanded the U.S. 7th Armored Division in the Battle of the Bulge in December 1944 and holds the distinction of being relieved of command and reinstated in the same day.

Hashimoto, Kingoro (–1957)

Japanese Army colonel. He was one of the leaders of an attempted coup by the military in 1936 to take over the Japanese government. To get him out of Japan, Hashimoto was sent to China, where he ordered the attack on the U.S.S. *Panay* in December 1937. At the end of the war, he was sentenced to life in prison for promoting a war of aggression, only to be freed after ten years (1955). Hashimoto died of cancer in 1957.

Hashimoto, Mochitsura

Japanese Navy lieutenant commander. He was the torpedo officer on the submarine *I-24* that launched the midget submarine at Pearl Harbor December 7, 1941, which carried Kazuo Sakamaki, the first prisoner of war for the U.S. Hashimoto later commanded *I-58*, which sank the U.S. cruiser *Indianapolis* in July 1945, in the last major disaster of the U.S. Navy in World War II. After the war, Hashimoto became a high-ranking officer in the new Japanese Defense Force Navy.

Haugland, Vern

Correspondent for the Associated Press during World War II. In 1942 the aircraft he was on was forced down in the jungles of New Guinea, where he survived for forty-three days. Haugland was awarded the Silver Star medal on October 3, 1942, by General Douglas MacArthur, making him the first civilian so honored.

Haupt, Herbert Hans (1919–1942)

German spy who landed in Florida from *U-584* on June 17, 1942, as part of *Operation Pastorius*. He had lived in Chicago from 1932 to 1941. Haupt's father was a loyal Nazi who had served in the German Army during World War I. Young Haupt joined the Nazi Bund, and worked for a company that manufactured parts for the Norden bomb sight. He escaped to Germany via Mexico City and was later awarded the Iron Cross for running the British blockade. After undergoing training, he returned to the U.S. and was picked up by the FBI, tried, found guilty of espionage, and executed on August 8, 1942. His birthday was December 7.

Hausser, Paul (1880–1972)

German S.S. general. In the old Reichswehr, he had been a lieutenant general before retiring. With the rise of the Nazi party, Hauser joined the S.S. and commanded troops on every fighting front for the Germans. He was the first S.S. officer to command an army, when he took over the German Seventh Army at Normandy in June 1944.

Hawkins Field

Name that the Americans gave to the captured Japanese airfield on Betio, Tarawa. It was named after William Hawkins, a Marine

Corps first lieutenant who was killed during the fighting for Tarawa and won the Congressional Medal of Honor posthumously.

Hawkins, Jack (1910–1973)

British actor. He enlisted in the Royal Welsh Fusiliers in 1940 and served throughout the war in Southeast Asia. Hawkins was discharged in 1946 as a colonel.

Hayakawa, Sessue (1890–1973)

Japanese-born Hollywood actor who was nominated for an Academy Award for the 1958 movie *The Bridge on the River Kwai*. He lived in Paris during World War II, where he helped the French underground.

Hayate

Japanese destroyer that was sunk off Wake Island, December 11, 1941, by U.S. Marine Corps shore batteries. It was the second Japanese ship sunk in World War II. The first was the *Kisaragi*, sunk minutes previously off Wake.

Hayden, Sterling (1916–   )

Hollywood actor and author. He was recruited by William Donovan, head of OSS, to go to England for commando and parachute training with COI in November 1941. On his eleventh jump, Hayden broke his ankle, tore some cartilage in his knee, and injured the base of his spine. He returned to the United States, where he became a test skipper for PT boats in New York harbor. Hayden then joined the Marine Corps as an enlisted man under the name John Hamilton (his real name) and was selected for officer training. After receiving his commission, he joined the OSS and was sent to command a supply base at Monopoli, Italy, that ran arms and equipment across the Adriatic to Yugoslavian partisans. Hayden was in charge of over four hundred guerrillas and twenty-two boats and made several trips himself behind the German lines. He was discharged as a captain. After the war, he became a member of the Communist party because of his experiences with the Tito partisans, but he later renounced his membership before the House Un-American Activities Committee.

Hayes, Ira Hamilton (1923–1955)

Pima Indian who enlisted in the U.S. Marine Corps at the age of seventeen. He fought on Iwo Jima and was one of the five Marines who participated in the second flag-raising over Mt. Suribachi, which was photographed by Joe Rosenthal, and became world-famous. Hayes was acclaimed as a national hero, but he could not adjust to civilian life, becoming an alcoholic. He helped dedicate the Iwo Jima Monument in Washington, D. C., and acted in the John Wayne movie *Sands of Iwo Jima* (1949). He died of exposure while intoxicated when he was 32 years old.

MOVIE PORTRAYAL:
The Outsider (1961), by Tony Curtis
Lee Marvin portrayed Ira Hayes on the March 27, 1960 episode of TV's "Sunday Showcase", titled *The American.*

Hayes Lodge
Name of General Dwight Eisenhower's official residence in London for Operation Overlord, the invasion of Normandy.

Hayes, Peter Lind (1915–)
American comedian. He enlisted in the U.S. Army Air Force in July 1942 and appeared in 620 U.S.O. shows throughout the South Pacific. Hayes was awarded a Bronze Star and two battle stars before being discharged on December 25, 1945.

Hayes, Woodrow "Woody" (1913–)
American football coach. During World War II, he was in charge of the exercise programs for U.S. Navy recruits at Norfolk, Virginia. Hayes was discharged in 1946 as a lieutenant commander.

Hayward, Louis (1909–)
Hollywood actor. During World War II, he fought with the U.S. Marine Corps in the Pacific and was awarded the Bronze Star medal for heroism.

HE100
Designator of a Heinkel fighter, which was designed to surpass the ME109 in Germany before World War II. The HE100 was thirty knots faster, had a stronger undercarriage, and was more stable on the ground than the ME109, but the Luftwaffe had already decided on the ME109 as its main fighter aircraft. Ironically, Russia purchased six of the prototypes and copied them. Japan also bought several and the twelve remaining aircraft were used for propaganda purposes. The Luftwaffe took many pictures of them, each time repainting them, so that it appeared that the Luftwaffe had hundreds in operational status to fool Allied intelligence. The twelve aircraft served only as fighter protection for the Heinkel factories.

Hearn, Thomas (1891–1980)
U.S. Army major general. He was Chief of Staff to General

Joseph Stilwell and walked with him out of Burma when it fell to the Japanese in 1942.

Hearse

Slang term that U.S. Navy men gave to German submarines during World War II. The U-boat crewmembers were called pallbearers.

Heavy water

Name given to deuterium oxide, which was used by the Germans to moderate and control any attempted atomic reactions. It weighed eleven percent more than normal water and was only produced at the Norsk Hydro Electric Plant in Norway.

Heath, Edward (1916–)

British Prime Minister. During World War II, he served with the Royal Artillery and saw action on the continent of Europe. Heath was discharged with the rank of lieutenant colonel in 1946 after being awarded the M.B.E. (Member of the British Empire) medal.

Heckling Hare

Name of a B-25, commanded by Captain Walter H. Greer, on which Lyndon Johnson flew on June 9, 1942. It was attacked by Japanese Zeroes and for the action Johnson was awarded the Silver Star medal.

Hedgehog

Name given to one of the most effective antisubmarine devices developed during World War II. The U.S. Navy invented the hedgehog, which consisted of twenty-four separate charges that were fired in one salvo from the front of the launching ship, detonating only if they struck a submarine. A destroyer could track a submarine with sonar at a slow speed, fire the hedgehogs, and, since they only detonated if they hit, continue to follow it and fire again. If a charge did detonate, it sympathetically exploded the other charges in the pattern. The first submarine to be sunk by a hedgehog was the Japanese submarine *I-175* on February 5, 1944.

Hedgerows

Name given to barriers that divided up the fields of Normandy. They were three to four feet thick and three to five feet high and were constructed of trees, roots, and rocks, forming an impenetrable barrier. Hedgerows turned each field into a small fortress for the Germans and made it significantly more difficult for the Allies to capture the Normandy area.

Hedman, Duke

American pilot with the Third Pursuit Group of the Flying Tigers. He became the first ace of the Flying Tigers when he shot down his fifth Japanese aircraft over Rangoon on Christmas Day, 1941. Gregory "Pappy" Boyington said that he was the first American ace of World War II, but "Buzz" Wagner actually was the first, for combat in the Philippines.

Heflin, Van (1910–1971)

Hollywood actor and Academy Award-winner in 1942. He joined the U.S. Army as a second lieutenant of Artillery during World War II.

Hefner, Hugh (1926–)

Owner and editor of *Playboy* magazine founded in 1953. He served in the U.S. Army from 1944 to 1946 as a clerk typist at Fort Meade, Maryland.

Heglund, Svein

Norwegian fighter pilot who shot down fourteen and one half enemy aircraft during World War II. Heglund flew with the Royal Air Force and was the leading ace of Norway.

Heiden, Konrad (1901–)

German-born author and journalist. He went to Nazi rallies as a student in the early 1920's, a time when they called themselves *Nasos*, an abbreviation of National Socialist. Heiden coined the term *Nazi* from a Bavarian word for "simpleton" and the name stuck. He was forced to flee Germany in 1933 because of his anti-Hitler stand and later wrote a bestseller about Hitler and the rise of Nazism called *Der Fuehrer.*

Heights

five feet	Joseph Goebbels
five feet, two inches	Fiorello La Guardia
	Haile Selassie
	Julius Streicher
five feet, three inches	Francisco Franco
	Victor Emmanuel III
	Isoruku Yamamoto
five feet, four inches	Joseph Stalin
	Hideki Tojo
five feet, five inches	James Devereaux
five feet, six inches	Charlie Chaplin
	George C. Kenney
	Erich Raeder

five feet, seven inches	Wilhelm Frick
	Benito Mussolini
five feet, eight inches	Chiang Kai-shek
	Winston Churchill
	King George VI
	Adolf Hitler
	Ernie Pyle
	Joseph Tito
five feet, nine inches	William F. "Bull" Halsey
	Alfred Jodl
	Harry S Truman
five feet, ten inches	Claire Chennault
	Dwight Eisenhower
	Hans Frank
	Hermann Goering
five feet, eleven inches	Alfred Rosenberg
	Arthur Seyss-Inquart
six feet	Sir Kenneth Anderson
	Douglas Fairbanks, Jr.
	Joseph Clark Grew
	George C. Marshall
six feet, one inch	Ronald Reagan
	Quentin Reynolds
	Joachim von Ribbentrop
	Wendell Willkie
six feet, two inches	Mark Clark
	Franklin D. Roosevelt
	Jimmy Stewart
six feet, three inches	Howard Hughes
	Henry Monore Giraud
	Albert Speer
six feet, four inches	Charles de Gaulle
	Sir William Ironside
	Ernst Kaltenbrunner
	Wilhelm Keitel
	Sir Oliver Leese
	Louis Mountbatten
	Otto Skorzeny
six feet, five inches	Paul von Hindenburg
six feet, six inches	David Sterling
six feet, seven inches	Richard Tregaski

Heimdal

Name of the personal yacht of King Haakon of Norway. It brought him back to Norway on June 7, 1945, after he spent the war years in exile in England.

Heinck, Heinrich (1907–1942)

German spy who landed on Long Island on June 13, 1942, from the submarine *U-202* as part of Operation Pegasus. He had lived in the U.S. from 1927 to 1939 and went back to Germany where he was trained in espionage and sabotage. Shortly after his arrival, he was picked up by the FBI, tried, and was executed August 8, 1942.

Heinkel, Ernst (1888–1958)

German aircraft designer and manufacturer. He was highly critical of the Luftwaffe leadership and was therefore, in perpetual disfavor with the Nazis. Heinkel was involved in one of several anti-Hitler resistance groups; this evidence caused Allied charges against him for war crimes to be dropped after the war.

Heinrich

Name of Heinrich Himmler's private armored train.

Heintges, John (1912–)

U.S. Army officer. As a lieutenant colonel, he led the U.S. 7th Infantry Regiment of the 3rd Division in the capture of Berchtesgaden and Hitler's house. Heintges's father had been a German officer and was killed in World War I.

Held, Alfred (–1939)

Luftwaffe fighter pilot. He was the first German to shoot down a Royal Air Force aircraft in World War II when on September 7, 1939, he downed a Wellington bomber that was attempting to bomb the cruiser *Gneisenau*. Held was awarded the Iron Cross Second Class and flew an ME109 of JG77. He was killed in a midair collision on November 2, 1939.

Helen

Code name given to Makin Island, the target of Operation Galvanic in November 1943.

Helena, U.S.S.

U.S. Navy cruiser that was damaged at Pearl Harbor. Later repaired, the *Helena* was with the carrier U.S.S. *Wasp* when it was sunk in September 1942. The *Helena* was also the first U.S. Navy ship to open fire in the Battle of Cape Esperance and the Battle of Guadalcanal in 1942. It was also the first to receive the

Navy Unit Commendation. *Helena* was sunk in the Battle of Kula Gulf on July 6, 1943.

Helicopters

The first U.S. helicopter was built and flown by Igor Sikorsky in 1939. The second one was built by Frank Piasecki in 1943.

Hell Boats

German nickname for their E-boats, or motor torpedo boats.

Hellcat

Name given to the Grumman F6F fighter aircraft. It was the first U.S. aircraft that could outperform the Japanese Zero. It could fly, climb, and dive faster, was more maneuverable, and had better firepower.

Hell's Angels

Nickname adopted by the 3rd Pursuit Squadron of General Claire Chennault's A.V.G. (Flying Tigers). It was made up of pilots from all three U.S. services.

Hell's Highway

Name given to the stretch of highway held by the U.S. 101st and the 82nd Airborne Divisions for Operation Market-Garden in September 1944.

Helms, Richard (1913–)

Head of the CIA. As a correspondent for United Press, he met and interviewed Hitler during the 1936 Nuremberg Rallies. Helms was assigned to the OSS by the U.S. Navy in 1943 because he spoke German; this was the beginning of his life-long career with American intelligence services.

Hemingway, Ernest (1899–1961)

Two-time Pulitzer Prize-winning American author. During World War II, he was a war correspondent and landed with the fifth assault wave at D-Day on June 6, 1944. Hemingway participated in the liberation of Paris and told everyone he was a general in command of a resistance movement. Earlier in the war, he had heavily armed his private yacht, *Pilar,* in the hopes of being able to attack a German submarine, but the opportunity never arose.

Hendaye

Spanish town on the border with France. It was the site of a conference between Hitler and Francisco Franco on October 23, 1940, when Hitler attempted to get Franco to sign a treaty to join the Axis powers, beginning in January 1941. Franco continued to decline, causing Hitler to comment after the meetings that talking him into doing anything was like pulling teeth.

Henderson Field

Airfield partially completed by the Japanese on Guadalcanal and captured by the U.S. Marine Corps on August 8, 1942. It was the first airfield captured by U.S. forces in World War II and was named after Major Lofton Henderson. The Japanese attacked the airfield so many times in the next six months that the runway was called "Bull's Eye."

Henderson, Lofton B. (–1942)

U.S. Marine Corps major and pilot. He commanded sixteen SBD-2's from Midway Island that attacked the Japanese carrier *Hiryu* during the Battle of Midway in June 1942. He was shot down and killed by Japanese aircraft.

Henderson, Lyle "Skitch" (1918–)

Orchestra leader who was the musical director of Steve Allen's "Tonight Show." During World War II, he piloted B-29's in the Pacific Theater with the U.S. Army Air Force. He had been serving with the Canadian Air Force until the U.S. entry into the war, then transferred to the U.S. Army Air Force.

Henderson, Sir Neville (1881–1942)

British statesman and ambassador to Berlin from 1937 to 1939. After the outbreak of the war, he became a group commander in the Home Guard as a colonel. Henderson died on December 29, 1942, in London after writing his book *Failure of a Mission*.

Hencke, Melburn

U.S. Army private first class. He was officially the first American soldier to land on British soil during World War II, when he stepped off a transport on January 26, 1942.

Henlein, Konrad (1898–1945)

Nazi head of the Sudeten Germans in Czechoslovakia before 1938. He was instrumental in fomenting unrest just prior to the Nazi takeover of the country. Henlein became the Gauleiter of the Sudetenland. He surrendered at the end of the war but committed suicide immediately afterwards, using a razor blade he had hidden in a cigarette case.

Henry-Haye, Gaston (1889–)

Vichy French ambassador to the U.S. appointed in September 1940. He believed the real enemy of France was England, as a result of which he was pro-Nazi. Henry-Haye collected intelligence against the British and sent it back to Vichy, from where it was sent on to Germany.

Herbert, Don (1917–)

Television actor who became popularly known as Mr. Wizard. During World War II, he enlisted in the Army Air Force as a private and volunteered for flight school. Herbert became a B-24 pilot and flew fifty-six missions with the Fifteenth Air Force. He was awarded the Distinguished Flying Cross and the Air Medal with three oak-leaf clusters.

Herlihy, Joseph L. (1902–1980)

U.S. Navy commodore and later rear admiral. He was in charge of fuel supplies for the Pacific fleet during the Pearl Harbor attack. Herlihy later became supply officer for Admiral Chester Nimitz.

Hermann, Hajo (1913–)

Luftwaffe officer and night-fighter ace. He flew 320 bomber missions, sinking twelve ships. Hermann then transferred to fighters and became Inspector of German Air Defenses. He was captured by the Russians and held prisoner until 1955.

Hermann, Kurt J.

U.S. Army Air Force technical sergeant. He was the first person to take part in bomber missions on all three Axis capitals and the first person to fly 108 missions. Hermann began the war in the Merchant Marine and was torpedoed, spending twenty-six days on a life raft. After being rescued, he enlisted in the Army Air Force in August 1942 and was sent to the Twelfth Air Force in North Africa as a waist gunner on a B-17. He shot down an ME109 on his first mission and later downed three more enemy aircraft while in B-26's. He participated in a July 1943 raid on Rome and ultimately flew 50 missions before he was furloughed. Herman then requested duty with the Eighth Air Force in England, a request that was personally approved by General "Hap" Arnold. He completed twenty-five missions by April 1944, including night missions as an observer on British aircraft over Berlin. He then asked for and was posted to a B-29 unit on Saipan from which he flew over Tokyo. He was listed as missing in action when his B-29 failed to return from a bombing mission toward the end of the war.

Hermes

The only British destroyer in the German Navy. It was originally built for the Greeks and was captured by the Germans, who used it to fight in the Mediterranean during World War II.

Hermes, H.M.S.

British aircraft carrier weighing 10,850 tons. It was sunk April 9, 1942, off Ceylon by Japanese aircraft and was the last major British ship to be lost in World War II.

Herr Wolf

Name Hitler used prior to his rise to power when he did not wish to be identified. He was originally introduced to Eva Braun as Herr Wolf.

Hersey, John (1914–)

Author and journalist. During World War II, he was a correspondent for *Time* and *Life* magazines. Hersey served at Guadalcanal, North Africa, and Italy.

Hess, Rudolph (1896–)

Hitler's party secretary. He had been an early convert to Nazism and stood by Hitler during the lean years. Hess wrote *Mein Kampf* as dictated by Hitler in Landsberg prison in 1924 and was nicknamed "the Brown Mouse" by his associates. He parachuted into Scotland on May 11, 1941, the day that Hitler had planned to invade Russia, in an attempt to talk the British into coming to terms with Hitler so that there would be no two-front war for Germany. Hess intended to see the Duke of Hamilton, whom he claimed to have met at the 1936 Olympics. The British imprisoned him in the Tower of London ("The Bloody Tower"); he was the last man ever to be imprisoned there. After the war, he was sentenced to life in prison by the Nuremberg tribunal and is the last man still held at Spandau prison.

MOVIE PORTRAYAL:

The Hitler Gang (1944), by Victor Varconi

Inside the Third Reich (1982 ABC TV miniseries), by Maurice Reeves

Heston, Charlton (1924–)

Hollywood actor. He enlisted in the Army Air Force in 1942 and served as a radio operator on B-25 bombers with the Eleventh Army Air Force in the Aleutians. Heston was discharged in 1945.

Heydrich, Reinhard (1904–1942)

German S.S. general and Protector of Czechoslovakia. He joined the S.S. after being kicked out of the German Navy for getting a girl pregnant and refusing to marry her. He said that if she was that easy, she was not good enough for him. Heydrich became the number two man to Heinrich Himmler and some believed him to be the successor to Himmler. In 1936 he engineered the Stalin purges by forging thirty-two documents that made it appear as though the top figures of the Russian military were plotting against Stalin. As a result, more than half of the Russian officer corps of 35,000 were either executed or exiled. Heydrich was noted for his ruthlessness in dealing with the Jews of Germany; it is rumored that his fanaticism had to do with the fact he was half Jewish. As Protector of Czechoslovakia, he attempted to use tact and diplomacy to gain the confidence of the Czechs and to get more production out of them. The British feared that he might be successful and so parachuted a team into Czechoslovakia to assassinate him, which they accomplished in June 1942. As a result, the Germans killed over 15,000 Czechs in reprisals that acted to sway the Czechs actively against the Nazis. Rumors have it that Heydrich repented on his deathbed of having betrayed his people, the Jews.

MOVIE PORTRAYAL:
Hitler's Madmen (1943), by John Carradine
Holocaust (1978), by David Warner

von der Heydte, Freiherr (1907–)

German officer. He was awarded a Carnegie Fellowship prior to World War II. During the war, he fought in France as the commander of an armored reconnaissance unit. Von der Heydte then joined the German parachute corps, where he became instrumental in the development of new techniques and equipment. He fought at Crete, North Africa, Leningrad, and Normandy. During the Battle of the Bulge, he commanded a unit that jumped behind the U.S. lines, only to be captured south of Eupen on December 17, 1944. He spent the rest of the war as a prisoner.

Heyerdahl, Thor (1914–)

Norwegian-born explorer and author. He served during World War II with the Free Norwegian Air Force and later with a parachute unit of the Norwegian Army.

Hiei

Japanese battleship sunk by U.S. Navy aircraft from the carrier *Enterprise* ten miles north of Savo Island, November 13, 1942. Previously damaged in the Battle for Guadalcanal, it was the first battleship that the Japanese lost in World War II.

Higgins, Andrew Jackson, Jr. (1886–1952)

U.S. ship builder in World War II who was known for a Navy

landing craft called a "Higgins boat." During Prohibition, he built fast boats for bootleggers, but he made sure to build faster boats for the U.S. Coast Guard. He invented the Higgins boat, which could beach itself, back off the beach by its own power, and return for more men and supplies. Higgins involved himself in all types of projects and his industries produced landing craft, PT boats, Liberty ships, cargo ships, aircraft (the C-116), helicopters, water purifiers, smoke generators, explosives, and amphibious bridges.

Higgins, Gerald J. (1909–)

U.S. Army officer and member of the 101st Airborne Division. He was promoted to brigadier general in 1944, making him, at age thirty-four, the youngest general in the U.S. Army. (General James Gavin was 36 when he was given his first star.)

Higgins, Marguerite (1920–1966)

New York Herald Tribune war correspondent. In World War II she traveled with the U.S. 7th Army in Europe and wrote front page stories about Buchenwald and Dachau.

Highet, Gilbert

Husband of British author Helen MacInnes. During World War II, he worked with BSC, the British intelligence branch, in New York.

High Flight

Famous poem recited at the end of the broadcast days of television stations across the U.S. It was written by John G. McGee, Jr., an American pilot with the Royal Air Force. He was killed in aerial combat on December 11, 1941. The first line of the poem reads "Oh! I have slipped the surely bonds of earth . . .".

High Wycombe

Headquarters in Great Britain of the U.S. Eighth Army Air Force in World War II.

Hijackings

According to the FBI the top three items that were hijacked during World War II to be sold on the black market were liquor, rayon, and shoes.

Hill, Arthur (1922–)

Canadian-born Hollywood actor. He served in the Royal Canadian Air Force as an airframe mechanic during World War II.

Hill, David "Tex"

Fighter pilot who flew with the A.V.G. (Flying Tigers) in China. He shot down twelve confirmed Japanese aircraft.

Movie portrayal:
God Is My Co-Pilot (1945), by John Ridgely

Hill, George Roy (1922–)

American movie director. He served as a U.S. Marine Corps transport pilot in the South Pacific in World War II.

Hill, Gladwin

Reporter for the Associated Press. He flew in a B-26 that buzzed the Normandy invasion on June 6, 1944, and was able to file the first eyewitness account of D-Day.

Hill, Ted

U.S. Army Air Force major general. He was the head of an air section of the U.S. military liasion mission to Russia during World War II. As such, Hill set up the staging fields for-shuttlebombing runs of U.S. bombers from England and Italy to Poltava.

Hillary, Sir Edmund (1919–)

World-famous mountain climber and explorer. He served as a navigator on Catalina aircraft for the Royal New Zealand Air Force in the South Pacific in World War II. Although severely wounded in the war, Hillary took up mountaineering after the war, becoming the first person (with Tenzing Norkay) to conquer Mount Everest on May 20, 1953.

Hillary, Richard (1918–1943)

Royal Air Force pilot officer of No. 603 Squadron. He was shot down on September 3, 1940, off the coast of Kent and was rescued by a lifeboat from the Royal National Lifeboat Institution, an organization founded by one of his relatives, Lieutenant Colonel Sir William Hillary. After recovering from burns, Hillary was posted to a night-fighter squadron but was killed on January 7, 1943, while on a training mission.

Hillsinger, Loren B. (1909–1966)

U.S. Army officer. He was the first American ground casualty of the European Theater in World War II; he lost his foot while on board a British destroyer during the Dieppe Raid in August 1942. Later Hillsinger was the air officer with British Combined Operations on the destroyer H.M.S. *Berkeley* when it was attacked and sunk.

Himmelbett

Name of a German defensive belt around the continent that utilized radar, search lights, and flak to detect enemy aircraft and bring night fighters in to attack. It positioned one fighter in each area on the theory that enemy aircraft would be in a concentrated zone for three to four minutes en route to and returning from a target. It was successful as long as the bombers were strung out. The system became overloaded, though, when bombers concentrated and overwhelmed the single fighter per area.

Himmler, Heinrich (1900–1945)

German head of the S.S. and one of the most feared men of history. He was a one-time chicken farmer and joined the Nazi party in its early days. Himmler carried the flag for S.A. leader Ernst Roehm in the 1923 Beer Hall Putsch in Munich. His wartime address was Berlin S.W. 11, Prinz Albrecht Strasse 8. Himmler was captured by the British at the end of the war in a private's uniform. He admitted his identity but committed suicide by biting a cyanide capsule while being searched.

MOVIE PORTRAYALS:
Hitler's Madness (1943), by Howard Freeman
That Nazty Nuisance (1943), by Wedgewood Nowell
The Hitler Gang (1944), by Luis van Rooten
The Magic Face (1951), by Sukmann
Operation Eichmann (1961), by Luis van Rooten
Hitler (1962), by Rick Traeger
The Eagle Has Landed (1977), by Donald Pleasance
Holocaust (1978 TV miniseries), by Tom Bell
The Bunker (1980 TV movie), by Michael Sheard

von Hindenburg, Paul (1847–1934)

German President who brought Hitler into the government in 1933. When he died in 1934, he and his wife were buried against their wishes at Tannenberg, the site of his greatest victory in World War I against the Russians. On January 23, 1945, the cruiser *Emden* removed von Hindenburg's and his wife Gertrude's bodies from Königsberg so that the advancing Russians would not get them. After the war, the Americans reburied them at Elisabeth Church in Marburg, along with Frederick Wilhelm I and Frederick II.

MOVIE PORTRAYALS:
The Hitler Gang (1944), by Sig Ruman
Fraulein Doktor (1969), by Walter Williams

Hinge of Fate

Name given by Winston Churchill to the Battle of Stalingrad. He believed that it was the turning point of World War II.

Hingle, Pat (1924–   )

Hollywood actor. He enlisted in the U.S. Navy in December 1941, dropping out of the University of Texas. Hingle served on the destroyer U.S.S. *Marshall* in the Marshall Islands during the war.

Hipper

German cruiser that sank seven ships out of a nineteen-ship convoy in the mid-Atlantic in 1941. The *Hipper* was limited by its short range but could steam at thirty-two knots.

Hired Man of 150 Million People

Phrase used by President Harry S Truman to refer to his role in the world scene.

Hirohito (1901–   )

Emperor of Japan since 1926. He remained aloof from the process of governing Japan until the last days of the war, when he let his true feelings be known. This resulted in the military finally agreeing to surrender to the Allies.

MOVIE PORTRAYALS:
Star Spangled Rhythm (1942), by Richard Loo
The Emperor and the General (1968), by Koshiro Matsumoto
MacArthur (1977), by John Fujioka

Hirohito Highway

Nickname given by U.S. bomber crews to the route from their bases in the Marianas to their targets in Japan.

Hiroshima University

Site of the clock tower so often photographed in Hiroshima. Its hands are permanently frozen at 8:15, the time the atomic bomb detonated on August 6, 1945. Ironically, this did not occur because of the bomb; the clock had stopped several days previously for no explainable reason.

Hirt, Al (1922–   )

Jazz musician. He served in the U.S. Army from 1942 to 1946, playing in the 82nd Army Air Force Band.

Hiryu

Japanese aircraft carrier weighing 17,300 tons. It participated in the strike on Pearl Harbor, December 7, 1941, and was sunk by aircraft from the carrier U.S.S. *Yorktown* during the Battle of Midway in June 1942.

His

Name of President D. Roosevelt's pistol, which he kept under his pillow while sleeping. Eleanor also had a pistol that she carried; it was called "Hers."

Hiss, Alger (1904–)

American lawyer and foreign affairs expert in the U.S. State Department. He attended the Dumbarton Oaks meeting to organize the United Nations and was a delegate at the Yalta conference as an adviser to President Roosevelt. Hiss was the temporary Secretary General of the United Nations conference in San Francisco in April 1945.

Hitaka

Japanese carrier which was torpedoed and damaged by the submarine U.S.S. *Trigger* June 10, 1943 outside Tokyo Bay while on its maiden voyage.

Hitchcock, Tommy (1900–1944)

Athlete who, for the twenty years prior to World War II, was considered the greatest polo player in the United States. In 1941, he received a commission in the Army Air Force at the age of forty-one and eventually attained the rank of lieutenant colonel. Hitchcock was killed in his P-51 Mustang, which crashed near Salisbury, England.

"Hit 'em where they ain't"

Phrase epitomizing General Douglas MacArthur's strategy of attacking only lightly defended or nondefended territories behind Japanese lines, leaving the well-fortified posts to wither away due to lack of supplies. This master plan cost the U.S. fewer casualties than if they had met the Japanese army head-on. The U.S. suffered more casualties in the Battle of the Bulge in Europe than MacArthur suffered in the entire Pacific campaign.

"Hit hard, hit fast, hit often"

Admiral William F. "Bull" Halsey's battle cry during World War II.

Hitler, Adolf (1889–1945)

German dictator. He was actually not a German but was born and raised in Austria. Hitler's father was illegitimate and probably half-Jewish, having been conceived while Hitler's grandmother worked as a maid for a Jewish family, the Frankenbergers, who paid support for the son until he was fourteen years old. When the

Germans annexed Austria, Hitler had the area of his father's birthplace, Dollersheim, and the grave of his grandmother, designated a tank-training ground, thus destroying all evidence forever. Although Hitler's later career revolved around his hatred of Jews, his earlier life was full of acquaintances who were Jews. His father's parentage probably made Hitler one-quarter Jewish. His mother's doctor, who treated her until she died on December 21, 1907, was Jewish. Hitler received his First Class Iron Cross in World War I from a Jew, First Lieutenant Hugo Gutmann. He borrowed his psychology of the masses from Sigmund Freud, a Jew. Eva Braun, his mistress, was saved after her second suicide attempt by a Jewish doctor, Martin Marx; his vegetarian cook, Marlene von Exner, was part Jewish. And finally, one of Hitler's Allies in the war, Francisco Franco, was half-Jewish, a fact carefully hidden from him by Hitler's advisers.

Although Hitler's name is synonymous with Nazism, if you consider the name of the party, Hitler was not a Nazi in the true sense of the word. The term stood for NSDAP, National Socialist German Workers' Party. Hitler was not a nationalist; his willful destruction of Germany toward the end of war proves this. He was not a Socialist, as he killed off the Socialists of the Party during the Roehm purge in 1934. He was born in Austria therefore he was not German, and he never was a member of the working class.

Hitler was selected by *Time* Magazine as the Man of the Year for 1938 (the criteria was "news impact not moral worth"). The 1941 *Who's Who* listed his phone number as #11 6191 and his mailing address as Wilhelmstrasse 77, Berlin W. 8 or at Ober Salzburg, Berchtesgaden, Bavaria. Hitler committed suicide on April 30, 1945, and was officially declared dead by a German court in Bonn, October 25, 1956.

MOVIE PORTRAYALS:
The Great Dictator (1940), by Charlie Chaplin* (as Hynkel)
The Devil with Hitler (1942), by Bobby Watson
Star Spangled Rhythm (1942), by Tom Dugan
That Nazty Nuisance (1943), by Bobby Watson
Strange Death of Adolf Hitler (1943), by Ludwig Donath
Miracle of Morgan's Creek (1944), by Bobby Watson

---

*Both Adolf Hitler and Charlie Chaplin were born in April 1889.

The Hitler Gang (1944), by Bobby Watson
The Magic Face (1951), by Luther Adler
Rommel—The Desert Fox (1951), by Luther Adler
The Story of Mankind (1957), by Bobby Watson
On the Double (1961), by Bobby Watson
Hitler (1962), by Richard Basehart
Is Paris Burning? (1966), by Billy Frick
What Did You Do in the War Daddy? (1966), by Carl Ekberg
Battle of Britain (1969), by Rolf Stiefel
Which Way to the Front? (1970), by Sidney Miller
Hitler: the Last Ten Days (1973), by Alec Guinness
Undercover Heroes (1975), by Peter Sellers
Ring of Passion (1978 TV movie), by Barry Dennen
The Bunker (1981 TV movie), by Anthony Hopkins
Inside the Third Reich (1982 TV miniseries), by Derek Jacobi

Hitler and Napoleon comparisons:

Both had photographic memories.

Both were foreigners to the countries they headed.

Both were contemptuously called "carpet chewers."

Napoleon was 5′7″ tall and Hitler was 5′8″.

Napoleon's coup d'etat of Bramaise was on November 9, 1799; Hitler's attempted Putsch in Munich was on November 9, 1923.

Both started planning their invasions of Russia while still preparing for an invasion of Britain.

Napoleon crossed the Niernan River en route to Moscow on June 22, 1813; Hitler launched his invasion of Russia on June 22, 1941.

Napoleon captured Vilna on June 24, 1813; Hitler captured it on June 24, 1941.

Napoleon took eight weeks to advance nearly to Moscow and was thrown back to his starting point in half that time, four weeks. Hitler took two summer campaigns to advance nearly to Moscow and was thrown back in half that time, one summer campaign.

At the end of the Napoleonic wars, Russian troops threw Napoleon's banners at the feet of Czar Alexander I.

The Russians at the end of World War II threw flags of captured German units at the foot of Lenin's tomb in a mass ceremony.

Napoleon died on May 5; Hitler attempted to hold out in Berlin until May 5, but committed suicide April 30, 1945.

Hitler, Hans

Nephew of Adolf Hitler. He fought at Stalingrad and escaped back to German lines before the fall of Stalingrad.

Hitler, Heinz

Nephew of Adolf Hitler. He was the son of Hitler's half-brother Alois Jr. and fought at Stalingrad, where he was captured by the Russians, dying in Soviet captivity.

Hitler, William Patrick

Nephew of Adolf Hitler. He was the son of Hitler's half-brother Alois Jr. He served in the U.S. Navy in World War II and now lives under an assumed name in the New York City area.

Hiwis

Name given by the Germans to Russians who volunteered to help them fight Stalin. Most of these actually did not participate in combat but performed support functions like driving trucks and cooking to release Germans for combat. The majority of Hiwis, when captured by the Red Army, were shot automatically.

Hiyo

Japanese carrier that was converted from a merchant ship. It was sunk on June 20, 1944, during the Battle of the Philippine Sea, by Lieutenant George B. Brown and Lieutenant Warren Omark, flying Avengers from the new U.S.S. *Yorktown*.

Hoare, Sir Samuel (1880–1959)

British ambassador to Spain in World War II. His job was to keep Spain out of the war. In 1935, as foreign secretary, Hoare and French foreign minister Pierre Laval secretly agreed not to object when Italy conquered Ethiopia. He was forced to resign as a result of the public outcry when the news was finally known.

Hobby, Oveta Culp (1905–   )

U.S. Army colonel. She was the head of the Women's Army Corps (WAC's) serving as its first member. Her nickname was "Miss Spark Plug" because of her way of getting things done.

Hobgoblin

Code name of the island of Pantelleria used in conjunction with the capture of the island in Operation Corkscrew.

Hodges, Courtney H. (1887–1965)

U.S. Army general. He commanded the U.S. First Army from 1944 to 1945, becoming one of the best Allied commanders of World War II. Hodges had failed out of West Point Military Academy in his first year.

Hodges, Gil (1924–1972)

Major League baseball player and sportscaster. During World War II, Hodges rose to the rank of sergeant while serving with the U.S. Marine 16th Antiaircraft Artillery Battalion at Pearl Harbor, Tinian, and Okinawa.

Hoess, Rudolph (1900–1947)

Nazi commandant of Auschwitz concentration camp. He testified at the Nuremberg trials in 1946. Hoess was tried and sentenced to death by a Polish people's court. He was hanged at Auschwitz.

MOVIE PORTRAYAL:
Operation Eichmann (1961), by John Banner

Hoff, Charles

Norwegian pole vaulter. During World War II, he collaborated with the Germans as director of Nazi athletics in Norway.

Hoffman, Heinrich (1885–1957)

Hitler's personal photographer. He was responsible for introducing Hitler and Eva Braun, who was his photographic assistant in Munich. Hoffman also brought Dr. Theodor Morell into contact with Hitler. Hoffman experimented with color photography in the very early days of color, and the majority of his pictures of Hitler and Nazi party history were in color. After the war, he buried the negatives in carefully sealed cans and only dug them up a couple of years before he died.

Holbrook, Hal (1925–   )

Hollywood actor. He served in the U.S. Army Corps of Engineers from 1943 to 1946 and was stationed in Newfoundland as a private.

Holcomb, Thomas (1879–1965)

U.S. Marine Corps officer. He was Commandant of the Marine Corps from 1936 to 1944 and was the first Marine officer to be promoted to four-star general. After retirement, Holcomb became the U.S. ambassador to South Africa.

Holden, William (1918–1981)

Hollywood actor. He enlisted in the U.S. Army in 1942 and graduated from Officer Candidate School in Florida. Holden spent the next three years of his enlistment entertaining troops in the states. It was while in the service that he legally changed his name from William Beedle, Jr. to William Holden.

Holland, Sir Lancelot (1887–1941)

British vice-admiral. He was the commander of the H.M.S. *Hood* and the *Prince of Wales* in their engagement with the German pocket battleship *Bismarck*. Holland went down with the *Hood* on May 24, 1940.

Movie portrayal:
Sink the Bismarck (1960), by Walter Hudd

Holloway, Sterling (1905–)
First Hollywood actor to be drafted into the U.S. Army during World War II. He was discharged on medical grounds after a horse kicked him.

Hollywood in Uniform
Name of a ten-minute film made by Columbia Pictures in 1943 showing the actors Clark Gable, Tyrone Power, James Stewart, John Payne, and Alan Ladd in their military uniforms.

Holohan, William V. (–1944)
U.S. Army major and head of the OSS Operation Chrysler mission in Northern Italy. His job was to see that arms got to the partisans who were fighting the Germans. Holohan believed the communists were not fighting, so he would not authorize shipments to them. He was subsequently assassinated by his second-in-command, Lieutenant Aldo Icardi, on the night of December 6, 1944, and his body dumped into a lake. Icardi then was able to request airdrops to the communists and money for himself that was earmarked for the Resistance. He, two Italian accomplices, and another American were subsequently tried in Italy after the war. All were found guilty and sentenced to life imprisonment, both Americans *in absentia*.

Holt, Tim (1918–1973)
Western actor who during World War II flew as a bombardier on B-29's in the Pacific Theater. He completed twenty-two missions, many of them over Tokyo, and was awarded the Distinguished Flying Cross, an Air Medal with three clusters, the Victory Medal, and the Asiatic Pacific Medal. Holt was discharged with the rank of major. His aircraft was named *Reluctant Dragon*.

Home Guard
British people's army taught by Thomas H. Wintringham to be used as a final defense against a German invasion in 1940.

Homma, Masaharu (1887–1946)
Japanese lieutenant general. He had been a Japanese Army observer with the British Army in World War I and was the military attaché in London in 1930. Homma was a recipient of the Military

Cross of the British Empire. He was commander of the Japanese Fourteenth Army that invaded the Philippines on December 22, 1941, and was responsible for the Bataan Death March. For this he was sentenced to death by a U.S. military tribunal in Manila in February 1946.

MOVIE PORTRAYAL:
Back to Bataan (1945), by Leonard Strong

Honolulu, U.S.S.

U.S. Navy cruiser. It was the first casualty of the Leyte invasion of October 22, 1944, when it was hit by a torpedo from a Japanese aircraft.

Hood H.M.S.

British battle cruiser that was sunk by the *Bismarck* on May 24, 1941, northeast of Iceland. There were only three survivors, the senior man being Midshipman W. J. Dundas. The *Hood* was Britain's largest battle cruiser.

Hooligan Navy

Name given to volunteer yachtsmen who aided the U.S. Navy in its search for German submarines off the eastern seaboard in the early days of World War II. Ernest Hemingway was a member, using his yacht *Pilar.*

Hope, Bob (1903–   )

London-born Hollywood actor and comedian. He traveled over a million miles entertaining Allied troops during World War II.

Hopkins, Harry L. (1890–1946)

U.S. statesman. He was Executive Assistant and adviser to President Franklin D. Roosevelt during World War II. His youngest son, eighteen-year-old Stephen P. Hopkins, was killed in action as a U.S. Marine PFC in the Marshall Islands.

MOVIE PORTRAYAL:
Churchill and the Generals (1982 TV movie), by Robert Arden
Eleanor and Franklin: The White House Years (1977 TV movie), Donald Moffat

Horii, Tomatore (1890–1942)

Japanese lieutenant general. Horii conquered Rabaul in 1942 and also led troops on the Kokoda Trail across the Owen Stanley Mountains of New Guinea to capture Port Moresby. He was ordered to withdraw, although he was within sight of his objective, because the Japanese needed more troops at Guadalcanal. Horii was drowned during the retreat back to Buna.

Horikoshi, Jiro (1903–)

Japanese aeronautical engineer. He designed the Zero fighter which was one of the most revolutionary fighter aircraft of its time (1940).

Hornet, U.S.S. (CV-8)

U.S. aircraft carrier weighing 20,000 tons. It was commissioned in 1941 and launched the B-25s of Doolittle's Raiders in their attack on Tokyo, April 18, 1942. President Franklin D. Roosevelt referred to the ship as *Shangri-La* in telling about the raid. The captain of the *Hornet* at the time was Marc "Pete" Mitscher, who became an admiral and important contributor to the defeat of Japan. The *Hornet* participated in the Battle of Santa Cruz, where it was sunk October 26, 1942 (Navy Day). It was initially struck by two apparent suicide dives, the first by Lieutenant Commander Mamoru Seki, who crashed through the flight deck; and then by Lieutenant Jiichiro Imajuku, who crashed near the forward elevator. The *Hornet* was severely damaged by these two Kamikaze attacks and finally sunk by the Japanese destroyers *Makikumo* and *Akigumo*.

Hornet, U.S.S. (CV-12)

U.S. aircraft carrier launched August 30, 1943, the namesake of CV-8. It displaced 27,000 tons of water and fought in many of the Pacific battles in the latter half of the war. The *Hornet* spent fifty-two days under Japanese attack and never received so much as a dent from a machine gun bullet, but succeeded in destroying 742 Japanese aircraft on the ground, 688 in the air, one Japanese cruiser, one carrier, ten destroyers and forty-two cargo ships. It was finally damaged June 5, 1945, when a typhoon caused the collapse of the forward section of the flight deck.

Horrified

Code name used for Sicily in the planning of Operation Husky, the invasion of Sicily in July 1943.

Horrocks, Sir Brian (1895–)

British Army lieutenant general. He had spent nearly all of World War I as a prisoner of war. Horrocks commanded the British XXX Corps in Operation Market-Garden in September 1944.

MOVIE PORTRAYAL:

A Bridge Too Far (1977), by Edward Fox

Horse Racing

Horse racing and auto racing were the only two sports to be banned in the U.S. during World War II. Horse racing was ruled nonessential to the war effort and car racing was banned because of its use of rubber and gas, both of which were in short supply.

Horst Wessel

Name of a square-rigged windjammer used by the German Navy to train its ensigns prior to and in the early part of World War II.

Horthy, Miklas (1868–1957)

Hungarian Regent and admiral. He was the virtual dictator of Hungary from 1920 to 1944 and allied himself with Hitler until he was arrested by the Gestapo in 1944 for attempting to withdraw from the war. The Germans imprisoned him in Dachau concentration camp where he was liberated by the Americans in 1945. Horthy's son, Stephen, was killed while a member of the Hungarian Air Force on the Russian front in 1942. His other son Nicholas was kidnapped by Otto Skorzeny in October of 1944 under orders from Hitler to use his safety as blackmail to assure Horthy's support.

Hosho

Japanese aircraft carrier. It was the world's first aircraft carrier to be built from the keel. The *Hosho* was used as support for the Battle of Midway in June 1942.

Hoskins, John M. (1899–1964)

U.S. Navy officer. As a captain, he was given orders to command the carrier *Hornet* (CV-8), which was sunk October 26, 1942. Hoskins was later given command of the *Princeton*, but while he was on board in preparation for the change of command, the carrier was sunk by Japanese bombs during the invasion of Leyte in October 1944. Hoskins lost a leg in the battle and had to fight the Navy to stay in, arguing with Admiral William F. Halsey that the Navy did not train a man to think with his leg. He was given command of the new *Princeton* at the end of the war and retired as an admiral.

MOVIE PORTRAYAL:
The Eternal Sea (1955), by Sterling Hayden

Hotrocks

Apropos code name given to Mount Suribachi during the Battle of Iwo Jima in 1945 by U.S. Marines.

Houk, Ralph (1919–　　)

Major league baseball manager. During World War II, he served in the U.S. Army and fought at Normandy and across Europe. Houk aided in the destruction of six German tanks in Waldbillig,

Luxembourg, for which he was awarded the Silver Star medal. He was discharged in 1945 as a major, with the Bronze Star and Purple Heart.

House of Savoy

Name of the ruling family of Italy. During World War II, Victor Emmanuel III served as the King of Italy.

Houseman, John (1902–)

American producer, director, and actor. He produced the *Voice of America* radio propaganda program during World War II.

Howard, John (1913–)

Hollywood actor. While serving in the U.S. Navy in World War II, he was awarded the Navy Cross and the French Croix de Guerre for valor.

Howard, Leslie (1893–1943)

British actor who played Ashley Wilkes in the 1939 classic movie *Gone with the Wind*. He was aboard BOAC 777, a British Overseas Airways flight from Algiers to London, when it was shot down by German fighters over the Bay of Biscay in June 1943. Aboard the same flight was Alfred Chenfalls, a double for Winston Churchill. The British knew from Ultra intercepts beforehand that the Germans intended to shoot the plane down, but did not warn any of the crew so as not to tip the Germans off that their codes were broken. Howard's last movie was *The First of the Few* (1942) about Reginald Mitchell, the designer of the Spitfire.

MOVIE PORTRAYAL:
Bogie (1980 TV movie), by Stephen Keep

Howard, Trevor (1916–)

British actor. In World War II, he served as an officer with the 6th Airborne Division, fighting in Sicily and Norway. Howard was medically discharged in 1943 as a captain, having received the Military Cross for valor.

HOWE

Code name used for General Dwight Eisenhower when he was on Gibraltar in November 1942 to oversee Operation Torch, the invasion of North Africa.

Howie, Thomas D. (–1944)

U.S. Army officer known as the "Major of St. Lo." He commanded the 3rd Battalion, 116th Infantry Regiment of the 29th Division in the assault on St. Lo and was killed. Howie became the symbol for the thousands of American casualties in the attack. His body was carried into the destroyed city and placed on a pile of rubble with an American flag draped over it.

Hozumi, Ozaki

Japanese communist and adviser to Prince Konoye. He gave top secret information to the Russian spy Richard Sorge that was then sent back to the Kremlin.

HR 1776

Official designator of the Lend-Lease Bill signed March 11, 1941, that allowed the U.S. to give aid to Britain.

Hradčany Castle

Nazi headquarters of the Protectorate of Bohemia in World War II. It was also the official residence of Reinhard Heydrich as the Reichs Protector.

HS 293

Designator of the German wire-guided bomb that sank the Italian battleship *Roma* as it attempted to surrender to the Allies in 1943.

Hube, Hans (1890–1944)

German general. He was the only one-armed general in the German Army and fought in the Battle of Stalingrad, where he commanded the 16th Panzer Division of the Sixth Army. Hube was ordered out of encircled Stalingrad to take command of a Panzer Army. He received the Knight's Cross with oak leaves, swords, and diamonds, Germany's highest decoration, and died of injuries sustained in a plane crash.

Hudson, Rock (1925–)

Hollywood actor. After he graduated from New Trier High School in Winnetka, Illinois, in 1944, he enlisted in the U.S. Navy as an aircraft mechanic. One of his instructors in boot camp was Lieutenant Robert Taylor, the actor. After boot camp, Hudson was stationed in the Philippines where he was responsible for the collision of two aircraft on the ground that resulted in serious damage to one of them. Needless to say, his career as an aviation mechanic came to an abrupt halt. Hudson was discharged in 1946.

Huff Duff

Name given to the system of High Frequency Direction Finding (HFDF), which was used by the Allies in World War II to locate German submarines in the Atlantic. It consisted of an arc of land-based radio stations in the Americas that used triangulation to pinpoint submarines. The network was built by IT&T's Federal Telephone and Radio Corporation.

Huff, Paul B.

U.S. Army soldier. He was the first American paratrooper to win the Congressional Medal of Honor. Huff was awarded the medal for fighting at Anzio in 1944.

Hughes, James Joseph (1898–)

U.S. Navy officer. As a lieutenant commander, he commanded the U.S.S. *Panay,* a gunboat on the Yangtze River in China, when it was attacked by Japanese aircraft on December 12, 1937.

Hughes-Hallett, John (1901–1972)

British Naval officer. He commanded the Naval forces for the ill-fated Dieppe Raid in 1942. In December 1943, Hughes-Hallett was in charge of the cruiser *Jamaica,* which participated in the sinking of the German cruiser *Scharnhorst.* It was he who suggested the use of artificial harbors to aid in the invasion of Normandy in June 1944.

Hughes, Howard (1895–1976)

U.S. businessman and movie producer. In 1936, he designed the H-1, a unique racing aircraft, many features of which are reputed to have been copied by the Japanese and incorporated into the Zero. In World War II, Hughes worked with Kelly Johnson, chief designer for Lockheed.

MOVIE PORTRAYALS:
Caught (1949), by Robert Ryan
Hughes and Harlow: Angels in Hell (1977), by Victor Holchak
The Amazing Howard Hughes (1977 TV movie), by David Schulman (boy), Tommy Lee Jones (middle age), Ben Pollock (old man)
Melvin and Howard (1981), by Jason Robards, Jr.

Hull, Cordell (1871–1955)

U.S. Secretary of State from 1937 to 1944. Hull was an idealist and refused, prior to World War II, to negotiate with the Japanese until they removed their troops from China and Southeast Asia, thus giving them the impression of American intransigence. During the war, he put pressure on Chiang Kai-shek to work with the Communists against the Japanese and it was largely his work that created the United Nations.

MOVIE PORTRAYALS:
Sergeant York (1941), by Charles Trowbridge
Mission to Moscow (1943), by Charles Trowbridge
Tora! Tora! Tora! (1970), by George Macready

Hun Sleds

Nickname that Dutch Resistance personnel gave to the radio detection cars used by the Gestapo to track down clandestine radio transmitters during the German occupation.

Hunt, Walter "Pee Wee" (1907–)

Musician whose biggest-selling record was "Twelfth Street Rag" in 1948. He served for a short time in the Merchant Marine during World War II.

Hunter, Alberta (1895–)

Blues singer who, during World War II, formed the first black rhythm-and-blues unit to travel overseas with the U.S.O.

Hunter, Evan (1926–)

American writer who served on board a U.S. Navy destroyer in the Pacific. It was while in the service that he wrote his first short story, *The Void*.

Hunter, Ross (1924–)

Hollywood producer who served for two years during the war with U.S. Army intelligence and was given a medical discharge because of a serious injury.

Hurban, Vladimir (1883–1949)

Czechoslovakian minister (1936–1943) and ambassador to the United States (1943–1946). In 1939, he refused to surrender his embassy in Washington, D. C., to the Germans and became a symbol of resistance to the Nazis.

Hurd, Peter

American artist who painted the official U.S. presidential portraits. During World War II, he flew on bombing missions in North Africa, Italy, and Germany, and on missions over South America and India to make sketches and paintings for *Life* magazine.

Hurtgen Forest

Heavily wooded area southeast of Aachen. It was known as the Argonne of World War II because it was the site of one of the costliest battles of the war. It was attacked by the U.S. 9th and 28th Infantry Divisions; of 120,000 troops, there were 33,000 casualties.

Hush Hush, U.S.S.

Name of Admiral Chester Nimitz's battleship-gray jeep, which was given to him by the Army.

Husky Number One

Code name for the American airborne operation on Sicily in July 1943. It was led by General James Gavin.

Husky Number Two

Code name of the second drop of American airborne forces on Sicily, which took place after the beachheads were secured.

Husseini, Amin el (1893–1974)

Arab Grand Mufti of Jerusalem who was pro-Nazi and anti-Semitic. He was forced to flee to Germany after the British invaded Iraq in 1941 and Hitler appointed him head of the Arab Bureau. Hitler backed him because he had red hair and blue eyes and appeared to be Aryan. With the defeat of Germany, Husseini fled to Egypt and was given sanctuary.

Huston, John (1906–)

Hollywood director and writer. He enlisted in the U.S. Army in 1942 to film war documentaries. Huston produced *Report from the Aleutians*, *Battle of San Pietro*, and *Let There Be Light*. He was discharged in 1945 as a major.

Movie portrayals:
Marilyn—The Untold Story (1980 TV movie), by John Ireland
Moviola (1980 TV miniseries), by William Frankfather

Huxley, Julian

British zoologist who invented a plastic explosive that looked like cow dung. It was planted on the roads leading to the Normandy beachhead to destroy the tires of enemy vehicles.

HYPO

Name for the U.S. Navy's codebreaking unit at Pearl Harbor. It was commanded by Tom Dyer who was the communications officer of the 14th Naval District.

Hyuga

Japanese hybrid carrier. It was part battleship and part carrier with room for twenty-four aircraft on a small flight deck. The *Hyuga* was used as a battleship in the Battle of Leyte Gulf in October 1944 since no aircraft were available. It was damaged during the battle and was finally sunk in July 1945.

I

I-6

Japanese submarine that torpedoed and damaged the carrier U.S.S. *Saratoga* on January 11, 1942, putting it out of commission.

I-8

Japanese submarine under Commander Tatsunoke Ariizumi that sank the Dutch ship *Tsijalak* and the U.S. ship S.S. *Richard Hovey* in March 1944 in the Indian Ocean, then machine-gunned the survivors.

I-15

Japanese submarine that torpedoed and damaged both the battleship *North Carolina* and the destroyer *O'Brian* on September 15, 1942.

I-17

Japanese submarine under Commander Kozo Nishino that surfaced off the coast of California, February 13, 1942, and fired thirteen shells into an oil tank farm at Goleta.

I-19

Japanese submarine commanded by Takaichi Kinashi that sank the carrier *Wasp* on September 15, 1942. The *I-19* was later sunk by the destroyer *Radford* while attempting to aid the defenders of Tarawa, November 25, 1942.

I-24

Japanese submarine that dropped a midget submarine off Hawaii on December 7, 1941, to penetrate the defenses of Pearl Harbor. The *I-24* was commanded by Hiroshi Hanabusa and was lost in June 1943, during the evacuation of Japanese forces from Kiska.

I-25

Japanese submarine that launched a special aircraft on September 9 and September 29, 1942, to bomb the forests of Oregon. The pilot was Nobuo Fujita, the only person ever to bomb the U.S. The I-25 was commanded by Meiji Tagami and while en route back to Japan, he sank the Russian submarine *L-16* northwest of Seattle on October 11, 1942. The *I-25* was sunk in the vicinity of Espiritu Santo in August 1943, while under the command of Lieutenant Commander Masaur Kobiga.

I-26

Japanese submarine commanded by Minoru Yokota. It made the first Japanese submarine kill of World War II when it sank the *Cynthia Olson* 750 miles northwest of Seattle on December 7, 1941. On August 31, 1942, the *I-26* put two torpedoes into the carrier U.S.S. *Saratoga* in the Solomons, damaging it. Several months later off Guadalcanal, it sank the *Juneau*, in what was one of the worst disasters in U.S. Naval history. *I-26* was sunk on October 24, 1944, in Leyte Gulf by the U.S.S. *Rowell*.

I-29

Japanese submarine that traveled to Germany in July 1944, to pick up a shipment of German technical material. U.S. codebreakers monitored the return route and set the U.S. submarine *Sawfish* on an intercept course. *Sawfish* was commanded by Alan B. Banister, who sighted and sank *I-29*.

I-58

Japanese submarine commanded by Mochitsura Hashimoto, which sank the U.S. cruiser *Indianapolis* on July 30, 1945. It left Kure on July 16, 1945, the same day that the *Indianapolis* departed San Francisco. The sinking was the last success of the Japanese during World War II. Several days later, on August 12, 1945, Hashimoto launched the last *Kaiten* (suicide torpedo) of the war.

I-70

Japanese submarine sunk off Oahu December 10, 1941, by aircraft from the carrier *Enterprise*. It was the first Japanese combat vessel to be sunk in World War II by a U.S. Navy ship.

I-168

Japanese submarine under Lieutenant Commander Yahachi Tanabe that torpedoed and sank the carrier U.S.S. *Yorktown* at the end of the Battle of Midway in June 1942. It was the only decisive naval action by the Japanese at Midway. The *I-168* was later sunk by the

U.S. submarine *Scamp* on July 27, 1943, in a submarine duel in which both fired torpedoes at the same time.

I-169

Japanese submarine, 330 feet long, that could do twenty-three knots on the surface and eight knots submerged. During an American air attack on Truk lagoon in 1944, in its haste to dive and escape, the *I-169* was sunk and lost because a crewmember failed to close a forward torpedo door, resulting in the flooding of the forward compartments. Japanese rescue teams attempted to save the crew or to raise the submarine from the 160 feet of water into which it settled, but both efforts were unsuccessful and the crew suffocated. The *I-169* was named *Shinohara*.

I-173

The first Japanese submarine to be sunk by an American submarine during World War II. The constant radio traffic between the I-173 and Japan allowed U.S. Navy codebreakers at Pearl Harbor to plot its course from the west coast of the U.S. to Midway, then to project its course to Kwajelien. They then guided the U.S.S. *Gudgeon* onto an intercept course that allowed it to sink *I-173* on January 27, 1942. *I-173* therefore was also the first ship to be sunk exclusively as a result of intelligence from radio intercepts.

I-175

Japanese submarine under Lieutenant Commander Sunao Tabata that sank the U.S. aircraft carrier *Liscombe Bay* on November 24, 1943. *I-175* was subsequently sunk on February 5, 1944, by hedgehogs fired from a U.S. Navy surface vessel; it was the first submarine to be sunk by hedgehogs (see Hedgehogs).

I-176

Under Lieutenant Commander Kosaburo Yamaguchi, *I-176* was the only Japanese submarine to sink a U.S. submarine in World War II. It torpedoed the U.S.S. *Corvina* on November 16, 1943, south of Truk.

I-373

Japanese submarine under Lieutenant Commander Yukio Inaba. It was the 134th and last Japanese submarine lost in World War II when it was torpedoed by the submarine U.S.S. *Spikefish* August 13, 1945.

Icicle

Code name of the instructor who taught the assassins of Reinhard Heydrich.

Ida

Code name of the Luftwaffe radio beacon located at Aachen, Germany, that was used to assemble night fighters for attacks against British bombers.

Ie Shima

Island off Okinawa. It was captured by the U.S. 77th Infantry Division on April 16, 1945. Ernie Pyle was killed on Ie Shima on April 18, 1945, by a Japanese machine gunner, four months before it was the landing site of the Japanese surrender delegation on August 19, 1945, as he was en route to Manila to meet with General Douglas MacArthur.

Iffy

Name given to a device carried in Allied aircraft that emitted a signal picked up by ground radar stations to indicate that the aircraft was not enemy. The device was designated *IFF* for "Identification Friend or Foe."

Ikazuki

Japanese destroyer sunk by the U.S. submarine *Harder* in April 1944. Commander Sam Dealy stated, "Range 900 yards, commenced firing. Expended four torpedoes and one Jap destroyer."

Ike Jacket

U.S. Army uniform jacket designed by Michael Popp, General Dwight Eisenhower's Army tailor who cut out the waist-length coat after Ike complained about his bulky officer's jacket. A civilian version was manufactured by Lord and Taylor with the tag line, "Even if he's 4F, he can feel like a hero."

Ilfrey, Jack

U.S. Army Air Force major. He became an ace, with eight enemy aircraft to his credit, while flying with the Twelfth Army Air Force and later with the Eighth Army Air Force from England. Ilfrey was promoted to major and on the same day reduced to a second lieutenant because of infractions of the rules. He was promoted back to major a step at a time in one week. Ilfrey once knocked down an ME109 with his wingtip and was himself shot down over Caen. In order to hide out, he was forced to work for the German Army until he was able to escape back to Allied lines. Once he was forced by low fuel to land in neutral Portugal, but he gassed up and hastily departed before he could be interned.

Illegitimati non carborundum

Latin motto of General Joseph Stilwell. It means, "Don't let the bastards grind you down."

Ilmen and Kola

Names of two Soviet ships that were sunk on February 17, 1943, off Kyushu by the U.S. submarine *Sawfish*. Its commander Eugene Thomas Sands mistook them for Japanese vessels. The incident caused considerable embarrassment for the State Department.

Imredy, Bela (–1946)

Hungarian Premier and finance minister during World War II. He was found guilty of collaborating with the Germans and shot by a firing squad in Marko Jail, Budapest, on February 28, 1946.

Independence

Name of President Harry S Truman's personal aircraft, a DC-6, which was piloted by Henry T. Myers.

Independence, U.S.S. (CVL-22)

U.S. Navy aircraft carrier weighing 11,000 tons. It was originally designed to be the cruiser *Amsterdam* but was converted to a small, fast, and armored carrier. The *Independence* was one of the ships used for the atomic bomb tests at Bikini Atoll in 1946 and survived both bomb blasts.

Indianapolis, U.S.S. (CA-35)

U.S. cruiser that depended solely on speed to evade submarines, since it had no antisubmarine detection gear on board. In 1936, it carried President Franklin Roosevelt to the Pan American Conference at Buenos Aires. The *Indianapolis* was the flagship for Admiral Raymond Spruance's Fifth Fleet and was selected to deliver the atomic bombs to Tinian before they were dropped on Japan. It set a new world speed record traveling from the Farallons to Diamond Head, Hawaii, a distance of 2,091 miles, which it covered in 74.5 hours on the outbound leg of its journey. After delivering the bombs, the *Indianapolis* was torpedoed and sunk on July 30, 1945, by the Japanese submarine I-58. I-58 had left Kure on the same day that the *Indianapolis* left San Francisco, July 16, 1945. The sinking of the *Indianapolis* was the greatest sea disaster in U.S. Navy history; it was also the last major ship lost in World War II. The commander, Captain Charles McVay, was the only commanding officer to be court-martialed for the loss of his ship in wartime in U.S. Navy history.

Indian National Government

Japanese-sponsored Indian nationalist movement aimed at casting off British imperialism in India. It was led by Subhas Chandra Bose, who recruited from Indian prisoners of war for the Indian

National Army. At one time this army had 40,000 men, but only 7,000 ever actually saw combat. The Germans also sponsored an Indian nationalist movement, called the Free Indian Legion.

Indians (American)

Lieutenant Ernest Childers—Congressional Medal of Honor
Lieutenant Jack Montgomery—Congressional Medal of Honor
PFC Ira Hayes—participated in the flag-raising in Iwo Jima
Leroy Himlin—member of the first squad to meet the Russians
Major General Patrick J. Hurley—U.S. ambassador to China
Harvey Natchees—first U.S. soldier to enter the heart of Berlin during the war

Inggs, Lee (1897–1980)

Personal pilot of South African Field Marshall Jan Smuts during World War II. Inggs was the first person to log over one million miles in the air.

Ingram, Jonas H. (1886–1952)

U.S. Navy admiral in charge of the Atlantic Fleet from November 1944 to the end of the war. He had won the Congressional Medal of Honor in the 1915 Battle of Vera Cruz.

Inouye, Daniel

U.S. Senator from Hawaii who lost his right arm in combat in World War II. He was a member of the Japanese-American 442nd Regimental Combat Team.

Intrepid

Code name of the Chief of the British Intelligence Network (BSC) in New York, Sir William Stephenson, during World War II. He was a close friend of Ian Fleming.

Intrepid, U.S.S. (CV-11)

U.S. Essex-class aircraft carrier which was launched in 1943. It is credited with the destruction of 650 enemy aircraft and eighty ships. The *Intrepid* was in dry dock so often that she was sometimes called the "Decrepit," sometimes the "Dry I." The carrier was hit by so many kamikaze aircraft that it was also called the "Evil I."

I Operation

Designator of Japanese Admiral Isoruku Yamamoto's proposed plan to knock out the U.S. carrier force by striking at Midway in 1942. The plan might never have been approved, except that the Doolittle Raid of April 18, 1942, caused the Japanese to seek revenge and also brought home to them the importance of the aircraft carrier.

Iowa, U.S.S.

U.S. Navy battleship. At the time (1942) it was the heaviest hull ever launched. Although planned for 45,000 tons, it actually weighed 52,000 tons when fully loaded. It took 45 tons of grease for the ways. The *Iowa* was the only battleship at the time that could fight the German pocket battleship *Tirpitz* singlehandedly and had 200,000-horsepower engines, which enabled the vessel to do 33 knots. It took President Franklin Roosevelt to the Casablanca Conference in 1943 and later served in the Pacific. The *Iowa,* which came to be called the "First Lady of the Third Fleet," never lost a man to enemy action, although she was attacked many times.

Iron Annie

Nickname given to the JU-52 tri-motor transport of the Luftwaffe in World War II.

Iron Bottom Sound

Name given to the body of water between Tulagi and Guadalcanal. It was so named because of the number of ships sunk during naval engagements to protect Guadalcanal. So many vessels were on the bottom that magnetic compasses became unreliable in the area.

Iron Cross

Most well-known of all German military decorations. It was established in 1813 and awarded in every war since then. During World War II, there were eight classes through the Knight's Cross.

Iron Curtain

Phrase referring to the Communist borders with the West. It was supposedly coined by Winston Churchill but was actually used first by Joseph Goebbels in a propaganda article called "The Year 2000," written early in 1945.

Iron Gates

Name given to the rapids of the Danube River in Rumania that Hitler used as the eastern frontier of the Greater German Reich.

Iron Guard

Rumanian Fascist party that was closely aligned with the Nazis. However, when Hitler decided he wanted Rumania on his side, he backed Marshall Ian Antonescu, who imprisoned most of the Iron Guard. They remained locked up until Antonescu's overthrow in 1944.

Ironside, Sir Edmund (1880–1959)

British Field Marshall and Chief of the Imperial General Staff from 1939 to 1940. He had fought in the Boer War and was the first British officer to land in France during World War I. Ironside also commanded the Allied forces in Archangel, Northern Russia, in 1918. During World War II, he was not able to cope with modern warfare tactics and was relegated to lesser positions after 1940.

MOVIE PORTRAYAL:
Churchill and the Generals (1982 TV movie), by Noel Coleman

Ise

Japanese hybrid aircraft carrier. It had been a battleship but was restructured with the addition of a small flight deck and hangar that could accomodate twenty-four aircraft. Due to the shortage of aircraft the *Ise* participated as a battleship in the Battle of Leyte Gulf in October 1944, where it was damaged.

I Shall Return

Famous propaganda phrase of General Douglas MacArthur that promised his return to and liberation of the Philippines after he was ordered to leave in 1942. He had the letters I.S.R. for "I Shall Return" printed on cigarettes, candy, matches, leaflets, and other items that were sent to the Filipino guerrillas to be distributed to the population.

Isley Field

Name of the airfield on Saipan. It had been captured from the Japanese, who called it *Aslito,* and renamed after the carrier *Lexington*'s torpedo plane commander Robert H. Isely. Isely had been hit by flak over the field two days before the invasion, on June 15, 1944, crashing into the field. The name was actually misspelled but remained spelled that way through repetition.

Ismay, Hastings L. (1887–1965)

British Army general. He was Chief of Staff to Winston Churchill throughout World War II.

MOVIE PORTRAYAL:
Churchill and the Generals (1981 TV movie), by Paul Hardwick

The Issue Is In Doubt

Message sent from Wake Island by Marine Corps Major James Devereaux just prior to the Japanese takeover of the island in December 1941.

Is-Was

Name of a plastic circular slide rule used on U.S. submarines to plot targets. It had concentric circles of different diameters representing the compass rose. By plotting where a target *is*, the crew could figure out where it *was* and then establish where it shortly would be.

Italian Army

Attacked France on June 10, 1940, as the French Army crumbled and the Nazis entered Paris. Mussolini sent 32 Italian divisions against six demoralized French divisions, who promptly stopped the Italians, then proceeded to push them back into Italy. The fall of France was the only thing that saved Mussolini.

It appears the peacock will be on time. Fan his tail.

Message sent by Admiral William F. Halsey to Admiral Marc Mitscher on Guadalcanal as permission to proceed in the plan to shoot down Japanese Admiral Isoruku Yamamoto April 18, 1943.

Itaya, Shigeru

Japanese Navy lieutenant commander. He was the first pilot to take off from the carrier *Akagi* to bomb Pearl Harbor on December 7, 1941. In order to be the first to depart, Itaya took off just prior to "getting the flag," the signal to take off.

"I Threw a Kiss in the Ocean"

Song written by Irving Berlin for the United States Navy Relief in World War II. It was introduced by Kate Smith in 1942.

Ito, Seiichi (1890–1945)

Japanese vice-admiral. He commanded the last sortie of the Japanese Imperial Navy on April 6, 1945, when the battleship *Yamato*, the light cruiser *Yahagi*, and eight destroyers left Japan for Okinawa. Ito could only obtain 2,500 barrels of oil, just enough for a one-way trip, after which he hoped to beach the ships and add their firepower to the defense of Okinawa. His force was attacked by U.S. carrier aircraft on April 7, 1945, and he went down with the *Yamato*.

Ives, Burl (1909–)

U.S. entertainer. He was singing on NBC on June 22, 1940, when he was cut off so that the fall of France could be announced. Ives was drafted into the U.S. Army in April 1942, after appearing in the movie *This Is the Army*. After entertaining troops around the country, he was medically discharged in October 1943.

Ivory Tower

Nickname given to the Government House in Port Moresby that was the headquarters of General Douglas MacArthur.

Iwo Jima

Japanese island assaulted by U.S. Marines in February 1945. It was needed as an emergency airfield for B-29's returning from attacking Japan. Iwo Jima was commanded by Lieutenant General Tasamichi Kuribayashi. Of 19,000 Japanese defending forces, fewer than 200 prisoners were captured. The first bomber to land there was piloted by Raymond Malo, after which nearly 2,400 others made emergency landings.

J

Jabara, James (1923–1966)
U.S. Army Air Force officer. He enlisted in the Army Air Force in 1942 and flew 108 missions as a fighter pilot with the Eighth and Ninth Army Air Forces. Jabara later became the first jet ace of the U.S. when he shot down 15 aircraft during the Korean War.

Jabo
German nickname for Allied fighter bombers. Several prominent victims were Field Marshalls Erwin Rommel and Fedor von Bock.

Jack the Tanker Killer
Nickname conferred on the U.S. submarine *Jack* when she sank four Japanese tankers in one day on February 19, 1944, in the South China Sea.

Jacob Jones, U.S.S.
U.S. destroyer that was the second ship to bear the name. The first was torpedoed and sunk in World War I. The second *Jacob Jones* suffered the same fate 24 years later, when it was torpedoed on February 28, 1942, by *U-578*. There were only twelve survivors from a crew of 122. It was the first U.S. warship ever to be torpedoed and sunk in home waters in World War II; it went down off Cape May, New Jersey.

Jade Amicol
Code name of the head of British Intelligence in France, Colonel Claude Ollivier, who had his headquarters in a convent in Paris.

James, Daniel Jr. (1920–   )
U.S. Air Force officer and first black four-star general in U.S. military history. During World War II, he flew 179 missions as a

pilot of a C-47. James also fought in Korea, where he logged 78 combat missions.

Janfu

Superlative that stood for Joint Army-Navy Foul-Up (used in place of expletive deleted).

Jannings, Emil (1884–1950)

Swiss-born, German-raised actor who won the first Academy Award for Best Actor in 1927. In 1929, he returned to Germany, where he made propaganda films for the Nazis and was personally presented a medal by Joseph Goebbels, the head of the Propaganda Ministry.

January 12, 1893

Birthdates of both Hermann Goering and Alfred Rosenberg.

Japanese aces

Hiroyoshi Nishizawa (102)
Shoici Sugita (80)
Saburo Sakai (64)
Waturo Nakamichi (55)
Naoshi Kanno (52)
Yasuhiki Kuroe (51)
Temei Akamatsu (50)
Kinsuke Muto (50)
Toshio Ota (50)

Japanese aircraft

Name	*Type*	*Manufacturer*
Betty	Navy torpedo bomber	Mitsubishi
Fran	Navy bomber	Nakajima
Francis	Navy bomber	Nakajima
Frank	Army fighter	Nakajima
Jake	Navy reconnaissance bomber	Aichi
Jill	Navy torpedo bomber	Nakajima
Judy	Navy dive bomber	Aichi
Kate	Navy torpedo bomber	Nakajima
Oscar	Army fighter	Nakajima
Nick	Army fighter	Kawasaki
Sally	Army fighter	Mitsubishi
Tojo	Army fighter	Nakajima
Tony	Army and Navy fighter	Mitsubishi
Val	Navy dive bomber	Aichi
Zeke	Navy fighter	Mitsubishi

Japanese aircraft carriers at the beginning of the war

Akagi—Red Castle
Kaga—Increased Joy
Hiryu—Flying Dragon
Soryu—Green Dragon
Shokaku—Soaring Crane
Zuikaku—Happy Crane

Japanese People's Volunteer Corps

Japanese last-ditch defense units that organized all males between the ages of fifteen and sixty and all females from seventeen to forty. It was envisioned that they would face the Allied invasion of the home islands with sharpened bamboo poles. The German equivalent was the *Volksturm* and the British had their Home Guard.

Japanese Relocation Centers

In 1942 Japanese-Americans on the West Coast of the United States were forcibly incarcerated in camps to prevent any sabotage or espionage. These camps were:

Gila River (Arizona)
Granada (Colorado)
Heart Mountain (Wyoming)
Jerome (Arkansas)
Manzanar (California)
Minidoka (Idaho)
Poston (Arizona)
Rohwer (Arkansas)
Topaz (Utah)
Tule Lake (California)

Japanese ships involved in the Pearl Harbor attack force

Carriers: *Akagi, Hiryu, Kaga, Shokaku, Soryu, Zuikaku*
Battleships: *Hiei, Kirishima*
Cruisers: *Chikuma, Tone*
Misc.: three submarines, nine destroyers, and eight tankers

Japanese surrender ceremony

United Nations signators on board the U.S.S. *Missouri*, September 2, 1945:

General Sir Thomas Blamey (Australia)
Colonel L. Moore-Cosgrave (Canada)
Lieutenant General Kuzma N. Dereyyanko (USSR)
Admiral Sir Bruce Fraser (UK)
Admiral C. E. L. Helfrich (Netherlands)

Vice-Admiral Leonard M. Isitt (New Zealand)
General Jacques Leclerc (France)
General Douglas MacArthur (U.S.)

Japanese delegates:
Shunichi Kase, Government Information Bureau
Lieutenant General Shuichi Miyakozi, Army General Headquarters
Katsuo Okezaki, Central Liaison Office
Mamoru Shigemitsu, Foreign Minister
Rear Admiral Todatoshi Tomioka, Naval General Headquarters
General Yoshijiro Umezo

Jeanie

Name of Bill Mauldin's jeep, which he converted into a complete artist's mobile work studio.

Jedburgh

Code name for teams of Allied agents that were parachuted behind German lines prior to the Normandy invasion of D-Day. They worked with the Resistance forces to help divert German troops from the invasion site. The team was usually made up of one American, one Englishman, and one Frenchman, in keeping with the Allied effort. William E. Colby, future head of the CIA, was a Jedburgh agent.

Jeep

All-inclusive Army nickname for anything judged to be insignificant from a raw draftee to an observation plane. The name was eventually applied to a 2,200 pound, four-wheel-drive vehicle with the versatility needed by the different branches of the army. The vehicle was supposedly named after the pet of Popeye's adopted son, Swee'Pea. Another story suggests that the name came from the initials *G.P.* which stood for "general purpose."

Jensen, Jackie (1927–1982)

Major league baseball player who is one of the only two people* to play in both a World Series Game and in a Rose Bowl football game. He scored two touchdowns in the 1949 Rose Bowl game and was voted the American League's Most Valuable Player in 1958. During World War II, Jensen spent a short time in the U.S. Navy as a physical fitness instructor for court-martialed prisoners in Idaho.

---

*The other player was Chuck Essegian, who played for the 1959 Dodgers and with Stanford University in 1952.

Jeremiah O'Brian, S.S.

Last Liberty ship in existence. In 1980, it was refurbished at Pier 3, Fort Mason, San Francisco, as a memorial to all those who fought at sea in World War II. It was built between May and June, 1943, at New England Shipbuilding Company in South Portland, Maine.

Jerry

British nickname for Germans (it was also the name of a chamber pot). The French called them *Boche* and the Americans used "Krauts."

Jerry Can

Nickname given to a standardized German can used for fuel or water and which could be attached to vehicles.

Jervis Bay, H.M.S.

British armed merchant cruiser. In November 1940, while guarding a thirty-seven-ship convoy in the North Atlantic, the *Jervis Bay* engaged the German pocket battleship *Admiral Scheer* to protect the convoy but was sunk after 22 minutes. Her captain, E. S. Fogarty-Fegen, was awarded a posthumous Victoria Cross.

Jeschonnek, Hans (1899–1943)

German Air Force colonel-general and Chief of Staff. He replaced General Wever after his death in 1936, becoming an advocate of dive bombers and medium bombers in place of heavy four-engine bombers. Jeschonnek was influenced by economic factors which forced him to preach economy of material. He was caught between Hitler and Goering; though he attempted to do what he believed to be right for the Luftwaffe, he was continually made the scapegoat by Goering for the failures of the Luftwaffe. On August 18, 1943, the Allies launched a major strike at Peenemunde after neutralizing German defenses; because of this, Jeschonnek shot himself. Goering and official propaganda put the date of his death at August 19 so that it would not coincide with the Peenemunde attacks.

MOVIE PORTRAYAL:

Battle of Britain (1969), by Otto Alberty

Jester, Maurice D.

U.S. Coast Guard lieutenant. He was the first Coast Guard officer to receive the Navy Cross in World War II for sinking a German submarine off the Carolina coast on June 4, 1942.

Jewish Brigade

British Army unit made up primarily of Palestinian Jews. It was much like the unit that fought under Montgomery, consisting of German Jews who had escaped from the Nazis before the outbreak of World War II. All of them spoke fluent German and conducted espionage and spy missions behind German lines. Many times they wore German Army uniforms allowing them to infiltrate German units in order to gain intelligence. After the surrender of Germany, the Jewish Brigade were used as the occupation forces of Holland.

Jingle Jangle

Name of General Elliott Roosevelt's B-17 *Flying Fortress* during World War II. He named it for the 1942 song, "Jingle Jangle Jingle," made popular by Kay Kyser.

Jinyo

Japanese aircraft carrier weighing 21,000 tons. It was sunk November 17, 1944, by the submarine U.S.S. *Spadefish,* commanded by Gordon Underwood.

Jodl, Alfred (1890–1946)

German Army colonel-general who was the last Chief of Staff of the German army. He was wounded in the July 20, 1944, assassination attempt against Hitler and later signed the surrender document at Rheims on May 7, 1945. Jodl was found guilty of war crimes at Nuremberg and hanged October 16, 1946.

MOVIE PORTRAYALS:
Rommel: The Desert Fox (1951), by Jack Baston
The Longest Day (1962), by Wolfgang Lukschy
Hitler (1962), by Walter Kohler
Is Paris Burning? (1966), by Hannes Messemer
Patton (1970), by Richard Munch
Hitler: The Last Ten Days (1973), by Phillip Stone
Ike (1979 TV movie), by Wolfgang Preiss
The Bunker (1980 TV movie), by Tony Steedman

Joel, Billy (1949–)

Highly successful rock 'n' roll singer of the 1970's and 1980's. His father survived the concentration camp at Dachau in World War II.

John Fitch, S.S.

World War II Liberty ship that was launched only 24 days after the keel was laid.

John Harvey, S.S.

U.S. Liberty ship that was bombed while at anchor in Bari, Italy, on December 2, 1943. It carried 100 tons of mustard gas bombs that were to be stored in Italy in case the Germans resorted to gas attacks. The Luftwaffe bombs caused the wide dispersal of the mustard gas, which resulted in most of the casualties in and around the harbor. It was the worst accident of World War II involving poison gas.

John, Otto (1909–   )

German Resistance member and one of the few survivors of the ill-fated attempt on Hitler's life on July 20, 1944. He was a lawyer with the Lufthansa Foreign office and the day after the attempt was able to board a Lufthansa aircraft bound for Madrid. John joined the British as an intelligence officer for the remainder of the war. In postwar Germany, he headed the West German intelligence organization and on July 20, 1954, was either forced or had chosen to defect to East Germany. Eighteen months later he escaped back to the West, where he served a prison sentence.

Johnson, James "Johnnie" (1916–   )

British fighter pilot and wing commander. He was the second-highest-scoring ace of the Royal Air Force in World War II, with 38 enemy aircraft shot down.

Johnson, Lyndon Baines (1908–1973)

Thirty-sixth President of the United States. He was the first U.S. Representative to join the military after the U.S. entry into the war, being sent to the South Pacific in May 1942 as President Franklin Roosevelt's personal representative. Johnson was a lieutenant commander in the U.S. Navy and went along on a B-25 named *Heckling Hare* on a bombing mission of New Guinea. A *New York Times* dispatch said the aircraft returned with engine trouble, but Johnson said they were attacked by Japanese aircraft. No one on board had been injured, yet General Douglas MacArthur presented Johnson with the Silver Star. Johnson was the only one on board who received it.

MOVIE PORTRAYAL:

King (1978 TV movie), by Warren Kemmerling

The Private Files of J. Edgar Hoover (1978), by Andrew Duggan

Johnson, Robert S. (1920–   )

U.S. Army Air Force fighter pilot. He was the top-scoring ace of the European Theater, with twenty-eight victories. Johnson had failed to pass gunnery school and so theoretically never qualified as a fighter pilot.

Johnstone, Stanley

Australian newspaperman who worked for the *Chicago Tribune*. He shared the cabin of the U.S.S. *Lexington*'s commander Captain Frederick C. Sherman when the *Lexington* was sunk by the Japanese at the Battle of the Coral Sea on May 8, 1942. Upon returning to Chicago, he and a cohort, Wayne Thomis, leaked a story that included the names of the Japanese ships at the Battle of Midway. This information had come from a secret message which Johnstone had seen aboard the transport that had returned him to the States. The U.S. Navy codebreakers were afraid the story would reveal their top-secret ability to read Japanese codes, but it did not. Johnstone had been recommended for a Navy medal, but this was revoked. He later wrote the book *Queen of the Flattops*.

Joint Chiefs of Staff

The American commanders of all branches of the military. During World War II they were Army Generals George C. Marshall and Henry H. Arnold, and Fleet Admirals William D. Leahy and Ernest King.

Joint Staff Missions

Representatives of the British Chiefs of Staff in Washington, D.C., as the liaisons with the American Chiefs of Staff. They were Field Marshall Sir John Dill; Rear Admiral W. R. Patterson; Lieutenant General G. N. MacReady; and Air Marshall Douglas C. S. Evill.

Jones, Alan W.

U.S. Army major general. He commanded the green 106th Infantry Division that fell apart during the German attack in the Battle of the Bulge in December 1944. Jones was subsequently relieved of command.

Joseph Conrad

Name of General Jonathan Wainwright's jumping horse. The horse was eaten when rations ran out on Bataan in 1942.

Joseph N. Teal, S.S.

U.S. Liberty ship launched in Kaiser's Portland, Oregon shipyards in October 1942. It was the first ship ever to be launched ten days after the keel was laid. It was launched by Anna Roosevelt Boettinger, the daughter of President Franklin Roosevelt, who watched the ceremony.

Joseph P. Kennedy, Jr., U.S.S. (DD850)

U.S. destroyer commissioned toward the end of World War II. It was named after Joseph P. Kennedy, Jr., brother of President John F. Kennedy, who was killed August 12, 1944, on a secret mission over England. The destroyer was christened by a sister, Jean Kennedy, and another brother, Robert F. Kennedy, served aboard it.

Jourdan, Louis (1920–)

French actor who served on a work gang building roads during the German occupation of France in World War II.

Joyce William (1906–1946)

Brooklyn, New York-born propaganda broadcaster for the Nazis in World War II known as "Lord Haw Haw." He emigrated to England in 1921, where he became a member of Sir Oswald Mosley's British Union of Fascists as well as other pro-Hitler groups. Joyce had a falling-out with Mosley and left for Germany in 1937. He broadcast from 1939 to 1945 and was also known as the Humbug of Hamburg. Joyce, who got his name "Lord Haw Haw" from the British radio columnist Jonah Barrington, was arrested by British troops at the end of the war. He was tried for treason, found guilty, and hanged by Arthur Pierrpoint.

MOVIE PORTRAYAL:

Passport to Destiny (1944), by Gavin Muir

JU-52

German tri-motor transport aircraft of World War II. Originally designed as a bomber, it proved too slow and was given the nickname "Iron Annie."

JU-87

German dive bomber more commonly known as a *Stuka*. It was designed as aerial artillery for close support of ground forces. It was very successful in the early phases of the war in Poland and the Low Countries but was highly vulnerable to fighters when it started an attack.

JU-88

German twin-engine bomber of medium range. It was designed in 1936 by an American, Alfred Gassner, and by a German, W. H. Evers. Although it proved to be well-suited for missions over Poland and France, it was overextended for use over England.

Jubilee

Code name given to the Dieppe raid in 1942. It was also called "the Great Deception."

Juin, Alphonse-Pierre (1888–1967)
French general. He was born in Algeria and later graduated with Charles de Gaulle from the French military academy of St. Cyr. Juin was a Vichy commander in North Africa until the Allied invasion of November 8, 1942, after which he switched sides to fight with the Free French.

July 4, 1944
Date of a national salute of 1,100 shells fired at exactly noon by the U.S. Armed forces in Europe. It was the largest national salute in U.S. Army history.

July 20, 1944
Date of the attempted assassination of Hitler by a faction of German intellectuals. Berlin radio cut its regular broadcast schedule to announce the attempted assassination. The scheduled program was a lecture on the extermination of rats. (July 20 was also the day Hideki Tojo resigned as the Japanese Premier.)

June 6, 1944
Date of the D-Day landings of Normandy. It was also the graduation day of John Eisenhower from West Point Military Academy; the birthday of Field Marshall Erwin Rommel's wife; the birthday of German General Marcks who commanded the 84th Corps defending Normandy; the anniversary of U.S. Admiral Ernest King's commissioning in the U.S. Navy.

Juneau, U.S.S.
U.S. cruiser that was sunk on November 13, 1942, off Guadalcanal by the Japanese submarine *I-26*. The five Sullivan brothers lost their lives, and only eleven of the crew of 687 survived.

Junge, Gertrude (Traudl)
Hitler's personal secretary. She was with him in the bunker in Berlin where she witnessed the wedding of Hitler and Eva Braun. Her maiden name was Humps before she married one of Hitler's valets, Hans Junge, in June 1943. He was killed on the Eastern Front in late 1944.

MOVIE PORTRAYAL:
The Bunker (1980 TV movie), by Sarah Marshall.

Junior
Name of a small Junkers aircraft that was fitted with a 650-pound rocket engine in 1936. It was the first attempt at jet-propelled flight.

Junkin, Sam F.
U.S. Army Air Force second lieutenant. He is officially credited

with being the first American military pilot to shoot down a German aircraft (FW190). He did so while flying escort over the Dieppe Raid on August 19, 1942, was subsequently wounded, and had to bail out on his return to England. Junkin was picked up in the Channel and returned to England by barge.

Junkroom

Code name used by the Germans to initiate the launching of the V-weapons against London. It was scheduled for June 16, 1944.

Juno Beach

Designator of the D-Day beach assaulted by the Canadian 3rd Infantry Division, the Canadian 2nd Armored Division, and the 4th Special Service Brigade Commando on June 6, 1944.

Junyo

Japanese light aircraft carrier. It was damaged in the Battle of the Philippine Sea on June 20, 1944, but survived the war.

Jurika, Stephen

U.S. Navy lieutenant commander. He was U.S. Naval attaché in Tokyo before World War II. As executive officer of the carrier U.S.S. *Hornet*, Jurika briefed the officers that participated in the Doolittle Raid on Tokyo, April 18, 1942.

K

K

British foreign office identifier for German Admiral Wilhelm Canaris.

K

Designator painted on all vehicles of German Field Marshall Paul von Kleist's Panzer group in Russia. It was used as an easy means of identification for the forces in the field and was copied from General Heinz Guderian, who had a white *G* painted on his vehicles.

K-74

Designator of the only U.S. Navy blimp to be shot down by a submarine during World War II. On July 18, 1943, under Commander Nelson R. Grills, the *K-74* located a German submarine on radar and attacked, but its bombs failed to release; the submarine shot it down, resulting in the loss of one crewmember. The submarine was later sunk by surface ships off the Florida coast near Miami.

KA-17-10

Serial number of the landing craft that transported General Douglas MacArthur to the beach at Aitape, New Guinea, on April 23, 1944.

Kaga

Japanese aircraft carrier weighing 38,200 tons. It was originally to be a 39,000-ton battleship, but was converted to a carrier in accordance with the disarmament treaty of 1921. The *Kaga* participated in the attack on Pearl Harbor on December 7, 1941, and was sunk during the Battle of Midway in June 1942 by aircraft from the U.S. carrier *Enterprise*. (On March 2, 1942, it was thought to have been damaged by torpedoes from the U.S.S. *Sailfish* and was therefore believed to be the first Japanese carrier of the war to be hit. In reality the *Sailfish* torpedoed and sank an aircraft-ferry, *Kamagawa Maru.)*

Kaholm

Site of a Norwegian fortress guarding the narrows into Oslo Fiord. Using turn-of-the-century Krupp guns, the fortress forces fired on the severely damaged German cruiser *Blucher* on April 9, 1940, which resulted in its sinking.

Kain, Edgar J. (Cobber) (1918–1940)

British fighter pilot and first Royal Air Force ace of World War II. He was a New Zealander who flew with No. 73 Squadron and was the first British airman in France to be awarded the Distinguished Flying Cross, in April 1940. Kain carried a *tiki* as a good luck charm and is officially credited with shooting down seventeen enemy aircraft before he was killed while ''beating-up''* his airfield before leaving France.

Kaiser, Henry J. (1882–1967)

U.S. industrialist who became the greatest shipbuilder of the war. He used assembly-line methods that other shipbuilders did not believe would work, and that allowed him to produce thirty percent of the country's wartime merchant shipping as well as fifty percent of small aircraft carriers. At one point Kaiser was building one Liberty ship per day, launching 1,490 vessels by the end of the war.

MOVIE PORTRAYAL:

The Amazing Howard Hughes (1978 TV movie), by Garry Walberg

Kaitens

Japanese human suicide torpedoes. The name meant ''turning the tide''; once launched, the crew was committed and could not get out. The torpedoes were fifty-four feet long, carried a warhead weighing three thousand pounds, and could travel up to thirty miles at slow speed and for twelve miles at a top speed of forty knots. The Kaiten was designed from the Type 93 torpedo by Lieutenant Nishina, Lieutenant Kuroki, and Naval architect Hiroshi Suzukawa. It was first piloted operationally at Ulithi Atoll on November 20, 1944, by coinventor Nichina. Several were fired

---

*Engaging in high-speed, low flight indicating a victorious mission.

from the submarine *I-47* under Lieutenant Commander Zenji Orita, but the only ship to be sunk was the U.S. tanker *Mississinewa.*

Kajioka, Sadamichi

Japanese rear admiral. He led the capture of Wake Island in 1941 as well as the invasion forces attacking Port Moresby during the Battle of the Coral Sea in 1942.

Kako

Japanese destroyer. It was the first major combat vessel sunk by U.S. submarines in World War II, when it was torpedoed by the *S-44* under John Raymond Moore, on August 10, 1942. Moore was awarded a Navy Cross for the sinking.

Kakwichi, Takahashi

Japanese Navy pilot. He commanded the dive bombers that attacked Pearl Harbor on December 7, 1941.

Kaltenbach, Frederick W. (1895–)

Axis propaganda broadcaster who was born in Dubuque, Iowa. He had been a second lieutenant in the U.S. Coast Artillery during World War I. Kaltenbach had been with William Shirer at the French surrender of Compiegne in June 1940.

Kaltenborn, H. V. (1879–1965)

Radio news commentator for CBS until 1940, when he joined NBC. He was of German descent and was a baron by birthright. The H. V. stood for "Hans von" and he was known as "the Voice of Doom."

Kaltenbrunner, Ernst (1902–1946)

German S.S. lieutenant general who commanded the Reich Main Security Office (RSHA). Kaltenbrunner, whose party number was 300,179, was sentenced to death at Nuremberg and executed on October 16, 1946.

Kamikaze

Japanese suicide planes. The name, which stood for "Divine Wind," was originated by Vice-Admiral Takejiro Onishi. The name *Kamikaze* referred only to Navy aircraft, while the Army called theirs *Tokko Tai*. In World War II, the Japanese used 1,228 of these aircraft, which sank thirty-four U.S. ships.

Kammhuber Line

Name of a defensive line stretching from northern Germany to Sicily. It was named after General Josef Kammhuber, who was the head of the German night fighters. The Kammhuber Line contained a belt of searchlights and radar sites to aid night fighters in shooting down enemy aircraft.

Kappler, Herbert (1908–)

German S.S. colonel and the embassy's police attaché in Italy. He was sentenced to life imprisonment for the massacre of 335 Italians at the Ardeatine Caves in Rome, becoming the last German war criminal to remain in Italian captivity. In 1978, Kappler's wife smuggled him out of his prison cell stuffed into a suitcase, with one of the Italian guards even helping her to carry it.

Karinhall

Elaborate hunting lodge built by Hermann Goering and named after his first wife. When he left it for the last time on April 22, 1945, en route to Berchtesgaden, Goering personally pushed the plunger that blew the lodge up.

Karl

Name of the siege mortar used by the Germans at the siege of Sebastopol in 1942. It was also known as *Thor.*

Karl Borromaeus Church

Prague church where the assassins of Reinhard Heydrich attempted to hide on May 26, 1942. They were betrayed and subsequently killed in the crypt.

Karlshorst

Suburb of Berlin. It was the site of the official German surrender on May 8, 1945, which was held in a former engineering college of the German Army.

Kasserine Pass

Site of the first defeat of the Americans at the hands of the Germans when Field Marshall Erwin Rommel's Korps attacked U.S. forces, inflicting serious casualties in February 1943. U.S. General Lloyd Fredenhall was relieved of command of the II Corps because one of his regimental commanders had grouped his forces in a valley of the pass and left the sides undefended, thus allowing the Germans to break through easily. The Germans finally withdrew because the British Eighth Army were threatening both the Mareth Line and their rear.

Katusha

Name of a Soviet multiple-rocket launcher that was known to the Germans as Stalin Organs. Having the effect of forty mortars, it was invented by Russian General Kostchow from a description of a ten-barrel pistol used in an assassination attempt on Louise Philippe in 1835.

Katyn Forest

Site of the massacre of an estimated 4,000 to 15,000 Polish officers on the banks of the Dnieper river near Smolensk during the spring of 1940. In April 1943, the Germans allowed an International Medical Commission to investigate and perform autopsies, which established that the Russians had killed the officers.* The Russians used this charge to sever diplomatic relations with the London-based Polish Government in exile and set up their own. At Nuremberg it was alleged by the Russians that the Germans had killed the Poles. In 1952 the U.S. House of Representatives set up a committee to settle the controversy; they established that the NKVD (Soviet secret police) had murdered the Poles in an attempt to rid Poland of all intellectual leadership.

Kauffman, Draper (1911–1979)

U.S. Navy admiral, called the father of underwater demolition teams (UDT). Prior to the U.S. entry into the war, he was a civilian ambulance driver in Paris, was captured by the Germans, and escaped two months later through Spain to England. Kauffman served in the Royal Navy until accepted into the U.S. Naval Reserves a month prior to Pearl Harbor. After the December 7 attack he recovered and disassembled a Japanese 500-pound bomb for which he was awarded the Navy Cross. Kauffman later commanded UDT teams in Saipan, Tinian, Guam, Iwo Jima, and Okinawa.

Kavanaugh, Ken (1916–)

Chicago Bears quarterback. During World War II, he served as a captain in the U.S. Army Air Force, flying B-17's in Europe. Kavanaugh's bombardier was Kenneth O'Donnell who later became President John F. Kennedy's appointment assistant.

Kawabe, Tokoshiro (1890–1960)

Japanese lieutenant general and Vice-Chief of the Imperial General Staff. He headed the surrender delegation that flew to Manila on August 19, 1945, to meet with General Douglas MacArthur.

Kawakita, Tomaya

Japanese interpreter in a prisoner-of-war camp in Japan. He had been raised in the U.S. and held American citizenship. Kawakita

---

*However the Commission's coroners only dissected eight of the bodies, and one coroner abstained from giving a judgement because his examination indicated that the bodies weren't decayed enough for the amount of time that was supposed to have passed.)

was known as the "Meatball" because of his brutality to the U.S. prisoners. After the war, he was tried, found guilty of treason, and imprisoned.

Kawato, Masajiro

Japanese fighter pilot who shot down U.S. Marine Corp ace Gregory "Pappy" Boyington.

Kaye, Danny (1913–)

Hollywood comedian. Although an avid dancer, he was 4F in World War II due to back trouble and entertained troops instead. In one six-month period, Kaye sold over a million dollars' worth of war bonds.

Kazan

Secret German base in Russia where tanks and their tactics were tested with the aid of the Russians prior to 1933 to circumvent the Versailles Treaty.

Kazan, Elia (1909–)

Hollywood actor and director. He was the first civilian consultant of the U.S. Army Special Services Office. Kazan was appointed to study the entertainment needs of soldiers overseas, and to that end, spent nearly three months in 1943 in New Guinea and the Philippines.

KDHP

Morse code shorthand message used in World War II by merchant ships to say "I have been torpedoed."

Kearby, Neel (–1944)

U.S. Army Air Force officer. He flew a P-47 named *Fiery Ginger* and was the first American to shoot down six enemy aircraft in a single day, October 11, 1943. Kearby was awarded the Congressional Medal of Honor.

Kearny, USS

U.S. destroyer which was torpedoed on October 17, 1941, by a German submarine off the coast of Iceland. It was the first casualty of the U.S. Navy in World War II, although it was actually torpedoed before the U.S. entry into the war. With eleven men killed, the *Kearny* made it back to Iceland, and later fought at both North Africa and Anzio.

Ked Plan

Name given by the French Resistance to the plan to cut German military telephone lines in support of the D-Day landings of June 6, 1944. The Allies called it Operation Violet.

Keeshan, Bob (1927–)

Television actor and producer who has played both Clarabell the Clown and Captain Kangaroo. In June 1945, after graduating from high school, he joined the U.S. Marine Corps, with which he served until September 1946.

Keitel, Wilhelm (1882–1946)

German Field Marshall and Chief of the High Command of the Armed Forces. He was the son-in-law of Field Marshall Werner von Blomberg and aided in von Blomberg's downfall by passing on a police dossier on his new wife to Goering. Keitel was nicknamed "Lackey" because of his willingness to do Hitler's bidding. He was found guilty of war crimes at Nuremberg and hanged October 16, 1946.

MOVIE PORTRAYALS:
Rommel: The Desert Fox (1951), by John Hoyt
Hitler (1962), by Carl Esmond
Hitler: The Last Ten Days (1973), by Gabriele Ferzetti
The Bunker (1980 TV movie), by John Paul

Kelly, Charles E. (1921–)

U.S. Army sergeant known as Commando Kelly for exploits that won him the Congressional Medal of Honor in Italy.

Kelly, Colin P., Jr. (1915–1941)

U.S. Army Air Force captain. He was America's first hero of World War II and was the first West Point graduate to be killed in action. Kelly was piloting a B-17 and attacked Japanese shipping that was invading the Philippines; legend has it that he dropped bombs on the battleship *Haruna,* which he supposedly sank. In fact he achieved no hits and was instead shot down on the return flight on December 10, 1941, by Japanese ace Saburo Sakai. Kelly held the plane level so that the crew could bail out but could not get out himself. He died in the crash of the first B-17 to be lost in combat in World War II. Myth also had it that he was awarded a Congressional Medal of Honor. In actuality he received a posthumous Distinguished Service Cross. President Franklin D. Roosevelt wrote a letter addressed to the future 1956 President Eisenhower to appoint Colin Kelly III to West Point. Young Kelly graduated in 1963, and served as a chaplain with the rank of major.

Kelly, Gene (1912–)

Hollywood dancer and actor. In November 1944, he enlisted in the U.S. Naval Air Service after playing a sailor in the 1944 movie *Anchors Aweigh*. Kelly received a commission and worked at the photographic center in Washington, D. C., where he produced a number of documentaries for the Navy.

Kelly, H.M.S.

British destroyer commanded by Lord Louis Mountbatten. At the beginning of World War II, it struck a mine off Newcastle and was later torpedoed off the coast of Germany. *Kelly* was finally sunk by Stuka dive bombers off Crete's north coast May 23, 1941. The ship was used as the model for Noel Coward's H.M.S. *Torrin* in his 1942 movie, *In Which We Serve*, in which Coward wore Mountbatten's hat in his role as captain of the destroyer.

Kempeitai

Japanese Army secret police that controlled Japanese citizens, in a manner very much like that of the Gestapo of Nazi Germany or the KGB of Soviet Russia.

Kempka, Erich (1910–1975)

Hitler's personal chauffeur during World War II. He was personally ordered by Hitler to divorce his wife because she did not look German. Kempka did so but continued to live with her outside the Reich chancellery area.

Kendleigh, Jane

Navy ensign. She was the first Navy flight nurse to set foot on a battlefield, when she landed at Iwo Jima at the height of the fighting, March 6, 1945. Her aircraft came under mortar fire and was delayed eight minutes while other aircraft attacked the nearby mortar positions.

Kennedy, Arthur (1914–   )

Hollywood actor. He enlisted in the U.S. Army Air Force in 1943, shortly after completing the movie *Air Force*.

Kennedy, Douglas

Editor of *True* magazine. In World War II, he commanded the PT500 at Normandy during the D-Day landings.

Kennedy, Edward (1905–1963)

Associated Press correspondent who prematurely leaked the news of the German surrender at Rheims, on May 7, 1945. He released the story twenty-four hours prior to the time established by Allied headquarters at SHAEF, saying it was a story the world needed to know. European correspondents had a gentleman's agreement not to divulge the information until May 8, 1945, when it could be officially released.

Kennedy, George (1926–   )

Hollywood actor. He served under General George S. Patton in World War II. As an officer, Kennedy became a technical adviser to the Phil Silvers TV show and was given walk-on parts when the producers needed extras. This launched his acting career, in which he portrayed General Patton in the 1978 movie *Brass Target*.

Kennedy, John Fitzgerald (1917–1963)

Thirty-fifth President of the United States. During World War II, he commanded PT boats in the Pacific and was the skipper of *PT109* when it was rammed and sunk by the Japanese destroyer *Amagiri* in 1943. Kennedy was awarded the Navy and Marine Corps Medal "for extremely heroic conduct" in aiding the rescue of his crew. The citation was personally signed by Admiral William F. "Bull" Halsey.

MOVIE PORTRAYALS:

PT109 (1963), by Cliff Robertson
The Missils of October (1974), by William Devane
Young Joe The Forgotten Kennedy (1977 TV movie), by Sam Chew, Jr.
Johnny We Hardly Knew Ye (1977 TV movie), by Paul Rudd
King (1978 TV movie), by William Jordan
Jacqueline Bouvier Kennedy (1981 TV movie), by James Franciscus

Kennedy, Joseph R., Sr. (1888–1969)

U.S. ambassador to Britain. He was pro-Nazi and anti-British and told the King of England shortly after war was declared that it would bankrupt the country and that England should get out as soon as possible. In his travels to the U.S., Kennedy said that there were no moral issues involved, stating that Hitler would win the war. Kennedy was replaced in 1941 because of his defeatist attitude. He had exclusive distribution rights to Haig & Haig Whiskey and Gordon's Gin from Britain to the U.S., and the Russians felt he was influenced in his attitude by his quest for the dollar. His stand was so radical that his son John F. Kennedy was forced to clear himself of complicity during the race for the Presidency in 1960.

MOVIE PORTRAYAL:

Young Joe, The Forgotten Kennedy (1977 TV movie), by Stephen Elliott
Johnny, We Hardly Knew Ye (1977), by William Prince

Kennedy, Joseph P., Jr. (1915–1944)

Oldest brother of John F. Kennedy and son of Joseph P. Kennedy. He flew as a U.S. Navy lieutenant on antisubmarine patrols with the British Coastal Command. Kennedy volunteered for Operation Aphrodite after completing two full combat tours and was killed on August 12, 1944, when the explosive-laden B-24 he was flying blew up in the air. He was intending to aim the ship and bail out, leaving another aircraft to guide the B-24 via remote control to a German submarine pen on the French coast; it apparently exploded when he armed the switches. The photograph chase plane had President Franklin Roosevelt's son, Elliott Roosevelt, on board. Therefore, the son of one President watched the brother of a future President die. Kennedy was awarded a posthumous Navy Cross.

MOVIE PORTRAYAL:

Young Joe, The Forgotten Kennedy (1977 TV movie), by Peter Strauss (Lance Kerwin at age 14)

Kennedy, Robert F. (1925–1968)

Brother of John F. Kennedy. He dropped out of Harvard to join the U.S. Navy in World War II and served aboard the destroyer *Joseph P. Kennedy Jr.* which was named after his brother.

MOVIE PORTRAYALS:

The Missiles of October (1974 TV play), by Martin Sheen

Francis Gary Powers: The True Story of the U-2 Spy Incident (1976 TV movie), by Jim McMullen

The Private Files of J. Edgar Hoover (1977), by Michael Parks

Young Joe, The Forgotten Kennedy (1977 TV movie), by Lance Kerwin (Shane Kerwin as a boy)

King (1977 TV movie), by Cliff De Young

Tail Gunner Joe (1977 TV movie), by Sam Chew, Jr.

Kenney Cocktail

Nickname given to a bomb devised by General George C. Kenney, which was a standard 100-pound bomb filled with white phosphorus. When it burst, flaming material was hurled 150 feet in every direction, which was devastating both to aerodromes and to personnel.

Kenney, George C. (1889–1977)

U.S. Army Air Force general who commanded all Air Force units in the southwest Pacific in World War II. He had joined the Army as an enlisted man and progressed through the ranks to become an officer and fighter pilot. His flight on October 9, 1918, shot down Hermann Goering, and it is believed that Kenney was the one who actually hit Goering's airplane. During World War II, he devised such innovations as low-level parachute fragmentation bombs and skip bombing of Japanese shipping. Kenney was responsible for the complete reorganization of General Douglas MacArthur's air arm into a successful striking force. He was called "The Beast" by Radio Tokyo. His birthday was August 6, the day that the atomic bomb was dropped on Hiroshima.

MOVIE PORTRAYAL:
MacArthur (1977), by Walter O. Miles

Keppler, Wilhelm

Hitler's economic advisor throughout World War II. He was sentenced to ten years' imprisonment by the military tribunal at Nuremberg in 1946.

Kerling, Edward (1909–1942)

German spy who was landed in Florida on June 17, 1942, by *U-584* as part of Operation Pastorius. He had joined the Nazi party in 1928 and a year later emigrated to the U.S. Kerling returned to Germany in July 1940 and was trained as a spy. He was picked up by the FBI and executed on August 8, 1942.

Kerr, Ralph (–1940)

Royal Navy captain. He commanded the H.M.S. *Hood* when it was sunk by the *Bismarck* on May 24, 1940.

MOVIE PORTRAYAL:
Sink The Bismarck (1960), by John Stuart

Kersten, Felix (1898–1960)

Personal masseur to Heinrich Himmler. He lived in Stockholm, traveled to Berlin once a month, and was credited with saving tens of thousands of lives by interceding with Himmler. He supposedly saved three million Dutch men from deportation because he convinced Himmler that the strain would ruin his health. For this, Kersten was awarded Holland's highest medal after the war. Unfortunately, it has subsequently been proven that he fabricated the claims of saving lives in order to sell a book he had written.

Kesselring, Albert (1887–1960)

Luftwaffe general who commanded all Axis forces in Italy. He was a very versatile commander who was in charge of Luftwaffe units in the Battles of Britain and North Africa and later conducted an excellent defense of Italy. Kesselring was tried and convicted by the British for his part in the massacre of 335 Italians at Ardeatine Caves in Rome on May 23, 1944. He was sentenced to death, but this was commuted to twenty years' imprisonment. He only served five years, having been released in 1952 on medical grounds.

Movie portrayal:
Battle of Britain (1969), by Peter Hager

Kessler, Horst
German Navy commander of the submarine *U-704*. In late 1942, he fired four torpedoes at the *Queen Elizabeth* but missed due to the speed of the ocean liner. It was probably the only attempt of the war to sink a superliner.

Ketcham, Hank (1920–)
Cartoonist who created the comic strip *Dennis the Menace** in 1951. During World War II, he enlisted in the U.S. Navy and spent four years making animated cartoons to help sell war bonds.

Keyes, Geoffrey (1917–1941)
British Army lieutenant colonel and son of Admiral Roger Keyes, the head of British commandos. Young Keyes led a commando raid on Afrika Korps headquarters on November 17, 1941, in an attempt to kill Field Marshall Erwin Rommel. The raid failed because Rommel was in Athens, and Keyes was killed. Keyes was awarded the Victoria Cross posthumously.

Keyes, Roger (1872–1945)
British Admiral of the Fleet. He founded and headed the British commandos early in the war but was replaced in 1941 by Lord Louis Mountbatten.

"Khaki Bill"
Division song to which the U.S. 28th Infantry Division marched down the Champs Elysées in Paris on August 29, 1944. The Parisians wanted a victory parade and the 28th was en route to a battle on the other side of the city, so they were diverted through the city.

Khan, Aly (1911–)
Pakistani prince and United Nations Representative. He enlisted in the French Foreign Legion as a second lieutenant at the beginning of World War II but deserted after the French surrender to the

---

*In 1977 when actor Jay North, who had played Dennis the Menace on the successful TV series, joined the U.S. Navy, he was sworn in by Reserve Navy Captain Jackie Cooper.

Germans. Khan then joined the British Army intelligence unit in Jerusalem. He later became the liaison officer with the Free French Army and the U.S. Sixth Army and was discharged as a lieutenant colonel in 1945. At one time (1949–1951), he was married to actress Rita Hayworth.

Khozedub, Ivan N. (1920–)

Soviet Air Force major. He was the highest-scoring Russian ace of World War II, with 62 aircraft shot down.

Khomyakova, Valeria I.

Russian pilot. She was the first female ever to shoot down a bomber when, in September 1942, she downed a JU-88 over Saratov on the Volga river.

Khrushchev, Nikita (1894–1971)

Russian premier. During World War II, he was the political commissar responsible for the district around Stalingrad during the Battle of Stalingrad. Khrushchev later became a political member of the military council of the southern part of Kursk.

MOVIE PORTRAYAL:

The Missiles of October (1974 TV movie), by Howard da Silva

Francis Gary Powers: The True Story of the U-2 Spy Incident (1976 TV movie), by Thayer David

Kiangya, S.S.

Chinese steamer weighing 1,200 tons, which was sunk on December 3, 1948, by a Japanese mine left over from World War II. It killed nearly 3,000 people (see Chimara).

Kidd, Isaac Campbell (1884–1941)

U.S. Navy rear admiral who was the first admiral killed in action in World War II. As the commander of the battleships at Pearl Harbor, he was on the bridge of the U.S.S. *Arizona* when it was hit and exploded on December 7, 1941. His body still rests with the sunken ship, and he was awarded a posthumous Congressional Medal of Honor.

Kilroy Was Here

Graffiti used by American GI's around the world during World War II. It could be found on fences and buildings all over Europe. Kilroy was supposedly a U.S. Army sergeant who, after checking equipment, would write on it "Kilroy was here." In 1947, Jackie Cooper starred in the movie *Kilroy Was Here*.

Kimigayo

Title of the Japanese national anthem.

Kimmel, Husband E. (1882–1968)

U.S. Navy rear admiral. He commanded the U.S. Pacific Fleet at Pearl Harbor during the Japanese attack of December 7, 1941. A military investigation charged him and Lieutenant General Walter Short, his Army counterpart, with unpreparedness; both were relieved of command and retired shortly thereafter. Kimmel believed he was a scapegoat of a maneuver by President Franklin Roosevelt to get the U.S. into the war.

MOVIE PORTRAYAL:
Tora! Tora! Tora! (1970), by Martin Balsam

Kimmel, Manning (–1944)

Son of Admiral Husband Kimmel and nephew of Admiral Thomas Kinkaid. He served on U.S. submarines in World War II and commanded the U.S.S. *Robalo,* which struck a mine on July 26, 1944, in Balabac strait. Kimmel and several crewmembers made it to Palawan, where they attempted to find friendly guerrillas. Instead they were captured by the Japanese and imprisoned. After an Allied air attack, the infuriated Japanese pushed him and the others into a ditch, poured gasoline over them, and set them on fire.

Kimmel, Thomas

Son of Admiral Husband Kimmel. He served on submarines, made five war patrols aboard the *S-40*, and was later engineering officer on the U.S.S. *Balao*. He was removed from sea duty as a result of the loss of his brother Manning.

Kinashi, Takaichi (–1944)

Japanese Navy commander. He was the top-scoring Japanese commander of World War II and sank the carrier U.S.S. *Wasp*, as well as damaging the battleship U.S.S. *North Carolina* and the destroyer U.S.S. *O'Brian*. The *O'Brian* was lost while trying to get back to the U.S. for repairs. Kinashi was lost while trying to take *I-29* to Germany and back again in July 1944. He had made it as far as Singapore but was sunk four days after leaving it, when he was torpedoed by the submarine U.S.S. *Sawfish*.

King, Edward P. Jr. (1884–1958)

U.S. Army major general. He commanded all troops on Bataan and surrendered his forces to the Japanese on April 9, 1942. He was the cellmate of General Jonathan Wainwright in a Japanese prisoner-of-war camp.

King, Ernest J. (1878–1956)

U.S. Navy admiral. He was overall commander of U.S. Naval operations in World War II and held the dual posts of Chief of Naval Operations and Commander in Chief of the U.S. Fleet.

MOVIE PORTRAYALS:
The Gallant Hours (1960), by Tyler McVey
MacArthur (1977), by Russell D. Johnson

King George V, H.M.S.

British battleship that rammed the destroyer *Punjabi* accidentally, causing depth charges aboard the destroyer to explode under the *King George*, severely damaging it.

Kingpin

Code word used to refer to General Henri Giraud when he was moved from Gibraltar to North Africa in 1942.

King's Ransom

Name of the twelve-year-old whiskey that was the only whiskey served at the Potsdam Conference in July 1945. It was stocked by General Dwight Eisenhower's commissary and was therefore available for Potsdam.

King, William N.

U.S. Army enlisted man. He was the first U.S. soldier to become a paratrooper (1941).

Kinkaid, Thomas C. (1888–1972)

U.S. Navy Vice-Admiral. He commanded the Naval forces for the invasion of Attu Island on May 12, 1943, and later the U.S. Seventh Fleet in the Pacific. (He was the brother-in-law of Admiral Husband Kimmel.)

Kirby, George (1924–)

American black comedian who served in both Europe and the South Pacific during World War II.

Kirishima

Japanese ship that was the only battleship sunk in World War II by another battleship. The *Kirishima* was attacked November 15, 1942, by the U.S.S. *Washington* in the Battle of Guadalcanal.

Kirk, Alan G. (1888–1963)

U.S. Navy admiral. He was the Chief of Staff for U.S. Naval forces in Europe during World War II and commanded the U.S. Navy in the D-Day landings of June 6, 1944, from the cruiser *Augusta*. Kirk had been naval attaché in London from 1939 to 1941.

MOVIE PORTRAYAL:
The Longest Day (1962), by John Mellon

Kisaragi

First Japanese destroyer sunk in World War II. It was bombed and sent to the bottom by Grumman fighters during the battle of Wake Island on December 11, 1941. A bomb detonated the depth charges stored on deck. The second ship sunk was the *Hayate*.

Kiser, Walter W.

U.S. Marine Corps second lieutenant. He was the first American parachute officer killed in action in World War II; he died on Gavutu in 1942.

Kiska

Aleutian island. It was taken by the Japanese in 1942 and in return invaded by U.S. forces, who expected a major battle, on August 15, 1943. Rear Admiral Masatomi Kimura had used two cruisers and six destroyers to evacuate the 5,200 Japanese troops in less than an hour on July 28, 1943, in thick fog. When U.S. troops landed there was nothing left of the last Japanese foothold in North America.

Kissinger, Henry A. (1923–   )

U.S. Secretary of State. He and his family fled Nazi Germany in 1933. Kissinger served in the U.S. Army in World War II as a German interpreter for the commanding officer of the 84th Infantry Division during the Battle of the Bulge. He later served with military intelligence and was awarded a Bronze Star. He was discharged in 1946 as a sergeant. His serial number was 32-816-775.

Kisters, Gerry

U.S. Army sergeant. He was the first person to win both a Congressional Medal of Honor and a Distinguish Service Cross. The DSC was awarded by General George C. Marshall in May 1943, for combat in North Africa. Kister was awarded the CMH by President Franklin D. Roosevelt on June 21, 1943, for fighting in Sicily.

Kittel, Otto (1917–1945)

Luftwaffe fighter pilot and fourth-highest-scoring ace in history with 267 victories, all of which were on the Eastern Front. He was killed on February 14, 1945, in aerial combat.

Kitty

Name that Anne Frank gave to her diary. She began each entry with "Dear Kitty."

Kitty Salon
Name of a brothel set up in Berlin by the S.S. for foreign dignitaries. The S.S. bugged the rooms and received valuable intelligence from the customers' indiscretions. Count Ciano, the Italian Foreign Minister, was one who paid with his life for talking too much at the Kitty Salon.

Klakring, Thomas B.
U.S. Navy officer and commander of the submarine U.S.S. *Guardfish*. He is credited with the longest torpedo shot of the war; he fired 7,500 yards to sink a Japanese freighter anchored in a harbor on September 4, 1942.

Klaus, Josef (1910–)
Chancellor of Austria. During World War II, he served as a lieutenant in the German infantry and ended up as an Allied prisoner of war. His father, Mathias Klaus, had been a POW in World War I.

Kleindienst, Richard G. (1923–)
Former Attorney General of the U.S. In World War II, he served as a navigator with the Fifteenth Army Air Force in Italy.

von Kleist, Paul (1881–1954)
German field marshall who commanded German forces in France, Russia, and Yugoslavia. Von Kleist was captured in 1945 in Mitterfels by two GI's from the 26th Infantry Division. In 1948, he was tried before a Yugoslavian court for war crimes and sentenced to fifteen years' imprisonment. Shortly after the verdict, he was turned over to the Russians; he died in a Soviet prison on November 5, 1954.

Klim
Name given to the powdered milk used by American forces throughout World War II. *Klim* is *milk* spelled backwards.

von Kluge, Hans G. (1882–1944)
German field marshall. He was removed by Hitler on August 18, 1944, due to the rapidly deteriorating situation in France. Von Kluge wrote a note advocating ending the war and then shot himself.

Knatchbull-Hugessen, Sir Hughe (1886–1971)
British ambassador to Turkey during World War II. He was the person who dispatched the declaration-of-war telegram to Germany on August 3, 1914. His valet was Elyesa Bazna, one of the most successful spies of the war, who was known to the Germans as Cicero.

Knickebein Beacon

Name given to a German guidance system for bombers used early in the war. It emitted medium-frequency radio beams for the bombers to follow. They released their bombs when two beams crossed, indicating that they were over their targets. The British, using the Germans' own system, developed a direction finder that told them what the German target would be. The British also developed a method of deflecting the beams so that the Germans would release their bombs over unpopulated areas. The name Knickebein was taken from a German fairy-tale character, a crow that could fly at night.

Knight, Eric (1897–1943)

Novelist who wrote *Lassie Come Home* in 1940. He had been a private in the Canadian Army during World War I and enlisted in the U.S. Army in World War II. Major Knight was killed in a plane crash in 1943 while en route to North Africa.

Knight, Ted

Television actor born Tadewurz Wladziu Konopka. He was awarded five Bronze Stars while serving in World War II.

Knight's Cross

Highest decoration awarded by Germany in World War II. Hitler had said that anyone who had been awarded the oak leaves to the Knight's Cross would be given an estate in conquered countries after the war.

Knox, Alfred Dilwyn (–1943)

Britain's chief cryptographer. He discovered the position of the German pocket battleship *Bismarck* while sick in bed but still decoding intercepted German messages.

Knox, Frank (1874–1944)

U.S. Secretary of the Navy. He had been one of Teddy Roosevelt's Rough Riders in the Spanish-American War of 1898 and also fought in France in World War I. His daughter Elyse Knox was a movie actress from 1921 to 1950 and married football star Tom Harmon.

MOVIE PORTRAYAL:

Tora! Tora! Tora! (1970), by Leon Ames

Knox, Jean (1908–   )

Commander of the British Auxiliary Territorial Service in World War II. She was the first female to become a major general in British history.

Knutsford Affair

Name given to General George S. Patton's indiscretion of referring to the American and British "destinies to rule the world" after World War II. By a slip of the lip, he left both France and Russia out and, therefore, insulted both. For this Patton was severely reprimanded by General Dwight Eisenhower.

Koch, Ilse (1907–1967)

Wife of the Nazi camp commandant of Buchenwald concentration camp. She was known as the "Bitch of Buchenwald" due to her cruelty to the prisoners and was sentenced to life imprisonment after the war. Koch committed suicide in Aichach women's prison in Bavaria in September 1967.

Koch, Karl (–1945)

Nazi commandant of Buchenwald concentration camp from 1937 to 1942. He was convicted of graft and corruption by the Nazis in 1945 and was executed by his fellow S.S. men.

Koenig, Pierre (1898–1970)

French Foreign Legion General. He commanded Foreign Legionnaires in Norway in 1940 and later in France. Koenig escaped from collapsing France in 1940 via Normandy and commanded the Free French Forces at the Battle of Bir Hacheim. He later commanded the French Resistance.

Koischwitz, Max Otto

Nazi and propagandist during World War II. He had become a naturalized U.S. citizen in 1935 but returned to Germany in 1939. Koischwitz broadcast under the aliases of "Dr. Anders" and "Mr. O.K." He was indicted by a Federal Grand Jury in July 1942.

Kokoda Trail

Name of the route across the Owen Stanley Mountains of New Guinea from Buna to Port Moresby. The Japanese landed at Buna on July 22, 1942, and began crossing the rugged mountains toward Port Moresby. Their advance was stopped short because troops were needed at Guadalcanal, so that they withdrew to Buna.

Kokorev, D. V.

Soviet sub-lieutenant who is credited with the first heroic act of the Russo-German War. As a pilot with the 124th Fighter Regiment flying Rata fighters, Kokorev rammed an ME-110 in a dog fight after his guns jammed.

Kolbe, Fritz

Member of the German Foreign Ministry. Under the code name "Wood," he supplied information to Allen Dulles in Bern that concerned itself with German diplomatic and Wehrmacht intelligence.

Komet

German auxiliary armed merchant ship that accounted for 31,005 tons of Allied shipping in the Atlantic and Pacific Oceans in World War II. It was commanded by Captain Robert Eyssen from July 3, 1940, until November 30, 1941, when the *Komet* returned to Hamburg. Captain Ulrich Brocksien took command on October 14, 1942, for its second voyage which ended with its sinking off Cap de la Hague. The Germans designated it as HSK VII or Ship 45.

Kondor Mission

Code name given to a German intelligence network set up in Cairo behind British lines. Two agents, John Eppler and Peter Monkaster, were aided by the Egyptian Free Officers' Movement in sending information back to Field Marshall Erwin Rommel that contributed to his numerous defeats of the British Army. They established their headquarters on a river boat in the Nile and used the novel *Rebecca* by Daphne du Maurier as their cipher base. The British eventually apprehended the pair and imprisoned them. After the war, Eppler took the West German Government to court for back wages but was never paid for his services.

Konev, Ivan S. (1897–1973)

Marshall of the Soviet Union. He was one of Russia's most capable generals of World War II and commanded the Second Ukrainian front in 1943. Konev also was in charge of the forces that captured Prague in 1945.

Kongo

Japanese battleship that participated in the attack on Pearl Harbor on December 7, 1941. It also fought in the Battle of Leyte Gulf in 1944. The *Kongo* was sunk by the U.S. submarine *Sealion*, commanded by Eli Reich, on November 21, 1944, while en route to Japan. It was the only Japanese battleship sunk by a U.S. submarine in World War II.

Konstantinov

Code name used by Marshall Zhukov in personal correspondence to Joseph Stalin.

Koons, Franklin M.

U.S. Army corporal. He was the first American to land in

France in World War II and the first one to kill a German when he landed as a U.S. Ranger with the Dieppe Raid in 1942. Koons was awarded the British Military Medal for bravery.

K Operation

Japanese plan to bomb Hawaii. Two flying boats flew from Japan to the French Frigate Shoals between the Marshall Islands and Hawaii, where they refueled from submarines. On March 3, 1942, they flew to Oahu where they were to bomb a pier; but due to cloud cover, one dropped his bombs at sea and the other dropped his to the east of Honolulu. Both planes escaped safely.

Koralle

Name of Admiral Karl Doenitz's headquarters complex twenty miles east of Berlin.

Korensky, Elizabeth (–1943)

U.S. Seaman Second Class. She was the first WAVE killed in the line of duty, when a load of depth charges were set off by a fire on a trailer at Norfolk Naval Air Station in September 1943.

Kormoran

German Naval auxiliary cruiser that sank eleven ships for a total of 68,274 tons. It was known to the Allies as "Raider G" and designated by the Germans as HSK VII or Ship 41. On November 19, 1941, the *Kormoran* deceived the Australian heavy cruiser *Sydney* into coming alongside for a search of her cargo and engaged the cruiser at close range. The *Kormoran* sank the *Sydney* but was so heavily damaged that it had to be scuttled.

Korten, Gunther (1898–1944)

German Luftwaffe general. He replaced General Hans Jeschonnek as Chief of Staff of the Luftwaffe after his suicide in 1943. Korten was killed by the bomb that was meant for Hitler on July 20, 1944.

Kos

Island in the Aegean Sea off the coast of Turkey. It was occupied by British troops, who were then attacked by German paratroopers and mountain troops in October 1943. The British were finally forced to surrender on November 16, 1943. It was the last time British troops surrendered to German paratroopers. The loss of the island kept Turkey from joining the Allies, because they still viewed Germany as a dangerous military force.

Kosciusko Division

Polish Division that fought with the Russians in World War II. It was recruited from former Polish prisoners of war and Polish citizens living in exile in the USSR.

Kraft durch Freude

"Strength through joy." This was the name of the Nazi workers' organization that replaced unions and gave the workers many socialist benefits. One of the most noteworthy of the organization's plans was the provision of vacations to other areas of Europe for German workers who would not have been able to afford them on their own.

Kragujevac

Yugoslavian town where 7,000 men, women, and children were massacred by the Germans on October 21, 1941, in reprisal for their attacks on the Germans.

Kramer, Josef (1906–1945)

German S.S. commandant of Belsen concentration camp. He was known as the "Beast of Belsen" and was tried for war crimes and executed in November 1945.

Kramer, Stanley (1913–   )

Hollywood producer. He enlisted in the U.S. Army in 1942 and made training films for the Signal Corps. Kramer was discharged as a first lieutenant.

K Ration

Designator of U.S. field rations originally designed for use by airborne forces. They consisted of a breakfast box, a dinner box, and a supper box, each containing concentrated foods. Each box had fortified biscuits, canned meat, malted milk tablets, and chewing gum, as well as coffee and sugar in the breakfast box, boullion paste in the dinner box, and lemonade powder in the supper box. The K Ration was named by American physiologist Ancel Keyes.

Krebs, Hans (1898–1945)

German general. He was the last Chief of Staff of the Wehrmacht and committed suicide by taking potassium cyanide in the Reich Chancellery in Berlin in May 1945.

MOVIE PORTRAYAL:

Hitler: The Last Ten Days (1973), by Adolfo Celi

Kreipe, Karl

German general who was a divisional commander on Crete. He was kidnapped from occupied Crete in April 1944 by Major Patrick Leigh-Fermor and Captain W. Stanley Moss, who then drove past German sentries in the general's staff car wearing his hat. Kreipe was later spirited off to Cairo after hiding out for twenty days on Crete. After the war, Kreipe was quite thankful for the kidnapping because his two fellow generals were both executed by the Greeks.

Kreisau Circle

Name given to an anti-Hitler conspiracy group led by Helmuth von Moltke. It met on his estate of Kreisau. The members advocated the overthrow of Hitler but not the use of violence. Most of them were killed by the S.S. after the abortive July 20, 1944, attempt on Hitler's life.

Kretschmer, Otto (1912–)

German lieutenant commander and top-scoring submarine ace of World War II. Kretschmer is credited with sinking forty-four ships, including a destroyer, for a total of 266,629 tons. While attacking the convoy HX112 in March 1941, he was forced by the H.M.S. *Walker* to the surface, where gunfire disabled his submarine, the *U-99*. Kretschmer and thirty-nine other men were taken prisoner. He was sent to a prisoner-of-war camp in Canada, where he was awarded the swords to the Knight's Cross by the camp commandant of the Bowmanville POW camp. Kretschmer returned to Germany in 1948.

Kriegies

Nickname that Allied prisoners of war called themselves while in German captivity. It came from the German word for prisoner of war, *Kriegsgefangener.*

Kriegsmarine

Name of the German Navy.

Krueger, Walter (1881–1967)

U.S. Army general. He commanded the U.S. Sixth Army in the Pacific and masterminded fifteen amphibious landings from New Guinea to the Philippines. Krueger was born in Prussia and entered the U.S. Army as a private during the Spanish-American War. He was not from West Point but rather graduated from the U.S. Naval War College and was a very conservative, even overly cautious commander. General Douglas MacArthur threatened to relieve him on several occasions.

Movie portrayal:
MacArthur (1977), by Everett Cooper

Krupp, Alfried (1908–1967)

German industrialist. He was head of the Krupp Works from 1943 until the end of the war and was sentenced to twelve years' imprisonment at Nuremberg for taking over industrial concerns in occupied countries and for exploiting foreign workers, POW's, and concentration camp inmates. Krupp was released in the early 1950's because of the tensions of the Cold War and the need of the Allies for a strong Germany. He began manufacturing weapons again as his family had done for generations.

K Sites

British decoy airfields constructed around England to draw German aircraft away from real airfields.

K Tablet

Designator of a drug used by the OSS to knock out its victims but not kill them.

Kube, Wilhelm (–1943)

German commissioner general of Byelorussia during the German occupation. He was notorious for his attitude of treating the Russians as sub-human, yet he kept a harem of Russian women as part of his entourage. One of these women, Galya Mazanik, in September 1943, as a protest for her spurned love, put an antipersonnel mine in his bed that blew him away.

Kubelwagen

German name for the Volkswagen jeep used extensively throughout World War II. It meant "roadster."

Kublis, Jan (–1942)

Czechoslovakian who was trained in England to assassinate Reinhard Heydrich. Kublis and Joseph Gablitz were parachuted into Czechoslovakia in 1942 and attacked Heydrich in Prague on May 26, 1942. Although they failed to kill him initially, he did die as a result of internal injuries several days later. Kublis and Gablitz hid out in Charles Borremeau Church in Prague, were betrayed by Korel Curda, and died in a battle with the Germans. Curda was later killed by the Czech underground.

Kuhl, Charles H. (1916–1971)

U.S. Army private who was slapped by General George S. Patton on August 3, 1943, on Sicily. He was the first of two soldiers whom Patton attempted to shame into returning to the battle. He thought they were malingering, but afterwards Kuhl was found to have had a temperature of 102.2°, diarrhea, and malaria. His serial number was ASN 35536908. (The second person slapped was Private Paul Bennett.)

MOVIE PORTRAYAL:
Patton (1970), by Tim Considine

Kuhn, Fritz (1896–1951)

American Nazi and head of the German American Bund prior to World War II. He was imprisoned during the war and deported to Germany afterwards.

Kuhn, Otto

German who worked as a spy for the Japanese in Pearl Harbor. He was recruited in Tokyo in 1936 and went to Hawaii where he was a dormant spy until October 1941; he then began sending information on U.S. Navy ships and installations back to the Japanese.

Kukris

Name of the official knife carried by the Gurkhas in the British army. Once it was taken out of the sheath, it had to draw blood before it could be replaced. The Gurkhas, if asked to see the knife, would cut their own thumbs so that they could put it back.

Kummetz, Oskar

German Navy rear admiral and inspector of torpedoes. At the outbreak of the war, German torpedoes had at least a thirty percent failure rate. Ironically, Kummetz was on board the cruiser *Blucher* when it was sunk by two Norwegian torpedoes in Oslo Fiord in April 1940.

Kursk

Russian railway junction and industrial center. It was the site of the greatest clash of armor in history, July 5 to July 22, 1943, which involved over 1,300,000 men, 3,600 tanks, 20,000 guns, and 3,130 aircraft. The Germans used over one hundred divisions and lost over a half-million men and 1,500 tanks. The Russians were able to set up a defense in depth at the point of attack because of information received from the Lucy spy ring in Switzerland. The battle marked the real turning point on the Eastern Front; the Russians went on the offensive and the Germans were reduced to defensive maneuvers until the end of the war.

Kurusu, Saburo (1888–1954)

Japanese special envoy to Washington in November 1941 who attempted to convince the U.S. to accept Japanese dominance in the Far East. As the Japanese ambassador to Germany, Kurusu had signed the Tripartite Pact of September 27, 1940, whereby

Japan joined the Axis powers. Kurusu was married to an American; after the outbreak of the war, his son, who was a Japanese military pilot, made a forced landing with mechanical problems and was beaten to death by Japanese peasants who thought he was an American pilot.

Kusaba, Sueki

Japanese major general. He commanded the Japanese effort to bomb the U.S. using high-altitude ballons launched into the jet stream from Japan. Known as FUGO, this constant threat was the second-best-kept secret of World War II by the Allies. The first was the atomic bomb.

Kutschera, Franz

S.S. commander of Warsaw who was sentenced to death in the middle of the war by the Polish Home Army. Nine men assassinated him, using machine guns and grenades.

Kuznetsov, Nikolai G. (1902–1974)

Soviet Admiral and Commander in Chief of the Navy in World War II.

Kwajelein

Island of the Marshall Islands group. It is the largest atoll in the world and was a Japanese possession for twenty-four years prior to its assault by U.S. forces on January 31, 1944, as part of Operation Flintlock.

L

L

Designator of the largest Japanese espionage ring in the world. Located in Mexico City, it was headed by Tsuneo Wachi, the Naval attaché. It was the job of L to keep an eye on the U.S. Fleet maneuvers in the Atlantic ocean. Wachi later commanded Japanese Naval forces on Iwo Jima from February to October 1944.

Laconia

British ship that was sunk September 12, 1942, by the German submarine *U-156* while transporting between 1,400 and 1,800 Italian prisoners of war to Canada. Captain Hartenstein of the *U-156* decided to rescue as many of the survivors, who included many women and children, as possible, and began broadcasting in plain language asking for assistance from any ships in the area. He also displayed a Red Cross banner and took several lifeboats in tow but was attacked by a B-24 and nearly sunk. Another German submarine was also bombed later while trying to save some of the people. From this time on German submarines made no attempts to rescue shipwrecked survivors.

Ladbroke

Code name of the British airborne attack on Sicily in July 1943 that included a glider landing near Syracuse.

Ladd, Alan (1913–1964)

Hollywood actor, five feet, four inches tall, who was drafted into the U.S. Army Air Force at the height of his career. Cecil B. DeMille announced his induction over the "Lux Radio Theater" on January 25, 1943. Ladd made training and propaganda films while in the service, in addition to conducting savings bond drives. He was medically discharged in November 1943 as a corporal, never having left the States.

Lady Be Good

Name of a B-24* of the Ninth Army Air Force in World War II. It was piloted by Lieutenant William J. Hatton and, on the crew's first mission from Soluch to Naples, was given a bum steer from a ground-based d.f. and crashed in the Libyan desert on April 4, 1943. The crew survived the crash but died of thirst, and were listed as missing in action. On November 9, 1953, the aircraft was sighted by a geologist, Ronald MacLean, and found in nearly perfect condition. The disappearance of the *Lady Be Good* and its crew was finally solved and the bodies of the men given military burials.

Ladybird

Name of a British gunboat on the Yangtze River that was attacked by Japanese aircraft during the attack on the U.S.S. *Panay* in December 1937.

Lady Lex

Nickname given to the U.S. aircraft carrier *Lexington*.

Lafayette, U.S.S.

New name given to the French ocean liner *Normandie* before it burned at dockside in New York harbor on February 9, 1942.

Laffey, U.S.S.

U.S. destroyer that was hit by six *kamikaze* aircraft and four bombs in 80 minutes on April 16, 1945, off Okinawa. It survived.

La Guardia, Fiorello (1882–1947)

Mayor of New York City whose nickname was "the Little Flower." He was a U.S. aviator in Italy during World War I and made many radio broadcasts to the Italians during World War II, asking them to overthrow Mussolini and join the Allies.

MOVIE PORTRAYAL:

The Amazing Howard Hughes (1978 TV movie), by Sorrell Booke

Lamarr, Hedy (1915–   )

Hollywood actress who coinvented a torpedo guidance system that was evaluated by the U.S. Navy in World War II but never adopted. While a young actress in Europe, Hedy Lamarr, born

*Named for the 1941 musical movie *Lady Be Good* directed by Norman Z. McLeod and starring Eleanor Powell, Ann Sothern, and Robert Young.

Hedwig Eva Maria Kiesler, had been present at parties attended by both Adolf Hitler and Benito Mussolini.

Lammerding, Heinz (1905–1971)

German general in command of the S.S. Division *Das Reich*. He was sentenced to death *in absentia* after the war for the massacre of French civilians at Oradour-sur-Glane in 1944. Lammerding disappeared at the end of the war and was finally located in Bad Tolz. France repeatedly asked for his extradition but it was refused by the West German government.

Lammers, Hans H. (1879–1962)

Chief of the Reich Chancellery in Berlin until 1945. He was sentenced to twenty years in prison at Nuremberg, but was released in 1952.

L'Amour, Louis (1908–)

Prolific writer of western stories. During World War II, he served as a member of the U.S. Army and landed at Normandy on D-Day, June 6, 1944. L'Amour was an officer in charge of a tank destroyer.

Lancaster, Burt (1913–)

Hollywood actor who was drafted into the U.S. Army in 1942 and was assigned to the Special Services Division of the Fifth Army as an entertainer. Lancaster served in North Arica, Italy, and Austria until 1945.

Landing Craft Designators (U.S. Navy)

LCA—landing craft, assault
LCC—landing craft, control
LCF—landing craft, flak
LC (FF)—landing craft, flotilla flagship
LCI—landing craft, infantry
LCI (L)—landing craft, infantry (large)
LCM—landing craft, mechanized
LCP—landing craft, personnel
LCR—landing craft, rubber
LCS—landing craft, support
LCS (S)—landing craft, support (small)
LCT—landing craft, tank
LCT (R)—landing craft, tank (rocket)
LCV—landing craft, vehicle
LCVP—landing craft, vehicle, personnel
LSD—landing ship, dock
LSM—landing ship, medium

LSM (R)—landing ship, medium (rocket)
LST—landing ship, tank
LST (H)—landing ship, tank (hospital)
LSV—landing ship, vehicle
LVT—landing vehicle, tracked

Landry, Tom (1924–)

Football coach of the Dallas Cowboys. During World War II, he flew as a copilot in bombers with the Eighth Army Air Force in England, recording thirty combat missions over Europe. Landry survived a crash landing of his B-17 in France that sheared off both of the aircraft's wings.

Lang, Herman

German-born final inspector of the top secret Norden bombsight in the Carl L. Norden Incorporated plant in Manhattan. He turned the plans over to the Germans in 1938, so that one of the most guarded secrets of the U.S. in World War II was actually known by the enemy long before the war.

Langley, U.S.S. (CV–1)

The U.S. Navy's first aircraft carrier, which was converted from the collier U.S.S. *Jupiter* in 1920 by the addition of a flight deck. By the beginning of World War II, the *Langley* was old and slow and the Navy cut her flight deck in half and made her into a seaplane tender, which could haul aircraft but not launch them. Early in 1942, the *Langley* was packed with aircraft and sent to Java to aid the Dutch but it was torpedoed and crippled by the Japanese submarine *I-25*. Japanese bombers found and sank her on February 27, 1942. The *Langley* was affectionately called "Old Covered Wagon."

Langsdorff, Hans (1890–1939)

German admiral in command of the pocket battleship *Graf Spee*. He attacked and sank many British merchant ships without a single loss of life. The *Graf Spee* was attacked by three British cruisers in the Battle of the Plate River in December 1939 and Langsdorf sought refuge in Montevideo Harbor, Uruguay. After being ordered to leave the harbor, Langsdorff scuttled the ship and committed suicide on December 19, 1939.

Lansdowne, U.S.S.

U.S. Navy destroyer that took the eleven Japanese delegates from Tokyo to the battleship U.S.S. *Missouri* for the signing of the surrender on September 2, 1915. It was named after Commander Zachary Lansdowne, the officer in charge of the U.S. Navy dirigible *Shenandoah* who was killed in its crash in September, 1925.

Lanikai, U.S.S.

Schooner commissioned into the U.S. Navy December 4, 1941, in Manila by order of President Franklin Roosevelt. The *Lanikai* was commanded by Lieutenant Kemp Tolley and manned by both Filipino and U.S. Navy personnel. It was assigned to Cam Ranh Bay, Vietnam, to serve as a picket ship to keep a watch on the Japanese fleet. It is believed that Roosevelt hoped the Japanese would fire on the *Lanikai* and provoke an incident so that the U.S. could enter the war. The mission became superfluous after the attack on Pearl Harbor on December 7, 1941.

Lanphier, Charlie

Brother of Tom Lanphier (see below). Charlie Lanphier was shot down in his Marine Corsair on September 11, 1943, during a raid of Kahili airfield near the spot where Yamamoto was killed. Lanphier died in a prison camp at Rabaul two weeks before it was liberated by U.S. Marines.

Lanphier, Thomas G. (1915–)

U.S. Army Air Force captain who is credited with shooting down Admiral Isoruku Yamamoto's Betty bomber April 18, 1943. In the confusion of the air battle, it was questionable whether Lanphier or Lieutenant Rex T. Barber actually shot down the aircraft, but Lanphier was given the credit and awarded the Navy Cross. When he landed after the mission, one of those present in the crowd was Lieutenant (j.g.) John F. Kennedy.

MOVIE PORTRAYAL:

The Gallant Hours (1960), by William Schallert

Lashio

Western terminus of the Burma Road which was occupied by the Japanese on April 29, 1942, thus cutting off all Allied overland supplies to China.

Last and First

Colonel Walter Bayler—last American off Wake Island in 1941; the first American to return in 1945.

Larry Lesueur—last American to broadcast from a free Paris in June 10, 1940; the first American to broadcast from a liberated Paris August 25, 1944.

Raymond Sarniguet—man who lowered the last French flag on the Eiffel Tower June 13, 1940, and raised the first French flag from the Eiffel Tower August 25, 1944.

Last D-Day

Name given to the assault on Balikpapan, Borneo, July 1, 1945.

"Last Time I Saw Paris, The"

Ballad written by Oscar Hammerstein II and Jerome Kern in 1940 and inspired by the Nazi invasion of Paris that same year.

Latham, Mrs. Wales,

Woman who founded the organization Bundles for Britain on January 15, 1940.

Laval, Pierre (1883–1945)

Vichy French premier under Marshall Philippe Petain during World War II. He had refused to volunteer for service in World War I because of varicose veins. He did, however, collaborate with the Nazis throughout World War II. Laval was shot by a would-be assassin in 1941 but survived. After the war he fled to Spain but voluntarily returned to France because he felt he had done nothing wrong. Laval was tried and sentenced to death, attempted suicide by biting a cyanide capsule but was revived so that he could be shot an hour later on October 15, 1945, wearing a white tie, which had been his personal symbol.

Lawson, Ted W. (1917–)

U.S. Army Air Force captain. He flew the seventh plane to depart the carrier *Hornet* as part of the Doolittle Raid on Tokyo on April 18, 1942. He flew a B-25 named *Ruptured Duck*. It had a picture of Donald Duck with crutches, which proved prophetic for Lawson because his leg had to be amputated as a result of injuries sustained in the crash of his aircraft. He wrote the book *Thirty Seconds over Tokyo* and served as a consultant on the 1944 movie of the same name. Van Johnson portrayed Lawson in the film.

Laycock, Sir Robert E. (1907–1980)

British major general who organized one of the first commando forces in the British army in 1940, known as Layforce. He led the unit on raids behind enemy lines in Greece, Crete, and North Africa. Laycock commanded the assassination attempt against Field Marshall Erwin Rommel for which Geoffrey Keyes was awarded a posthumous Victoria Cross. Laycock and a sergeant were the only survivors. He took over command of Combined Operations from Lord Mountbatten, becoming the youngest major general in the British Army (see "Wind in the Willows").

LCT (R)

Landing craft developed after the Dieppe Raid of 1942. It could fire 1,080 rockets onto a beachhead in 26 seconds, thereby matching the firepower of 80 Naval cruisers firing simultaneously.

L Detachment

Designator of the British unit set up by David Sterling in North Africa in 1941 to harass the enemy by conducting commando raids behind their lines. It was part of SAS, Special Air Service, which did not really exist at the time but was a dummy unit to deceive the enemy.

L Documents

Telegrams sent by Allen Dulles from Switzerland to inform key people about the progress of the Schwarze Kapelle in their conspiracy against Hitler.

Leahy, William (1875–1959)

U.S. Navy fleet admiral. He served as Chief of U.S. Naval Operations in 1937, ambassador to Vichy France from 1940 to 1941, and later Chief of Staff to Presidents Franklin Roosevelt and Harry S Truman in World War II.

MOVIE PORTRAYAL:
MacArthur (1977), by John McKee

Lear, Norman (1922–   )

Hollywood television producer. During World War II, he served as a radio operator in the Fifteenth Army Air Force at Foggia, Italy. Lear flew 57 combat missions.

Leatherneck

Slang term for a U.S. Marine.

Leber, Julius

German socialist who was executed in the aftermath of the attempt on Hitler's life of July 20, 1944. He greatly influenced a young boy whom he believed showed potential. The boy was Willy Brandt, who fled to Norway from the Nazis and became in 1968 the first Socialist chancellor of Germany since 1930.

LeClerc, Philippe (1902–1947)

French major general. LeClerc was not his real name but was assumed to protect his wife and six children in German-occupied France. His real name was Philippe François Marie LeClerc de Hautecloque and he commanded the Free French 2nd Armored Division that liberated Paris in August 1944. LeClerc also was the French representative on board the U.S.S. *Missouri* for the Japanese surrender Spetember 2, 1945. He was born on November 28 and died in a plane crash on November 28.

MOVIE PORTRAYAL:
Is Paris Burning? (1966), by Claude Rich

Ledo Road

Road from China to India built by Lieutenant General Lewis Andrew Pick, who was Chief of the U.S. Army engineers. It was built to establish a land route to Kunming and was opened on January 26, 1945. General Pick led the first convoy, so the troops nicknamed it Pick's Pike. Chiang Kai-shek renamed it the Stilwell Road after General Joseph Stilwell.

Lee, Christopher (1922–)

British actor. He flew with the Royal Air Force in World War II and was decorated by the Czech, Yugoslavian, Polish, and British governments.

Lee, Ernest (Tex)

U.S. Army officer. As a captain, he was aide to General Dwight Eisenhower in World War II.

MOVIE PORTRAYAL:
Ike (1979 TV movie), by Paul Gleason

Lee, John C. H. (1887–1958)

U.S. Army general. He was deputy theater commander to General Dwight Eisenhower for the D-Day landings and commander of the Allied supply network. Lee was nicknamed "Courthouse Lee" by his staff and "Jesus Christ Himself" by the troops, taken from his initials.

Lee, William C. (1895–1948)

U.S. Army major general called the father of American airborne forces.

Lee, Willis A., Jr. (1888–1945)

U.S. Navy admiral credited with saving Guadalcanal while in command of a task force. He later became second-in-command to Admiral William F. Halsey and was nicknamed "Ching Lee" by his men. Lee died of a heart attack on board his ship on August 25, 1945.

von Leeb, Wilhelm Ritter (1876–1956)

German field marshall. He commanded the Bavarian artillery unit that stopped Hitler and the Munich Beer Hall Putsch in 1923. Von Leeb commanded an Army unit in the takeover of Czechoslovakia, Army Group C in the invasion of France, and Army Group North for the attack on Russia. He was retired after failing to capture Leningrad. Von Leeb was sentenced to three years' imprisonment by the Nuremberg Tribunal in 1948 and released because he had already been in prison for three years awaiting trial.

Leese, Sir Oliver W. H. (1894–1978)

British general. He escaped from Dunkirk in 1940 and commanded British forces in North Africa, Sicily, and Italy. Leese was one of the most capable generals the British had. From 1944 to 1945, he commanded in Southeast Asia.

Legion of Merit

U.S. medal established July 20, 1942, by Congress. It was awarded in four grades with the top two grades going only to foreign dignitaries. Chiang Kai-shek received the first Chief Commander medal. Brazillian General Amaro Bettencourt received the first Commander medal. U.S. Army Captain Ralph B. Praeger received the first medal. Lieutenant Colonel Westray Battle Boyce was the first woman to be awarded the Legion of Merit.

Lehand, Marguerite "Missy" (–1944)

Nurse to President Franklin Roosevelt. According to his son Elliott Roosevelt, Lehand was also FDR's mistress. She died of a stroke eight months before FDR died from the same thing.

MOVIE PORTRAYAL:
Eleanor and Franklin: The White House Years (1977 TV movie), by Priscilla Pointer

Leigh-Mallory, Trafford (1892–1944)

British Royal Air Force Vice-Marshall. He commanded No. 12 Group that protected the midlands of England during the Battle of Britain. He advocated employing large wings of fighters to attack German formations. This was in opposition to Air Vice-Marshall Keith Park, who used small groups in order to save his fighters. Leigh Mallory later replaced Park as commander of No. 11 Group as the Battle of Britain decreased in ferocity. He was killed in an aircraft crash in France in 1944 while en route to a new command in Southeast Asia.

MOVIE PORTRAYAL:
Battle of Britain (1969), by Patrick Wymark

Leipzig

German light cruiser that was torpedoed on December 13, 1939, by the British submarine H.M.S. *Salmon*. It made it back to port, where it was repaired. The *Leipzig* was accidentally rammed by the *Prinz Eugen* and nearly cut in half on October 15, 1944, in the Baltic. It survived the war only to be sunk by the British in the North Sea with a load of poison gas.

Leiser, Ernest

Newspaperman for *Stars and Stripes* in World War II. He went with Mack Morris into Berlin riding in a jeep in the third week of April 1945, but encountered no opposition. Their escapade made it appear possible for U.S. forces to have captured Berlin before the Russians.

Lemay, Curtis (1906–   )

U.S. Army Air Force general. He commanded bomber forces in England and the Pacific in World War II. In England, he concluded that too many bombers were missing targets by zigzagging away from flak, so he led the next mission over Saint-Nazaire. LeMay held his aircraft in a straight line through the flak which he simply ignored. The next day he ordered his planes to no longer take evasive action on the final bomb run. Losses increased but so did bombing accuracy. LeMay led the first shuttle bombing mission from England to North Africa and bombed Regensburg while en route, August 17, 1943. In Japan, he removed the defensive guns and gunners from B-29's and overloaded them with fire bombs to be dropped from extremely low altitudes. This was very unpopular with the crews but highly effective. LeMay usually had a cigar clenched in his mouth because it helped to cover a slight facial paralysis as a result of an old wound.

MOVIE PORTRAYAL:
Above And Beyond (1953), by Jim Backus

Lemmon, Jack (1925–   )

Hollywood actor who served as communications officer on the aircraft carrier U.S.S. *Lake Champlain* in the closing days of World War II. His commanding officer was Captain Logan C. Ramsey, who during the attack on Pearl Harbor is supposed to have sent out the message, "Air Raid Pearl Harbor, This Is No Drill." Lemmon was discharged in the summer of 1946.

Lemp, Fritz-Julius

German Navy lieutenant. He commanded the submarine *U-30* that sank the *Athenia* on September 3, 1939, the first ship sunk in World War II.

Lend-Lease Bill

Name of a bill passed March 11, 1941, that gave President

Franklin Roosevelt the power to "sell, transfer, exchange, lend, lease, or otherwise dispose of defense materials for the government of any country whose defense the President deems vital to the defense of the United States."

Leningrad

Russian city that was besieged by the Germans for 880 days from August 30, 1942, to January 27, 1944. It is estimated that between 1.3 and 1.5 million people died.

Lesueur, Larry

CBS broadcaster. He was the last American to broadcast from free Paris on June 10, 1940, and the first American to broadcast from a free Paris on August 25, 1944. He used a French transmitter for the broadcast. (It was believed that Charles Collingwood was the first but in fact he transcribed in advance a broadcast on a wire recorder; it was accidentally aired before the liberation of Paris, a fact he had a difficult time living down.)

Levanitis, Steven L.

U.S. Navy ensign in PT boats in the Pacific during World War II. He was formerly from Boston College and played pro football for the Philadelphia Eagles.

Lever Brothers

U.S. soap manufacturers. They owned the coconut groves on Guadalcanal and received seven million dollars from the Allies for damages during the fighting for the island.

Lewis, Sinclair (1885–1951)

American author. In 1930 he became the first American to be awarded the Nobel Prize in Literature. His son, Lieutenant Wells Lewis, was killed in action in France in 1944.

Lexington, U.S.S. (CV-2)

U.S. aircraft carrier. It was originally planned as a 43,000-ton battle cruiser but was later converted to a 33,000-ton carrier. It was commissioned in 1927 and ironically had 1,927 enlisted men assigned to it. The *Lexington* was heavily damaged in the Battle of the Coral Sea and had to be sunk by the destroyer U.S.S. *Phelps* on May 8, 1942, becoming the first U.S. carrier lost in World War II. The last man off the ship was Captain Frederick C. Sherman.

Lexington, U.S.S. (CV-16)

U.S. Essex-class carrier, launched June 16, 1942, and named after the *Lexington* (CV-2) which was lost the month before. The new carrier was nicknamed "the Blue Ghost" because it was not camouflaged like other carriers.

Ley, Robert (1890–1945)

Nazi labor leader. He was also the director of the Union of Germans Abroad, head of the Strength through Joy organization, and finally, commander of the Adolf Hitler Volunteer Corps of guerrilla fighters. Ley was captured by the U.S. 101st Airborne Division on May 16, 1945, near Berchtesgaden. He was later tried as a war criminal at Nuremberg, where he committed suicide. His wartime address was Berlin W57, Postdamstrasse 75, Germany.

Leyte Gulf

Site of a battle on October 22 to October 27, 1944, that put an end to the Japanese fleet as an offensive force. More ships and aircraft participated than in any other battle of Naval history (321 ships and 1,996 aircraft).

Levzacky

Name of a Czechoslovakian town that was destroyed on June 24 along with Lidice in reprisal for the assassination of Reinhard Heydrich in 1942.

Liberty Cabbage

Name that Americans used in referring to sauerkraut after the declaration of war by the United States.

Liberty Ship

Name given to a specially designed cargo ship widely used in World War II. Copied from a British tramp steamer, it was 441 feet long, 57 feet wide, displaced 14,100 tons, and could carry 10,000 tons of cargo. The ship was designed for rapid construction at minimum cost and utilized welded hulls, which were faster to produce than riveted hulls. It also used reciprocating engines since turbine engines were needed for Navy ships. Two thousand seven hundred seventy Liberty ships were built, each with a life expectancy of only five years. The first one launched was the S.S. *Patrick Henry.* The S.S. *Joseph N. Teal* was the first ship to be launched ten days after the keel was laid, and the S.S. *Booker T. Washington* was the first ship to be commanded by a black. The last Liberty ship built was the S.S. *Benjamin Warner.*

Liberty Steak

New term for German-sounding "hamburger." The name coincided with a new wave of awareness by Americans of the crisis in Europe prior to U.S. involvement in World War II.

Lice

Scourge of infantrymen on the Eastern Front in World War II. They were called various names by the Russians depending on the area: Vlasov's Men—Northern Donets area; Faustniks—Vistula river area; tommygunners—Stalingrad front.

Liddell-Hart, Sir Basil (1985–1970)

British military theorist. He fought in World War I and developed the idea of mechanized warfare to replace the stalemate warfare he encountered. Liddell-Hart's ideas were rejected by the British Army, but they were adopted as the foundation of the German *blitzkrieg*. He worked for General Dwight Eisenhower as a captain in assessing the German commanders' abilities and personalities. After the war, he interviewed many of the high-ranking Germans.

Lidice

Name of a Czechoslovakian village that was destroyed by the Germans on June 9, 1942, in reprisal for the assassination of Reinhard Heydrich. Every male over fifteen years old was shot, every female was sent to a concentration camp, where she was killed, and all children were sent to Germany for adoption. The city was blown up and the ground was salted so that nothing would grow there again. In memorial, towns in both Mexico and the United States changed their names to Lidice.

Lightoller, Charles

British second officer on the R.M.S. *Titanic* in 1912. During the Dunkirk evacuation of 1940, he helped evacuate 130 men on his sixty-foot yacht *Sundowner.*

"Lili Marlene"

Sentimental song that enchanted troops of both sides during World War II. It was written by Hans Liep, who had served in World War I. He composed the song about two girlfriends, Lili and Marlene, whom he never saw again after going to the front. It was put to music by Norbert Schultze, who still receives $4,000 per year in royalties. "Lili Marlene" was used as the theme song for the German Army Radio's record show that came on every night at 10 P.M. and was sung by Lale Andersen. In North Africa, on a quiet evening, soldiers in the German and British lines could hear the program from both sides.

Lillyman, Frank L.

U.S. Army officer. He was the commander of a pathfinder detachment of the 101st Airborne Division and was the first Allied paratrooper on French soil on D-Day, June 6, 1944.

Lily

Name given to a British airport that was designed by R. M. Hamilton to float on the ocean. It was constructed of buoyant metal cans that were linked together to be flexible in the swells of the ocean and also to withstand the weight of an aircraft. It was hoped that the Lily's could be used off Normandy for close fighter support of the invasion of France, but they never became operational.

Limpet

Name of a mine developed by the OSS in World War II. It could be attached to the hull of a ship by magnets and detonated after a determined span of time.

Lindbergh, Charles A. (1902–1974)

First person to fly the Atlantic solo in 1927. He was involved in aircraft development and visited Germany several times. As a guest of Hermann Goering, Lindbergh was present at the opening ceremonies of the 1936 Olympics in Berlin and was later decorated by Goering with a Nazi medal. He advocated U.S. isolationism up until the Japanese attacked Pearl Harbor. Lindbergh became a civilian employee of the United Aircraft Corporation and was also a technical representative to the U.S. Army Air Force. As such, he flew over fifty missions in the Pacific and shot down several Japanese aircraft. He downed one aircraft while flying P-38's, in addition to teaching Air Force pilots the techniques of fuel conservation for long flights. Lindbergh was the only person to win both the Congressional Medal of Honor and a Pulitzer Prize.

MOVIE PORTRAYALS:

The Spirit of St. Louis (1958), by James Stewart

The Lindbergh Kidnaping Case (1976 TV Movie), by Cliff De Young

Lindemann, Ernest (–1941)

German Navy officer. He was the captain of the *Bismarck* when it was sunk on May 27, 1941.

MOVIE PORTRAYAL:

Sink The Bismarck (1960), by Carl Mohner

Lindsay, John V. (1921–)

Mayor of New York City and U.S. Representative. During World War II, he served as a gunnery officer aboard the destroyer U.S.S. *Swanson*, which supported the Sicily landings of 1943. Lindsay received five battle stars and was discharged in 1946 as a lieutenant, senior grade.

Lingayen Gulf

Gulf located on the west coast of Luzon, the Philippines. It was a shallow gulf ideally suited for amphibious operations and opened onto a broad plain stretching all the way to Manila. Lingayen Gulf was assaulted by the Japanese Fourteenth Army under General Masaharu Homma in December 1941, which led to the fall of the Philippines.

Linge, Heinz (1913–1980)

German S.S. officer. He was Hitler's personal valet from 1935 to 1945 and claimed to be the last person to see Hitler alive. Linge later stated that Hitler had committed suicide with a pistol instead of cyanide as claimed by the Russians.

Linz

Austrian city where Hitler grew up. He intended to make it the new capital of the German Reich after the war.

Lion

Nickname given to Admiral Karl Doenitz by his submarine crews in World War II.

Lion Has Wings, The

Name of the first British film that used World War II as a setting. It was produced in 1940.

Lions Express

Name given to an Allied supply network that ran from Bayeux to Brussels. It primarily supplied the British forces in the same manner as the Red Ball Express.

Lipes, Wheeler B.

U.S. Navy pharmacist mate on board the submarine U.S.S. *Seadragon*. While on a combat patrol, he successfully operated on Seaman Darrell Rector for appendicitis, although he had no formal training.

Lipetsk

Russian airfield where the German Army trained airmen secretly, in violation of the Versailles Treaty, until 1933. Russians guarded the field but everything else was under German authority. It was here that they tested fighter aircraft and light bombers in preparation for the day when a new German Air Force would arise.

Lipski, Joseph (1894–1958)

Polish foreign ambassador to Germany until September 1, 1939, when the Germans attacked.

Lisbon Report

Name of a series of documents that were given to British MI-6 in

Lisbon by the German Abwehr on August 7, 1943. They pinpointed Peenemunde as the rocket-test site for German terror weapons. Eleven days later it was bombed by the Royal Air Force.

Liscombe Bay, U.S.S.

U.S. aircraft carrier that was sunk on November 24, 1943, twenty miles from Makin Island by the Japanese submarine *I-175*. It went down in less than thirty minutes with the loss of nearly 650 men, including Rear Admiral H. M. Mullinix and Captain I.D. Wiltsie.

List, Wilhelm (1880–1971)

German Field Marshall. He commanded German forces in Poland, France, and Russia, but was dismissed by Hitler in 1942. List was tried at Nuremberg and given life imprisonment for war crimes, but was released after serving five years.

Little Bill

Nickname given to William Stephensen, head of British intelligence in New York, to differentiate him from William Donovan, head of OSS in Washington. Donovan was called "Big Bill."

Little Blitz Week

Name given to a week of concentrated bombing attacks by the U.S. Eighth Air Force in July 1943. Sixteen targets in Norway and Germany, including Hamburg, were bombed.

Little Boy

Name of the atomic bomb (Uranium 235) dropped on Hiroshima by the *Enola Gay*. It was 120 inches long and 28 inches in diameter, weighed 9,000 pounds and had an explosive yield of 20,000 tons of TNT. The bomb had originally been named *the Thin Man,* after President Franklin D. Roosevelt.

Little Entente

Alliance between Czechoslovakia, Yugoslavia, and Rumania prior to World War II in mutual defense against Hungary. With the German takeover of Czechoslovakia, the Little Entente lost most of its importance and power.

Little Maginot Line

Name of the French defense line built along the Italian border.

Litvak, Lilya (–1943)

Russian air force lieutenant. She was the top-scoring female ace of World War II with twelve German aircraft shot down. Litvak flew a Yak 1 fighter and was awarded the Order of the Red Banner and the Order of the Patriotic War, before she was killed in action in September 1943.

Litvinov, Maxim (1876–1951)
Soviet Foreign Minister until May 1939. He was removed because he was a Jew, as Stalin did not want to endanger Soviet-German relations. Litvinov was replaced by Molotov and then became the Russian ambassador to the U.S. until 1943.

Livadia Palace
Site of the Yalta Conference in 1945. It was built in 1911 as a summer palace for Czar Nicholas II.

Lloyd-George, David (1863–1945)
British Prime Minister from 1916 to 1922 and signatory of the Treaty of Versailles ending World War I. He was a member of Parliament until 1944.

Lockard, Joseph L.
U.S. Army private. He was a radar operator who spotted the Japanese planes inbound to Pearl Harbor on December 7, 1941. Lockard attempted to warn the military, but when he notified the officer on duty, Lieutenant Kermit Tyler, he was told "Well, don't worry about it." Lockard was later awarded a Distinguished Service Medal and sent to Officer's Training School.

Lockwood, Charles A., Jr. (1890–1967)
U.S. Navy admiral. He graduated from the Naval Academy in 1912, after which he went into the submarine branch of the Navy in 1914. He was the U.S. Naval attaché in London in 1940 and took command of U.S. submarines in Australia in April 1942. Lockwood was the first high-ranking officer to realize that torpedoes were defective and to set up tests to prove it. He later commanded the U.S. Pacific Fleet submarine force.

MOVIE PORTRAYAL:
Hellcats of the Navy (1958), by Maurice Manson

Lodge, Henry Cabot II (1902–)
First U.S. Senator to see action since the Civil War when, as a lieutenant colonel, he commanded a tank force in North Africa in 1942. Shortly after this, Lodge returned to the Senate.

Lodz
First Jewish ghetto to be established by the Germans in Poland and the last to be liquidated.

Logan, Joshua (1908–)
Broadway and movie producer. He was drafted into the U.S. Army on June 10, 1942, and served as a public relations and

intelligence officer with the 405th Fighter Group in Europe. Logan was discharged as a captain.

Logan, Mary Lee

Sister of producer Josh Logan. She flew B-25's from the States to overseas bases as a member of Jaqueline Cochran's WASP's.

Logan, Sam

U.S. fighter pilot. He was the first American to get reinstated to flight duty with an artificial leg. Logan had bailed out over Guadalcanal in an incident in which a Japanese pilot attempted to shoot him while he hung in his parachute. When the pilot was finally out of ammunition he tried to ram Logan. As a result, Logan's foot had to be amputated.

Loge

Code name used by the Luftwaffe for London in its first attack on September 7, 1940.

Lohr, Alexander (1885–1947)

German Air Force colonel-general. In 1936, he was the commander of the Austrian Air Force and became part of the German Air Force after the Austrian Aushluss of 1938. Lohr commanded the forces that attacked Coventry in 1940 and the Fourth Air Fleet over Stalingrad in 1942, and became Luftwaffe commander in the Balkans. After the war, he was convicted of war crimes by a Yugoslavian court and hanged March 16, 1947.

Lombard, Carole (1908–1942)

Hollywood actress and wife of Clark Gable. She was the first woman killed in action in World War II when her plane, a TWA DC-3, crashed into Table Mountain near Las Vegas, January 16, 1942, while she was on a government bond drive.

MOVIE PORTRAYALS:
Gable and Lombard (1976), by Jill Clayburgh
Moviola (1980 TV miniseries), by Sharon Gless

London

Selected as the site of the 1944 Olympic games, which never took place.

London After Dark

Edward R. Murrow's CBS network radio program that provided some of the best early war reporting available to the American public.

London Cage

Name given to the best-known interrogation depot for prisoners of war in England, commanded by Colonel A. P. Scotland. It was located on the corner of Kensington Park Gardens and Bayswater Road. A favorite tactic was to dress a Russian-speaking British officer in a Russian uniform and have him present for the interrogation of a prisoner. If the POW was hesitant to answer questions, a threat to turn him over to the Russians usually brought quick results. The London Cage was also used for the questioning of high-ranking POW's like German Generals von Thoma and Crewell, who were both captured in North Africa.

London Controlling Section (LCS)

Name of a British unit established by Winston Churchill to devise schemes in order to deceive the Axis powers as to the true intentions of Allied operations. Located at 2 Great George Street, London, it was commanded by Colonel John Bevin.

Lone Eagle

Nickname given to aviation pioneer Charles Lindbergh.

Lone Eagles

Nickname given to the black fighter pilots of the 99th Pursuit Squadron. Founded at Tuskegee Institute, the squadron fought in Italy in World War II.

Longest Day, The

Name given to D-Day by Field Marshall Erwin Rommel when he said "The invasion will be decisive. For the Allies, as well as for Germany, it will be the longest day." The name was used as the title of Cornelius Ryan's book on D-Day and also for the 1962 movie, which was the most expensive black-and-white movie ever filmed.

Long, Luz

German athlete against whom Jesse Owens competed in the 1936 Olympics. The two became good friends and corresponded with one another until Long was killed during the fighting in North Africa in World War II.

Long Pounce

Name of a purported operation as revealed by Joseph Stalin, whereby German S.S. officer Otto Skorzeny would attempt to assassinate President Franklin Roosevelt at the Teheran Conference. Stalin arranged to have Roosevelt stay within the Russian compound for safety.

Long, Russell (1918–   )

U.S. Senator from Louisiana. During World War II, he was an ensign in the U.S. Navy, commanding landing craft in the invasion of North Africa (1942), Sicily (1943), Anzio (1944), and southern France (1944). Long was awarded four battle stars.

Lonsdale, Gordon (1922–1970)

Soviet agent caught in England in 1961. In 1943, he was dropped behind German lines to set up partisan units near Minsk. Lonsdale became the radio operator for another future Soviet spy, Rudolph Abel, who was caught in the U.S. and later exchanged for U-2 pilot Francis Gary Powers.

Lord Haw Haw

Nickname given to William Joyce, who broadcast propaganda for the Germans in World War II. The name was coined by British Professor Arthur Lloyd James, who taught pronunciation to BBC announcers. Other variants were "Lady Haw Haw," who was Jane Anderson, and the "American Lord Haw Haw," Douglas Chandler.

Lord, Walter (1917–   )

Author of nonfiction *(The Day of Infamy, The Incredible Victory,* and *A Night To Remember)*. During World War II, he served with the OSS along with Arthur Schlesinger, Jr.

Loren, Sophia (1934–   )

Academy Award-winning Italian actress. As a little girl, she lived in Naples at the time that the Allies were bombing the city. Her sister Maria married Benito Mussolini's son.

Lorient

French coastal port. It was the site of the first German submarine base established in western France. The first submarine to enter the base was the *U-30*, under Lieutenant Fritz-Julius Lemp on July 5, 1940. The German garrison of the city held out against the Allies until the end of the war.

Lothian, Lord (1882–1940)

British ambassador to the U.S. His real name was Philip Kerr, eleventh Marquess of Lothian.

Loughlin, Charles Elliott

U.S. Navy officer and commander of the submarines *S-14* and *Queenfish* in World War II. He had previously been an All-American basketball player.

Love Day

U.S. Marine Corps euphemism for the assault on Okinawa on Easter Sunday, April 1, 1945. It had been designated L-Day and because of the initial lack of Japanese opposition, was called *Love* by the Marines.

Love, Nancy Harkness (1914–)

U.S. female aviation pioneer and test pilot. She organized the WASP's, the Women's Air Service Pilots, during World War II.

Loveitt, Ray

British flying officer with No. 42 Squadron. He torpedoed the German cruiser *Lutzow* on June 13, 1941, putting it out of action for six months. His was the first Royal Air Force torpedo launched at the enemy in World War II.

Louis, Joe (Joseph Louis Barrow) (1914–1981)

American heavyweight boxing champion from 1937 to 1949. In order to help the U.S. Navy Relief Society, he fought against Buddy Baer in a championship fight on January 19, 1942, and won the fight after 2 minutes and 56 seconds. That evening Louis learned that he had been drafted into the U.S. Army. He served throughout World War II as a sergeant, giving boxing demonstrations for the troops. He is buried in Arlington National Cemetery in Washington, D.C., although he never saw combat (a special waiver was given to his burial).

Low, David (1891–)

British political cartoonist for the *Evening Standard*. He was the creator of Colonel Blimp, who poked fun at the traditions of British society.

Low, Francis S. (1894–1964)

U.S. Navy rear admiral. As operations officer on Admiral Ernest King's staff, he thought up the idea of using medium bombers launched from an aircraft carrier that became the Doolittle Raid on Tokyo in April 1942.

L Pills

Designator of potassium cyanide pills carried by Allied agents in occupied countries in case of capture.

LST

Designator of a U.S. Navy ship intended to land vehicles directly on a beach during an invasion. The letters stood for Landing Ship Tank but crewmembers humorously said that they meant Large Slow Target.

LST 779

U.S. Navy landing ship that contributed the flag used for the second flag raising on Mount Suribachi, Iwo Jima. It was this flag raising that was made famous by photographer Joe Rosenthal.

Lucas, John P. (1890–1949)

U.S. Army general. He commanded the Anzio landings of February 1944, but was relieved of command for being overly cautious. Lucas maintained that he was ordered by General Mark Clark to be cautious in expanding the beachhead. He was sent back to the U.S. and took command of the Fourth Army, actually a promotion for him, since an Army is larger than a Corps, which he had commanded in Anzio.

Lucius

OSS code name for Ho Chi Minh while he supplied intelligence on Japanese forces to the Allies in World War II. An OSS medic saved his life by treating him for tropical fever with the then revolutionary sulfa drugs.

Lucky

Code name that General George S. Patton gave his Third Army. His advance headquarters was called *Lucky Forward*.

Lucky Strike Green Has Gone to War

Advertising slogan authored by George Washington Hill, President of the American Tobacco Company. The dyes used for the green emblem on packs of Lucky Strike cigarettes were needed for the war effort. The color red was thus adopted and has been used up to the present.

Lucy

Code name of Rudolph Roessler, who supplied information to the Russians during World War II from Lucerne, Switzerland. He maintained that he received his intelligence material from ten high-ranking Wehrmacht officers whose identities have never been divulged. Roessler passed the verbatim plan for the German invasion of Russia, and is credited with the information that led to the Russian encirclement of the Germans at Stalingrad. He also was the first to mention the V-1 and V-2 rockets and made progress reports on German jet development.

Ludendorff Bridge

Name of the railway bridge across the Rhine River located at Remagen. It was captured by U.S. forces on March 7, 1945.

Ludendorff, Erich (1865–1937)

German general in World War I. He joined the Nazi Party and marched with Hitler on the 1923 Munich Beer Hall Putsch, for which he was tried for treason and acquitted.

MOVIE PORTRAYAL:
The Hitler Gang (1944), by Reinhold Schunzel

Ludlow-Hewitt, Edgar R. (1886–1973)

British Royal Air Force officer. He was the head of bomber command from 1939 to 1940 and planned the first bombing raids on Germany. Ludlow-Hewitt later became the Inspector General of the RAF.

Luftflotte 1

German Luftwaffe unit that was stationed in Rumania during World War II to protect the Ploesti oil fields. It was commanded by General Kurt Pflugbeil.

Luftflotte 2

German air fleet based in Holland, Belgium, and northern France. Field Marshall Albert Kesselring was in command during the Battle of Britain in 1940.

Luftflotte 3

German Luftwaffe unit that was stationed in France. It was commanded by Field Marshall Hugo Sperrle during the Battle of Britain.

Luftflotte 4

German Luftwaffe unit stationed in Greece and commanded by General Alexander Lohr. It was involved in the capture of Crete in 1941.

Luftflotte 5

German Luftwaffe unit commanded by Colonel General Hans Jurgen Stumpff and stationed in Norway throughout World War II.

Lufthansa

German airline owned and operated jointly by the government and private business. It was created in 1926 to train German bomber pilots in violation of the Versailles Treaty. The Chairman of the Board was Erhard Milch, who became a Luftwaffe general when the Nazis took power.

Luftwaffe

German Air Force commanded by Hermann Goering. Adolf Galland was the General of Fighters; Josef Kammhuber was General of Night Fighters; and Werner Baumbach was the General of Bombers.

Luftwaffe aces

Ninety-four pilots accounted for 13,997 enemy aircraft. Thirty-four German pilots shot down over 150 enemy aircraft in World War II, and sixty pilots downed between 100 and 150. The top twenty aces were

Eric Hartmann (352)
Gerhard Barkhorn (301)
Gunther Rall (275)
Otto Kittel (267)
Walter Nowotny (258)
Wilhelm Batz (242)
Theodor Weissenberger (238)
Erich Rudorffer (222)
Heinrich Baer (220)
Heinrich Ehrler (220)
Hans Philipp (213)
Walter Schuck (206)
Anton Hafner (204)
Helmut Lipfert (203)
Hermann Graf (202)
Walter Krupinski (197)
Anton Hackl (192)
Joachim Brendel (189)
Joachim Kirschner (188)
Werner Brandle (180)

Luftwaffe formations
Geschwader (Group): 100–120 aircraft or three Gruppe
Gruppe (Wing): thirty to thirty-six aircraft or three Staffel
Staffel (Squadron): nine to twelve aircraft or three Schwarm
Schwarm: three or four aircraft or two Rotte
Rotte: two aircraft

Luftwaffe stomp
Name given by U.S. fighter pilots to a turn used in combat to evade pursuers. It involved stalling the aircraft and turning at the same time. The maneuver was very effective in allowing the pilot to come out on the tail of a German fighter and therefore with a good chance of shooting it down.

LuJack, Johnny (1925–)
Pro football player. In World War II, he was an officer on a U.S. Navy submarine chaser in the Atlantic Ocean and along the coast of Europe.

Luneburg Heath
Site near Hamburg of the surrender of German forces in northern Germany to British Field Marshall Bernard Montgomery on May 4, 1945.

Lummus, Jack (–1945)
All-American football player for Baylor University who was killed on Iwo Jima. He had played one year (1941) for the New York Giants.

Lupino, Ida (1918–)
Hollywood actress. During World War II, she served with the American Ambulance Corps as a lieutenant.

LUT
German torpedo developed to overcome the difficulty for submarines of getting within range of a convoy late in the war. This torpedo was extremely long-ranged.

Luth, Wolfgang (1913–1945)
German Navy's second-highest-scoring submarine commander of World War II, with forty-three ships and one submarine to his credit, totaling 225,712 tons. He survived the terrible odds at sea and numerous submarine patrols from 1940 to the end of 1943, only to be accidentally killed on May 14, 1945; he failed to answer the call of a sentry who was guarding the headquarters of Grand Admiral Karl Doenitz. Luth had been awarded the diamonds as well as the oak leaves and swords of the Knight's Cross and was the first naval officer so honored.

Lutjens, Gunther (1889–1941)
German admiral. He commanded the battleship *Bismarck* and the cruiser *Prinz Eugen* in May 1941, when they attempted to break out into the Atlantic and attack British convoys. Lutjens went down with the *Bismarck* on May 27, 1941.

MOVIE PORTRAYAL:
Sink The Bismarck (1960), by Karl Stephanek

Lutze, Viktor (1890–1943)
German Chief of Staff of the S.A. (Brown Shirts) after Ernst Roehm was shot in 1934. Lutze was killed in an auto accident while returning from a black market expedition; he was given a hero's funeral by Hitler.

Lutzow
German 10,000-ton pocket battleship, formerly named the *Deutschland*. The name was changed by Hitler because he feared the effect on morale if the ship were to be sunk. The *Lutzow* had its propellers and rudder blown off by a torpedo from the British submarine *Spearfish* on April 11, 1940, off Norway. After repairs it was put to sea and on June 13, 1941, was torpedoed by Ray Loveitt,

which put it out of action for six more months. The *Lutzow* was finally sunk by the British, using six-ton bombs, but it settled evenly to the bottom, with its decks and guns above water, and continued to shell the advancing Russians until May 4, 1945, when it was finally blown up.

Lynde, Paul (1926–1981)
Hollywood comedian. His brother Cordy was reported missing in action during the Battle of the Bulge in December 1944. Upon hearing of her son's probable death, Mrs. Lynde died.

Lyon, Ben (1901–1979)
Hollywood actor. He flew as a combat pilot in World War II with the Royal Air Force and was discharged with the rank of lieutenant colonel.

Lysander
British single-engine aircraft used primarily by the SOE to insert and remove agents from occupied Europe. The airplane was very slow on takeoffs and landings but could land in a short space, making it ideal for secluded areas.

M

MacArthur, Douglas (1880–1964)

U.S. General of the Army. He commanded U.S. Armed Forces in the Far East in 1941 and was Supreme Commander of Allied Forces in the Southwest Pacific in 1942. MacArthur was awarded a Congressional Medal of Honor. His father had won the CMH in the Civil War, and they were the first and only father and son to be so honored.

MOVIE PORTRAYALS:

They Were Expendable (1945), by Robert Barrat

An American Guerrilla in the Philippines (1950), by Robert Barrat

The Court Martial of Billy Mitchell (1955), by Dayton Lummis

Collision Course (1976), by Henry Fonda

MacArthur (1977), by Gregory Peck

Inchon (1982), by Laurence Olivier

MacArthur was much admired by Henry Luce, who put him on the cover of *Time* magazine seven times.

Machine Parts

Label on packing cases sent from secret German training bases in Russia back to Germany and containing the bodies of Germans killed in training exercises before 1933. The training was primarily in two fields, tank and aircraft, both expressly forbidden by the Versailles Treaty that ended World War I.

MacIntyre, Donald

Canadian Royal Navy commander. He was in charge of the destroyer HMS *Walker* when it sank the German submarine *U-99* in March 1941 and the destroyer HMS *Vanoc* when it sank the *U-100* in the same month. MacIntyre commanded the HMS *Hesperus* in March 1943 when it sank *U-191* with hedgehogs.

MacKall, John T. (1920–1942)

U.S. Army enlisted man. He was the first American paratrooper killed in action in World War II. While en route to the invasion of North Africa on November 8, 1942, his aircraft was attacked by a French fighter and he was killed. MacKall was buried in Gibraltar.

von Mackensen, August (1849–1945)

German field marshall who fought in battles in eastern Europe in World War I. He was a member of the Death's Head Hussars, who were used by Hitler as a means of demonstrating respectability for the Nazis. Von Mackensen was captured by U.S. forces in April 1945 and died on November 8, 1945, in the British Zone.

Mackerel

German code name for Ireland. They unsuccessfully attempted several times to cause the Irish to actively oppose the British in World War II.

Mackie, Thomas Robert

U.S. Navy language officer who was sent from Tokyo to Cavite, Philippines, just before World War II. He was assigned to the CAST crypto unit and intercepted what was called the Winds Code, which stated "East Wind Rain," meaning that war was imminent with the U.S. Because the message was sent in Chinese characters, his superiors would not believe him. Mackie was evacuated from Corregidor via the submarine U.S.S. *Permit* on March 16, 1942. In Melbourne, he decoded and translated a message that said that the Japanese would strike Port Moresby across the Owen Stanley Range in New Guinea. Mackie's decoding gave General Douglas MacArthur time to set up a defense of Port Moresby.

Madagascar Plan

Last plan of the Nazis to rid Germany of the Jews without killing them. The plan was devised before the war and revived when France capitulated, because Madagascar was a French colony. It was proposed that all German Jews be shipped there and held as hostages to ensure the good graces of the U.S. Due to lack of transport and the continuation of the war, the plan was discarded.

Madeleine

Code name of Noor Inayat Khan (1914–1944), an Indian princess who was dropped into France as a British agent of SOE on June 17, 1943. She had been born in Russia, schooled in France, and was captured by the Germans shortly after landing. They imprisoned her at Dachau concentration camp and executed her on September 14, 1944. The indications are that the British knew the group she joined had been infiltrated by the Gestapo but sent Khan anyway so that the Germans would not suspect that the British were reading their codes.

Madman of St. Malo

Nickname given to German Colonel von Aulock who commanded the garrison of Saint Malo on the north Breton coast. He refused to surrender because it was "not compatible with the honor of a German soldier." Von Aulock was finally forced to surrender on August 17, 1944, after a four-day siege.

McGee, James C. (1883–   )

U.S. Army general. He was the Surgeon General of the Army during World War II.

Magic

Code name given to Japanese messages that were decoded by cipher personnel of the U.S. Navy Intelligence Service from September 1940 onward. They primarily worked on the Purple Code, the Japanese diplomatic signals.

Magic Carpet Fleet

Name given to the U.S. Navy carriers that were used at the end of World War II to transport servicemen back to the States.

Maginot Line

French defensive barrier that stretched from Switzerland to Belgium along the German border. It was built between 1930 and 1935 by the French Minister of War, Andre Maginot, and was supposedly impenetrable; however, it proved futile when the German tanks outflanked the line by attacking through the Ardennes of Belgium. The Maginot Line did not cover the Ardennes because Marshall Philippe Pétain had judged them to be impassable.

Magnet

Code name for U.S. forces in Ireland in World War II.

Mailer, Norman (1923–   )

Pulitzer Prize-winning American author. He was drafted into the U.S. Army in January 1944 and served in an intelligence section of an Infantry Regiment in the Philippines. Mailer also participated in the invasion of Luzon.

Mainila Incident

Excuse used by the Soviets to attack Finland. The Russians claimed that the Finns had shelled the Russian border village of Mainila with artillery on November 26, 1940, killing four people. Actually it was Soviet artillery that shelled the town, as the Finns had no artillery near the border.

Maisky, Ivan (1884–1975)

Soviet diplomat. He was Ambassador to Britain from 1932 to 1943.

Maisy

Name of a German coastal gun on the cliffs overlooking Omaha Beach that was captured by U.S. Rangers on June 6, 1944.

Makin Island

Island of the Gilbert chain that was the target of a hit-and-run attack August 17, 1942, by Carlson's Raiders. The men were dropped off by the submarines U.S.S. *Nautilus* and the U.S.S. *Argonaut* in an attempt to divert Japanese attention from the Guadalcanal operations. The attack force, with USMC Major James Roosevelt as second-in-command, killed 350 Japanese and destroyed a seaplane base. The raid cost over thirty Marines, nine of whom were captured and later beheaded. The attack was a fiasco and caused the Japanese to fortify other islands that, until then, were unfortified. As a result, many American and Japanese soldiers later lost their lives. Makin was finally captured between November 20 and November 23, 1943, by the U.S. Army.

Malan, Adolph G. (1910–1964)

British Royal Air Force fighter pilot. Malan, who was nicknamed "Sailor," was the third-highest-scoring British ace of World War II, with thirty-five aircraft shot down. Malan, a South African, was the first pilot to be awarded the Distinguished Service Order and the Distinguished Flying Cross with bars. Winston Churchill became the godfather of his son.

Malaparte

Code word of the anti-Hitler conspirators for their proposed overthrow of Hitler on July 20, 1944.

Malden, Karl (1914–)

Hollywood actor. He served in the U.S. Army in World War II and was part of Moss Hart's *Winged Victory* show. Malden was discharged in 1945 as a corporal.

Malinovsky, Rodion (1898–1967)

Soviet Marshall. He fought at Stalingrad and commanded the

Russian units that captured Bucharest in August 1944, the first European capital liberated by the Red Army.

Malitna Tunnel

1,400-foot-long main tunnel on Corregidor where General Douglas MacArthur and later General Jonathan Wainwright set up headquarters before the surrender of Corregidor. In 1945, after Japanese troops retreated into Malitna Tunnel, U.S. forces blew up the main entrances, sealing them inside.

Malmedy

Site of a massacre of captured U.S. soldiers during the Battle of the Bulge in December 1944. Over one hundred were killed by an S.S. unit. In 1946, 73 Germans, including Sepp Dietrich and Joachim Peiper, were put on trial at Dachau and all were found guilty. Forty-three were sentenced to death, but their defense counsel, William Meade Everett, Jr., discovered that torture and kangaroo courts had been used to coerce the prisoners into confessions that were in many cases false. An investigating board reversed the death penalties of thirty-one and commuted the other twelve to life sentences.

Malo, Raymond (–1945)

U.S. Army Air Force lieutenant. Against orders, he piloted the first aircraft to land on Iwo Jima, March 4, 1945, when he landed a B-29 named *Dinah Might*. The runway was too short and fighting was still heavy, but his fuel systems were defective, giving him the choice of Iwo Jima or the Pacific Ocean. Malo departed after his crew hand-poured over 2,000 gallons of gasoline into the aircraft. He and all but one of the crew members were killed just six weeks later.

Maloney, Margaret Helen

U.S. Women's Army Corps private. She was the first WAC to receive the Soldier's Medal, which she received for saving the life of Private Kenneth J. Jacobs from a fire in North Africa.

Malta

Island astride the main supply route between Italy and North Africa. The British viewed it as an unsinkable aircraft carrier from which their aircraft attacked convoys destined for Field Marshall Erwin Rommel's Afrika Korps. The Germans laid siege to it from the air for two and a half years, losing as many airmen as there were casualties on the ground. Malta was the first air siege in history.

Manchester, William (1922–   )
U.S. author *(American Caesar: Douglas MacArthur, Glory and the Dream,* etc.). He enlisted in the U.S. Marine Corps and served in the intelligence section of the 29th Regiment, fighting on Guadalcanal, Tarawa, Saipan, and Okinawa. Manchester's grandfather had been wounded and left for dead during the Civil War but was still alive when found. His father, during World War I, was wounded and removed to an aid station and left to die, but lived. Manchester was wounded on Okinawa and left for dead for four hours, but was later discovered to be still alive. He spent five months in hospitals recovering.

Mancini, Henry (1924–   )
Academy Award winner, musician, and composer. He was drafted in 1943 into the U.S. Army Air Force and served overseas during World War II.

Manhattan Project
Code name for the American development of the atomic bomb in World War II. It was taken from the first office in New York City that was part of the Manhattan Engineer District. Brigadier General Leslie Groves commanded the project throughout the war.

Mann, David (1916–   )
Musician and composer. He served in the U.S. military during World War II and was the official pianist for President Harry S Truman.

Mann, Thomas (1875–1955)
German-born author. He fled Nazi Germany because his wife was Jewish.

Mannerheim, Carl (1867–1951)
Finnish Field Marshall. He was born in Sweden and joined the Russian Army in 1889, becoming a lieutenant general by 1917. Mannerheim commanded the Finnish troops that held off over a million Russians during the Russo-Finnish War of 1940. He received intelligence information from the Swedes that helped him fight the Russians with only 175,000 men.

Mannerheim Line
Name given to a system of fortifications that stretched eighty-eight miles across the Karelian Isthmus to protect Finland from Russia. It was built continuously, beginning in the early 1920's.

Manston
Royal Air Force fighter base located northeast of Dover. It was the easternmost forward base and therefore easily accessible to the

German Luftwaffe. The British cover name for Manston was "Charlie Three."

Manzanar

Relocation camp in the Owen Valley of California where Japanese-Americans were incarcerated in World War II. It is listed as the U.S.'s largest concentration camp and encompassed over 5,000 acres.

Maquis

Name of the French Resistance forces in World War II.

Marat

Soviet battleship weighing 23,600 tons. It was attacked on September 23, 1941, while at anchor at Kronstadt, by German Stukas and was sunk by Hans Ulrich Rudel. The *Marat* was the first battleship ever sunk by dive bombers.

Marceau, Marcel (1923–)

French pantomimist. His father was taken as a hostage by the Germans and executed. Marceau and his brother joined the French underground in 1944.

"Marching Through Berlin"

Song adapted by Belford Hendricks to the tune of the German national anthem. Ethel Merman introduced the tune in the 1943 musical movie *Stage Door Canteen*.

Marchwind

Code name used by Allied officers of field rank and above to make long-distance calls in England prior to D-Day.

Marciano, Rocky (1923–1969)

Heavyweight boxing champion. He was drafted into the U.S. Army on March 4, 1943, and served with the 150th Combat Engineers stationed in Wales. It was while in the Army that he took up boxing seriously; he was discharged in 1947.

Marcks, Erich (1891–1944)

German general. He was the commander of the 84th Corps defending Normandy during the D-Day assault on June 6, 1944, which occured on his birthday. Marcks had lost a leg on the Russian front and was fitted with an artificial limb. He had been a friend of General Kurt von Schleicher, who was killed by the Nazis in 1934, and was not favored by the Nazis; he was tolerated because he was a highly capable and efficient officer. Marcks was killed on June 12, 1944, by Allied fighter aircraft.

Marco Polo Bridge

Site of an incident on July 7, 1937 (7-7-37), when Japanese troops were supposedly fired on by Chinese troops. The Japanese forces used this as an excuse to attack the Chinese. This was the start of the major fighting between Japan and China. The bridge was over 800 years old and was named after the first Westerner to cross it, Marco Polo. U.S. General Joseph Stilwell, who was present, set up an intelligence network to evaluate the strength of the Japanese Army.

Marcos, Ferdinand E. (1917–)

The Philippines' most decorated soldier of World War II. As a third lieutenant, he won two Distinguished Service Crosses, two Silver Stars, and two Purple Hearts. Marcos later became the President of the Philippines.

Marcus, David "Mickey" (1902–1948)

U.S. Army colonel born on Washington's birthday in 1902. Marcus jumped with the 101st Airborne Division in Normandy on June 6, 1944, being one of only two to jump on D-Day without prior parachute training. (Walter Winchell said that Marcus was the sixth person to land at Normandy.) After World War II, he helped the Israelis win their independence and became the first Israeli General of the Army in 2,000 years, since Biblical times. Marcus was accidentally killed on June 10, 1948 (the very day that author Don McCombs was born), by one of his own sentries because he did not speak Hebrew. He is the only person killed while fighting under a foreign flag to be buried at West Point.

MOVIE PORTRAYAL:

Cast a Giant Shadow (1966), by Kirk Douglas

Mare Island

U.S. Navy base in San Francisco Bay that was the site of a mutiny in 1944 of fifty black enlisted men who refused to load ammunition on ships bound for the Pacific fighting. The refusal was prompted by the Port Chicago explosion on July 17, 1944, that killed over 300 people. All the mutineers were sentenced to fifteen years' hard labor and dishonorable discharges, but this was overturned in 1946 and all were allowed to return to active duty. They were subsequently given honorable discharges.

Marfak No. 1

Designator of canned butter shipped to U.S. troops overseas in World War II.

Marge

Name of Richard Bong's P-38. He was the top-scoring American ace of World War II, with 40 victories.

Marianas Turkey Shoot

Name given to an air battle on June 19, 1944, as part of the larger Battle of the Philippine Sea. This engagement virtually destroyed Japanese naval power for the rest of the war. The Japanese lost 328 carrier-based aircraft and another fifty land-based aircraft, while the Americans lost twenty-three aircraft, plus six more destroyed operationally.

Mark

Code name of U.S. General Mark Clark on his secret trip to North Africa to talk with the representatives of Vichy French forces preparatory to the North African invasion, Operation Torch, on November 8, 1942.

Mark 3

Designator of a Japanese secret weapon developed in World War II. It was a naval shell weighing one ton that was to be fired from a battleship. Inside the casing were over 300 artillery shells. The plan was to fire the larger projectile to a height of 100,000 feet, where it would detonate, spraying the smaller shells over an enemy formation. The Japanese hoped that one salvo would destroy an entire task force. On June 8, 1943, the battleship *Mutsu* blew up in the Inland Sea and it was believed that the Mark 3's on board had accidentally detonated. The Mark 3's were never carried again because it was felt they were too dangerous.

Mark I

Designator of a U.S. Navy experimental electrical torpedo conceived in 1915. It was built by a persistent technician in the 1920's but lost in a test-firing exercise.

Mark II

U.S. Navy electrical torpedo that was developed in 1941 with the help of both the General Electric Company and Exide. It was not a practical weapon because there were too many machined parts.

Mark VI

Designator of a magnetic warhead developed by the U.S. Navy that was to be used with the Mark XIV torpedo. It was supposed to detonate beneath a ship, breaking the keel and splitting open the bottom, thus sinking the ship. The Mark VI was pushed into use by Admiral Ralph Christie, but was never tested with a real warhead. This proved to be a major mistake of the U.S. Navy in the early days of World War II because of the high number of failures.

Mark XIV

Principal U.S. Navy torpedo of World War II. It was steam-driven, which left a distinctive trail in the water, and it carried a 500-pound warhead. The Mark XIV could travel for 4,500 yards at forty-six knots or nearly 9,000 yards at thirty-one and five-tenths knots. At the beginning of the war, it was found to be defective, running deeper than it was set for, thus making U.S. submarines ineffectual in the first year of operations.

Mark XVI

U.S. Navy torpedo that was developed experimentally in the 1920's and 1930's using compressed oxygen and hydrogen peroxide as a propellant. The work was done by Ralph Christie, who believed that it would carry a 500-pound warhead for 15,000 yards at fifty knots with no tell-tale trail. The Mark XVI met with a negative response because the Navy did not want hazardous materials on board ships in case they were hit by enemy shells or were in a fire. The torpedo for surface ships was the Mark XVII.

Mark XVIII

U.S. Navy electric torpedo built by Westinghouse in mid-1942. It was copied from a German electric torpedo and was rated as one of the most important accomplishments of U.S. torpedo history.

Markey, Gene (1896–1980)

Hollywood writer. He served as an infantry officer in World War I in France. Markey was an admiral on Admiral William F. Halsey's staff in World War II and was married at different times to actresses Joan Bennett, Hedy Lamarr, and Myrna Loy. Admiral Halsey was best man at his 1946 wedding to actress Myrna Loy.

Marks, Johnny (1909–)

Composer of the Christmas classics "Rudolph the Red-Nosed Reindeer" and "Rock Around the Christmas Tree." During World War II, he served under General George S. Patton in Normandy, where he won a Bronze Star for leading twenty soldiers in an attack that captured a castle with over 100 German soldiers.

Mark Twain

Name given to a bomb sight devised by Captain Charles R. Greening for the Doolittle Raid on Tokyo on April 18, 1942. Something was needed to replace the Norden bomb sight, which was not accurate for low-level missions and which they also did not carry for fear it might fall into the hands of the Japanese. The Mark Twain was made from twenty cents' worth of metal and proved to be surprisingly accurate.

Mars

Name of a U.S. Navy flying boat built by Martin. Weighing 140,000 pounds, it was the first flying boat to be launched like a ship, on November 8, 1941. The *Mars* had a 200-foot wingspan and was powered by four 2,000-horsepower engines. The aircraft designator was XPB2M-1.

Marseille, Jans Joachim (1919–1942)

German Luftwaffe fighter pilot known as "the Star of Africa." He shot down a total of 158 Allied aircraft before being killed on September 30, 1942. Marseille shot down an unprecedented seventeen aircraft in a single day on September 1, 1942, a feat that attests to his remarkable ability as a fighter pilot. He was killed when his ME109 (#14) developed an engine fire; he bailed out, only to be hit by the tail of his aircraft. Marseille flew with JG-27 and was awarded the diamonds to the oak leaves and swords of the Knight's Cross.

Marshall, George C. (1880–1959)

U.S. Army officer and Chief of Staff from 1939 to 1945. He commanded the world-wide war effort of the U.S. Army during World War II. In World War I, he served as an aide to General John Pershing who called him the finest Army officer of World War I. Marshall's stepson, Allen T. Brown, was killed in action in Italy in 1944. When a new five-star rank was proposed, several titles were recommended. One was General of the Armies, but Marshall decided that Pershing should be the only one to hold that rank. Another suggestion was Field Marshall but he squelched this one, saying he did not want to be called Marshall Marshall. The title finally selected was General of the Army, and he was one of those chosen to wear the fifth star. Marshall received the Nobel Peace Prize in 1953 for the Marshall Plan that helped Europe after the war.

MOVIE PORTRAYALS:
Tora! Tora! Tora! (1970), by Keith Andes
MacArthur (1977), by Ward Costello
Tail Gunner Joe (1977 TV movie), by John Anderson
Ike (1979 TV movie), by Dana Andrews
Churchill and the Generals (1981 TV movie), by Joseph Cotten

Marshall, S.L.A.

U.S. Army brigadier general. He was the chief historian in the European Theater in World War II and had previously served in World War I. Marshall was present at the liberation of Paris, along with General LeClerc's 2nd French Armored Division and Ernest Hemingway, in August 1944.

Marston Mat

Name of perforated-steel planks used by the U.S. military to surface airfields for rapid use. Enough matting to cover a 3,000-foot runway, 150 feet wide, weighing 1,200 tons, could be installed by 100 unskilled men in ninety hours. The matting got its name from the 1941 Army maneuvers near Marston, North Carolina, where it was originally used.

Martian Room

Name given to a room located at Storey's Gate, St. James Park, London, that housed a British intelligence group. The unit was commanded by John L. Austin and assigned the job of gathering information from across the English Channel that could eventually be used for an invasion of the continent.

Martians

Code name of the intelligence committee of COSSACK/SHAEF. It was also the code used to classify any information that might be useful for future invasion plans. Martians naturally worked in the Martian Room.

Martin, Barton, and Fish

Isolationist trio of U.S. Congressmen who opposed American entry into World War II and were constantly at odds with President Franklin D. Roosevelt. They were Republicans Joseph W. Martin, Jr., of Massachusetts, Bruce Barton of New York, and Hamilton Fish, also of New York. (Fish's birthday was December 7.)

Martin, Frederick Leroy

U.S. Army major general. He commanded the Hawaiian Air Force at the time of the Japanese attack on Pearl Harbor on December 7, 1941, and was relieved of command.

Martin, John

Telephone code name of Prime Minister Winston Churchill when he called President Franklin Roosevelt at the White House in World War II.

Martin, Neil

Fighter pilot with General Claire Chennault's Flying Tigers in the early days of World War II. He was the first Flying Tiger to die in battle.

Martin, William

Fictitious name of the "Man Who Never Was." The British dropped a body off the coast of Spain from the submarine H.M.S. *Seraph* on April 30, 1943, carrying papers stating that the Allies would invade the Balkans rather than Sicily. The information got back to the Germans, who then fortified the Balkans rather than Sicily, making the Allied landings there easier. The true identity of the body was never known and it was given the name Martin, the rank of Major in the Royal Marines, and the serial number 09560. The tombstone gives the date of birth as March 29, 1907, and date of death as April 24, 1943.

Marty, Andre

Frenchman who founded the International Brigades that fought against Franco during the Spanish Civil War. He was a highly incompetent communist.

Marvin, Lee (1924–   )

Hollywood actor. He enlisted in the U.S. Marine Corps when he was seventeen years old and assaulted twenty-one beaches in the Pacific from Kwajelein to Saipan as a member of I Company, 24th Marine Regiment, 4th Division. In the battle for Saipan, of 247 in his company, only he and five others survived. Marvin was wounded on Saipan, was evacuated on the hospital ship *Solace*, and spent thirteen months hospitalized. He still receives a one hundred percent disability for his injuries. At the time Marvin was fighting in the Pacific, his father fought in Europe as an Army sergeant.

Mary

Code name given by the Germans to William "Wild Bill" Donovan, who was President Roosevelt's personal envoy and later head of the OSS in World War II.

Maryland, U.S.S.

U.S. battleship weighing 31,500 tons. It was damaged during the Japanese attack on Pearl Harbor on December 7, 1941, and was one of the first ships to be repaired so that it could rejoin the fleet. The *Maryland* fought in the Battle of Leyte Gulf on October 20, 1944.

Mary Q

Name of General Omar Bradley's personal C-47. Piloted by Major Alvin E. Robinson, it was named after his wife.

Maschwitz, Eric

American song writer. He was hired to direct the forging of documents and nearly froze to death when his transport flight to Britain was forced down in Iceland.

Maskelyne, Jasper

British magician. He was selected to create illusionary weapons to deceive the Germans and almost died of oxygen starvation while being ferried across the Atlantic in a stripped-down bomber.

Mason, Donald Francis

U.S. Navy pilot. While flying a twin-engine Lockheed Hudson bomber on a return to Newfoundland from a routine submarine patrol in March 1942, he sighted the wake of a periscope going toward an unescorted cargo ship. Mason dropped his bombs and after sighting debris, radioed back "Sighted sub, sank same." He sank another submarine a month later and became a national hero. The two were among the first submarines sunk in the war.

Mason-MacFarlane, Sir Frank (1889–1953)

British lieutenant general. He was educated at Freiburg University in Germany, afterwards becoming military attaché in Berlin until 1939. He devised a scheme to assassinate Hitler using a high-powered rifle, but the British government vetoed the idea as "unsportsmanlike." In 1941, Mason-MacFarlane was the head of the British military mission to Moscow and later he became the commander of Gibraltar. In 1943, he traveled secretly to Rome in an attempt to negotiate an Italian surrender.

Massachusetts, U.S.S.

U.S. battleship. It was nicknamed "Big Mamie" and fought in thirty-five sea battles in World War II and lost not a single man.

Massey, Raymond (1896–   )

Canadian-born actor. He served in World War I as a lieutenant in the Canadian Field Artillery and was wounded at Ypres in 1916. Massey was then sent to the U.S. as a gunnery instructor at Yale and Princeton Universities. He fought with the Siberian Expeditionary Force in 1918 and 1919. Massey rejoined the Canadian Army in November 1942 as a major and was discharged in the middle of 1943 for medical reasons.

Masterman, Sir John (–1977)

Director of British, and later Allied, counterintelligence units during World War II. Part of this was the Twenty Committee which caught German spies and fed them carefully planned information, which they sent back to Germany. This was also known as "Double Cross" and was very effective in making the Germans believe Calais would be invaded instead of Normandy.

Mastroianni, Marcello (1924–   )

Italian actor. During World War II, he drew maps for the Germans and was sent to a forced labor camp in the Alps in 1943. He and a friend later escaped, going into hiding until the American occupation.

Matapan

Battle in the Mediterranean where Admiral Andrew Cunningham defeated the Italian fleet on March 28, 1941. It was the first time that radar was used by the Royal Navy. Three Italian cruisers (*Pola, Fiume,* and *Zara*), and two destroyers were sunk, and the battleship *Vittorio Veneto* was damaged.

Matthau, Walter (1920–   )

Hollywood actor. He enlisted in the U.S. Army Air Force in April 1942, winning six battle stars while serving as both a gunner and a radio operator in the European theater. Matthau was discharged in October 1945 as a staff sergeant.

Mathieu, Simone (1909–1980)

French Resistance heroine. She was the head of General Charles de Gaulle's women volunteers in the Free French Movement in London during World War II. This was known as the French WAC's.

Mature, Victor (1916–   )

Hollywood actor. He enlisted in the U.S. Coast Guard on July 2, 1942, and served for fourteen months on a Coast Guard cutter in the North Atlantic. Mature also served in recruiting and, after V-E Day, on the U.S.S. *Admiral Mayo,* a troop transport taking soldiers from Europe to the Pacific. He was discharged in November 1945 as a chief boatswain's mate.

Mauldin, William "Bill" (1921–   )

American cartoonist. He created the characters Willie and Joe to represent U.S. soldiers in World War II. Mauldin was a sergeant in the 45th Infantry Division in Sicily and Italy and drew the characters at first for the division newspaper. He later became a staff member of *Stars and Stripes* and won a Pulitzer Prize for his cartooning.

Mauthausen

Nazi concentration camp located near Hitler's home town of Linz, Austria.

Max Heiliger

Cover name of the secret bank account set up in the Reichsbank, where all gold from the Jews was deposited and credited to the account of the S.S.

May, Andrew Jackson

U.S. Congressman. He was a member of the House Military Affairs Committee and proudly announced to the press in June 1943 that the Japanese were setting their depth charges to explode at too shallow a depth to affect U.S. submarines. This information was printed, after which the Japanese began using deeper settings. Admiral Charles Lockwood, commander of U.S. submarines in the Pacific, attributed the loss of at least ten submarines and over 800 men to this thoughtless statement.

McAfee, Mildred (1900–)

U.S. Navy captain. She was the director of the WAVES in World War II. McAfee christened the carrier U.S.S. *Franklin* on October 14, 1943.

McAuliffe, Anthony C. (1898–1975)

U.S. Army brigadier general. He was the temporary commander of the 101st Airborne Division during the Battle of the Bulge in December 1944. When the division was surrounded by the Germans at Bastogne, he replied "Nuts" to a surrender demand by the German commander.

McAuliffe, Leon

Steel guitar player with Ernest Tubbs's Texas Playboys. He was a pilot for the U.S. Army Air Force in World War II.

McCain, John S. (1884–1945)

U.S. Navy vice-admiral who commanded the Third Fleet's carrier task force from August 1943 until the end of the war. McCain took part in the Japanese surrender ceremony on the U.S.S. *Missouri* in Tokyo Bay on September 2, 1945, but died at home soon afterwards on September 6.

McCampbell, David (1910–)

U.S. aviator. He was the Navy's leading ace of World War II, with thirty-four enemy aircraft shot down, and was awarded the Congressional Medal of Honor.

McCandless, Bruce (1912–1968)

U.S. Navy officer. As a thirty-year-old lieutenant commander on the cruiser U.S.S. *San Francisco* during the Battle of Guadalcanal in November 1942, McCandless was knocked unconscious by a direct hit that killed or severely wounded all superior officers. When he came to, he took command of the ship, attacked a superior Japanese force, and achieved a major U.S. Naval victory.

McCandless was awarded a Congressional Medal of Honor and later promoted to rear admiral.

McCarthy, Kevin (1915–)

Hollywood actor and brother to author Mary McCarthy *(The Group)*. He joined the U.S. Army in 1942 and served throughout World War II.

McCarthy, Joseph C.

Royal Air Force flight lieutenant. Born an American, he flew with No. 617 Squadron on the Dam Buster Raid of May 16, 1943. McCarthy's target was the Sorpe Dam and his was the only one of five attacking aircraft that successfully bombed the dam. He flew a Lancaster bomber (*T* for Tommy) and was awarded the Distinguished Service Order.

McCarthy, Joseph (1909–1957)

U.S. Senator. During World War II, he served in the U.S. Marine Corps as a gunner on aircraft and was awarded the Distinguished Flying Cross and the Air Medal.

MOVIE PORTRAYAL:
Tail Gunner Joe (1977 TV movie), by Peter Boyle

McCloy, R. C.

U.S. Navy ensign. He was a lookout on the minesweeper U.S.S. *Condor* off Pearl Harbor on December 7, 1941. McCloy was the first American to sight the enemy in World War II, when he spotted the conning tower of one of the Japanese midget submarines attempting to enter Pearl Harbor. His sighting caused it to be sunk by the U.S.S. *Ward*.

McCluskey, Wade

U.S. Navy commander. He was a graduate of the U.S. Naval Academy in 1926 and was in charge of Air Group Six from the carrier U.S.S. *Enterprise* during the Battle of Midway in June 1942. McCluskey is credited by many writers with winning World War II because he continued to search for the Japanese carriers past his estimated fuel allotment, finally sighting them. His flight attacked the *Kaga* and when he returned, it was found that he had only two gallons of gas left. McCluskey was awarded the Navy Cross.

McCombs, Charles

U.S. Navy lieutenant commander who was in charge of the destroyer U.S.S. *Monnsen*, which was sunk during the Battle of Savo Island in 1942.

McCoy, Tim (1891–1978)
Hollywood Western actor. During World War II, he was awarded a Bronze Star.

McGee, Frank (1922–1974)
NBC newscaster. During World War II, he was a journalist in London and occasionally dated Kay Summersby, General Dwight Eisenhower's aide and driver.

McGovern, George (1922–)
U.S. Senator and Presidential candidate. During World War II, he flew as a pilot of a B-24 with the U.S. Army Air Force. McGovern's aircraft was named *Dakota Queen* and was part of the 455th Bomb Group of the Fifteenth Air Force. He was awarded a Distinguished Flying Cross for a mission to the Skoda works at Pilsen, Czechoslovakia, on December 20, 1944.

McGowan, Lieutenant Colonel
Code name given to Robert Murphy, the U.S. representative to Vichy France in North Africa, as he traveled between the U.S. and England preparing for Operation Torch, the invasion of North Africa on November 8, 1942.

McGuire, Thomas Jr. (1920–1945)
U.S. Army Air Force major. He was the second-highest-scoring American ace of World War II with thirty-eight aircraft shot down. He flew P-38's with the Fifth Air Force in the southwest Pacific. When McGuire reached the score of thirty-eight aircraft, General George Kenney grounded him because his rival, Major Richard Bong, was returning to the States as the top-scoring ace with 40 aircraft and Kenney did not want Bong to arrive only to find out that he was now number two. On January 6, 1945, Bong reached the U.S., and Kenney allowed McGuire to fly again. The next day he was killed in action over Los Negros, Philippines, while engaging Japan's number two ace Shoici Sugita, when he tried to turn at low altitude with drop tanks, stalling his aircraft. McGuire had been awarded the Congressional Medal of Honor and McGuire Air Force Base in New Jersey was named after him.

McIntyre, Ross T. (1889–1959)
U.S. Navy vice-admiral. He was the Surgeon General of the U.S. Navy during World War II and was personal physician to President Franklin D. Roosevelt.

McKeogh, Mickey
U.S. Army sergeant. During World War II, he was General

Dwight Eisenhower's orderly. He wrote letters once a week to Mamie Eisenhower and helped Ike with his clothes every morning, even to the point of helping him put on his shorts. Before the war, McKeogh had been a bellboy at the Plaza Hotel in New York.

MOVIE PORTRAYAL:
Ike (1979 TV movie), by Vincent Marcello

McLain, Raymond S. (1890–1954)

U.S. Army major general. He commanded the XIX Corps and was the only American Corps commander in World War II who was a National Guardsman.

McMahon, Ed (1923–)

Announcer for Johnny Carson's "Tonight Show." He was a U.S. Marine Corps fighter pilot in World War II. Out of 150 recruits in his class, only he and one other successfully completed training and received their wings. McMahon flew for four years and at one time was stationed aboard the carrier U.S.S. *Guadalcanal* in the Pacific.

McMillan, Oden

Bandleader aboard the battleship U.S.S. *Nevada* at Pearl Harbor on December 7, 1941. He continued to lead the band through the "Star Spangled Banner" even as Japanese aircraft attacked.

McNair, Lesley J. (1883–1944)

U.S. Army lieutenant general. He commanded the Army Ground Forces in the continental U.S. in charge of training. McNair went to Europe in 1944 as a War Department observer in order to view the U.S. soldiers in combat and to evaluate the effectiveness of the training they had received in the States. General Omar Bradley said McNair also served a dual purpose as a "decoy commander," to make the Germans think a new Army group was being formed to invade the Pas de Calais instead of Normandy. McNair was killed in July 1944, by Allied carpet bombing when bombs fell short of their targets and onto U.S. positions. He was the highest-ranking U.S. Army officer to be killed in action in World War II.

McNaughton, Andrew G. (1887–1966)

Canadian Army general. He commanded the Canadian forces overseas in World War II.

McQueen, William

Father of actor Steve McQueen. He left his wife six months before the birth of son Steve and during World War II flew as a fighter pilot with General Claire Chennault's Flying Tigers in China. (Steve McQueen's first wife, Neile Adams, had been a civilian prisoner of the Japanese for eighteen months in the Philippines during World War II.)

McTureous, Robert M., Jr. (1924–)

U.S. Marine Corps private. He was awarded the last Congressional Medal of Honor to be issued during the war years for fighting on Okinawa on June 7, 1945. McTureous singlehandedly took on a series of Japanese-held caves that were firing on stretcher bearers.

McVay, Charles Butler III

U.S. Navy officer and captain of the cruiser *Indianapolis*, which was sunk on July 30, 1945, by the Japanese submarine *I-58*. McVay was court-martialed because of failure to take appropriate security measures, becoming the only commanding officer ever court-martialled for the loss of his ship in wartime in U.S. Navy history.

ME109

Main Luftwaffe fighter aircraft of World War II. Over 33,000 of these planes were produced; they were designed so that the engines could be changed and the aircraft ready to fly in twelve minutes as opposed to twenty-four to thirty-six hours for most U.S. fighters at the beginning of World War II. The ME109 could outclimb and was faster than the Spitfire during the Battle of Britain but was limited in effectiveness because it only had a ninety-minute fuel supply. The first ME109's used operationally had British-manufactured wing slats and American propellers.

ME110

Luftwaffe twin-engine fighter. It was used early in World War II but did not have the ability to oppose British fighters in daytime and was thus converted to a night fighter role. It was equipped with four machine guns and two 20mm cannons firing forward and a single 7.9mm machine gun firing to the rear.

ME209

Luftwaffe special test aircraft that was built along the lines of an ME109, except with smoother air flow and a smaller design. It set a new world speed record on April 26, 1939, of 469.22 M.P.H. German propaganda attributed this to their standard ME109 to make the world believe that their fighters were far superior. In reality the ME209's top speed could only be attained for a few seconds because the engine only had a half-hour supply of coolant that burned up after running for sixty seconds.

ME262

World's first operational jet aircraft. The first flight, on July 18, 1942, was flown by Fritz Wendel, test pilot for Messerschmitt. The flight only lasted twelve minutes but broke the world speed record when it flew over 500 M.P.H. The ME262 was finally demonstrated for Hitler on November 26, 1943, who decreed it should be built as a bomber to conduct retaliatory raids on England. The aircraft was redesigned and strengthened, with auxiliary fuel tanks added that upset the stability in flight. It also lacked an adequate bomb sight because of its speed. After many delays, the engineers and Luftwaffe pilots finally went against Hitler and revamped the plane as a fighter; but of 1,294 built, only about a quarter ever engaged the enemy.

Medals

The U.S. Army in the European Theater of Operations gave 82.32% of all decorations to the Air Force, 9.3% to the infantry, 3.5% to the Artillery, 1.5% to the medical corps, and 3.38% to all others.

Meeks, George

Black orderly to General George S. Patton in World War II. Every time Patton was promoted, Meeks received another stripe.

MOVIE PORTRAYAL:
Patton (1970), by, James Edwards

Meier, Karl Heinrich (–1940)

German spy who, along with Jose Waldberg, was the first German spy executed in Great Britain in World War II. Both were hanged in December 1940.

Meine Ehre Heisst Treue

"My honor is loyalty." It was the motto of the German S.S. and was found on the blade of all S.S. daggers. The phrase was coined by Himmler from a speech made by Hitler to the S.S. in 1931.

Mein Kampf

"My Struggle." It was the title of Adolf Hitler's book, in which he outlined his Nazi philosophy, including his anti-Semitism and his plans to conquer Eastern Europe and Russia. The book actually was composed of two parts: "A Reckoning," which was written in cell number seven in Landsberg prison in 1925 and dictated to Rudolph Hess, party secretary; and "The National Socialist Movement," which was added after Hitler's release from prison. Every newlywed couple in Germany was given a special presentation copy and the royalties made Hitler a millionaire

Memel

Baltic port that was ceded to Lithuania after World War I. Unlike the other ports of the Baltic, Memel did not freeze over in the winter. Also, it had good docks and warehouses. Hitler seized it on March 22, 1939, but it was recaptured by the Russians on January 28, 1945.

Memphis Belle

Name of the first B-17 to complete twenty-five missions over Europe in World War II. A documentary film was produced by Lieutenant Colonel William Wyler in 1944 about the *Memphis Belle*.

Mengele, Josef (1911–　　)

German S.S. doctor. He was known as the "Angel of Auschwitz" because of his cruel medical experiments at Auschwitz concentration camp during World War II. Mengele was the chief medical officer and designated new arrivals for slave labor or the crematorium. He escaped to South America after the war, where he probably still lives in hiding.

MOVIE PORTRAYALS:
Marathon Man (1976), by Laurence Olivier (as Christian Szell)
The Boys From Brazil (1978), by Gregory Peck
Playing for Time (1980 TV movie), by Max Wright

Menzies, Sir Stewart (1890–1968)

British Army major general. He was the head of MI-6, the British Secret Intelligence Service, from 1939 until 1951 and is said to be the model for "M," the boss of James Bond, created by Ian Fleming. Menzies was sent in World War I to Spain to kill or kidnap a German agent, Wilhelm Canaris, who became his counterpart in German intelligence in World War II.

Merchant Marine

U.S. maritime agency that carried cargo to all fronts during World War II. It suffered the most casualties in relation to the number of men of any of the U.S. armed forces in World War II. The Merchant Marine had to deliver ten tons of cargo space for each person to go overseas in addition to one and a half tons a month to supply him while stationed there.

Meredith, Burgess (1909–)

Hollywood actor. He served in the U.S. Army Air Force as a captain during World War II.

Merrill, Frank D. (1903–1955)

U.S. Army brigadier general. He commanded the first American infantrymen to fight in Asia, the 5307th Composite Group, better known as Merrill's Marauders. Merrill trained his group in guerrilla warfare and penetrated deep behind Japanese lines in Burma. Merrill later commanded the joint Chinese-American effort, Operation Galahad, to push the Japanese out of Burma and clear the Burma road so that supplies could get to China. In late 1944, he became aide to General Joseph Stilwell and pinned on Stilwell's fourth star when he was promoted to full general on August 7, 1944.

MOVIE PORTRAYAL:
Merrill's Marauders (1962), by Jeff Chandler

Merrill's Marauders

Name of the 5307th Composite Group; coined by *Time-Life* correspondent James Shepley.

Merriman, Robert Hale (1906–1938)

American commander of the Abraham Lincoln Battalion at the Battle of Jarama during the Spanish Civil War. Ernest Hemingway used him as the model for Robert Jordan in his novel *For Whom the Bell Tolls*. Merriman was killed in March 1938 in battle.

Mers-el-Kebir

Site of a British attack on the French fleet in June 1940 near Oran to prevent it from falling into the hands of the Germans. The British believed the Germans would use the French Navy to invade England. It is said by the French that the British killed more Frenchmen in this one attack than the Germans did in the entire invasion of France.

Mersigs Book

Name given to a khaki-colored book that was used to brief convoy captains on the signal procedures used in convoy.

Metaxas, John (1871–1941)

Greek general and premier at the time of the Italian invasion. He had been appointed Prime Minister in 1936, later becoming a dictator. Metaxas died suddenly in 1941.

Meteor

British jet fighter that was used in combat a month before the German ME262. It was flown against V-1's as early as July 1944 and was the Allies' only jet fighter used operationally during World War II.

Metox

Device installed aboard German submarines that detected the approach of aircraft before they could get within striking range. This enabled the submarine to dive to safety. Metox received radar pulses emitted from the aircraft.

Mexico

One of two Latin American countries that actually sent fighting forces to the battle zones of World War II. (The other was Brazil.) Mexico sent Squadron 201 to the Pacific toward the end of the war, flying P-47's in combat in the Philippines and Formosa. Eight Mexican pilots were killed in action.

Meyer, John C. (1919–1975)

U.S. Army Air Force lieutenant colonel. He became an ace with twenty-four enemy aircraft shot down. Meyer flew a P-51 named *Petie*.

Meyer's Hunting Horn

Nickname that Germans gave to air raid sirens. It was taken from the time when Goering proclaimed that if a bomb ever fell on the Reich, his name would be Meyer.

Mga

Obscure Russian town that was captured by the Germans on August 30, 1941. This cut the last overland link between Leningrad and the rest of the Soviet Union and began the siege of Leningrad.

MI-5

Designator of the British counterintelligence agency. It searched for Axis spies and set up the Twenty Committee to turn them against their masters.

MI-6

Designator of the British secret intelligence service headed by Sir Stewart Menzies that conducted all espionage activity.

MI-9

Designator of a British organization to help Allied personnel to escape from occupied Europe back to England. Lines of communication criss-crossed the continent and helped escaped POW's, as well as newly shot-down airmen. Airey Neave, himself an escaped POW, headed MI-9.

Michel

Name of a German auxiliary cruiser or armed merchant ship. It accounted for the loss of 121,994 tons of Allied shipping or a total of 17 ships on two voyages. The first trip was under Lieutenant Commander von Ruckteschell and ended March 2, 1943, at Kobe, Japan. The same day that the *Michel* set sail under the command of Captain Gunther Gumprich, it was sunk by the submarine U.S.S. *Tarpon*. It was the first German ship sunk by a U.S. submarine in World War II. The Germans had also designated *Michel* HSK IX or Ship 28.

Michelin

French tire manufacturer who published road guides to France that were used by the Germans in the 1940 invasion. Michelin maps were also used by the British Expeditionary Forces to find their way to Dunkirk because the B.E.F. could not get adequate tactical maps from the War Department. One officer, Major Cyril Barclay, bought 80 maps in one of the small French villages and successfully led his unit to Dunkirk, but the War Office refused to reimburse him because "regulations offer no provision for an officer to buy maps on active service."

Michener, James A. (1907–)

Pulitzer Prize–winning American author. He waived his Quaker status exempting him from military service and enlisted in the U.S. Navy during World War II. Michener served as an officer in charge of aviation maintenance in the Solomon Islands, where he wrote his first book, *Tales of the South Pacific*. He was discharged as a lieutenant commander.

MOVIE PORTRAYAL:

Men of the Fighting Lady (1954), by Louis Calhern

Mickey

Name given to an American radar bomb sight that allowed navigators to find their designated targets even under conditions of zero visibility and to bomb accurately through cloud cover or in the dark.

Mickey Mouse

Password used by U.S. forces on D-Day, June 6, 1944.

Mickey Mouse

Walt Disney character that was painted on the side of an ME109 flown by one of Germany's leading aces, Adolf Galland.

Midway

U.S. Naval refueling station and airbase 1,136 miles west of

Hawaii. It was the target of Japanese Admiral Isoruku Yamamoto in an attempt to draw out and destroy the last U.S. carriers from Hawaii. The Japanese outnumbered the U.S. with eight carriers, eleven battleships, eighteen cruisers, and sixty-five destroyers to the U.S.'s three carriers, no battleships, eight cruisers, and fifteen destroyers; yet they were defeated June 4–6, 1942, because of the American ability to read their codes. The defeat of Midway was the first Japanese Naval defeat since 1592 (at the hands of the Koreans) and it marked the end of the threat from Japanese carriers. For the U.S., the victory equalized the Japanese and American fleets and allowed the U.S. to move from a defensive to an offensive role in the Pacific. As in the Battle of the Coral Sea, there was no exchange of gunfire; aviation accounted for all the attacking. The Japanese lost the carriers *Akagi*, *Kaga*, *Hiryu*, and *Soryu*, while the U.S. lost the *Yorktown*.

MIG-1

Designator of a Soviet fighter that was first used in 1940. It was designed by Artem Mikoyan and Mikhail I. Gurevich.

Mihajlovic, General Draza (1893–1946)

Yugoslavian war minister and colonel in the Royal Yugoslavian Army. When the Germans invaded Yugoslavia, he set up a band of guerrillas called the Chetniks to resist the Nazis, for which he was hailed as the first Resistance leader in occupied Europe. Mihajlovic represented the old regime upon the return of the royalists and was selected as both a general and Commander in Chief by the exiled Yugoslavian government. He later fought against the other guerrilla leader, Josef Tito, and aided the Nazis when it suited his needs. After the war, he was tried by the Communist government on charges of treason and of aiding the enemy, for which he was shot by a firing squad on July 17, 1946. (His son and daughter both fought with Tito in World War II.)

MOVIE PORTRAYAL:

Chetniks (1943), by Philip Dorn

Mighty Mo

Nickname given to the U.S. battleship *Missouri* in World War II.

Mighty Moo

Nickname given to the U.S. light aircraft carrier U.S.S. *Cowpens* (CVL-25), which was named after a Revolutionary War battle.

Mikado

Name of a Michigan town that changed its name to MacArthur after the Japanese attack on Pearl Harbor on December 7, 1941.

Mikoyan, Artem I. (1905–1970)

Soviet aircraft designer. He was the brother of Soviet politician Anastas Mikoyan.

Mikuma

Japanese heavy cruiser. In the Battle of the Java Sea, it fired torpedoes at the U.S.S. *Houston,* missed, and sank instead four Japanese transports in Bantam Bay, Batavia, February 27, 1942. The *Mikuma* participated in the Battle of Midway, where it was rammed and damaged by the cruiser *Mogami* and subsequently attacked by aircraft based at Midway. U.S. Marine Corps Captain Richard E. Fleming, who crashed into the turret behind the bridge thus crippling the cruiser, was later awarded a posthumous Congressional Medal of Honor. The *Mikuma* was finally sunk by aircraft from the carriers *Hornet* and *Enterprise* on June 6, 1942.

Milch Cow

Name given to the Type XIV German submarine. It carried every provision needed by the smaller submarines, including 432 tons of diesel oil to refuel them at sea, thus extending their time in combat areas. These submarines, being extremely large, were both vulnerable and not very maneuverable. Of the ten ''Milch Cows'' with which Germany began the war, the British succeeded in locating and sinking all.

Milch, Erhard (1891–1972)

German Air Force field marshall who was half-Jewish. The Nazis got around this by having his mother sign a statement that she had committed adultery. Milch was tried at Nuremberg in 1947 and sentenced to life imprisonment, but this was reduced to fifteen years. He was released in 1955.

MOVIE PORTRAYAL:

Inside the Third Reich (1982 TV miniseries), by Robert Vaughn

Milice

Name of the French fascist police under German occupation. There were 250,000 members headed by Joseph Darnand, who made Milice even more feared than the S.S.

Military Academies

Australia—Duntroon

Belgium—Ecole Royale Militaire
Britain—Cranwell (R.A.F.)
Sandhurst (Army)
Canada—Royal Military College
China—Whampoa
France—St. Cyr
Italy—Accademia Militare
Japan—Eta Jima (Navy)
Netherlands—Koninklijke Militaire Academie
Russia—Frunze
Spain—Academia General Militar
U.S.—Annapolis (Navy)
West Point (Army)

Milland, Ray (1907–)

Hollywood actor. In the 1920's, he had been a member of the British Royal House Guards and assigned to mounted guard duty at Whitehall. At the beginning of World War II, he attempted to join the U.S. Army Air Force but was rejected due to impaired use of his left hand. Instead, Milland became a civilian flight instructor for the Army, completing two tours of duty in the Solomon Islands. He also entertained troops as part of a U.S.O. group on Guadalcanal and Tulagi in 1944.

Miller, Dory (–1943)

U.S. Navy mess attendant on the U.S.S. *West Virginia* at Pearl Harbor. During the Japanese attack on December 7, 1941, he shot down two Japanese aircraft officially and six aircraft unofficially, for which he was awarded the Navy Cross. He was the first black to be so honored in World War II. Many accounts report Miller as having fought on the U.S.S. *Arizona,* but in fact he did not. He was killed on Thanksgiving Day, 1943, when the carrier *Liscombe Bay* was torpedoed.

Miller, Glenn (1904–1944)

American bandleader. He enlisted in the U.S. Army Air Force in 1942 as a captain (serial number 0505273) and head of an Air Force band. Miller was lost on a flight over the North Sea en route to Europe to entertain troops on December, 15, 1944. His musical arranger Glen Gray missed the flight because of a head cold.

MOVIE PORTRAYAL:
The Glenn Miller Story (1954), by Jimmy Stewart
The Five Pennies (1959), by Ray Daley

Miller, Henry J. F. (–1949)

U.S. Army major general. He graduated from West Point in 1915 with General Dwight Eisenhower, serving as quartermaster of the Ninth Army Air Force in England. Miller was responsible for one of the major security leaks of Operation Overlord when he stated at a party at Claridges on April 18, 1944, that D-Day would be prior to June 15. For this Eisenhower ordered him back to the States and reduced in rank to a lieutenant colonel.

Miller, Norman (1918–1946)

U.S. Navy captain. He was the most decorated Navy flyer of World War II and was called a one-man task force. Miller took his Liberator, named *Thunder Mug,* into Truk lagoon time after time at mast-top level, sinking or damaging more than sixty Japanese vessels.

Miller, William (1914–)

While in the U.S. Army during World War II, he was one of the assistant prosecutors at the Nazi war crimes trials at Nuremberg, serving under Supreme Court Justice Robert A. Jackson.

Mills, John (1908–)

British actor and father of actress Hayley Mills. During World War II, he joined the Royal Engineers and later received a commission in the Royal Monmouthshire Rifles but was medically discharged in 1942 because of ulcers.

Milne Bay

New Guinea port 230 miles from Port Moresby. The Japanese landed at Milne Bay August 25, 1942, but were stopped by General Douglas MacArthur because he had prior knowledge of their intentions from code intercepts. It was the first time a Japanese amphibious assault had been halted and forced to withdraw in World War II.

Milorg

Name of the Norwegian Resistance movement. It succeeded in tying down thirteen Wehrmacht divisions, 90,000 Kriegsmarine, and 6,000 S.S. by the end of the war. Milorg accepted the surrender of 400,000 Germans and liberated over 90,000 prisoners of war.

Minh, Ho Chi (1890–1969)

Vietnamese nationalist who gravitated toward the Communist party after disillusionment with right-wing parties and their lack of concern for Asian national interests. He returned to Vietnam in 1941 after 30 years of exile and set up the Viet Minh to oppose the Japanese. His guerrillas, who worked for the OSS, rescued seventeen downed U.S. airmen (see Lucius).

Mississinewa

U.S. fleet tanker anchored at Ulithi atoll where it was sunk in October 1944 by a Japanese Kaiten (suicide torpedo). The *Mississinewa* was the first ship to be sunk in this manner.

Miss Kimiko

Code name used by the Japanese to refer to President Franklin Roosevelt in telephone conversations between the Japanese embassy in Washington, D.C., and Tokyo, prior to December 7, 1941.

Missouri Mule

Name given to General Omar Bradley's Piper Cub observation aircraft. It was flown by Captain Delbert L. Bristol.

Missouri, U.S.S. (BB-63)

U.S. Navy battleship on which the Japanese signed the surrender terms in Tokyo Bay on September 2, 1945. It was nicknamed the *Mighty Mo* and is now located in Bremerton, Washington, in "the Mothball Reserves." After V-J Day, the *Missouri* was opened to the public in New York, but visitors did so much damage that it had to be sent to a Navy yard for repairs.

Miss Umeko

Japanese foreign ministry code name for U.S. Secretary of State Cordell Hull.

Mistresses

Martin Bormann—Manja Behrens
King Carol—Magda Lupescu
Adolf Eichmann—Margit Kutschera, Maria Masenbucher
Herman Fegelein—Mata O'Hara
Joseph Goebbels—Lida Baarova
Ritter von Greim—Hanna Reitsch
Heinrich Himmler—Hedwig Potthast
Adolf Hitler—Eva Braun
Josef Mengele—Irma Griese
Benito Mussolini—Clara Petacci
Juan Perón—Eva Duarte
Ezra Pound—Olag Rudge
Paul Reynand—Helene de Portes
Viktor Sokolov—Margarete Baraeza
Josef Stalin—Marina Raskova

Julius Streicher—Anni Seitz
Isoruku Yamamoto—Chioko Kawai

Mitchell, Cameron (1918–)

Hollywood actor. He flew as a bombardier during World War II.

Mitchell, George Washington (1879–1949)

Black doorman of the American embassy in Paris for over twenty-five years. He went to Europe prior to the turn of the century with Buffalo Bill's Wild West Show and remained to become an embassy landmark until the U.S. entered the war.

Mitchell, John (1913–)

U.S. Attorney General under President Richard Nixon. He served in the U.S. Navy during World War II as a commander.

MOVIE PORTRAYAL:
Blind Ambition (1979 TV movie), by John Randolph

Mitchell, Reginald (1895–1937)

British aeronautical engineer. He designed the Spitfire and was one of the few men with the foresight needed to save England. Mitchell died in 1937 before the first production model of his Spitfire flew.

MOVIE PORTRAYAL:
The First and the Few (1942), by Leslie Howard (his last movie)

Mitchum, Robert (1917–)

Hollywood actor. He was drafted into the U.S. Army in 1945 but was given a deferment to finish the World War II film *GI Joe*. After spending eight months as a private at Fort MacArthur and at Camp Roberts, Mitchum received a hardship discharge by claiming six dependents.

Mitscher, Marc A. (1887–1947)

U.S. Navy vice-admiral. He was the thirty-second Navy man to receive his pilot's rating and was a pilot of NC-1, the aircraft that made the trans-Atlantic crossing of May 1919. Mitscher was the first air officer on the U.S.'s first true aircraft carrier, the *Saratoga*, landing the first aircraft on its deck. In April 1942, Mitscher was captain of the U.S.S. *Hornet*, which launched the B-25's of Doolittle's Raid on Tokyo. He later commanded Carrier Task Force 58 in the Pacific Campaign.

Mitch's Squitch

Name of John W. Mitchell's P-38 that led the attack that shot down Japanese Admiral Isoruku Yamamoto's plane on April 18, 1943.

Model, Walther (1891–1945)

German field marshall. He was known as the "Fuehrer's Fireman" because Hitler shifted him from one difficult command to another. Model committed suicide after 320,000 Germans surrendered in the Ruhr pocket on April 18, 1945.

MOVIE PORTRAYAL:
Is Paris Burning? (1966), by Konrad Georg

Moelders, Werner (1913–1941)

German Luftwaffe ace. He was the top-scoring Luftwaffe ace of the Spanish Civil War, with fourteen aircraft shot down, and was the first fighter pilot of World War II to exceed Baron von Richtofen's World War I score of 80 aircraft. Moelders was also the first person in history to exceed 100 victories in the air and was the first recipient of the diamonds to the oak leaves and swords of the Knight's Cross. On June 5, 1940, he was shot down over France by French Second Lieutenant Pommier-Layrargues and was a prisoner of war until the fall of France. Moelders was an anti-Nazi but was tolerated because of his accomplishments. He was killed on November 22, 1941, while flying as a passenger in an HE111 to General Ernst Udet's funeral when his aircraft crashed in bad weather. He had shot down a total of 115 enemy aircraft at the time of his death.

Mogami

Japanese heavy cruiser that, during the Battle of Midway in 1942, accidentally rammed another cruiser, the *Mikuma*, which was disabled and later sunk by U.S. carrier aircraft. During the Battle of Leyte Gulf in 1944, the *Mogami* itself was rammed by another Japanese heavy cruiser, the *Nachi*, and subsequently sank.

Mohr, Johann (–1943)

German Navy lieutenant commander. He sank the British cruiser *Dunedin* on November 24, 1941, with two torpedoes, which he fired from over three miles away while commanding the *U-124*. Mohr was the seventeenth-ranked submarine ace of the war, having sunk twenty-seven Allied ships totaling 132,731 tons. He himself was sunk in April 1943.

Molotov Cocktail

Name given to a bottle filled with flammable liquid used to knock out tanks. Attached to the bottle was a wick, which was lit before the bottle was hurled against a tank. When the bottle broke, the wick ignited the liquid, setting the tank on fire. The name was first used by the Finns in the Russo-Finnish War of 1940, but Molotov Cocktails, which were named after the Soviet Foreign Minister, were actually used for the first time during the Spanish Civil War.

Molotov's Bread Basket

Name that the Finns gave to Soviet bombs. After Russia attacked Finland on November 30, 1940, they bombed Helsinki, a fact that the Finns broadcast to the world. The Russian radio called them liars, stating that the bombers were only dropping bread to the starving masses.

Molotov, V. M. (1890–   )

Soviet foreign minister. He replaced Litvinov as the Soviet negotiator with the Germans because Litvinov was Jewish. However, Molotov's wife was also Jewish, a fact kept secret from Hitler by his closest advisers. Molotov signed the Soviet-German Nonaggression Pact in 1939. After the German invasion of Russia in June 1941, he was also involved in negotiations with the U.S. President Franklin Roosevelt nicknamed him "Stone-Ass" because he seemed to be able to sit forever and continuously propose the same issue. In June 1943, Molotov traveled over 2,000 miles into German-occupied territory to confer with German Foreign Minister Joachim von Ribbentrop about a separate peace, but nothing came of the talks.

MOVIE PORTRAYAL:
Mission to Moscow (1943), by Gene Lockhart

von Moltke, Helmuth (1907–1945)

German intellectual. He was a former Rhodes scholar and was the leader of the anti-Hitler Kreisau Circle. Von Moltke was arrested in January 1944 by the Gestapo, who executed him a year later.

Monaghan, U.S.S.

U.S. destroyer that sank a Japanese midget submarine inside Pearl Harbor December 7, 1941. The submarine was from *I-16* and had Lieutenant Masaharu Yokoyama and Petty Officer Teiji Veda aboard. It was later used as fill for land reconstruction with both bodies still inside. The *Monaghan* shelled and damaged the Japanese submarine *I-7* on June 22, 1943, resulting in its being beached at Kiska. The *Monaghan* was capsized by a typhoon on December 17, 1944.

Monitors

Name given to bulletins released by the Operational Intelligence Center of SHAEF that included what was known about the German defenses opposing the D-Day landings.

Montagu, Ewen

British Navy commander. He was part of Naval Intelligence along with Ian Fleming. Montagu authored the plan for using a corpse to fool the Germans into believing that an invasion of the Balkans rather than Sicily was imminent.

MOVIE PORTRAYAL:

The Man Who Never Was (1956), by Clifton Webb (based on the book authored by Ewen Montagu)

Montana State

The only American college to lose its entire 1940-1941 eleven-man football team in World War II.

Dana Bradford—end	killed in plane crash
John Hall, Jr.—end	killed in plane crash
Albert Zupin—center	killed in plane crash
John Burke—tackle	killed in Italy
Newell Burke—tackle	killed in New Guinea
Bernard Cluzen—guard	killed in South Pacific
Joseph McGreever—guard	killed in Germany
Wendell Scabad—backfield	killed in action
John Phelan—backfield	killed in action
Alton Zempel—quarterback	killed in plane crash
Rich Roman—backfield	killed in Germany

Monte Cassino

Italian monastery bombed on February 15, 1944, as a result of one of the most controversial decisions of the war. The Benedictine Monastery was defended by German General von Senger und Etterlin, who was a lay member of the Benedictine Order. The Germans were not actually in the monastery, but British General Freyberg ordered it bombed anyway because of its strategic location. The Germans then moved into the rubble, which made it even more difficult to get them out since ruins are more easily defended than intact buildings. The only part of the Abbey that remained undamaged was the cell where St. Benedict had lived, died, and was buried. A heavy caliber artillery shell had landed a foot away from the tomb but did not explode.

Monterrey, U.S.S. (CV-26)

U.S. Navy light aircraft carrier on which President Gerald Ford served during World War II.

Montgomery

Name of the house General Dwight Eisenhower stayed in at Granville, France, after the D-Day landings.

Montgomery, **Bernard Law (1887-1976)**

British field marshall. He escaped from Dunkirk in 1940 and planned the Dieppe Raid. When it failed, he washed his hands of it, took command of the British Eighth Army in North Africa, and adapted the plans of General Auchinleck, which proved successful. Montgomery blamed all the failures on Auchinleck and his staff without giving them any credit for the successes. He had a high opinion of himself and felt he was the only one who could adequately control a battle. He would not attack until he had an overwhelming superiority in everything. Montgomery commanded forces in Sicily, Normandy, and Operation Market-Garden. He failed to take Caen in the allotted time, failed to clear the Scheldt Estuary to open the port of Antwerp, and masterminded Operation Market-Garden, which also failed. He was not well-thought-of by most Allied commanders because of his egoism; General Dwight Eisenhower referred to him as a "thorn in my side." Montgomery, whose two favorite books were *The Bible* and *Pilgrim's Progress*, himself wrote a book called *Infantry Manual*.

MOVIE PORTRAYALS:
I Was Monty's Double (1958), by E. Clifton James
The Longest Day (1962), by Trevor Reid
Desert Tanks (1968), by Michael Rennie
Patton (1970), by Michael Bates
Ike (1979 TV movie), by Ian Richardson
Churchill and the Generals (1981 TV movie), by Ian Richardson

Montgomery, George (1916–   )

Hollywood actor who enlisted in the U.S. Army during World War II and took part in the invasion of North Africa. While he was in the service, his wife at the time, Dinah Shore, made numerous U.S.O. appearances. Montgomery rose to the rank of corporal.

Montgomery, Robert (1904–1981)

Hollywood actor and father of actress Elizabeth Montgomery. On May 30, 1940, he arrived in Paris to serve as a volunteer in the American Field Services as an ambulance driver. He was to be there six months, but the fall of France caused him to leave aboard the Pan American Clipper for New York in June 1940. In August 1941, Montgomery enlisted in the U.S. Navy Reserve as Lieutenant (j.g.) Henry Montgomery, Jr., and became the assistant naval attaché in the U.S. embassy in London. After returning to Washington, D.C., in November 1941, he requested and received sea duty as a PT-boat commander, first in Panama, then in Guadalcanal and the Marshall Islands. Montgomery contracted malaria and returned to the U.S. in April 1943, becoming soon afterwards an operations officer and lieutenant commander aboard a destroyer. He fought in support of the D-Day landings and was one of the first people to enter the captured port of Cherbourg, for which he received a Bronze Star. Montgomery returned to the U.S. where he starred as PT commander John Brickley in the 1945 movie *They Were Expendable*. He was discharged shortly thereafter as a commander. In 1947, he received the French Legion of Honor for his service as an ambulance driver back in 1940. Montgomery became an adviser to President Dwight Eisenhower and directed the movie *The Gallant Hours* about Admiral William F. Halsey, whom Montgomery greatly admired.

Montgomery Ward and Company

U.S. mail-order company. The U.S. Army seized the Chicago plant on April 26, 1944, after Chairman Sewell Avery refused to follow a War Labor Board directive regarding a CIO contract. The Army withdrew on April 29, and Montgomery Ward submitted a bill to the U.S. government for $480,000 for damages incurred while it was under Army management.

Monti, Martin James

U.S. Army Air Force lieutenant. He defected to the Germans in October 1944 by flying his P-38 to Vienna to fight the Russians. The Germans did not fully trust him but placed him in charge of an American S.S. unit. In January 1948, Monti was tried in Brooklyn Federal Court and charged with twenty-one overt acts including treason, theft of U.S government property, and being an agent of the enemy, and was sentenced to twenty-five years in prison and given a $10,000 fine.

Montini, Giovanni Battista (1897–1978)

Catholic monsignor during World War II. He was the Vatican Undersecretary of State for Current Affairs and as such passed intelligence information to the OSS about bombing targets in Tokyo. The world knew him later as Pope Paul VI.

Moonlight Sonata

Code name for the German raid on Coventry, England, on November 14, 1940.

Moonshine

Code name of the U.S. equipment used to produce false readings on German radar. It was developed by Dr. Joan Cockburn and first tested on April 6, 1942, for its ability to simulate bombers approaching Cherbourg. Moonshine was used extensively during the D-Day landings to generate the impression of a fictitious fleet approaching the Pas de Calais so that the Germans would not move reinforcements to Normandy.

Moon Squadrons

Special Royal Air Force units that specialized in clandestine activity over Europe. By D-Day they had flown 2,562 missions and dropped over 1,000 agents and 40,000 containers of equipment.

Moore, George (1887–1949)

U.S. Army major general. He commanded the forces on Corregidor when it fell to the Japanese in 1942. Moore surrendered along with General Jonathan Wainwright, spending three years as a prisoner of war after surviving the Bataan Death March. He committed suicide in 1949.

Moran, Charles (1882–1977)

British doctor and personal physician to Prime Minister Winston Churchill.

Moravec, Frantisek

Czech major general. He was an intelligence officer and escaped from Czechoslovakia on March 14, 1939, just prior to the German occupation. Moravec planned the assassination of Reinhard Heydrich in 1942.

Morell, Dr. Theodor (1887–1948)

German doctor who was the personal physician of Hitler. He had begun his career in the Merchant Marine treating venereal disease, becoming a V.D. specialist in Berlin. Morell was introduced to Hitler by Heinrich Hoffman, personal photographer to the Fuehrer, and became wealthy producing medicines under Hitler's good graces. He owned his own pharmaceutical company, one product of which was used exclusively by the military. It was a lice powder called "Russia." Morell was an addict of morphine and injected Hitler with drugs laced with atropine and strychnine. Many tried to warn Hitler of Morell's quackery but Hitler believed in him and would not hear any adverse talk.

MOVIE PORTRAYALS:
Hitler (1962), by John Wengraf
The Bunker (1980 TV movie), by John Sharpe

Morgan, Charles
British Royal Navy captain in command of H.M.S. *Valiant* on December 19, 1941, when it was badly damaged by an Italian two-man torpedo. The two Italians, Lieutenants Luigi Durand de la Penne and Bianchi were captured exhausted in the water before the explosion and brought to Captain Morgan but refused to divulge any information. After the battleship was damaged they were sent to a prisoner-of-war camp. In March 1945, Morgan, now an admiral, was stationed at the Italian Naval base of Taranto when the Italian Crown Prince came to award medals. Italy's highest decoration, a Gold Medal, went to de la Penne for damaging the *Valiant* and Admiral Morgan pinned it on him.

Morgan, Sir Frederick E. (1894–1967)
British Army lieutenant general. He drew up the initial plans for the Normandy invasion. After the war, Morgan headed the British atomic energy project and is considered the father of the British H-bomb.

Morgan, Henry (1915–1982)
Radio comedian. He enlisted in the U.S. Army Air Force in January 1943 and was discharged in the fall of 1945, having never left the States.

Morgenthau, Henry Jr. (1891–1967)
U.S. Secretary of the Treasury from 1934 to 1945. He devised the Lend-Lease program which gave Britain and other allies the much-needed weaponry to fight the Axis. Morgenthau also raised the funds needed to pay for the U.S. war effort. He drafted what became known as the Morgenthau Plan.

Morgenthau Plan
Scheme devised for the destruction of all German industrial capacity and a return of Germany to a pastoral society, thus destroying any chances of its ability to ever wage war again. Although, Morgenthau had his name put on the plan, it was actually authored by the Assistant Treasury Secretary Harry Dexter White, who was a Communist sympathizer.

Morison, Samuel Eliot (1887–1976)
Two-time Pulitzer Prize–winning author. He was a former professor of history at Harvard and was selected as the official historian

of the U.S. Navy in World War II. Morison was present as an observer at many of the famous battles of the war.

Morris, Howard (1919–)

Hollywood comedy writer, actor, and director. During World War II, he served as an Army first sergeant. One of the enlisted men who served with him was Carl Reiner.

Morris, Mack

U.S. newspaperman for *Yank* magazine. In the third week of April 1945, he and Ernest Leiser of *Stars and Stripes* magazine jeeped into Berlin without meeting any opposition. This was before the fall of the city to the Russians.

Morris, Wayne (1914–1959)

Hollywood actor. He flew as a U.S. Navy fighter pilot in the Pacific during World War II and was Hollywood's first ace with seven Japanese aircraft shot down. Morris flew fifty-seven combat missions and was awarded four Distinguished Flying Crosses. He was also credited with sinking two Japanese destroyers. He said his one big fear was that one of his movies might be shown on his ship. He was discharged in 1945 as a lieutenant commander. Morris died September 14, 1959, of a heart attack while aboard the aircraft carrier U.S.S. *Bonhomme Richard*, which was commanded by his wife's uncle, Captain David MacCampbell.

Mortal Storm

Film produced in 1940 by MGM. It was the first film to name Hitler specifically. Previous films had resorted to facsimile, as did Charlie Chaplin's *Great Dictator.* Word got back to the U.S. from the Swiss consulate that the Germans intended to punish everyone involved in the production of the film once Germany won the war.

Moscicki, Ignacy (1867–1946)

Polish President at the outbreak of the war. He fled to Paris just before the fall of Poland.

Mosconi, Willie (1913–)

Popular American billiards player. In 1944, he was drafted into the U.S. Army where he spent a year with the Special Services until his discharge.

Mosdale

Norwegian cargo ship that crossed the Atlantic more times (ninety-eight) than any other Allied ship in World War II. In June 1941, it had the distinction of transporting the first Canadian female to go to sea in World War II, when Fern Blodgett joined the ship's crew as a radio operator. She made seventy-eight crossings of the Atlantic with the ship and in July 1942, married the ship's captain, Gerner Sunde.

Mosley, Oswald E. (1896–1980)

British politician. He had been a member of Parliament in the 1920's. When the Depression struck England, Mosley founded the British Union of Fascists, which was also known as the Black Shirts. He modeled his organization after the Nazi party, thus keeping in touch with Hitler. Mosley was arrested in 1940 as a threat to security but released from prison in 1943 due to ill health.

Mosquito

British twin-engine aircraft that was made of plywood so that it could penetrate enemy radar. It was built by de Havilland without government backing because the British government believed that wooden airplanes were only for World War I minds. The Mosquito was used extensively on counterinsurgency missions behind enemy lines, as well as on pathfinder missions for Allied bombers. It was called "Termite's Delight" or the "Wooden Wonder."

Moss, Sanford Alexander (1872–1946)

U.S. research engineer who invented the supercharger for aircraft and automobile engines. B-29's in World War II equipped with his superchargers were able to climb to unprecedented heights, giving them a tremendous advantage over enemy forces.

Mostel, Samuel (Zero) (1915–1980)

Hollywood and Broadway actor. He was drafted into the U.S. Army in March 1943 but was discharged at the end of the year.

Mother of the WAVES

Nickname given to U.S. Senator Margaret Chase Smith because of her work in advancing the status of women in the U.S. Navy.

Mother's Cross

Nazi medal instituted by Hitler in December 1938 to encourage German women to have more children for the fatherland. The medal came in three grades: bronze for four children; silver for six or seven children; gold for eight or more children. It was awarded every year on August 12, the birthdate of Hitler's mother.

Moulin, Jean (1899–1943)

Head of the French Resistance Movement and General Charles de Gaulle's personal representative in France. His code name was Max, but he was nicknamed the "King of Shadows" because of his elusiveness. Moulin was finally captured by the Gestapo in

June 1943, was tortured, and died without revealing any information about the Resistance.

Mountbatten, Lord Louis (1900–1979)

British admiral who commanded Combined Operations and later the Southeast Asia Command. He was the second cousin of King George VI and was the first Englishman other than the King to hold rank in all three services simultaneously. Mountbatten began the war commanding a destroyer, the H.M.S. *Kelly*, which was sunk off Crete in 1941. He was one of the most capable commanders the British had during the war. In 1945 he accepted the surrender of Japanese land forces in Southeast Asia and signed the surrender at Singapore in September. Mountbatten was killed by a bomb of the Irish Republican Army on August 26, 1979, a sad end for one of Britain's real heroes of the war. (Another hero was Airey Neave, member of Parliament, who was also killed by the IRA.)

MOVIE PORTRAYALS:
In Which We Serve (1942), by Noel Coward (as Captain Kinross)
The Devil's Brigade (1968), by Patric Knowles

Mount Elbrus

The highest peak in the Caucasus Mountains at 18,480 feet. It was probably the highest point conquered by German troops in World War II, when the men of the First Mountain Division and the Fourth Mountain Division successfully scaled it on August 21, 1941.

Mount Emily

Oregon site of the first bombing of American soil during World War II. It was bombed on September 9, 1942, by Nobuo Fujita, who flew from the Japanese submarine *I-25* and was the only person ever to bomb the continental U.S. The attack started a forest fire that was quickly put out by forestry personnel.

Mousetrap

Name given to a U.S Navy rocket-propelled antisubmarine weapon. It was developed in 1943 and was similar to the hedgehog but lacked recoil. It took quite a bit of effort for a crew to become proficient in using it, so a practice rocket was developed that was called *Minnie Mouse*.

Moyzisch, L. C.

German attaché at the embassy in Ankara, Turkey, during World War II. He was also the chief of the S.S. Security Service and as such was the contact man for *Cicero* (see Bazna; Cicero).

MOVIE PORTRAYAL:
Five Fingers (1952), by Oscar Karlweis

Mr. P

Code name used by Prime Minister Winston Churchill at the Casablanca Conference in 1943.

Mrs. Miniver

President Franklin Roosevelt was so impressed with the closing speech given in the 1942 movie *Mrs. Miniver* that he had it printed on leaflets and dropped over Nazi-occupied Europe.

Mueller, Heinrich (1900–)

German S.S. chief of the Gestapo from 1936 to 1945. He was largely responsible for making the Gestapo the efficient terrorizing police force it became. Mueller was denied admission into the Nazi party until 1939 because as a Munich policeman he had worked against the party in its early days. After the war, it was rumored that he had defected to Russia and was working in their secret police. A tombstone was erected in his name over a grave in the American sector of Berlin, but when the grave was opened in 1963, it was found to contain the remains of three separate people.

MOVIE PORTRAYAL:
Holocaust (1978 TV movie), by Anthony Haygarth

Mulberries

Name given to prefabricated harbors that were floated across the English Channel to create sheltered areas for ships supporting the D-Day invasion. They were conceived by Lord Mountbatten and cost $96 million each. It took 20,000 men eight months to build each one from two million tons of concrete and steel. Two were built, one for the British at Arromanches and one for the Americans intended for Omaha Beach. The latter was destroyed on June 19, 1944, by a storm.

Mulloy, Gardner

U.S. tennis player. He was one of the winners of the U.S. National Doubles Championship in 1942, 1946, and 1948. During World War II, Mulloy commanded an LST and took part in the invasion of Salerno and Anzio.

Mulzac, Hugh

British West Indies-born black who became a U.S. citizen in 1918. He was the first black to hold a U.S. master's certificate in the Merchant Marine. Mulzac was also the first black to command a Liberty ship, the *Booker T. Washington*.

Munemori, Sadao (–1945)

U.S. Army private first class. He was the only Japanese-American to win the Congressional Medal of Honor in World War II. Munemori was a member of the 442nd Combat Team in Italy, where he threw himself on a grenade, saving the lives of his fellow soldiers. His mother was presented the medal while interned in Manzanar in the Owens Valley of California.

Murder Inc.

Nickname of a B-17 assigned to the 508th Squadron, 351st Bombardment Group of the Eighth Army Air Force. On November 26, 1943, the crew flew a spare bomber on a raid over Bremen and had to bail out. They had "Murder Inc." painted on the backs of their flight jackets. German propaganda used them as the example to portray the Americans as a bunch of gangsters.

Murders of the Rue Morgue

Novel by Edgar Allan Poe. A German translation surfaced along with other debris when the destroyer *George E. Badger* sank the submarine *U-613* on July 23, 1943.

Murphy, Audie (1924–1971)

Hollywood actor. He was officially listed as the most decorated soldier of World War II and is credited with killing or capturing 240 German soldiers. Murphy was awarded the Congressional Medal of Honor plus twenty-seven other medals, including the Distinguished Service Cross, three Silver Stars, Legion of Merit, Bronze Star, three Purple Hearts, Good Conduct Medal, Victory Medal, European Theater Medal, the American Theater Medal, the French Legion of Honor, and the Croix de Guerre.

Murphy, Robert (1894–1978)

U.S. diplomat. He was Acting U.S. Consul in Munich during Hitler's November 9, 1923, Beer Hall Putsch attempt. Murphy was also the U.S. representative in North Africa to the French Vichy government and was the underground chief of U.S. intelligence. He paved the way for Operation Torch, the North Africa invasion of November 8, 1942. Afterwards, Murphy became General Dwight Eisenhower's political adviser for the remainder of the war.

Murray, George D. (1890–1956)

U.S. Navy captain. He was in command of the carrier U.S.S.

Enterprise off Hawaii at the time of the Pearl Harbor attack by the Japanese.

Murray, Stuart S.

U.S. Navy captain. He commanded the battleship U.S.S. *Missouri* at the Japanese surrender ceremony in Tokyo Bay, September 2, 1945.

Murrow, Edward R. (1908–1965)

American broadcaster. He was the chief of CBS's European News Service and hired such people as William L. Shirer, Eric Sevareid, Charles Collingwood, and Howard K. Smith. Murrow flew over forty combat missions in Europe and was aboard a C-47 for the parachute drop of the U.S. 101st Airborne Division at Arnhem in September 1944. He was also present at the liberation of Buchenwald.

Murtaugh, Daniel (1917–1976)

U.S. major league baseball manager. He served with the U.S. Army in Europe during World War II.

Musashi

Japanese battleship. It took nineteen torpedoes and multiple bomb strikes before it sank during the Battle of Leyte Gulf in October 1944.

Musial, Stan (1920–   )

Major League baseball player. He enlisted in the U.S. Navy in 1945 and served at a training station in Maryland and later at Pearl Harbor.

Mussert, Anton (1894–   )

Dutch Nazi leader in World War II. He was jailed in the Hague at the end of the war.

Mussolini, Benito Juarez (1883–1945)

Italian dictator. His father was an admirer of the Mexican revolutionary Juarez and named Benito after him. He fought in World War I as a corporal, the same rank that Hitler held. After he came to power, Mussolini was made a British Knight of the Bath, but this was cancelled in August 1940 by King George VI. He had great aspirations for Italy as a world power but could never quite accomplish what he wanted. Hitler was constantly bailing him out of one predicament after another. In April 1945, Mussolini was arrested by Italian partisans at Lake Como while attempting to escape to Switzerland and was shot along with his mistress Clara Petacci. (His son Romano married actress Sophia Loren's sister Maria in a church built by Mussolini in 1934. Their daughter

Allesandra Mussolini, granddaughter of Benito, has appeared in several movies with Sophia Loren.)

Movie portrayals:
The Great Dictator (1940), by Jack Oakie (as Napaloni)
The Devil With Hitler (1942), by Joe Devlin
Star Spangled Rhythm (1942), by Paul Porcassi
That Nazty Nuisance (1943), by Joe Devlin
The Miracle of Morgan's Creek (1944), by Joe Devlin
Mussolini: Last Days (1974), by Rod Steiger
Lion of the Desert (1981), by Rod Steiger

Mussolini, Bruno (1918–1941)

Son of Benito Mussolini. He was a fighter pilot in the Regio Aeronautica and fought in the Spanish Civil War, where he commanded a fighter unit. He was killed while testing a bomber near Pisa, Italy.

Mussolini Wire

Name of a barbed-wire fence that was ten feet wide, three feet high, and stretched for 200 miles along the Libyan border. It was actually put up to keep the Libyans from escaping to territory not under Fascist rule.

Mutt and Jeff

Nickname that the British gave to the service ribbons awarded for World War I. At the outbreak of World War II, it seemed that everyone was entitled to wear the Service Medal and Victory Medal ribbons.

Mutsuki

Japanese destroyer. It was sunk on August 25, 1942, in Iron Bottom Sound by B-17's, becoming the first Japanese ship to be sunk by high-level bombing in World War II.

"My Day"

Name of Eleanor Roosevelt's daily column. It was syndicated across the U.S. beginning in 1936. Originally it was intended to be nonpolitical and aimed at women but after 1939, Eleanor gradually developed an approach to politics that complemented that of her husband, President Franklin Roosevelt.

Myers, G. A.

U.S. Navy seaman second class. He was on board the U.S.S. *Cachalot*, an old submarine, at Pearl Harbor during the Japanese attack on December 7, 1941, was hit by machine-gun fire from a Japanese aircraft, and recovered. Myers was the first submarine casualty of World War II and the only submarine casualty of the Pearl Harbor attack.

Myers, Henry T.

U.S. Army Air Force lieutenant colonel. He was the personal pilot of President Franklin Roosevelt's aircraft, *Sacred Cow,* and of President Harry S Truman's aircraft, *Independence.*

Myrtle

Name of a pet chicken of Lieutenant Glover that jumped with him at Arnhem in September 1944. Myrtle was later killed during the battle.

Mysels, Sammy (1906–   )

U.S. songwriter (''The Singing Hills'' and ''We Three''). He was wounded in combat, thus becoming the first member of the ASCAP union to be wounded in World War II.

N

Ninth Army Air Force

U.S. Air Force unit that was stationed in the Middle East and later in England in support of the invasion of Europe. Until D-Day, the Ninth flew support for the bombers of the Eighth Army Air Force; after D-Day it flew ground support missions for the advancing Allied armies.

92nd Infantry Division

U.S. Army black unit commanded by Major General Edward Almond. It fought in Italy and was used to hold the western end of the Allied line. The combat record of the 92nd was spotty and its personnel were described as having less-than-average literacy and above-average superstition. General Mark Clark in 1956 called it "the worst division I had."

93rd Infantry Division

U.S. Army black unit that fought at Bougainville, Solomon Islands, the Treasury Islands, Dutch East Indies, and the Philippines, maintaining a good combat record.

99th Fighter Squadron

U.S. Army Air Force all-black unit that flew P–51's in the Mediterranean Theater during World War II. The unit was awarded ninety-five Distinguished Flying Crosses, one Silver Star, one Legion of Merit, fourteen Bronze Stars, seven hundred forty-four Air Medals and eight Purple Hearts.

Nagato

Only Japanese battleship to survive World War II. It was used as one of the ships at the atomic bomb tests in Bikini Atoll in July 1946.

Nagumo, Chuichi (1886–1944)

Japanese admiral. He commanded the fleet that attacked Pearl Harbor on December 7, 1941, but because he was not aviation-minded, he did not follow up the main attack and missed a chance to inflict a decisive blow on the U.S. Pacific Fleet. Nagumo also was in charge of the Japanese carriers during the Battle of Midway in June 1942, and his indecision cost the Japanese four carriers. He committed suicide when the Americans assaulted Saipan in the Marianas in 1944.

MOVIE PORTRAYALS:
Tora! Tora! Tora! (1970) by Eijiro Tono
Midway (1974), by James Shigeta

Naples

Italian city. It was the first major European city to be liberated in World War II, on October 1, 1943.

Narvik

Norwegian port on the western coast through which high-grade Swedish iron ore was shipped to Germany. It was captured on May 28, 1940, by the French Foreign Legion and was the first Allied land victory of the war. The Legionnaires were withdrawn as the rest of Europe became embroiled in the war; the British finally had to evacuate 24,500 troops between June 4 and June 8, 1940, although they had driven the Germans inland and virtually controlled Narvik.

Nashville, U.S.S.

U.S. cruiser that transported General Douglas MacArthur to the Philippines for his historic wade ashore on Leyte, on October 20, 1944.

Nasser, Gamal Abdel (1918–1970)

Egyptian president. As a young officer in World War II, he was an anti-British nationalist who allied himself with the Abwehr, the German secret service, in opposing the British. Nasser had been a weightlifter at the 1936 Olympic games in Berlin and admired the Germans. He helped the Kondor Mission get information to Field Marshall Erwin Rommel about the British Army until he was arrested and imprisoned.

Nathaniel Crosby, S.S.

U.S. Liberty ship launched in 1944. It was named after singer Bing Crosby's grandfather, who had pioneered the ocean routes from China to the U.S. west coast. He had also been one of the founders of Portland, Oregon and of Olympia, Washington.

National Geographic Magazine

President Franklin Roosevelt used a *National Geographic* magazine with a map of the Atlantic to divide the zones of defense for convoy protection between the British Navy and the U.S. Navy before the Pearl Harbor attack. Japanese Emperor Hirohito would often read *National Geographic* while in his air raid shelter in Tokyo. He had a collection of the magazines at his disposal.

National Redoubt

Name given to the area around Berchtesgaden where the Nazis proposed to set up a stronghold of resistance and carry on guerrilla warfare. The myth of the redoubt caused the Americans to drive toward Czechoslovakia and cut off the retreating Germans from the redoubt area rather than heading for Berlin.

NATO

Acronym used for the North African Theater of Operations during World War II.

Natushie

Japanese destroyer. It was sunk on February 8, 1942, by the U.S. submarine *S-37*, commanded by James Dempsey in the Flores Sea. The *Natushie* was the first confirmed Japanese destroyer sunk by a U.S. submarine in World War II.

Naujocks, Alfred

German S.S. officer. He is said to be the man who started World War II because he led the fake attack on a German radio station at Gleiwitz on August 31, 1939. This was used as the excuse to invade Poland the next day. Naujocks also conceived Operation Bernhard (the counterfeiting of British money) in an attempt to bankrupt England.

Naval Person

Code used to identify Winston Churchill in correspondence with President Franklin Roosevelt prior to World War II. Churchill was the First Lord of the Admiralty at the time.

Nazi

Name coined by journalist Konrad Heiden as a term of derision for members of Hitler's party. Originally the party members were called *Nasos*, an abbreviation of National Socialist. Heiden never dreamed his term would be so universally accepted.

Nazi Party Numbers

#3—Max Amann
#7—Adolf Hitler
#8672—Joseph Goebbels
#14,303—Heinrich Himmler
#31,981—Kurt Daluege
#60,508—Martin Bormann
#89,015—Sepp Dietrich
#248,256—Walter Darre
#300,179—Ernst Kaltenbrunner
#474,481—Albert Speer
#544,916—Reinhard Heydrich

Neale, Robert H.

U.S. fighter pilot. He was the top-scoring ace of the American Volunteer Group, better known as the Flying Tigers, with sixteen Japanese aircraft to his credit.

Neave, Airey (1916–1979)

British Army lieutenant colonel. He was captured in 1940 at Calais and escaped from the Germans, only to be recaptured and to escape again. He was finally caught and put in Colditz Castle, which was believed to be escapeproof; yet he succeeded in breaking out in January 1942 and made it back to England. Neave headed Room 900 of MI-9, which helped Allied servicemen escape from Europe throughout the war. Field Marshall Wilhelm Keitel personally put a price on his head; in turn Neave handed Keitel his indictment papers at Nuremberg after the war. Neave was an Irishman who became a member of Parliament, only to be killed by an Irish Republican Army bomb in 1979.

Nebe, Arthur (1896–1945)

German S.S. officer. He headed the Nazi Criminal Investigation Department (KRIPO) until January 1942, when he took command of an Einsatzgruppen that killed Jews in Russia. Nebe was designated to become the police chief of Moscow after it was captured. He became involved in the plot against Hitler and was arrested after the July 20, 1944, assassination attempt. Nebe was executed on March 3, 1945.

Nebelwerfer

Name of a German six-barreled rocket launcher that was used as a mortar. It was originally designed by the Russians who called it "Stalin's Organ." The American troops called it "Screaming Mimi" because of its distinctive sound.

NEGAT

Name of the Washington, D. C., branch of the U.S. Navy's codebreaking unit. NEGAT, which was headed by Laurence Safford, read the Japanese Purple Code throughout the war.

Negroes

Name given to German one-man torpedoes. The pilot sat in a cockpit with a clear bubble cover that stuck up eighteen inches out of the water. He maneuvered to the target, released a torpedo from under his compartment, and made a getaway. "Negroes" were used extensively during the D-Day landings but sixty to eighty percent failed to return. Their only success was the sinking of a British light cruiser.

Negro Units (U.S.)

2nd Cavalry
92nd Infantry Division (fought in Italy)
93rd Infantry Division (fought in the Pacific)
99th Pursuit Squadron (fought in Sicily and Italy)
104th Infantry (fought in Germany)
555th Parachute Infantry Company (never saw action)
614th Tank Destroyer Battalion (fought in Italy)
755th Field Artillery Battalion (Battle of the Bulge)
761st Tank Battalion
969th Field Artillery Battalion (Battle of the Bulge)

Nelson, Donald M. (1888–1959)

Head of the U.S. War Production Board (WPB) in World War II. He was largely responsible for putting the U.S. economy on a war footing. Nelson had been an executive of Sears, Roebuck and Company. (The British equivalent was Lord Beaverbrook and the German was Albert Speer.)

Nelson H.M.S.

34,000-ton British battleship. It struck a magnetic mine in November 1939 that had been dropped by the German submarine *U-31*, commanded by Lieutenant Johannes Habekost. The *Nelson* was severely damaged but survived to support the Normandy landings of June 6, 1944.

Neosho

American Naval tanker that was sunk by the Japanese just prior to the Battle of the Coral Sea in 1942. Japanese pilots mistakenly identified it as a carrier and battered her into a twisted hulk that did not sink till the day after the attack.

Neubauer, Herman Otto (1910–1942)

German spy who landed in Florida on June 17, 1942, from the submarine *U-584* as part of Operation Pastorius. He had lived in the U.S. from 1931 to 1940, when he returned to Germany and trained as an espionage agent. Neubauer was arrested by the FBI along with his cohorts and executed on August 8, 1942.

von Neurath, Constantin (1873–1956)

German foreign minister in Hitler's cabinet in 1933. He later became the protector of occupied Czechoslovakia after the assassination of Reinhard Heydrich in 1942. Von Neurath was tried and convicted as a war criminal at Nuremberg and imprisoned at Spandau Prison in Berlin. He was released in November 1954 due to ill health.

Neutrals

Only five countries of Europe were able to remain neutral throughout World War II. They were Switzerland, Sweden, Spain, Portugal, and Ireland.

Nevada, U.S.S.

U.S. battleship that was at Pearl Harbor during the Japanese attack on December 7, 1941. She was the only battleship able to get under way but was attacked and damaged. The *Nevada* was beached, later salvaged, and returned to action in support of the Normandy invasion on June 6, 1944. It also fought at Iwo Jima in 1945 and was used as a target ship for the atomic bomb tests at Bikini Atoll in 1946.

New Deal

President Franklin Roosevelt's name for his administration's effort to put the U.S. economy back on its feet after the Depression. In 1943 President Roosevelt declared that "Dr. New Deal" had been superseded by "Dr. Win-the-War."

New London

Connecticut port that was the site of the U.S. Navy's submarine school, which was established in 1916.

Newman, Edwin (1919–   )

NBC newscaster. He enlisted in the U.S. Navy in April 1942, where he was trained as a communications officer. Having never served overseas, Newman was discharged in October 1945 as a lieutenant.

Newman, Paul (1925–   )

Hollywood actor. He enlisted in the U.S. Navy shortly after the outbreak of World War II and went to the Naval Air Corps

Officers' Training School at Yale University. Color-blindness caused Newman to fail the physical, and he served the rest of the war as a radio man and gunner on torpedo planes in the South Pacific. He was discharged in April 1946, attended college on the GI Bill, and took up acting.

New Orleans, U.S.S.

U.S. Navy cruiser upon which Chaplain Howell M. Forgy uttered his now famous phrase "Praise the Lord and Pass the Ammunition," while under attack by the Japanese on December 7, 1941.

New Zealand

One of only three countries that sent troops to every theater of World War II. The other two were the United States and Britain.

Niblack, U.S.S.

U.S. destroyer. It was commanded by Lieutenant Commander E. R. Durgin and was the first U.S. Navy ship to use force in World War II, when on April 10, 1941, it attacked a suspected German submarine off the coast of Iceland. The submarine got away.

Nickles

British code for propaganda leaflets dropped from aircraft on German territory in the early days of the war. On the first night of hostilities, "nickles" were dropped on Bremen, Hamburg, and the Ruhr. Bomber crews did not like these missions and felt they only increased the amount of toilet paper available to the Germans. They called these raids "bumphlet raids."

Nicknames

Field Marshall Werner von Blomberg—Rubber Lion
Sir Alan Brooke—Wizard
Admiral Arleigh Burke—31-Knot
Admiral Daniel Callaghan—Uncle Dan
General Claire Chennault—Old Leatherface
General J. Lawton Collins—Lightning Joe
Admiral Sir Arthur Coningham—Maori
General Charles H. Corlett—Cowboy Pete
Sir Hugh Dowding—Stuffy
Admiral Frank Fletcher—Black Jack
General James Gavin—Slim Jim
General Heinz Guderian—Fast Heinz
Admiral William F. Halsey—Bull
Arthur Harris—Bomber Harris
Rudolph Hess—Brown Mouse
Colonel Oveta Hobby—Spark Plug

Field Marshall Wilhelm Keitel—Lackey
Field Marshall Albert Kesselring—Smiling Albert
Field Marshall Hans von Kluge—Clever Hans
General Curtis LeMay—Iron Ass
General Douglas MacArthur—Dugout Doug
V. M. Molotov—Stone Ass
Audie Murphy—Baby
Admiral Chester Nimitz—Cottonhead
General George S. Patton—Blood and Guts
General Holland Smith—Howlin' Mad
General Hideki Tojo—Razor
General Alexander Vandegrift—Sunny Jim
General Jonathan Wainwright—Skinny
Sir Henry Maitland Wilson—Jumbo

Nicholas Butler

Code name used by the Allies for physicist Niels Bohr, who kept forgetting to identify himself by it.

Nicholson, James B. (1917–)

Royal Air Force fighter pilot. He was the first British fighter pilot to win the Victoria Cross in World War II and was the only pilot to win the VC for the Battle of Britain. Nicholson was attacked in his first air battle by an ME110, which wounded him and set his Hurricane afire. He remained with his aircraft, turned on the German fighter, and shot it down. Nicholson then bailed out and was shot and wounded while in his parachute by an excited Home Guardsman.

Niemoller, Martin (1892–)

German Protestant pastor. He had been a submarine commander in World War I and was awarded Germany's highest medal, the *Pour le Mérite*. Niemoller at first staunchly supported the Nazi party but eventually turned anti-Nazi when he realized what Hitler intended to do. Niemoller refused to stop preaching against the Nazis and was consequently imprisoned in Sachsenhausen concentration camp for eight years. He was liberated by the U.S. Fifth Army.

MOVIE PORTRAYAL:
The Hitler Gang (1944), by Ivan Triesault

Night and Fog Decree

Order issued by Hitler on December 7, 1941, as a terror campaign to suppress anti-Nazi activity in Western Europe. It called for the arrest, usually at night, of suspects and for their quick disappearance into "night and fog," into Germany. Nothing more was to be heard by the families. Very few survivors of the Night and Fog arrests returned after the war.

Night, Clayton

American cartoonist who drew the comic strip *Ace Drummond*, which was created by Eddie Rickenbacker. Night was on board the U.S.S. *Missouri* at the time of the signing of Japan's surrender, September 2, 1945.

Night of the Long Knives

Name given to the purge of the S.A. on June 30, 1934. It was generally directed against Ernst Roehm but was used by Nazis all over Germany to even old scores. It is estimated that several hundred people were killed by the S.S.

Nimitz, Chester W. (1885–1966)

U.S. Navy rear admiral. Prior to World War I, he was in submarines and was instrumental in the U.S. Navy's adoption of the diesel engine in both submarines and surface ships. Nimitz lost a finger of his left hand to the Navy's first diesel engine, which he had built. He replaced Admiral Husband Kimmel as Commander of the Pacific Fleet after the Pearl Harbor attack. Nimitz masterminded the U.S. victory in the Pacific and was present on the U.S.S. *Missouri* for the Japanese surrender of September 2, 1945.

MOVIE PORTRAYALS:
Hellcats of the Navy (1957), by Selmer Jackson
The Gallant Hours (1960), by Selmer Jackson
Midway (1974), by Henry Fonda
MacArthur (1977), by Addison Powell

Nimitz, Chester W. Jr.

U.S. Navy officer. He was the son of Admiral Chester Nimitz and commanded the submarine U.S.S. *Haddo* in World War II.

Nisei

Name for second-generation Japanese-Americans. All civilian Japanese-Americans were forcibly interned during World War II, after being removed from a 150-mile strip along the West Coast. The evacuation was commanded by Colonel Karl Robin Bendetsen, who was awarded the Distinguished Service Medal for his contribution to the war effort. The Army set up two units of Nisei-Japanese, the 100th Infantry Battalion and the 442nd Regimental

Combat Group. The 100th Infantry was part of the 34th Division and won more awards than any other unit of its size, with nine Distinguished Service Crosses, forty-four Silver Stars, nine Legions of Merits, thirty-one Bronze Stars, and more than one thousand Purple Hearts. They and the 442nd had more than 9,000 casualties, with no AWOL's; six men were known to have escaped from hospitals to return to their units.

Nishizawa, Hiroyishi (1920–1944)

Japanese fighter pilot and the greatest ace of Japan with 104 aircraft to his credit. He flew escort for the first *Kamikaze* attack during the Battle of Leyte Gulf and witnessed the sinking of the carrier *St. Lo* in 1944. Nishizawa was shot down and killed by U.S. Hellcat fighters while flying an L2D (*Tabby*), which was a copy of the DC-3, on October 26, 1944.

Nissenthal, Jack

Canadian scientist who landed at Dieppe in 1942 to investigate German radar for technical advancements. He was accompanied by an Army enlisted man whose job it was to shoot him if it looked as though he would fall into the hands of the enemy.

Nitto Maru No. 3

Japanese patrol boat that was camouflaged as a fishing boat. It spotted the task force surrounding the U.S.S. *Hornet* en route to launch Doolittle's Raid on Tokyo on April 18, 1942. The *Nitto Maru* was sunk by the cruiser U.S.S. *Nashville* after it had successfully radioed a contact report.

Niven, David (1910–)

British actor. He graduated from Sandhurst, the British West Point, in 1927 and was commissioned as an officer in the British Army. Niven resigned in the 1930's to become an actor and rejoined the Army in 1940 as a second Lieutenant in a rifle brigade. He was one of the first commandos in the British Army and worked with the intelligence branch. It was Niven who contacted E. Clifton-James to act as a double for Field Marshall Bernard Montgomery in 1944. As a lieutenant colonel, Niven was assigned to the U.S. 1st Infantry Division and was one of the first to land at Normandy on D-Day. He then fought to the Rhine river and was one of only twenty-five British to be awarded the U.S. Legion of Merit medal. Niven portrayed William Stephensen in the TV movie *Intrepid*. Niven had known Stephensen during the war.

Nixon, Richard M. (1913–   )

Thirty-seventh U.S. President. During World War II, he enlisted in the U.S. Navy and served for a while at Quonset Point, Rhode Island. Nixon served from August 1942 until January 1946.

MOVIE PORTRAYAL:
Tail Gunner Joe (1977 TV movie), by Richard M. Dixon
The Private Files of J. Edgar Hoover (1977), by Richard M. Dixon
The Caymas Triangle (1977), by Anderson Humphreys
Born Again (1978), by Harry Spillman
Blind Ambition (1979 TV movie), by Rip Torn
Hopscotch (1980), by Richard M. Dixon

No. 10 Group

Designator of a Royal Air Force unit that protected southwestern England during the Battle of Britain. It was commanded by Air Vice-Marshall Sir Christopher Brand and was headquartered at Rudloe near Bath.

No. 11 Group

Royal Air Force unit that protected the southern part of England directly across the English Channel from France during the Battle of Britain. It bore the brunt of the battle and was commanded by Air Vice-Marshall Keith Park. Headquarters of No. 11 Group was at Uxbridge; one of its most difficult jobs was the protection of London.

No. 12 Group

Royal Air Force unit that had the job of protecting the midlands of England during the Battle of Britain. Air Vice-Marshall Trafford Leigh-Mallory commanded No. 12 Group, which was headquartered at Watnall near Nottingham.

No. 13 Group

Royal Air Force unit that protected northern England and Scotland. It was commanded by Air Vice-Marshall Richard E. Saul and was headquartered at Newcastle.

No. 603 Squadron (City of Edinburgh)

Royal Air Force fighter squadron that shot down the first German aircraft of World War II over the Firth of Forth in September 1939.

No. 617 Squadron

Special Royal Air Force bomber squadron organized by Guy Gibson to carry out the raid on the Ruhr Dams in May 1943. It also sank the *Tirpitz* toward the end of the war.

Nobel Peace Prize

World's most respected award that was not given from 1939 to 1943 because no candidates could be found. It was awarded in 1944 to the International Red Cross and again in 1945 to Cordell Hull, the U.S. Secretary of State under President Roosevelt.

Nobarovig, Jesse Roper (1942–)

Name of a baby born in a lifeboat launched from the torpedoed passenger ship *City of New York,* which sank in March 1942 off the east coast of the U.S. The destroyer U.S.S. *Jesse Roper* picked up the survivors; hence the baby's name.

Nomura, Kichisaburo (1887–1964)

Japanese admiral and ambassador to the U.S. at the outbreak of World War II. He had been naval attaché to the U.S. in World War I and was a delegate to the Versailles Peace Treaty Conference of 1919, as well as the Washington Naval Conference in 1922. It fell to Nomura to deliver the note to Cordell Hull, severing diplomatic relations with the U.S. He presented the note an hour after the attack on Pearl Harbor. After repatriation to Japan in 1942, Nomura retired from public life.

MOVIE PORTRAYAL:

Tora! Tora! Tora! (1970), by Shogo Shimada

Norden bomb sight

Top secret bomb sight of the U.S. Army Air Force in World War II. It was only twelve inches by nineteen inches, yet was very complex; using it, the Air Force claimed, they could drop a bomb into a pickle barrel from any altitude. Each unit cost over $10,000. Despite the top-secret classification, the Germans had received complete drawings of the bomb sight from a German sympathizer, Herman Lang, who worked in the Norden plant on Long Island, New York, in 1938.

Norden, Carl L. (1880–1965)

Java-born Dutch inventor of the Norden bombsight. He was not a U.S. citizen, yet he also designed the arresting gear and catapults on the U.S. aircraft carriers *Lexington* and *Saratoga.*

Nordling, Raoul (1882–1962)

Swedish Consul General in Paris. He was responsible for saving 4,213 political prisoners held by the Gestapo and also for negotiating the surrender of the city by German General von Choltitz in August 1944. Choltitz disobeyed Hitler's order to destroy the city if the Germans were defeated. Nordling had a heart attack just before he was to cross the lines and instead sent his brother Rolf to convince General Dwight Eisenhower to enter Paris rather than bypass it.

MOVIE PORTRAYAL:
Is Paris Burning? (1966), by Orson Welles

Norfolk, H.M.S.

British cruiser that shadowed the *Bismarck* after it sank H.M.S. *Hood* in May 1941. It later participated in the sinking of the *Scharnhorst* in December 1943 and returned King Haakon to Norway in June 1945.

Norfolk House

Headquarters of General Dwight Eisenhower as Supreme Commander of the Allied Expeditionary Force in the invasion of North Africa. It was located in St. James Square, London, and was the birthplace of King George III.

Normandie

French ocean liner that was the largest and most luxurious one afloat at the outbreak of World War II. It was 1,029 feet long, 119 feet wide, displaced 85,000 tons of water, and could travel at 35 knots. When France collapsed, the *Normandie* was docked in New York and placed under "protective custody" by the U.S. In November 1941 *Time* magazine published a report that said in case of war the U.S. would seize the *Normandie* and convert it to an aircraft carrier. It further stated that conversion would be relatively simple since her stacks were fed by flues that ran up the sides and the four passenger elevators, which were located in a single shaft, could be combined to form an aircraft elevator. In February 1942, the U.S. Navy began converting it to a troop ship, rechristening it the U.S.S. *Lafayette*. The liner caught fire due to sparks from a welding unit that ignited some kapok life vests, and she capsized. The ship was finally cut up for scrap.

Normandie Dock

Dock located at St. Nazaire, France, for the ocean liner *Normandie*. After the Germans occupied France, it was used to berth one of the German pocket battleships. The British rammed the dock on March 28, 1942, with the H.M.S. *Campbeltown*, which was loaded with explosives and a delay fuse, effectively putting it out of commission for the rest of the war.

Normandie Squadron

Name of a French fighter squadron that served in Russia in

World War II. Formed in 1942, the pilots were given their choice of any aircraft. They chose the YAK because they were fighting with Russia and felt they should therefore use Russian equipment. Eventually the French pilots made up three squadrons and they are credited with shooting down 188 German aircraft. They flew over 1.200 combat missions, lost forty-one pilots, and had two members receive the Order of Lenin for heroism.

Normandy

French coastal area assaulted by the Allies on D-Day, June 6, 1944. Overall commander was General Dwight Eisenhower. Field Marshall Bernard Montgomery was in charge of all Allied ground troops, with General Omar Bradley over the Americans. Air operations were under Air Vice-Marshall Sir Trafford Leigh-Mallory and General Miles Dempsey commanded the British and Canadian troops.

Norseman

Type of aircraft (C-64) that disappeared over the North Sea on December 15, 1944, while in flight from Bedford, England, to Paris, France. Bandleader Major Glenn Miller was aboard and was listed as missing in action.

Norsk Hydro Electric Plant

Norwegian plant that was the world's only producer of heavy water at the beginning of World War II. The Germans needed the heavy water for their atomic energy research, and the Allies made several attempts to put it out of action.

North Carolina, U.S.S.

U.S. battleship. It was the first battleship built since the Washington Treaty of 1922; it was also the first U.S. battleship of the superdreadnought class, weighing 35,000 tons.

Northrop, John (1895–1981)

American aeronautical engineer. He was both president and chief designer of Northrop Aviation and designed the P-61 Black Widow, a lightweight anchor for the Navy, in addition to a highly efficient artificial arm for amputees.

Norton, John (1918–)

U.S. Army officer. As a lieutenant colonel in the 82nd Airborne Division, he was the youngest G-3 of any American combat division in World War II. Norton fought in Operation Market-Garden and retired from the Army in 1975 as a lieutenant general.

No Runs, No Hits, No Errors

Report given by Admiral Oscar Badger when he successfully led Task Force 31 through the mined entrance of Tokyo Bay on August 30, 1945 in advance of the occupation forces.

Novikov, Alexander A. (1900–1976)

Soviet Commander in Chief of the Red Air Force. He was the first Marshall of the Air Force and was in charge of the air operations over Leningrad and Stalingrad.

Nowotny, Walter (1920–1944)

German Air Force major. He was the fifth-highest-scoring ace of all time, with 258 enemy aircraft shot down. Nowotny was killed November 8, 1944, when the ME262 jet he was flying flamed out and he unsuccessfully attempted to fight P-51's that were waiting for him to land.

NSDAP

Abbreviation of the Nazi party. The letters stood for National Socialist German Workers Party, which was founded in 1918 in Munich by Anton Drexler and joined by Adolf Hitler in 1919.

Numbers

The Third Reich (Germany) defeated the Third Republic (France); Churchill became the resident of 10 Downing Street on May 10; Hitler was Nazi party member number seven and was jailed in cell number seven in Landsberg prison;

The First U.S. Army met the First Ukrainian Army at Torgau in April, 1945;

U.S. Number Two ace, Thomas McGuire, was killed in combat by Japan's Number Two ace, Shoici Sugita.

Nuremberg

German city where the International War Crimes trials were held. War criminals whose crimes were not localized were tried in the Palace of Justice; those who committed crimes exclusively in a local area were handed over to the appropriate country. Of 199 men put on trial, thirty-six were sentenced to death, twenty-two were given life imprisonment, 103 received shorter sentences, thirty-eight were acquitted, and five committed suicide before the end of the trials.

Nuremberg defendants' sentences

Hermann Goering—death
Joachim von Ribbentrop—death
Wilhelm Keitel—death
Ernst Kaltenbrunner—death

Alfred Rosenberg—death
Hans Frank—death
Wilhelm Frick—death
Julius Streicher—death
Fritz Saukel—death
Alfred Jodl—death
Arthur Seyss-Inquart—death
Rudolph Hess—life imprisonment
Walter Funk—life imprisonment
Eric Raeder—life imprisonment
Baldur von Schirach—twenty years
Albert Speer—twenty years
Constantin von Neurath—fifteen years
Karl Doenitz—ten years
Hjalmar Schacht—acquitted
Franz von Papen—acquitted
Hans Fritzsche—acquitted
Robert Ley—committed suicide awaiting trial
Martin Bormann—death in absentia

Nuremberg judges

France	Henri Donnedieu de Vabres
	Robert Fako (alternate)
Great Britain	Geoffrey Lawrence
	Norman Birkett (alternate)
Russia	I. T. Nikitchenko
	A. F. Volchkov (alternate)
U.S.	Francis Biddle
	John J. Parker (alternate)

Nuremberg prosecutors

France	François de Menthon
Great Britain	Sir David Maxwell-Fyfe
	Sir Hartley Shawcross
Russia	General R.A. Rudenko
U.S.	Justice Robert Jackson

Nürnberg

German Navy cruiser. It was the only major ship of the German Navy still afloat at the end of the war. The *Nürnberg* was transferred to the Russians, who renamed her *Admiral Makarov.*

"Nuts"

Reply given by General Anthony McAuliffe to a German request for the surrender of the 101st Airborne Division, who were surrounded at Bastogne during the Battle of the Bulge in December 1944. Several versions say he used obscene words, but this is not true. McAuliffe was persuaded to use ''Nuts'' by his G-3, Colonel Harry Kinnard, Jr.

Nygaardsvold, Johan

Norwegian Premier at the time of the German invasion in 1940.

O

1,364 days, 5 hours, 44 minutes
Length of the war between the U.S. and Japan from December 7, 1941, to September 2, 1945.

$1,000,000
Amount of the reward offered in 1940 by the American humanitarian Samuel Harden Church for the capture of Adolf Hitler alive and unharmed. He wanted to turn Hitler over to the League of Nations for trial. Church died in 1943 with Hitler still at large.

$1,000,000 wound
GI nickname for any wound in combat that was serious enough to ensure the return to the States of the "lucky" person.

Oak Ridge, Tennessee
Site of U.S. atomic bomb research. This community of 50,000 people did not have a funeral home during World War II because of the secrecy of the research. The garbage companies only hired illiterates so that if they found any classified material, they would not be able to read it.

Obersalzberg
6,400-foot mountain in southern Bavaria near the Austrian border. It was the site of Hitler's house, the *Berghof.*

Oboe
British system of directing bombers to their targets at night. It consisted of transmitting from England two radio beams that intersected over the selected target. The pilot flew along one beam until he met the crossing beam, then released his bombs, knowing that he was over the target.

O'Brien, U.S.S.

U.S. destroyer. It was damaged by the Japanese submarine *I-15* while firing torpedoes at the aircraft carrier *Hornet* on September 15, 1942. The battleship U.S.S. *North Carolina* was also hit and damaged.

O'Brien, George (1900–)

Hollywood actor. During World War II, he served as a commissioned officer in fifteen invasions.

O'Brien, Hugh (1925–)

Hollywood actor. He dropped out of college during World War II to join the U.S. Marine Corps. O'Brien served as a drill instructor and at age eighteen was one of the youngest in Marine Corps history. He was shipped overseas but saw no action and was discharged in 1945.

OB Sued

Designator of Field Marshall Albert Kesselring's headquarters, which was located in Frascati, ten miles south of Rome. It was the headquarters of all German forces in the Mediterranean.

O'Callahan, Joseph (1904–1964)

U.S. Navy chaplain. He was the only chaplain to have been awarded a Congressional Medal of Honor since the Civil War. O'Callahan was aboard the carrier U.S.S. *Franklin* when it was struck by two Japanese bombs in March 1945. He ministered to the wounded, manned fire hoses, and went into oven-hot turrets to cool off ammunition so that it could be thrown overboard.

O'Connell, Arthur (1908–1981)

Hollywood actor. During World War II, he served as an instructor at West Point Military Academy.

O'Connor, Carroll (1924–)

Hollywood actor. He served with the Merchant Marine during World War II, sailing on fourteen different ships in the North Atlantic.

O'Connor, Richard (1889–)

British general. He commanded British forces in Egypt and was one of the most promising of British generals. O'Connor was captured by the Afrika Korps at Derna in April 1941 and imprisoned in Italy. He escaped in 1943, making it back to Allied lines, and later commanded the British VIII Corps at Normandy.

Octagon

Code name of the Quebec Conference on September 11, 1944,

between President Franklin Roosevelt and Prime Minister Winston Churchill.

Ode to Autumn

Name of a poem by the French poet Paul Verlaine. The second line, "Pierce my heart with a dull languor," was the key phrase broadcast by the BBC to inform the French underground that the D-Day invasion would take place. The Germans intercepted the message but would not believe that the Allies would be so stupid as to broadcast news of the invasion over the BBC.

O'Donnell, Emmett, Jr. (1906–1971)

U.S. Army Air Force major general. He piloted the B-29 that dropped the first bomb of the first land-based raid on Tokyo on November 24, 1944. The aircraft was named *Dauntless Dottie*.

Oertel, Albert

German Abwehr operative who went to England in 1927, where he became a citizen. He set up a jewelry shop near the British Naval base at Scapa Flow. He supplied the charts that depicted the absence of torpedo nets around the battleship *Royal Oak*, thereby aiding the German submarine *U-47* to torpedo it October 14, 1939.

Office of Production Management (OPM)

U.S. government agency set up in January 1941 to ensure that the arms needed for the Lend-Lease program would be available. The OPM represented both the unions and the employers and attempted to alleviate friction between them.

Ofuna

Name of a Japanese prisoner-of-war camp near Yokosuka. It was only for special or exceptionally high-ranking prisoners of whose capture the Japanese did not notify the International Red Cross. U.S. Marine Corps ace Gregory "Pappy" Boyington was one of those held at Ofuna.

O'Hare, Edward H. (1914–1943)

U.S. Navy lieutenant. He became the Navy's first ace by shooting down five Japanese aircraft in one day, February 20, 1942. He was also the first American to shoot down five aircraft in a single mission and is credited with saving the carrier *Lexington*. O'Hare was awarded the Congressional Medal of Honor. He was killed in 1943, while joining a U.S. Navy TBF aircraft at night. The rear gunner thought he was a Japanese and shot him down. O'Hare Field in Chicago is named in his honor.

O'Hara, Mata

Pseudonym of an Irish woman who was the mistress of S.S. General Hermann Fegelein and who worked for Allied intelligence. O'Hara gave information about the coming Ardennes offensive, but no one believed her. She also conveyed intelligence about the last months in Berlin that was used on Soldatensender Calais and broadcast back to the Germans. Hitler was furious about this leak from his inner circle but never knew who it was. O'Hara disappeared in the closing days of the war and her real name and whereabouts are not known.

OHIO

Acronym used prior to December 7, 1941, to typify U.S. Army recruits' view of Army life. It stood for "over the hill in October," i.e., to desert.

Ohio, S.S.

U.S. tanker that is credited with saving the island of Malta. The tanker, loaded with aviation gas, was hit and disabled, but two destroyers towed it into Malta on August 15, 1942. The island at the time was out of aviation gas and had no fighter cover to protect it. Captain Dudley Mason of the *Ohio* was awarded the British George Cross.

Ohka

Name of a Japanese glider bomb. The 2,000-pound warhead was carried by a Betty bomber, released, then guided by rocket boosters to its target. It was one of the many suicide weapons developed by the Japanese in World War II. Of over 800 that were built, fewer than 50 were ever used; of these, only three successfully sank ships. The first mission was flown on March 21, 1945, to Okinawa and all were either jettisoned so that Betty could escape, or destroyed by U.S. fighters. American sailors called it the Baka ("stupid") Bomb.

Ohnishi, Takijiro (1891–1945)

Japanese Vice-Admiral. He devised the idea of kamikaze forces while in command of the First Air Fleet in Manila on October 17, 1944, in order to make up for the heavy losses the air arm had sustained. Ohnishi felt that unorthodox means were needed to compensate for the U.S.'s overwhelming superiority. He committed suicide in 1945.

O'Kane, Richard H. (1911–   )

U.S. Navy officer. Commander of the U.S.S. *Tang*, he was the leading U.S. submarine ace of World War II, having sunk 227,800 tons of enemy shipping. He is also credited with the best patrol of the war, when he sank ten ships totaling 39,100 tons in June 1944. The *Tang* was sunk on October 24, 1944, by one of its own torpedoes, and O'Kane and seven other survivors spent the rest of the war as prisoners of the Japanese. He was awarded the Congressional Medal of Honor after the war, which he added to his three Navy Crosses, three Silver Stars, and Legion of Merit. In 1977 he authored the book *Clear the Bridge*.

Okinawa

Japanese territory that was assaulted on Easter Sunday 1945 by U.S. forces. The Japanese commander was Lieutenant General Mitsuru Ushijima, who had nearly 100,000 troops. Okinawa was also the site of the main kamikaze attacks in a last-ditch effort to stop the Allied drive on the home island.

Oklahoma, U.S.S.

U.S. battleship that capsized after being struck five to seven times by Japanese aircraft on December 7, 1941, at Pearl Harbor. It was finally righted by twenty-one land-mounted winches on June 16, 1943, and refloated. Shortly thereafter the *Oklahoma* was sold for scrap for $46,000. It was lost during a storm at sea 500 miles northeast of Hawaii on May 17, 1947, while being towed back to the U.S. for salvage. It never fired a shot in battle.

OKW

Initials standing for Oberkommando der Wehrmacht, the German Armed Forces Supreme Command, located in Berlin. The OKW was formed on February 4, 1938, by Hitler so that he would have more control in running the armed forces and be able to restrict the Commander in Chief, Field Marshall von Blomberg.

Old 98—Little Butch

Name of football star Tom Harmon's bomber that crashed in the jungles of South America in June 1943. Of a crew of six, Harmon was the only survivor. Ninety-eight was the number of his Michigan State football jersey, and "Little Butch" was the nickname of his future bride Elyse Knox, daughter of Frank Knox, U.S. Secretary of War during World War II. Tom and Elyse were married on August 26, 1944, and her wedding dress was made from the parachute he used to bail out of a burning

P-38 over China on November 30, 1943. Singer Rick Nelson later became his son-in-law when he married his daughter Kristin.

Oldendorf, Jesse B. (1887–   )

U.S. Navy admiral. He commanded naval forces during one part of the Battle of Leyte Gulf in October 1944 and successfully "crossed the T" in a classic naval maneuver that virtually destroyed a major Japanese strike force.

Older, Charles H.

Judge of the Charles Manson trial. He was a U.S. Army Air Force lieutenant colonel during World War II. Older had been a fighter pilot with the original Flying Tigers and later flew with the 23rd Fighter Group of the Fourteenth Army Air Force in China. He is officially credited with shooting down twenty-three enemy aircraft.

MOVIE PORTRAYAL:
Helter Skelter (1976 TV movie), by Skip Homeier

Old Exterminator

Name of U.S. Army Air Force Colonel Robert L. Scott's P40 in the early days of World War II. The serial number of the aircraft was 41-1496. Scott wrote about his experiences in his 1944 book, *God Is My Co-Pilot*, which became a 1945 movie of the same name.

Oldfield, Barney (1878–1946)

U.S. auto racer and world speed record holder in 1910. During World War II, he enlisted in the U.S. Army as a captain and became a public relations officer with the Seventh Service Command, headquartered in Omaha, Nebraska.

Olejnik, Robert

German fighter pilot. He was the first Luftwaffe pilot to shoot down a Russian aircraft on June 22, 1941. He was flying an ME109.

Olivier, Sir Laurence (1907–   )

British actor and husband of actress Vivien Leigh. He quit show business to enlist in the Royal Navy air arm as a pilot in 1941. Olivier had learned to fly on his own in the U.S. and became a lieutenant and instructor-pilot until 1943. He was released from duty to return to the U.S. as a goodwill representative.

Olympiad

Documentary film produced by Leni Riefenstahl about the 1936

Olympics in Germany. It was made to present the Nazis and Nazi Germany in a favorable light to the world. Riefenstahl maintained that the film was financed by private concerns, but it is believed that Hitler personally put up the capital so that the world would see a peaceful Germany.

Olympics, 1936

Mussolini's sons participated in the opening ceremonies with Hitler. Charles Lindbergh was also present as a guest of Goering. Two Jews represented Germany, Helene Mayer in fencing and Rudi Ball in soccer. The Olympic Village was built by Wolfgang Furstner, a Jew who later committed suicide.

Olympics, 1940 and 1944

The 1940 Olympic games were scheduled to be held in Tokyo and the 1944 games in London, but both were cancelled due to the war.

Omaha Beach

Code name of the Normandy beach assaulted by the U.S. V Corps on D-Day, June 6, 1944. It was a difficult beach to attack because the tide rose and fell nineteen feet, exposing over a quarter of a mile of defensive area for the Germans. Also, its sloped beaches were more heavily defended than the other D-Day beaches. The difficulties of terrain were compounded by the errors of the attacking force. Most of the landings were inaccurate and many units were misplaced. The naval bombardment was not very effective, leaving many German batteries still operational, and once ashore, many of the troops were pinned down. Omaha was assaulted by the U.S. 1st and 29th Infantry Divisions and defended by the German 352nd Infantry Division. The beach was divided into areas designated *Charlie, Dog Green, Dog Red, Dog White, Easy Green, Easy Red, Fox Green*, and *Fox Red*.

One-eyed people in World War II

Moshe Dayan—Israeli soldier
Peter Falk—actor
John Ford—director
Rex Harrison—actor
Kichisaburo Nomura—Japanese ambassador to U.S.
Saburo Sakai—Japanese fighter ace
Colonel Claus von Stauffenberg—German army colonel
Archibald Wavell—British field marshall

O'Neill, James H.

U.S. Army chaplain attached to the U.S. Third Army. General George S. Patton ordered him to write a prayer for better weather during the Battle of the Bulge. O'Neill protested that it didn't seem right to ask God for better weather to kill your fellow man, but Patton insisted. O'Neill wrote the prayer and the weather cleared up shortly thereafter. Patton awarded him the Bronze Star.

MOVIE PORTRAYAL:
Patton (1970), by Lionel Murton

One-Ship Fleet, The

Nickname given to the heavy cruiser U.S.S. *Salt Lake City* because of her fighting record in the Pacific in World War II. Shortly after the Japanese attack on Pearl Harbor, *Salt Lake City* attacked Wotje Atoll in the Marshall Islands and was the first U.S. Navy ship to carry the war back to the Japanese.

Operation 7

German Admiral Wilhelm Canaris's ploy to send a number of Jews to safety to Switzerland, ostensibly as agents of the German secret service, the Abwehr.

Operation 157

Japanese reinforcement of their forces on New Guinea in January 1943, with the idea of mounting future attacks on Port Moresby.

Operation A

Japanese plan in April 1943 to eliminate all U.S. airpower in the Solomon Islands and New Guinea.

Operation Accolade

Allied plan to capture the Aegean island of Rhodes after the fall of Sicily. It was never carried out, although Winston Churchill was a primary advocate.

Operation A-Go

Japanese operation in 1944 to counterattack the U.S. Fleet in their attempt to seize the Marianas. It developed into the Battle of the Philippine Sea.

Operation Aida

German offensive in North Africa in May 1942 that was aimed at the capture of Egypt and the Suez Canal.

Operation Alarich

German contingency plan for a withdrawal of German forces in southern Italy and the occupation of the north if Italy dropped out of the war.

Operation All One Piece

German attack on Wolverhampton in November 1940.

Operation Alpine Violet

German operation proposed in 1940 to help the Italians break out of Albania into Greece. It was canceled.

Operation Anakim

British plan to use amphibious forces against Rangoon in early 1944. It was abandoned due to a lack of necessary equipment.

Operation Annie

Name of an underground radio station operated by the U.S. Twelfth Army Group from Luxembourg during the last five months of the war in Europe. The station pretended to be inside Germany and pro-German to win the Nazis' confidence. Many times it deceived the Germans into surrendering well-fortified positions.

Operation Anvil

Tentative name of the Allied invasion of the French Riviera to draw off as many Axis forces from Normandy as possible. The name was changed to *Operation Dragoon* because Winston Churchill felt he had been forced into approving it. The invasion took place on August 15, 1944.

Operation Aphrodite

Allied attempt to guide explosive-laden bombers via remote control to difficult-to-hit German targets. A pilot and an engineer put the plane in flight, armed it in the air, and bailed out, letting another aircraft take over by remote control. Joseph Kennedy, Jr., was killed on one of these missions when his aircraft exploded in midair.

Operation Apostle I

Allied return to Norway after the fall of Germany on May 10, 1945.

Operation Apostle II

Planned Allied return to Norway after the surrender of German forces in Norway, although fighting might continue in the rest of Europe.

Operation Argument

U.S. Army Air Force plan to destroy all German factories that produced fighters. It began on January 11, 1944, and was to be completed by March 1, 1944, in preparation for the D-Day landings.

Operation Attila

Proposed German occupation of Vichy France and the capture of the French Fleet and Air Force. It was nearly implemented on December 10, 1940, in response to the British victory against the Italians in North Africa. Operation Attila was carried out on November 11, 1942, as a result of the Allied invasion of North Africa.

Operation Avalanche

Amphibious invasion of Italy at Salerno by the U.S. Fifth Army on September 9, 1943.

Operation Axis

Hitler's plan to either capture or destroy the Italian Fleet after Mussolini's fall in 1943. It was along the same idea as Operation Alarich.

Operation Backbone

Allied contingency plan to occupy Spanish Morocco if necessary during the North African invasion in Operation Torch in November 1942.

Operation Barbarossa

German attack on Russia on June 22, 1941. Over three million Germans assaulted a 1,000-mile front with 750,000 horses, 600,000 vehicles, 7,200 guns, 3,000 tanks, and 1,800 aircraft. Stalin had been warned by Winston Churchill, the U.S. government, Richard Sorge, the spy, and the Lucy spy ring, but discounted the warnings as British propaganda. He did not want to provoke Hitler and he even went so far as to order Soviet antiaircraft batteries not to fire on attacking German planes. When the full impact struck Stalin, he locked himself in his room for five days, leaving Russia leaderless.

Operation Barney

U.S. Navy operation of sending nine submarines into the Sea of Japan in June 1945. It was planned by Admiral Barney Sieglaff in Pearl Harbor; the submarines sank twenty-eight Japanese ships in twelve days.

Operation Battle-axe

British attack by Field Marshall Archibald Wavell on Sollum, June 15, 1941. The Afrika Korps counterattacked and defeated the British.

Operation Baytown

British amphibious invasion of Italy opposite Messina, September 3, 1943. The British Eighth Army conducted the assault commanded by Field Marshall Bernard Montgomery.

Operation Beggar

Scheduled U.S. Army Air Force drop of arms and ammunition to the French Resistance during the Paris uprising of August 23, 1944. It was canceled at the last minute; instead coal and food were flown into the beleaguered city.

Operation Bernhard

German S.S. plan to counterfeit British pound notes and flood foreign banks in an attempt to devalue British currency. It was expected to disrupt the British economy and was masterminded by Walter Schellenberg.

Operation Bertram

Code name of the British cover operations to protect Field Marshall Bernard Montgomery's El Alamein offensive in October 1942, which was known as Operation Lightfoot. This was later used as a basis for the D-Day deceptions.

Operation Big Saturn

Russian attempt to destroy the Italian Army and the German forces in the Caucasus after Stalingrad was encircled at the end of 1941.

Operation Black

One of Hitler's plans to occupy Italy after Mussolini's imprisonment in 1943.

Operation Blue

German attack called for by Hitler in Directive 41 of April 5, 1942. The intention was to capture the Russian oil fields of the Caucasus and destroy the Red Army in the Don Basin. It resulted in the Battle of Stalingrad.

Operation Bodyguard

Code name of the Allied deception of the Germans about the site of the D-Day landings.

Operation Bodyline

Allied investigation of the German secret weapons that developed into the V-1 and V-2. It became Operation Crossbow headed by Duncan Sandys.

Operation Bolero

American logistical operation to transport supplies and men to

England, which were needed for the cross-channel invasion of Operation Overlord.

Operation Booty

Soviet appropriation of German factories and their removal to Russia. This had already been implemented as the Red Army advanced in 1945.

Operation Brassard

Allied operation staged from Corsica on June 17, 1944, to capture the island of Elba.

Operation Brewer

U.S. assault on the Admiralty Islands in the Pacific, begun February 19, 1944

Operation Bridge Building

German relief of II Corps which was encircled at Demyansk in March 1942. It was to be met by Operation Gangway.

Operation Brimstone

Allied capture of the island of Sardinia, September 18, 1944.

Operation Bronx Shipments

Code name for the U.S. shipment of atomic bomb parts to Tinian in July 1945.

Operation Buccaneer

Proposed Allied amphibious operation to recapture the Andaman Islands in March 1944. It was canceled because landing craft were needed in the Mediterranean.

Operation Buttress

Allied assault across the Straits of Messina from Sicily to Italy. It was divided into the American Operation Avalanche and the British Operation Baytown.

Operation Carpetbagger

Code name for the supply of equipment and personnel to the underground forces of western Europe by the U.S. Army Air Forces.

Operation Cartwheel

Combined operation of General Douglas MacArthur and Admiral William F. Halsey beginning in June 1943. It lasted for nine months, with Halsey's forces attacking New Georgia Island in the Solomons at the same time that MacArthur occupied the islands of Woodlark and Kiriwina off New Guinea.

Operation Catapult

British attack on the French fleet at Mers-el-Kebir, July 3, 1940.

The British had orders to either seize or disable the French ships to keep them from being used in a possible invasion of England by Hitler.

Operation Catchpole

U.S. capture of Eniwetok Island on February 17, 1944. Eniwetok is the northernmost island of the Marshalls.

Operation Catherine

Proposed British Naval offensive in the Baltic Sea in 1939. It was proposed by Prime Minister Winston Churchill, but he was dissuaded by the Imperial Naval Staff.

Operation Cerberus

German name for the Channel breakthrough of the battle cruisers *Scharnhorst, Gneisenau,* and *Prinz Eugen* on February 11, 1942.

Operation Choker I

Proposed Allied airborne assault on the Siegfried Line near Saarbrucken, Germany. It never took place.

Operation Choker II

Proposed Allied airborne assault across the Rhine River near Frankfurt. It never took place.

Operation Chrysler

OSS parachute drop of Major William V. Holohan, Lieutenant Aldo Icardi, and two others into Italy on September 26, 1944. Their mission was to evaluate Italian partisan potential and to supply weapons and material to units that were actively engaged against the Germans.

Operation Citadel

German attack on the Russian salient of Kursk on July 4, 1943. The Germans planned to encircle over one million Russian troops in a classic pincers movement used so successfully in the past. The Russians knew of the impending attack via Ultra intercepts and also from the Lucy spy ring, which enabled them to prepare defenses in depth.

Operation Clarion

Massive Allied air assault on February 22, 1945, that involved over 9,000 aircraft. They struck German strategic points in front of Field Marshall Bernard Montgomery's Army to clear the way for his big push, which occurred a month later. The attack attempted to knock out the German transportation system.

Operation Clausewitz

German defense of central Berlin at the end of April 1945.

Operation Cobra

U.S. First Army breakout of the Normandy area toward *St. Lo*, on July 25, 1944. It was preceded by a massive artillery and aerial bombardment. General Omar Bradley called it "the most decisive battle of our war in western Europe."

Operation Cockade

Plan of the Allies to deceive the Germans into thinking that an invasion of western Europe was imminent in 1943, so that they would withdraw forces from the Eastern Front, thereby relieving pressure on the Russians.

Operation Compass

British code name for the attack on the Italians in North Africa on December 7, 1940.

Operation Copperhead

British use of a double, actor E. Clifton-James, for Field Marshall Bernard Montgomery in an attempt to have the Germans believe that southern France was the target of D-Day. Clifton-James nearly ruined the cover while flying en route to Gibraltar by getting drunk on board the aircraft. The people with him sobered the actor up by holding his head in a freezing blast of air from a tiny window. Later, in North Africa, it was rumored that Montgomery, who was a nonsmoker, was seen with a cigar. Clifton-James was subsequently spirited back to London and into obscurity. The plot was also called *Operation Hambone*.

Operation Corkscrew

Allied capture of the island of Pantelleria on June 11, 1943. The operation was actually begun May 18, 1943, with heavy air attacks.

Operation Coronet

Proposed U.S. invasion of Honshu, Japan, by the Eighth Army. It was planned for December 1, 1945, but the Japanese surrender made it unnecessary.

Operation Crossbow

Allied air attacks on the German V-1 sites. The operation began on August 17, 1943, with the Royal Air Force attack on the test grounds of Peenemunde.

Operation Crossroads

Code name of the American detonation of two atomic bombs at Bikini Atoll in July of 1946. It was designed to test the effectiveness of atomic bombs on ships and was made up of Test Able, July 1,

1946, which was an air detonation; and Test Baker, July 25, 1946, to test an underwater blast.

Operation Crusader

British Field Marshall Sir Claude Auchinleck's attack on November 18, 1941, against the Axis in North Africa to relieve Tobruk.

Operation Culverin

Proposed Allied assault on the Japanese-occupied Netherlands East Indies. It was planned for 1943 but never undertaken.

Operation Decision

Planned Japanese attack on U.S. forces on Okinawa to be launched from the homeland in late 1945.

Operation Demon

British evacuation of Greece from April 24 to May 1, 1940.

Operation Desecrate

U.S. invasion of the Palau Islands on March 31, 1943.

Operation Detachment

U.S. invasion of Iwo Jima to provide a forward air base for fighter aircraft escorting bombers attacking the Japanese home islands. The battle lasted from February to March 1945.

Operation Dexterity

U.S. invasion of New Britain, December 26, 1943.

Operation Diadem

Code name of the Allied offensive in Italy in June 1944, planned in conjunction with the D-Day landings in Normandy.

Operation Donar

German effort to eliminate all resistance and espionage activity in France in 1944. Over 800 Resistance members were captured.

Operation Downwood

Royal Air Force raid on the Ruhr Dams of Moehne, Eder, and Sorper in May 1943. It was planned by Dr. Barnes Wallis and led by Guy Gibson, who was awarded the Victoria Cross.

Operation Dracula

Allied operation aimed at the capture of Rangoon on May 3, 1945.

Operation Dragoon

Allied invasion of southern France on August 15, 1944. Originally called *Operation Anvil,* it was contested bitterly by the British, who did not want to weaken the Allied drive in Italy.

Operation Dynamo

British evacuation of Dunkirk in 1940 involving the use of 860 vessels, of which nearly 250 were sunk. The name *Dynamo* was chosen because the Naval Operations Room in Dover Castle, Kent, had once been an electrical plant.

Operation Eagle

German Luftwaffe effort to destroy the Royal Air Force preparatory to Operation Sea Lion. It commenced on August 13, 1940, with an attack of 1,500 German aircraft.

Operation Eastwind

Forced repatriation of former Soviet citizens from Allied camps in Italy to Russia on May 8, 1947, as part of Operation Keelhaul. Many of the Russians committed suicide rather than go back to the Communists.

Operation Eclipse

American operation to be carried out in case of a rapid collapse of Germany; it called for an airborne assault to capture Berlin. Planned by General James Gavin, the operation was never enacted.

Operation Effective

Proposed airborne assault of airfields near Bisingen, Germany, by the First Allied Airborne Army.

Operation Elkton

General Douglas MacArthur's plan to send ground forces along the coast of New Guinea, to be timed with amphibious assaults at Lae and Madang in 1943.

Operation Exporter

Allied occupation of Syria between June 8 and June 12, 1941, by British and Free French forces.

Operation Fanfare

Collective code name for all Allied operations in the Mediterranean during the latter half of the war.

Operation Felix

Proposed German assault on the British base of Gibraltar planned for November 1940. Admiral Wilhelm Canaris, head of the Abwehr, talked Hitler out of enacting the assault.

Operation Firebrand

Allied occupation of the island of Corsica that lasted from September to October 1943.

Operation Flash

Code name for the conspiracy to assassinate Hitler and take over the German government. The unsuccessful attempt occurred on July 20, 1944.

Operation Flax

Allied effort to cut Field Marshall Erwin Rommel's supply lines to

North Africa from Italy in April 1943. U.S. fighters intercepted Luftwaffe transport aircraft ferrying supplies and shot down as many as possible (see Palm Sunday Massacre).

Operation Flintlock

U.S. attack on the Marshall Islands in 1944.

Operation Flying Elephant

Japanese attempt to bomb the U.S. northwest forests with hydrogen-filled balloons which were launched from Japan and carried across the Pacific by the jet stream. Nearly 10,000 balloons were launched, but very few actually made it to the U.S.

Operation Forager

Allied operation in June 1944 to capture the Marianas Islands by assaulting Saipan first, then Guam and Tinian.

Operation Fortitude

Allied plan to deceive the Germans into believing that the Normandy landings were merely a feint so that the real assault force could land on the Pas de Calais.

Operation Fortitude North

Allied plan to make the Germans believe that the D-Day invasion would be directed against Scandinavia.

Operation Fortitude South

Allied plan to convince the Germans that D-Day would be against Belgium and the north coast of France.

Operation Fortitude South II

Allied plan to convince the Germans that Belgium and northern France were still the main targets of the invasion of D-Day, even after the Normandy landings.

Operation Frantic

Code name of the shuttle-bombing from England to Russia of American bombers. The first mission was held in June 1944, and the effort lasted until August 1944, but was stopped due to the difficulty of supplying the turnaround points and the changing tactical situation.

Operation Freshman

British attempt on October 18, 1942, to land two teams of paratroopers in Norway to destroy the heavy-water plant at Norsk. The gliders carrying the troops crashed in the bad weather and all of the soldiers were captured by the Germans. The paratroopers were all executed, although they wore their British uniforms.

Operation Fuller
British plan to maintain a constant night and day aerial reconnaissance of the English Channel in order to spot any German capital ships attempting to break out either to the Atlantic or the North Sea.

Operation Gaff
Code name for the Allied plot to either kill or kidnap Field Marshall Erwin Rommel in France in 1944.

Operation Galahad
Allied operation to reopen the Burma Road and drive the Japanese out of Burma in 1944.

Operation Galvanic
U.S. effort to capture the Gilbert islands from the Japanese in 1943.

Operation Gangway
Attempt by encircled German forces at Demyansk in March 1942 to break out and link up with Operation Bridge Building, which was fighting to relieve them.

Operation Garden
Ground portion of the thrust by Field Marshall Bernard Montgomery to seize the bridge of Arnhem on September 17, 1944.

Operation Giant II
Planned airborne assault by the U.S. 82nd Airborne Division on three airfields north of Rome on September 8 and 9, 1943, in conjunction with the Salerno landings. The operation depended on massive help from the Italians, who promised to fulfill their commitments but in reality could not. The operation was called off in the last few minutes prior to the aircraft departing Sicily.

Operation Glimmer
Code name of the program to convince the Germans that an invasion fleet was situated off the coast of Boulogne on D-Day, June 6, 1944. This was accomplished by a device called *Moonshine*, which generated false radar echoes.

Operation Golden Eye
Plan of Prime Minister Winston Churchill to seal off Gibraltar in the event that Spain entered the war on the side of the Axis. Ian Fleming, the creator of James Bond, was involved in this operation as a member of British Naval Intelligence. He later gave the name "Golden Eye" to his estate in Jamaica where he wrote his James Bond novels.

Operation Goldfake

Movement of Canadian troops from the Mediterranean to England in February 1944 to prepare for the D-Day invasion.

Operation Gomorrah

Name given to the aerial attack on Hamburg beginning July 24, 1943. The British bombed the city by night and the Americans by day for a week. They dropped over 9,000 tons of explosives, which created a fire storm that killed over 30,000 people, destroyed 280,000 buildings, and gutted 6,000 acres of the city.

Operation Goodwood

Field Marshall Bernard Montgomery's attempted breakout from the Normandy stalemate of July 18, 1944. When the attack failed, Montgomery stated that he really had no intentions of a breakout but only of tying down more Germans. Operation Goodwood was followed by the American breakout attempt, Operation Cobra, which succeeded.

Operation Green

Hitler's takeover of Czechoslovakia on March 12, 1938. It was also known as *Case Green* and *Plan Green.*

Operation Grief

German operation during the Battle of the Bulge in December 1944 to infiltrate the American lines with Germans dressed in U.S. uniforms in order to spread confusion and terror behind the lines. S.S. officer Otto Skorzeny commanded the infiltrators and became known as the "Most Feared Man of Europe."

Operation Grenade

Thrust of the U.S.. Ninth Army toward the Rhine River on Feburary 23, 1945. It was begun in conjunction with the Canadian attack of Operation Veritable.

Operation Grubworm

Allied airlift of two Chinese Army divisions from Burma to China to aid in the defense of Kunming, which was attacked by the Japanese in 1945.

Operation Gunnerside

Name of the second attempt by the British to knock out the heavy water plant at Norsk, Norway. The British employed specially trained Norwegians, organized as a commando team, to land on February 16, 1943. They succeeded in disabling the plant and destroying nearly 2,000 pounds of heavy water needed for nuclear research, but the Germans had it back in operation by April 1943.

Operation Gymnast

Name given to the planned invasion of French North Africa. Since the French were anti-British, the invasion was originally intended to involve only the Americans, who would land outside the Mediterranean. This later was changed to Operation Torch, which included the British in a landing within the Mediterranean.

Operation Hailstone

U.S. aircraft carrier strike on the Japanese anchorage of Truk on February 16 and 17, 1944, in support of the Eniwetok invasion. The raid devastated Truk, in a battle that became known as the "Japanese Pearl Harbor."

Operation Hambone

British deception to make the Germans think that southern Europe was the D-Day invasion target instead of Normandy. They used an actor, E. Clifton-James to impersonate Field Marshall Bernard Montgomery. It was also called *Operation Copperhead*.

Operation Hammer

Proposed British operation against the Norwegian port of Trondheim in 1940. It was cancelled in the last few days because it would have required almost all of the British Home Fleet.

Operation Harborage

Plan for the capture of the German cities of Hechingen, Bisingen, and Haigerloch during the last days of the war. All three cities, which were the centers of German atomic research, were to fall within the French zone of occupation. The Americans initiated Operation Harborage to capture the towns before the advancing French and collect any intelligence information about the German atom bomb.

Operation Harpoon

Code name of an attempt to get a six-ship convoy through enemy lines to relieve Malta in June 1942. The ships sailed from Gibraltar in conjunction with Operation Vigorous, which sailed from the east. Only two ships made it through.

Operation Heinrich

Code name of the strategic withdrawal of German forces into the French port of Cherbourg ahead of Allied pressure from Normandy in July 1944.

Operation Hellbound

Planned attack by the U.S. Fifteenth Army Air Force from Italy on Berchtesgaden from which Hitler was controlling the defense of Normandy in June 1944. It was canceled, possibly for fear that it would endanger further Ultra intercepts; the information about Hitler's whereabouts had come from the decoding of German secret messages.

Operation Hermann

Name given by Luftwaffe pilots to the support missions flown on January 1, 1945, in conjunction with the Battle of the Bulge. Operation Hermann consisted of a series of surprise attacks on Allied airbases in the Netherlands, Belgium, and France.

Operation Hercules

Proposed German capture of the island of Malta that was planned for the summer of 1942 in support of Field Marshall Erwin Rommel's offensive against Egypt. It was canceled by Hitler because the plan depended on action from the Italian Navy and Hitler believed that as soon as the British fleet headed for Malta the Italians would turn tail and run.

Operation Highjump

Forced repatriation after the war by the British of Croatian nationals, who had sided with the Germans during the war against Titoist forces in Yugoslavia. Operation Highjump was part of Operation Keelhaul. Most of the Croats were killed by the Yugoslavians.

Operation Himmler

Name given to a raid staged by the Germans on the radio station at Gleiwitz, August 31, 1939. It was purported to have been attacked by Polish forces, but the raid was in fact conducted by the S.S. dressed in Polish uniforms. The raid was used as the pretext for Hitler to invade Poland the next day.

Operation Hotfoot

Proposed raid by Admiral William F. Halsey's Task Force 38 on the Japanese mainland in October 1944. It was to be the first carrier strike against Japan since the Doolittle Raid of April 18, 1942, and was intended to catch the Japanese fleet at anchor as well as cripple the aircraft industry. The attack was called off because of unexpected resistance on Leyte.

Operation Humbug

American effort to collect the German scientists and their notes and equipment on nuclear research in Hechingen, Germany.

Operation Husky

Allied invasion of Sicily on July 10, 1943.

Operation Hydra
Royal Air Force night bombing attack on the German rocket test site of Peenemunde, August 18, 1943.

Operation I (I Go)
Japanese attempt from April 1 to April 15, 1943, to reinforce their airbases in the Solomon Islands.

Operation Iceberg
U.S. invasion of Okinawa on Easter Sunday, April 1, 1945.

Operation Independence
Plan of the Allies to clear the French port of Bordeaux. It later became Operation Venerable.

Operation Infatuate
Allied capture of the Walcheren Islands on November 1, 1944, to clear the Scheldt Estuary and open up the Belgian port of Antwerp.

Operation Influx
Proposed British occupation of Sicily in 1941.

Operation Ironclad
British assault on Madagascar on May 3, 1942, to prevent the Vichy government in control of the island from letting it fall into the hands of the Japanese. The British were thereby able to ensure the safe passage of their India-to-Egypt convoys.

Operation Ironside
Allied deception plan to make the Germans believe that the port of Bordeaux would be invaded. It was part of Operation Fortitude South.

Operation Isabella
Proposed German occupation of the Atlantic coast of Spain in 1941.

Operation Jericho
Royal Air Force attack by Mosquito aircraft on the German prison at Amiens, France, February 18, 1944. The raid freed over 250 prisoners awaiting execution at the hands of the Gestapo.

Operation Jubilant
Planned Allied protection of prisoner-of-war camps in Germany that would fall to the First Allied Airborne Army in Operation Eclipse.

Operation Jubilee
Allied raid on Dieppe, August 11, 1942, ostensibly to test landing-craft techniques, but in reality to capture top-secret German radar equipment for evaluation.

Operation Juggler

Combined assault by the U.S. Ninth Army Air Force from North Africa on Wiener Neustadt and the Eighth Army Air Force from England on Regensburg on August 14, 1943, to knock out German fighter production.

Operation Juno

German Navy offensive in northern Norway to relieve pressure on Narvik, using the battle cruisers *Gneisenau, Scharnhorst,* and *Hipper* in June 1940. During the offensive the British lost the carrier *Glorious.*

Operation Jupiter

Proposed British invasion of Norway advocated by Prime Minister Winston Churchill.

Operation Ka

Japanese reinforcement of their troops on Guadalcanal in August 1942.

Operation Keelhaul

Allied forced repatriation of Soviet citizens after the war to comply with the Yalta agreements. The majority of these people had fled Communism and sought political asylum, but they were forcibly handed back to the Russians, who executed many of them on the spot. There were a number of cases of British soldiers killing many of these people to get the others to return to the Soviets.

Operation Kettledrum Roll

German Grand Admiral Karl Doenitz' submarine offensive into American waters in January 1942. He sent five submarines to carry the war to the U.S. and in ten days they sank twenty-five ships, totaling over 200,000 tons.

Operation Knight's Gambit

German plan by Vice-Admiral Otto Schniewind to halt the Allied convoys of PQ-17 en route to Russia and PQ-13 returning from Russia by using the *Tirpitz, Admiral Scheer,* and *Hipper* in July 1942. The German ships did not locate either convoy, but the threat caused the British Admiralty to order PQ-17 dispersed. The individual ships were then picked off by the Luftwaffe and submarines in one of the worst convoy disasters of the war.

Operation Knight's Move

German attempt to capture Marshall Josef Tito on May 25, 1944.

They landed glider troops near Tito's headquarters at Drvar, but all they brought back was his dress uniform.

Operation Kon

Japanese reinforcement of Biak islands after the U.S. forces had invaded them on May 27, 1944.

Operation Land of Fire

German effort to smuggle gold and art treasures to Argentina toward the end of the war. Martin Bormann ordered the transfers, beginning in the latter part of 1943, by submarine.

Operation Lightfoot

Code name of Field Marshall Bernard Montgomery's El Alamein offensive in October 1942. It was the last purely British victory of World War II and did not have to be fought because of the impending North African landings of Operation Torch. With the Americans landing to his rear, Field Marshall Erwin Rommel would have been forced to evacuate Egypt and El Alamein anyway.

Operation Little Saturn

Russian response to Field Marshal Erich von Manstein's attempt to rescue the encircled Sixth Army at Stalingrad (Operation Winter Storm). The Russians were able to stop von Manstein and then tighten the pressure on the Germans at Stalingrad.

Operation Lobster

German intelligence chief Admiral Wilhelm Canaris's efforts to gain information about the British in conjunction with the proposed invasion of England (Operation Sea Lion).

Operation Long Jump

Attempted assassination of Josef Stalin, Franklin D. Roosevelt, and Winston Churchill at the 1943 Teheran conference. It was to be carried out by the S.S. intelligence service, the S.D. Because of the tight security of the Russians the mission never took place.

Operation Longsuit

U.S. Marine Corps 2nd Division's invasion of Tarawa on November 20, 1943. It was part of the larger Operation Galvanic.

Operation Ludlum

Allied bombing of the abbey of Cassino in March 1944. It was named after Captain David Ludlum, the U.S. Army Air Force weather officer who allowed the attack to proceed after a week of postponements due to weather.

Operation Lumberjack
Attacks between Koblenz and Cologne north of the Moselle River on February 23, 1945, by the U.S. First and Third Armies.

Operation Luster
British movement of troops from Egypt to Greece in March 1941. It weakened the British position in Egypt and did little to save Greece.

Operation Lusty
U.S. Army Air Force effort in June 1945 to capture German scientists who could contribute to the development of U.S. aviation.

Operation Luttich
German counteroffensive of August 1944 in Normandy.

Operation Magic Carpet
U.S. effort after the victory in Europe to transport servicemen back to the U.S. from Europe.

Operation Majestic
Proposed Allied plan to capture the main island of Kyushu, Japan.

Operation Manna
Mercy missions flown by Allied bombers from April 29, 1945, until May 8, 1945, dropping food to the Dutch. The Germans had cut off all food shipments into Holland and put the Dutch on the verge of starvation. The bombers flew completely unarmed because of an agreement between Brigadier General Walter Bedell-Smith, Eisenhower's Chief of Staff, and Reichskommissar Dr. Artur Seyss-Inquart, whereby the Germans would not interfere with the missions.

Operation Marita
German attack on Greece in April 1941 to bail Mussolini out of his Balkan predicament and to prevent the establishment of an Allied base of operation that could threaten his forces during the Russian invasion.

Operation Market-Garden
Allied offensive to penetrate deeply into German territory by capturing the Arnhem Bridge in the Netherlands in September 1944.

Operation Marston
British parachute attack on the Primosole Bridge in Sicily in July 1943. The jump was made by the 1st Parachute Brigade of the 1st Airborne Division.

Operation Matador
British plan to move troops to Thailand in order to occupy Thai

ports so that they could defend the Malay peninsula. The British were hesitant to violate Thai independence and had to abandon the operation when the Japanese landed at the Kra Isthmus on December 7, 1941.

Operation Matterhorn

Code name of the U.S. effort to bomb Japan from Chinese bases using B-29's. It was not successful because of the difficulty of sending supplies over the Himalayas.

Operation Maurice

Allied attempt to capture Trondheim in Norway in 1940.

Operation Meeting House

U.S. Army Air Force fire bombing of Tokyo on March 9, 1945, using B-29's commanded by General Curtis LeMay.

Operation Menace

Code name of the attempted occupation of Dakar in 1940 by the British and the Free French under General Charles de Gaulle. It was hoped other French colonies of Africa would fall, but French indiscretions tipped off the Germans, causing heavy Allied task force losses. The British never again allowed the French to enter into war plans.

Operation Mercury

German capture of Crete in May 1941 combining airborne troops with an assault from the sea.

Operation MI

Japanese attack on Midway in June, 1942. It was devised by Admiral Isoruku Yamamoto to engage the U.S. fleet in a decisive battle in hopes of defeating it. The Japanese had planned the attack but had been reluctant to implement it until the Doolittle Raid on Tokyo on April 18, 1942, demonstrated to them that the U.S. was far from finished.

Operation Mickey Mouse

S.S. commando Otto Skorzeny's plan on October 15, 1944, to kidnap the son of Admiral Horthy of Hungary to prevent that country from defecting to the Allies.

Operation Mike I

U.S. amphibious assault of Lingayen Gulf on Luzon on January 9, 1945. It was part of Operation Musketeer III, the overall plan of General Douglas MacArthur for the reconquest of the Philippines.

Operation Millennium

British thousand-plane raid on Cologne on May 30, 1942, planned by Air Marshall Sir Arthur Harris and personally approved by Winston Churchill. In actuality only about nine hundred planes reached the target.

Operation Mincemeat

Code name of the plot to deceive the Germans into thinking that the Balkans would be the next invasion site rather than Sicily. A body purported to be Major Martin of the Royal Marines was dropped off the coast of Spain on April 30, 1943, from the submarine H.M.S. *Seraph.* Major Martin had documents on him that were passed on to the Germans by Spanish sympathizers. As a result Hitler moved a panzer division from France to Greece, sent a number of ships from Sicily to southern Greece, and mined the waters along the coasts of Greece.

Operation MO

Japanese plan originally devised as a thrust against Australia but modified due to a shortage of occupation troops. They then attempted to cut off Australia by conquering the New Hebrides and New Caledonia.

Operation Neptune

Planned Allied capture of the French port of Cherbourg in 1944.

Operation Nestegg

Allied occupation of the Channel Islands on May 9, 1945.

Operation Northwind

New Year's Eve, 1945, German thrust to reopen the deadlocked Ardennes offensive.

Operation Oak

Hitler's plan for the rescue of Benito Mussolini by S.S. commando Otto Skorzeny. It was to be followed by Operation Student.

Operation Olympic

Projected invasion of Kyushu, one of the main Japanese islands, by the U.S. Sixth Army. It was planned for September 1, 1945, but the Japanese surrendered.

Operation One (Ichi Go)

Japanese operation in eastern China to eliminate the American airbases of General Claire Chennault. The effort was started April 18, 1944, and lasted into 1945. General Joseph Stilwell had argued for years the possibility of the Japanese attacking the airbases, but because Chennault had the favor of Chiang Kai-shek, Stilwell's warnings went unheeded.

Operation Otto

German occupation of Austria on March 12, 1938.

Operation Overcast

American project to send German rocket scientists to the U.S. so that they could aid in the war against Japan. One of the first group of seven was Dr. Wernher von Braun.

Operation Overlord

Allied invasion of Europe on June 6, 1944 (D-Day). The name was coined by Winston Churchill.

Operation Overthrow

Deception plan of the Allies to convince the Germans that an invasion of western Europe would occur in 1942.

Operation Panzerfaust

S.S. Commando Otto Skorzeny's plan for October 16, 1944, to seize the Citadel, seat of the Hungarian government in Budapest, in a coup to prevent the Hungarians from surrendering to the Russians.

Operation Paperclip

Program designed to capture German scientists and send them to the U.S. before the Russians located them and sent them to Russia. The operation derived its name from the fact that cards were filled out on each scientist; those cards containing information indicating that the individual fulfilled certain requirements had a paperclip attached.

Operation Pastorius

German Abwehr mission to infiltrate eight saboteurs into the U.S. aboard the submarines *U-202* and *U-584* in May 1942. It was named after Franz Pastorius, who was the first German immigrant to America in 1683. *U-202* carried Georg Dasch, Ernest Burger, Richard Quirin, and Heinrich Heinck. *U-584* brought Edward Kerling, Hermann Heubauer, Werner Thiel, and Herbert Haupt.

Operation Pedestal

Code name of the August 1942 convoy to resupply Malta. The ships were diverted from the Murmansk run for this convoy; of fourteen transports, only four got through. The carrier H.M.S. *Eagle* was also lost on this operation when it was sunk by U-73.

Operation Penitent

Proposed Allied operations along the Yugoslavian coast toward the end of World War II.

Operation Platinum Fox

German attempt to cut Murmansk off from the rest of Russia to prevent Allied supplies that were landing in the port from getting to the Russian Army. Three infantry divisions were used, one attacking the port itself and the other two cutting the 650-mile railway line in June 1941. Both attempts failed because of the distances involved.

Operation Plunder

Allied crossing of the Rhine River north of the Ruhr on March 23, 1945.

Operation Pointblank

All-out Allied bombing effort against Germany in preparation for D-Day.

Operation Porto II

German plan of deception by Field Marshall Kurt von Rundstedt to make the British believe Dieppe was only lightly defended with poor troops prior to the Dieppe raid in 1942.

Operation Punishment

German attack on Belgrade in retaliation for Yugoslavia not permitting the Germans to march through the country. Over 17,000 people were killed on April 6, 1941, in the attack.

Operation Quicksilver

Code name of the overall deception of the Germans that the Pas de Calais was the D-Day target.

Operation Rankin A

Projected plan of the Allies in the event that Germany collapsed prior to the D-Day landings. The U.S. First Army was to put everything it could onto the continent and take advantage of the vacuum created.

Operation Rankin B

Projected plan of the Allies to invade the continent if the Germans withdrew from either Norway or France prior to D-Day.

Operation Rankin C

Projected Allied plan to land on the continent if the Germans surrendered unconditionally prior to D-Day.

Operation Reckless

Bold scheme of General Douglas MacArthur to bypass the strongly defended Hansa Bay and Wewak, so that he could attack Hollandia on April 22, 1944, before it could be reinforced. The attack was a resounding success because the Japanese support troops on Hollandia broke and ran.

Operation Retribution

Allied plan to destroy any Axis ships that attempted to evacuate the surrounded Afrika Korps from Tunis to Sicily in 1943.

Operation Road's End
Allied scuttling of the Japanese ships in February 1946 that had survived the war.

Operation Roundup
General George C. Marshall's initial plan for the invasion of Europe in 1943. It was finally scrapped because of Field Marshall Erwin Rommel's successes in North Africa.

Operation Roundhammer
Allied contingency plan for a cross-channel invasion prior to May 1, 1944.

Operation Royal Flush
Plan of deception whereby the Allies approached the Spanish to gain the use of Barcelona as a port for the shipment of supplies and the evacuation of wounded from a projected invasion of southern France.

Operation Rusty Project
U.S. Army Air Force aerial mapping of North Africa early in 1942 in preparation for Operation Torch. One of the two intelligence officers selected was Captain Elliott Roosevelt, son of President Franklin Roosevelt.

Operation Rutter
Proposed Allied raid on Dieppe planned for July 1942. It was postponed and later renamed *Operation Jubilee*.

Operation Schwarz (Black)
German campaign to eliminate Yugoslavian guerrillas in May 1943. It was launched after the failure of Operation White, but failed.

Operation Scorcher
British occupation of Crete in May 1941 and the subsequent defense against German airborne forces.

Operation Sea Lion
Hitler's proposed invasion of England. He gradually lost interest while planning for the invasion of Russia in Operation Barbarossa.

Operation Seaside
Proposed Luftwaffe concentrated attack on Warsaw immediately after the outbreak of hostilities on September 1, 1939. It was cancelled due to fog but reinstated September 13, 1939.

Operation Shingle
Allied landing at Anzio on January 22, 1944, that was planned to coincide with a frontal attack on the Gustav line by the U.S. Fifth

Army and the British Eighth Army in an attempt to break the stalemate in Italy.

Operation Sho

Japanese plan to engage the U.S. Naval Fleet in a decisive battle. This finally led to the Battle of Leyte Gulf in October 1944, which was the death knell of the Japanese Fleet. Japan lost three battleships, four carriers, nine cruisers, thirteen destroyers, and five submarines. (*Sho* is Japanese for "victory.")

Operation Sickle

U.S. buildup of the Eighth Army Air Force in England.

Operation Skorpion

German plan of S.S. officer Gunter d'Alquen to give Russian General Andrei A. Vlasov command of all Russians under German control in September 1944. It was formulated because the Germans began to fear an uprising of eastern peoples in Germany as the fighting lines approached their borders.

Operation Skye

British deception plan to make the Germans believe that an invasion of Norway was imminent in 1944. The British created a fictitious Fourth Army of 350,000 men as part of Operation Fortitude North.

Operation Sledgehammer

Allied plan to reduce the pressure on the Russians by seizing a small beachhead across the channel with the limited resources available in 1942. It was only intended to be used if the situation on the Eastern Front grew desperate.

Operation Soapsuds

Allied bombing raid on the oil fields of Ploesti, Rumania, on August 1, 1943 by the U.S. Ninth Army Air Force. The name was changed to *Tidal Wave,* which was the code name for Ploesti.

Operation Sonnie

U.S. Army Air Force operation between March and December 1944, to repatriate nearly 900 American airmen who had been interned in neutral Sweden. The project was commanded by the Norwegian Bernt Balchen, who had won a Congressional Medal of Honor as pilot for the Byrd Expedition to Antartica. Unmarked B-24's flew 110 missions in bad weather to elude the Luftwaffe in order to free the airmen.

Operations Staff Rosenberg

Nazi agency set up during the attack on Russia. It was originally established as a compiler of information about the Jews but was expanded into a government to administer the conquered lands. The operation was headed by Alfred Rosenberg, who planned on turning Russia into a pastoral society.

Operation Stalemate II

U.S. Navy occupation of the Palaus commanded by Admiral Chester Nimitz.

Operation Starkey

Allied deception plan to lure the Luftwaffe out to battle over the English Channel in 1943. The Allies used simulated large-scale amphibious assaults as bait, but the Germans did not fall for the trick.

Operation Starvation

U.S. operation to plant mines around the coasts of Japan from March 1945 until the end of the war.

Operation Strangle

U.S. Army Air Force attempt to cut the supply lines north of Rome during the Battle of Cassino in 1944.

Operation Student

Hitler's plan for the occupation of Rome and the reinstatement of Mussolini after his rescue in Operation Oak.

Operation Sunrise

Effort of Allen Dulles, head of the OSS in Switzerland, to negotiate a surrender of all German troops in Italy in the last days of the war. It culminated in the surrender of over two million Germans. (Churchill called it *Operation Crossword*.)

Operation Sussex

Allied operation to parachute intelligence teams into France in preparation for D-Day. The British teams were called *Brissex* and the Americans were called *Ossex*.

Operation Swordhilt

Allied effort to capture the port of Brest. After success at a heavy cost, the port was never used for supplies.

Operation Taxable

Operation to make the Germans believe that an invasion fleet lay off the Cap d'Antifer on D-Day. This was done with *Moonshine*, false radar echoes.

Operation Thunderbolt

German breakout of the battle cruisers *Scharnhorst*, *Gneisenau*, and *Prinz Eugen* from Brest on February 12, 1942.

Operation Thunderclap

Allied attack on Berlin that lasted for three continuous days and nights in early 1945. It was planned by General Carl Spaatz to lower German morale.

Operation Thunderclap

Planned German breakout of Field Marshall von Paulus's encircled Sixth Army from Stalingrad. However, he did not have the supplies necessary by the time it was to be undertaken.

Operation Thunderstorm

Gestapo dragnet to arrest the conspirators after the July 20, 1944, attempt on Hitler's life.

Operation Thursday

March 1944 Allied airborne operation aimed at Myitkyina to drive the Japanese out of Burma.

Operation Tidal Wave

Ninth Army Air Force attack on the oilfields of Ploesti on August 1, 1943. Five Congressional Medals of Honor were awarded for the operation, which was the highest number for any single mission of World War II.

Operation Tiger

British operation to run a convoy of five ships loaded with tanks through the Mediterranean to Egypt in May 1941. Only one ship was lost and that was to a mine.

Operation Tindall

Deception plans to make the Germans believe that an Allied invasion of Norway would be launched in 1943. It was part of Operation Cockade.

Operation Titanic

Code name of the phony parachute drops north of Normandy on D-Day. Dummies were used that were activated when they hit the ground, exploding a series of blank cartridges to simulate ground fire in order to confuse the Germans.

Operation Torch

Code name of the Allied invasion of North Africa on November 8, 1942. General Dwight Eisenhower was the overall commander of the landings.

Operation Torture

Support operations of the French Resistance to disrupt German road travel at the time of the D-Day invasion. The French called it Operation Turtle.

Operation Totalize

Field Marshall Bernard Montgomery's operation on August 7,

1944, using the Canadian II Corps in an unsuccessful offensive to capture Falaise.

Operation Turtle

French Resistance cover for the interdiction of all German road traffic in support of D-Day. It was known to the Allies as Operation Torture.

Operation Transportation

Campaign by the British Bomber Command in support of the D-Day landings to bomb eighty major rail centers in western Europe over a period of ninety days, to prevent the Germans from bringing up tanks and troops to oppose the beachhead.

Operation Treacle

British Naval operation in August 1941 to move the Polish Carpathian Brigade into Tobruk to relieve the Australian 18th Brigade.

Operation Typhoon

German operation begun on October 2, 1941, and aimed at the capture of Moscow by Army Group Center of Field Marshall Fedor von Bock.

Operation Umbrella

German air force attack on the English industrial center of Birmingham in November 1940.

Operation Undertone

Allied operation south of the Moselle River on March 15, 1945, to approach the Rhine south of Koblenz. (North of the Moselle was Operation Lumberjack.)

Operation Uranus

Code name of the Russian encirclement of the German Sixth Army at Stalingrad. It was planned by Stalin and Marshalls Zhukov and Vasilevsky.

Operation Valkyrie

New German code name for the overthrow of the Nazi regime that replaced Operation Flash. The name was selected by Count Claus von Stauffenberg, who attempted to kill Hitler with a bomb on July 20, 1944.

Operation Varsity

Airborne assault across the Rhine River by the American 17th Airborne Division and the British 6th Airborne Division. It was the largest single parachute drop by either side during the war.

Operation Vendetta

Deceptive operation to make the Germans believe that the Allies would strike southern France. It was part of Operation Fortitude South.

Operation Venerable

Allied operation to open the port of Bordeaux on April 14, 1945. It was formerly Operation Independence.

Operation Vert

D-Day support operation of the French Resistance to disrupt railways so that the Germans could not bring up reinforcements.

Operation Vigorous

British attempt to supply besieged Malta in June 1942 with eleven supply ships sent from Egypt. Only two vessels made it to Malta.

Operation Violet

D-Day support operations by the French Resistance to disrupt German communications. (It was also known as the *Ked Plan*.)

Operation Wadham

Proposed Allied invasion of Brittany in 1943 to deceive the Germans. It was part of Operation Cockade.

Operation Watchtower

Official code name for the U.S. assault on Guadalcanal and Tulagi on August 7, 1942. Admiral Robert Ghormley called it *Operation Shoestring*, since it was put together in haste with limited forces.

Operation Weiss (White)

Joint German-Italian campaign to eliminate Yugoslavian partisans in January 1943.

Operation White

Attempted British reinforcement of tne fighter aircraft on Malta, November 15, 1940. Fighters were launched from the aircraft carrier H.M.S. *Argus*, which was commanded by Admiral Sir James Somerville. Due to bad weather, only five of fourteen aircraft reached Malta.

Operation Wilfred

British Naval attempt to mine the waters along the coast of Norway on April 8, 1940.

Operation Winter Storm

German attempt to relieve the encircled Sixth Army at Stalingrad on December 12, 1942. The Russians knew of this attempt via the Lucy spy ring in Switzerland and were able to prevent the breakthrough.

Operation Yellow

Hitler's plan for the invasion of the West. It was originally planned for the autumn of 1939 but was postponed until the spring of 1940. The principal tactic was an armored thrust through the Ardennes planned by General Erich von Manstein. The German Army was only given three weeks' supplies to accomplish the defeat of France.

Operation Z

Japanese attack on Pearl Harbor on December 7, 1941. It was planned by Admiral Isoruku Yamamoto and was based on the success of the British torpedo attack on the Italian fleet at Taranto a year earlier.

Operation Zeppelin

German attempt to infiltrate agents into Russian partisan bands to gather information during the war.

Operation Zeppelin

Deceptive operation to make Hitler believe that the next Allied steps after the invasion of North Africa would be assaults on Greece and southern France, rather than on Sicily and Italy.

Oppenheimer, J. Robert (1904–1967)

U.S. physicist in charge of the atomic bomb laboratory at Los Alamos. As such, he was largely responsible for the development of the atomic bomb.

MOVIE PORTRAYAL:

The Beginning of the End (1946), by Hume Cronyn

Oppenheimer (1982 PBS miniseries), by Sam Waterston

Oradour-sur-Glane

French village that was destroyed by the S.S. Division Das Reich in July 1944. The Germans shot all the men, locked the women and children in a church, and burned it down in reprisal for sabotage directed at them along their route toward Normandy. They had actually intended to massacre the inhabitants of another village, Oradour-sur-Vayres, which was a few kilometers away. There were only ten survivors from the 652 villagers.

Oralloy

Security designator for the U-235 produced at Oak Ridge, Tennessee, for the Manhattan Project. The first two letters were from the location, *O*ak *R*idge.

Oran

Site of the British Naval attack on the French Fleet on July 3,

1940. The British, commanded by Admiral Sir James Somerville, attempted to get the French to surrender; when their commander, Admiral Gensoul, refused, the British opened fire. This was one of many of the reasons for French antipathy toward the British during World War II.

Orange

Code word used by the U.S. military in referring to general officers.

Order of the Winged Boot

Special organization consisting of Allied airmen who had been shot down over enemy territory, successfully evaded capture, and managee to escape back to Allied lines. The unofficial emblem was a winged boot on a patch.

Order of Victory

Russian decoration given to General Dwight Eisenhower and Field Marshall Bernard Montgomery at the end of the war. The medal was made of platinum and covered with diamonds and rubies. In 1945, it was valued somewhere between $20,000 and $100,000.

Orion

German armed merchant ship of 7,021 tons. The *Orion* sank ten Allied ships, totaling 62,915 tons, between April 6, 1940, and September 23, 1941, when it returned to Bordeaux. Captain Kurt Weyher commanded the ship on its successful cruise. It was designated HSK 1 or Ship 36 by the Germans.

Orion, H.M.S.

British cruiser. It was the flagship for the Normandy landings of June 6, 1944, and was the first to open fire at 5:10 A.M.

Orita, Zenji (1910–   )

Japanese Naval officer. He was the executive and torpedo officer of the submarine *I-15* on picket duty off Pearl Harbor on December 7, 1941. He commanded the submarine *RO-101* and later *I-177*. On April 14, 1944, as commander of *I-47*, Orita launched the first kaiten suicide torpedo ever used in combat.

Oscar

Black cat rescued from the German battleship *Bismarck* by British sailors in 1941 when the *Bismarck* was sunk. Oscar was then on board the destroyer H.M.S. *Cossack* when it was sunk and was again rescued, and later on the carrier H.M.S. *Ark Royal* when it was sunk. Apparently, this cat really did have nine lives.

Oscar

Name of the statuettes awarded annually to Hollywood personalities for achievement in the film industry. The Academy Awards were first given out in 1927 and are constructed of a mixture of copper, tin, and antimony, electroplated with gold, nickel, and copper. During the war years, 1941 to 1945, Oscar gave up his metal content for the war effort and was made of plaster, which could be exchanged after the war.

Oshima, Hiroshi (1886–1975)

Wartime Japanese ambassador to Germany. He was tried as a war criminal after the war and sentenced to life imprisonment. Oshima was released in 1955.

Oslo Report

Name given to a package of documents in German that was left at the British embassy in Oslo on November 4, 1939. It contained information on Nazi developments in acoustic torpedoes, blind bombing devices of the Luftwaffe, radar, and rocket testing. Eventually, the British believed Admiral Wilhelm Canaris had passed the material to them, although this has never been proven.

Osmena, Sergio (1878–1961)

Philippine Vice-President under Manuel Quezon and President after Quezon's death in 1944. Osmona hated General Douglas MacArthur, and it took quite a bit of effort to convince him to accompany MacArthur on the walk ashore at Luzon in 1944.

Osprey, U.S.S.

U.S. minesweeper which struck a mine and sank off the coast of Normandy during the D-Day invasion. Six crewmembers were killed in this, the first naval loss of the invasion.

OSS

Office of Strategic Service. It was the first true American secret service, founded in June 1942, and headed by William Donovan. OSS headquarters was located in Temporary Building Q in Washington, D.C., next to the reflecting pool between the Lincoln Memorial and the Washington Monument. Uniforms were made by Brooks Brothers and supplies (i.e., sleeping bags, air mattresses, etc.) were provided by Abercrombie and Fitch.

OSS Branches

SO—special operations (conducted sabotage and aid to resistance groups in occupied countries.)

OG—operational groups (conducted harassment behind enemy lines by guerrillas)

MO—morale operations (disseminated propaganda to weaken enemy morale)

MV—maritime units (dealt with naval sabotage)

SI—secret intelligence (gained information needed to conduct operations)

Ossex

Name given to American intelligence teams that were parachuted into occupied France prior to D-Day in 1944.

Ossewa Brandweg

"Ox wagon sentinels." This was the fascist organization in the Union of South Africa that conducted acts of sabotage against South Africa throughout World War II. The slogan of the organization was "one people, one country, one tongue."

Oster, Hans (1888–1945)

Chief of Staff of the Abwehr, the German intelligence service. He was one of the primary figures in the opposition against Hitler. Oster had a close friend killed by the S.S. during the Night of the Long Knives in the 1934 purge of the S.A. He also was the one to deliver the order of dismissal to Field Marshall Werner von Blomberg on trumped-up charges. Oster was arrested by the Gestapo in connection with the July 20, 1944, assassination attempt against Hitler and was executed on April 9, 1945.

Ott, Elsie S.

U.S. Army Nurse Corps second lieutenant. She was the first woman to receive the Air Medal, March 26, 1943, for a medical evacuation flight from India to Washington, D.C., between January 17 and 23, 1943.

Ott, Eugene (1890–1966)

German general. He was the ambassador to Japan from 1938 to 1942 and inadvertently contributed to the defeat of Germany by giving information to a close friend, Richard Sorge. Sorge was the Soviet spy who provided the intelligence material that saved Moscow in 1942. Ott resigned his post after Sorge was discovered and arrested.

Otto

Code name of the Luftwaffe radio beacon at Frankfurt, which was used as a homing beacon for fighter aircraft.

Outerbridge, William W.

U.S. Navy officer. He was the commander of the destroyer U.S.S. *Ward* that sank the Japanese midget submarine off Pearl Harbor on December 7, 1941. The incident occurred on the first night of his first patrol of his first command, and the *Ward* was the first ship to fire on the Japanese at Pearl Harbor.

Owens, Alfred George

Canadian who worked for the German Abwehr as a spy in England. He was arrested by British Intelligence MI-6 the day after war was declared. Owens was given a choice of either being hanged or of sending back controlled information to the Germans. He chose to work for the British; because of this, every new German agent sent to England was caught.

OWI

Office of War Information. It was the official U.S. agency for the control of information to the public in World War II. Elmer Davis was the head of the OWI.

Oxford

English university town. It was never bombed by the Germans throughout World War II, possibly because Hitler intended to make it the capital of occupied England when he conquered the island.

Oxley, H.M.S.

British submarine. Ironically, it was the first ship sunk by the British Navy in World War II, when a sister submarine, the H.M.S. *Triton*, accidentally torpedoed it on September 10, 1939, off the Norwegian coast.

Oyster

Code name to identify the telephone exchange for the Allied Strategic Air Forces at St. Germain in Normandy. Oyster was commanded by General Carl Spaatz.

Ozawa, Jisaburo (1886–1966)

Japanese admiral who swore there would be no British Dunkirk-type evacuation of Singapore and used his fleet to destroy boats loaded with civilian refugees.

P

P-38

U.S. Army Air Force twin-engined fighter. It was originally designed as a high-performance bomber interceptor in 1937 when the prevailing military thought was that the bombers would always get through. The P-38 was not designed to oppose other fighters, but it could outclimb and outdive nearly every enemy fighter. It was first named the *Atlanta*, which was changed by the British to *Lightning;* the U.S. followed suit. The P-38 was the first fighter with two engines, the first fighter with tricycle landing gear, and the first American plane to shoot down a German aircraft after the U.S. entered the war. The P-38 shot down more Japanese aircraft than any other fighter of World War II. Lockheed built 9,323 Lightnings and Vultee built 113. The first Japanese aircraft was shot down by Robert Faurot and Lieutenant Elza Shahan downed the first German plane from P-38s.

P-39

U.S. Army Air Force single-engine fighter. It was designed primarily as a ground-support, short-range aircraft to defend the U.S. from an invading power. The P-39 was never meant to oppose other fighter aircraft, yet this was its main U.S. role in World War II. The engine was mounted behind the pilot and the propeller shaft passed between his legs. The Russians received over half the P-39's built and used them for ground support missions very effectively. The name of the P-39 was *Aircobra.*

P-40

U.S. Army Air Force single-engine fighter. It was designed only for ground support missions to protect the coasts of the U.S. from invasion, but was pressed into service in the early days of the war in aerial combat. The P-40 was the aircraft used by the Flying Tigers in China, who realized its shortcomings and used it very effectively against the Japanese.

P-47

U.S. Army Air Force single-engine fighter. It was named the *Thunderbolt* and nicknamed the "Jug" because of its size. The P-47 was designed by Alexander Kartveli and was one of the best and most versatile fighters the U.S. had in its arsenal. It did well in aerial combat and was an extremely good ground-support aircraft.

P-51

U.S. Army Air Force single-engine fighter. The first models had Allison engines and were not high-performance aircraft. Rolls Royce Inc. believed that the P-51 needed more power and equipped them with Rolls Royce-Packard engines, which turned them into some of the best-performing aircraft of the war. When equipped with auxiliary fuel tanks, the P-51 could escort bombers into the heart of Germany and back, thus becoming the first fighter able to give continuous protection to Allied bombers. It was first named the *Apache*, but the British named their purchased models *Mustang* and after awhile that name was used for all P-51's.

P-400

Designator of the export model of the P-39. A few ended up in the Pacific because of the shortage of aircraft. The pilots that flew the P-400 named them "Klunkers."

Parr, Jack (1918–)

U.S. comedian. During World War II, he entertained troops in the South Pacific, serving with the U.S. Army 28th Special Service Company. At one time during the fighting on Guadalcanal, he and Jackie Cooper lived in the same tent.

PAC

Parachute and cable. It was a British experiment that consisted of a rocket with a cable attached that was fired in front of low-flying enemy aircraft. The cable then fell slowly back to earth on a parachute. It was hoped that the aircraft would strike the cable and crash. The British used this to protect their aircraft industries.

Pact of Steel

Name given to the alliance between Germany and Italy which was signed in Berlin on May 22, 1939.

Paddock

Code name given to emergency underground facilities near Hampstead, England, to be used as a headquarters for the British War Cabinet if their London offices were destroyed.

Paddock, Charles W. (1900–1943)

Track star who was known as "the world's fastest human" during the 1920's. He was a participant for the U.S. in the 1924 and 1928 Olympic games. During World War II, he served in the U.S. Marine Corps as an officer. Paddock was killed in a plane crash in Alaska on July 21, 1943.

Page, George Nelson

American propaganda broadcaster for the Italians in World War II. He was the nephew of the U.S. ambassador to Italy and became an Italian citizen. Page served for a time in the Italian Army before the war and became a friend of Count Ciano. Because of this, he was able to get a high office in the Italian Propaganda Ministry.

Palazzo Venezia

Fifteenth-century building in the center of Rome. It was the headquarters of Benito Mussolini.

Palm Sunday Massacre

Name given to an attack on April 18, 1943, when P-40's of the U.S. Ninth Army Air Force attacked nearly one hundred JU-52 transports off Cape Bon, North Africa. The transports were taking men to reinforce Field Marshall Erwin Rommel and over half were lost to the U.S. fighters. This attack was part of Operation Flax.

Panama Canal

It was called the "Achilles Heel" of the American defense in World War II.

Panay, U.S.S.

450-ton U.S. gunboat sunk by Japanese planes on December 12, 1937, on the Yangtze River. The ship was built in 1927, named after a Philippine island, and commanded by Lieutenant Commander James J. Hughes. The Japanese aircraft attacked it on a Sunday, although it was well-marked with the U.S. flag, and killed one sailor, Charles L. Ensminger, and an Italian journalist, Sandro Sandri. The Japanese government called it an accident and apologized profusely.

Panda Bears

Nickname of the 2nd Pursuit Squadron of General Claire Chennault's Flying Tigers. It consisted mostly of U.S. Navy pilots.

Panki

Name of a Polish border village. It was the first case of direct support of the German Luftwaffe for the infantry in World War II on September 1, 1939. The first squadron was led by Captain Otto Weiss, the second squadron by Adolf Galland.

Pannell, Ernest W.

U.S. Navy ensign on PT boats in the Pacific during World War II. He was a former All-American tackle from Texas A & M and a pro football player for the Green Bay Packers.

Pantaloon

Allied code name for Naples, Italy.

Pantelleria

Italian island between Tunisia and Sicily. It was defended by 10,000 troops and had an airdrome with underground hangars that could accommodate eighty fighters. Pantelleria was attacked from the air and from the sea in a massive assault as part of Operation Corkscrew. It surrendered on June 11, 1943, and was the first defended place to do so as a result of both aerial and naval bombardment. The only casualty occurred when a British soldier was bitten by a mule.

Panther Tank

Fifty-ton German medium tank that was equipped with a high-velocity 75mm gun. It was designed to be able to take on the Russian T-34, but had a shorter range and was slower than the T-34. However, because of the gun, it could shoot farther.

Papandreou, George (1888-1968)

Greek Premier of the government in exile in Cairo during World War II.

von Papen, Franz (1889–1969)

German politician. He is probably one of the best examples of a bungling idiot who continued to survive. In World War I, he was the German military attaché to Washington and was the head of German espionage and sabotage in the U.S. In 1915, von Papen was exposed by a British female secret agent and expelled. While searching his luggage, the U.S. customs confiscated 126 check stubs that were receipts for payments to all his American agents. He served for a time on the Western Front, then was sent to Palestine as Chief of Staff to the Turkish Army, which was defeated by British General Allenby. Von Papen hastily fled, and secret documents were found that he forgot to destroy or take with him. When London was asked about the papers, it said, "Forward papers. If von Papen is captured, do not intern, send him to a lunatic asylum!" Between the wars, he was a politician and became Chancellor in 1932. He dissolved the Reichstag before it could vote him out of office. Von Papen then helped Hitler come to power and became Vice-Chancellor on January 30, 1933, under Hitler with the hopes of being able to control him. In June 1934, he made a speech at the University of Marburg in which he questioned the Nazi suppression of freedom of speech. At the end of the month the S.S. purged the S.A. and several assassins went to his office to kill him, but he was not there. Von Papen was forced to resign on July 3, 1934, thus allowing him to become the ambassador to Austria. In 1939, he was appointed ambassador to Turkey and inadvertently did much to keep Turkey from joining the Axis powers. The Russians sent a team of Bulgarians to Ankara to assassinate him, but they only succeeded in blowing themselves up. He was captured on April 10, 1945, in the Ruhr by U.S. Ninth Army glider troops, tried at Nuremberg for war crimes, and acquitted.

MOVIE PORTRAYALS:
The Hitler Gang (1944), by Walter Kingsford
Five Fingers (1952), by John Wengraf

Parachute troops

The Russians were the first nation reported to have used parachute forces in battle, when they dropped small detachments of infantry at Petsamo in northern Finland during the Finno-Russian War in 1940.

Parakeet owners

German General Gunther Blumentritt and Field Marshall Bernard Montgomery.

Park, Keith (1892–1975)

British Air Vice-Marshall. As the commander of No. 11 Group of Fighter Command during the Battle of Britain, Park masterminded the defense around London and bore the brunt of the German attacks. He advocated sending up small fighter groups to break up German formations, and then attacking the bombers. Park was highly criticized for not using large fighter formations, but he believed that these would only increase his losses at a time when he needed a strong reserve in case of a German invasion. He was replaced, went on to Malta, commanded the air defenses there, and later went to Southeast Asia.

MOVIE PORTRAYAL:
Battle of Britain (1969), by Trevor Howard

Parks Bert (1914–   )
Hollywood celebrity. He enlisted in the U.S. Army in 1942 and rose from private to captain. While a second lieutenant, Parks was once lost behind Japanese lines for ten days while fighting in Burma.

Parry, Sir William E. (1893–1972)
Royal New Zealand Navy officer. He was the captain of the cruiser *Achilles* that fought against the *Graf Spee* on December 13, 1939.

Parsons, William S. (1901–1953)
U.S. Navy captain. He flew on the *Enola Gay* and assembled the atomic bomb in the air while en route to Hiroshima on August 6, 1945. Parsons was awarded a Distinguished Service Medal and a Silver Star.

MOVIE PORTRAYALS:
Above and Beyond (1953), by Larry Gates
Enola Gay (1980 TV movie), by Robert Pine

Pash, Boris T.
U.S. Army lieutenant colonel. He was head of the Alsos mission that searched for German scientists before the Russians could capture them at the end of World War II.

Patch, Alexander M. (1889–1945)
U.S. Army lieutenant general. He commanded U.S. Army forces on Guadalcanal in 1942 and the U.S. Seventh Army in southern France in 1944.

Patent No. 2,026,077
Patent awarded to James True, founder of the America First Fascist organization, for his invention called a "kike killer," which was a small club. It came in two sizes, one of which was especially designed to be used by women.

Pathfinder
Term used to refer to special air force units that guided bomber formations and parachute troops to their target areas.

Patrick Henry, S.S.
Name of the first Liberty ship. It was 441 feet long, displaced 14,100 tons of water, took 244 days to build, and was launched on December 30, 1941. The first captain of the *Patrick Henry* was

Richard Gailard Ellis. The coauthor's father, Arlie "Bud" McCombs, was transported to Italy in 1943 on the *Patrick Henry.*

Patrol Plane 4

Japanese patrol plane launched from the cruiser *Tone* that spotted the American carriers at Midway in June 1942.

Pattle, Maraduke E. (1914–1941)

Royal Air Force squadron leader. He was the top-scoring RAF ace of World War II with fifty-one aircraft to his credit. Pattle downed thirteen enemy planes while flying Gladiators and the rest while in Hurricanes. All victories were in the Middle East and Greece. He was killed in action on April 20, 1941, during the Battle of Athens while trying to rescue another pilot.

Patton 75

Name of a drink served at General George S. Patton's villa in Sicily. It consisted primarily of champagne and brandy but often had other alcoholic ingredients to give it "body."

Patton 75

Name given to a World War I artillery piece, the 75mm Howitzer, that was originally called the *French 75*. It was named after General George S. Patton because of its strong recoil.

Patton, George S. (1885–1945)

U.S. Army general. He had been a participant in the 1912 Olympics in Stockholm, Sweden as the first American to enter the Pentathlon (he finished fifth), and was well known for his equestrian ability. Patton, nicknamed "Blood and Guts," commanded the U.S. Third Army in the fighting across Europe. He died as a result of injuries in a postwar auto accident and is buried at Diekirch, Luxembourg. Many postwar publications have erroneously attributed to him the Congressional Medal of Honor.

MOVIE PORTRAYALS:
Miracle of the White Stallions (1963), by John Larch
Is Paris Burning? (1966), by Kirk Douglas
Patton (1970), by George C. Scott
Brass Target (1978), by George Kennedy
Ike (1979 TV movie), by Darren McGavin

Paul Revere

Radio name used by former Hearst newsman Douglas Chandler, who was a propaganda broadcaster for Germany during World War II. He was known as the "American Lord Haw Haw" and began each broadcast with "Misinformed, misgoverned friends and compatriots."

Paulus, Friedrich von (1890–1957)

German field marshall. He was sent to North Africa to observe Field Marshall Erwin Rommel's disposition of troops during the first siege of Tobruk in 1941. Paulus recommended withdrawal, but Rommel continued to attack in a battle that lasted 221 days. Von Paulus was placed in command of the ill-fated Sixth Army and concentrated his German forces in Stalingrad, leaving his flanks to Rumanians and Hungarians, whom the Russians were able to defeat easily. After the fall of Stalingrad in 1942, von Paulus collaborated with the Russians in opposition to Hitler. When the war was over he returned to East Germany but refused to cooperate with the Communists by acting as a figurehead.

Pavelitch, Dr. Ante (1889–1959)

Yugoslavian leader of the fascist Ustachi under German occupation. He was reported to be responsible for over 850,000 deaths but escaped arrest at the end of the war aboard an Italian passenger vessel. Pavelitch fled to Argentina disguised as a monk, living there until a Yugoslavian assassination team attempted to kill him in 1957. He survived, although he was badly wounded, and traveled to Spain, where he died in 1959 as a result of his injuries.

Pavlichenko, Liudmila

Russian woman sniper who was credited with killing 309 Germans along with two Rumanians during World War II.

PAYE

"Pay As You Earn." Name given to the British income tax during World War II. The scheme of "paying as you earn" was devised by Sir Kingsley Wood and implemented by the Chancellor of the Exchequer, Sir John Anderson.

Payne, Robert (1911–   )

American author and historian. He was a reporter in the Spanish Civil War and was involved in a 1938 plot to assassinate Hitler. In 1973, Payne wrote *The Life and Death of Adolf Hitler*, a biography of Hitler.

PB4Y

U.S. Navy version of the B-24 which was used for antisubmarine patrols.

P. C. Bruno

Code name used by the French cryptographic service prior to the fall of France in June 1940. It was headquartered at the Chateau Vignoble twenty-five miles from Paris.

Peabody, Eddie (1901–1970)

U.S. musician once known as the "Banjo King." He served with the U.S. Navy in both World War I and World War II and held a high officer's rank at the Great Lakes Naval Training Center, where he was in charge of entertainment.

Pearl Harbor

Name of a secret radio station set up by the first OSS agents to infiltrate Europe during World War II. The team landed at Corsica on December 14, 1942, from the French submarine *Casablanca*, and worked until the summer of 1943.

Pearl Harbor Attack Witnesses (December 7, 1941)

Edgar Rice Burroughs—author
Webley Edwards—radio announcer
Leif Ericson—Hollywood actor
James Jones—author
Jason Robards, Jr.—Hollywood actor
Jackie Robinson—athlete (as a civilian)
Robert Trumbull—newspaper reporter
Carl "Bobo" Olson—future Middleweight Champion of the World (Bobo was eleven years old at the time)
Dave Guard—original member of the Kingston Trio (Guard was seven years old at the time)

Pearl Harbor Battleships

Battleships anchored at battleship row during the Japanese attack.

U.S.S. *Arizona*—sunk
U.S.S. *California*—sunk (salvaged)
U.S.S. *Maryland*—damaged
U.S.S. *Nevada*—beached (salvaged)
U.S.S. *Oklahoma*—sunk
U.S.S. *Pennsylvania*—damaged
U.S.S. *Tennessee*—damaged
U.S.S. *Utah*—sunk
U.S.S. *West Virginia*—sunk (salvaged)

The Japanese unwittingly sowed the seeds of their own destruction by forcing the U.S. Navy to resort to the aircraft carrier, since the majority of the battleships were unserviceable. Prior to this, the top Navy brass had been in favor of the battleship as the main weapon in their arsenal.

Pearson, Drew (1897–1969)

American newspaper columnist whose articles appeared in over 600 papers. He was second in journalistic power only to Walter Winchell. It was Pearson who leaked the story on his radio program on November 21, 1943, of General George S. Patton slapping a soldier in a field hospital in Sicily. Many other journalists were aware of the incident but had agreed not to reveal the information to the public at the express wishes of General Dwight Eisenhower. Pearson did not believe he was bound by this gentlemen's agreement. He died on September 1, 1969, exactly thirty years after Germany's invasion of Poland started World War II.

MOVIE PORTRAYAL:
Tail Gunner Joe (1977 TV movie), by Robert F. Simon

Peashooters

Name given to U.S. fighters by the bomber crews during World War II.

Peck, James Lincoln (1912–)

First American after World War I to shoot down a German aircraft. He did so during the Spanish Civil War, in which he became an ace, with two German and three Italian aircraft to his credit. Peck offered his experience to the U.S. Army as an instructor but was ignored because he was black. He became a writer for aviation publications for the duration of World War II.

Peenemunde

Secret German rocket-test base on the Baltic. Security was so tight that there was one S.S. man for every one of the 40,000 inhabitants. It was bombed by the Royal Air Force on August 17, 1943, and put out of operation for quite a while. The British had actually learned of the existence of Peenemunde from Ultra intercepts but to protect this fact they attributed its discovery to 1) a photo-reconnaissance analysis WAAF, Constance Babington-Smith; 2) the Lisbon Report; 3) the Lucy spy ring; 4) the Oslo Report; 5) Charles Coward, a British prisoner of war interned near Auschwitz, Poland.

Pegasus Bridge

Drawbridge over a canal near Benouville, Normandy, which was captured on June 6, 1944, by the British 6th Airborne Division. It was renamed after the unit insignia of the Division, which was a flying Pegasus.

Peggy

Name of a British Army mule from whose grave in Italy *Time* magazine printed the epitaph, "In memory of Peggy, who in her lifetime kicked one brigadier, two colonels, four majors, ten captains, twenty-four lieutenants, forty-two sergeants, sixty corporals, 436 other ranks, and one bomb."

Peiper, Joachim (1915–1976)

German S.S. colonel and head of Kampfgruppe Peiper, which spearheaded the assault of the 1st S.S. Panzer Division in the Battle of the Bulge in December 1944. His unit massacred nineteen American prisoners of war at Housfeld, fifty at Bullingen, and eighty-six at Malmedy, and shot about 200 other Americans and 100 Belgian civilians in isolated instances. Peiper was tried after the war at Dachau and given the death sentence, but this was later commuted to life imprisonment. Peiper was finally released from Landsberg Prison on December 22, 1956, and moved to Traves in eastern France, where he led a low-key life until he was attacked and murdered in his home in 1976. The killer or killers were never apprehended.

Pendleton, Walton B.

U.S. Navy lieutenant commander. He was captain of the destroyer U.S.S. *England*, which sank six Japanese submarines in twelve days. Pendleton was called by Zenji Orita "...the deadliest enemy it [the Japanese submarine service] ever met during the war...."

Peniakoff, Vladimir (1897–1951)

Belgian-born Russian businessman in Cairo at the outbreak of World War II. He had fought in the French Army in World War I and had been a student at Cambridge, England, between the wars. Peniakoff, known as "Popski" for short, joined the British Army in Cairo as an officer and commanded a Long Range Desert Group that became known as Popski's Private Army or PPA. It specialized in attacks on Field Marshall Erwin Rommel's supply lines hundreds of miles in the rear.

Peninsula Hotel

Hotel on mainland China across the tiny strait from Hong Kong. It was the site of the surrender of Hong Kong by the governor, Sir Mark Young, to the Japanese on December 23, 1941. Hong Kong was the first British territory in the Pacific to be lost in World War II.

Pennsylvania, U.S.S.

U.S. Navy battleship that served as the flagship of the Pacific Fleet at Pearl Harbor. It was damaged by the Japanese attack of December 7, 1941, but was refurbished and fought at the Battle of Leyte Gulf on October 20, 1944. The *Pennsylvania* was used as the target ship for the atomic bomb tests at Bikini Atoll in 1946 but did not sink. It was finally sunk in 1948 by shellfire.

Pentagon

Five-sided building in Washington, D. C., that is the site of the U.S. military headquarters complex. The building was opened in January 1943. Its construction was commanded by Major General Leslie Groves, who later headed the Manhattan Project.

People's Court

Nazi judicial organization headed by Dr. Roland Freisler that tried and convicted the conspirators in the July 20, 1944, assassination attempt on Hitler.

Percival, Arthur E. (1887–1966)

British lieutenant general who commanded Malaya. He refused to erect fortifications for defense on the north end of Singapore because he thought it would be bad for the morale of the civilians and troops. When he did begin defensive operations, his actions were ineffectual. Percival ignored the evidence of a Japanese assault on the northwest part of Singapore and failed to take countermeasures. He surrendered to General Tomoyuki Yamashita on February 15, 1942, and was imprisoned in Mukden, Manchuria. Percival was selected to be a witness to the Japanese surrender aboard the U.S.S. *Missouri* in Tokyo Bay on September 2, 1945.

Per Videm Volo

"By Faith I Fly," inscription on the side of the P-47 fighter flown by Dean E. Hess out of Belgium in 1944.

Perón, Juan (1895–1975)

President of Argentina. He took over the government in a 1943 coup to insure that the country would remain pro-Axis.

MOVIE PORTRAYAL:

Evita Peron (1981 TV movie), by James Farentino

Pershing, John J. (1860–1948)

U.S. General of the Armies during World War I. In 1940, he advocated the transfer of fifty obsolete U.S. destroyers to the British to help them fight Germany. Pershing, although bedridden through most of World War II, was a highly respected adviser to American generals and statesmen.

MOVIE PORTRAYALS:
Sergeant York (1941), by Joseph Gerard
Court Martial of Billy Mitchell (1955), by Herbert Hayes

Petacci, Clara (1912–1945)

Mistress of Benito Mussolini who was executed with him on April 28, 1945, by Italian partisans. After Mussolini's capture, he asked that a message be sent to her, which resulted in her capture also. Petacci requested to be shot with Mussolini, and both were killed by Walter Audisio.

MOVIE PORTRAYAL:
Mussolini: Last Days (1974), by Lisa Gastoni

Pétain, Henri (1856–1951)

French marshall and head of the Vichy government during World War II. He had been the French ambassador to General Francisco Franco in Spain prior to the war. Pétain was put on trial for collaborating with the Germans and was sentenced to death after World War II, but this was commuted to life imprisonment by General Charles de Gaulle because they had served in the same unit in World War I.

Peterson, Chesley Gordon

American who commanded the Royal Air Force No. 71 Squadron, the first Eagle Squadron, for nearly a year. He had been thrown out of the U.S. Army Air Force because he was too young and enlisted in the R.A.F. as a fighter pilot a year and four months prior to the attack on Pearl Harbor. After the U.S. entered the war, Peterson became executive officer of the 4th U.S. Fighter Group and was then only twenty-two years old.

Petropavlovsk

Name given a cruiser presented to the Russian government by Hitler in January 1940. The 10,000-ton ship was involved in the harassment of the retreating German forces along the shores of the Gulf of Finland in 1944.

Phelps, U.S.S. (DD–360)

U.S. Navy destroyer that sank the carrier *Lexington* after it was badly damaged at the Battle of the Coral Sea on May 8, 1942. The *Phelps* had been present at Pearl Harbor, but was not damaged in the Japanese attack of December 7, 1941.

Philadelphia Story

Movie of 1940 starring Cary Grant, Katharine Hepburn, and James Stewart. It was the movie playing at the Cathay Building in Singapore in February 1942 when the city surrendered to the Japanese.

Phillips, Sid (1907–1973)

British musician and composer who was known as England's "King of the Clarinet." He served in the Royal Air Force during World War II.

Phillips, Sir Tom (1888–1941)

British admiral. He was commander of the *Prince of Wales* and the *Repulse* when they were sunk by Japanese aircraft in December 1941. Phillips went down with his flagship the *Prince of Wales*. He was known as "Tom Thumb" because of his short stature.

Philpot, Oliver

Royal Air Force pilot who flew Beauforts with the No. 42 Squadron. He was shot down and captured by the Germans, yet escaped with Eric Williams via the "Wooden Horse," one of the most clever and unique escapes in the history of World War II (see Wooden Horse).

Phoebe

Name of the P-38 flown by Tom Lanphiers, who was credited with shooting down Admiral Isoruku Yamamoto on April 18, 1943.

Phoenix

Code name for the Mulberries and Gooseberries, which were concrete barges sunk off the Normandy coast after the D-Day invasion to create a breakwater to protect the landing operations.

Phoenix, U.S.S. (CL-46)

U.S. Navy cruiser that was present in Pearl Harbor on December 7, 1941, during the Japanese attack, but did not sustain any damage. During fifteen months of battle throughout World War II, the *Phoenix* participated in twenty different engagements, earning nine battle stars, and lost only one man. Because of her record she attained the nickname "Luckiest Ship in the Navy."

Phonetic Alphabet

Used by the U.S. forces during World War II.

Phonetic Alphabet

Able	Charlie	Easy
Baker	Dog	Fox

George	Oboe	Victor
How	Peter	William
Jig	Queen	X-Ray
King	Roger	Yoke
Love	Sugar	Zebra
Mike	Tare	
Nan	Uncle	

Phony War

Name given to the period from September 3, 1939, to April 9, 1940, when the Germans and Allied land forces faced each other across the borders with no attempt by either side to attack. The term was attributed to the U.S. isolationist Senator William E. Borah. The Phony War ended on April 9 with the German invasion of Denmark and Norway. It was also referred to as the *Sitzkrieg*.

Piasecki, Frank N. (1920–   )

U.S. aeronautical engineer. At the age of twenty-three, he designed and flew the U.S.'s second helicopter, which he built from discarded car parts. It was designated the PV-2, nicknamed "the aerial jeep," and was intended for reconnaissance work. (The first helicopter was built by Igor Sikorsky.)

Pick, Lewis Andrew (1890–1956)

U.S. Army lieutenant general. He was chief of the engineers and commanded the building of the Ledo Road, which was nicknamed "Pick's Pike."

Pier 88

Site where the French ocean liner *Normandie* was docked in New York, caught fire, and capsized in 1942.

Pierce Brothers

John Reeves Pierce and George Ellis Pierce, both U.S. Navy officers in command of submarines during World War II. John Pierce, captain of the U.S.S. *Argonaut,* went down with his vessel; George Pierce commanded the U.S.S. *Tunney.*

Pierce, Clinton A.

U.S. Army brigadier general. He was the first American general to be wounded in action in World War II, February 4, 1942, on Bataan. Pierce became a prisoner of war with the surrender of Bataan to the Japanese.

Pierrepoint, Arthur

Chief executioner of England during World War II. He hanged William Joyce, "Lord Haw Haw," in 1946.

Pierson, Reginald K. (1891–1948)
British aeronautical engineer. He designed the twin-engine Wellington bomber.

Pigboat
Slang term for U.S. Navy submarines. It was coined because early submarines did not have periscopes, so an attack on a ship was conducted with a bobbing motion similar to that of a porpoise, which was known as a "sea pig."

Pike, James (1913–1969)
Episcopalian bishop. He served in World War II as a lieutenant in the U.S. Navy.

Pilar
Name of the yacht owned by Ernest Hemingway. He armed the *Pilar* in hopes of sighting a German submarine in the Caribbean and attacking it. The *Pilar* was named after one of his characters in the Spanish Civil War novel, *For Whom the Bell Tolls*.

Pilots
Julius Barr—Chiang Kai-shek
Hans Baur—Adolf Hitler
Herman Giesen—Field Marshall Erwin Rommel
Larry Hanson—General Dwight Eisenhower
Len Iggs—Field Marshall Jan Smuts
Royal Leonard—Chiang Kai-shek
Lionel Marmier—General Charles de Gaulle
Henry T. Myers—President Franklin Roosevelt
Henry T. Myers—President Harry Truman
Alvin E. Robinson—General Omar Bradley
Harold C. Rutter—General Harold "Hap" Arnold

Pilot's General
Nickname conferred on U.S. Army Air Force Lieutenant General Elwood R. Quesada, who commanded the Ninth Air Force in World War II. He was the first American airman to land on Corsica.

Pinetree
Code name for the headquarters of the U.S. 8th Bomber Command, which was originally set up by General Ira Eaker at High Wycombe in Buckinghamshire, England.

Pink Lady
Name of torpedo fluid that PT boat crews drained and distilled into 190 proof alcohol, which they then mixed with grapefruit juice to make a potent drink.

Pinquin

German armed merchant ship. It was the most successful of all the auxiliary cruisers of World War II, sinking thirty-two Allied ships totaling 154,619 tons. The *Pinquin* was finally sunk by the H.M.S. *Cornwall* on May 8, 1941, off Seychelles. It had been designated HSK V or Ship 33 by the Germans.

Pin-Up Girls

The two most popular American pin-up girls of World War II were Betty Grable and Rita Hayworth.

Piper, USS

Last U.S. Navy submarine to return from a combat patrol at the end of World War II. It was commanded by Edward Beach.

Pius XI (–1939)

Roman Catholic Pope. He died on February 10, 1939, after receiving an injection from Dr. Francesco Petacci, father of Clara Petacci, the mistress of Benito Mussolini. Pius XI was very anti-Fascist and was going to denounce Fascism in a speech to be given several hours after Dr. Petacci's visit. It was alleged by Cardinal Eugene Tisserant, who was head of the College of Cardinals at the time and therefore the number two person in the Vatican, that Pius XI was assassinated at the instigation of Mussolini.

Plan A-Go

Japanese operation to lure the U.S. fleet into a decisive naval engagement.

Plan D

Operation advocated by French General Maurice Gamelin to counter a German drive through Belgium.

Plan E

Alternate to Plan D, it was an Allied proposal to counter a German attack through Belgium.

Plan Eclipse

Code name for the occupation and rule of the American sector of postwar Germany. The first phase was strictly a military government with a gradual transition to some form of civilian government under Allied supervision. Plan Eclipse was divided into three parts, punitive, political, and propagandistic.

Plan Green

Hitler's attack on Czechoslovakia.

Plan Jael

Plan of deception devised by the Allies to throw Hitler's High

Command off the D-Day objective of Normandy. The name was later changed to Operation Bodyguard.

Plan Kon

Japanese operation to reinforce the island of Biak in the Palaus on May 30, 1944, as part of Plan A-Go. The first attempt was called off when the Japanese ships were sighted by U.S. submarines while en route. A second attempt was driven back to port by Admiral Thomas Kinkaid's 7th Fleet. A third expedition that included the battleships *Yamato* and *Musashi*, along with five cruisers, seven destroyers, and several support ships, was postponed when the U.S. attacked the Marianas islands.

Plan Orange

U.S. military contingency plan in the event of war with Japan. It was thought that Japan would attack the vulnerable Philippines and that U.S. forces there could fight a delaying action to Bataan, holding out for not more than six months. During this time the U.S. fleet would sail across the Pacific, engage and defeat the Japanese fleet, then set up a blockade of the home islands. Plan Orange governed naval theory between the wars and influenced ship designs tremendously. It was revamped by ABC-1 to Rainbow 5 in 1941.

Ploesti

Site of Rumanian oil fields that covered nineteen square miles and supplied one third of all fuel oil needed by the Germans. It was the first target in Europe bombed by American aircraft, thirteen B-24's led by Colonel Harry A. Halverson, on June 11, 1942. Ploesti was attacked again by the Ninth Army Air Force in Operation Soapsuds on August 1, 1943.

Plunger, U.S.S.

First U.S. submarine to be attacked by the Japanese Navy in World War II when it was depth-charged off the coast of Japan in January, 1942. The *Plunger* survived the attack.

PLUTO

Code word for *P*ipe*l*ine *U*nder *t*he *O*cean. PLUTO was the Allied plan to lay a pipeline across the English Channel to carry fuel to the invasion forces after the D-Day invasion. Over sixty percent by weight of all battle supplies consisted of oil and gasoline. PLUTO was first proposed by Lord Louis Mountbatten in 1942, and, after completion, it delivered one million gallons of fuel a day.

Pocket Blitz

Name given to the period from January to March, 1944, when the Luftwaffe began bombing London again. The raids were very light compared to the efforts of 1940.

Pocket Patton

Name given to U.S. General Ernest Harmon, who commanded the U.S. XXII Corps at the end of the war. He acquired the nickname because he was short and carried pearl-handled pistols like those of General George S. Patton.

Plan R 4

British operation to occupy the Norwegian ports of Narvik, Trondheim, Bergen, and Stavanger in April 1940.

Plan Red

German armored thrust across the Somme and into the heart of France in June 1940.

Plan White

Hitler's invasion of Poland on September 1, 1939.

Plan Z

German plan in 1938 to build up the Navy to a point where it could take on the British Navy on equal terms. The strategists envisioned over 200 submarines, eight superbattleships, four aircraft carriers, twelve pocket battleships, plus numerous heavy and light cruisers and support vessels.

Play Ball

Code phrase used to indicate to American forces participating in the landings in North Africa on November 8, 1942, to attack the French. "Play Ball" followed the code phrase "Batter Up," which indicated that the French were resisting the landings.

Pleasance, Donald (1919–   )

British actor. He enlisted in the Royal Air Force after having declared himself a conscientious objector. Pleasance was shot down over France and spent twelve months in a prisoner-of-war camp. Ironically, he would play a prisoner of war in the 1963 movie *The Great Escape*.

Podhajsky, Alois (1898–1973)

Director of the Vienna Spanish Riding School from 1939 to 1965. He had been an Olympic medal winner for equestrian events. At the end of World War II, Podhajsky asked General George S. Patton, also an Olympic equestrian participant, to help him save the Lipizzan horses from the advancing Russians. Patton sent a task force into Czechoslovakia to help the horses cross into the western Allied territory.

Pointe du Hoc

German strong point situated on the lime cliffs overlooking both Omaha and Utah beaches that were assaulted on D-Day. At one time, the Pointe had six 155mm guns, making it a primary target for Allied bombers in preparation for D-Day. The site was assaulted by U.S. Rangers of the 2nd Battalion under Lieutenant Colonel James Rudder on June 6, 1944. The Germans put up a heavy defense but were hindered by 200 Russians in their ranks who fled. When the Rangers took the strong point, they found that the guns had been removed, so the assault on the Pointe was not really necessary.

Point System

Name given to a system devised by the U.S. military to equitably rotate forces overseas back to the States for discharge. Points were given so that those who had served the longest overseas would be released first.

1 point for every month of service
1 point for every month overseas
5 points per battle star

Congressional Medal of Honor winners could be discharged whenever they chose.

Poitier, Sidney (1924–)

American actor. During World War II, he enlisted in the U.S. Navy, lying about his age. Poitier was assigned to the 1267th Medical Detachment, which was an all-black unit stationed in Northport, Long Island, at a veterans' hospital for psychiatric patients. Poitier was discharged one year and eleven days after enlisting—all prior to his eighteenth birthday.

Pokryshkin, Alexander (1913–)

Russian Air Force ace. He was possibly the second highest scorer of the Red Air Force, having downed fifty-nine enemy aircraft during World War II. Pokryshkin, who was shot down three times himself, later became a lieutenant general.

Poland

Crimes against the Poles by Stalin:

1) In 1938, Stalin killed nearly the entire leadership of the old Polish Communist Party.

2) Stalin-Hitler Pact of 1939.
3) Massacre of 10,000 Polish officers in the Katyn forest.
4) Failure of Russia to aid underground Polish armies.
5) Deliberate stand-off of the Red Army during the Warsaw uprising in 1944.

Polonsky, Abraham (1910–)
Hollywood director. He served with the OSS during World War II.

Polar Bear
Emblem of the Northern Waters Flotilla, which was the German submarine unit that attacked the Murmansk convoys that were taking military supplies to the Russians. The submarines, which were painted white, were nicknamed "Ice Devils."

Pollywog
U.S. Navy slang term for anyone who has never crossed the equator. A person who had crossed was called a "shellback."

Pony Editions
Name given to special issues of magazines sent to U.S. servicemen overseas during World War II. These editions did not have any advertising. *Time* magazine was the primary Pony Edition publication.

Poole, Noel
British Army lieutenant. He is credited with being the first Allied soldier on the Normandy beaches on D-Day. Poole officially jumped at 12:11 A.M. and set up record players to broadcast battle sounds to add to the Germans' confusion. This was part of Operation Titanic.

Popov, Dusko (1919–)
Yugoslavian who became a double agent in World War II. Under the code name *Tricycle*, he fed information provided by British intelligence back to the German intelligence service. Four months prior to the Pearl Harbor attack, Popov was requested to gather information about the Pearl Harbor defenses and warned the U.S. of the special interest the Axis were taking in Hawaii, but he was ignored. Popov was a high-living playboy after whom it is believed that Ian Fleming modeled James Bond.

Popp, Michael (–1968)
General Dwight Eisenhower's personal Army tailor. He made the first Ike jacket, which was to become the symbol of GI's all over the world.

Popski's Private Army
British Army long-range reconnaissance unit of approximately

200 men. Commanded by Vladimir Peniakoff, they penetrated enemy lines in North Africa and Italy to gather information as well as to destroy enemy supplies. The unit used armored jeeps for rapid mobility.

Porsche, Ferdinand (1875–1971)

German automobile designer. During World War II, he was in charge of Volkswagen production as well as tank assembly.

Port Chicago

Small town on the Sacramento River forty miles northeast of San Francisco, California. It was the site of a U.S. Navy ammunition depot that shipped munitions to the Pacific battle zones. On July 17, 1944, an accidental explosion occurred that is estimated to have been equal to the force of a five-kiloton atomic bomb. It killed 323 people, destroyed five ships, a diesel engine, sixteen boxcars, and the town, besides damaging twelve other communities as far away as seventy-five miles. It was one of the worst disasters in maritime history and slowed up the flow of supplies to Saipan, which had just been invaded.

Poston, Tom (1927–   )

Television comedian and actor. He served in World War II as an Army Air Force pilot in Air Transport Command.

Potomac

President Franklin D. Roosevelt's personal yacht from 1936 until his death in 1945. Roosevelt wrote his Four Freedoms Doctrine on board and ostensibly the Atlantic Charter was signed on it. Prior to the official entry of the U.S. into World War II, the *Potomac* was armed with two 50-caliber machine guns. (Elvis Presley owned the *Potomac* at one time.)

Potsdam Conference

International meeting at the end of World War II in Europe (July 17 to August 2, 1945). It was attended by U.S. President Harry S Truman, Russian Premier Joseph Stalin, and the British Prime Minister Winston Churchill, who was replaced by Clement Attlee in the middle of the conference. Potsdam is a suburb of Berlin and former home of the kings of Prussia.

POTUS

Code word used to identify President Franklin Roosevelt in correspondence with Winston Churchill prior to World War II. Churchill's code was "Naval Person" since he was the First Lord of the Admiralty at this time.

Pound, Sir Dudley (1877–1943)

British admiral. He was the First Sea Lord from 1939 to 1943 and died on Trafalgar Day, October 21, 1943.

Pound, Ezra (1885–1972)

American poet. He broadcast for Mussolini throughout the war and could be heard every morning on Radio Roma's *American Hour.* Pound served as an anti-Semitic propagandist and was captured at the end of World War II. He was tried for treason, pronounced insane, and committed to St. Elizabeth's Hospital in Washington, D. C., from 1945 until 1958, when the charges against him were dropped. Pound returned to Italy to continue his self-imposed exile.

Pour le Mérite

Germany's highest military decoration for World War I. Some famous World War II personalities who were awarded the Pour le Mérite were

General Hans Baur
Field Marshall Werner von Blomberg
Field Marshall Fedor von Bock
General Alexander von Falkenhausen
Reichsmarschall Hermann Goering
Field Marshall Ritter von Greim
Pastor Martin Niemoller
Lieutenant General Theo Osterkamp
Field Marshall Erwin Rommel
Field Marshall Ferdinand Schorner
Field Marshall Hans von Seckt
General Ernst Udet

Powell, Lee (–1944)

Hollywood actor who played the Lone Ranger in the 1938 Republic serial *The Lone Ranger.* In July 1944, Powell was killed in action in the invasion of Tinian. (Actor George Montgomery was Powell's stunt double in the serial.)

Power, Tyrone (1914–1958)

Hollywood actor. He enlisted in the U.S. Marine Corps as a private on August 24, 1942 (the same day that Henry Fonda enlisted in the U.S. Navy), went to Officers Candidate School, and was commissioned. Power took flight training at El Toro, California, and graduated in April 1943 at Corpus Christi, Texas. In February 1945, he was assigned to Squadron 353 of the Marine

Transport Command stationed at Okinawa and Guam. Power was one of the first pilots to land on Iwo Jima while transporting supplies to the Marines fighting there. He returned to the U.S. in November 1945 aboard the U.S.S. *Marvin MacIntyre* and was discharged as a first lieutenant on January 14, 1946.

POW #1

Kazuo Sakamaki, Japanese midget submarine officer who was captured on December 7, 1941, at Pearl Harbor.

POW's (Prisoners of War)

During World War II, the U.S. interned 5,413 Japanese, 51,156 Italians, and 371,683 German prisoners of war within the continental U.S. Over 1,800 Axis prisoners attempted to escape, and by the end of the war twenty-eight Germans and fifteen Italians were still at large. In Europe, American Military Police handled 3,239,484 German prisoners of war up to V-E Day, a number that was greater than the total number of Americans in the European Theater of Operations on V-E Day.

POW Jargon

Slang of Americans held by the Germans:

Appell—roll call held to count prisoners

Ferrets—Germans who wandered through the compound to catch prisoners in escape attempts

Goons—name given to the Germans and also anything associated with them, i.e., goon boxes were guard boxes; goon-baiting was antagonizing the Germans, etc.

Goonskins—fake German uniforms made by the prisoners for escape attempts

Penguins—prisoners who dispersed dirt and sand from tunnels

Stooges—prisoners who kept an alert eye for Germans and warned other prisoners.

POW ships (Japanese) sunk in World War II

Arisan Maru—sunk on October 24, 1944, off the coast of China by the U.S. submarine *Shark*. Only five Allied prisoners of the 1,790 prisoners of war aboard survived.

Enoura Maru—sunk on September 12, 1944, by the U.S. submarine *Sealion*, killing over 1,000 Australian and British prisoners of war.

Oryoku Maru—sunk on December 15, 1944, in Subic Bay, Philippines, by Allied aircraft. Over 900 prisoners died out of 1,800 aboard.

Shinyo Maru—sunk on September 7, 1944, off Mindanao by the submarine U.S.S. *Barb*, killing all but eighty-two of the 750 Allied prisoners on board.

PQ-1

Designator of the first Allied convoy to Murmansk. Ten ships sailed in September 1941 to haul supplies to the Russians.

PQ-5

Designator of the first Murmansk convoy to lose a ship from a German attack. The *Waziristan* was sunk January 2, 1942, by the submarine *U-134*, commanded by Lieutenant Rudolph Schendel.

PQ-13

Murmansk convoy that sailed in March 1942. Of nineteen ships, two freighters were sunk by German aircraft, three by submarines and destroyers.

PQ-14

April 1942 Murmansk convoy that lost one ship to the German submarine *U-403*, but had sixteen of twenty-four others damaged by ice floes, forcing the convoy to return to Iceland.

PQ-15

April 26 to May 7, 1942 Murmansk convoy. Three ships were lost to German torpedo aircraft out of a convoy of twenty-five ships.

PQ-16

Murmansk convoy that sailed in May 1942. Out of thirty-five ships, seven were sunk by over 100 aircraft of KG30 and KG26. Many other ships were damaged. The convoy lost 770 vehicles, 147 tanks, and 77 aircraft on the ships sunk, but the rest were able to deliver 2,507 vehicles, 321 tanks, and 124 aircraft to the Russians.

PQ-17

Designator of a Murmansk convoy in July 1942. The Germans put together a concentrated effort to stop supplies to Russia and the convoy of thirty-six ships lost ten to submarines and thirteen to aircraft, with two turning back. The British made several major mistakes that caused the disaster. In an effort to deceive the Germans, the British made them believe that Norway would be invaded, causing Hitler to withdraw all his submarines from the Atlantic to Norway—the right place to intercept the convoy. The second mistake was made when the German pocket battleship *Tirpitz* was rumored to be ready to attack the convoy. The British admiralty withdrew all the protective escort vessels from the convoy, leaving the unarmed merchant ships to fend for themselves. The Allies lost 3,350 vehicles, 430 tanks, and 210 aircraft.

PQ-18

Last Murmansk convoy. It was protected by fifty-one British warships and two British submarines. This was the first time an escort carrier, the *Avenger,* was used to protect a convoy. PQ-18 was attacked both by aircraft and submarines and, though defended, still lost a total of thirteen ships out of thirty-nine freighters, three tankers, and one rescue ship making up the convoy.

Praeger, Ralph B. (–1944)

U.S. Army captain. He was awarded the first Legion of Merit medal which was given posthumously for service as a guerilla fighter in the Philippines in the early days of the war. Praeger was captured by the Japanese in August 1943 and executed in Manila on December 31, 1944.

Prague

Capital of Czechoslovakia. It was the only European capital of the countries involved in World War II that was never bombed. Prague also had the distinction of being liberated from the Germans by Russians who had been fighting against the Germans in German uniform—the Vlasov Army.

Praise the Lord and Pass the Ammunition

Phrase attributed to Chaplain William A. McGuire during the Japanese attack on Pearl Harbor on December 7, 1941. He later denied ever saying it. A popular song was written from the saying.

Pratt and Whitney

Largest U.S. producer of piston engines for aircraft in World War II.

Preddy, George F.

U.S. Army Air Force officer and ace of World War II. He was credited with shooting down twenty-six enemy aircraft and downed six German planes over Hamburg in August 1944 within six minutes. Preddy was killed when American flak gunners shot his aircraft down by mistake as he pursued a German fighter.

President Coolidge, S.S.

American transport ship weighing 22,000 tons. It struck a mine on December 12, 1942, in the Solomon Islands. Captain Henry Nelson ran the vessel onto a coral reef but it slid off and capsized. As a result of his efforts, only two lives out of over 4,000 troops on board were lost.

President Harrison, S.S.

U.S. transport that was captured by the Japanese on December 8, 1941, in the Philippines. They renamed the ship *Kachidoki Maru*. It was sunk on September 12, 1944, by the U.S. submarine *Sealion*, killing over one thousand Australian and British prisoners of war en route to Japan.

President Roosevelt and Cordell Hull

Name of two Spitfire fighter planes sent to the British by Warner Bros. studios to help fight the Battle of Britain in September 1940.

Preston Robert (1917–)

Hollywood actor. He enlisted in the U.S. Army Air Force in 1943, becoming a captain in intelligence for the Ninth Army Air Force stationed in England. Preston gave intelligence briefings to the pilots before missions over the continent.

Prien, Gunther (1908–1941)

German Navy officer and tenth top-scoring submarine commander of World War II. He sank twenty-eight Allied ships, totaling 160,939 tons, as commander of *U-47* and was the first Naval officer to be awarded the Knight's Cross. Prien penetrated the British defenses at their anchorage of Scapa Flow October 14, 1939, and sank the battleship H.M.S. *Royal Oak*. He fired seven torpedoes at the ship, five of which were duds. On July 2, 1940, he sank the 15,501-ton passenger ship *Arandora Star*, which was carrying Italian and German prisoners of war to Canada. Prien and the *U-47* were sunk on March 7, 1941, by the destroyer H.M.S. *Wolverine* as he attempted to attack convoy OB-293 in the mid-Atlantic.

MOVIE PORTRAYAL:

Lt. Commander Prien (1967), by Dieter Eppler

Priller Josef (1915–1961)

German Luftwaffe ace with 101 Allied aircraft to his credit. He was commander of JG-26 and had been awarded the Knights Cross, Oak Leaves, and Swords. Priller and his wingman Feldwebel Heinz Wodarczyk were the only two pilots to attack the D-Day beaches on June 6, 1944.

Primaflex

German-made camera used by U.S. submarines for photo reconnaissance missions because U.S. Navy cameras were unsuitable.

The cameras had to be acquired through want ads in trade journals because the cameras were not available otherwise.

Primasole Bridge

Sicilian bridge. It was the site of one of the most unusual coincidences of World War II when British paratroopers and German paratroopers were both dropped at the same time in an attempt to reach the same objective. Each group overshot their drop zones and ended up on opposite ends of the bridge from where they were intended to be, yet they still opposed each other.

Prince of Wales, H.M.S.

British battleship weighing 35,000 tons. It was the newest and fastest ship in the British fleet and transported Prime Minister Winston Churchill across the Atlantic to Newfoundland for the Atlantic Charter meeting with President Franklin Roosevelt in 1941. The *Prince of Wales* was sunk by Japanese aircraft off Malaya on December 10, 1941. The Japanese then sent divers down to recover the radar units on the ship, which were sent back to Japan and used to develop the Japanese radar systems.

Princeton U.S.S. (CVL-23)

U.S. aircraft carrier. The keel was originally laid for the light cruiser U.S.S. *Tallahassee*, but the ship was converted to a carrier. The *Princeton* was bombed in the Battle of Leyte Gulf in October 1944 and so severely damaged that it had to be sunk by the destroyer U.S.S. *Reno*. It was nicknamed the "Peerless P."

Prinz Eugen

German heavy cruiser weighing 10,000 tons. It was torpedoed on February 23, 1942, by the British submarine H.M.S. *Trident* and had twenty feet of the stern blown off, yet survived. The *Prinz Eugen* was used as a test ship for the Atomic bomb blasts at Bikini Atoll in July 1946.

Program A-4

Hitler's planned attack on England using V-1 rockets. It was scheduled for November 1943, but a British attack on Peenemunde in August 1943 caused the Germans to postpone the assault until June 1944.

Project A

Designator of the U.S. Army Air Corps endeavor in 1933 to design and build a heavy bomber that could fly 5,000 miles at 200 miles per hour. The Air Corps planned on an aircraft that could protect Hawaii and Alaska and also be able to fly to Europe and back nonstop. The XB-15 was developed as a result of Project A and was the forerunner of the B-17.

Project A

Code name of Japan's atomic energy research which was the equivalent to the U.S. Manhattan Project. Project A was started shortly after Pearl Harbor but abandoned a year later because of the vast resources it required.

Project B

Japanese effort to develop radar and the proximity fuse in World War II.

Project Matterhorn

U.S. Army Air Force attempt to bomb the Japanese main islands using B-29's based in China. It was a failure because of the supply problems associated with flying everything over the Himalayas.

Project Plough

Code name for the establishment of a joint Canadian-U.S. military unit to be used as a guerrilla commando unit. It was designated the First Special Services Force and was initially to be used in Norway. Eventually the force fought in Italy, where they were known as the Devil's Brigade.

Propaganda Slogans on U.S. war posters

A Careless Word . . . A Needless Loss
A Careless Word . . . Another Cross
A Careless Word . . . A Needless Sinking
Save Your Cans . . . Help Pass the Ammunition
Salvage Victory—Throw Your Scrap Into the Fight
The Slip of a Lip May Sink a Ship
Idle Gossip Sinks Ships
Enemy Ears Are listening
Loose Talk Costs Lives

Proserpina

Tanker weighing 5,000 tons. Field Marshall Erwin Rommel put his hopes on this vessel to supply the gasoline needed to continue the Battle of El Alamein. The *Proserpina* was torpedoed on October 26, 1942, by Ralph Manning off the coast of Tobruk as German officers watched from the cliffs. Rommel then began his withdrawal.

Proximity Fuse

Antiaircraft artillery shell detonator that would explode the shell close to a target and scatter fragments through the air. It was originally designed by the Americans to be used against Japanese kamikaze aircraft and was found to be useful against ground targets. In Europe, the use of the proximity fuse was restricted to use over water, only because it was feared that the Germans might be able to find a dud intact and copy it for use against the Royal Air Force and the Eighth U.S. Air Force. This restriction was cancelled on December 16, 1944, just in time for the Battle of the Bulge.

PSP

Pierced steel planking. PSP were perforated steel sheets that were used for rapid construction of runways for aircraft.

PT Boats

Plywood torpedo boats used by the U.S. Navy in World War II. They were designed by a British engineer, Hubert Scott-Paine, to be lightly armed and to depend exclusively on speed for defense. Walt Disney drew the insignia for the PT boats—a mosquito astride a torpedo. The first PT boat squadron was set up in November 1940 and was commanded by Lieutenant Earl Stevens Caldwell, who was the youngest and lowest-ranked squadron commander in the Navy. The Navy attitude toward PT crews in World War II was that if someone graduated from Navy boot camp and was incapable of recognizing various knots, they were assigned to PT boats. If the PT's were sent out on patrol and did not return, the Navy then knew where the enemy was located.

PT-6

First motor torpedo boat of the U.S. Navy, built by Higgins Industries of New Orleans, Louisiana.

PT-10

Flagship of the first PT boat squadron commanded by Lieutenant Earl Caldwell.

PT-41

Boat on which General Douglas MacArthur was evacuated from the Philippines on March 11, 1942. It was commanded by Lieutenant John D. Bulkeley. Other PT boats in the escape were *PT-32*, *PT-34*, and *PT-35*.

PT-109

Lieutenant John F. Kennedy's torpedo boat, which was rammed by the Japanese destroyer *Amagiri* and sunk in the Solomons in 1943. Kennedy commanded *PT-101* before *PT-109* and *PT-59* after.

PT-373

PT boat that returned General Douglas MacArthur to Corregidor March 2, 1945 in a reversal of *PT-41*'s role.

PT Boat Congressional Medals of Honor

Lieutenant John D. Bulkeley and Lieutenant Arthur M. Preston

Ptchelintzev, Vladimir

Russian sniper who was credited with killing 152 Germans with 154 shots in the course of the war.

Pulitzer Prize

Award given to Americans annually for achievement in journalism, letters, and music. Presentations during the war were:

General Reporting
1939—Thomas Lunsford Stokes
1940—S. Burton Heath
1941—Westbrook Pegler
1942—Stanton Delaplane
1943—George Weller
1944—Paul Schoenstein
1945—Jack S. McDowell

General Correspondence
1939—Louis P. Lochner
1940—Otto D. Tolischus
1941—group award
1942—Carlos P. Romulo
1943—Hanson W. Baldwin
1944—Ernie Pyle
1945—Harold V. Boyle

Also in 1945, Bill Mauldin was given the Pulitzer Prize for cartoons and Joe Rosenthal for photography.

Puller, Lewis B. "Chesty" (1898–1971)

U.S. Marine Corps general. He was the most decorated Marine officer of World War II. Puller fought on Guadalcanal as a lieutenant colonel.

Purple Code

Designator of Japan's highest-level code. It was broken through the joint efforts of William Friedman of the U.S. Army and Laurence Stafford of the Navy prior to the attack on Pearl Harbor. The Purple Code was used by the Japanese from 1937 to the end of the war because the Japanese believed it was unbreakable.

Purple Heart

U.S. decoration originally instituted by George Washington as an award for merit. It was redesigned in the shape of a gold heart with a purple insert and ribbon; it is awarded for wounds sustained in action against the enemy.

Purvis, Melvin

FBI agent who shot John Dillinger. During World War II, he was an assistant to Kim Philby, who was head of the MI-5 Iberian subsection and was later discovered to be a Russian spy. Purvis became a colonel in U.S. Army intelligence and put together much of the evidence used at the Nuremberg trials. Purvis committed suicide using the same gun with which he shot Dillinger.

MOVIE PORTRAYALS:

Dillinger (1973), by Ron Johnson
Melvin Purvis: G-Man (1974 TV movie), by Dale Robertson
Story of Pretty Boy Floyd (1974 TV movie), by Geoffrey Binney
The Kansas City Massacre (1975 TV movie), by Dale Robertson
The Private Files of J. Edgar Hoover (1978), by Michael Sachs

PWOP

U.S. military casualty abbreviation for "Pregnant Without Permission."

Pyke, Geoffrey N. (1894–1948)

British inventor. He devised the idea of forming a unit for guerrilla warfare in Norway known as *Project Plough*. Pyke also developed a special vehicle to travel in snow, which became the *Weasel*.

Pyle, Ernie (1900–1945)

Pulitzer Prize-winning war correspondent. He witnessed the Blitz of London in 1941 and saw action in North Africa, Sicily, Italy, France, and the Pacific and reported the story of the average GI. Pyle was killed by a Japanese machine gun on Ie Shima off Okinawa on April 18, 1945.

MOVIE PORTRAYAL:

The Story of GI Joe (1945), by Burgess Meredith

Q

QLA

Designator of a short-range sonar developed for U.S. submarines to detect mines. It was also called FM sonar because it was frequency-modulated. QLA gave off a gong sound as a warning of mine detection that the crews nicknamed Hell's Bells. The U.S.S. *Tinosa* was the first submarine equipped with QLA; it detected a minefield off Okinawa that was not previously known.

Quadrant

Code for the conference between President Franklin Roosevelt and Prime Minister Winston Churchill held in Quebec in August 1943.

Quakers

Paul H. Douglas
Herbert Hoover
James A. Michener
Richard M. Nixon
Drew Pearson

Quandt, Harold (1921–)

Stepson of Joseph Goebbels. He was the son of Frau Goebbels by a previous marriage and was a prisoner of war in Canada in 1945.

Quayle, Anthony (1913–)

British actor. He rose to the rank of major with the Royal Artillery during World War II. Quayle also was involved in a number of secret missions for the Allies. At Gibraltar, he personally met General Dwight Eisenhower, Winston Churchill, and Charles de Gaulle.

Queen

Code name given to Sword Beach, which was assaulted on D-Day, June 6, 1944.

Queen Elizabeth

British ocean liner weighing 83,000 tons. It was the sister ship of the *Queen Mary* and was launched in 1940 with her maiden voyage to New York cloaked in secrecy. The *Queen Elizabeth* was the largest passenger liner ever built and transported troops across the ocean throughout World War II. She held the record for the most GI's carried on a single crossing by transporting the entire 1st U.S. Infantry Division of 15,028 troops.

Queen Elizabeth, H.M.S.

British battleship dating from World War I. It was damaged by Italian human torpedoes who affixed charges to the hull after penetrating the harbor defenses of Alexandria, Egypt, on December 19, 1940.

Queen Elizabeth and Queen Mary

Two passenger liners that carried twenty-four percent of the total U.S. troops transported to Europe during World War II. They made a combined total of thirty-seven Atlantic crossings.

Queen Mary

British Ocean liner weighing 80,000 tons. Her maiden voyage was from Southampton to New York in May 1936. During World War II, the *Queen Mary* served as a troop transport and carried a total of 510,000 soldiers across the Atlantic.

Queen Mary

Nickname given to President Franklin Roosevelt's black limousine used for official functions.

Quesada, Elwood R. (1904–   )

U.S. Army Air Force major general. He commanded the U.S. Ninth Army Air Force that performed tactical support for the D-Day landings and the advance across Europe.

Quezon, Manuel (1878–1944)

President of the Philippines from 1935 to 1944. He was evacuated with MacArthur when he left the Philippines in 1942 and never returned.

Quill, Jeffrey

Test pilot for Vickers Aircraft Company. He was the first person to fly a Spitfire fighter in 1936 and flew with No. 65 Squadron in the Battle of Britain.

Quincy, U.S.S.

U.S. Navy cruiser that was the first ship to fire on the Normandy beaches on D-Day on June 6, 1944. In 1945, the *Quincy* transported President Franklin Roosevelt to Malta en route to Yalta and returned him from Egypt to the U.S. after the conference.

Quirin, Richard (1908–1942)

German spy who was landed on Long Island from the German submarine *U-202* on June 13, 1942, as part of Operation Pastorius. He had lived in the U.S. from 1927 to 1939. Quirin was tried by a military court-martial and executed on August 8, 1942, in the electric chair.

Quisling, Vidkun (1887–1945)

Norwegian collaborator with the Nazis during World War II. He was a general staff officer and had been Norwegian Minister of War from 1931 to 1933. Quisling was captured at the end of the war, held in Oslo prison, and executed. He contributed his name to all collaborators in World War II.

Quislings

Name for those who helped the Nazis to take over their countries:
Konrad Henlein—Czechoslovakia
Adrian Mussert—Netherlands
Vidkun Quisling—Norway
Arthur Seyss-Inquart—Austria
Josef Tiso—Slovakia

Quonset Hut

Prefabricated single-story steel buildings used throughout World War II by U.S. forces around the world. They were recognizable by their half-circle shape and rippled metal construction and were named after the town of manufacture, Quonset Point, Rhode Island.

Quotable Quotes

German Foreign Minister Joachim von Ribbentrop who at a dinner party with Winston Churchill said loudly, "The next war will be different, for we will have the Italians on our side!" Churchill just smiled and answered "That's only fair—we had them last time."

In 1946, after a German soccer team beat the British 53rd Division team, a German spectator yelled "You don't know what this victory means to Dusseldorf. For the first time we have beaten you at your national game." A Tommy called back "That's all right. We've already beaten you at yours!"

Q Ships

Name given to merchant ships that were converted to armed antisubmarine trawlers to act as decoys in luring submarines in close so they could be sunk. Q ships were equipped with sonar, concealed guns, depth charges, and other devices, to seek out and destroy submarines. The first Japanese Q ship was the *Delhi Maru*. The U.S.S. *Atik* was the first U.S. Navy Q ship.

R

Radar

Acronym coined by the U.S. Navy in 1942 to stand for Radio Detection and Ranging. The father of radar was U.S. scientist Albert Hoyt Taylor, but the first practical system was developed by Sir Robert Watson-Watt, a British scientist. Radar allowed the British to economize their efforts in the Battle of Britain. It was first used by the Royal Navy in the Battle of Matapan when they defeated the Italian Navy. The German battleship *Bismarck* was the first ship to use radar for gun control in a night battle.

Radcliffe, Taylor

U.S. Army captain who is credited with leading the first Allied penetration into Rome at 6 A.M., June 4, 1944.

Radio Bari

Italian radio station that broadcast propaganda to the Arab countries in an attempt to gain their allegiance for the Axis powers against the British.

Rado, Alexander

Chief of Russian intelligence in Switzerland. He sent much of the information from the Lucy spy ring back to the Russians. Rado's real last name was Radolfi and he served as the director of a geographical firm in Geneva. Hungarian-born, Rado held the rank of colonel in the Red Army.

Raeder, Erich (1876–1960)

German Navy Grand Admiral. He was the person who talked Hitler into invading Norway and getting involved in the Mediterranean and North Africa. Raeder lost favor with Hitler due to the heavy losses sustained in Norway and because of his failure to halt the Allied convoys to Russia. He was replaced with Grand Admiral Karl Doenitz in 1943. Raeder was tried at Nuremberg and sentenced to life imprisonment but was released in 1955 due to ill health. He died in 1960 as a mental patient.

Raguet, Conde R. (1915–1945)

U.S. Navy officer and graduate of the Naval Academy at Annapolis in 1938. He commanded the submarine U.S.S. *Tuna*, which was sunk by Japanese aircraft on February 4, 1945, off Palawan. At age thirty, Raguet was the youngest submarine skipper lost with his submarine in World War II.

Raider C

British designator for the German armed merchant raider *Atlantis*.

Raider F

British designator of the *Pinguin*, an armed merchant ship commanded by Captain Ernst-Felix Kruder.

Raider G

British designator for the German commerce raider (auxiliary cruiser) *Kormoran*.

Raider J

British designator for the *Stier*, a German armed commerce raider.

Rainbow 5

American strategy devised by the ABC-1 conference to provide a course of action in case of war with Germany and Japan. It called for a defensive action in the Pacific until the defeat of Germany.

Rainbow Order

Message sent out to the German Navy in the last days of the war that called for all ships to be scuttled to prevent them from falling into the hands of the enemy. Upon the receipt of the code word "Rainbow" all were to be destroyed. The order was subsequently cancelled by Admiral Karl Doenitz.

Rainier III, Prince of Monaco (1923–)

Ruler who enlisted in the French Army at the outbreak of World War II as Lieutenant Grimaldi. He was cited for bravery and offered the rank of colonel but declined the promotion.

Rall, Gunther (1918–)

German Luftwaffe fighter pilot. He was the third-highest-scoring ace of World War II, shooting down 275 Allied aircraft and flying over 600 combat missions. Rall survived the war and was captured by the Americans. He had been awarded the Knight's Cross, Oak Leaves, and Swords.

Ramage, Lawson P. (1920–   )

U.S. Navy commander. He was in charge of the submarine U.S.S. *Parche* and was awarded the Congressional Medal of Honor on July 31, 1944. Ramage was the third submariner to be given the CMH and one of four to survive the war.

Ramrod

Name given by U.S. fighter pilots to escort missions for bombers over the continent of Europe.

Ramsay, Sir Bertram (1883–1945)

British admiral. He organized the evacuation of Dunkirk in 1940. Ramsay was the naval commander for the D-Day landings of June 6, 1944. It was his job to insure that the invasion forces got to the beaches and to guarantee reinforcements afterwards. Ramsay was killed in an aircraft accident while attempting to take off from SHAEF headquarters at Versailles in 1945.

MOVIE PORTRAYALS:
The Longest Day (1962), by John Robinson
Churchill and the Generals (1981 TV movie), by Noel Johnson

Ramsey, Logan C.

U.S. Navy officer who sent out the famous message alerting the world to Japanese attack when he broadcast "Air Raid. Pearl Harbor. This is no drill." In 1937, he had written an article entitled "Aerial Attacks on Fleets at Anchor." Toward the end of the war, Ramsey, as a captain, commanded the carrier U.S.S. *Lake Champlain* on which actor Jack Lemmon served as communications officer.

Randall, Tony (1924–   )

Hollywood actor. He served in the U.S. Army Signal Corps during World War II. Randall was discharged in 1946 as a first lieutenant.

Ranger, U.S.S. (CV-4)

U.S. Navy aircraft carrier weighing 13,800 tons. It was the first U.S. ship specifically designed as a carrier in 1933. The *Ranger* was too small and slow for Pacific operations and was used instead in the Atlantic. She survived the war and was cut up for scrap in 1947.

Rankin, Jeanette (1880–1973)

First woman to serve in the U.S. Congress and the only member to vote against U.S. entry into both World War I and World War II. She was elected to Congress in 1916, four years before women received the right to vote and opposed entry into World War I by maintaining that the war was being fought for democracy, yet women had not been granted their share of democracy. Rankin was defeated in 1919 due to her antiwar stand. She was reelected in 1941 but served only one term, again because of her antiwar views.

Movie portrayal:
Wilson (1944), by Hilda Plowright

Ranville

First French village liberated by the Allies. It was captured at 2:30 A.M. on June 6, 1944, by the 13th Lancashire Battalion of the 5th Parachute Brigade commanded by Major General Richard Gale.

Rasher, U.S.S.

U.S. submarine credited with being the second-highest-scoring submarine in the U.S. Navy in World War II with 99,901 tons of enemy shipping sunk. (The top-scoring submarine was the U.S.S. *Flasher.*)

Rastenburg

Site in East Prussia of Hitler's headquarters through most of World War II. It was called the "Wolf's Lair" (*Wolfsschanze*).

Rath, Ernest von (–1938)

German secretary in the embassy in Paris who was assassinated by a Jew, Herschel Grynzspan, on November 10, 1938. This became the excuse for the reprisals against the Jews of Germany known as *Kristallnacht* ("the Night of the Broken Glass"). Grynzspan selected von Rath at random, and ironically, he was the only person in the embassy who was against the Nazi anti-Semitism. Because of this, he was under Gestapo investigation.

Rathbone, Basil (1892–1967)

British actor. He attempted to join the British military in 1939 but was turned down because of his age. He was forty-seven.

Rationed Items in the U.S.

rubber	January 5, 1942
civilian cars	February 2, 1942
typewriters	March 24, 1942
sugar	May 6, 1942
bicycles	May 15, 1942
gasoline	May 15, 1942
farm machinery	September 15, 1942
rubber boots	October 5, 1942

fuel oil	October 22, 1942
milk cans	November 11, 1942
farm fences	November 11, 1942
coffee	November 29, 1942
oil and coal stoves	December 18, 1942
shoes	February 7, 1943
processed foods	March 1, 1943
firewood	March 1, 1943
canned milk	June 2, 1943
soft cheese	June 6, 1943

Rattle

Code name given to a top-secret conference held in Scotland between the American, British, and Canadian military on June 28, 1943. It was attended by twenty generals, eleven air marshalls and commodores, and eight admirals, and was headed by Lord Louis Mountbatten. The conference resolved the issue of the target for Operation Overlord, choosing Normandy rather than the Pas de Calais.

Raubal, Geli

Niece of Hitler, rumored to have been his mistress for a time. She committed suicide due to his jealousy toward her.

MOVIE PORTRAYALS:
The Hitler Gang (1944), by Poldy Dur
Hitler (1962), by Cordula Trantow

Raubal, Leo

Nephew of Adolf Hitler and brother to Geli Raubal. He fought with the German army at Stalingrad, was captured by the Russians, survived Soviet captivity, and was repatriated to Germany in 1955.

Ravensbrück

Nazi concentration camp in Mecklenburg specifically designed for women prisoners. The camp commandant was S.S. Major Fritz Suhrens.

Rawalpindi, H.M.S.

British auxiliary cruiser weighing 16,697 tons. It had been a passenger liner and was converted to an armed merchant vessel commanded by Captain E. C. Kennedy. The *Rawalpindi* was sunk on September 23, 1939, by the German cruiser *Scharnhorst* and was the first victim in World War II of the *Scharnhorst*.

RDF

Radio Detection Finding. This was the early name for radar.

Reagan, Ronald (1911–)

Fortieth President of the United States and former Hollywood actor. He enlisted in the U.S. Army on April 14, 1942, and was discharged with the rank of captain December 9, 1945, having never left the States. It was Reagan who signed Major Clark Gable's discharge papers in Culver City in June 1944. Reagan was disqualified from combat duty because of poor eyesight.

Reaper, H.M.S.

British aircraft carrier that transported German aircraft such as ME262's to the U.S. on July 20, 1945, for experimentation after victory in Europe.

Rebecca

Novel by Daphne du Maurier which was used as the code base by German agent Johannes Eppler to send intelligence to Field Marshall Erwin Rommel from Cairo. Eppler was eventually captured by the British and spent the rest of the war in prison. In the 1960's, he sued the West German government for $60,000 back pay, which he said was owed him since his capture in 1942. The 1940 film version of the novel *Rebecca* was the first American movie directed by Alfred Hitchcock.

Rector, Darrell D.

U.S. Navy seaman first class. He was stricken with appendicitis while on a combat patrol aboard the submarine U.S.S. *Seadragon*. Rector was operated on by Pharmacist Mate First Class Wheeler B. Lipes, who used bent spoons for retractors and other jerry-rigged instruments, all sterilized in torpedo alcohol. The operation was a success and became widely publicized.

Red Ball Express

Name given to the supply route from Normandy inland to the rapidly advancing Allied armies. It began operations on August 25, 1944, and transported supplies via two main roads, one of which was used for inbound traffic and the other for outbound traffic. The Red Ball Express transported over 410,000 tons of supplies in its four months of existence. (Other supply networks were ABC Express, Green Diamond, Lions Express, and White Ball Express.)

Red Beret

Name given to the British paratroopers of World War II because of their distinctive head gear, a red beret. Actors Richard Todd and Trevor Howard were both Red Beret members.

Red Bible

Book compiled by Reinhard Gehlen, the head of German intelligence on the Eastern Front, which included intimate details about the personal lives of prominent Russians.

Red Code

Designator given to a Japanese naval code by U.S. intelligence codebreakers. The U.S. obtained the code by breaking into the Japanese consulate in New York City and photographing their naval codebooks. These were then translated by a Quaker missionary, Dr. Emerson J. Haarworth, who wrote in a red notebook, thus the name Red Code.

Red Devils

Nickname of British parachute troops in World War II. The name came from their red berets.

Redfish, U.S.S.

U.S. submarine that sank the 27,000-ton Japanese aircraft carrier *Unryu* on December 19, 1944.

Redhead

Name of the pet cat aboard the cruiser U.S.S. *Houston*.

Redheads

Otto Abetz—Nazi ambassador to France
Ion Antonescu—Rumanian dictator
Henry G. Bennett—Australian Lieutenant General
Brendan Bracken—Irish author
Harold "Pinky" Bull—British General
James Cagney—actor
Winston Churchill—British Prime Minister
Frank Fay—actor
Arthur Godfrey—radio commentator
Hermann Goering—Nazi Reichsmarschall
Lewis B. Hershey—head of U.S. Selective Service
Patrick J. Hurley—US ambassador to China
Amin el Hussein—Grand Mufti of Jerusalem
Van Johnson—actor
Joseph P. Kennedy—US ambassador to England
Sinclair Lewis—author
Magda Lupescu—mistress of King Carol
Ezra Pound—poet
Vidkun Quisling—Norwegian traitor

Quentin Reynolds—war correspondent
Ginger Rogers—actress
Duncan Sandys—British scientist
Red Skelton—comedian
Don McCombs—this book's co-author

Red Gremlin

Name of a B-17 piloted by Major Paul Tibbets that flew General Dwight Eisenhower from England to Gibraltar on November 6, 1942, to command the invasion of North Africa.

Red Line

Outer defense line around Tobruk.

Red Orchestra

Name of a Communist spy ring in Paris headed by Leonard Trepper that sent thousands of intelligence reports back to Moscow before the ring was broken by the Germans in 1942.

Reese, Harold "Pee Wee" (1918–)

Shortstop for the Brooklyn Dodgers. He served in the U.S. Navy from 1943 to 1945 and was discharged with the rank of chief petty officer.

Reeves, Joseph Mason (1873–1948)

U.S. Navy admiral. He was an early advocate of naval airpower and was the first Commander in Chief of the U.S. Fleet to wear wings (he was an observer). During World War II, Reeves served as the Navy's Lend-Lease liaison officer to Britain and later was a member of the Pearl Harbor investigating committee.

Reggie's Reply

U.S. Army Air Force ace John T. Godfrey's P-51 mustang when he flew with the 4th Fighter Group of the Eighth Army Air Force. It was named after his brother, who was killed when the U.S. Navy ship upon which Reggie Godfrey served was sunk by a German submarine in the Atlantic.

Reggio di Calabria

Site of the first Allied landing on the Italian mainland when troops of the British Eighth Army crossed the Straits of Messina September 3, 1943.

Regia Aeronautica

Name of the Italian Air Force in World War II.

Reichelderfer, Francis W. (1895–)

Chief Meteorologist of the U.S. from 1939 to 1945. His birthday was August 6.

von Reichenau, Walther (1884–1942)

German Field Marshall. He was the first German general to become a Nazi party member and it was he who devised the oath of allegiance to Hitler in 1933. Von Reichenau commanded the Sixth Army on the Eastern Front until his death in January 1942 of a heart attack. He cooperated with the S.S. in the extermination of the Jews and attempted to get the army to help.

MOVIE PORTRAYAL:
The Hitler Gang (1944), by Arthur Loft

Reichstag Fire

February 27, 1933, conflagration that Hitler used as an excuse to suppress the Communists of Germany. The Nazis accused Georgi Dimitrov and a Dutchman, Marinus von der Lubbe; Dimitrov proved his innocence in court and von der Lubbe was found guilty and hanged.

Reid, Jewell H.

U.S. Navy ensign. He was a pilot of a Catalina flying boat which was the first reconnaissance aircraft to spot the Japanese fleet approaching Midway in May 1942.

Reid, Pat

British soldier who was captured by the Germans, but in October 1942 escaped from Colditz Castle, which was purported to be escapeproof. Reid made it to Switzerland where he became the assistant military attaché. He is the author of two books on his period of internment in Colditz—*Escape from Colditz* and *Men of Colditz*.

Reilly, Mike

White House Secret Service chief under President Franklin Roosevelt.

Reinberger, Helmut

German Luftwaffe major who was head of the paratrooper school at Stadel. He and Major Erich Hoenmanns crash-landed in Belgium on January 9, 1940, carrying top-secret German plans for the invasion of the West. The Allies believed that they were planted by the Germans and took no measures to oppose the attack. They were flying in an ME108 Taifun.

Reiner, Carl (1922–   )

Hollywood actor and producer. He enlisted in the U.S. Army in 1942 and served with an entertainment unit touring the South Pacific. Reiner was discharged in 1946.

Reitsch, Hanna (1912–1979)

German aviatrix. She was the first woman to fly a glider over the Alps, the first female helicopter pilot, the first female German pilot to win a captain's license, the first female test pilot, and the first and only woman to receive the Iron Cross First Class in World War II. Reitsch was a favorite of Hitler and was chosen by Luftwaffe General Ritter von Greim to fly into Berlin in the last days of the war because she could fly a helicopter. The helicopter to be used was damaged so she had to fly a conventional aircraft. Reitsch was one of the last people to see Hitler alive.

Movie portrayals:
Operation Crossbow (1965), by Barbara Rutting
Hitler: The Last Ten Days (1973), by Diane Cilento

Remagen

German town twelve miles south of Bonn on the Rhine River. It was the site of the capture by the Allies of a railway bridge across the Rhine River that opened the final barrier to the heart of Germany in March 1945. The bridge was actually named the Ludendorff Bridge but was mistakenly called the Remagen Bridge.

Remarque, Erich Maria (1898–1970)

German antiwar writer, author of *All Quiet on the Western Front*. He fought with the German Army in World War I. Remarque's books were banned by the Nazis, who took away his citizenship in 1938. In 1939, he immigrated to the U.S., becoming an American citizen.

"Remember Pearl Harbor"

Song composed by Don Reid and Sammy Kaye in 1942 and recorded by Sammy Kaye and his orchestra.

Remer, Otto Ernst (1912–)

German Army major at the time of the July 20, 1944, attempted assassination of Hitler. Remer commanded the Guards Regiment in Berlin, crushed the officers' revolt, and became the Nazi hero of the day, being promoted to Major General. In 1949, Remer ran for office in West Germany as part of the neo-Nazi Socialist Reich Party.

Remington Typewriter Company

Manufacturer of a large number of weapons for the U.S. Army in World War II. They produced mostly Garand rifles.

Remondino, Aldo

Italian Air Force major. He was the first non-German to fly the

ME-109 in July 1937, at the Zurich International Flying Meet. He later became the vice-president of Alitalia airlines.

Renault, Louis (1877–1944)

French automobile manufacturer. He collaborated with the Nazis and was arrested on September 23, 1944, by the Free French, dying before he could be brought to trial.

Rennie, Michael (1909–1971)

British actor. He served as a pilot with the Royal Air Force in World War II as an instructor of American pilots in Georgia. He portrayed Field Marshall Montgomery in the 1968 movie *Desert Tanks*.

Reno, U.S.S.

U.S. Navy destroyer that sank the carrier U.S.S. *Princeton* after it was severely damaged in the Battle of Leyte Gulf in October, 1944.

Repenting War Criminals

Only two Nazi war criminals repented of their crimes before their deaths: Hans Frank while imprisoned at Nuremberg, and Reinhard Heydrich as he lay dying in 1942. Heydrich was half-Jewish and felt he had betrayed his people.

Report From the Aleutians

Documentary film produced by Army Captain John Huston in 1943.

Republicans

There were only two Republicans in President Franklin Roosevelt's wartime cabinet, Frank Knox, the Secretary of the Navy, and Harry L. Stimson, the Secretary of War.

Repulse, H.M.S.

British Navy cruiser of 32,000 tons. It was torpedoed and sunk along with H.M.S. *Prince of Wales* by Japanese aircraft on December 10, 1941, in one of the worst British sea disasters in World War II.

Retreats (British "strategic withdrawals")

Andalsnes—May 1940
Namsos—May 1940
Dunkirk—May 1940
Narvik—June 1940
Somaliland—August 1940
Crete—1941
North Africa—numerous occasions

Reuben James, U.S.S.

U.S. Navy destroyer and the first U.S. warship lost in World War II. It was sunk off Iceland by the German submarine *U-562* on October 31, 1941, prior to the U.S. entry into war. There were 115 lives lost out of a crew of 160. The sinking became the subject of the folk song "The Sinking of the Reuben James," by the Almanac Singers.

Reynaud, Paul (1878–1966)

French premier when France was overrun by the Germans in 1940. He was arrested in September 1940 and sent to Germany where he spent the war in Oranienburg and Itter concentration camps.

MOVIE PORTRAYAL:

Churchill and the Generals (1981 TV movie), by Jacques Duby

Reynolds, Quentin (1902–1965)

War correspondent for *Colliers* magazine. He was in France in 1940, leaving Paris just ahead of the advancing Germans. Reynolds witnessed the London Blitz and narrated the popular film *London Can Take It* (1940). He traveled to Moscow after the German invasion and to North Africa to report on the campaigns against Rommel. Reynolds was a participant in the Dieppe Raid in 1942 and was with the U.S. invasion forces on Guadalcanal. His books include *The Wounded Don't Cry* (1941), about the fall of France and London Blitz; *Only the Stars Are Neutral* (1942), about North Africa fighting; *Dress Rehearsal* (1943), on the Dieppe Raid.

MOVIE PORTRAYALS:

The Private Files of J. Edgar Hoover (1978), by George Plimpton*

Rheims

Advanced headquarters of General Dwight Eisenhower's staff. It was the site of a German surrender on May 7, 1945. In attendance were: Germans—Admiral Hans Georg von Friedeburg, Colonel General Alfred Jodl, and Major General Wilhelm Oxenius; Allies—Lieutenant General Sir F. E. Morgan (Britain), General François Sevez (France), Lieutenant General Walter Bedell Smith (U.S.), Lieutenant General Carl Spaatz (U.S.), General Ivan Susloparov (USSR) and Air Vice-Marshall J. M. Robb (Britain). The surren-

---

*George Plimpton himself was portrayed by Alan Alda in the 1968 movie *Paper Lion*.

der was later repudiated by the Russians, who demanded another ceremony in Berlin. The Russian signer General Susloparov was hustled away in Berlin and disappeared because he did not have Stalin's permission. The Russians did not acknowledge the Rheims surrender in their history books until 1956.

Rhine Exercise

Code name of the breakout of the German battleship *Bismarck* and the cruiser *Prinz Eugen* into the Atlantic in May 1941.

Rhine River Crossings

British Field Marshall Bernard Montgomery crossed the Rhine in a set-piece maneuver with tremendous forces in contrast to Generals Patton's and Hodges's crossings which were impromptu. Montgomery also sustained far more casualties.

Rhino

Name of an attachment welded to the front of Sherman tanks toward the end of the war. It consisted of prongs of steel that dug into the hedgerows of Normandy, cutting a path. Otherwise the tank would climb over the hedgerow, exposing its vulnerable underside and pointing its gun into the air. The Rhino was invented by Sergeant Curtis G. Culin, Jr., out of the scrap steel from a German roadblock. Later these were made from the underwater obstacles that littered the beaches of Normandy.

Rhubarb

Name given by Royal Air Force crews to low-level nuisance raids conducted over the continent of Europe in World War II. They sought targets of opportunity rather than a specified target. The first raid was conducted on December 20, 1940, by two Spitfires.

von Ribbentrop, Joachim (1893–1946)

German ambassador to England from 1936 to 1938 and Foreign Minister from 1938 to 1945. He was a former champagne salesman who added the "von" to his name after marrying a girl of nobility. He was nicknamed "von Ribbensnob." Sir Neville Henderson, in a 1941 interview, said, "If I were given a gun and told to take two shots, I would shoot Himmler, then Ribbentrop, and brain Hitler with the butt of the rifle." Von Ribbentrop was captured at the end of the war and locked up in ASHCAN, a high-ranking prisoner detention center where he was listed as POW #31G35002. He was tried and convicted at Nuremberg of war crimes and executed in 1946.

MOVIE PORTRAYAL:

Mission to Moscow (1943), by Henry Daniell

Richardson, Elliot (1920–)
U.S. attorney general who took part in the Normandy invasion and was awarded a Bronze Star and two Purple Hearts.

von Richthofen, Freiherr (1895–1945)
German Luftwaffe Field Marshall. He commanded the Condor Legion during the Spanish Civil War. At one time he believed that dive bombers did not stand a chance against flak and that any bomb released below 6,000 feet was suicide for the pilot. Von Richthofen later changed his mind and became one of the strong advocates of the Stuka dive bombers for close support. He devised the idea for attaching high-pitched whistles to the wings as a terror tactic. Baron von Richthofen, the Red Baron of World War I fame, was his cousin.

Rickenbacker, Eddie (1890–1973)
Top-scoring U.S. ace of World War I. He was a special civilian observer for General "Hap" Arnold during World War II. At one time his B-17 crashed in the Pacific where he and his companions spent twenty-seven days in life rafts before being saved. They were rescued on November 11, 1942, twenty-four years to the day after the armistice ending World War I.

MOVIE PORTRAYALS:
Captain Eddie (1945), by Fred MacMurray
The Court Martial of Billy Mitchell (1955), by Tom McKee

Ricketts, James B. (1902–1979)
U.S. Navy rear admiral. He was the supply officer aboard the U.S.S. *Augusta* when President Franklin Roosevelt and Prime Minister Winston Churchill signed the Atlantic Charter in 1941. Ricketts helped Admiral Richard Byrd survey the South Pacific for potential Navy bases after the Pearl Harbor attack. He founded the Navy's first aviation supply office in Philadelphia in 1943 and served during the war on the U.S.S. *Oklahoma,* the U.S.S. *Maryland* and the U.S.S. *Omaha*.

Rickles, Don (1926–)
Hollywood comedian and actor. During World War II, he served with the U.S. Navy and was stationed aboard the PT boat tender U.S.S. *Cyrene* in the Philippines.

Ridgway, Matthew B. (1895–)
U.S. Army officer. He graduated from the U.S. Military Academy at West Point in 1917. Ridgway commanded the U.S. 82nd Airborne Division in Sicily, Italy, and Normandy. In August 1944

he took command of the XVIII Airborne Corps that fought in the Battle of the Bulge.

Riefenstahl, Leni (1902–   )

German actress and film producer. She was a favorite of Hitler, producing several propaganda films for the Nazi party although she never became a member. Riefenstahl made a documentary on the Nuremberg party rallies called *Triumph of the Will* that met with wide acclaim. She also did a documentary on the 1936 Olympics that is still recognized for its artistry. Riefenstahl was constantly at odds with Joseph Goebbels because Hitler gave her free reign over her productions and Goebbels wanted her to fall under the control of the propaganda ministry. It was rumored that she was a mistress of Hitler and this was the reason for his favoritism (she emphatically denies this). In the 1936 film on the Olympics, she appears in a nude scene but is only seen from behind. It has been said that in a private showing, Hitler sat up and said "Leni!" when it was shown.

Riggs, Bobby (1918–   )

Professional U.S. tennis player. He served in the U.S. Navy in the South Pacific during World War II. Riggs was discharged in November, 1945.

Rio Conference

January 1942 conference where Latin American countries bonded together for a common defense by either declaring war on the Axis powers or severing diplomatic relations.

Riom

French city that was the site of a court set up by the Vichy government to put on trial the people it believed were responsible for the defeat of France at the hands of the Germans. On trial were, among others, Reynaud, Daladier, Blum, and Gamelin.

Ripcord Plus Twenty-Four

Code phrase sent out by General Dwight Eisenhower to postpone the D-Day assault scheduled for June 5, 1944, by twenty-four hours.

Ritchie, Douglas (1905–   )

BBC Director of the European News Department. After the outbreak of World War II, he began broadcasting to occupied Europe under the title "Colonel Britton," encouraging the populace to signify their resistance to the Germans by using the first notes of Beethoven's Fifth Symphony as morse code for *V* for "victory."

Ritchie, Seil M. (1897–)

British general. He commanded the British Eighth Army for a time in North Africa and advocated World War I ideas of a rigid defense line to stop Field Marshall Erwin Rommel. Ritchie sent his tanks out piecemeal to the infantry units and set up a solid line ending at Bir Hacheim with no defense to the south. Rommel used his mobility to turn the line and force the British into retreat. Ritchie was then relieved of command and replaced by Auchinleck.

Rizzuto, Phil (1918–)

New York Yankees shortstop. He served for three years with the U.S. Navy, contracting malaria in New Guinea, where he saw action.

RLB

Reichsluftshutzbund. This was the German air raid service for World War II.

RO-501

German-built submarine that was turned over to the Japanese on April 30, 1944 so that they could copy German technology. It was commanded by Lieutenant Commander Sadatoshi Norita but was sunk in the Atlantic in May 1944 by the destroyer U.S.S. *Robinson*.

Road to Morocco

Movie of 1942 starring Bob Hope, Bing Crosby, and Dorothy Lamour. It was viewed by General Dwight Eisenhower and his staff ironically the night before they departed for the North African landings of Operation Torch.

Robards, Jason, Jr. (1922–)

American actor and son of actor Jason Robards, Sr. He enlisted in the U.S. Navy in 1940, serving as a radio operator at Pearl Harbor on December 7, 1941. During the war, he fought in thirteen major engagements in the South Pacific, had two cruisers torpedoed out from under him, and was awarded a Navy Cross for valor. Robards became a member of Admiral Raymond Spruance's staff and was discharged at the end of the war. He appeared in the 1970 movie *Tora! Tora! Tora!*, which recreated the Japanese attack on Pearl Harbor.

Robert Brothers

Three British brothers who were stationed aboard the H.M.S. *Hood* and were killed when it was sunk by the *Bismarck* in May 1941. They were the British version of the Sullivan Brothers.

(Their story was seen in a newspaper headline in the 1979 movie *Yanks*.)

Robert E. Perry, S.S.

Liberty ship constructed in four days and fifteen hours. Built at the Kaiser Ship Yards, Richmond, California, it was the fastest ship construction job in history. Ten days after the keel was laid, the ship, captained by Roy Neill, sailed through the Golden Gate with a full load of cargo.

Robertson, Cliff (1925–)

Hollywoood actor. He was disqualified from the draft as 4F due to a weak left eye, so enlisted in the Merchant Marine. The ship on which he served, the S.S. *Admiral Cole*, was bombed and disabled by Japanese aircraft off the Philippines.

Robin Moor, S.S.

First U.S. merchant ship sunk by a German submarine during World War II. It was sunk on May 21, 1941, in the South Atlantic by the *U-69* while en route to Cape Town, South Africa, from New York. No one was killed.

Robinson, Bernard W.

First black to be commissioned into the U.S. Navy. He was a medical student at Harvard, quitting to become an ensign in the U.S. Navy Reserve in 1942.

Robinson, Jackie (1919–1972)

Black football and baseball player. He was on board a ship leaving Pearl Harbor on December 7, 1941, from which he heard the Japanese attack. In April 1942, he was drafted into the U.S. Army and became a Cavalry officer in charge of morale. Robinson was given limited duties because of ankle injuries from his football days. He was discharged in 1945 as a first lieutenant.

Rochefort, Joseph J.

U.S. Navy lieutenant commander. He was the chief code breaker for Admiral Chester Nimitz at Pearl Harbor and was responsible for deciphering the Japanese submarine codes that resulted in the tracking and sinking of *I-173* by the submarine U.S.S. *Gudgeon* on January 27, 1942. Because of the knowledge about Japanese submarines gained from the intercepts, ships were routed around them for the rest of the war and many of them were sunk, making the Japanese submarine force ineffectual. Rochefort also found out that Midway was the intended target of the Japanese by having the garrison at Midway send out a message saying that they were short of drinking water. Japanese Admiral Yamamoto intercepted the message and told his forces that AF, the Japanese identifier for Midway, was short of water, thus confirming Rochefort's theory. This led to the victory at Midway by the U.S. forces.

Rockefeller, Nelson A. (1908–1979)

U.S. Vice President. During the early days of World War II, Standard Oil of New Jersey was supplying oil equally to both the British and the Germans. Rockefeller discovered this and immediately put a stop to all German shipments. He later was in charge of U.S.–Latin American Affairs.

Rock Happy

U.S. Marine Corps euphemism in the Pacific in World War II for combat fatigue.

Rockwell, George Lincoln (1918–1967)

Founder and fuehrer of the American Nazi Party in 1958. He had been a U.S. Navy fighter pilot in World War II in the Pacific and the Korean War. Rockwell, who believed Hitler to have been one of the greatest minds in 2,000 years of history, was assassinated by his vice-fuehrer, who was a closet Jew.

MOVIE PORTRAYAL:

Roots: The Next Generations (1979 TV mini series), by Marlon Brando

Rodney, H.M.S.

British ship that became the only battleship in history to torpedo another battleship, the *Bismarck*, in May 1941.

Roehm, Ernest (1887–1934)

Leader of Hitler's Brown Shirts, the S.A., in the early days of the Nazi Party. He advocated a continuation of the Nazi revolution toward socialist aims. Hitler had him shot in the Night of the Long Knives in June 1934 so that the Army would support the party. In 1928, Roehm penned his autobiography, entitled *Story of a Traitor.*

MOVIE PORTRAYALS:

The Hitler Gang (1944), by Roman Bohmen
Hitler (1962), by Berry Kroeger

von Roenne, Alexis (–1944)

German Army colonel. He was the head of FHW, the German Army intelligence services for the West, and was a member of the conspiracy against Hitler. Von Roenne was executed in 1944 as a result of the failure of the July 20, 1944, attempt on Hitler's life. His counterpart was Reinhard Gehlen who headed FHO, the Eastern intelligence service.

Roessler, Rudolf (1897–1958)

Name of the spy known by the code name Lucy. He accurately warned the Allies of every invasion from Poland to Russia but was not believed. In pamphlets that were written under the pseudonym of Hermes prior to World War II, Roessler outlined Hitler's plans for world conquest (see Lucy).

Rogers, Will, Jr. (1911–   )

Son of humorist Will Rogers. He served in World War II in the 814th Tank Destroyer Battalion and fought in most of the major battles of France and Germany, including the Battle of the Bulge. Rogers was discharged in November 1945 as a first lieutenant after being awarded the Bronze Star and Purple Heart medals.

"Roger Young"

Title of a song composed by Frank Loesser during World War II about twenty-five-year-old Congressional Medal of Honor winner infantryman Roger Young, who was killed in 1943 while attacking a Japanese pillbox.

Rogers, Charles "Buddy" (1904–   )

Hollywood actor, band leader, and husband of actress Mary Pickford, who served in the military during World War II.

Rogge, Bernhard

German Navy captain who commanded the auxiliary cruiser *Atlantis* in the early years of World War II.

MOVIE PORTRAYAL:

Under Ten Flags (1960), by Van Heflin (as Reger).

Rogstad, Henrik (–1945)

Chief of the Norwegian S.S. security police. He committed suicide at the end of the war.

Rokossovsky, Konstantin (1896–1968)

Russian general and victor in the battles of Stalingrad, Moscow, and Warsaw. He was a Pole by birth and was the general who refused to aid the Polish insurgents at Warsaw in 1944. Rokossovsky wore a set of stainless steel false teeth as a result of his imprisonment and torture by the NKVD, the Soviet secret police.

"Roll Out The Barrel"

Polka song played by the U.S. Navy band to greet each returning submarine to base at Pearl Harbor in World War II.

Roma

Italian 35,000-ton battleship which was sunk by German aircraft on September 8, 1943, after the Italian surrender to the Allies. The Germans used a guided missile called the 1400 FX missile which was launched from a bomber and controlled to the target by the bombardier. It struck the magazines and blew up the ship, which sank in just twenty-one minutes, taking the Italian Naval Commander in Chief. This was the first case of a battleship being sunk at sea exclusively by bombs.

Rommel Asparagus

Name given to a device thought of by Field Marshall Erwin Rommel to protect inland areas along the Atlantic Wall from parachute and glider attacks. They consisted of poles planted in the ground with wires strung along the tops to set off grenades and mines if the wires were disturbed.

Rommel, Erwin (1891–1944)

German field marshall. He fought in World War I, was captured by the Italians, and escaped from a prisoner-of-war camp. Rommel was one of the best field commanders in the German Army in World War II and distinguished himself in the battles for North Africa, where he was known as the "Desert Fox." The goggles he wore in all photographs were not German issue as believed, but were taken from British General O'Connor's command vehicle, which was captured at Derna. Rommel was the youngest of the German field marshalls and was later implicated in the plot to assassinate Hitler in July 1944. For his involvement he was persuaded to commit suicide and retain his status as a hero, rather than stand trial.

MOVIE PORTRAYALS:
Five Graves to Cairo (1943), by Erich von Stroheim
Rommel—The Desert Fox (1951), by James Mason
The Desert Rats (1953), by James Mason
Hitler (1962), by Gregory Gay
The Longest Day (1962), by Werner Hinz
Night of the Generals (1967), by Christopher Plummer
Patton (1970), by Karl Michael Vogler
Raid on Rommel (1971), by Wolfgang Preiss

Rommel, Juliuscz

Polish general. He was the senior Polish officer in Warsaw who surrendered the city to the Germans on September 27, 1939.

Romulo, Carlos (1901–)

Filipino press aide to General Douglas MacArthur at the beginning of World War II. He escaped with MacArthur from Bataan in 1942, after which he was promoted to brigadier general in Australia. Romulo was one of those in the photographs of MacArthur wading ashore in the Philippines in 1944.

Room 39

Office of British Naval Intelligence in the Admiralty building in London. This was where Ian Fleming, the creator of James Bond, was assistant to Admiral John Godfrey, the head of Naval intelligence.

Room 101

Room of the U.S. Army Hospital in Heidelberg, Germany, where General George S. Patton was taken after the auto accident of December 9, 1945, in which he broke his neck. He died three weeks later without once leaving Room 101.

Room 301

Hospital room at the Mayo Clinic where Harry Hopkins, confidante of President Franklin Roosevelt, spent his time after stomach surgery in April 1944.

Room 351

Room at the Mayflower Hotel in Washington, D. C., into which Georg Dasch, German spy, checked on June 18, 1942, in order to surrender to the FBI.

Room 900

Secret office located in the British War Office in London. It was the headquarters of MI-9, the escape apparatus for the continent of Europe. It aided in the escape of over 5,000 Allied soldiers and airmen from occupied Europe and was headed by Airey Neave, who himself had escaped from Colditz Castle.

Room 3603

Headquarters of the British Security Coordinator, the British intelligence service in North America. Headed by William Stephensen, it was located at 630 Fifth Avenue, Rockefeller Center, New York.

Rooney, Andrew "Andy" A. (1919–)

CBS "60 Minutes" writer. In World War II, he was the staff writer for the *Stars and Stripes* and interviewed Congressional Medal of Honor winner Major James H. Howard in January 1944.

Rooney, Mickey (1920–)

Hollywood actor. He was drafted into the U.S. Army in 1943 and was sent to Europe with an entertainment unit. Rooney was discharged in 1946.

Roosevelt, Archibald B. (1894–1979)

Last surviving son of President Teddy Roosevelt. He fought in World War I and was wounded as a captain with the 26th Infantry Division. He was the oldest battalion commander in World War II and, as a lieutenant colonel, was in charge of the 162nd Infantry Battalion on New Guinea. Roosevelt received a Silver Star and Purple Heart.

Roosevelt, Elliott (1910–)

Son of President Franklin D. Roosevelt. He had been a private pilot before World War II but could not pass the flight physical to become a pilot with the U.S. Army Air Force, so he enlisted as an administrative officer. In 1941, just prior to the U.S. entry into the war, Roosevelt flew as an observer on the first aircraft ever flown over the Greenland icecap, in a B-24 of Ferry Command. He became commander of a photo reconnaissance unit that did work in North Africa, the Arctic, Iceland, Britain, and later Normandy. By 1945, he was a brigadier general and was one of the few Army Air Force generals to get his rank without being pilot-rated. Roosevelt almost did not receive the promotion because at the time his name was forwarded to Congress, an incident made the newspapers that involved his dog Blaze. Several military men were bumped from a flight across the U.S. so Blaze could be transported. Roosevelt was not aware that his dog would be given priority, but it nearly cost him his star. He won the Distinguished Flying Cross and the Air Medal for service in World War II.

MOVIE PORTRAYAL:
Eleanor and Franklin: The White House Years (1977 TV movie), by Don Howard

Roosevelt, Franklin D. (1882–1945)

U.S. President from 1933 to 1945. He was the first president since Lincoln to visit a battle theater, the first president to leave the U.S. during wartime, the first to go to Africa, the first to travel in an airplane, and the first to make a foreign-language broadcast (it was to the French on November 7, 1942, concerning Operation Torch).

MOVIE PORTRAYALS:
Yankee Doodle Dandy (1942), by Captain Jack Young
This Is The Army (1943), by Captain Jack Young

The Beginning of the End (1946), by Godfrey Tearle
Sunrise at Campobello (1960), by Ralph Bellamy
The Pigeon That Took Rome (1962), by Richard Nelson
First to Fight (1967), by Stephen Roberts
Eleanor and Franklin (1976 TV movie), by Edward Hermann
Eleanor and Franklin: The White House Years (1977 TV movie), by Edward Hermann
The Rebel General (1977), by Dan O'Herlihy
MacArthur (1977), by Dan O'Herlihy
The Private Files of J. Edgar Hoover (1978), by Howard Da Silva
Ring of Passion (1978 TV movie), by Stephen Roberts
Ike (1979 TV movie), by Stephen Roberts
Backstairs at the White House (1979 TV miniseries), by John Andersen
Enola Gay (1980 TV movie), by Stephen Roberts
FDR: The Last Year (1980 Play), by Jason Robards
Churchill and the Generals (1981 TV movie), by Arthur Hill
Annie (1982), by Edward Hermann

Roosevelt, Franklin D., Jr. (1914–   )

Son of President Franklin D. Roosevelt. He joined the U.S. Navy in World War II and was executive officer of the destroyer U.S.S. *Mayant* during the North African invasion. Roosevelt later commanded the escort destroyer *Ulvert H. Moore* and sank a Japanese submarine off Mindoro, Philippines, on January 30, 1945, the night of his father's birthday.

MOVIE PORTRAYAL:
Eleanor and Franklin: The White House Years (1977 TV movie), by Joseph Hacker

Roosevelt, James (1907–   )

Eldest son of President Franklin D. Roosevelt. He became a U.S. Marine Corps officer and was the executive officer of Carlson's Raiders during the Makin Island raid in August 1942. As a lieutenant colonel, Roosevelt was an adviser to the U.S. Army's 165th Infantry, 27th Division, that assaulted Makin in November 1943. By April 1945, he had been promoted to full colonel and been awarded a Navy Cross for bravery.

MOVIE PORTRAYAL:
Eleanor and Franklin: The White House Years (1977 TV movie), by Ray Baker
Eleanor, First Lady of the World (1982 TV movie), by Peter White

Roosevelt, John A. (1916–1981)

Youngest son of President Franklin D. Roosevelt. He served in the U.S. Navy in World War II as an ensign on the carrier U.S.S. *Hornet*.

MOVIE PORTRAYAL:
Eleanor and Franklin: The White House Years (1977 TV movie), by Brian Patrick Clarke

Roosevelt, Kermit (1889–1943)

Son of President Theodore Roosevelt. He held the rank of major in both the British and the American armies.

Roosevelt, Quentin (1918–1948)

U.S. Army captain. He fought in North Africa, Italy, and France. As G-2 of the U.S. 1st Division, he led a party to repatriate a group of German nurses during a ceasefire on June 26, 1944, also conducting another exchange on July 9. It is speculated that more than just the exchanges were going on, possibly negotiations with high-ranking German officers. After the war Roosevelt was killed in an aircraft crash near Hong Kong.

Roosevelt Sausage

Nickname the Russians gave to Spam, which was shipped to them in tremendous quantities throughout World War II as part of Lend-Lease.

Roosevelt, Theodore, Jr. (1887–1944)

U.S. Army brigadier general and son of President Theodore Roosevelt. He was the acting assistant division commander of the U.S. 4th Infantry Division during the Normandy invasion of June 6, 1944, and was awarded the Congressional Medal of Honor. Roosevelt died of a heart attack on July 13, 1944, becoming the third of Roosevelt's four sons to die serving his country.

MOVIE PORTRAYAL:
The Longest Day (1962), by Henry Fonda

Rose, Billy (1899–1966)

U.S. songwriter. He was Bernard Baruch's stenographer in World War I and began writing songs in the 1920's. In World War II, Rose wrote many songs for the war effort.

Rosenberg, Alfred (1893–1946)

Nazi Commissar of the Occupied Eastern Territories. He was the chief anti-Jewish ideologist for Hitler and carried out an active campaign to exterminate the Jews. Rosenberg was found guilty of war crimes and sentenced to death at Nuremberg in 1946. He was the only Nazi executed by the Tribunal who had no last words to say.

MOVIE PORTRAYAL:
The Hitler Gang (1944), by Tonio Selwert

Rosenthal, Joe (1911–)

Civilian photographer for the Associated Press who took the photographs of the second flag-raising on Mount Suribachi, Iwo Jima, March 15, 1945. He was awarded the Pulitzer Prize for the photograph of the event, which was restaged so he could get a better picture. Rosenthal had been classified 4F because of bad eyesight. After the publication of the picture, his draft board in San Francisco reclassified him 2-AF, essential deferment.

Rosie the Riveter

World War II character created to inspire the women working in the factories of the U.S. Supposedly she was based on the aircraft worker Rosina B. Bonavita, who, with a coworker, riveted 3,345 rivets on the wing of a Grumman Avenger in six hours. Rosie was portrayed in the 1944 movie *Rosie the Riveter* by Jane Frazee.

Ross, Barney (1909–1967)

World champion boxer in the mid-1930's. He fought in World War II with the U.S. Marine Corps, being awarded a Distinguished Service Cross and the Silver Star for killing twenty Japanese soldiers on Guadalcanal.

MOVIE PORTRAYAL:
Monkey on My Back (1957), by Cameron Mitchell

Rossi, Guido

Italian fighter ace. In May 1943, an American P-38 landed on Sardinia where it was captured by the Italians. Rossi received permission from Mussolini to use the captured P-38 to shoot down unsuspecting stragglers from Allied bomber missions. He would fly alongside a crippled bomber and offer to fly protection for them, then fall behind and shoot them down. Harold Fisher was the only survivor of Rossi's numerous kills. Fisher set up a specially armed and armored B-17 to decoy him into attacking so he could be shot down. Fisher had a picture of Rossi's wife painted on the B-17 and named it *Gina* after her. When Rossi appeared, Fisher told him over the radio how nice it was to live with her. This so infuriated Rossi that he abandoned his normal rear attack and set up for a head-on pass. The B-17 succeeded in shooting him down. Rossi was picked up by Allied air-sea rescue and spent the rest of the war as a prisoner.

Rostok, Max

German S.S. captain. He was in charge of the destruction of the Czechoslovakian village of Lidice in reprisal for Reinhard Heydrich's assassination in June 1942.

Roth, Ludwin (–1967)

German rocket scientist who designed the V-1 buzz bomb. He was brought to the U.S. in 1945 as part of the Alsos Mission.

Rotte

Designator of a Luftwaffe tactical formation of two aircraft developed during the Spanish Civil War. Two Rotte made up a *schwarme*.

Rotterdam

Dutch city bombed by the Luftwaffe on May 14, 1940. The Dutch commander of the city, Colonel Sharoo, had already agreed to surrender the city to the Germans, but the city was bombed anyway, in an action that was a tremendous propaganda victory for the Allies. The German officer who had accepted the surrender to save the city was Dietrich von Choltitz, who in 1944, surrendered Paris to the Allies rather than see it destroyed.

Rouen–Sotteville

French railroad yards. It was the first target attacked by the U.S. Eighth Army Air Force (August 17, 1942). Twelve B-17's led by General Ira C. Eaker took part in the attack and all returned. Some of the planes involved were: *Alabama Exterminator, Baby Doll, Berlin Sleeper, Big Stuff, Birmingham Blitzkrieg, Butcher Shop, Johnny Reb, Peggy D*, and *Yankee Doodle*.

Rover

Code name for Eleanor Roosevelt during World War II because of her numerous trips around the country and the globe. The name was given by Harry Butcher, naval aide to General Dwight Eisenhower, when she was planning a visit to England in October 1942, and it remained with her from then on.

Rover Joe

Nickname given to U.S. Army Air Force personnel who traveled with the infantry on the ground to act as coordinators between support aircraft and the advancing battle lines in World War II.

Rowan, Dan (1922–)

Hollywood comedian. He flew as a fighter pilot with the U.S.

Fifth Army Air Force in the Southwest Pacific in World War II. Rowan was injured in a crash landing.

Rowe, Hartley

Chief engineer for the United Fruit Company who invented the amphibious D.U.K.W.

Rowehl Geschwader

Top-secret Luftwaffe squadron that conducted high altitude photo-reconnaissance flights deep into Russia to gather military intelligence for the German invasion of Operation Barbarossa. It was set up by Lieutenant Colonel Rowehl in October 1940 by direct order of Hitler and was the forerunner of the U.S. U-2 flights of the 1960's. One group flew from Insterberg over the Baltic States using special DO-215's equipped with high-altitude engines. A second unit flew out of East Prussia and used HE111's while a third flew between Minsk and Kiev in JU88's and JU86's. All flew at between 33,000 and 39,000 feet, enabling them to photograph every Red Air Force base.

Royal Hawaiian Hotel

Hotel on the beach of Waikiki that was reserved exclusively for U.S. submarine personnel as a rest camp after they returned from a combat patrol.

Royal Oak, H.M.S.

British battleship. It was torpedoed on October 14, 1939, while at anchor in Scapa Flow, by the German submarine U-47, which was commanded by Gunther Prien. The *Royal Oak* displaced 29,000 tons of water and suffered 810 killed in the first British Naval loss of World War II.

RRR

Emergency distress signal for merchant ships to indicate that they were under attack by an enemy surface raider.

Rubber

First commodity to be rationed by the U.S. in World War II.

Rubble

Nickname that the U.S. Navy pilots gave to the Japanese stronghold of Rabaul because of the constant aerial attacks that it had sustained.

Rudd, Hughes (1921–)

CBS anchorman of the "Morning News." He was a U.S. Army artillery spotter during World War II and was awarded a Silver Star, six Air Medals, and a Purple Heart.

Rudder, James

U.S. Army lieutenant colonel. He commanded the 2nd Ranger Battalion that assaulted and captured Pointe du Hoc overlooking Utah and Omaha beaches on D-Day June 6, 1944.

Rudel, Hans Ulrich (1916–)

German Luftwaffe Stuka dive bomber pilot. He was the highest decorated member of the Luftwaffe in World War II, flying over 2,000 missions. Rudel was the first pilot to sink a battleship with a dive bomber when he bombed the Russian battleship *Marat* on September 23, 1941. He is also credited with sinking two cruisers and destroying 532 tanks. In January 1945, he was awarded the Gold Oak Leaves to the Knight's Cross, which had been specially minted for him. Rudel lost his right leg to flak toward the end of the war but continued to fly. Rudel was shot down thirty times and wounded five times yet survived the war. In 1958 Rudel wrote his autobiography, *Stuka Pilot*.

Rudorfer, Erich (1917–)

German Luftwaffe major. He was the eighth-top-scoring ace of World War II with 222 aircraft shot down. Rudorfer was awarded the Knight's Cross, Oak Leaves and Swords and was himself shot down sixteen times. Twelve of his victories were while flying the ME262 jet fighter.

Ruhr Dams

Target attacked on May 16, 1943, by the Royal Air Force in an attempt to halt production in the industrial Ruhr. The dams, the Mohne, Eder, and Sorpe, were attacked by Lancaster bombers of No. 617 Squadron led by Guy Gibson using a special bomb devised by Dr. Barnes Wallis. The bombs, which were shaped like oil drums, skipped across the water to the dams, where they sank to a predetermined depth and exploded against the dam itself. Gibson was awarded the Victoria Cross.

Ruminoel

German oil mission in Rumania to ship oil from the Ploesti oil fields to Germany.

Rundstedt, Karl Gerd von (1875–1953)

German Field Marshall. He engineered the breakthrough of Sedan in 1940, the attack on the Ukraine in 1941, and commanded the Battle of the Bulge offensive in 1944. Von Rundstedt spoke four languages and was a personal friend of French General Maurice Gamelin. He was captured in 1945 at Bad Tolz, where he was being treated for heart disease.

MOVIE PORTRAYALS:
Rommel The Desert Fox (1951), by Leo G. Carroll
The Longest Day (1962), by Paul Hartmann
A Bridge Too Far (1977), by Wolfgang Preiss

Ruptured Duck

Name of the B-25 piloted by Captain Ted W. Lawson during Doolittle's Raid on Tokyo, April 18, 1942. It had a picture of Donald Duck on crutches painted on the side.

Ruptured Duck

Name given to a lapel pin awarded to veterans of the armed forces for honorable service between September 8, 1938, and December 31, 1946. It was designed by a German, Franz Sales Meyer, who modeled it from an eagle used by the Roman Legions.

Russell, Donald H.

Second civilian to receive the Silver Star medal from the Navy. He was awarded the medal on March 22, 1945, for services aboard the carrier *Franklin* when it was attacked by Japanese aircraft.

Russell, Harold (1914–)

Canadian-born handicapped commander of the American Veterans of World War II. He joined the U.S. Army in 1942, becoming a parachute instructor at Fort Benning, Georgia. While a demolition instructor at Camp Mackill, North Carolina, Sergeant Russell lost both hands in a grenade accident that occurred on June 6, 1944 (D-Day). After his discharge, he appeared in a Signal Corps film, entitled *Diary of a Sergeant*, about his accident and recovery. Hollywood director William Wyler saw the film and cast Russell as the handicapped sailor, Homer Parrish, in the 1946 movie *The Best Years of Our Lives*. Russell received two Oscars for the role, one for Best Supporting Actor and one an honoring award. He is the only person ever to receive two Oscars for the same role.

Russhon, Charles "Rush"

U.S. Army Air Force captain and photographer who took the first low-level pictures of Hiroshima and Nagasaki after the atomic bombs. He was also the first American to set foot on Japanese soil at Atsugi airbase on August 28, 1945, at 0945 GMT. He photographed the deplaning of a general of MacArthur's staff, who is erroneously believed to be the first. (The second to deplane was Lieutenant Ben Reyes, assistant to Russhon.) Russhon flew 226 combat missions in the course of World War II in the CBI

(China-Burma-India Theater). He was a model for Milt Caniff's character "Charlie Vanilla" in *Terry and the Pirates*. He also appeared in the James Bond movies *Goldfinger* (1964) and *Thunderball* (1965). In *Goldfinger* a sign on a tower read "Welcome to Fort Knox—General Russhon." He appeared as a two-star general in *Thunderball*.

Russian aces of World War II

Major Ivan N. Khozedub—62
Colonel Alexander I Pokryshkin—59
Captain Dimitri B. Blinka—56
Captain Nikolai Gulayer—56
Captain Grigori A. Rechkalov—53
Captain Sirill A. Yevstigneyer—52
Lieutenant Arsenii V. Vorozheikin—52
Captain Alexander F. Klubov—50
Lieutenant Ivan M. Pilipenko—48
Lieutenant Vasili N. Kubarev—46
Captain Nikolai M. Skomorokhov—46
Captain Pavel N. Kamozhin—46
Lieutenant Alexander I. Koldunov—46
Sergei D. Lugansky—43
Lieutenant Vladimir Bobrov—43
Major Vitaliy I. Popkov—40
Captain Kistilev—40
Captain Lapanskii—40

Russian military

Headed by almost 10,000 generals at the close of World War II.

Ryan, Lieutenant

U.S. Navy Seabees officer who stepped out of the jungle at New Caledonia in World War II to greet U.S. Marines assaulting the beach, stating "The Seabees are always glad to welcome the Marines ashore."

Ryan, Cornelius (1920–1974)

American author and historian. He was a war correspondent during World War II and is known for his trilogy of the war: *The Longest Day; The Last Battle;* and *A Bridge Too Far.*

MOVIE PORTRAYAL:

A Private Battle (1980 TV movie), by Jack Warden

Ryan, Paddy

Inventor who designed the modern bomb sight. He was portrayed loosely by Pat O'Brien in the 1943 movie *Bombardier* as Major Chick Davis.

Ryan, Robert (1909–1973)

Hollywood actor. He enlisted in the U.S. Marine Corps in 1943, serving as a Camp Pendleton instructor until he was discharged in 1945. His movies on World War II were:

Bombardier (1943)
The Sky's the Limit (1943)
Behind the Rising Sun (1943)
Tender Command (1943)
Marine Raiders (1944)
Flying Leathernecks (1951)
The Longest Day (1962)
The Battle of the Bulge (1965)
The Dirty Dozen (1967)

Ryti, Risto Heikki (1889–1956)

President of Finland during World War II. He was imprisoned after the war for allying Finland with the Axis powers.

Ryujo

Japanese aircraft carrier weighing 11,700 tons that was sunk by carrier aircraft from the U.S.S. *Saratoga* August 24, 1942, in the Battle of the Eastern Solomons.

RZM

Reichzeugmeisterei. It was the Nazi Party Department of Ordnance and was responsible for all items manufactured for the party. The offices were located in Munich and dictated all prices and quality.

S

Sixth U.S. Army Air Force

Established February 5, 1942, to protect the Panama Canal Zone and the Caribbean.

Sixteen

Number of B-25's in Doolittle's Raid on Tokyo on April 18, 1942. Only one aircraft succeeded in landing intact at Vladivostok, where it was interned by the Russians. The other fifteen aircraft were lost after they shot down three Japanese fighters.

Sixteen

Number of P-38's that took part in the mission to shoot down Japanese Admiral Isoruku Yamamoto on April 18, 1943, one year to the day after Doolittle's Raid. They also shot down three Japanese fighters. Whereas the bombers of Doolittle's force had only one land safely and lost the rest, the P-38's lost one and had the remainder return to base.

69th US Infantry Division

Unit commanded by Major General Emil F. Reinhardt. It was the first western Allied unit to make contact with the Russians on April 25, 1945, at Torgau.

Seventh US Army Air Force

Established February 5, 1942, to operate in the Central Pacific north of the equator.

Seventeen

U.S. standing in the world in 1939 regarding total Army and Air Force strength.

Italy—7,633,000 Russia—7,150,000
Germany—7,188,000 Japan—6,271,000

France—5,480,000
China—3,001,500
Yugoslavia—1,840,000
Rumania—1,800,000
Great Britian—1,130,000
Spain—990,000
Belgium—842,000
Turkey—710,000
Hungary—700,000
Bulgaria—670,000
Netherlands—660,000
Sweden—626,000
U.S.—615,256

17F

Ian Fleming's code identifier as aide to the British Chief of Naval Intelligence during World War II.

77 Chester Square

London residence of Dutch Queen Wilhelmina who escaped to Britain in May 1940. She returned to the Netherlands on May 2, 1945, nearly five years to the day after the Germans had invaded Holland.

7:45

Time at which the watch of Admiral Yamamoto had stopped, as was discovered when his body was recovered after his plane was shot down on April 18, 1943.

761st Tank Battalion

First U.S. black armored unit to see combat in World War II. It landed at Omaha Beach shortly after D-Day.

S-25

U.S. submarine loaned to the British in April 1942. They rechristened it H.M.S. *P-551*, then in turn loaned it to the Polish Free Forces, who again renamed it *Jastrazab*. It was accidentally sunk by Allied forces off the coast of Norway on May 2, 1942.

S-36

Second U.S. submarine lost at sea in World War II. The S-36 ran aground on an uncharted reef in Makassar Strait in January 1942 and had to be scuttled by her crew. (The first submarine lost was the U.S.S. *Shark*.)

S.A.—Sturm Abteilung

Nazi Brown Shirts. It was the first paramilitary organization of the Nazi party founded on November 4, 1921, in Munich at a Beer Hall rally. Membership was voluntary, and under the leadership of Ernst Roehm, it took on the characteristics of a military alternative to the German Army. In order to break the increasing power of the SA, Hitler had Roehm and 150 other S.A. leaders shot in June 1934. From then on, it primarily functioned as a training unit for other Nazis.

St. Croix-sur-Mer
First airfield liberated by the Allies in France after D-Day.

St. Lo, U.S.S.
U.S. Navy escort carrier. It was sunk during the Battle of Leyte Gulf in October 1944, with the distinction of being the first ship to be sunk by a kamikaze attack. The Japanese pilot whom it is believed dived into the *St. Lo* was Lieutenant Yukio Seki.

St. Louis, U.S.S.
U.S. passenger ship that transported 937 Jews from Hamburg, Germany, to Havana, Cuba, in May 1939, only to have the U.S. deny the Jews entry. The ship then returned to Germany where Nazi propaganda portrayed the incident as an example of the Jews not being wanted anywhere in the world. The incident became the subject of the 1978 movie *Voyage of the Damned*.

St. Nazaire
French port that was the only Atlantic port large enough to drydock the German battleship *Tirpitz*. It was attacked by British commandos in March 1942 and disabled for the remainder of the war.

St. Paul's Cathedral
London cathedral built after the London fire by Sir Christopher Wren between 1675 and 1710. It was the only building in the heart of old London to survive the German incendiary attack of December 29, 1940. St. Paul's became the symbol for British resolve during the Battle of Britain. The fire bombing was known as the Second London Fire (the first was in 1666).

St. Valentine's Day Massacre
Name given to a U.S. Army Air Force attack in February 1943 on Kahili airfield in Bougainville. The U.S. lost two B-24's, two P-40's, two Corsairs,and four P-38's; the Japanese lost only three aircraft.

SABS
Stabilizing Automatic Bomb Sight. This was a highly accurate bomb sight invented by the British in 1941 that used a gyroscope for stability. Once the bomb sight was set up, it could guide the pilot over a target via an indicator in the cockpit and even released the bomb itself. No. 617 Squadron was given the sight and specially trained in its use after the Dam Buster Raid of 1943.

Sabu (1924–1963)
Indian actor, born Sabu Dastagir. He enlisted in the U.S. Army Air Force on January 4, 1944, the same day he became a U.S.

citizen. Sabu, as Sergeant Dastagir, flew 42 missions as a tail gunner on B-29's in the Pacific. He was awarded the Distinguished Flying Cross and the Air Medal with four clusters.

Sachsenhausen

Nazi concentration camp located near Berlin.

Sacred Cow

Name of President Franklin Roosevélt's personal aircraft which was piloted by Henry T. Myers. Put into service in 1944, it was the first official presidential airplane. *The Sacred Cow,* serial number 2107451, was named by Bernard Baruch.

Sad Sack's Catechism

If it moves, salute it;
If it doesn't move, pick it up;
If you can't pick it up, paint it.

Safeguarding Military Information

Ten-minute training film made during World War II, starring Ginger Rogers.

Stafford, Laurence F. (1894–1973)

U.S. Navy captain. He was the head of the Communications Security Unit whose job it was to decode Japanese messages intercepted through Magic. Safford is the father of U.S. Navy codebreaking.

Sagan Order

Order issued by Ernst Kaltenbrunner, head of the German Gestapo, after the recapture of all but three prisoners of war of the seventy-six who had escaped from Stalag Luft III on March 25, 1944, in what became known as "the Great Escape." The order called for more than half of the recaptured prisoners to be executed while being transported back to Sagan.

Sahl, Mort (1927–)

U.S. comedian. He enlisted in the U.S. Army Air Force in 1944 and served at Elmendorf Field in Anchorage, Alaska. Sahl was discharged in 1947 and continued his education on the G.I. bill.

Sailfish, U.S.S.

U.S. Navy submarine formerly named *Squalus*. In 1939 the *Squalus* sank in over two hundred feet of water, but through superhuman efforts by the Navy, better than half of her crew were rescued. The sub was salvaged, repaired, rechristened *Sailfish*, and sent to the Asiatic Fleet in the Philippines. It was considered a jinxed ship and the fears of many were not allayed when the commander, Morton C. Mumma, Jr., had a nervous breakdown while under attack from Japanese depth charges shortly after the outbreak of World War II. He was replaced by Richard Voge, who on December 3, 1943, sighted and sank the Japanese carrier *Chuyo*. Unfortunately, the carrier had on board survivors of another U.S. sub, the U.S.S. *Sculpin,* which had been sunk off Truk. It was the *Sculpin* that had aided in the rescue of the crew members of the *Squalus* in 1939. There were no survivors.

Sailor's Delight

Name of General Dwight Eisenhower's private hideaway ten miles outside Algiers. It was probably so named because it was located by Ike's naval aide Harry Butcher.

Sainte-Mere-Eglise

French village. It was the target of the U.S. 82nd Airborne Division on D-Day on June 6, 1944, and was occupied at 4:30 A.M. by the 3rd Battalion of the 505th Regiment. It was said to be the first French town liberated on the Western Front, but in fact British paratroopers had liberated Ranville two hours earlier.

Saipan

Island of the Marianas that was assaulted by the U.S. Marine 2nd and 4th Divisions and the U.S. Army's 27th Infantry Division on June 16, 1944. Overall commander was U.S. Marine Corps General Holland "Howlin" Smith, who relieved the Army commander Major General Ralph Smith from command of the 27th Infantry because he lacked aggressive drive. The 27th was a New York National Guard unit that was poorly trained and led and was not able to keep up with the Marines. The battle for Saipan lasted until July 9, 1944, and its capture forced the resignation of General Hideki Tojo as Premier of Japan (see Gabaldon, Guy).

Sakai, Saburo (1916–   )

Japanese fighter ace and the highest-scoring ace to survive World War II. He had been educated at Aoyama Gakuin, a school set up by American missionaries. Sakai shot down sixty-four aircraft in over 200 air battles, including the B-17 of Captain Colin Kelly on December 10, 1941, over the Philippines. (Kelly was the first American hero of World War II.) Sakai was seriously wounded in the first aerial battle over Guadalcanal and lost an eye as a result. He then returned to Japan to recuperate and train new pilots.

Sakamaki, Kazuo

Japanese Navy ensign and only survivor of the midget submarine attack on Pearl Harbor on December 7, 1941. He became the first U.S. prisoner of war. Sakamaki was dropped off by the *I-24* whose torpedo officer was Mochitsura Hashimoto, who sank the cruiser *Indianapolis* in the last days of World War II. Sakamaki lost control of his submarine due to a malfunction and was forced to abandon it. He was washed up on the beach unconscious. He was interned at Camp McCoy, Wisconsin, and repatriated in December 1945. The American press said he was the first Japanese fighting man to pass through the Golden Gate.

Sakamoto, Akira

Japanese lieutenant who commanded twenty-five dive bombers that attacked Pearl Harbor on December 7, 1941. He dropped the first bomb of the attack.

Sales, Soupy (1926–   )

Television comedian, born Milton Hines. During World War II he served on the U.S.S. *Randall*, flagship of the Seventh Fleet, which took part in the invasion of Okinawa on April 1, 1945.

Salinger, Pierre (1925–   )

White House Press Secretary under President John F. Kennedy. During World War II, he was the commanding officer of a sub chaser in the Pacific, holding the distinction of being one of the youngest men ever to command a U.S. Navy vessel. In 1945, Salinger helped to rescue fifteen sailors during a typhoon off Okinawa, for which he was awarded the Navy and Marine Corps medal.

Salmon

British admiralty code word for the German cruiser *Scharnhorst*.

Salmon, H.M.S.

British submarine under Lieutenant Commander E. O. Bickford. On December 13, 1939, it torpedoed and damaged the German cruisers *Nürnberg* and *Leipzig*.

Salo Republic

Name given to Mussolini's resurrected Fascist government in Northern Italy that was maintained in power due to German influence.

Sambo

Code name radioed back to England by Guy Gibson to indicate that he had successfully breached the Moehne Dam in the Ruhr in May 1943. It was the name of his dog, a black labrador that was killed by a car on May 15, 1943, the day before the raid.

San Antonio I

Code name of the first B-29 bombing mission of Tokyo in World

War II, on November 24, 1944. The raid was led by the B-29 *Dauntless Dotty.*

Sand, Eugene T.

U.S. Navy officer. As the commander of the submarine U.S.S. *Sawfish* in February 1943, he mistakenly sank two Russian freighters, the *Ilmen* and the *Kola,* while patroling in the Sea of Japan—an incident that did not endear the U.S. to its Russian ally. The Soviets, by agreement with Japan, were sending ships out via the Sea of Japan because the northern ports and passages were blocked by ice.

Sandhurst

British military academy equivalent to West Point in the U.S. Prominent graduates were:

Sir Harold Alexander
Sir Winston Churchill
Ian Fleming
Lord Gort
King Hussein of Jordan
Bernard Montgomery
David Niven
Sir Archibald Wavell

Sandys, Duncan

Son-in-law of Winston Churchill. He commanded the first rocket-equipped antiaircraft regiment in Britain. At the end of 1942, Sandys was appointed to investigate reports of German rocket development, in what was called Operation Bodyline.

MOVIE PORTRAYAL:
Operation Crossbow (1965), by Richard Johnson

San Francisco, U.S.S.

U.S. cruiser that was the flagship during the Battle of Savo Island on November 13, 1942. The cruiser was severely damaged but continued to fight. Three Congressional Medals of Honor were given members of its crew: Rear Admiral Daniel Callaghan, Commander Bruce McCandless, and Commander Herbert E. Schonland. The submarine *I-26* was actually shooting at the *San Francisco* when it sank the *Juneau* during the battle.

San Marino

Tiny republic of 14,000 people in northern Italy. On September 17, 1940, it revoked its declaration of war on Germany made in

1915, and instead declared war on England. On September 21, 1944, San Marino again declared war on Germany and threw the weight of its 900-man army behind the Allies.

Saratoga, U.S.S. (CV-3)

U.S. aircraft carrier that was originally planned to be built as a 43,500-ton battle cruiser but was converted to a 33,000-ton carrier. It fought throughout World War II in the Pacific, being struck by torpedoes on January 11, 1942, and again on August 31, 1942, near Guadalcanal. The *Saratoga* was also attacked and damaged by kamikazes off Iwo Jima in February 1945. At war's end, it was the Navy's oldest and largest aircraft carrier. The *Saratoga* was used as a test ship at the Bikini Atoll atomic bomb experiments in July 1946 and sunk as a result. The nickname of the ship was "Sara Maru."

Sarniquet, Raymond

French fire captain in Paris. He lowered the Tricolor flag from the Eiffel Tower for the last time on June 13, 1940, just prior to the German occupation. On August 25, 1944, Sarniquet raised the first Tricolor over the Eiffel Tower after the liberation of Paris, an honor for which he had to race two other people to the top of the monument.

Sartre, Jean Paul (1905–   )

French playwright and philosopher. He was part of the French Resistance uprising in Paris in August 1944 in and around the Theatre Comédie Française. Sartre had served in the French Army at the outbreak of World War II as a private but was captured by the Germans. He served nine months as a prisoner of war and returned to Paris, where he became a journalist in the Resistance.

SAS

Special Air Service. It was a British commando-type unit founded by Colonel David Stirling that operated behind enemy lines. At one time he was in command of one regiment and his brother Bill commanded the second, prompting many to say that the initials SAS stood for Stirling and Stirling. Their motto was "Who Dares, Win."

Sauckel, Fritz (1894–1946)

Early Nazi party member. During World War II, he commanded the slave labor program in Germany. He was sentenced to death at the Nuremberg trials and was hanged on October 16, 1946.

Saul, R. E.

British Royal Air Force Air Vice-Marshall. He commanded No.

13 Group, which protected northern England and Scotland during the Battle of Britain.

Saundby, R. H.

British Air Vice-Marshall. It was his responsibility to choose the Royal Air Force code names for bombing targets and operations during World War II.

Savalas, Aristotle "Telly" (1924–)

Hollywood actor. He enlisted in the U.S. Army while still underage and was critically wounded in action. Savalas was crippled for over a year and was told by doctors that he would never walk again.

Savo Island

Island off Guadalcanal in the Solomons. It was the site of the worst ocean defeat in U.S. Navy history on August 9, 1942, when it lost four cruisers. Japanese Admiral Mikawa sank the U.S.S. *Quincy,* U.S.S. *Vincennes,* U.S.S. *Astoria,* and the H.M.A.S. *Canberra.* The Japanese called this the First Battle of the Eastern Solomons.

Sawbuck

Code name used by President Franklin D. Roosevelt when he traveled to the Yalta conference in January and February, 1945. He crossed the Atlantic on the U.S.S. *Quincy* and flew from Malta to Yalta aboard the presidential airplane *The Scared Cow.*

SC-2

Designator of the first Allied convoy attacked by a German submarine wolf pack in September 1940. It was en route from Canada to England and lost five ships out of the fifty-three in the convoy.

Schacht, Hjalmar Horace Greeley (1877–1970)

Nazi finance minister under Hitler. His father gave him his middle name after American journalist Horace Greeley. Schacht manipulated the German economy so that the increased growth of armaments and the reconstruction of the military was done without a significant inflationary increase. He was the primary person responsible for German rearmament prior to World War II. Schacht, who was never a member of the Nazi party, was arrested after the July 20, 1944, attempt on Hitler's life and imprisoned at Flossenburg concentration camp, until he was liberated by the Americans in 1945. He was tried at Nuremberg for war crimes but acquitted.

MOVIE PORTRAYAL:
Mission to Moscow (1943), by Felix Basch

Schaffhausen

Swiss town mistakenly bombed by U.S. aircraft on April 1, 1944, killing fifty people and wounding 150. The U.S. paid $3.2 million in damages after the war.

Scharnhorst

German 31,000-ton battle cruiser and sister ship of the *Gneisenau*. It was commissioned on January 7, 1939, and participated in several engagements in the early days of World War II. The *Scharnhorst* sank the British auxiliary cruiser *Rawalpindi* and participated in the destruction of the carrier H.M.S. *Glorious*. It was finally sunk on December 26, 1943, while attempting to attack an Allied convoy going to Murmansk with supplies for the Eastern Front. The British battleship *Duke of York*, commanded by Sir Bruce Fraser, sank the *Scharnhorst* during the Battle of the North Cape. There were only thirty-six survivors out of 1,900 crew members.

Scheldt Estuary

Area between the port of Antwerp and the sea. The Allies captured the port but could not use it because the Germans, commanded by General Daser, held both sides of the narrows and denied its use to the Allies for nearly three months. (This ensured that the Russians and not the Western powers reached Berlin first.)

Schellenberg, Walter (1911–1952)

German S.S. General. He was the head of the foreign intelligence section of the S.S. and was the youngest general in the Nazi party. Schellenberg was responsible for the kidnapping of two British agents in the Venlo Incident, the counterfeiting of British money at Oranienburg to disrupt the British economy, the manipulation of Cicero, and the establishment of the Kitty Salon bordello in Berlin. He was sentenced in 1949 to not more than four years' imprisonment.

Schepke, Joachim

German Navy officer and eleventh-top-scoring submarine ace of World War II, sinking thirty-nine ships totaling 159,130 tons. Schepke's submarine *U-100* was rammed by the H.M.S. *Vanoc* on March 7, 1941, while attempting to attack the convoy HX-112. Only seven crew members were rescued.

Schibanoff, Alex

U.S. Navy ensign who served in PT boats in the Pacific during World War II. He was formerly a football player for the Detroit Lions.

Schirach, Baldur von (1907–1974)

Hitler Youth leader. He took part in the French campaign, then became Governor and Gauleiter of Vienna in 1940. After World War II, von Schirach went into hiding and served as an interpreter for the Americans, using the name Richard Falk. He voluntarily turned himself in and was sentenced to twenty years' imprisonment by the Nuremberg Tribunal for deporting Jews and organizing forced labor. Von Schirach was released from Spandau in 1966.

Schlabrendorff, Fabian von (1906–1980)

German Army officer who attempted to assassinate Hitler in 1943 by placing a bomb aboard Hitler's aircraft. The bomb was from British materials with a German detonator, but failed to explode. Von Schlabrendorff was arrested after the July 20, 1944, attempt on Hitler's life and sent to a concentration camp. He was being tried in the Nazi People's Court when American B-17's attacked Berlin; a bomb fell on the courtroom, causing a beam to kill Judge Roland Feisler. Von Schlabrendorff was one of the few conspirators to live through Hitler's wrath.

Schlageter, Albert Leo (–1923)

German Free Corps Volunteer who was executed by the French for sabotage during the Ruhr occupation on May 26, 1923. The Nazis made him into a martyr; May 26 was celebrated as a memorial day throughout Germany.

Schleswig–Holstein

German cruiser that, at 4:45 A.M. on September 1, 1939, fired the first shots of World War II when it shelled the Polish outpost in Danzig Harbor. The cruiser was sunk by Allied aircraft in 1945 in the Baltic.

Schlieben, Karl von (1894–1964)

German lieutenant general who commanded the defenses of Cherbourg. After the Americans captured most of the city, Schlieben told an American officer that he would be dishonored if he surrendered because he could still oppose an infantry attack. Von Schlieben admitted that he had no antitank weapons and was unable to resist an armored attack. A single tank was moved up and he surrendered on June 26, 1944.

Schlief, Captain

German fighter pilot who shot down a Polish P-11 aircraft on September 1, 1939, for the first German aerial victory during World War II.

Schmeling, Max (1905–   )

Germany's most famous boxer. Former heavyweight champion of the world (1930–1932), Schmeling was a paratrooper during World War II and jumped on Crete with the 1st Battalion Pararegiment under Lieutenant Colonel von der Heydte. He developed a severe case of diarrhea and had to be hospitalized, according to von der Heydte, but Goebbels used false accounts to create a propaganda campaign that resulted in his being awarded a medal.

MOVIE PORTRAYALS:
The Joe Louis Story (1953), by Buddy Thorpe
Ring of Passion (1978 TV movie), by Stephen Macht

Schmid, Al

U.S. Marine machine gunner who was blinded by a Japanese grenade during the fighting for Guadalcanal in 1942. Prior to his injury, he reportedly killed over 200 Japanese soldiers.

MOVIE PORTRAYAL:
Pride of the Marines (1945), by John Garfield

Schmid, Bepo (1901–   )

Luftwaffe major general in charge of intelligence for the Battle of Britain in 1940. He continually underestimated British strength.

Schmidt, Anton (–1942)

German Army sergeant. He supplied Jewish partisans in Poland with forged papers and equipment from October 1941 until March 1942, when he was arrested and executed.

Schmidt, Arthur (1895–   )

German general. He was Chief of Staff of the encircled Sixth Army at Stalingrad. Schmidt was not liked by other officers, but he was a highly capable planner. He was captured by the Russians and not repatriated to Germany from Siberia until 1955.

Schmidt, Helmut (1918–   )

German Social Democratic Chancellor of the Federal Republic. He joined the Hitler Youth in 1933 and was drafted into the Army in 1937. Schmidt became a first lieutenant in a flak artillery unit and won an Iron Cross for fighting on the Russian front. He also participated in the Battle of the Bulge in December 1944, where he was captured.

Schmidt, Paul (1899–1970)

Chief of the German Foreign Office press relations. He joined the Nazi party in 1943 and was the official interpreter for Hitler and

Joachim von Ribbentrop. Schmidt was captured in Salzburg by the Americans, only to be released.

Schmitt, Aloysius (–1941)

First priest to die in action in World War II. He was aboard the U.S.S. *Oklahoma* on December 7, 1941, and was killed during the Japanese attack on Pearl Harbor.

Schnaufer, Heinz-Wolfgang (1922–1950)

Luftwaffe major and most successful night fighter pilot of history. He only flew 164 combat missions but shot down 121 Allied aircraft, for which he was awarded the Knight's Cross, Oak Leaves, Swords, and Diamonds. The British greatly admired him, calling him the "Night Ghost of Saint-Trond" (he was based in Belgium). Schnaufer's aircraft tail with the victory marks is on display in the Imperial War Museum in London. He was killed in an automobile accident in 1950.

Schneider, Karl F.

Chief garage mechanic at the Chancellory in Berlin throughout World War II.

Schnorkel

Name of a breathing tube for German submarine diesel engines so that the submarines did not need to surface. It was a major breakthrough in submarine development because it allowed them to remain submerged for long periods of time.

Schuhart, Otto

German Navy officer. As commander of the submarine *U-29*, he sank the British aircraft carrier H.M.S. *Courageous* on September 17, 1939.

Schultze, Herbert

German Navy lieutenant commander. He was the sixth-top-scoring submarine ace of World War II, sinking twenty-six ships totaling 171,122 tons. Schultze commanded *U-48*.

Schultz, Lester R.

U.S. Navy lieutenant and assistant naval aide to President Franklin D. Roosevelt. He took the intercepted Japanese message warning other Japanese commands of impending war with the U.S. to Roosevelt the night before the Pearl Harbor attack.

Schulz, Charles M. (1922–)

American cartoonist and creator of the *Peanuts* comic strip. He was drafted into the U.S. Army in 1943, serving with the 20th Armored Division in France and Germany. Schulz was a sergeant of a light machine-gun squad.

Schuschnigg, Kurt von (1897–1977)

Austrian chancellor at the time of Hitler's Anschluss joining Austria to Germany in 1938. He was then arrested by the Gestapo and spent the war in Flossenburg concentration camp. After being liberated, von Schuschnigg became a college professor in the U.S.

Schutze, Victor

German Navy captain. He was the fifth-top-scoring submarine commander of World War II, with thirty-four ships totaling 171,164 tons to his credit. Schutze commanded *U-25* until May 1940 and *U-103* until July 1941.

Schwarme

German Air Force tactical formation developed during the Spanish Civil War. It consisted of two *Rotte* for a total of four aircraft.

Schweinfurt

German industrial city attacked by the U.S. Army Air Force to knock out ball-bearing production on August 17, 1943. Over 200 B-17's dropped 1,200 tons of bombs that reduced ball-bearing output by thirty-five percent, while losing thirty-six aircraft. On October 15, 1943, the Air Force attacked again with 228 aircraft, 62 of which were shot down and 138 heavily damaged. This was the last deep penetration of Germany by the U.S. Army Air Force without fighter escort.

Scorpion

Name of a British tank with a flail on the front in order to detonate mines. It was used in North Africa but could only travel a half mile per hour. An improved version called a Crab was used for D-Day.

Scott, George C(ampbell) (1927–   )

American actor who won an Academy Award for the title role in the 1970 movie *Patton*. He enlisted in the U.S. Marine Corps in 1945 with hopes of fighting in the Pacific but instead spent four years stateside teaching a creative writing correspondence course. Scott also participated in burial details at Arlington National Cemetery.

Scott, Robert (1908–   )

U.S. Army Air Force officer. He was a graduate of West Point in 1932 and gained fame flying a P-40 named *Old Exterminator* as part of Chennault's Flying Tigers. Scott shot down twelve Japanese planes and terrorized troop movements on the Burma Road. He wrote a book about his experiences called *God Is My Co-Pilot*.

Later in the war, Scott tested rockets fired from aircraft on Japanese shipping off Okinawa.

MOVIE PORTRAYAL:
God Is My Co-Pilot (1945), by Dennis Morgan

Scott-Paine, Hubert

British engineer who designed the prototype for U.S. Navy PT boats.

"Scratch One Flattop"

Message that Lieutenant Commander Robert Dixon radioed back to the carrier *Yorktown* after planes from his squadron sank the Japanese carrier *Shoho* on May 7, 1942.

Sculpin, U.S.S.

U.S. submarine sunk off Truk on November 18, 1943. A majority of the crew were captured by the Japanese and put aboard the aircraft carrier *Chuyo* for return to Japan. The carrier was then sunk by the U.S.S. *Sailfish (Squalus)* on December 4, 1943, with the loss of all hands. Ironically, *Sculpin* had helped in the rescue of the crewmembers of the U.S.S. *Squalus* in 1939.

Scuttlebutt

Slang term for a rumor in the U.S. Navy. It was also the name of a drinking fountain on a ship (where all rumors were spread).

Scuttle-car

Nickname given by German troops to Volkswagen jeeps used by German officers after the Normandy invasion. Most of the time, the doors were removed so that the occupants could get out quickly in case of fighter aircraft attacks. General Meindl traveled nine miles and had to hurriedly evacuate his vehicle over thirty times in July 1944.

SD

Designator of an early radar set used on U.S. submarines at the outbreak of World War II. It had a limited range of six to ten miles and was useful for picking up enemy aircraft before the submarine surfaced. SD gave off a very strong signal that could be picked up by regular radio direction finding (RDF) gear.

Seagraves, Gordon (1897–1965)

American doctor known as the "Burma Surgeon." He practiced medicine for the remote native tribes of northern Burma and was one of the world's foremost experts on tropical disease. Seagraves became a major in the U.S. Army and accompanied General Joseph Stilwell on his retreat from Burma in 1942.

Seal, H.M.S.

British 1,520-ton submarine commanded by Lieutenant Commander Rupert P. Lonsdale. While laying mines on May 5, 1940, in Norwegian waters, the submarine struck a mine and sank. After several hours on the bottom, the crew was able to resurface the sub and slowly proceeded to neutral Swedish waters. En route it was attacked by two German Arado aircraft flown by Lieutenant Gunther Mehrens and Karl Schmidt. After the planes had dropped their bombs and achieved a near miss, the *Seal* surrendered. The German pilots radioed for a ship, which towed the submarine to Frederikshaven.

Sealion, U.S.S.

First U.S. submarine lost in World War II. It was hit by bombs while in Cavite, Philippines, and damaged so badly it had to be scuttled. (The first submarine sunk by the Japanese was the U.S.S. *Shark*.)

Sealion, U.S.S.

U.S. Navy submarine recommissioned in 1943 and commanded by Eli Reich. It sank the Japanese battleship *Kongo* on November 21, 1944, with electric torpedoes in the East China Sea.

Seals

Name of a German two-man submarine weighing fifteen tons. Over 250 were built.

Seawolf, U.S.S.

Only U.S. submarine lost to Allied forces in the Pacific during World War II. The *Seawolf* was commanded by Al Bontier and was attacked in a safety zone while en route to Samar to deliver seventeen Filipino guerrillas along with ten tons of supplies. The U.S. destroyer *Rowell*, under Harry Allan Barnard, Jr., ignored both the safety zone and the recognition signal from the *Seawolf*, and continued to attack her until he sank the *Seawolf* on October 4, 1944, with the loss of all hands.

Secretaries

Secretaries	*Their Bosses*
Margaret Blank	Joachim von Ribbentrop
Gerda Christian	Adolf Hitler
Trudy Junge	Adolf Hitler
Else Kruger	Martin Bormann
Pokrebyshev	Joseph Stalin
Hedwig Potthast	Heinrich Himmler
Christa Schroeder	Adolf Hitler

Mary Shearburn	Winston Churchill
Ingeborg Sperr	Rudolph Hess
Johanna Wolfe	Adolf Hitler

Seeger, Pete (1919–)

American folk singer who was drafted into the U.S. Army in 1942. He spent the next three and a half years entertaining troops as a member of the Special Services. Prior to being drafted, Seeger, Lee Hays, and Woody Guthrie sang anti-Fascist songs broadcast by the Office of War Information (OWI).

Seekt, Hans von (1866–1936)

German colonel-general who, between the wars, laid the groundwork for a resurgent German military. Von Seekt was visionary enough to appreciate the role of tanks and aircraft. He hid all preparations from the victors of World War I because of the prohibitions imposed by the Treaty of Versailles.

Seki, Yukio (–1944)

Japanese lieutenant and commander of the first kamikaze attack squad. It consisted of pilots from the 201st Air Group stationed at Mabalacat Field, Philippines (part of Clark Field) and was used in Operation Sho in October 1944. Seki was the first kamikaze to strike when he dove into the carrier U.S.S. *St. Lo*, which was sunk as a result of the attack.

Selassie, Haile (1892–1975)

Emperor of Ethiopia. He was born Ras Tafari and set out to modernize his country. Selassie drew up the first penal code in 1930, the first written constitution the following year, and attempted to abolish slavery, which was still widespread. Selassie, who was known as the Black Napoleon, was forced to flee before the advancing Italians in 1936.

Sellers, Peter (1925–1980)

British actor. He served as a corporal in the Royal Air Force in World War II with the serial number 222-3033.

Semper Fidelis

"Always Faithful"; motto of the U.S. Marine Corps.

Semper Paratus

"Always Ready"; motto of the U.S. Coast Guard.

Send Us More Japs

Propaganda slogan attributed to the defenders of Wake Island in the opening days of World War II. However, it did not originate on Wake Island. The survivors of the Japanese prison camps first heard of it on their release at the end of 1945. The phrase was used in the 1942 movie *Wake Island* by Brian Donlevy as Major Devereaux.

Senger und Etterlin, Frido von (1891–1963)

German general who commanded the forces at Monte Cassino in Italy. He was a former Rhodes Scholar, an Anglophile, and ironically, a lay member of the Benedictine order, which was the order at the Abbey of Cassino.

Senshi

Name of the highest honor for a Japanese soldier, death in battle. His soul would then be enshrined in the Yasukuni Temple in Tokyo.

Sent to Switzerland Without Shoes

Phrase used by both the Allies and the Axis in Italy to indicate people who had been captured by the Gestapo and executed.

Sequoia

Presidential yacht, anchored in the Potomac River, on which Secretary of War Frank Knox lived.

Seraph, H.M.S.

British submarine, number P-219, commanded by Lieutenant N.L.A. Jewell. In October 1942, it took French General Henri Giraud from southern France to Gibraltar prior to the North African landings of Operation Torch. The *Seraph* also dropped off U.S. General Mark Clark in North Africa for his secret mission to negotiate with the French to prepare for the invasion. On April 30, 1943, it launched the body of Major Martin off the coast of Spain to dupe the Germans into believing that the Balkans rather than Sicily would be the next target of invasion.

Sergeant York

Movie of 1942 starring Gary Cooper as Sergeant Alvin York. It was the film watched by pilot John W. Mitchell at the Carolina Theater in Charlotte, North Carolina on December 7, 1941. Only after leaving the theater did he learn about the Japanese attack on Pearl Harbor. It was also the movie being shown on Corregidor when it was attacked by Japanese planes several days later (see Mitchell, John W.).

Sergeyev, Lily (1918–   )

German spy who worked in the British ministry offices. She transmitted her reports from a house in Hampstead and was in reality a double agent working for the British. She used the code name *Treasure*.

Serling, Rod (1925–1975)

Television writer, producer, and host who as a U.S. Army private in the 11th Airborne Division in the Pacific jumped at Tagaytay in the Philippines and was later seriously wounded during the liberation of Manila. While in the hospital he began his studies to become a writer.

Sevareid, Eric (1912–)

CBS-TV news anchorman who was a war correspondent during World War II. At one point he bailed out of a crippled aircraft over the Himalayas and lived with a tribe of headhunters for a month. Sevareid was also present at the liberation of Paris in August 1944.

Sevastopol

Black Sea Russian naval base which fell to the Germans on July 3, 1942. The loss seriously restricted the movement of the Black Sea Fleet and was the last major German victory of World War II.

Seydlitz, Walther von (1888–1976)

German general of artillery who commanded the II Corps at Stalingrad. He repeatedly advocated a breakout and withdrawal although Field Marshall von Paulus had orders to stay. After the fall of Stalingrad in February 1942, von Seydlitz was captured by the Russians and became the head of the League of German Officers, which was part of the National Committee of Free Germany, a Communist organization for the overthrow of the Nazis. The Nazis forced his wife to divorce him because of his anti-Nazi stand. After the war, he refused to become a member of the East German Communist government and was sentenced to twenty-five years in prison. He was released in 1955.

Severity Order

Command issued by German Field Marshall Walter von Reichenau to the Sixth Army prior to his death in January 1942. It called for Army participation in the extermination of the Jews but was rescinded by the new commander, General Frederick von Paulus.

Seyffardt, Hendrik (1872–1943)

Dutch lieutenant general until 1934 when he retired. When the Germans occupied Holland, he agreed to command a volunteer corps, the Vrijkorps, and fought on the Eastern Front against the Communists. Seyffardt was the only Dutch general to collaborate with the Germans and was assassinated on February 5, 1943, in the Hague by SOE-sponsored gunmen.

Seyss-Inquart, Arthur (1892–1946)

Early Nazi party member and Gauleiter of the Netherlands in World War II. He suggested a truce with the Allies in April 1945 because General Dwight Eisenhower was reluctant to attack since the war was nearly over. Seyss-Inquart was captured by Canadian troops, tried at Nuremberg, and sentenced to death for war crimes.

Sextant

Code name for the Cairo Conference of November and December, 1943, between President Franklin D. Roosevelt, Prime Minister Winston Churchill, and Generalissimo Chiang Kai-shek.

SHAEF

Supreme Headquarters Allied Expeditionary Force. It was the name of General Dwight Eisenhower's headquarters for the D-Day invasion and the battle across Europe. In London SHAEF was located at 20 Grosvenor Square.

Shahan, Elza

U.S. Army Air Force lieutenant. As a P-38 fighter pilot he was the first American fighter to shoot down a German aircraft in World War II, when he downed an FW200 Condor near Iceland on August 14, 1942. The Condor was a long-range reconnaissance aircraft gathering weather and sending data for the German Navy. Shahan, as a member of the 27th Fighter Squadron, 1st Fighter Group, was at the time ferrying his aircraft to England and on a layover in Iceland. He later fought in North Africa.

Shakespeare, H.M.S.

British submarine that acted as a beacon to guide the Salerno invasion fleet to the beaches to assault Italy.

Shangri-La

Name of President Franklin D. Roosevelt's retreat in the Catoctin Mountains of Maryland. Today it is called Camp David.

Shangri-La

Mythical point of departure for the bombers of Doolittle's Raid on Tokyo on April 18, 1942. The name was chosen by President Franklin Roosevelt to hide the fact they had departed from the aircraft carrier *Hornet*. He chose the name from James Hilton's classic novel *Lost Horizon*. (In 1944 a carrier named *Shangri-La*, CV-38, was launched by Mrs. James Doolittle.)

Shangri-La

Name of U.S. Army Air Force ace Captain Don Gentile's P-51 Mustang. He flew with the 4th Fighter Group of the Eighth Army

Air Force. On his last mission before being removed from combat, news cameramen were waiting at the airfield. Gentile did a high-speed low approach that ended when he caught the propeller and crashed, destroying the airplane. Luckily he escaped without injury.

Shapely, Alan (1903–1973)

U.S. Marine Corps officer who commanded the eighty-three-man Marine detachment stationed aboard the U.S.S. *Arizona* on December 7, 1941. Only Shapely and eight other Marines survived the Japanese attack. He was awarded a Silver Star for heroism. He later was promoted to general.

Shark, U.S.S.

First U.S. submarine sunk by Japanese forces in World War II. Commanded by Louis Shane, the *Shark* went down in the vicinity of Molucca Passage in January 1942. (The first lost in the war was the *Sealion* and the second lost at sea was *S-36*.)

Shaw, U.S.S.

U.S. destroyer that exploded during the December 7, 1941, attack on Pearl Harbor. The photograph of the explosion is one of the most famous of World War II. The *Shaw* was not destroyed and was put back into service in the South Pacific, where it fought in the Battle of Santa Cruz on October 26, 1942.

"Sheik of Araby, The"

Novelty song by Spike Jones and the City Slickers that was adopted by the crew of a U.S. aircraft carrier during World War II. The song was played whenever planes were being launched.

Shellburst

Name of General Dwight Eisenhower's headquarters in Normandy. It was later moved to Granville where Ike's house was called Villa Montgomery. Shellburst was moved as the armies advanced so that Eisenhower could stay in contact.

Shelley, Norman (1903–1980)

British actor who, while working for the BBC, imitated Churchill's voice for a recording session after the evacuation of Dunkirk and defiantly said "We shall fight on the beaches . . . we shall fight in the hills; we shall never surrender." It was heard by millions around the world. That it was Shelley and not Churchill who uttered the lines was one of the best kept secrets of World War II, only being revealed in 1979.

Sheng, Wong Hai

Chinese cameraman nicknamed "Newsreel." It was his photograph of a crying burned baby sitting in the middle of the Shanghai railroad station that became one of the most dramatic photos of the war. Sheng escaped the fall of Singapore one day before the Japanese occupation.

Shepard, Alan B. Jr. (1923–   )

U.S. astronaut. He graduated from the U.S. Naval Academy of Annapolis in 1944 and served aboard the destroyer U.S.S. *Cogswell* in the Pacific in World War II. Shepard became a pilot only after the war.

Shepardson, Whitney

First chief of the OSS in London in World War II. He later became president of the CIA-funded Free Europe Committee from 1953 to 1956.

Sheridan, Martin

Reporter for the *Boston Globe* during World War II. He was the only correspondent allowed on a U.S. submarine on a war patrol when he went on the U.S.S. *Bullhead* into the South China Sea in April 1945. Sheridan had the distinction of being on the submarine when it was mistakenly attacked by a B-24, which dropped three bombs that barely missed the vessel.

Sherman, Allan (1924–1973)

Writer and comedian who was medically discharged from the U.S. Army for asthmatic allergies five months after he enlisted in December, 1942.

Sherman, Forrest P. (1896–1951)

U.S. Navy admiral. He commanded the aircraft carrier *Wasp* when it was attacked and sunk in the Solomons in 1942. Sherman always had a plan, and when the carrier was hit by torpedoes, he maneuvered the ship so that the stern was clear of flaming gasoline in the water; 2,054 men escaped through the lane he had cleared. He became a major planner of the Pacific campaign as Deputy Chief of Staff to Admiral Chester Nimitz and developed the leapfrog technique of capturing Japanese territory.

Sherman Tank

American thirty-four-ton medium tank. It was notorious among the tankers for the ease with which it could be set on fire, for which it was nicknamed the "Ronson." The *Sherman* had gasoline engines and the high-octane fuel burned easily when the engine was hit. (This did not happen with diesel engines.) It was no match for the more heavily armored and armed German

Panther or Tiger, but it was more dependable and it outnumbered and outflanked the German forces.

Shigehura, Murata

Japanese commander of the torpedo planes that attacked Pearl Harbor on December 7, 1941.

Shigemitsu, Mamoru (1881–1957)

Japanese foreign minister who headed the surrender delegation on the U.S.S. *Missouri,* on September 2, 1945. He had a wooden leg due to an assassination attempt by a Korean in Shanghai in 1932. Shigemitsu was sentenced to seven years in prison for war crimes after the war.

Shigeru, Itaya

Japanese Naval officer who commanded the fighter aircraft in the Pearl Harbor attack on December 7, 1941.

Schilling, Erikson E.

Group Photo Officer for the Flying Tigers in China. He devised the scheme to paint the famous shark's teeth on the P-40's, because he believed that the Japanese were superstitious and would remain clear of the evil-looking American aircraft.

Shimizu, Mitsumi

Japanese Vice-Admiral who commanded submarine forces in the early days of World War II. He was wounded at Kwajelein on February 1, 1942, and was eventually relieved of command.

Shimpu Attack Corps

Name selected for the first kamikaze unit organized at Mabalacat airfield, Philippines, to support Operation Sho, the attack on the U.S. Fleet at Leyte Gulf on October 19, 1944. The unit consisted of twenty-four volunteers and was conceived by Admiral Takijiro Ohnishi.

Shinano

Japanese carrier that was sunk by the U.S. submarine *Archerfish* two hours after it was launched on November 29, 1944. It was constructed on a hull comparable to the battleship *Yamato* and was 861 feet long. In reality it was to be a sister ship of the *Yamato* and the *Musashi,* the two largest battleships ever built. The first B-29 raids on Tokyo made the Japanese uneasy and the high command ordered it moved to the safer Inland Sea. The *Shinano* was commanded by Captain Toshio Abe, who along with most of his crew was untrained. Many of the watertight doors had not been installed and there were no fire pumps on board. Abe and 500 of the crew were killed.

Shinyo Maru
Japanese ship sunk off Mindanao on September 7, 1944, with the loss of 668 Filipino and American prisoners of war.

Ship 10
German designator for the auxiliary cruiser *Thor.*

Ship 16
German designator of the auxiliary cruiser *Atlantis.*

Ship 21
German designator for the auxiliary cruiser *Widder.*

Ship 23
German designator for the auxiliary cruiser *Stier.*

Ship 28
German designator for the auxiliary cruiser *Michel.*

Ship 33
German designator for the auxiliary cruiser *Pinquin.*

Ship 36
German designator for the auxiliary cruiser *Orion.*

Ship 41
German designator for the auxiliary cruiser *Kormann.*

Ship 45
German designator for the auxiliary cruiser *Komet.*

Ship Designators of the U.S. Navy

BB—battleships
CA—heavy cruisers
CC—battle cruisers
CL—light cruisers
CL (AA)—light cruisers (antiaircraft)
CV—aircraft carriers
CVA—attack aircraft carriers
CVB—large aircraft carriers
CVE—escort aircraft carriers
CVL—light aircraft carriers
DD—destroyers
DE—destroyer escorts
SS—submarines

Ship Names in the U.S. Navy

Aircraft Carriers—Battles
Ammunition Ships—Gods of Mythology
Battleships—States
Destroyers—Deceased War Heroes

Submarines—Fish
Tugs—Indian Tribes

Shirer, William L. (1904–)

Writer and broadcaster. In 1934, he traveled to Germany as a reporter for Hearst's *Universal News Service* but changed to CBS prior to World War II. He reported on the Nazi rise to power and the conditions in Germany in the early days of World War II. Shirer is best known for his books *Berlin Diary* (1941) and *The Rise and Fall of the Third Reich* (1960). He portrayed himself in the 1951 movie *The Magic Face.*

Shkuro, Andrey (–1947)

Cossack general who was awarded the British Commander of the Order of the Bath for services to the British cause in World War I. A Russian emigré, he had never returned to Russia after the Communist Revolution. Shkuro commanded the Cossacks, who fought with the Germans against Stalin in World War II. The British turned him over to the Soviets at Judenburg, Austria, on May 29, 1945, along with other officers; he was hanged in January 1947.

Shoho

Japanese escort carrier sunk in the Battle of the Coral Sea on May 7, 1942, by aircraft from the *Yorktown* and *Lexington*. The *Shoho* was the first enemy aircraft carrier sunk by U.S. aircraft and the first carrier lost in the war in the Pacific.

Shokaku

Japanese carrier that participated in the attack on Pearl Harbor on December 7, 1941. It was severely damaged during the Battle of the Coral Sea in May 1942. The *Shokaku* was sunk by the submarine U.S.S. *Cavalla* on June 19, 1944, in the First Battle of the Philippine Sea. *Shokaku*'s sister carrier, the *Taiho*, was sunk the same day by the sister submarine of the *Cavalla*, the *Albacore*, which was also in the area.

Shomo, William A.

U.S. Army Air Force captain in the Fifth Air Force in the Pacific in World War II. On January 11, 1945, on his first air combat mission, Shomo shot down seven Japanese aircraft over the Philippines, becoming the first U.S. pilot to do so. He was awarded the Congressional Medal of Honor by General George C. Kenney. Shomo's wingman, Lieutenant Paul M. Liscombs, downed three aircraft during the same battle and received a Distinguished Service Cross.

Shore, Dinah (1917–)

American singer and talk show host. In December 1941, she was to have met a sailor friend who was due for a furlough on December 8, only to find out that he was one of the many killed at Pearl Harbor the day before. She entertained troops around the U.S. throughout World War II and was made an honorary private first class by the Chico, California, Air Force Training base. Shore also had a B-17 named after her. (She originally was a brunette and was persuaded to change her hair to blond by the Warner Bros. Studios.) During the war she undertook much work for the U.S.O. In 1943 Dinah Shore married actor George Montgomery, who was serving in the U.S. Army.

Short, Walter C. (1880–1949)

U.S. Army lieutenant general who commanded all U.S. forces at Pearl Harbor during the Japanese attack on December 7, 1941. He was relieved of command after being charged with unpreparedness. Short was demoted to major general and retired shortly afterwards. He ended a forty-year career by returning to the states a few weeks later and worked throughout the war for Ford Motor Company as a traffic engineer.

MOVIE PORTRAYAL:

Tora! Tora! Tora! (1970), by Jason Robards

Shoumatoff, Elizabeth

American artist who was painting a portrait of President Franklin D. Roosevelt when he died on April 12, 1945, in Warm Springs, Georgia.

Shoup, David M. (1904–)

U.S. Marine Corps officer. As a colonel, he commanded the 2nd Marine Division on Tarawa and was awarded the Congressional Medal of Honor for heroism. In 1929, when Shoup was a lieutenant, his first ship was the U.S.S. *Maryland,* which was later the flagship for the Tarawa invasion. He also fought on Guadalcanal, New Georgia, Saipan, and Tinian. Shoup participated in the 1949 John Wayne movie *Sands of Iwo Jima.*

Shriver, R. Sargent (1915–)

Brother-in-law of President John F. Kennedy and U.S. Ambassador to France, as well as Democratic Vice-Presidential candidate in 1972. During World War II he served on the submarine U.S.S. *Sandlance.* Shriver also served aboard a battleship and was discharged in 1945 as a lieutenant commander.

Shute, Nevil (1899–1960)

Author and aircraft designer. In 1924, he helped engineer the airship R-100 and flew with it from England to Canada and back. Shute became a lieutenant commander in the Royal Navy in 1942. Two of his novels are *No Highway in the Sky* and *On the Beach*. His full name is Nevil Shute Norway.

Sicily

Italian island assaulted on July 10, 1943, in Operation Husky. Over 467,000 Allied troops were opposed by 60,000 Germans, two-thirds of whom escaped to Italy with their equipment. The beaches at Sicily were designated Cent, Dime, and Joss. Cent was assaulted by Troy Middleton and the 45th Division, Dime by Terry Allen and the 1st Division, and Joss by Lucian Truscott and the 3rd Division.

Siegfried Line

German defense line facing the French Maginot Line. It was a continuous line of fortifications from Switzerland to Belgium, nine miles deep in many places. The Germans called it the "Westwall."

"Sieg Heil Sieg Heil"

One of the marches used by Adolf Hitler and the Nazis to rally audiences. The tune was taken from the Harvard University "Fight, Fight, Fight" song.

Signal

German Army propaganda magazine in World War II. It depended heavily on color photography to appeal to its readers.

"Sighted Sub, Sank Same"

Ensign Donald Mason's famous one-sentence radio message after he sank a German submarine on January 28, 1942.

Sigmund, Carl (1909–   )

Popular songwriter who penned such classics as "Ebb Tide," "What Now My Love?" and "It's All In the Game."* He served in the 82nd Airborne Division in World War II, receiving six combat stars as well as a Bronze Star. Sigmund also composed the 82nd Airborne's marching song "The All-American Soldier."

Sikorski, Wladyslaw (1881–1943)

Polish general and Premier of the Polish government in exile in England in World War II. It was felt he endangered Allied

---

*The song was based on a melody written by U.S. Vice-President Charles Dawes.

solidarity by accusing the Russians of the Katyn forest massacre of Polish officers discovered in 1942. Sikorski was killed when his aircraft AL-523 crashed less than a mile from its departure point at Gibraltar on July 4, 1943, in an incident that has been very controversial ever since. The prevailing feeling is that the British had him killed to get him out of the way.

Sikorsky, Igor (1889–1972)

U.S. aircraft designer who was born in Russia. Sikorsky designed the first American helicopter in 1939.

Silverplate

U.S. Army's code name for the training of fifteen bomber crews to drop the first atomic bomb. The 393rd Heavy Bombardment Squadron trained at Wendover, Utah, and was headed by Colonel Paul Tibbets.

Simonds, Guy (1903–1974)

Canadian general and the leading field commander for Canada in World War II. He went to Europe in 1939 and became a general in 1941, thus becoming Canada's youngest general at thirty-nine. Simonds led the Canadian 1st and 2nd Divisions in Africa and Italy and the II Corps in the assault on Antwerp to open the Belgian port.

Simpson, Eva Best (1905–1966)

U.S. Marine Corps major. She commanded the first Marine Women's Reservist unit sent to the Pacific in World War II.

Sinclair, Sir Hugh

British admiral. Referred to as "C," he was the chief of the British Secret Intelligence Service until 1939, at which time he was replaced by Sir Stewart Menzies.

Singapore

Malayan capital and key British base in the Far East called "the Gibraltar of the East." It was captured on February 15, 1942, by the Japanese after a seventy-day siege in the greatest debacle of British history. Singapore was connected to the Malaya mainland by a causeway across the Straits of Johore. It was armed with fifteen-inch guns that faced only toward the sea with a limited traverse and were supplied only with armor-piercing shells. British military forces were not unified and there was a tremendous rivalry and jealousy among the three services. British General Arthur Percival did not fortify the northern approach to Singapore because he believed it would be bad for morale. When he did move troops, it was to the wrong places. The naval base at the north end of the island was abandoned before the end of fighting, leaving millions of dollars' worth of equipment for the advancing Japanese. Many more casualties occurred because no air raid shelters had been provided for civilians.

Singer

U.S. sewing machine company and one of the primary suppliers of M-1 Garand rifles to the U.S. Army in World War II.

Siren Suit

Special one-piece pullover outer garment worn by Winston Churchill during World War II. One of these is on display at Churchill's birthplace, Blenheim Castle, in England.

Site S

Code name of Alamagordo, New Mexico, where the first atomic bomb was detonated July 16, 1945. In Spanish the area was called Jornado del Muerto or "tract of death."

Site Y

Code name for Los Alamos, New Mexico, where research was conducted on atomic bombs in the Manhattan Project.

Sitzkrieg

Derisive name given to German military methods during the period of the Phony War.

Siwash

Name of a duck, mascot of a U.S. Marine artillery battalion in the Pacific. The duck participated in the assaults on Tarawa, Saipan, and Tinian, returning to the U.S. in October 1944, allegedly for laying an egg. It appears that the marine mascot was a female.

Six, Dr. Frank

Former dean of political science at Berlin University. He was selected to be in charge of Nazi-occupied Britain after the success of Operation Sea Lion. It was one post he never got to hold.

SJ

Designator of an improved radar for U.S. submarines that replaced SD sets. It could give range and bearing to a target and was used as a surface search radar to spot ships both at night and in bad weather.

Skalski, Stanislaw

Top-scoring Polish ace of World War II with eighteen enemy aircraft to his credit.

Skelton, Red (1913–)

Comedian who was drafted into the U.S. Army on March 9, 1945, entertaining troops in Italy until his discharge in September

1945. He once stated that he was the only celebrity who went in and came out a private.

Skipjack, U.S.S.

U.S. Navy submarine on which John S. McCain, Jr., served in World War II. He later became an admiral and the U.S. Navy Commander in Chief in the Pacific. The *Skipjack* was later used in the atomic bomb tests at Bikini Atoll in 1946 and sunk.

Skorzeny, Otto (1908–1975)

Austrian-born, S.S. colonel known for his daring exploits in World War II. He rescued Mussolini in an airborne assault on Gran Sasso on September 12, 1943, and was head of Operation Grief during the Battle of the Bulge, in which Germans dressed in American uniforms infiltrated and confused the U.S. Army. Skorzeny, called "the most dangerous man in Europe," was tried at the end of the war and acquitted because a British commando officer testified on his behalf that the British used German uniforms in secret missions. Skorzeny lived in Spain until his death in 1975.

Skunk

U.S. Navy code name for an unknown surface ship. The term is similar to "bogey" for an unknown aircraft.

Sky Pilot

U.S. military slang term for a chaplain.

Slayton, Donald K. "Deke" (1924–   )

U.S. astronaut. He enlisted in the U.S. Army Air Force in 1942 where he was trained as a bomber pilot, flying fifty-six missions in Europe and seven over Japan in B-25's. Slayton was discharged in 1946.

Slim, Sir William J. (1891–1970)

British general and commander of the Fourteenth Army in Burma. Lord Louis Mountbatten said he was the finest general produced by World War II.

Slogans

"Home Alive in '45"
"Out of the sticks in '46"
"From hell to heaven in '47"
"Golden Gate by '48"

Slovik, Eddie D. (–1945)

U.S. Army private (#36896415) who was executed on January 31, 1945. He was the only U.S. soldier to be executed for desertion since 1864. Forty-nine Americans were sentenced to death in World War II for desertion, but he was the only one executed, in one of the great controversies of the war. (Over 25,000 Germans were executed for desertion.)

MOVIE PORTRAYALS:
The Victors (1963), by James Chase
Execution of Private Slovik (1974 TV movie), by Martin Sheen

Smersh
Soviet counterintelligence section in World War II headed by General Ivan Serov. The name meant "death to spies" and was immortalized in Ian Fleming's James Bond novels.

Smigly-Rydz, Edward (1886–1943)
Polish Army marshall. He was the inspector general of Polish Armed Forces at the outbreak of World War II. Smigly-Rydz escaped to Rumania with the collapse of Poland and returned to fight in the Polish underground. He was believed to have been killed by the Germans in 1943.

Smith, Baldwin B
U.S. Army colonel who served as a double for General Dwight Eisenhower during the Battle of the Bulge in December 1944. It was believed that the Germans, disguised in American uniforms and commanded by Otto Skorzeny, would attempt to assassinate Eisenhower. Smith traveled around SHAEF headquarters at Versailles to try and draw fire.

Smith, Holland M. (1882–1967)
U.S. Marine Corps major general. He commanded all Marine landing forces in the invasion of the Gilbert Islands, Saipan, Iwo Jima, Tarawa, Namur, and Kwajalein. He was nicknamed "Howling Mad."

Smith, Ian (1919–   )
Prime Minister of Rhodesia. During World War II, he flew with the 237th Squadron as a fighter pilot and was once shot down over North Africa. Smith was hospitalized for several months in Cairo, where his face was reconstructed by plastic surgery. After resuming his flight duties, he was shot down again, this time over Italy. He was discovered by Italian partisans, whom he joined to fight the Germans. They conferred the rank of major on him.

Smith, John L. (1914–1972)
U.S. Marine Corps officer. As a fighter pilot with VMF223 at Guadalcanal, Smith earned the Congressional Medal of Honor, officially shooting down nineteen Japanese aircraft.

Smith, Julian C. (1885–1975)
U.S. Marine Corps major general. He commanded the 2nd Marine Division during the Battle of Tarawa and was one of the primary developers of amphibious tactics in the Pacific in World War II.

Smith, Kate (1909–   )
U.S. singer. In 1939, she introduced Irving Berlin's "God Bless America" on Armistice Day and has donated all royalties from the song to the Boy and Girl Scouts of America. During World War II, Smith traveled nearly 520,000 miles entertaining U.S. troops. She is also responsible for selling more U.S. Savings Bonds than anyone else, for a total of nearly $600,000,000.

Smith, Leonard (1915–   )
U.S. Navy ensign. He was the copilot of a British PBY which spotted the *Bismarck* after it had disappeared in the Atlantic in May 1941. Smith's contact report telling of the position of the *Bismarck* resulted in the concentration of British forces that sank it. He was one of seventeen Navy pilots selected to train the British of Coastal Command in the use of PBY's for search missions before the U.S. entry into the war. On December 7, 1941, Smith was en route from Pearl Harbor to an aircraft carrier when the Japanese attacked the U.S. Pacific Fleet. He was awarded a Distinguished Flying Cross in 1943 for his role in the hunt for the *Bismarck* and retired as a Captain in 1962.

Smith, Margaret Chase (1897–   )
U.S. Senator from Maine. She was the first woman ever to be elected to the Senate for three consecutive terms. During World War II, Smith became the first woman ever to sail on a destroyer during wartime (she was a member of the Naval Affairs Subcommittee).

Movie portrayal:
Tail Gunner Joe (1977), by Patricia Neal

Smith, Ralph (1893–   )
U.S. Army major general. He commanded the U.S. 27th Infantry Division in the seizure of Makin Island and the battle for Saipan. Smith was relieved of command by Marine Corps General Holland Smith because of his lack of aggressive drive. The 27th had been placed between the Marine 2nd and 4th Divisions and failed to advance with them.

Smith, Walter Bedell (1895–1961)
U.S. Army officer. He was Chief of Staff to General Dwight

Eisenhower in Europe although he had never attended West Point. His secretary throughout World War II tried to keep the British from hyphenating his name, as in Bedell-Smith, which was not his last name. After the war, Smith became ambassador to Russia and head of the CIA from 1946 to 1949.

MOVIE PORTRAYALS:
The Longest Day (1962), by Alexander Knox
Patton (1970), by Edward Binns
Ike (1979 TV movie), by J. D. Cannon

Smothers Brothers

Hollywood comedians, Tommy (1937–) and Dick (1939–). Their father, Major Thomas B. Smothers, died as a prisoner of war on a Japanese prison ship en route to Japan in World War II.

Smuts, Jan C. (1870–1950)

South African Prime Minister and Field Marshall. He was a close friend of Winston Churchill and was the only person to be present at both the Versailles Peace Conference of 1919 and at the signing of the 1946 Versailles peace agreement.

SN-2

German airborne radar, known as Lichenstein, that was used by night fighters. It had a much wider angle of search (120 degrees), was impervious to jamming by window, and had a better operating range than the older sets. SN-2 began to be used in March 1944, but production was hindered by Allied bombing raids on Berlin that disrupted the factories that assembled it.

SNAFU

American superlative that stood for "situation normal, all fouled up" (see superlatives).

Snead, Sammy (1912–)

U.S. golfer. He was drafted into the U.S. Navy in 1942 after winning the Professional Golfers Association (PGA) Open for that year. Snead was discharged in September 1944 due to a bad back.

Snipers (Russian)

Liudmila Pavlichenko—309 Germans and two Rumanians killed
Vassili Zaitsev—242 Germans killed
Vladimir Ptchelintzev—152 Germans killed

Snowballs

Name which Londoners gave to American military police after General Eisenhower transformed them from the typically sloppy

Yanks into smartly dressed soldiers wearing white helmets, white pistol belts, white gloves, and white leggings.

SO 1

Designator of the subversion section of British MI-6.

SO 2

Designator of the sabotage section of British MI-6.

SOB

Small book carried by U.S. General Joseph Stilwell in which he recorded people and events that he did not like.

SOE

Special Operations Executive. It was a British organization to encourage guerrilla activities behind enemy lines in World War II. SOE was established in November 1940 under Hugh Dalton. Major General Colin Gubbins later took command.

Soedermann, Harry

Chief of the Stockholm Criminal Investigation Department and one of the best criminal investigators of Europe. He was called in by the Nazis to study the Reichstag Fire and after doing so placed the blame on Hermann Goering. Soedermann was immediately hustled out of Germany.

Sokolov, Viktor

Soviet intelligence agent in Brussels, code-named Kent. He fed accurate information back to Stalin about Operation Barbarossa. Sokolov was finally captured in November 1942 in Marseilles and agreed to work with the Germans to save his mistress Margarete Baraza. He was also called Petit Chef. (The Grand Chef was Leopold Treffer.)

Soldier's Medal

U.S. Army decoration given for risking one's life to save someone else in other than a combat situation. The first award to a female was to a WAC, Private Margaret H. "Peewee" Maloney in November 1943 for saving a soldier's life in North Africa.

Solo One

Cover story put together by General Mark Clark prior to the North African invasion to make the Axis powers believe Norway was the objective.

Solo Two

Cover story devised to make Allied troops believe the objective of Operation Torch was other than North Africa, so that the enemy would not be tipped off in case of security leaks.

Somervell, Brehon B. (1882–1955)
U.S. Army lieutenant general. He was the chief of the army Services of Supply in World War II.

Somerville, Sir James (1882–1949)
British admiral. He commanded Force H that sank the French fleet at Oran rather than allow it to fall into German hands. Somerville also participated in the sinking of the *Bismarck* in 1941 and the *Scharnhorst* in 1943.

SONAR
Acronym for Sound Navigation and Ranging which was the American version of ASDIC. It was used to locate submarines under water.

Sonobuoy
Buoy dropped in the water from aircraft to detect submarines. It used sound waves to plot the range and bearing of the submarine, then transmitted this information to Allied aircraft. The Japanese submarine *I-52*, while en route to Germany, was one victim of a sonobuoy in the Bay of Biscay.

Soong Sisters
Ching-ling, Ai-ling, and Mei-ling, Daughters of Chinese millionaire Charles Soong. Ching-ling married Dr. Sun Yat-sen, the father of the Chinese Republic. Ai-ling married H. H. Kung, a direct descendant of Confucius and one of the wealthiest people in China. Mei-ling married Chiang Kai-shek, the unifier of China.

Soong, T. V. (1894–1971)
Chinese foreign minister. He was the brother of Madame Chiang Kai-shek.

Sorge, Richard (1895–1944)
Soviet spy in World War II. He was the grandson of Karl Marx's secretary and the Tokyo correspondent for the *Frankfurter Zeitung*. Because Sorge pretended to be a loyal Nazi, Berlin had asked him to be the Fuehrer of all Nazis in Japan, an honor he declined. He told Stalin that the Japanese intended to attack the U.S.; this knowledge allowed Stalin to move Mongolian troops from Siberia to defend Moscow, thus saving the capital. Sorge was captured by Colonel Ozaki, head of the Japanese counterintelligence, via triangulation of his radio signals, and was hanged November 7, 1944.

Soryu
Japanese aircraft carrier that participated in the attack on Pearl

Harbor on December 7, 1941. It fought in the Battle of Midway where it was sunk on June 6, 1942, by aircraft from the U.S. carriers *Yorktown* and *Enterprise*.

SOS

Emergency signal for ships in distress. In World War II, ships also sent out *SSS* to signify "under submarine attack"; *AAA* to warn of aircraft attack; and *RRR* to indicate "surface raider attack." (The first vessel to officially use the SOS was the *Titanic*, when it fatally hit an iceberg the evening of April 12, 1912.)

South Dakota, U.S.S.

U.S. Navy 35,000-ton battleship launched in 1942. It was nicknamed "Old Nameless."

Southwick House

Site of the D-Day Operations Room. The room is just as it was on June 6, 1944.

Sovine, Woodrow Wilson "Red" (1918–)

Popular country singer. He was a prisoner of war during World War II, an experience that inspired his hit song "Soul of a Convict."

Spaatz, Carl (1891–1974)

U.S. Army Air Force officer. In World War I, he was a fighter pilot credited with shooting down three German aircraft. In 1925 he was a defense witness at the court martial of Billy Mitchell. At the outbreak of World War II, Spaatz, as a colonel, was sent to England to evaluate the German military, sitting on rooftops during the Blitz to observe German tactics. He was promoted to general, commanding the U.S. Strategic Air Forces in Europe and later the Pacific. Spaatz was the first Chief of Staff of the independent U.S. Air Force.

MOVIE PORTRAYAL:

The Court Martial of Billy Mitchell (1955), by Steve Roberts

Spaatzwaffe

Nickname given to U.S. Army Air Force in England after General Carl Spaatz took command in 1942.

Spahn, Warren (1921–)

U.S. major league baseball pitcher considered by many to have been the greatest left-handed pitcher in baseball history (he won over 300 games). During World War II, Spahn served in the U.S. Army in Europe, taking part in the Battle of the Remagen Bridge in March 1945. He received a Purple Heart after being wounded in the foot by shrapnel during the battle. Spahn was discharged in 1946 with a Bronze Star and holds the distinction of being the only major league baseball player during the war to receive a battlefield commission. After the war, Spahn returned to baseball and pitched in the 1948 World Series.

Spam

Canned meat consisting of chopped ham and pork shoulders introduced in 1937 by the Hormel Meat Company. The advertising campaign was conducted by George Burns and Gracie Allen in one of the first singing commercials. Spam gained worldwide fame in World War II because of its mass distribution to GI's overseas; ironically, though, the product provided by the Army was not true Spam, but a cheap imitation concocted by the U.S. Army Quartermaster Corps.

Spamland

Nickname given to England because of the amount of Spam consumed by the English as part of Lend-Lease. They referred to it as "Escallope of Spam."

Spam Man

Nickname of Jay Catherwood Hormel, head of the Hormel Meat Company that offered Spam as one of over 300 products.

Spandau

West Berlin prison where the seven prisoners sentenced by the Nuremberg Tribunal were incarcerated. They were Rudolph Hess, Walter Funk, Karl Doenitz, Erich Raeder, Baldur von Schirach, Konstantin von Neurath, and Albert Speer. All but Rudolph Hess have been released.

Spearfish, H.M.S.

British submarine under Lieutenant Commander J. H. Forbes that torpedoed and damaged the German cruiser *Lutzow* on April 11, 1940.

Special Group R

Top secret section of the Reichswehr that trained in Russia with weapons denied by the Treaty of Versailles; the *R* stood for "Russia." Training was carried out on tanks, airplanes, chemical warfare, and submarines.

Special Liaison Units (SLU)

Special groups set up by F. W. Winterbotham to protect the secret that the British were reading the German secret codes. These units were attached to the highest levels of British and American commands.

Speedy

Designator for the U.S. II Corps in Sicily under General Omar Bradley in 1943.

Speer, Albert (1905–1981)

German Reichs Armaments Minister after the death of Fritz Todt in 1942. Speer's address was No. 53 Pariser Platz, Berlin. He was sentenced to twenty years in prison by the Nuremberg Tribunal and released in 1966. He died September 1, 1981 exactly 42 years after the start of World War II. Ironically, he died in London.

MOVIE PORTRAYAL:
The Bunker (1980 TV movie), by Richard Jordan
Inside the Third Reich (1982 TV miniseries), by Rutger Hauer

Speidel, Hans (1897–   )

German lieutenant general and Chief of Staff to Field Marshall Erwin Rommel. It was Speidel who talked Rommel into joining the anti-Hitler conspiracy. Speidel was arrested in July 1944 for complicity in the July 20 attempt on Hitler's life. He escaped from a Gestapo prison in Berlin, hiding for the rest of the war. After the Federal Republic was founded, Speidel was instrumental in building the new German Army.

Spence, Sir Basil

British architect (he later designed Coventry Cathedral) who designed and built a fictitious oil dock at Dover that spread out over three square miles to make the Germans believe Pluto was aimed at the Pas de Calais instead of Normandy.

Sperrle, Hugo (1885–1953)

German Field Marshall. As a general, he commanded the Condor Legion during the Spanish Civil War. Sperrle later was in charge of Luftflotte 3 based in France during the Battle of Britain.

Spikefish, U.S.S.

U.S. Navy submarine. It sank the last Japanese submarine to fall victim to a U.S. submarine in World War II on August 13, 1945.

Spitfire

British fighter designed by R.J. Mitchell. It was one of the mainstays of British defense during the Battle of Britain. In 1940, the Spitfire could turn tighter than the ME109, but it lacked the ME109's firepower.

Spock, Dr. Benjamin (1903–   )

Controversial pediatrician and Olympic gold medal winner for rowing. During World War II, he served with the medical corps of the U.S Naval Reserve as a psychiatrist holding the rank of lieutenant commander.

Sponeck, Count Hans von (1888–1944)

German lieutenant general. He commanded the XLIII Corps on the Kerch Peninsula of the Black Sea, becoming the first German general to be court martialed for disobeying an order. Von Sponeck had commanded the 22nd Airborne Division in the 1940 capture of Holland, for which he was awarded the Knight's Cross. At Kerch, he gave the order for retreat to a division being attacked by two Russian armies. His court-martial, which was presided over by Hermann Goering, resulted in a sentence of a reduction of rank, surrender of all awards and decorations, and execution, but Hitler commuted his death sentence to seven years' imprisonment. After the July 20, 1944, attempt on Hitler's life, an overzealous execution squad of Himmler's shot him without sentence.

Spruance, Raymond (1886–1969)

U.S. Navy admiral who commanded the Central Pacific Force in World War II.

MOVIE PORTRAYAL:
Midway (1974), by Glenn Ford

Spruce Goose

Name given to the aircraft designed and built by Howard Hughes in World War II. Nicknamed "the flying lumberyard," it was the largest airplane ever built, with a 320-foot wingspan and an 85-foot tail. The official designator was HK-1 for *Hughes Kaiser.* The aircraft, built of wood (birch, not spruce) because of the shortage of metal, could carry 700 troops. It flew only once, with Howard Hughes at the control, on November 2, 1947.

Squalus, U.S.S.

U.S. Navy submarine that was sunk on May 23, 1939, in 243 feet of water, drowning twenty-three of her crew. Thirty-three others were rescued by a McCann Rescue Chamber. The submarine was salvaged and recommissioned as the *Sailfish*.

Squire of Hyde Park

Nickname given to President Franklin D. Roosevelt.

S.S.

German elite bodyguards of Adolf Hitler in the early days of the Nazi party. It was originally formed in 1925 as a sub-unit of the S.A. and grew under Heinrich Himmler into the most feared section of the Party. All members had to prove their Aryan ancestry to 1750 A.D. and meet certain physical requirements. The S.S. was intended to be the aristocracy of Nazi Germany.

S.S. Generals

Thirty-two were killed in action
Four died of wounds
Two were executed by Hitler
Fourteen were executed by the Allies
Five died of unknown causes
Nine died of natural causes on duty
Eight died in jail
Four were executed by the West German government
Sixteen committed suicide

SSS

Emergency signal for ships in distress to indicate that the ship was under submarine attack.

Stack, Robert

U.S. Army brigadier general. He was the first U.S. officer of field rank to meet Hermann Goering (May 6, 1945) after his capture by American forces. Stack shook Goering's hand, for which he was later reprimanded by General Dwight Eisenhower.

Stack, Robert (1919–)

Hollywood actor. He served as a gunnery officer for the U.S. Navy for three and a half years in World War II. At one time, he taught gunnery at Pensacola.

Stage Door Canteen

British organization for servicemen of all ranks and services located in London. Founded by comedienne Beatrice Lillie, it was the British equivalent of the American U.S.O.

Stagg, John M. (1900–1975)

British Royal Air Force group captain and chief meteorologist for SHAEF. He interpreted weather charts for Normandy, influencing General Dwight Eisenhower to go ahead with the D-Day operations on June 6, 1944.

Stalag II A

German camp for Allied prisoners of war located 100 miles north of Berlin at Neubrandenburg.

Stalag VIII B

Largest prisoner-of-war camp in Germany in World War II. It was originally built in 1915 at Lamsdorf to house British prisoners during World War I and again held British POW's in World War II.

Stalag XX

German camp located at Thorn, Poland. Airey Neave was moved here along with other POW's in protest against alleged ill-treatment of German officers in Canada. Neave later escaped.

Stalag Luft I

German Luftwaffe prisoner-of-war camp located in Barth on the Baltic Sea. Noteworthy prisoners were Francis Gabreski, Gerald Johnson, Herb Zemke, and Duane Beeson, all top-ranked U.S. Army Air Force fighter aces.

Stalag Luft III

Luftwaffe prisoner-of-war camp for Allied airmen. It was located at Sagan between Berlin and Breslau in Silesia and was built at the express orders of Reichsmarschall Hermann Goering who claimed that it was completely escapeproof. This boast went the way of most of Goering's statements when seventy-six prisoners succeeded in escaping at one time in March 1944. Three of these succeeded in returning to Allied lines. Of the rest who were captured, fifty were shot outright by the Gestapo. This episode was immortalized through Paul Brickhill's book and the 1963 movie *The Great Escape*. Another famous escape, immortalized in the book *The Wooden Horse* by Eric Williams, also took place in this camp.

Stalag Luft III A

German Luftwaffe prisoner-of-war camp located at Luckenwalde, thirty-five miles south of Berlin.

Stalin, Jokov (–1943)

Eldest son of Joseph Stalin. He was captured by the Germans at Smolensk in 1941 and put in Sachsenhausen concentration camp. The Germans attempted to exchange him for any comparable German prisoner, but Stalin would have nothing to do with the offer. Jakov Stalin reportedly threw himself on the electrical wire surrounding the camp on April 14, 1943, and was killed.

Stalin, Joseph (1879–1953)

Soviet premier and dictator. He was *Time* magazine's Man of the Year for both 1939 and 1942. During the battle for Moscow in December 1941, Stalin locked himself in his room in the Kremlin, leaving Russia leaderless for five days.

MOVIE PORTRAYALS:
Mission to Moscow (1943), by Mannart Kippen
Truman at Potsdam (1976), by Jose Ferrer

Stamp Collectors

Ernest Borgnine
King Carol of Rumania
General Mark Clark
King George VI of England
Herbert Hoover
Harold Ickes
Adolphe Menjou
King Michael of Rumania
Ezio Pinza
Lily Pons
Franklin D. Roosevelt
Simon Wiesenthal

Stangl, Franz (1908–1971)

German S.S. commandant of Treblinka. He was arrested in Austria after World War II by American troops but escaped to South America. Stangl was captured in Brazil in 1967 and returned to Germany, where he was sentenced to life imprisonment by a West German court for the deaths of 400,000 Jews, although he never personally mistreated anyone.

Stanmore

Site of British Fighter Command operations during the Battle of Britain.

Stark, Harold R. (1880–1972)

U.S. Navy admiral. He was the Chief of Naval Operations at the time of the Pearl Harbor attack. Stark was given command of all U.S. Naval Forces in Europe until 1945.

MOVIE PORTRAYAL:
Tora! Tora! Tora! (1970), by Edward Andrews

Stars and Stripes

GI newspaper in World War II. It was launched with 5,000 copies in London on April 18, 1942, the day Doolittle bombed Tokyo, and ended the war with a circulation of 1,200,000. An illustrated supplement was called *Warweek*.

Stassen, Harold E. (1907–)

U.S. politician and former governor of Minnesota. He resigned his office to serve in the U.S. Navy in April 1943, serving as an aide to Admiral William Halsey. Stassen was promoted to captain in September 1945 and was a delegate to the San Francisco

Conference while on leave. He was discharged November 15, 1945.

Staubwasser, Anton

German Army colonel. He was intelligence officer for Field Marshall Erwin Rommel in Normandy.

von Stauffenberg, Claus (1907–1944)

German Army colonel who planted the bomb at Rastenburg July 20, 1944, in an attempt to kill Hitler. Von Stauffenberg had participated in the conquest of Poland, France, and the fighting in North Africa, where he lost an arm and an eye. He was executed the night of the failed plot against Hitler.

Movie portrayals:
Rommel: The Desert Fox (1951), by Eduard Franz
Hitler (1962), by William Sargent

Stavka

Name of the Red Army High Command in Moscow in World War II.

Steelhead, U.S.S.

U.S. Navy submarine on which the temporary head of the FBI, L. Patrick Gray, served in World War II.

Steiger, Rod (1925–)

Hollywood actor. He lied about his age and enlisted in the U.S. Navy in 1941, serving in the South Pacific as a torpedoman on the destroyer U.S.S. *Taussig*. Steiger was involved in the Battles of Iwo Jima and Okinawa, among others, being medically discharged for acute skin disease twenty-four hours after the Japanese surrendered.

Stephen Hopkins, S.S.

U.S. Liberty ship commanded by Paul Buck. It was one of the first built and after being put into service was intercepted by the German raider *Stier* in the South Atlantic on September 27, 1942. Captain Buck decided to fight rather than surrender his ship, engaging the more heavily armed *Stier* in a running gun battle. The *Stephen Hopkins* eventually was sunk but not before it had inflicted such damage on the German ship that it too eventually sank.

Stephensen, William

British head of the BSC, the British intelligence network in the U.S. during World War II. Stephensen, code-named Intrepid, flew as a tail gunner in a bomber over Normandy on D-Day. He was a superior of Ian Fleming. After reading the manuscript for Fleming's *Casino Royale*, about the exploits of James Bond, he said it would never sell.

MOVIE PORTRAYAL:
A Man Called Intrepid (1979 TV movie), by David Niven

Stettinius, Edward R. (1900–1949)
U.S. Secretary of State (1944–1945) under President Franklin Roosevelt.

Steubenville
Ohio town that *Time* magazine claimed had the largest red light district of any city east of the Mississippi River in World War II. (Actor Dean Martin is from Steubenville.)

Stevens, E. E.
Royal Air Force squadron leader of No. 603 Squadron (City of Edinburgh). He is credited with shooting down the first German aircraft over British soil since the end of World War I, when he downed a JU-88 piloted by Captain Helmut Pohle, on October 16, 1939. Pohle was attempting to bomb ships in the Firth of Forth. It was the first German bombing mission over Britain of World War II.

Stevens, R. Henry
British captain in the intelligence service. He and Captain S. Payne Best were the two senior MI-6 officers in the continent at the outbreak of World War II. They were kidnapped on November 8, 1939, at Venlo, Holland, by German S.S. men under Walter Schellenberg for supposedly masterminding the attempt on Hitler's life at a Munich beer hall the same day. Stevens and Best were supposedly negotiating with a group of German dissidents who were in reality S.S. men. Both men spent the remainder of the war in concentration camps.

Stewart, Jimmy (1908–   )
Hollywood actor and Academy Award winner for 1940. He enlisted in the U.S. Army Air Corps eight months prior to the Pearl Harbor attack, becoming the first actor to do so. Stewart had been deferred from the draft because he was underweight (140 pounds) for his height (6′2½″), so he put on ten pounds to barely qualify for enlistment. For a while, he became a bombardier instructor at Moffet Field, California. In 1943 Stewart was transferred to England to the 445th Bombardment Group of the Eighth

Army Air Force, flying twenty-five combat missions in a B-17 named *Four Yanks and a Jerk*. He returned to the States in 1945 with the Distinguished Flying Cross, Air Medal, and Croix de Guerre, and remained in the Air Force Reserve, where he became a general.

Stier

German auxiliary cruiser of World War II. It was the last armed merchantman to break out of the British blockade unscathed in May 1942. Under Captain Horst Gerlach, it sank four Allied ships, totaling 29,409 tons, in the Atlantic from May 20 until September 27, 1942, when it attacked the Liberty ship *Stephen Hopkins*. Although *Stier* sank the ship, she suffered such extensive damage herself that she also sank. The *Stier* was equipped with six 5.9-inch guns as well as 37mm and 20mm antiaircraft guns. The Germans designated it HSK VI or Ship 23, and she was known to the Allies simply as "Raider J."

Stilwell, Joseph W. (1883–1946)

U.S. Army lieutenant general. He was Commander in Chief of the China-Burma-India Theater and Chief of Staff to Chiang Kai-shek. Stilwell had to retreat 140 miles on foot through the jungles of Burma in 1942 ahead of the advancing Japanese. Yet he turned around and beat the Japanese in 1944 in Burma. Stilwell was contemptuous of Chiang, calling him "the Peanut." He was placed in command of the U.S. Tenth Army on Okinawa in 1945. Stilwell, who was nicknamed "Vinegar Joe," was well known for saying what was on his mind. He did not think much of the British and could not understand why we had to help them regain their empire.

MOVIE PORTRAYALS:
Objective Burma (1945), by Erville Anderson
Merrill's Marauders (1962), by John Hoyt
1941 (1979), by Robert Stack

Stimson, Henry L. (1867–1950)

U.S. Secretary of War. He had fought in France in World War I and had been Secretary of War under President Taft. Stimson believed that in World War II Churchill and the British commanders were influenced too much by the experience at Dunkirk in 1940 to effectively head a cross-channel invasion, so he advocated having an American as commander. He drew the first number (158) for the draft of 1940.

MOVIE PORTRAYALS:
Tora! Tora! Tora! (1970), by Joseph Cotten
Churchill and the Generals (1981 TV movie), by Alexander Knox

Stirling
British heavy four-engine bomber weighing forty tons. It was the first heavy bomber to strike Germany in World War II. Unfortunately the Stirling was handicapped with slow speed and a low service ceiling and had many blind spots, making it highly vulnerable to fighter attack.

Stirling, David (1915–)
British Army colonel who founded the L Detachment commandos in North Africa (L Detachment later developed into SAS, supported by the Long Range Desert Group). He was captured at Thala by the Tunisians, who traded him to Field Marshall Erwin Rommel for eleven pounds of tea. The Germans called him the "Phantom Major" because of his exploits behind their lines. Stirling was imprisoned in Colditz Castle.

Stormovik
Russian Ilyushin that was a low-flying, heavily armored, close-support airplane. The Germans called it "flying death" because it was armed with eight rockets under each wing, two heavy cannon, and four machine guns. The Stormovik was used primarily as an antitank close-support aircraft for the Red Army.

Stoyanov, Stoyan
Bulgarian pilot who shot down fourteen aircraft during World War II to become the leading ace of Bulgaria.

Straight Flush
Name of the B-29 photographic and weather plane (#91) that photographed the atomic bomb explosions on Hiroshima and Nagasaki in August 1945. Major Claude Eatherly piloted the *Straight Flush*.

Stranahan, Frank R. (1922–)
U.S. golfer. He was drafted into the U.S. Army, trained as a bomber pilot, and flew over 800 hours in World War II. Stranahan was discharged in October 1945.

Strasbourg
French city liberated by French General Philippe LeClerc's armored force. He announced that five Germans would be shot for every French soldier killed by snipers. The Germans retaliated by saying they would abandon the international rules of warfare.

Eisenhower finally stepped in, giving orders that no Germans would be harmed.

Strasser, Gregor (–1934)

Adolf Hitler's first gauleiter. His secretary was Heinrich Himmler. Gregor and his brother Otto went into the publishing business in the early days of the Nazi party, hiring Joseph Goebbels. Gregor was later executed in the Nazi purges of 1934.

MOVIE PORTRAYALS:
The Hitler Gang (1944), by Fritz Kortner
Hitler (1962), by John Banner

Strasser, Otto (1897–1974)

Brother of Gregor Strasser and leader of the socialists of the early Nazi party. He openly broke with Hitler, fled Germany, and headed a German Fifth Column opposed to Hitler. Goebbels called him Hitler's Public Enemy Number One.

Strathallen, S.S.

American troop transport torpedoed and sunk off Oran in November 1942. General Dwight Eisenhower's driver, Kay Summersby, as well as *Life* magazine photographer Margaret Bourke-White, survived the sinking.

Stratton, Dorothy C. (1899–)

U.S. Coast Guard captain. She commanded the U.S. Coast Guard Women's Reserves (SPARS) in World War II, having been Dean of Women at Purdue University prior to the war.

Strawberries

Name that U.S. paratroopers gave to red marks on the back of the neck received when the parachute opened and the risers struck the skin.

Streeter, Ruth Cheney (1895–)

U.S. Marine Corps Reserve Colonel. She was the director of the Marine Corps Women's Reserve in World War II. Streeter was the first woman to become a Marine major (January 29, 1943); the first to be promoted to lieutenant colonel (November 22, 1943); and the first to wear the rank of colonel (February 17, 1944).

Strehla

Town in Saxony on the Elbe River that was the actual site of the first meeting of the Russians and Americans in the closing days of World War II. A U.S. patrol led by First Lieutenant Albert Kotzebue met a Russian patrol under Lieutenant Colonel Alexander T. Gardiev, but because Kotzebue was not positive of his position, his superors would not give him credit. Instead the first meeting was attributed to the U.S.-Russia meeting at Torgau on April 27, 1945.

Streib, Werner

German Air Force first lieutenant. As a pilot of an ME-110, he shot down a British Whitley bomber on July 20, 1940, in what was the first night fighter victory for the Luftwaffe in World War II. Streib went on to become the fifth-ranking night fighter ace of the war with sixty-six enemy aircraft shot down.

Streicher, Julius (1885–1946)

German anti-Jewish propagandist for the Nazi party. He was an early party member known for his extremism against the Jews and for his pornography collection. Streicher was found guilty at Nuremberg and executed in October 1946.

MOVIE PORTRAYAL:
Hitler (1962), by Theodore Marcuse

Strike Ox

Code name of the British effort to prevent iron ore from being shipped to Germany from Northern Sweden. The secondary objective was the destruction of the heavy water needed to create a German atomic reaction.

Strobing, Irving

U.S. Army radio operator on Corregidor who kept a continuous signal going that told of the conditions and hardships in the last days before the fall of the island to the Japanese in 1942.

Strong, Kenneth (1900–)

British Army brigadier general. He was the chief of intelligence for General Dwight Eisenhower in World War II. Strong was from the Royal Scots Fusiliers and had been deputy military attaché in Berlin prior to the war.

Student, Kurt (1890–1978)

Father of the German parachute branch of the Luftwaffe. He had served as a pilot in World War I, also masterminding the airborne operations in the early days of World War II. Student was accidentally shot in the head during the invasion of Holland in 1940 by a member of the Adolf Hitler Waffen S.S. unit.

von Stuelpnagel, Karl-Heinrich (1886–1944)

German general and military governor of France. As one of the conspirators against Hitler on July 20, 1944, he was arrested and executed by the Gestapo in August 1944.

MOVIE PORTRAYALS:
Rommel: The Desert Fox (1951), by John Goldsworthy
Night of the Generals (1967), by Harry Andrews

von Stuelpnagel, Otto (–1948)
German general and commander in Paris. He was wanted for war crimes in France during World War I, but was never brought to trial. Von Stuelpnagel was arrested for war crimes after World War II, but hanged himself while awaiting trial in Paris in 1948.

Stuka (JU-87)
German dive bomber modeled after a design of the U.S. Navy. It was acclaimed as the wonder weapon of the Luftwaffe. The Stuka prototype was tested in exercises in Russia prior to World War II by the "Black Reichswehr" to circumvent the Versailles treaty. It was armed with two 37mm antitank cannons and was used as a substitute for artillery in close support of the advancing military in World War II. The Stuka was highly vulnerable to fighter aircraft; the British took a high toll in the Battle of Britain.

"Sturgeon No Longer Virgin"
Message sent by Lieutenant Commander W. L. Wright of the submarine *Sturgeon*, when, on the night of January 22, 1942, it torpedoed its first Japanese ship of World War II.

SU-122
Designator of a Soviet tank first used in the Battle of Kursk in July 1943. The SU-122 outclassed all German tanks of the time. It had a 122mm gun mounted on a T-34 chassis, weighed thirty tons, had a range of 375 miles, and could travel thirty-four miles per hour. The SU-122 was the most effective tank destroyer for the Russians in World War II.

SU-152
Soviet tank that weighed forty tons and mounted a 152mm gun.

Submarine Designators (U.S. Navy)
SM—minelaying submarine
SS—submarine
SSA—cargo-carrying submarine
SSK—antisubmarine hunter
SSO—submarine oiler
SSP—troop-carrying submarine

Submarine Prefixes
H.M.A.S.—Australian
H.M.S.—British

I—Japanese
S—United States
U—Germany

Submarine shellings by Japanese of U.S. West Coast

I-17 shelled Goleta, California, on February 13, 1942
I-26 shelled Estewan Point, Vancouver, B.C., on June 20, 1942
I-25 shelled Fort Stevens, Oregon, on June 21, 1942

Suckling, Michael (–1941)

Royal Air Force pilot officer and member of a photo-reconnaissance unit. While flying a Spitfire over Bergen, Norway, May 21, 1941, Suckling spotted and photographed the German battleship *Bismarck*, starting one of the most intensive sea chases in naval history. Suckling was killed exactly two months later on July 21, 1941, on a photo-reconnaissance mission over La Rochelle.

Sudeten Germans

Name given to the German nationals residing in Czechoslovakia. They were used as the pretext by Hitler to annex part of Czechoslovakia, although they did not actually live in Sudetenland, which was northeast of the German settlements.

Sugar

Last food item still rationed by the U.S. government after World War II.

Sugita, Shoici

Japanese number two ace of World War II with eighty aircraft to his credit. He was involved in a dog fight with the U.S. number two ace Thomas McGuire that resulted in McGuire's death on January 7, 1945.

Sullivan Brothers

Five sons of Mr. and Mrs. Thomas E. Sullivan of Waterloo, Iowa. They were killed aboard the U.S.S. *Juneau* on November 14, 1942. The *Juneau* was sunk in the Battle of Guadalcanal. After this tragedy, the U.S. government did not allow brothers to serve on the same ship.

MOVIE PORTRAYALS: *The Sullivans* (1944)

As Sailors	*As Children*
Frank (John Campbell)	(Marvin Davis)
George (James Cardwell)	(Buddy Swan)
Matt (John Alvin)	(John Calkins)
Al (Edward Ryan)	(Bobby Driscoll)
Joe (George Offerman, Jr.)	(Billy Cummings)

Sultan, Daniel I. (1885–1947)

U.S. Army lieutenant general and Inspector General of the Army. He relieved General Joseph Stilwell as commander of the India Burma Theater in 1944. Sultan was the first soldier to receive four Distinguished Service Medals.

Summersby, Kay (1908–1975)

Chauffeur and secretary to General Dwight Eisenhower during World War II. She was the only civilian member of his staff until October 14, 1944, when she joined the U.S. Women's Army Corps (WAC's). Summersby was the first female aide to a five-star general in U.S. Army history and the first British female to enter Berlin. She was also one of three women to witness the German surrender ceremony at Rheims in May 1945. Summersby added to the problems of security for the Normandy invasion because she was born in Ireland. As such, she was not qualified for contact with Bigot personnel, yet she was privy to all top secret information.

MOVIE PORTRAYAL:
Ike (1979 TV movie), by Lee Remick

Sundays

September 3, 1939	Britain declared war on Germany
December 7, 1941	Japanese attack on Pearl Harbor
June 22, 1941	Germany invades Russia
November 9, 1942	North African invasion by the Allies
April 18, 1943	Admiral Yamamoto shot down
September 17, 1944	Operation Market-Garden offensive
April 1, 1945	Invasion of Okinawa
July 1, 1945	Invasion of Balikpapan, Borneo

Superlatives

FUBAR—fouled* up beyond all recognition
FUMTU—fouled* up more than usual
JANFU—joint army navy foul* up
SNAFU—situation normal, all fouled* up
TARFU—things are really fouled* up

Supreme Allied Commanders

Sir Harold Alexander—Mediterranean
Chiang Kai-shek—China
Dwight Eisenhower—Europe

---

*"fouled" being used in place of an expletive deleted.

Douglas MacArthur—Southwest Pacific
Lord Louis Mountbatten—Southeast Asia
Chester Nimitz—Central Pacific

Surcouf

French submarine that was the largest submarine ever built. It displaced 2,880 tons of water, could cruise for 12,000 miles, and carried a seaplane in a hangar located behind the turret. The *Surcouf* was seized by the British on July 3, 1940, and turned over to the Free French. She sank on February 18, 1942, after colliding with a merchant ship in the Caribbean.

Suribachi

Extinct 556-foot volcano on Iwo Jima that was known as the "Japanese Gibraltar." It was the site of two flag raisings by U.S. Marines during the battle for Iwo Jima. The first flag was raised on February 23, 1945, by men of the 3rd Platoon, Company E, 28th Marines. They were Corporal Charles W. Lindberg, First Lieutenant Harold G. Schrier, Sergeant Henry O. Hansen, and Platoon Sergeant Ernest I. Thomas. The flag, taken from the transport *Missoula*, which had taken the platoon to Saipan, measured only 28 by 54 inches and was raised on a piece of Japanese water pipe found by Private First Class Leo J. Rozek. The scene was photographed by Staff Sergeant Louis Lowery of *Leatherneck* magazine. Because the flag was hard to see, another flag was obtained from LST779 on the beach and a second flag raising was staged for photographer Joe Rosenthal. Involved were marines John H. Bradley, Michael Strank, Harlon H. Block, Franklin R. Sousley, Rene A. Gagnon, and Ira H. Hayes.

Susloparov, Ivan

Russian major general of artillery. He represented the Soviet forces at the Rheims surrender of the Germans. Susloparov had been the head of the Russian mission to France and did not have permission from Stalin to sign the papers. He subsequently was called to Berlin and hustled off into oblivion by Soviet secret police.

Sussex

Name of intelligence teams parachuted into France prior to D-Day to harass the Germans. British teams were called Brissex and the American teams Ossex. Over one hundred teams were used.

Susskind, David (1920–)

TV producer. In World War II, he served as a communications officer on a U.S. Navy attack transport and participated in the invasions of Iwo Jima and Okinawa. Susskind was discharged in 1946.

Sutherland, Richard K. (1893–1966)

U.S. Army major general. He was chief of staff to General Douglas MacArthur in World War II.

MOVIE PORTRAYAL:

MacArthur (1977), by Ivan Bonar

Suttill, Francis

British major parachuted into France on October 1, 1942, to set up Resistance units. He worked under the code name *Prosper* and the cover name François Despree until captured and executed by the Germans.

Sutton, Frank (1923–1974)

Hollywood actor who played Marine Sergeant Vince Carter on the TV series ''Gomer Pyle, USMC.'' He actually served in the U.S. Army as a sergeant during World War II.

Swallow

Code name of four Norwegian agents dropped into Norway to disrupt the Norsk Hydro Plant's production of heavy water, which was needed by the Germans to create an atomic bomb.

Swanson, Gloria (1897–)

Hollywood actress. Her son, William, was killed in World War II while a member of the Royal Canadian Air Force.

Swastika

Symbol of Nazi Germany. The design dates back to prehistoric times, with the word itself derived from Sanskrit meaning ''good luck.'' Hitler adapted the symbol from earlier German anti-Jewish organizations that had used it to cover up the Star of David. Nearly every ancient religion of the world used the swastika or a variation.

Swayback Maru

Nickname of the U.S cruiser *Salt Lake City.*

Sweeney, Charles Michael (–1963)

American soldier of fortune. He was admitted as a cadet to West Point in the class of 1904 but dropped out prior to graduation. Sweeney had been a private in the U.S. Army during the Spanish-American War and went on to fight in seven wars under five flags. He joined the French Foreign Legion, rejoining the American Army as a major in World War I. He served in the Turkish Army and the Polish Army as a general. Sweeney went back to the

French Foreign Legion and eventually became a major general. He fought in the Spanish Civil War. When the Russians invaded Finland, he intended to form an American air unit to help the Finns, but the war ended before he could do so. He then organized thirty pilots into a French Air Force unit, which was driven back across the English Channel to England. There he joined the Royal Air Force to become the commanding officer of an Eagle Squadron.

Sweeney, Charles W. (1919–   )

U.S. Army Air Force major. He flew the B-29 *Great Artists*, which accompanied the *Enola Gay* over Hiroshima on August 6, 1945. Three days later, Sweeney piloted *Bock's Car,* which dropped the atomic bomb on Nagasaki.

Sweetheart of Okinawa

U.S. Marine Corps nickname on Okinawa for the Corsair fighter, which served as a close-support aircraft, dropping napalm and rockets on Japanese positions.

Sweet Pea

U.S. Navy nickname for the cruiser *Portland*.

Swett, James E.

U.S. Marine Corps captain. He shot down seven Japanese aircraft over Guadalcanal on April 7, 1943, on his first combat mission. Swett was the first American to shoot down seven enemy aircraft in a single mission, a feat that won him the Congressional Medal of Honor.

Swiss Army

In 1939, the Swiss Army consisted of 400,000 men, 600 rounds of ammunition per man, 44 antiaircraft guns, 835 antitank guns, 121 reconnaissance aircraft, and 86 fighters. Most of the equipment was obsolete, leading to the belief that the army could only hold out for one week. The Swiss embarked on a program to build up their Army so that they could hold out for two years against invaders if necessary.

Switzerland

Country that does not have a Navy. It does, however, have a port, Basle, on the Rhine River.

Swoose

Name of U.S. Army Air Force General George H. Brett's B-17 in the early days of World War II. *Swoose* was the last plane to leave the Philippines.

Sword Beach

D-Day beach assaulted by the British 3rd Division, the 27th Armored Brigade, and the 1st Special Service Brigade Commando on June 6, 1944. It was subdivided into Green Queen, White Queen, and Red Queen; the city of Caen was the objective.

Swordfish

Single-engine British biplane nicknamed "Stringbag." It was primarily used as a torpedo plane, carried a crew of three, had a radius of 200 miles, and could cruise at eighty-seven knots. The Swordfish was used against the *Bismarck*, the *Scharnhorst*, and the *Gneisenau*, and accounted for thousands of tons of Axis shipping in the Mediterranean in World War II.

Swordfish, U.S.S.

U.S. submarine that evacuated Philippine President Manuel Quezon and members of his family and government from Corregidor to Panay in 1942.

Symbol

Allied code name for the January 14–23, 1942, conference at Casablanca between Winston Churchill and Franklin D. Roosevelt.

T

Two Pounds
Amount in British sterling promised to the first person aboard the cruiser H.M.S. *Sheffield* to spot the elusive German battleship *Bismarck* on May 26, 1940.

Three "D" 's of Potsdam
Name given to the Allied policy toward defeated Germany: *d*enazification, *d*emilitarization, and *d*eindustrialization.

Ten Million Crowns
Reward (equal to $403,000) offered by the Gestapo for the capture of the assassins of Reinhard Heydrich in May 1942.

Tenth U.S. Army Air Force
Unit established on February 12, 1942, to command the China-Burma-India Theater.

Twelfth U.S. Army Air Force
Unit established August 20, 1942, to fight in North Africa. The first commander was Lieutenant General James Doolittle.

Thirteenth U.S. Army Air Force
Unit established January 13, 1943 to oppose the Japanese in the Solomon Islands and the Bismarck Archipelago.

20 Grosvenor Square
Address in London of General Dwight Eisenhower's headquarters. In February 1944, it was moved down the street to 47 Grosvenor Square.

263 Prinsengracht
Address of the Amsterdam house in which Anne Frank and seven other Jews hid from the Nazis for two years and one month (1942–1944). It is now the site of the Anne Frank Museum.

(Shelley Winters's Oscar for Best Supporting actress for the 1959 movie *The Diary of Anne Frank* can be seen at the museum.)

2419D

Serial number of the French dining car in which the Germans surrendered in Compiegne at the end of World War I. It was the same car in which Hitler insisted that the French sign their capitulation to Germany on June 22, 1940. The car was later ordered destroyed by Hitler.

Third Front of World War II

Name given to the power of radio during the war. (The other "fronts" were military and economic.)

Third Reich

Adolf Hitler's official designator for the Nazi government of Germany. He maintained it would last for a thousand years.

Third Republic

Official designator of the government of France at the time of its defeat by the Germans in June 1940.

323

Number on the rudder of the Betty bomber in which Admiral Isoruku Yamamoto was shot down on April 18, 1943.

34th Infantry Division

Unit commanded by Major General Russell P. Hartle that was the first U.S. Army unit to be assigned to Great Britain during World War II.

$300,000,000

Reparations agreed to be paid to the Soviet Union by Rumania (September 13, 1944); Finland (September 19, 1944); Hungary (January 21, 1945).

T-34

Soviet tank that was invulnerable to all antitank guns except the German 88mm. It was specially designed to cope with the unique terrain of Russia and was equipped with the extremely wide nineteen-inch treads for traction in mud and snow. The T-34 was the wonder tank of the early days of World War II, amazing the Germans, who had believed that their tanks were superior to all others. They eventually incorporated design features of the T-34 into the Panther and Tiger tanks. The T-34 weighed 54,000 pounds, had a top speed of thirty-three miles per hour, and was protected by sloped armor to ward off antitank rounds. It carried seventy-seven shells of which generally nineteen were armor-piercing, fifty-three were high-explosive, and five were shrapnel.

A major drawback, though, was that only nine shells were readily accessible in racks in the turret; the remainder were under floor mats. The T-34 crews also had problems shifting into high gear; each tank was equipped with a large hammer stored next to the gear shift to pound it into gear.

T-124

British Naval form that civilians were required to sign in order to participate with their boats in the evacuation of Dunkirk. It officially made them volunteers of the Royal Navy for one month.

Taffy 3

Designator of the six CVE escort carriers and seven escort vessels in support of the Leyte landings October, 1944. They fought in the Battle of Samar which was part of the larger Battle of Leyte Gulf. The CVE's were *Fanshaw Bay, St. Lo, White Plains, Kalinin Bay, Kitkun Bay,* and *Gambier Bay.*

Tague, James R.

U.S. Navy captain. He was the only U.S. officer in World War II both to be born in Japan and to become the captain of a U.S. Navy ship, the carrier U.S.S. *Antietam* (CV-36). Tague was born in Kobe on Honshu Island of Methodist missionary parents.

Taiho

Japanese 31,000-ton aircraft carrier. It was the largest Japanese carrier afloat and second only to the U.S.S. *Saratoga*. The *Taiho* was sunk by the submarine U.S.S. *Albacore* on June 19, 1944, when a single torpedo ruptured her fuel tanks. The crew attempted unsuccessfully to pump fuel overboard and a damage control officer ordered vents opened to disperse the fumes, which were then sucked throughout the ship. A spark blew up the carrier, killing 1,500 members of the crew. (Her sister carrier *Shokaku* was sunk by the sister submarine U.S.S. *Cavalla* on the same day in the same area.)

Taiyo

Small Japanese carrier weighing 20,000 tons that was sunk on August 18, 1944, by the submarine U.S.S. *Rasher* under the command of Henry G. Munson.

Takahashi, Kuichi (–1942)

Japanese Navy lieutenant commander who led the dive bombers that attacked Hickam Field and the U.S. Naval Air Station at Pearl Harbor on December 7, 1941. He later led the attack on the destroyer U.S.S. *Sims* and the tanker *Neosho,* sinking both in the opening phase of the Battle of the Coral Sea on May 6, 1942.

Takahashi also led the strike against the carrier U.S.S. *Yorktown* in the same battle and was killed.

Tallboy

A 12,000-pound bomb invented by Barnes Wallis as a scaled-down version of the earthquake bomb. When dropped, it fell faster than the speed of sound and was fitted with fins, making it spin and stabilize itself like a gyroscope. The first use of the Tallboy was by No. 617 Squadron to knock out a railway tunnel, the Saumur Tunnel near the Loire, through which a panzer division was to travel to counterattack the Normandy invasion forces. It was also used to sink the battleship *Tirpitz*.

Tally Ho

Cry devised by Air Vice-Marshall Keith Park for fighter pilots to announce over the radio that they had spotted enemy aircraft. They then gave the type, number, direction of flight, and altitude of the enemy aircraft.

Tanabe, Yahachi

Japanese Navy lieutenant commander. He was in charge of the submarine *I-168* that torpedoed the U.S. carrier *Yorktown* at Midway in June 1942. Tanabe was given command of the *I-176*, which torpedoed and damaged the cruiser U.S.S. *Chester* on October 20, 1942.

Tang, U.S.S.

U.S. submarine commanded by Dick O'Kane that in the short span of only one year (1944) sank twenty-four Japanese ships. It was in turn sunk by one of its own torpedoes on October 24, 1944, when the last torpedo on board malfunctioned and circled back. Nine crew members survived, including O'Kane (see *Tullibee;* H.M.S. *Trinidad*).

Tank, Kurt

German aircraft engineer. He was the technical director of the Focke-Walf complex and designed the FW-190 fighter. After the war, Tank escaped to Argentina, where he helped design jet aircraft.

Taranto

Italian Naval base attacked by British carrier aircraft on November 11, 1940. The British used special shallow-running torpedoes to destroy much of the Italian fleet as it lay at anchor in the shallow harbor, at a cost of only two aircraft. The attack was extensively studied by the Germans and Japanese because it proved that aircraft could sink battleships in shallow waters. The Japanese applied the British techniques to the attack on Pearl Harbor, December 7, 1941.

Tarawa

Atoll of the Gilbert Islands which was needed by the U.S. as a bomber base en route to Tokyo, which was 2,900 miles away. Tarawa was assaulted on November 20, 1943, by U.S. Marines commanded by Colonel David Shoup during Operation Longsuit. The battle cost three times as many American lives as had the initial landings in North Africa a year before. Of 5,000 Japanese defenders, only three prisoners were taken.

Tarfu

American superlative for "things are really fouled up."

Target 42

Designator used by the Germans to indicate London as the target of V-1 attacks.

Target 105

Russian Army designator for the artillery bombardment of the Reichstag building in Berlin.

Target 106

Russian Army designator for the Reich Chancellery building in Berlin.

Tarpan, U.S.S.

U.S. submarine commanded by Tom Wogan. It sank the first German ship to be sunk by an American submarine in World War II, when it torpedoed the auxiliary cruiser *Michell* on March 2, 1943.

Task Forces (U.S. Navy)

#00-09—commanded by the Sea Frontiers
#10-19—part of the First Fleet
#20-29—part of the Second Fleet
#30-39—part of the Third Fleet
#40-49—part of the Fourth Fleet
#50-59—part of the Fifth Fleet
#60-69—part of the Sixth Fleet
#70-79—part of the Seventh Fleet
#80-89—part of the Eighth Fleet
#90-99—part of the Ninth Fleet

Task Force 16

U.S. Navy force commanded by Admiral William F. Halsey, which launched Doolittle's Raid on Tokyo on April 18, 1942. The two carriers were the *Hornet* and the *Enterprise*.

Task Force 17

U.S. Navy unit comprised of the carriers *Yorktown* and *Lexington* under Rear Admiral Frank Fletcher that fought in the Battle of the Coral Sea on May 3, 1942, inflicting the first setback of the war on the Japanese.

Task Force 141

Designator of the planning group that developed the invasion of Sicily in July 1943. It was so named because the members met in Room 141 of the Hotel St. George in Algiers.

Task Force Komet

One of three German groups involved in the capture of Crete in 1941 with the western objectives of Maleme airfield. General Eugene Meindle commanded the force.

Task Force Mars

Second of three German groups that assaulted Crete in 1941. It had the central objectives of Conea, Galatas, and Retino.

Task Force Orion

Third German group involved in the capture of Crete in 1941 with the eastern objective of the town of Heraklion and the nearby airfield. Colonel Hans Brauer was in charge.

Task Force Peiper

Designator of the spearhead of the Sixth Panzer Army in the Battle of the Bulge in December 1944. It was commanded by S.S. Colonel Joachim Peiper, who was later tried for war crimes after part of Task Force Peiper massacred a number of American prisoners at Malmedy, Belgium.

Task Group 16.2

Designator of the U.S. carrier *Hornet* plus escort ships that took Doolittle's Raiders within reach of Japan. It departed Alameda, California, on April 2, 1942, and joined with the *Enterprise* and her support ships (designated Task Group 16.1) to become Task Force 16.

Tattersalls

U.S. code name for the island of Saipan in planning the invasion of Operation Forager.

Tautog, U.S.S.

First U.S. Navy submarine to destroy anything Japanese in World War II when it shot down a Japanese plane during the initial attack on Pearl Harbor. The *Tautog* survived the war and sank more Japanese ships than any other submarine (twenty-six).

Tawi Tawi
Site of the last amphibious operation of World War II on July 1, 1945.

Taylor, Albert Hoyt (1879–1961)
U.S. scientist known as the "father of radar."

Taylor, Maxwell D. (1901–)
U.S. Army major general and commander of the 101st Airborne Division. In 1943, he slipped through German lines while wearing his uniform and traveling to Rome for armistice talks with Italian Premier Pietro Badoglio.

Taylor, Napoleon E.
U.S. Army private and orderly of Major Charles S. Ward of the 41st Engineers. Taylor is credited with being the first American to land in North Africa on June 17, 1942.

Taylor, Robert (1911–1969)
Hollywood actor. He enlisted in the U.S. Navy in February 1943 as Lieutenant Spangler Arlington Brugh, his real name. Taylor became a flight instructor since he was too old for combat flying and was discharged in November 1945. He narrated the 1944 movie *The Fighting Lady.*

MOVIE PORTRAYAL:
Moviola (1980 TV miniseries), by Terrance McNally

T Card
U.S. gas rationing card that entitled the holder to unlimited gasoline. Truckers fell under this category.

TD Tablet
OSS drug used to force prisoners to talk under interrogation.

Teague, Olin (1911–1981)
U.S. Congressman from Texas. In World War II, he served as a colonel and was highly decorated for bravery.

Tedder, Sir Arthur (1890–1967)
British Air Marshall and Deputy Supreme Allied Commander under General Dwight Eisenhower. He devised the method of "carpet bombing," using hundreds of aircraft to bomb a path for ground troops through German minefields and fortifications.

MOVIE PORTRAYALS:
Patton (1970), by Gerald Flood
Ike (1979 TV movie), by Terrence Alexander

Teetotalers
Richard Bong—U.S. ace

James Doolittle—U.S. General
Albert Einstein—physicist
Henry Ford—industrialist
Adolf Hitler—dictator
Bernard Montgomery—British Field Marshall
Benito Mussolini—Italian dictator
Edward Stettinius—U.S. Secretary of State
Henry Wallace—U.S. Vice-President

Teheran

Site of an Allied conference in Iran attended by Franklin Roosevelt, Winston Churchill, and Joseph Stalin. Prior to this, it had been the headquarters of all Axis espionage in the Middle East.

Telegraph Cottage

Name of General Dwight Eisenhower's retreat and hideaway outside London in World War II. It was selected by Ike's naval aide Harry Butcher, who did not know that a half mile away was a decoy to lure German bombers from their intended targets, so that they would drop their bombs "harmlessly" away from London.

Telek

Name of General Dwight Eisenhower's Scottie dog given to him by his staff as a birthday present. He was named after Telegraph Cottage and Kay Summersby, Ike's chauffeur. His mate was Caacie (pronounced Khaki) after Canine Auxiliary Air Corps and was purchased in Washington by Harry Butcher. Their offspring were Junior and Rubev.

Teller, Edward (1908–)

Hungarian-born father of the H-bomb. He fled Europe because of the anti-Semitism of the Nazis.

Tenaru River

Intended site of major battle on Guadalcanal. It was actually fought on the Ilu River, where U.S. Marines wiped out the Japanese troops of the Ichiki detachment, led by Kiyano Ichiki. Ichiki committed hara-kiri.

Tennessee, U.S.S.

U.S. battleship that was damaged at Pearl Harbor on December 7, 1941. It was repaired and fought in the Battle of Leyte Gulf on October 20, 1944.

Terboven, Josef (1898–1945)

Nazi commissioner for Norway during World War II. He is said to have blown himself up with dynamite at the end of the war.

Terminal

Code name for the Potsdam Conference, July 17, 1945, to August 2, 1945, between Truman, Stalin, and Churchill.

Terrible Three

Name given by the Germans to three U.S. Army Air Force fighter aces, Hubert Zemke, Francis Gabreski, and David Schilling. All flew P-47's with the 56th Fighter Group of the U.S. Eighth Army Air Force in England.

Terry and the Pirates

Cartoon strip in World War II drawn by Milton Caniff. Colonel Flip Corkin is believed to be modeled after U.S. Brigadier General Philip C. Cochran.

Texas, U.S.S.

U.S. battleship that fought in support of the D-Day landings. It was damaged by return fire while shelling the forts of Cherbourg on June 25, 1944. The *Texas* also supported the invasions of North Africa, Southern France, Iwo Jima, and Okinawa.

Texas, Nevada, and Arkansas

Three U.S. battleships present at Normandy on June 6, 1944. The *Nevada* had also been present at Pearl Harbor on December 7, 1941.

Thach, John Smith (1905–   )

U.S. Navy captain. He was serving aboard the carrier *Saratoga* at the outbreak of World War II, then transferred to the *Lexington* for the Battle of the Coral Sea. Thach devised fighter tactics, among them the "Thach Weave," in which fighters flew across the path of other fighters to give better protection.

There Are No Atheists in Foxholes

Slogan made famous by *Reader's Digest* magazine. It also appeared in the 1942 movie *Wake Island*.

Theresienstadt

Nazi concentration camp in Czechoslovakia reserved for privileged Jews exempted from extermination camps. These included Jews who had won the First Class Iron Cross, senior civil servants, those with foreign reputations or influential foreign friends, etc. It was the only camp directly commanded by Adolf Eichmann and visited regularly by the International Red Cross.

Thiel, Werner (1907–1942)

German spy who landed in Florida from the submarine *U-584* on June 17, 1942, as part of Operation Pastorius. He had lived in the

U.S. from 1927 to 1939, then returned to Germany where he joined the Abwehr. Thiel was executed on August 8, 1942.

"This Is Jairmany Calling"

Opening phrase of William Joyce's evening propaganda broadcast from Germany to the British Isles.

"This Is London"

Opening line of Edward R. Murrow's evening CBS radio news show during World War II.

"This Is the Army"

Broadway play that opened on July 4, 1942. It toured the U.S., then went to military bases in Europe, Africa, and Australia. Irving Berlin sang "Oh, How I Hate to Get Up In the Morning" in his World War I uniform. Two other songs that were made popular were "This Is the Army, Mr. Jones," and "I Left My Heart at the Stage Door Canteen."

This Is the Army

Warner Bros. movie of 1943 starring George Murphy and Joan Leslie which was based on the Irving Berlin Broadway play. In the movie, George Murphy played the father of Ronald Reagan. The film was described by the *New York Times* as "the freshest, the most endearing, the most rousing musical tribute to the American fighting man that has come out of World War II." The movie and play made over $10,000,000, which was donated to the Army Emergency Relief fund.

Thomas, Charles

U.S. Army captain. He was the first living black to be awarded the Distinguished Service Cross in World War II. Thomas was given the medal in March 1945.

Thompson, John N.

First war correspondent ever to accompany U.S. parachute troops on a combat mission. He jumped in Algeria and later in Sicily as a reporter for the *Chicago Tribune*.

Thompson, Robert L.

U.S. Army technical sergeant who was driving the Army GMC truck that collided with General George S. Patton's Cadillac on December 9, 1945, resulting in Patton's broken neck. Thompson was driving without orders and joyriding after a night of beer drinking.

Thor

Name of a German armed merchant raider commanded by Captain

Otto Kahler. *Thor* operated in the Atlantic from June 6, 1940, to April 30, 1941, accounting for twelve Allied ships totaling 96,602 tons. It also sank the British armed merchant ship *Voltaire* and damaged the *Alcantara* and *Carnarvon Castle*. The Germans designated the *Thor* HSK IV or Ship 10.

Thor

Name of a 24.2-inch siege mortar with a sixteen-foot barrel used by the Germans in the attack on Sevastapol to fire a shell that weighed two and a quarter tons. It was also used in the siege of Brest-Litovsk and Stalingrad. After gathering dust in a Berlin warehouse, *Thor* was moved to Paris in 1944 in order to defend or destroy Paris, whichever was needed. *Thor* was also called "Karl" after its inventor, General Karl Becker.

Thorpe, Elizabeth

Spy for the BSC in the U.S. who was credited with obtaining the Naval codes from the Italian embassy that resulted in a series of British victories in the Mediterranean. Thorpe, code-named Cynthia, was also responsible for getting the French Naval codes in preparation for Operation Torch.

MOVIE PORTRAYAL:
A Man Called Intrepid (1979), by Gayle Hunnicutt

Thresher, U.S.S.

First U.S. submarine attacked by friendly forces in World War II. It was fired on by surface vessels and bombed by aircraft outside Pearl Harbor shortly after the Japanese attack on December 7, 1941. The *Thresher* later served as a weather-reporting ship in Tokyo Bay for the Doolittle Raid of April 18, 1942.

Thunderbolt IV

Name of Lieutenant Colonel Creighton Abrams's tank during his drive to relieve Bastogne during the Battle of the Bulge.

Thunder From Heaven

Motto of the U.S. 17th Airborne Division in World War II.

Thurmond, J. Strom (1902–   )

Governor of South Carolina. He enlisted in the U.S. Army on December 11, 1941, serving in the 82nd Airborne Division. Thurmond was wounded at Normandy. After V-E day, he transferred to the Pacific where he was stationed in the Philippines. Thurmond was discharged as a lieutenant colonel in January 1946, having been awarded the Legion of Merit, Purple Heart, Bronze Star, and several foreign decorations.

Thyssen, Fritz (1873–1951)

German industrialist who had been an early supporter of Hitler and the Nazi party. He fled to Switzerland at the beginning of World War II, was tried by the Allies after the war for his minor role in the rise of the Nazis, and found guilty. Thyssen fled to Argentina, where he later died.

MOVIE PORTRAYAL:
The Hitler Gang (1944), by Lionel Royce

Tibbets, Paul, Jr. (1915–   )

U.S. Army Air Force colonel who flew the B-29 *Enola Gay* that dropped the atomic bomb on Hiroshima on August 6, 1945. He piloted the first B-17 to cross the English Channel and bomb German-occupied Europe in the Rouen-Sotteville Raid, which was the first mission of the Eighth Army Air Force of World War II. As a major, Tibbets flew General Mark Clark to Gibraltar so he could board the H.M.S. *Seraph* en route to secret meetings in North Africa. On November 5, 1942, he transported General Dwight Eisenhower to Gibraltar preparatory to the invasion of North Africa in a B-17 named *Red Gremlin*. Tibbets also piloted the first B-17 to bomb North Africa during the Allied invasion of November 1942.

MOVIE PORTRAYALS:
The Beginning or the End (1947), by Barry Nelson
Above and Beyond (1953), by Robert Taylor
Enola Gay (1980), by Patrick Duffy

Tiger

Code name of a practice maneuver by the U.S. 4th Infantry Division to ascertain its effectiveness in an amphibious landing. This was to prepare for the Normandy invasion of D-Day, June 6, 1944.

Tiger P

Porsche version of the Tiger tank or Mark VI built by the Krupp Works. It lacked secondary armament of machine guns and was therefore highly vulnerable to infantry.

Tiger Tank

German heavy tank weighing sixty-three tons. It carried an 88mm gun, was protected by seven-inch-thick armor on the front, and could outgun any Allied tank in the field. On the other hand, the Tiger was only equipped with a 650-horsepower engine, giving it a range of only sixty miles and a top speed of twelve miles per hour. It frequently broke down.

***Time* magazine Man of the Year**

1938—Adolf Hitler
1939—Joseph Stalin
1940—Winston Churchill
1941—Franklin D. Roosevelt
1942—Joseph Stalin
1943—George C. Marshall
1944—Dwight D. Eisenhower

Timoshenko, Semyon (1895–1970)

Soviet Marshall. He became the first World War II hero of Russia when he prevented the German capture of Moscow. Timoshenko then took over command of the southern sector, where he failed to stop the German advance into the Crimea. He was thus transferred to a quieter area. Timoshenko was later downgraded to a position at Stalin's headquarters.

Timmerman, Karl

U.S. Army second lieutenant. He was the first officer to cross the bridge at Remagen over the Rhine River in March 1945. Timmerman was a high school graduate of West Point, Nebraska.

Tin Can

U.S. Navy slang term for a destroyer.

Tin Fish

U.S. Navy slang term for a torpedo.

Tinian

Island of Micronesia where U.S. B-29s were based that bombed Hiroshima and Nagasaki in August 1945. Tinian had been invaded on July 23, 1944, taking nine days for its capture.

Tinker, Clarence L. (–1942)

First American major general missing in action in World War II. He disappeared on a flight off Midway on June 7, 1942, during the Battle of Midway. Tinker was posthumously awarded a Distinguished Service Medal.

Tinker, Frank G.

First American to shoot down an ME-109 on July 13, 1937, in Spain. He was flying a Rata fighter in a squadron primarily made up of Russians who fought for the Loyalists in the Spanish Civil War.

Tiny Tim

Name given to the largest rocket developed by the Allies in World

War II. Weighing 1,824 pounds, it was ten feet long and eleven and three-quarters inches in diameter. The Tiny Tim was designed to be fired from an aircraft. It gave a group of Grumman Hellcat fighters the same firepower as a division of heavy cruisers.

Tirpitz

German battleship weighing 42,000 tons that was launched on April 1, 1939. It had 138,000-horsepower engines, could do thirty-one knots and carried a crew of 2,500 men. The British pursued the *Tirpitz* from the time it was commissioned in 1941 until November 12, 1944, when it was sunk by the 12,000-pound bombs of No. 617 Squadron off Tromso Harbor in northern Norway. Over 1,400 members of her crew died, including the captain. In three and a half years of existence, the *Tirpitz* failed ever to sink a ship.

Tirpitz Pier

Name of the jetty into the Bay of Kiel from which German submarines departed at the beginning of World War II. It was named after the founder of the modern German Navy, Admiral Alfred von Tirpitz.

Tiso, Josef (1887–1946)

Prime minister of an independent Slovakia under the auspices of Nazi Germany. Tiso, who was also a Catholic priest, was tried after the war for collaborating with the Germans and hanged on December 3, 1946.

Tito, Josip Broz (1892–1980)

Communist partisan leader in Yugoslavia during World War II. During the Spanish Civil War, he had gone to Paris as an undercover communist agent to supply volunteers to fight for Loyalist Spain. Tito traveled with forged papers as a Czech named Jaromir Havlicek, sending 1,500 Yugoslavian volunteers to Spain. The Russians gave him the code name Valter.

Tobiason, Reba (1920–1981)

U.S. Army nurse. She is believed to be the only American female captured by the Germans in World War II. Tobiason was assigned to the Ninth Army Air Force, when her aircraft was shot down near Aachen on September 27, 1944. She was sent to a solitary cell at Stalag Luft 9 because the Germans had no facilities for female prisoners of war. Tobiason was finally included in an exchange of prisoners in February 1945, after which she was awarded the Air Medal and the Purple Heart.

Tobruk

Libyan harbor and fortress that became prominent as a key to the fighting in North Africa. It was captured by the British along with 25,000 Italian prisoners on January 22, 1941. The Axis began a counteroffensive that lasted from mid-April to December 10, 1941, when the British, in a second drive through North Africa, pushed the Axis forces back across Libya. Rommel began his own counter-offensive and subsequently captured Tobruk after a four-day siege ending June 21, 1941, in the capture of 33,000 British troops.

Todd, Mike (1907–1958)

Movie producer and one-time husband of actress Elizabeth Taylor. Todd was the first American civilian to enter Berlin in 1945, just after the fall of Nazi Germany.

Todd, Richard (1919–)

British actor. In World War II, he served six years with the British Army as a commando, an armored cavalryman, and a paratrooper. Todd jumped at Normandy and was one of the first British airborne officers to land on D-Day. He fought across France and Germany, serving in Palestine after the war. He was discharged in June 1946.

Todt, Fritz (1891–1942)

German engineer. He was the reorganizer of German industry and was the builder of the well-known *autobahns* and the West Wall. Todt was killed in an aircraft accident in February 1942, when his airplane attempted to take off from Hitler's headquarters at Rastenburg.

Togo, Shigenori (1882–1950)

Japanese foreign minister under Premier Hideki Tojo. He had been a delegate to the Versailles Peace Conference in 1919. Togo was put on trial by the Allies for war crimes and sentenced to 20 years' imprisonment. He died in prison.

To Hell And Back

Title of the autobiography of actor Audie Murphy, the most decorated U.S. soldier of World War II. Audie Murphy portrayed himself (Gordon Gebert played Murphy as a boy) in the 1955 movie *To Hell and Back,* which was based on the book of the same name.

To hell with Roosevelt, to hell with Babe Ruth, to hell with Roy Acuff.

Insult yelled by Japanese soldiers to American GI's during World War II.

Tojo, Hideki (1884–1948)

Wartime Premier of Japan. He had commanded Japanese troops in Manchuria prior to World War II. He was made Chief of Staff of the Kwantung Army in June 1937, Minister of War in July 1940, and Prime Minister from October 1941 until July 1944. Tojo was in a light plane on an inspection tour of military bases when Doolittle's Raiders bombed Tokyo on April 18, 1942. A B-25 came so close that he could see the pilot, although the American bomber never fired a shot. Tojo and his entire cabinet was forced to resign because of the fall of Saipan, and he was placed on the list of retired Army officers on July 20, 1944, the day of the attempted assassination of Hitler half a world away. After the war, he attempted to kill himself using an American 38-caliber pistol. Ironically, his life was saved by an American doctor, who gave him a blood transfusion with American blood. In the end, he was found guilty of war crimes and executed by the Americans in 1948.

MOVIE PORTRAYAL:
Tora! Tora! Tora! (1970), by Asao Uchida

Tokyo

Japanese capital that was firebombed the nights of March 9 and 10, 1945, by 334 B-29's. Over one million people were left homeless and between 83,000 and 125,000 were killed. Over a quarter of Tokyo was destroyed in a raid that completely overwhelmed the Japanese defenses. The raid had been planned by General Curtis LeMay, without official approval or permission.

Tokyo Express

Name given to the Imperial Japanese Navy's nightly runs between Rabaul and Guadalcanal to reinforce and supply the Japanese troops fighting there. The name originally was Cactus Express, but correspondents thought that American readers would not associate Cactus with Guadalcanal and coined the term *Tokyo Express*.

Tokyo Military Tribunal

Allied military trial of twenty-eight Japanese war criminals. It was held in the building that had been the Japanese War Ministry on a hill behind the Emperor's palace. Eleven nations were represented and the trial cost nine million dollars and used 100 tons of paper. Seven of the defendants were sentenced to death, including Tojo; sixteen others received life imprisonment, one was sent to a mental hospital, and two died in prison. Those sentenced to death were

General Hideki Tojo—Premier of Japan
General Kenji Doihara—engineered the Mukden Incident of 1931
General Heitaro Kimura—commander of Manchuria
General Iwane Matsui—commanded troops in the Rape of Nanking
General Akira Muto—Chief of Staff, Philippines
Koki Hirota—Premier (1936–1937)
Seishiro Itagaki—War Minister

Tokyo Rose (1916–)

Pseudonym of Iva Ikuo Toguri d'Aquino, who broadcast English programming to Allied troops in the Pacific as part of Japanese propaganda. When she first began broadcasting, she went by the name Ann, which was short for announcer. D'Aquino was pardoned by President Gerald Ford on his last day in office, January 19, 1977.

Tokyo Rose

Name of a reconnaissance version of a B-29 that was the first American aircraft over Tokyo since the Doolittle Raid in 1942. *Tokyo Rose* was flown by Captain Ralph D. Steakley on November 12, 1944, taking over 700 pictures in thirty-five minutes over the city. Steakley was awarded a Distinguished Flying Cross for this mission.

Tolbukhin, Fedor I. (1894–1949)

Marshall of the Soviet Union. His Army broke through German lines in November 1942 to complete the encirclement of the German Sixth Army at Stalingrad. Tolbukhin later helped drive the Germans out of the southern Ukraine and the Balkans.

Tolley, Kemp

U.S. Navy officer. As a lieutenant at the outbreak of World War II, he commanded the U.S.S. *Lanikai* and later became the assistant military attaché in Moscow. Tolley was a 1929 graduate of Annapolis and became an admiral.

Tompkins, Peter

OSS chief of the Naples section. He infiltrated into Rome on January 21, 1944, and was protected by a Fascist police officer as he gathered intelligence. Tompkins's code name was Pietro.

Tom Thumb

Nickname of five foot, four inch tall British Vice-Admiral Tom Phillips, who commanded the *Prince of Wales* and *Repulse* when they were sunk by Japanese aircraft on December 10, 1941. He went down with his ship, the *Prince of Wales*.

Tonan Maru II

Japanese merchant ship sunk twice by American submarines, the first time by the *Amberjack* on October 10, 1942. After being salvaged, she was again torpedoed and sunk on August 21, 1944, by the *Pintado*. Coincidentally, Captain Bernard "Chick" Clarey, the *Pintado*'s commander, had been executive officer aboard the *Amberjack* when it first sank the *Tonan Maru II*.

Topp, Erich (1914–)

German Navy officer. He was the third-top-scoring submarine ace of World War II, having sunk thirty-four ships totaling 193,684 tons, including a destroyer. Topp commanded *U-57* from July 1940 to September 1940 and *U-552* from February 1941 until August 1942.

Tora! Tora! Tora!

Signal sent by Mitsuo Fuchida back to the carrier *Akagi* to let the Japanese fleet know that total surprise had been achieved at Pearl Harbor on December 7, 1941. Because of unusual atmospheric conditions, this message skipped across the Pacific and was received in Tokyo as well as aboard Admiral Yamamoto's flagship at anchor in Hiroshima Bay.

Toraplane

Name of a flying torpedo developed to be released at 1,500 feet and fly into the water at a predetermined entry angle.

Torgau

Officially recognized site of the first meeting of the Russian and American armies in the closing days of the war in Europe. The U.S. 69th Infantry Division met the Russian 58th Guards Division on April 25, 1945, on a bridge over the Elbe River. The U.S. patrol members were Second Lieutenant William D. Robertson, Sergeant James J. McDonnell, Corporal Frank B. Huff, and Corporal Paul Staub. All were promoted one grade by General Dwight Eisenhower. The first real meeting of the Russians and Americans took place earlier at Strehla, just up the river (see Strehla).

Torpedo Juice

Alcohol (160-proof) which many submarine crews drained from torpedoes and then strained through bread to rid it of a chemical added to render it undrinkable.

Torpedo Junction

Name given to the area in the Coral Sea between Espiritu Santo and Guadalcanal. The battleship *North Carolina* and the destroyer *O'Brian* were torpedoed and damaged on September 15, 1942, while the carrier *Wasp* was torpedoed and sunk on the same day.

Torsk, U.S.S.

Submarine that fired the last shot (a torpedo) of World War II, 2117 GMT, August 14, 1945, sinking a Japanaese ship.*

Toulon

French port and anchorage of the French fleet. The Germans attempted to seize it on November 27, 1942, but all ships were scuttled under the orders of French Admiral de Laborde. As a result, 230,000 tons of naval shipping were sunk, including three battleships, seven cruisers, twenty-eight destroyers, and twenty submarines. The battleships were the *Dunkerque*, *Strasbourg*, and *Provence*. The cruisers were the *Algerie*, *Colbert*, *Foch*, *Dupleix*, *Jean de Vienne*, *La Galissonnaire*, and *La Marseillaise*.

Tower of London

British prison and fortress on the Thames river in London. German agent Eddie Chapmann was a red-coated guard of the Tower before the war. From 1933 to 1938, Norman Baillie-Stewart, known as the "officer in the Tower," was imprisoned there for selling secrets to the Germans. Rudolf Hess was imprisoned there after his flight to England on May 10, 1941. The Traitor's Gate, a well-known portion of the Tower, was damaged by V-1 flying bombs in 1944. The moat around the fortress was plowed up in World War II and planted with vegetables to alleviate the food shortage.

Towers, Jack

U.S. Navy vice-admiral who commanded U.S. Navy aviation in the Pacific during World War II. In 1913, he taught P.N.L. Bellinger to fly. (Bellinger commanded Navy aviation in the Atlantic during World War II.) Towers commanded NC-3 on the historic Atlantic crossing of May 1919.

Towers, John Henry (1885–)

U.S. Navy admiral and chief of the Bureau of Aeronautics. He

---

*Although Torsk was the last U.S. submarine to sink a Japanese vessel during World War II, it was not the last U.S. submarine to sink a Japanese ship. On April 8, 1981, the nuclear submarine *George Washington* accidentally collided with and sank the Japanese freighter *Nissho Maru* in the East China Sea.

had been taught to fly by Glenn Curtis, becoming the number three Navy aviator.

Towle, John R. (–1944)

U.S. Army private and only Congressional Medal of Honor winner in World War II in the 82nd Airborne Division. (The only CMH winner for the 82nd in World War I was Sergeant Alvin C. York.) Towle received his medal for action in Holland during Operation Market-Garden on September 21, 1944. He was killed in action by a mortar while holding off German tanks with a bazooka.

Townsend, Peter (1914–)

Royal Air Force group captain. He was the first R.A.F. pilot to bring down a German plane on British soil, when on February 3, 1940, he shot down an HE-111 bomber. Townsend is credited with eleven enemy aircraft for World War II.

Tracers

Bullets with flammable material that left a trail so that the weapon firer could see where they went. The Americans used red for tracers and the Germans used silver.

von Trapp, Georg

Head of the von Trapp family made famous in the 1965 movie musical *Sound of Music*. His father-in-law, Robert Whitehead, invented the torpedo, and von Trapp fired the first torpedo used in a naval engagement in World War I. His first wife was Jewish, making his seven children half-Jews; this is why he and his family fled Austria after the Anschluss.

MOVIE PORTRAYAL:

The Sound of Music (1965), by Christopher Plummer

Trautloft, Hannes

German Air Force officer. He flew the first combat sortie of an ME-109 in Spain with the Condor Legion on January 20, 1937. Trautloft ended World War II as a colonel with fifty-seven aircraft to his credit.

Travis, Merle (1917–)

Country-western composer and singer who wrote "Sixteen Tons" and "Smoke, Smoke, Smoke That Cigarette." He served in the military in World War II and appeared in the 1953 movie *From Here to Eternity* as a soldier assigned to Scofield Barracks at the time the Japanese attacked Pearl Harbor. In the movie, Travis sang "Reenlistment Blues."

Travis, Robert F. (1904–1950)

U.S. Army Air Force general. He was killed in a crash of a B-29 in 1950 at Fairfield Suisun Air Base, which was later renamed Travis Air Force Base in his honor.

MOVIE PORTRAYAL:
The Wings of Eagles (1957), by James Todd

Treason

Six U.S. citizens who were tried and convicted of treason after World War II were Robert Best, Douglas Chandler, Iva d'Aquino, Mildred Gillars, Atooya Kawakita, and Martin Monti. The poet Ezra Pound was indicted but not put on trial, due to insanity.

Treasure

Code name of the XX Committee double agent Lily Sergeyev who fed information back to the Germans in World War II.

Treaty of Moscow

Treaty that ended the war between Finland and Russia on March 13, 1940. The Finns lost ten percent of their territory and thirteen percent of their economic base.

Treblinka

Nazi extermination camp located in a pine forest sixty-two miles northwest of Warsaw. It was ranked as fourth among the death camps, behind Auschwitz, Buchenwald, and Dachau. Over 700,000 people were sent to Treblinka, and there are only forty known survivors. It was commanded by Franz Stangl. The Germans attempted to erase all traces of the camp, even sending S.S. guards to fight Yugoslavian partisans with the hope that they would be killed.

Tregaskis, Richard (1916-1973)

American war correspondent for the International News Service on Guadalcanal and author of the bestseller *Guadalcanal Diary*. Tregaski later went to Italy where he was seriously wounded in the head in 1943.

MOVIE PORTRAYAL:
Guadalcanal Diary (1943), by Reed Hadley

Trenchard, Sir Hugh (1873–1956)

Royal Air Force air marshall who preserved the R.A.F. through the years of appeasement prior to World War II.

Trepper, Leopold (1904–)

Polish Jew who served as a Soviet agent in Paris in the early days of World War II. Trepper, who was also known as the "Grand

Chef,'' was the head of the spy ring Red Orchestra. Under the alias Gilbert, he fed very accurate information back to Stalin about Operation Barbarossa. The Germans moved in on the Red Orchestra, but Trepper fled to unoccupied France where he established another spy network. Trepper was captured by the Germans on November 16, 1942, agreed to become a double agent, escaped, and hid for the rest of the war.

Tricycle

Code name of German agent Dusko Popov. He agreed to become a double agent for the Allies and came to the U.S. to get information on the Pearl Harbor defenses for the Japanese. J. Edgar Hoover knew about the interest in Pearl Harbor, but paid no attention to it because he did not like Popov.

Trident

Code name of the Washington Conference between Winston Churchill and Franklin Roosevelt in May 1943.

Trigger, U.S.S.

U.S. submarine that torpedoed the Japanese carrier *Hitaka* on June 10, 1943, on its maiden voyage outside Tokyo Bay. Edward L. Beach was engineering officer on the *Trigger* at the time.

Trinidad, H.M.S.

British cruiser that, while guarding a Murmansk convoy in March 1942, fired a torpedo at a German destroyer, but the torpedo circled back and struck her. The *Trinidad* was put out of action but safely limped into Murmansk (see U.S.S. *Tang*).

Trinity

Code name of the first atomic bomb test. It was held at Alamogordo, New Mexico, at 5:30 A.M. on July 16, 1945, the dawn of the atomic age.

Tripartite Pact

Agreement signed on September 27, 1940, between Germany, Italy, and Japan to last for ten years. It included economic, political, and military provisions and gave Germany control over Europe, Italy control over the Mediterranean, and Japan control of the Orient. The signators were Hitler for Germany, Count Ciano for Italy, and Saburo Kurusu, the Japanese ambassador to Germany. The Tripartite Pact was joined by Hungary on November 20, 1940, and by Rumania on November 23, 1940.

Triton, H.M.S.

British submarine that sank its sister submarine H.M.S. *Oxley* on September 10, 1939, off the Norwegian coast. Ironically, the

Oxley was the first ship sunk by the British Navy in World War II.

Trout

Royal Air Force code word for the thousand-plane raid of Cologne on May 30, 1942, in Operation Millennium. Actually, only about 900 planes bombed the target, but the British didn't let that fact stand in the way of a good propaganda campaign.

Trout, U.S.S.

U.S. submarine that carried twenty tons of gold and silver as ballast from the Philippines to Pearl Harbor in 1942, to keep it from falling into the hands of the Japanese. Michael Fenno, commander of the *Trout*, had attempted to get twenty-five tons of sandbags for ballast, but the sandbags were needed by the besieged Allied forces. They offered him the gold and silver instead. At a time when good news was rare, this made the headlines; Fenno was awarded the Army Distinguished Service Cross and the rest of *Trout*'s crew were given Silver Stars. On August 28, 1942, *Trout*, now under Lawson P. Ramage, torpedoed and damaged the Japanese light carrier *Taiyo* near Truk. It was the first Japanese carrier hit by a U.S. submarine in World War II.

Truan, Fritz G. (–1944)

World championship cowboy (rodeo rider). He was a sergeant in the U.S. Army in World War II and died on Iwo Jima.

Truant, H.M.S.

British submarine that, on April 9, 1940, torpedoed the German cruiser *Karlsruhe* off the Norwegian coast, damaging it so badly that it had to be abandoned.

Truk

Japanese anchorage in the Carolines. It was attacked February 17–18, 1944, by aircraft from Admiral Marc Mitscher's task force, who dropped thirty times the amount of explosives used by the Japanese on Pearl Harbor. The Japanese lost a major portion of their fleet, causing the attack to be known as the "Japanese Pearl Harbor."

Truman, Harry S (1884–1972)

Successor of Franklin D. Roosevelt as President of the U.S. He was sworn in on April 12, 1945, by Chief Justice Harlan Stone. On May 8, 1945, Truman was sixty-one years old; it was the day on which Germany surrendered.

MOVIE PORTRAYALS:

The Beginning of the End (1946), by Art Baker

The Man from Independence (1974), by Robert Vaughn
Give 'Em Hell, Harry (1975), by James Whitmore
Truman at Potsdam (1976 TV movie), by Ed Flanders
Collision Course (1976), by E. G. Marshall
MacArthur (1977), by Ed Flanders
Harry S Truman: Plain Speaking (1977), by Ed Flanders
Tail Gunner Joe (1977 TV movie), by Robert Symonds
Backstairs at the White House (1979 TV miniseries), by Harry Morgan
Enola Gay (1980 TV movie), by Ed Nelson
Eleanor, First Lady of the World (1982 TV movie), by Richard McKenzie

Truman, Louis W. (1908–)

Nephew of Harry S Truman. He graduated from the U.S. Military Academy of West Point in 1932 and served as Chief of Staff of the U.S. 84th Infantry Division in Europe from 1944 to 1946.

Trumbauer, Frankie (1900–1956)

Jazz musician of the 1920's and 1930's. During World War II he served as a test pilot.

Trumpets of Jericho

Name given to the sirens attached to the wings of Stuka dive bombers in order to terrorize the enemy.

Truscott, Lucian K. (1895–1965)

U.S. Army officer. He was the founder of the American Rangers and the ranking U.S. officer of the Dieppe Raid in 1942. Truscott later commanded the U.S. Fifth Army in Italy.

MOVIE PORTRAYALS:
Darby's Rangers (1958), by Willis Bouchey
Patton (1970), by John Doucette
Ike (1979), by Charles Gray

Truscott Trotters

Nickname given to the U.S. 3rd Infantry Division on Sicily because of the speed with which it advanced.

Tube Alloys

Code name of the British atomic bomb project in World War II.

Tuck, Robert Stanford (1916–)

Royal Air Force fighter pilot officially credited with twenty-nine aircraft. He was shot down and captured in 1942, but later escaped from Germany to Russia and eventually found his way back to Italy in 1945.

Tuesday

Day of the week on which the American public was urged to eat a meatless diet by the U.S. government to conserve meat during World War II.

Tullibee, U.S.S.

U.S. submarine that is believed to have sunk itself with a circular running torpedo on March 30, 1944, in the Palaus. The only survivor was Gunner's Mate C. W. Kuykendall, who was captured and beaten by the Japanese, spending the rest of the war in the copper mines in Ashio, Japan (see *Tang; Trinidad*).

Tupolev, Andrei N. (1888–1973)

Soviet General and aircraft designer. He spent five years in prison for defending a friend in the purge trials of 1936; he designed several Russian bombers while in prison.

Turkey

Mideast country that was the only source of chrome for Germany. It severed diplomatic relations with the Axis powers on August 2, 1944.

Turner, Richard Kelly (1885–1961)

U.S. Navy rear admiral. As a captain, he commanded the cruiser *Astoria* that returned the ashes of a Japanese ambassador to Japan. Turner, whose personal motto was "If you don't have losses, you're not doing enough!" commanded the amphibious forces at Guadalcanal.

Tweed, George Ray

U.S. Navy radioman who was one of 555 men on Guam at the outbreak of World War II. When the Japanese attacked, he escaped into the hills and successfully evaded capture for thirty-one months. Tweed was not well thought of by the natives because he had assured them that if his presence threatened their survival, he would surrender; but when several were killed by the Japanese, he continued to hide. When the U.S. Navy began its pre-invasion bombardment, he stood on the beach signaling with homemade flags that he had information for them and was picked up. (He collected $6,027 in back pay.)

MOVIE PORTRAYAL:
No Man Is an Island (1962), by Jeffrey Hunter

Twenty Committee

Name of the British double-cross system derived from the Roman numerals *XX* for "twenty." It effectively controlled German agents in Britain, feeding them information to be sent back to Germany.

Twining, Nathan Farragut (1897–   )

U.S. Army Air Force officer. He spent five days in the Pacific in an open raft after his B-17 ditched and was rescued on January 27, 1943. Twining was the first commander of the Fifteenth Army Air Force in Italy and later went to the Twentieth Army Air Force in the Pacific to replace General Curtis LeMay.

Tyler, Kermit

U.S. Army lieutenant who was the duty officer at the Fort Shafter Information Center on December 7, 1941, at Pearl Harbor. He received the call from Joe Lockard, the radar operator who picked up the incoming Japanese planes. Tyler told Lockard ". . . don't worry about it."

Type 92

Japanese electric torpedo developed in 1934 that propelled a 660-pound warhead 7,660 yards at a speed of thirty knots, but was seldom used because of the emphasis on the oxygen torpedo.

Type 93

Japanese torpedo designed by Vice-Admiral Toshihide Asaguma and Rear Admiral Kaneji Kichimoto. Oxygen-propelled, it was twenty-four inches in diameter, thirty feet long, weighed 6,000 pounds, and carried a 1,000-pound warhead. The Type 93 was named the "Long Lance" and was first used in the Battle of the Java Sea in February 1942.

Type 95

Oxygen-fueled Japanese torpedo that left no telltale wake. It had a top speed of forty-eight knots, a range of 5,500 meters, carried a 1,210-pound warhead, and was far superior to U.S. torpedoes.

Type VII

Designator of the standard German submarine of World War II. It had a range of 9,000 miles and displaced 770 tons. Six hundred ninety four were built throughout the war and accounted for over ninety percent of all Allied ships sunk.

Type XXI

Designator of a new streamlined German submarine that could do seventeen knots submerged. It was equipped with a snorkel so that it could charge its batteries under water using the diesel engine. Type XXI had all sorts of sophisticated electronic gear for early warning and plotting of enemy ships.

Typhoon

In December 1944, a typhoon hit Admiral William F. Halsey's Third Fleet in the Western Pacific. It seriously damaged twenty-eight ships, sank the destroyers *Spence*, *Hull*, and *Monaghan*, destroyed over two hundred aircraft, and killed over eight hundred men. Herman Wouk made mention of it in his Pulitzer Prize–winning novel *The Caine Mutiny.*

U

U-2 Flights (see Rowehl Geschwader)

U-29

German submarine under Lieutenant Shuhart that sank the British aircraft carrier H.M.S. *Courageous* on September 17, 1939, off the coast of Ireland. It was the first major U-boat success of World War II.

U-30

German submarine under Lieutenant Fritz-Julius Lemp that torpedoed and sank the passenger ship S.S. *Athenia* on September 3, 1939. The crew of the U-boat were sworn to secrecy by Hitler's orders so that he could state that it was a British ploy to get the U.S. into the war. The *U-30* was also the first U-boat to enter the newly captured French port of Lorient on July 5, 1940. The *U-30* was captured by the British toward the end of 1940 when the crew abandoned it, believing it was about to sink. The British recovered all code books and cypher machine; these were useful in combating the German submarine force in the Atlantic.

U-32

German submarine under Lieutenant Jenisch that sank the passenger ship *Empress of Britain* west of Ireland on October 26, 1940.

U-39

First German submarine sunk in World War II. Commanded by Lieutenant Gerhard Glattes, it tried to attack the H.M.S. *Ark Royal* on September 14, 1939, with magnetic torpedoes that prematurely detonated. British destroyers were alerted to the attack and depth-charged the submarine, forcing it to the surface, where the crew abandoned the U-39 and were rescued.

U-47

German submarine commanded by Lieutenant Gunther Prien that entered the heavily defended British base of Scapa Flow on October 13, 1939, and sank the battleship H.M.S. *Royal Ark*. Prien was welcomed as a hero by the Nazis. He and *U-47* were sunk by the destroyer H.M.S. *Wolverine* on March 7, 1941.

U-48

Most successful German submarine of World War II, commanded by Lieutenant Herbert Schultze.

U-73

German submarine commanded by Lieutenant Helmut Rosenbaum that torpedoed and sank the aircraft carrier H.M.S. *Eagle* in August 1941 while it was attempting to supply Malta under Operation Pedestal. Rosenbaum was awarded the Knight's Cross and later was killed in an aircraft crash in 1943 near the Black Sea.

U-81

German submarine under Lieutenant Friederich Guggenberger that sank the carrier H.M.S. *Ark Royal* in the Mediterranean on November 14, 1941.

U-85

First German submarine sunk by a U.S. Naval vessel in World War II. *U-85* was sunk by the destroyer U.S.S. *Roper* off Wimble Shoal near Hatteras on April 13, 1942. The destroyer then proceeded to kill all the survivors from the submarine with depth charges.

U-99

German submarine under Otto Krestschmer. After sinking six ships of the convoy HX112 in March 1941, *U-99* was driven to the surface and disabled by gun fire from the destroyer HMS *Walker*. Krestchmer and thirty-nine crew members were captured and spent the rest of the war in prisoner-of-war camps in Canada.

U-100

German submarine under ace Joachim Shepke that was rammed and sunk by the destroyer HMS *Vanoc* on March 17, 1941.

U-110

German submarine that was captured intact on May 9, 1940, off Greenland by H.M.S. *Bulldog* under Commander John Baker-Cresswell. The *U-110* sank while in tow, but not before the British removed all code books and the cypher machine, which helped in turning the tide of the antisubmarine campaign in the Atlantic.

U-156

German submarine under Werner Hartenstein that sank the passenger ship *Laconia* on September 12, 1942.

U-168

German submarine under Commander Pich that, while en route to Japan to deliver technical data, was sunk outside Surabaya on October 6, 1944, by a British-built Dutch submarine, the *Zwaardvisch*. Pich and nineteen others survived, but were interned for the rest of the war.

U-183

Third German submarine sunk in the Pacific in World War II and the second to fall victim to U.S. submarines. The *U-183* was torpedoed on April 23, 1945, off Surabaya by the U.S.S. *Besugo*, commanded by Herman E. Miller, who rescued the sole survivor.

U-202

German submarine that landed four German agents at Long Island on June 13, 1942. The *U-202* was commanded by Lieutenant Commander Lindner.

U-352

Second German submarine to be sunk off the U.S. east coast in World War II. The U.S. Coast Guard cutter *Icarus* attacked and sank the *U-352* on May 9, 1942, afterward picking up survivors.

U-435

German submarine that supposedly delivered Martin Bormann to Argentina in 1946, after which it was scuttled by the crew.

U-505

German submarine captured on June 4, 1944, by the destroyer U.S.S. *Pillsbury*. It was the first enemy ship captured by the U.S. Navy on the high seas since 1815. The *U-505* is now on display in Chicago.

U-511

German submarine that was given to the Japanese in May 1943 to copy so that the Japanese factories could manufacture similar vessels. It was rechristened *RO-500*.

U-537

German submarine sent to help the Japanese by conducting operations in the Indian Ocean. It was ineffective because U.S. Navy codebreakers kept track of it until it was sunk on November 10, 1944, by the U.S.S. *Flounder*, commanded by James E. Stevens. The *U-537* was the second German U-boat sunk in the Pacific.

U-556

German submarine commanded by Lieutenant Wohlfarth that was in a position to attack the H.M.S. *King George V* and the carrier H.M.S. *Ark Royal* in May 1941 while they were attempting to sink the *Bismarck*. Wohlfarth had expended all his torpedoes and could only watch as the targets sped across his bow.

U-584

German submarine that landed four German espionage agents at Ponte Verde Beach, Florida, on June 17, 1942, as part of Operation Pastorius. *U-584* was commanded by Lieutenant Commander Deeke.

U-656

First German submarine sunk by the U.S. Navy in World War II. It was destroyed on March 1, 1942, off Cape Race, Newfoundland, by Ensign William Tepuni, who was flying a Lockheed Hudson.

U-701

Third German submarine sunk off the east coast of the U.S. in World War II on July 7, 1942, by a B-24 flown by Second Lieutenant Harry J. Kane.

U-Boats

Most effective weapon of the German Navy in World War II. German submarines sank 2,828 Allied merchant ships and 145 warships with a loss of 785 U-boats out of 1,162 built.

U-Boat Aces

Otto Kretschmer (*U-23*, *U-99*)	44 ships/266,629 tons
Wolfgang Luth (*U-9*, *U-138*, *U-43*, *U-181*)	43 ships/225,712 tons
Erich Topp (*U-57*, *U-552*)	34 ships/193,684 tons
Karl Merten (*U-68*)	29 ships/186,064 tons
Victor Schutze (*U-25*, *U-103*)	34 ships/171,164 tons
Herbert Schultze (*U-48*)	26 ships/171,122 tons
Georg Lassen (*U-160*)	28 ships/167,601 tons
H. Lehman-Willenbach (*U-5*, *U-96*, *U-256*)	22 ships/166,596 tons
Heinrich Liebe (*U-38*)	30 ships/162,333 tons
Gunther Prien (*U-47*)	28 ships/160,939 tons
Joachim Schepke (*U-3*, *U-19*, *U-100*)	39 ships/159,130 tons
Werner Henke (*U-515*)	25 ships/156,829 tons
Carl Emmermann (*U-172*)	27 ships/152,656 tons

Heinrich Bleichrodt (*U-48, U-109*)	24 ships/151,319 tons
Robert Gysae (*U-98, U-177*)	25 ships/144,901 tons
Ernst Kals (*U-130*)	19 ships/138,567 tons
Johann Mohr (*U-124*)	27 ships/132,731 tons
Klaus Scholtz (*U-108*)	24 ships/132,417 tons
Engelbert Endrass (*U-46, U-567*)	22 ships/128,879 tons
Reinhard Hardegan (*U-147, U-123*)	23 ships/128,412 tons

Udet, Ernst (1896–1941)

World War I German ace with sixty-two victories, second only to Manfred von Richtofen. Between the wars he flew as a stunt pilot, developing the idea of dive bombing with a Curtiss Hawk that was manifested in the Stuka. Udet became a lieutenant general in charge of technical development. As the Luftwaffe failed to achieve its goals—i.e., knocking out Britain and bombing long-range targets in Russia—Udet became a scapegoat for each failure. General Milch took over part of his department and began firing staff members. Finally, one of these people returned and told Udet about the extermination of the Jews in the east. Udet subsequently shot himself on November 17, 1941. Goebbels announced that he died "while experimenting with a new weapon."

MOVIE PORTRAYAL:
Von Richtofen and Brown (1971), by Robert La Tourneaux

Ulbricht, Walter (1893–1973)

German Communist leader. He was drafted into the German Army in World War I but jumped from the train that was taking him to the Western Front, after which he was imprisoned for desertion. When Hitler became Chancellor in 1933, Ulbricht fled to Paris and later to Moscow. He returned to Berlin in 1945 to set up a Communist government in the Soviet Zone.

Ulithi Atoll

Site of the major U.S. deep-water anchorage in the Pacific in World War II. It was 400 miles southwest of Guam and could accommodate over 1,000 ships.

Ultra

Code name of intercepted messages between Adolf Hitler and his field commanders in World War II. The British were able to decipher the German codes; this knowledge allowed them to prepare for every major German attack, except the Battle of the Bulge in December 1944. At that point Hitler began to suspect that the Allies were reading his messages, so he stopped using the Enigma machines and startled the Allies with the Ardennes offensive.

Ulvert H. Moore, U.S.S.

U.S. Navy destroyer in the South Pacific commanded by Lieutenant Commander Franklin D. Roosevelt, Jr., son of President Franklin D. Roosevelt.

Umezu, Yoshijiru (1880–1949)

Japanese general and chief of the general staff. He was one of the signers of the surrender papers on September 2, 1945, aboard the U.S.S. *Missouri* in Tokyo Bay. Umezu was given life imprisonment at the Tokyo War Crimes Trial, dying of cancer in 1949.

Unconditional Surrender

Term first used at a luncheon in Casablanca attended by President Franklin D. Roosevelt, his son Elliott Roosevelt, Prime Minister Winston Churchill, and Harry Hopkins on January 23, 1943. Coined by FDR, it is thought by many to have prolonged the war, since it gave no alternative to the Axis powers.

United States

Only country fighting in World War II that conducted an election during the war. Franklin Roosevelt defeated Thomas Dewey in 1944.

US Army Air Force Aces

Richard Bong—40
Thomas B. McGuire—38
Francis S. Gabreski—28
Robert S. Johnson—27
Charles H. MacDonald—27
George E Preddy—26.83
John C. Meyer—24
David C. Schilling—22.5
Gerald R. Johnson—22
Neel E. Kearby—22
Jay T. Robbins—22
Frederick Christensen, Jr.—21.5
Raymond S. Wetmore—21.25
John J. Voll—21
Walker M. Mahurin—20.75
Thomas J. Lynch—20
Robert B. Westbrook—20
Donald S. Gentile—19.88

Glenn E. Duncan—19.5
Leonard K. Carson—18.5

US Army Air Force Aircraft

Bombers

Boeing	B-17	Flying Fortress
Douglas	B-18	Bolo
Douglas	B-23	Dragon
Consolidated	B-24	Liberator
North American	B-25	Mitchell
Martin	B-26	Marauder
Boeing	B-29	Superfortress
Vega	B-34	Ventura
Douglas	A-20	Havoc
Douglas	A-24	Dauntless
Curtis	A-25	Helldiver
Lockheed	A-29	Hudson
Martin	A-30	Baltimore
Vultee	A-31	Vengeance
Brewster	A-34	Bermuda
North American	A-36	Mustang

Fighters

Lockheed	P-38	Lightning
Bell	P-39	Aircobra
Curtis	P-40	Warhawk
Republic	P-47	Thunderbolt
North American	P-51	Mustang
Northrop	P-61	Black Widow
Bell	P-63	King Cobra
Douglas	P-70	Havoc

Liaison Aircraft

Taylorcraft	L-2	Grasshopper
Aeronca	L-3	Grasshopper
Piper	L-4	Grasshopper
Vultee	L-5	Sentinel

Observation

Vultee	O-49	Vigilant
Curtiss	0-52	Owl
Lockheed	O-56	Ventura
Taylorcraft	O-57	Grasshopper

Aeronca	O-58	Grasshopper
Piper	O-59	Grasshopper
Vultee	O-62	Sentinel

Trainers

North American	AT-6	Texan
Beech	AT-7	Navigator
Beech	AT-10	Wichita
Beech	AT-11	Kansan
Boeing	AT-11	Crewmaker
North American	AT-15	Harvard
Cessna	AT-17	Bobcat
Lockheed	AT-18	Hudson
Vultee	AT-19	Reliant
Fairchild	AT-21	Gunner
North American	BT-9	Yale
	BT-14	
Fleetwing	BT-12	Sophomore
Vultee	BT-13	Valiant
	BT-15	
Stearman	PT-13	Cadet
	PT-17	
Stearman	PT-18	Cadet
	PT-27	
Fairchild	PT-19	Cornell
	PT-23	
Fairchild	PT-26	Cornell
Ryan	PT-21	Recruit
	PT-22	

Transports

Beech	C-43	Traveller
Beech	C-45	Expediter
Curtis	C-46	Commando
Douglas	C-47	Sky train
Douglas	C-49	Skytrooper
	C-53	
Douglas	C-54	Skymaster
Lockheed	C-56	Lodestar
	C-60	
Lockheed	C-63	Hudson
Lockheed	C-69	Constellation

Curtis	C-76	Caravan
Consolidated	C-87	Liberator
Grumman	OA-9	Goose

U.S. Army Air Force Aircraft Designators

A—attack
AT—advanced trainer
B—bomber
BT—basic training
C—cargo
CG—cargo glider
F—photo reconaissance
G—glider
L—liaison
O—observation
P—pursuit
PT—primary trainer
R—rotary wing
TG—training glider
UC—utility cargo
X—experimental
Y—test aircraft
Z—obsolete

U.S. Army General Staff

G-1—personnel
G-2—intelligence
G-3—plans, training and operation
G-4—supply
G-5—civilian affairs

U.S. Army Organization

Army Air Forces—Air Corps and Air Force Combat Command
Army Ground Forces—Infantry, Cavalry, Field Artillery
Services of Supply—Quartermaster, Ordnance, Chemical Warfare

U.S. Army, Post Office Box 1663

Address of the scientists at the University of Chicago who were working on the Manhattan Project. This was the only address available to their families.

U.S. Marine Corps #037773

Serial number of major league baseball player Ted Williams, who flew as a Marine pilot in both World War II and the Korean War.

U.S. Marine Corps Aces

Gregory Boyington—28
Joseph J. Foss—26
Robert M. Hanson—25
Kenneth A. Walsh—21
Donald N. Aldrich—20
John L. Smith—19
Marion E. Carl—18.5
Wilbur J. Thomas—18.5
James E. Swett—16.5
Harold L. Spears—15

Archie G. Donahue—14
James N. Cupp—13
Robert E. Galer—13
William P. Marontate—13
Edward O. Shaw—13
Kenneth D. Frazier—12.5
John F. Bolt—12
Loren D. Everton—12
Harold E. Segal—12
Eugene A Trowbridge—12

U.S. Navy Aces

David S. McCampbell—34
Cecil E. Harris—24
Eugene A. Valencia—23
Patrick D. Fleming—19
Alexander Vraciu—19
Cornelius N. Nooy—18
Ira C. Kepford—17
Charles R. Stimpson—17
Douglas Baker—16
Arthur R. Hawkins—14
Elbert McCuskey—14
John L. Wirth—14
George C. Duncan—13.5
Roger W. Mehle—13.3
Daniel Charmichael—13
Roy W. Rushing—13
John R. Strane—13
Wendell Van Twelves—13
Clement Craig—12
Leroy Harris—12

U.S. Navy Aircraft Designators

VB—bomber
VF—fighter
VOS—observation
VPB—patrol bomber
VS—scout
VSB—scout bombers
VSO—scout observation
VTB—torpedo bomber

U.S. Navy Fleets

Even-numbered fleets served in the Atlantic, odd-numbered fleets operated in the Pacific.

Third Fleet—established March 15, 1943, from South Pacific Force

Fourth Fleet—established March 15, 1943, from Atlantic Force

Fifth Fleet—established April 26, 1944 from Central Pacific Force

Seventh Fleet—established February 19, 1943 from Southwest Pacific Force

Eighth Fleet—established March 15, 1943 from Northwest African Force

Tenth Fleet—established May 20, 1943 and directed US antisubmarine effort in the Atlantic

Twelfth Fleet—established March 15, 1943 from Naval Forces Europe

USO

Name of a B-17 of the Eighth Army Air Force on which newscaster Walter Cronkite flew a mission over Germany in 1943.

U.S. Production in World War II

296,429	aircraft	5,425	cargo ships
2,455,964	trucks	71,062	navy ships
102,351	tanks		

U.S Submarine Aces

Richard H. O'Kane (*Tang*)	31 ships/227,800 tons
Eugene B. Fluckey (*Barb*)	25 ships/179,700 tons
Roy M. Davenport (*Haddock*)	17 ships/151,900 tons
Slade D. Cutter (*Seahorse*)	21 ships/142,300 tons
Henry G. Munson (*S-38, Rasher*)	13 ships/113,400 tons
Reuben T. Whitaker (*S-44, Flasher*)	18 ships/111,500 tons
William S. Post Jr. (*Gudgeon, Spot*)	19 ships/110,900 tons
Charles E. Loughlin (*S-14, Queenfish*)	12 ships/109,400 tons
Walter T. Griffith (*Bowfin, Bullhead*)	17 ships/106,300 tons
Edward E. Shelby (*Sunfish*)	14 ships/106,200 tons
Thomas W. Hogan (*Bonefish*)	15 ships/105,500 tons
Eli T. Reich (*Sealion II*)	11 ships/101,400 tons
Dudley W. Morton (*R-5, Wahoo*)	17 ships/100,500 tons
Bernard A. Clarey (*Pintado*)	13 ships/98,600 tons
Robert E. Dornin (*Trigger*)	13 ships/96,500 tons
Anton R. Gallaher (*Bang*)	15 ships/94,000 tons
Norvell G. Ward (*Guardfish*)	14 ships/90,200 tons
Gordon W. Underwood (*Spadefish*)	14 ships/89,600 tons

Charles O. Triebel (*S-15*, *Snook*) 13 ships/83,300 tons
Henry C. Bruton (*Greenling*) 11 ships/82,600 tons

University of Chicago

Site of Enrico Fermi's plutonium pile. On a squash court of the University, the world's first nuclear chain reaction was initiated on December 2, 1942. For security reasons it was called the Metallurgical Laboratory.

University Specialties of World War II

California Institute of Technology—rocket research
Columbia—oceanography
Harvard—oceanography
Massachussetts Institute of Technology—radar
Pennsylvania University—hydraulic fluids
Princeton—ballistics
University of Chicago—nuclear fission
University of Michigan—explosives

Unryu

Japanese aircraft carrier of 18,500 tons. It was sunk on December 19, 1944, by the submarine U.S.S. *Redfish*, commanded by Sandy McGregor.

Unyo

Japanese escort carrier weighing 20,000 tons that was originally intended to be a merchant ship. It was sunk on September 16, 1944, by the U.S.S. *Barb* under Eugene B. Fluckey.

Upholder, H.M.S.

British submarine under Lieutenant Commander M. D. Wanklyn that sank two fully loaded troop ships bound for North Africa, the *Neptunia* and *Oceania*, totaling 19,500 tons. The *Upholder* made twenty-four war patrols, sinking a total of 97,000 tons of Axis shipping.

Urban, Matt (1920–   )

U.S. Army officer. He was awarded the second to the last Congressional Medal of Honor for the war, on July 19, 1980. As a captain in the 9th Infantry Division at St. Lô thirty-six years earlier, he had mounted a tank and fired at advancing Germans with a machine gun. Urban had been put in for the award at the time, but the Army lost his paperwork. He retired as a lieutenant colonel and was finally presented the medal by President Jimmy Carter.

Urbanowicz, Witold

Polish squadron commander of No. 303 Squadron (a Polish outfit) of the Royal Air Force. He was the highest-scoring Polish ace of the R.A.F. with seventeen victories. Urbanowicz later joined the U.S. Army Air Force as a pilot of the Fourteenth Army Air Force and shot down three Japanese aircraft. Serving as the Polish Air Attaché to the U.S. he finagled a tour in the Pacific.

Uris, Leon (1924–)

American writer. He enlisted in the U.S. Marine Corps and served at Guadalcanal and Tarawa as a radio operator. Uris was sent home after he caught malaria. His first novel was entitled *Battle Cry,* which in 1955 was made into a movie.

Urquart, Robert (1901–)

British major general who commanded the 1st Airborne Division in Operation Market-Garden in September, 1944.

MOVIE PORTRAYAL:
A Bridge Too Far (1977), by Sean Connery

USA-1

License plate of General Douglas MacArthur's car while he was in Australia during World War II.

Ustashi

Yugoslavian guerrillas and terrorists backed by Mussolini, who were opposed by Tito and his partisans.

Ustinov, Peter (1921–)

British actor. Between 1942 and 1946 he served in the Royal Sussex Regiment and the Royal Army Ordnance Corps. Ustinov served as Lieutenant Colonel David Niven's batman (orderly).

Utah Beach

Designator of a Normandy beach assaulted on June 6, 1944, by the U.S. First Army under General Omar Bradley. It had a broad flat area that was ideal for amphibious assault, but had limited exits through flooded marshlands. The 101st Airborne Division was to be dropped behind the beach to keep the Germans from blowing up the exits. The 82nd Airborne Division parachuted to the north of the 101st to prevent a German counterattack. Utah beach forces had Cherbourg as an objective.

Utah, U.S.S.

U.S. battleship used prior to December 7, 1941, as a target ship. It was attacked and sunk by Japanese aircraft and along with the U.S.S. *Arizona* still lies at the bottom of Pearl Harbor. Public enemy number one John Dillinger had been stationed on the U.S.S. *Utah* during his time in the Navy.

V

V

Letter used by the Allies in World War II to symbolize victory. The idea was created by a Belgian refugee, Victor de Laveleye, who, as a broadcaster for the BBC, asked the people in occupied Belgium to use the letter as a covert symbol of resistance. The upraised index and middle finger of the hand as a "V" is credited to Douglas Ritchie, another broadcaster for the BBC. Goebbels unsuccessfully attempted to tell Europe that the "V" stood for German victory.

V-1

Designator of a German flying bomb built by the Volkswagen works at Fallersleben. More than 32,000 were manufactured; each required 130 gallons of low-grade fuel and could fly 150 miles at a ceiling of 2,000 to 3,000 feet. Costing an average of $600 to produce, the V-1's were used as one of the vengeance weapons on which Hitler placed his hopes for victory. The V-1's were known to the Allies as "Buzz Bombs," "Doddle Bugs," and "Divers." The U.S. built an equivalent that was called "Yankee Doodle."

V-2

German rocket that took twelve years to develop. It was forty-six feet long and flew 230 miles to a height of 120 miles. The V-2 weighed five tons empty and carried eight tons of fuel, primarily alcohol and liquid oxygen, that propelled a 2,000-pound warhead. The V-2 made a crater thirty feet wide when it descended at over 2,000 miles per hour. The first operational V-2 was launched against Paris on September 8, 1944, with the next two fired against London. A total of 1,145 were aimed at London with

2,050 against Brussels, Antwerp, and Liege in Belgium. Production was halted for a time because Hitler had a dream that London would never be hit. It took both Dr. Wernher von Braun and General Dornberger to convince him to carry on with the offensive.

V-3

Little-known German vengeance weapon that was referred to as the "London Gun." It had a 416-foot barrel that could fire a shell up to 100 miles using a method of sequential explosive charges to propel the shell through the barrel. These guns were to be buried underground and aimed at London with each one firing six shells a minute, putting 600 tons of explosives on London each day. A series of twenty-five barrels were installed near Mimoyecques outside Calais but were never used.

Valiant, H.M.S.

British battleship damaged on December 19, 1941, while at anchor in Alexandria, Egypt, by Italian two-man torpedoes (see Morgan, Charles).

Vallee, Rudy (1901–)

Popular singer, musician, and movie actor of the 1930's and 1940's. During World War II, he enlisted in the U.S. Coast Guard, rising from chief petty officer to obtain a commission as a lieutenant senior grade. In 1943, Vallee became a bandmaster of the Eleventh Naval District, entertaining troops for the U.S.O. Previously in 1917, he had enlisted in the Navy to fight in World War I but was discharged because he was underage.

Valter

Code name of Yugoslavian partisan leader Tito in his dealings with the Russians during World War II.

Vance, Cyrus (1917–)

Former U.S. Secretary of State. During World War II, he served as a gunnery officer aboard the destroyers U.S.S. *Hale* and U.S.S. *Henderson* in the Pacific. Vance fought at Bougainville, Tarawa, Guam, and the Philippines before being discharged in 1946 as a lieutenant senior grade.

Vandegrift, Alexander A. (1887–1972)

U.S. Marine Corps general who commanded the 1st Marine Division on Guadalcanal, winning the Congressional Medal of Honor. He was the first Marine to win the CMH and the Navy Cross in World War II and the first to become a four-star general. On January 1, 1944, Vandegrift became Commandant of the Marine Corps.

Movie portrayal:
The Gallant Hours (1960), by Raymond Bailey

Vandenberg, Hoyt S. (1899–1954)
U.S. Army Air Force general who commanded the Ninth Army Air Force in World War II.

Van Dyke, Dick (1925–)
Hollywood actor and comedian who spent two years in the U.S. Army Air Force during World War II.

Van Falkenburgh, Franklin (–1941)
U.S. Navy captain who commanded the battleship U.S.S. *Arizona* on December 7, 1941. He was killed when the *Arizona* blew up after being attacked by Japanese aircraft. Van Falkenburgh was the first Navy captain killed in World War II and was posthumously awarded the Congressional Medal of Honor.

Van Heusen, Jimmy (1913–)
American songwriter and cofounder of Capitol Records, who served during World War II as a test pilot for Lockheed.

Vasilyev
Code name for Joseph Stalin in all correspondence in World War II.

Vasco
Nickname of British submarine navigators. They were so named after Vasco da Gama, the Portuguese navigator.

Vassar
Women's college in the eastern United States attended by both Nancy Harkness Love, head of the WASPS, and Mildred H. McAfee, head of the WAVES.

Vaughn, Harry H. (1893–1981)
U.S. Army major general and aide to President Harry S Truman. He and Truman had served together in World War I in the Field Artillery. When Truman was elected Vice-President in 1944 he requested a military aide, thus Vaughn became the first aide to a Vice-President.

V-Discs
Name given to a special series of phonograph records made for distribution to servicemen around the world during World War II. Over eight million were made, including classical, popular, and jazz music.

V-E Day
May 8, 1945, the day the war ended in Europe.

Veeck, Bill (1914–)

Imaginative owner of several professional baseball teams. He lost his right leg in 1946 as a result of an injury he incurred as an antiaircraft gunner with the U.S. Marine Corps in World War II.

Vekemans, Robert

Belgian Resistance man who served as an engineer lieutenant in the Belgian Army in 1940. He was largely responsible for the British capture of Antwerp relatively intact; he guided the advancing British tanks around strong points of German resistance that he had personally reconnoitered several days before.

Vengeance Weapons

Name given by Hitler to the V-1 and V-2 rockets. They killed about fifteen percent (9,000) of the total Britishers who died by German bombing in World War II (60,000).

Venlo Affair

S.S. officer Walter Schellenberg who masterminded the plot to capture two British intelligence officers. An S.S. group crossed the frontier at Venlo, Holland, on November 8, 1939, kidnapping Captain S. Payne Best and Major R. H. Stevens, whom the Germans accused of setting up an attempt on Hitler's life in a Munich Beer Hall the day before. Best and Stevens spent the remainder of the war in concentration camps.

Vercors

Natural fortress area located southwest of Grenoble in France. It became a center of the French Resistance from the end of 1942. The French mistakenly believed Allied help was imminent and arose to fight on June 13, 1944. Nearly 3,500 Resistance men were opposed by two German divisions, who killed most of them.

Verlaine, Paul (1844–1896)

French poet. His poem ''Ode to Autumn'' was broadcast over the BBC to warn the French Resistance of the coming Allied invasion. It was transmitted in two parts: the first message alerted them that the invasion was imminent and to monitor the BBC, the second portion indicated that the invasion would be within forty-eight hours. The Germans learned of this and successfully received both messages, but they could not believe that the Allies would actually announce over the BBC to the world the top-secret invasion. Believing it to be a hoax, the Germans chose to ignore the information.

Vian, Sir Philip (1894–1968)

British Admiral of the Fleet. He commanded the destroyer *Cossack* in the early days of World War II, taking it into neutral Norwegian waters on February 16, 1940, to board the German ship *Altmark* and rescue over 300 British prisoners of war. This gave the Britons one of the few victories that they could cheer about in 1940. Vian was in charge of the destroyer that maintained contact with the *Bismarck* in May 1941, after it was damaged by torpedoes. He commanded a convoy to Malta in March 1942 that resulted in an Italian defeat at the Second Battle of Sirte, and he later commanded one of the two naval task forces to be used on D-Day at Normandy. Vian went to the Pacific in the last year of the war, taking charge of British aircraft carriers. He is buried at St. Paul's Cathedral London along with Lord Nelson and the Duke of Wellington.

Vichy

Name of the unoccupied but pro-Nazi portion of France after the French surrender in July 1940. With Marshall Pétain as head of state, it was named after a spa in southern France.

Victor Emmanuele III (1869–1947)

King of Italy throughout World War II. He was five feet, three inches tall.

Victoria

Italian 14,000-ton merchant ship that was the pride of the Italian merchant fleet. It was sunk on January 23, 1943, while transporting troops and supplies to Rommel in North Africa in the first British Beaufort torpedo attack of the Mediterranean.

Victoria Cross

Britain's highest award for valor. It was awarded 182 times during World War II. Some notable recipients were

James Nicholson—first fighter pilot
Premindra Singh Bhagat—first Indian
Lord Syell—first peer
Harold E. Andrews—first officer
John Hannah—youngest winner (eighteen)

Victory

Magazine put out by the Office of War Information (OWI) during World War II that relied on pictures to propagandize the war effort.

Victory Bonds

Bonds sold by the U.S. government to raise money for the war effort. They matured after ten years.

Victory Gardens

Suggestion of Secretary of Agriculture Claude R. Wickard at the end of 1941, who said that since U.S. farmers would be too busy producing for the Army, civilians should grow their own food wherever possible. It is estimated that over twenty million Victory Gardens were planted during World War II, producing at least one third of all vegetables in the U.S. The gardens were planted in every available area, even on apartment rooftops and in parks.

Victory Girls

Name euphemistically given to women of less-than-pure morals who were available to servicemen on leave in the U.S. Many were married to other servicemen overseas; many more were merely single girls attempting to cope with the shortage of eligible males.

Victory Kitchens

Communal kitchens set up on the island of Malta at the height of the siege there. These kitchens usually served several city blocks.

Victory Program

Name given to President Franklin Roosevelt's overall plan to gear the U.S. economy for war. It was implemented in mid-1941.

Victory Ship

Specially designed cargo ships that were easily mass-produced and were intended to replace the Liberty ships. The Victory ship was conceived with long-term goals in mind; it was better than the Liberty ship in that it was faster and carried more cargo.

Victory Siren

Air raid alert siren designed in World War II by Bell Telephone Co. that could be heard for a ten-square-mile area. It was so powerful that it could rupture the eardrums of anyone within one hundred feet. The Army seriously experimented with it as a weapon.

Victory Suit

Name given to a men's suit designed to conserve material in World War II. It lacked cuffs, lapels, pockets, vest, and belt loops. Very little demand existed for the suits.

Victory Tax

Five percent tax added to the normal U.S. income tax as of November 1, 1942, on all incomes above $624 per year.

Victory Through Air Power

Documentary color film produced by Walt Disney in 1943.

Victory Walk

Name given to a dance invented by Arthur Murray in 1943 at the request of the Office of War Information. It was performed to march music but failed to become popular.

Victory Waste Paper Company

Name given to the U.S. war effort headed by Edwin S. Friendly to salvage used paper for recycling. Friendly collected over twelve million tons in only twenty-two months. Nearly forty percent of the paper used during World War II came from recycled material.

Vidal, Gore (1925–)

American author. Prior to World War II, he was staunchly opposed to the American involvement in the war. In 1943, upon graduation from Philips Exeter Academy, Vidal enlisted in the U.S. Army, serving as a warrant officer on an Army ship that carried supplies to the Aleutians.

Vigan, Philippines

Site of the first U.S. heavy bomber mission of World War II, in which the first enemy ship was sunk by U.S. aircraft. On December 10, 1941, five B-17's led by Major Cecil Combs attacked a Japanese convoy.

Viking Line

Name given to the Lucy spy ring located in Switzerland that sent military information to Russia throughout World War II.

Villa dar el Ouad

"Villa of the Family." Name of General Dwight Eisenhower's official residence in Algiers after the fall of North Africa.

VIP

Abbreviation for "very important person." Also used was VGDIP for "very god-damned important person," or VIPI, "very important person indeed."

Vireo

Tugboat that attempted to tow the damaged carrier U.S.S. *Yorktown* back to Pearl Harbor on June 6, 1942, after the Battle of Midway. The Japanese submarine *I-168* sank the *Yorktown* while it was in tow.

Virus House

Code name of Nazi Germany's first uranium pile. The name effectively scared the curious away.

Vita Nova Verlag

Rudolph Roessler's publishing house located in Lucerne, Switzerland, from which he conducted his spy network under the code name *Lucy.*

Vitousek, Royal

Honolulu lawyer who, with his son Martin, was flying in an Aeronca when Japanese fighters passed them on their way to attack Pearl Harbor on December 7, 1941.

Vittorio

OSS radio in Rome that was set up in October 1943 to supply information to the Allies on German troop movements. The OSS agents were betrayed by one of their Italian operatives on March 13, 1944.

V-J Day

Official end of the war with Japan. The U.S. recognizes September 2, 1945, but the British use August 15, 1945. Twenty-three years later to the day (1968), China and Japan signed a peace and friendship treaty officially ending their part of World War II.

Vlasov, Andrei A. (1900–1946)

Soviet lieutenant general who was one of the heroes of Russia in the defense of Moscow in 1941. He was later put in command of an army on the Volkov front in defense of Leningrad. Stalin would not allow him to retreat to a more defendable position, thus causing the annihilation of his army and his capture by the Germans. Vlasov gradually came to head the Russian Army of Liberation that fought with the Germans against Communism. He was an idealist who felt that Communism was worse than Hitler and hoped to set up a free Russia after the defeat of Stalin. Vlasov and his men were classified as renegades by the Western press and were returned to the Russians after the war. Nearly all were executed.

Vlotman, C.

Dutch pilot who shot down four German aircraft in the early days of World War II to become the leading fighter pilot of the Netherlands.

V-Mail

Name given to a process developed by Eastman-Kodak before World War II as a less bulky method of shipping mail by air. It consisted of photographing letters on 16mm film, which then was flown to its destination, enlarged, printed, and mailed to the address shown. Two thousand pounds of letters only weigh twenty pounds as film.

VMF-214

Designator of the U.S. Marine Corps fighter wing commanded by leading Marine ace Gregory "Pappy" Boyington during World War II. They became known as the Black Sheep Squadron.

Voice of Denmark

Name given to Aksel Schiotz, Danish opera and concert singer who, during the German occupation, refused to sing German compositions. He only performed Danish folk music and appeared to sing at the funeral of every person killed by the Nazis. Schiotz expected the Gestapo to arrest him at any time and kept a rope handy in order to escape from his bedroom if they came in the middle of the night. He was knighted by King Christian X in 1946.

Voice of Doom

Nickname given to American newscaster H. V. Kaltenborn in World War II.

Voice of Freedom

Name given to Carlos Romulo because of his broadcasts to the occupied Philippines in preparation for General Douglas MacArthur's return in 1944.

Voice of the Wehrmacht

Name given to German Lieutenant General Karl Ditmar, who broadcast radio commentaries on the German Army radio program in World War II.

Völkischer Beobachter

"People's Observer." The official Nazi party newspaper, purchased in the 1920's, was enlarged from a biweekly with 7,000 subscribers to a daily with a circulation of millions.

Volksjäger

"People's Fighter." Name given to the HE-162 jet fighter of the Luftwaffe. It was designed, built, and flown in sixty-nine days, first seeing action on December 6, 1944. The engineers designed the HE-162 to be built by semiskilled laborers using materials not essential to the German war effort—i.e., wood, duraluminum, and a little steel.

Volksturm

"People's Guard." The German home guard consisting of civilians organized for last-ditch fighting in the last days of Nazi Germany. All able-bodied males from sixteen to sixty were conscripted except those in the Todt Organization, police, or security units.

Volkswagen

"People's Car." Automobile designed by Ferdinand Porsche in the 1930's so that every worker could have his own car. The Volkswagen factory made a multipurpose vehicle throughout World War II, which was very similar to the U.S. jeep and was known as a *Kubelwagen*. (After the war the German government offered Ford Motor Company of America the Volkswagen for free so that it could be rebuilt, only to have Ford turn the offer down.)

von Manstein, Erich (1887–1973)

German field marshall. He drew up the plans for the reoccupation of the Rhineland in 1936 and also planned the attack through the Ardennes on France in 1940. Manstein managed to get permission from Hitler to retreat from around Stalingrad in 1942 and later from Kursk in 1943, but was relieved of command in March 1944 for advocating still another retreat. He surrendered to advancing British forces in May of 1945. He was tried for war crimes for allowing Einsatzgruppen to operate in his area but was exonerated. However, Manstein was convicted by the British in 1949 for war crimes in Russia and sentenced to eighteen years' imprisonment. This was later reduced to twelve years and later still to four years in prison.

von Manteuffel, Hasso (1897–1978)

German general. He was one of the most capable armored commanders that the Germans had and was in charge of the Fifth Panzer Army during the Battle of the Bulge in December 1944. At the end of the war, he surrendered to the U.S. Eighth Infantry Division.

Vonnegut, Kurt Jr. (1922–   )

American science fiction writer. He survived the Allied bombing of Dresden as a prisoner of war in an underground slaughterhouse. Vonnegut wrote *Slaughterhouse Five* based partially on his experiences. It was made into a movie in 1972.

Von Pannwitz, Helmut (–1947)

German lieutenant general. He was a Russian-speaking Balt and commanded the 15th Cossack Cavalry Corps that fought the Russians and later Yugoslavian partisans under Josef Tito. The Cossacks were Russian citizens who welcomed the Germans as liberators from Stalin. They fought hard against the Red Army and were commanded by German officers. After surrendering to the British at the end of the war, the Germans attempted to separate themselves from the Cossacks. Since they were not Russian, they did not fall under the forced repatriation of the Yalta agreement, yet the British turned von Pannwitz and the other Germans over to the Red Army at Judenburg, Austria, on May 28, 1945. *Pravda* announced on January 17, 1947, that von Pannwitz had been executed with many of his officers.

Von Seydlitz Division

Russian Army division formed by German General Walter von Seydlitz after he had been captured at Stalingrad. The unit was composed entirely of Germans opposed to Fascism. During the battle of Berlin they fought the Charlemagne S.S. Division made up of Frenchmen fighting Communism.

von Thoma, Wilhelm Ritter (1892–1948)

German general who served as Field Marshall Erwin Rommel's second-in-command of the Afrika Korps. During the Spanish Civil War, von Thoma had commanded armored forces in Spain and earned the title "Butcher of Guernica." He later commanded the Afrika Korps as successor to Rommel and was captured in late 1942 by the British at El Alamein. Von Thoma died in 1948 while still being held prisoner of war.

Voroshilov, Kliment E. (1881–1969)

Marshall of the Soviet Union. He was the Commander in Chief of the Red Army and responsible for the defense of all Russia.

Vraciu, Alex

U.S. Navy lieutenant and fourth-ranked Navy fighter ace of World War II. He is credited with shooting down nineteen enemy aircraft. During the Marianas Turkey Shoot on June 19, 1944, Vraciu downed six Japanese fighters in eight minutes, although his Hellcat had a rough-running engine and oil covered his windscreen. He was awarded the Navy Cross for his flying from the carrier *Lexington*.

VT

Designator of U.S. artillery shells that could be set to explode at preselected heights above the ground in order to shower troops in fox holes with shrapnel.

W

W-2

Code name of an underground command post built in 1940 for Hitler to oversee the Invasion of Britain.

WAAC

U.S. Women's Army Auxiliary Corps founded on March 14, 1942. The first director was Oveta Culp Hobby. The WAAC became the WAC on September 30, 1943.

WAC

U.S. Women's Army Corps established on September 30, 1943. At its peak in April 1945 the WAC's had 99,000 women in uniform.

Wachtel, Ulrich

German colonel who commanded the V-1 flying bomb regiment that launched the rockets against England.

Wade, Lance C. (–1944)

Top-scoring American ace in the Royal Air Force in World War II with twenty-five enemy aircraft shot down. Wade was killed in action in 1944.

Waffle Bottoms

Nickname given to businessmen who were continually seated in waiting rooms throughout Washington, D.C., in an attempt to gain government approval for contracts during World War II.

Wagner, Boyd D. (1916–1942)

U.S. Army Air Force officer and fighter pilot. He was the first Air Force ace of World War II for action on December 12, 1942, in the Philippines. Wagner was awarded a Distinguished Service Cross by General Douglas MacArthur for shooting down two aircraft and destroying twelve on the ground. He later fought in New Guinea and Guadalcanal as a lieutenant colonel. He flew P-39's and was officially credited with eight aircraft. Wagner was killed in a flying accident while on takeoff from Elgin Air Force Base in Florida.

Wagner, Walter (–1945)

Berlin municipal councillor and member of the *Volksturm*. He conducted the marriage ceremony of Eva Braun and Adolf Hitler on April 29, 1945. Wagner was selected at random; coincidentally, his last name was the same as Hitler's greatest musical love, Richard Wagner. Wagner was killed a half-hour after the ceremony while en route to his foxhole.

MOVIE PORTRAYAL:
The Bunker (1980 TV movie), by Robert Austin

Wagner, Winifred (1898–1980)

Daughters-in-law of German composer Richard Wagner who was the idol of Hitler. She directed the Bayreuth Wagner festivals from 1930 to 1944 that Hitler attended frequently. Wagner was a staunch supporter of Hitler; because of this, she was not allowed by the Allied occupation forces to participate in the festivals after World War II.

Wags

Name of U.S. Rear Admiral Frederick Sherman's black cocker spaniel that was aboard the carrier *Lexington* in the Battle of the Coral Sea in May 1942.

Wags

Nickname for the dogs in the U.S. Army K-9 Korps in World War II.

Wainwright, Jonathan (1883–1953)

U.S. Army lieutenant general. He was theater commander over Corregidor who, after surrendering to the Japanese, survived the Bataan Death March and three years of captivity at Mukden, Manchuria. Wainwright was present on the U.S.S. *Missouri* for the Japanese surrender on September 2, 1945, and was awarded a Congressional Medal of Honor by President Harry S Truman. Nicknamed "Skinny," Wainwright died September 2, 1953, exactly eight years to the day after the surrender ceremony.

MOVIE PORTRAYAL:
MacArthur (1977), by Sandy Kenyon

Waiter, Edward (–1945)

German S.S. officer and commandant of Dachau concentration camp. At the end of the war, he shot himself through the heart, lived, then shot himself through the head and died.

Wake Island

U.S. possession in the Pacific that was the only bright spot in the early days of World War II. The U.S. Marines, commanded by Major James Devereaux, held off several Japanese invasion attempts but finally succumbed to their overwhelming superiority. The last man off Wake, Colonel Walter Bayler, later became the first American to go back onto the island when it was recaptured September 4, 1945.

Wake Island

1942 Hollywood movie that realistically portrayed the Japanese assault. Starring Brian Donlevy, Robert Preston, and MacDonald Carey, the movie inspired Malcolm Scott Carpenter to become a U.S. Navy pilot and later one of the seven original astronauts.

Wake, U.S.S.

U.S. Navy gunboat moored at Shanghai and captured by the Japanese in a surprise move on December 7, 1941, while the crew slept. The Japanese rechristened the ship *Tataru*.

Wakefield, U.S.S.

U.S. Navy transport, formerly the luxury liner S.S. *Manhattan*, that caught fire while en route from Europe to New York on September 3, 1942.

Waldberg, Jose (–1940)

German agent who, along with Karl Meier, was the first German spy executed in Great Britain in World War II (December 1940).

Waldheim, Kurt (1918–)

Secretary General of the United Nations. During World War II, he served with the German Army as an officer on the Russian front. Waldheim received a medical discharge in 1943 after spending a year recuperating from a leg wound from a grenade.

Waldron, John C. (–1942)

U.S. Navy lieutenant commander and pilot, He commanded the ill-fated Torpedo Squadron 8 from the carrier *Hornet*, which was destroyed attempting to attack Japanese carriers.

Walker, Frederick J. (1896–1944)

British Naval captain credited as one of the primary U-boat killers in the Atlantic in World War II. The ships under his command sank twenty-one German submarines while escorting convoys. Walker, who died of a stroke July 9, 1944, was buried at sea.

Walker, HMS

Royal Navy destroyer under Commander Donald MacIntyre that sank the German submarine *U-99* commanded by Otto Kretschmer, one of the top-scoring aces of U-boats. Kretschmer, with thirty-nine of his crew, was rescued and interned.

Walker, Walton H. (1889–1950)

U.S. Army lieutenant general who commanded the U.S. XX Corps in World War II. The three-star insignia he wore had belonged to General George S. Patton before Walker and to Eisenhower before Patton. Walker was killed in Korea.

Wall, Robert W.

U.S. Navy seaman aboard the carrier U.S.S. *Hornet* who was accidentally thrown into the propeller of the last B-25 to depart for Doolittle's Raid on Tokyo on April 18, 1942. Wall's left arm was mangled by the propeller.

Wallace, George C. (1919–)

Governor of Alabama who during World War II served as B-29 flight engineer with the rank of sergeant. Today he still receives an allowance each month for "nervous disability" from the Veterans Administration; his disability is a fear of flying.

Wallace, Mike (1918–)

CBS newscaster. He served in the U.S. Navy during World War II as a communications officer in Hawaii, Australia, and aboard a submarine tender.

Wallach Eli (1915–)

Hollywood actor. He served in the U.S. Army Medical Corps during World War II.

Wallis, Sir Barnes (1887–1979)

Chief engineer for the British Vickers aircraft company. He designed the bombs used on the Mohne and Eder Dams of the Ruhr as well as the six-ton bombs, known as Tallboy, that were used to sink the German battleship *Tirpitz*. Wallis is also the designer of the Wellington bomber.

MOVIE PORTRAYAL:
The Dam Busters (1955), by Michael Redgrave

Walt Disney Studios

Hollywood production studios that drew many of the emblems used by Allied forces in World War II. The symbol of the Seabees and the Flying Tigers*—a Tiger jumping through a *V* for Victory—were designed by Walt Disney, as was the emblem for U.S. PT boats—a mosquito riding a torpedo.

Walter

Code name of Tito, the Yugoslavian partisan commander. Although he disliked the name, it was still used throughout World War II.

Walter, Hellmut

German inventor who designed the Panzerfaust antitank weapon, the Schnorkel for U-boats, and the first air-to-air missile, the HWK-509.

Waltzing Matilda of the Pacific Fleet

Nickname given to the carrier U.S.S. *Yorktown*.

War and Peace

Classic 1869 Russian novel written by Leo Tolstoy and used as the basis of a propaganda campaign. Soviet Ambassador to Britain Ivan Maisky convinced a British publishing firm to print a cheap edition of the novel to assure the British that the Russians would continue to fight against Hitler despite his early successes.

War Bonds

U.S. government-issued bonds to finance the war effort. The first Series E War Bond was sold on May 1, 1941, to President Franklin D. Roosevelt. At that time they were called Defense Bonds, but the name was changed after the Japanese attack on Pearl Harbor on December 7, 1941. The bonds were to yield 2.9% after a ten-year maturity. An imaginative Sioux Falls, South Dakota, purchaser listed as co-owners Hitler, Tojo, Laval, and Quisling.

Warburton, Adrian (–1944)

Royal Air Force squadron leader and photo-reconnaissance pilot. From below a cloud cover, he took the pictures of the Italian naval base at Taranto that later enabled British torpedo aircraft to attack the Italian fleet in 1940. Warburton then returned after the attack to photograph the damage, again at low altitude, only to have an Italian admiral throw a sword at him from the deck of a sunken battleship. Warburton was awarded a Distinguished Service Order as well as a bar to his Distinguished Flying Cross; he also was

---

* The actual designer of the Seabee and Flying Tiger insignia was Roy Williams, who later played Big Mousketeer on the TV series *The Mickey Mouse Club*.

given an American DFC. He was lost April 12, 1944, while on a photo-recon mission over the Alps.

War Criminals

By 1968, 6,192 war criminals had been convicted in West Germany, 16,000 to 18,000 alleged criminals were either awaiting trial or being investigated, and an estimated 17,000 undetected war criminals were still at large in West Germany alone.

War Declarations

September 3, 1939	Great Britain on Germany
September 3, 1939	Australia and New Zealand on Germany
September 6, 1939	South Africa on Germany
September 10, 1939	Canada on Germany
June 10, 1940	Italy on France and England
September 17, 1940	San Marino on England
June 22, 1941	Germany and Italy on Russia
December 6, 1941	Britain on Finland, Hungary, and Rumania
December 7, 1941	Dutch government in exile on Japan
December 7, 1941	Canada and Costa Rica on Japan
December 8, 1941	United States on Japan
December 8, 1941	Britain on Japan
December 8, 1941	China on Germany, Italy, and Japan
December 8, 1941	Free French on Japan
December 8, 1941	Honduras, Haiti, Dominican Republic, Guatemala, and El Salvador on Japan
December 9, 1941	Cuba and Nicaragua on Japan
December 11, 1941	Germany and Italy on the United States
December 11, 1941	United States on Germany and Italy
December 11, 1941	Cuba, Costa Rica, Dominican Republic, Nicaragua, and Guatemala on Germany and Italy
June 1, 1942	Mexico on Germany, Italy, and Japan
August 22, 1942	Brazil on Germany and Italy
September 21, 1944	San Marino on Germany
February 23, 1945	Turkey on Germany and Japan
February 26, 1945	Egypt on Germany and Japan
March 27, 1945	Argentina on Germany and Japan
July 18, 1945	Italy on Japan
August 8, 1945	Russia on Japan

Ward, James A. (–1941)

Royal Air Force sergeant and copilot of a Wellington bomber of No. 75 Squadron. On July 7, 1941, his aircraft was attacked by an ME-110 while he was bombing Munster, setting a wing on fire. As the crew attempted to fly back to England across the North Sea, Ward crawled out onto the wing and smothered the flames. He was awarded the Victoria Cross, England's highest decoration, but was killed two months later.

Ward, Orlando (1891–)

U.S. Army major general and West Point graduate. He was to be the senior American commander in Tunisia as head of the 1st Armored Division, but Eisenhower placed General Fredendall in charge. Ward and Fredendall did not get along and both were relieved of command after the defeat of Kasserine Pass in February 1943. Ward later returned to Europe as commander of the 20th Armored Division.

Ward, U.S.S.

U.S. Navy destroyer credited with having fired the first shot against the Japanese at Pearl Harbor. Commanded by William W. Outerbridge, the *Ward* attacked and sank a midget submarine an hour before the attack on Pearl Harbor. The midget submarine had been launched from the *I-22* and is believed to have had on board Lieutenant Naoji Iwasa and Petty Officer Naoharu Sasaki. The *Ward* was sunk three years later in Ormoc Bay, Leyte, during the invasion of the Philippines.

Warden, Jack (1921–)

Hollywood actor. He was a U.S. Army paratrooper in World War II with the 101st Airborne Division. On the last practice jump over England prior to D-Day, Warden broke his leg and injured his back, which prevented him from making the D-Day jump. In the 1980 TV movie, *A Private Battle,* he portrayed Cornelius Ryan, who as a correspondent did jump with the 101st Airborne Division at D-Day.

Ware, Keith L. (1915–1968)

U.S. Army officer who was drafted in 1941. He fought his way through North Africa, Sicily, southern Italy, and France. In December 1944, as a lieutenant colonel commanding a battalion of the 3rd Division, Ware was awarded a Congressional Medal of Honor for leading an attack near Sigolsheim, France. He eventually became a major general, commanding the 1st Division in Vietnam, where he was killed in a helicopter crash in 1968.

Warner, Jack L. (1892–1978)

Hollywood movie producer and head of Warner Bros. Studios. At the outbreak of World War II, he was commissioned as a lieutenant colonel in the Army Air Force. Due to his studios' proximity to the Lockheed aircraft plant, Warner had painted a huge sign on the rooftops of his sound stages pointing the way to Lockheed so that no one (the Japanese) would mistakenly bomb his facilities. The words "Lockheed thataway" were followed by an arrow. The sign was short-lived.

Warsitz, Erich

German test pilot for Heinkel aircraft. He was the first to fly the rocket-powered HE-176 on June 20, 1939, at the test site of Peenemunde. Warsitz also flew the HE-178, the world's first jet aircraft, on August 27, 1939.

Warspite, H.M.S.

British battleship. It was the only ship to fight in the Battle of Jutland in 1916 and later to support the D-Day landings at Normandy on June 6, 1944.

Washing Machine Charlie

Nickname given to a Japanese aircraft that flew over Guadalcanal every night at 3:30 A.M. to drop a single bomb on U.S. Marines.

Washington, U.S.S.

First U.S. Navy battleship to fire its main batteries at an enemy since 1898 when it participated in the Battle of Guadalcanal on November 15, 1942. The *Washington*, launched on June 1, 1940, was the first U.S. battleship to be launched in nineteen years.

Wasp, U.S.S.

U.S. aircraft carrier weighing 14,700 tons. In 1942 it made several trips to Malta delivering Spitfire fighters to the besieged island. During the Battle of the Coral Sea, September 15, 1942, the *Wasp* was struck by three torpedoes fired from the Japanese submarine *I-19* under Takaichi Kinashi, Japan's most successful submarine commander. It was damaged so severely that the destroyer U.S.S. *Landowne* had to sink it, making it the third U.S. carrier to be lost in World War II. The *Wasp,* nicknamed U.S.S. *Flatiron,* was commanded by Captain Forrest Sherman at the time.

WASP's

Women's Airforce Service Pilots, organized by Nancy Harkness Love and commanded by Jacqueline Cochran. The WASP's worked with U.S. Army Air Force Ferry Command to release men for combat duty. Between September 1942 and December 1944, over a thousand women were accepted into the program, flying nearly every aircraft in the U.S. inventory.

Watch on the Rhine

German code name for the December 1944 attack through the Ardennes. The western Allies called it the Battle of the Bulge. According to German General Hasso von Manteuffel, Stalin knew of the impending attack through a security leak in the German high command but failed to inform the Western powers. *Watch on the Rhine* was the name of Lillian Hellman's play; it was made into a movie in 1943 in which Paul Lukas won an Academy Award for Best Actor.

Watson's Whizzers

Name given to the U.S. Army Air Force's first unofficial jet squadron commanded by Colonel Harold E. Watson, who gathered up the latest German aircraft (Jet) as part of Operation Lusty. The pilots involved broke the propeller off their insignia to signify their new status.

Watson-Watt, Robert (1892–1973)

British scientist who was instrumental in the early stages of radar. He developed the world's first practical radar system which helped to defend Britain against the Germans in 1940.

Wavell, Archibald (1883–1950)

British field marshall who was highly competent but one of the unluckiest British commanders of World War II. He always appeared to have taken command of a theater just before the worst defeats, thus getting adverse publicity. In 1941 he replaced General Auchinleck in North Africa and was removed by Churchill for the subsequent British failures. Wavell was made Supreme Allied Commander of the Southwest Pacific just before the fall of Singapore and Burma. Wavell, who in June 1943 became the Viceroy of India, had only one eye, and often stated that he kept his good eye on the Japanese and his glass eye on India. He wrote a book called *Generals and Generalship* that German Field Marshall Erwin Rommel carried with him.

MOVIE PORTRAYAL:

Churchill and the Generals (1981 TV movie), by Patrick Magee

WAVES

"Women Accepted for Voluntary Emergency Service." It was the women's branch of the U.S. Navy established July 31, 1942, under Lieutenant Commander Mildred Helen McAfee.

Wayne, David (1914–)

Hollywood actor who enlisted in the American Field Service in World War II. The AFS was a volunteer group of ambulance drivers who served with the British Eighth Army in North Africa. Wayne was in Tobruk on June 21, 1942, when it fell to the Germans, was listed as killed in action, but safely escaped back to British lines.

Wayne, John (1907–1979)

Hollywood actor, born Marion Michael Morrison, who between 1942 and 1966 appeared in fourteen movies set in World War II, although he was 4F and exempt from military service. He starred in

Flying Tigers (1942)
Reunion in France (1942)
The Fighting Seabees (1944)
Back to Bataan (1945)
They Were Expendable (1945)
Sands of Iwo Jima (1949)
Operation Pacific (1951)
Flying Leathernecks (1951)
The Sea Chase (1955)
Blood Alley (1955)
The Wings of Eagles (1957)
The Longest Day (1962)
In Harm's Way (1965)
Cast a Giant Shadow (1966)

W-Day

Designator of the day of assault on Guam July 21, 1944.

Wead, Frank "Spig" (1895–1947)

U.S. Navy officer, a lieutenant commander, who advocated jeep carriers and pursuit planes prior to World War II. He fell down a flight of stairs, injured his spine, and subsequently became paralyzed from the waist down. Wead wrote the screenplay for the 1945 movie *They Were Expendable,* starring John Wayne and Robert Montgomery. John Wayne portrayed Wead in the 1957 movie *The Wings of Eagles.*

Weaver, Fritz (1920–)

Hollywood actor who worked as a conscientious objector serving at several Civilian Public Service work camps during World War II.

Webb, Jack (1920–   )

Hollywood actor and producer. He enlisted in the U.S. Army Air Force in 1943 where he was trained as a B-26 pilot. Webb was discharged in 1945 having never left the States.

Webling, Kurt

German general of artillery who was in charge of the defense of Berlin and surrendered the city to the Russians in May 1945.

"We Did It Before"

First war song written in the U.S. during World War II. It was composed on December 7, 1941, by Charles Tobias and Cliff Friend and appeared in the Broadway musical *Banjo Eyes*.

Weissenberger, Theodor (–1950)

German Air Force major. He is the seventh-top-scoring fighter ace of World War II, with 208 enemy aircraft shot down, 175 of them on the Eastern Front. Weissenberger was awarded the Knight's Cross, Oak Leaves, and Swords.

von Weizsacher, Ernst (1882–1952)

German Undersecretary of the Foreign Ministry. He was found guilty of preparing for an aggressive war as well as of crimes against humanity and received a sentence of seven years in prison, which was commuted in 1951. He died shortly afterwards.

Welch, George C. (–1954)

U.S. Army Air Force officer who shot down four Japanese aircraft at Pearl Harbor on December 7, 1941. General "Hap" Arnold recommended him for the Congressional Medal of Honor, but it was denied because Welch's commanding officer said he took off without orders. Instead he was given a Distinguished Service Cross. Welch was America's first air hero of World War II and finished the war with sixteen aircraft officially shot down. He was killed on October 11, 1954, in an aircraft accident.

Movie portrayal:
Tora! Tora! Tora! (1970), by Rick Cooper

Wellington

British twin-engine bomber in World War II. It burned easily when hit because it did not have self-sealing fuel tanks. It was nicknamed "Wimpy" after the Popeye cartoon character, J. Wellington Wimpy.

Wendel, Fritz

Chief test pilot for Messerschmitt in World War II. He set a new world's speed record on April 26, 1939, of 469.22 miles per hour in an ME-209. He was also the first to fly an ME-262 on July 18, 1942.

Wenneker, Paul

German Naval captain. He commanded the pocket battleship *Deutschland* in the early days of World War II, later becoming the naval attaché to Tokyo.

Werewolf

Code name of Hitler's headquarters located near Vinnitsa, Ukraine, when he visited the Eastern Front in July 1941.

"We're Off to See the Wizard"

Song composed by Harold Arlen for the 1939 classic movie *The Wizard of Oz*. This was used by Australian troops as a marching tune during World War II.

Wermuth, Arthur

U.S. Army captain known as "the One-Man Army of Bataan." He was one of the first heroes for the U.S. in World War II, credited with killing over 100 Japanese. Wermuth was captured while unconscious in a hospital and sent to Bilibid prison in Manila. In December 1944, Wermuth was sent on a Japanese prison ship to Manchuria, where he was liberated by Russian troops in 1945.

Werner, Oskar (1922–)

Viennese-born actor and director. He was drafted into the German Army in World War II, serving as a corporal with an artillery battery. Werner was wounded in an American bombing raid; after his discharge from the hospital, he deserted, hiding in the Vienna woods when the war only had three months to go.

von Werra, Franz (–1943)

Luftwaffe ace shot down over England on September 5, 1940, by Royal Air Force pilot Peterson Hughes of No. 234 Squadron. Von Werra made several unsuccessful escape attempts from English prisoner-of-war camps. He finally escaped in Canada and made his way through the U.S., Mexico, Central and South America back to Germany, where he was acclaimed a hero. Von Werra was instrumental in giving valuable information to German intelligence about British interrogation methods. He also visited German prisoner-of-war camps to inform the authorities of gaps in security. As a result of his visit to Colditz Castle, the prison system was tightened. Von Werra was killed in a sortie over the English Channel when his ME-109 apparently developed engine trouble.

MOVIE PORTRAYAL:

The One That Got Away (1959), by Hardy Krueger

Werth, Alexander (1901–1969)

British author and historian. During World War II, he served as a war correspondent on the Eastern Front, being one of the few Western reporters allowed to accompany the Red Army.

Werther

Code name given to the high-ranking German who supplied military information to the Lucy spy ring in Switzerland, who sent it on to the Russians. His identity has never been established although General Reinhard Gehlen, Walter Schellenberg, and Admiral Wilhelm Canaris all believed that Martin Bormann was actually Werther.

Wessel, Horst (–1930)

Berlin S.A. leader shot by communists in February 1930, making him a martyr for the Nazis. The S.A. marching song "Horst Wessel" was named after him. In actuality, Wessel had resigned from the Nazi party several weeks earlier because of his love for a prostitute. He was killed by her pimp.

West, Morris (1916–)

Australian writer (*Shoes of the Fisherman*). During World War II, he served with the Australian Imperial Forces and earned a commission. West was assigned to intelligence, where he worked as a cypher officer. In 1943 he was given a discharge so that he could become the secretary to former Prime Minister William Morris Hughes.

Westgate, Frederick (–1944)

British shelter warden, who on the night of June 12, 1944, became the first Londoner to die by a V-1 buzz bomb. He was the first of 5,864 Londoners to die in V-1 explosions.

Westmoreland, William C. (1914–)

U.S. Army officer and commanding general of U.S. forces in Vietnam. During World War II he served as the commanding officer of an artillery battalion in North Africa and Sicily. Westmoreland landed at Utah Beach on June 6, 1944, as the executive officer of the 9th Infantry Division.

Weston, E. C.

British general who took over the defense of Crete at the end of March 1941. He was the fifth Allied commander to do so since the Greek entry into the war, but he failed to cope with the situation. The defenses of the island were considered poor and it was believed that he did not have sufficient experience to defend it, so he was replaced by General Bernard Freyberg.

West Point

U.S. military academy founded on the Hudson River in New York in 1802. The graduating class of 1915 produced sixty generals, more than any other class in its history.

West Point, S.S.

U.S. ship that transported German and Italian consular officials from the U.S. to Europe in July 1941 after President Franklin D. Roosevelt closed the consuls.

West Virginia, U.S.S.

U.S. battleship sunk at Pearl Harbor on December 7, 1941. It was salvaged and later fought in the Battle of Leyte Gulf on October 20, 1944.

Wever, Walther (–1936)

Luftwaffe general and first chief of the general staff. He advocated the development of four-engine bombers to be used against Russia and England. Wever believed in long-range strategic bombing, but was killed in an aircraft crash on June 3, 1936, near Dresden, taking with him his far-sighted tactics. After his death Wever was replaced by General Hans Jeschonnek.

Wewelsburg Castle

German castle located near Paderborn in West Westphalia. It was the symbol of the S.S. ideology. In German mythology, it was said that a castle in Westphalia would survive an invasion from eastern Europe, and Himmler believed Wewelsburg would be the one.

Weygand, Maxime (1867–1965)

French Army general who was the Commander in Chief of French forces, taking over command from General Gamelin on May 19, 1940. Weygand's ancestry is unrecorded, although it is known that he was not French. It was believed that he was the illegitimate son of Leopold III of Belgium. At the end of World War I, Weygand accepted the German surrender in a railway car in the forest of Compiegne on November 11, 1918. On June 22, 1940, he appeared in the same railway car to surrender to the Germans.

Whampoa

Name of the Chinese military academy that was the equivalent to West Point in the U.S.

Wherley, Clifford R.

U.S. Army Air Force staff sergeant. He was a turret gunner on a Martin Marauder bomber, flying twenty-one missions in North Africa, which earned him an Air Medal with three oak-leaf clusters. Wherley was forcibly discharged when it was revealed that after serving one year, he was still only sixteen years old.

Whistling Death

Name of U.S. Marine Corps ace Gregory ''Pappy'' Boyington's Corsair fighter in World War II.

White bait

Royal Air Force code name for Berlin.

White Ball Express

Smaller version of the Red Ball Express. The White Ball Express supply route ran between Le Havre and Paris in 1944.

White Beach

Name of one of the beaches assaulted by U.S. forces near Tacloban, Philippines. It was here that General Douglas MacArthur waded ashore for his famous ''liberation of the Philippines'' photograph.

White, Byron R. "Whizzer" (1917–   )

All-American football star at Yale and later member of the U.S. Supreme Court. As a member of U.S. Navy intelligence in the Pacific in World War II, he wrote the report on the sinking of the *PT-109* commanded by John F. Kennedy.

"White Cliffs of Dover"

Song written in 1941 by Walter Kent and Nat Burton that became very popular in Britain during World War II. It was recorded by several bands that year, including Kay Kyser and Glenn Miller.

Whitehead, Edward (1908–   )

British business executive who appears in Schweppes beverage commercials. During World War II, Whitehead served in the Royal Navy where he first wore his famous beard. He was discharged after the war with the rank of commander.

White Palace

Yugoslavian Prince Paul's official residence in Belgrade. When the city was liberated, Tito took up residence there.

White Rabbit

Code name of Frederick F. Yeo-Thomas, head of the French section (F) of British SOE.

White Rose

Name of a German youth movement led by brother and sister Hans and Sophie Scholl. As Christians, they felt obligated to speak out against Nazism, which they did from 1939 until 1942, when they were arrested and tried before the People's Court. Judge Roland Feisler sentenced them to death by beheading. The name of the group came from the picture of a white rose on their printed literature.

White, Theodore H. (1915–)

Pulitzer Prize–winning U.S. journalist and author who was hired by *Time* magazine to cover the Asian front during World War II. He was present on the U.S.S. *Missouri* in Tokyo Bay for the Japanese surrender.

Whitley

British twin-engine bomber known as the Flying Barn Door. It was the first aircraft of World War II to bomb both Germany and Italy and was the first Allied aircraft over Berlin on leaflet raids.

Whitmore, James (1921–)

Hollywood actor. He served with the U.S. Marine Corps from 1942 to 1946 and fought both on Saipan and Tinian. Whitmore received a commission in the Pacific and was discharged in 1946.

MOVIE PORTRAYAL:

James Dean (1976 TV movie), by Dane Clark

Whittle, Frank (1907–)

British scientist and inventor of the British jet aircraft. He was a Royal Air Force group captain in World War II.

Widder

German armed merchant ship commanded by Lieutenant Commander H. von Ruckleschell. It accounted for ten Allied ships totaling 58,664 tons during a cruise from May 5, 1940, to October 3, 1940, when it returned to Brest. The German designators for the *Widder* were HSK III and Ship 21.

Widewing

Code name for the headquarters of the Eighth Army Air Force located at Bushy Park, Kingston, on the outskirts of London. In early 1944 it became SHAEF headquarters.

Wiedemann, Fritz

German Army captain. He was Hitler's commanding officer at the end of World War I in the 16th Bavarian Infantry Regiment. Wiedemann became the German consul-general in San Francisco from 1939 until July 1941. As such, he was in charge of transporting German nationals of military age back to Germany via Japan and Siberia. In 1940 he became an agent for the British. Wiedemann was expelled from the U.S., returned to Europe, then traveled to Argentina in September 1941 and to Tokyo the next month.

Wilder, Thornton (1897–1975)

Pulitzer Prize–winning American author. He enlisted in the U.S. Army in World War II and served as a major in Army Air Intelligence.

Wildflower

U.S. code name for Great Britain in World War II.

Wilhelm II (1859–1941)

Kaiser of Germany until 1918. He was exiled to the Netherlands where he died on June 4, 1941, at Doorn. When the Germans invaded, they bypassed Doorn out of respect for him and later placed a guard of honor at the entrance to his estate.

Wilhelm Gustoff

German passenger liner weighing 25,000 tons that was sunk by a Russian submarine in the Baltic on January 30, 1945. It was evacuating refugees from Danzig at the time and over 8,000 people died in the worst sea disaster in maritime history.

Wilhelm, Hoyt (1923–)

U.S. major league baseball player who hit the first and only home run of his career at his very first time at bat for the New York Giants. Wilhelm served in the U.S. Army as a staff sergeant during World War II, receiving a Purple Heart for the Battle of the Bulge.

Wilhelmina (1880–1962)

Dutch queen (full name: Wilhelmina Helena Pauline Maria) throughout World War II. She and Dutch Financier Deterding financed Hitler's rise to power on his promise to sponsor the sale of Shell oil and gasoline. Shell was a Dutch corporation.

MOVIE PORTRAYAL:
Soldier of Orange (1979), by Andrea Dombung

Wilhelmshaven

German Naval base and target of the first Royal Air Force air attack of World War II when on September 4, 1939, ten Blenheims led by Flight Lieutenant K. C. Doran of No. 110 Squadron attacked. The only damage inflicted was to the cruiser *Emden,* when an aircraft crashed into her forecastle, killing several Germans. Four other British aircraft were lost.

Willamette University

Oregon University football team who were visiting in Honolulu on December 7, 1941, during the Japanese attack. Immediately afterward the entire team dug trenches for the defense of Hawaii.

Willkie, Wendell L. (1892–1944)

American politican and opponent of President Franklin D. Roosevelt in the 1940 Presidential race. He travelled as a goodwill ambassador to China and Russia in August 1942 in a C-87 named *Gulliver.*

Williams, Al

U.S. Marine Corps major who was a personal friend of German Air Force General Ernst Udet. On July 15, 1938, he became the first American to fly an ME-109.

Williams, David M. "Carbine" (1901–1975)

American inventor of the 30-caliber M-1 carbine rifle used in World War II. He developed the rifle while in prison, prior to being pardoned in 1929. Williams held over seventy patents.

MOVIE PORTRAYAL:
Carbine Williams (1952), by James Stewart

Williams, Eric

British prisoner of war of the Germans held at Stalag Luft III who, along with two other prisoners escaped via "The Wooden Horse," a wood vaulting horse. It was one of the most ingenious escapes ever. He authored the book, *The Wooden Horse,* telling about the escape.

Williams, John B.

U.S. Navy lieutenant. He was a former Olympic swimmer from Oregon State, serving in PT boats in the Pacific during World War II.

Williams, Ted S. (1918–)

American professional baseball player. He joined the U.S. Marine Corps in May 1942, becoming a captain and fighter pilot in World War II. Williams flew over 1,100 hours between 1942 and 1945. His serial number was 037773.

Willie

Name of General George S. Patton's white English bull terrier. It had belonged to a Royal Air Force pilot killed over Germany. Patton purchased Willie from a London kennel, originally naming him after William the Conqueror.

MOVIE PORTRAYAL:

Patton (1970), by Abraxas Aaran

Willie and Joe

Names of Bill Mauldin's World War II GI cartoon characters.

MOVIE PORTRAYALS:

Up Front (1951), by Tom Ewell (Willie); David Wayne (Joe)

Back at the Front (1952), by Tom Ewell (Willie); Harvey Lembeck (Joe)

Willoughby, Charles

U.S. Army major general. He was evacuated from Corregidor on March 11, 1942, aboard *PT-35* along with other members of General Douglas MacArthur's staff. Willoughby later became chief of intelligence for MacArthur.

Wilmot, Chester

BBC correspondent who reported on the fighting in North Africa, Syria, Libya, and New Guinea. Wilmot jumped with British paratroopers on Normandy on June 6, 1944, and was present at the Nuremberg Trials after the war.

Wilson, Sir Henry M. (1881–1964)

British Field Marshall who was the Supreme Allied Commander for the Mediterranean Theater in the latter part of World War II.

MOVIE PORTRAYAL:

Churchill and the Generals (1981 TV movie), by Robert Raglan

Wimpy

Nickname for the British Wellington bomber in World War II, named for the hamburger-loving character Wellington J. Wimpy in the Popeye comic strip.

Winant, John G. (1889–1947)

U.S. ambassador to England who succeeded Joseph P. Kennedy in 1941. He committed suicide in 1947.

Winchell, Walter (1897–1972)

American newspaper columnist whose work appeared in over 800 newspapers across the country. He did much to gain American support for the British cause prior to Pearl Harbor. Winchell coined the phrase, "America, Love It or Leave It" in 1940 when referring to the German-American Bund.

Movie portrayals:
Okay America (1932), by Lew Ayres (loosely)
Sweet Smell of Success (1957), by Burt Lancaster (loosely)
Lepke (1976), by Vaughn Meader
The Private Files of J. Edgar Hoover (1978), by Lloyd Gough

Wind in the Willows

Children's book written by Kenneth Grahame in 1908. After an unsuccessful commando attack on Field Marshall Erwin Rommel's headquarters in 1941, British General Robert Laycock and the only other survivor, a Sergeant Terry, wandered in the North African desert for two weeks carrying *The Wind in the Willows*. Laycock read aloud from the book to Terry to pass the time until they were rescued two weeks later. Terry greeted his rescuers with "Thank God I shan't have to hear any more about the bloody Mr. Toad."

Window

Name given to an Allied radar-jamming technique of using small strips of aluminum foil dropped from aircraft to generate false returns on enemy radar and block reception. It was first used by the British over Hamburg on July 24, 1943, with such effectiveness that the British only lost twelve aircraft out of a force of 800. Window was also used at D-Day to make the Germans think a large fleet was off the Pas de Calais. Throughout World War II the US Eighth Army Air Force dropped over ten million pounds over Germany. To the Americans, Window was known as *chaff* and the Germans called it *Duppel*.

Winds Code

Japanese code phrases used to notify their diplomats abroad of the impending outbreak of war:
"East wind rain" meant war with the U.S.
"North wind cloudy" meant war with Russia
"West wind clear" meant war with England

Windsor Castle

Weekend home of King George VI outside London at the height of the Battle of Britain. Lord Beaverbrook used the grounds as temporary storage for fighter aircraft until they could be delivered to R.A.F. squadrons.

Windsor, Elizabeth (1926–   )

British Second Lieutenant in the Women's Auxiliary Territorial Service in World War II. She was a truck driver trained as a mechanic. Today the world knows her as Queen Elizabeth II.

Wingate, Orde (1903–1944)

British major general called the "Napoleon of Guerrilla Warfare." As a major, he organized Ethiopian partisans to harass the Italians from 1940 to 1941. Wingate later commanded a British airborne commando force in Burma. He was killed March 24, 1944, in a plane crash in the Burma jungle.

Wingate, Sir Ronald E. L.

British Army colonel and deputy director of the LCS (London Controlling Section). He was a cousin of Orde Wingate and T. E. Lawrence.

Winston Port

Name given the Mulberry artificial harbor at Arromanches, Normandy. It was constructed in England using sixty ships and 146 concrete blocks and towed across the Channel at a speed of four knots. The harbor took ten days to assemble and provided unloading facilities for 2,500,000 men, 500,000 vehicles, and four million tons of supplies in support of the D-Day invasion.

Winterbotham, Frederick W.

Chief of British air intelligence of MI-6. He had been a pilot with the Royal Flying Corps in World War I and worked for British secret intelligence from 1934 to 1939. Winterbotham devised a system months before the outbreak of war of flying a Lockheed aircraft into Germany, ostensibly on business trips, that was secretly equipped with special cameras to photograph military installations.

Winters, Jonathan (1925–   )

Hollywood comedian. He served in the U.S. Marine Corps from 1943 until 1946.

Wintringham, Thomas (1898–1949)

Instructor of the British Home Guard in World War II. He had been a dispatch rider, a machine gunner, and an aerial gunner in World War I in France. During the Spanish Civil War, Wintringham commanded a British Battalion of the Loyalist Army, fighting against General Francisco Franco. He authored the book *New Ways of War—A Homeowner's Guide to Killing People Without Getting Killed*.

Wiesenthal, Simon

Jewish survivor of Mauthausen concentration camp who heads the Jewish Documentation Center in Vienna, Austria, which still searches for Nazi criminals.

MOVIE PORTRAYAL:
The Boys From Brazil (1978), by Laurence Olivier (loosely)

von Witzleben, Erwin (1881–1944)

German Field Marshall who was involved in the anti-Hitler plot of July 20, 1944. Had the attempted assassination of Hitler been successful, he would have become the Commander in Chief of all German forces. Von Witzleben was condemned to death by the Nazi People's Court under Judge Freisler and executed.

Wodehouse, P. G. (1882–1975)

British author who created Jeeves, the typical English butler. During World War II, he was captured by the Germans and sent to a concentration camp. Wodehouse made several radio broadcasts for the Nazis poking fun at his experiences, for which he was branded a collaborator by many in England. After the war he exiled himself to the U.S. because of the ill-feeling toward him in Britain. Wodehouse returned to England in 1975 to be knighted by Queen Elizabeth II, at the same time as Charlie Chaplin. He died on St. Valentines Day, 1975.

Wolf, Johanna

Hitler's private secretary from 1940 until 1945. She testified as a witness at Nuremberg.

Wolf, Paula (1886–1960)

Spinster sister of Hitler who adopted the last name Wolf in the 1930's at Hitler's insistence and was the only member of his immediate family to outlive him.

Wolf, Samuel

U.S. Navy lieutenant commander. He was the defense counsel of the General Court Martial at the Brooklyn Navy Yard when the carrier U.S.S. *Franklin* arrived after sustaining major damage from kamikazes off Japan. Several junior officers were to be charged with deserting their posts; Wolf let it be known that if charges were made, he would include all the most senior officers of Task Force 58, who were aboard the carrier at the time for a briefing. They all hastily left the carrier during the attack. Shortly after Wolf's accusations, all charges were dropped and the Navy turned the *Franklin* into the most decorated ship and crew in history.

Wolff, Karl (1900–)

German S.S. general who negotiated with Allen Dulles to surrender northern Italy in the last days of World War II. He was captured by Italian partisans but rescued by Donald Jones and Emilio Daddario, two OSS agents. A few hours afterwards, Wolff surrendered all German forces in Italy. He was tried by a British court in 1949 and given four years' imprisonment. He was rearrested in 1962, tried by a German court, and sentenced to fifteen years.

Wolf's Canyon

Name of Hitler's personal headquarters in France.

Wolf's Lair

Name of Hitler's headquarters located in a forest near Rastenburg, East Prussia, site of the July 20, 1944, attempt on Hitler's life.

Wollenhaupt, August

Hitler's personal barber who was never allowed to shave the Fuehrer because Hitler could not stand to have anyone near his throat with a razor.

Wolverine, H.M.S.

British destroyer under Commander J. M. Rowland that sank the German submarine *U-47*, commanded by German U-boat ace Gunther Prien, on March 7, 1941.

Women's Land Army

Name of a U.S. government-organized cadre of 60,000 women who worked around the country as field hands to harvest crops during World War II. Part of the U.S. Crop Corps, it was intended to partially alleviate the manpower shortage.

Wood, George

Employee of the German Foreign Office in Berlin who turned over more than two thousand top secret documents to the OSS head in Switzerland, Allen Dulles, during World War II.

Wooden Horse

Name of a wooden vaulting horse constructed by Allied prisoners of war in Stalag Luft III and through which Eric Williams, Oliver Philpot, and Mike Codner made their escapes. They hid in the frame and dug a tunnel to freedom in one of the most unusual escapes of World War II. It became the subject both of a book, *The Wooden Horse* by Eric Williams, and of a 1951 movie of the same title.

Wooden, John (1910–)
UCLA basketball coach. During World War II, he served as a physical education instructor in the U.S. Navy. An emergency appendectomy interrupted his orders to report to the carrier U.S.S. *Franklin*. The officer that replaced Wooden was killed in a kamikaze attack.

Wooden Wonder
Nickname given to the Mosquito, a British aircraft made of wood, that was used as a night fighter and photo-reconnaissance aircraft in World War II.

Wood, Sir Kingsley
British Air Minister at the outbreak of World War II. When asked to bomb forests in Germany, he refused on the grounds that it was private property.

Woodring, Horace L. (1926–)
U.S. Army private first class who was the driver of the car in which General George S. Patton was injured on December 9, 1945. It was struck by an Army truck that apparently jolted Patton so harshly that he broke his neck. Patton died three weeks later.

Woods, John C.
U.S. Army master sergeant. He was the Army's chief executioner at the Nuremberg trials in 1946. In the preceding fifteen years, Woods hanged over 300 soldiers for various crimes in the Army.

Wouk, Herman (1915–)
Pulitzer Prize–winning American author. He enlisted in the U.S. Navy as an officer shortly after the Japanese attack on Pearl Harbor. Wouk served in the Pacific aboard the U.S.S. *Zane* where he wrote his first book to relieve the boredom.

Wounded Bear
Code name given the damaged Japanese carrier *Shokaku* after the Battle of the Coral Sea in 1942 when it began a slow trip back to Japan for repairs.

WRENS
British Women's Royal Naval Service. It augmented the Royal Navy, releasing men for other jobs. The WRENS were commanded by Vera Laughton Mathews.

Wright, Peter
American fighter pilot with the Flying Tigers in China who shot down the last Japanese plane to fall to a member of the AVG before it was disbanded in 1942.

Wurzburg

German radar that used ultra short wavelengths to identify the altitude, location, and course of enemy aircraft. It was first used by flak units to shoot down aircraft above cloud layers. Early sets were limited to a range of only twenty-two miles, but in 1942 a Giant Wurzburg was built that had a forty-five-mile range for night fighter aircraft.

Wyler, William (1902–1981)

Hollywood director who produced the 1944 movie *Memphis Belle*. He enlisted in the U.S. Army Air Force in 1942 as a major and was sent to the Eighth Army Air Force in England. Wyler flew five combat missions to obtain footage for the movie and was awarded an Air Medal. He then went to the Mediterranean to produce *Thunderbolt* (1945), documenting the fighters of the Twelfth Army Air Force in Italy. Wyler was discharged in 1945 and awarded a Legion of Merit medal.

Wynn, Keenan (1916–)

Hollywood actor, son of comedian Ed Wynn, who was drafted into the U.S. Army in 1945. A motorcycle accident on March 10, the day before he was to report, left him with a broken lower jaw, resulting in his being reclassified 4F.

Wyoming, U.S.S.

U.S. battleship refitted as a gunnery training ship stationed in Chesapeake Bay. It had several nicknames—"The Chesapeake Raider," "Back Every Friday," etc.

X

X

Designator of the beach assaulted fifteen miles west of Oran in the North Africa invasion of Operation Torch on November 8, 1942.

X-2

American counterintelligence branch of the OSS similar to the XX Committee of the British.

X-6

British midget submarine commanded by Donald Cameron that attempted to destroy the German battleship *Tirpitz* on September 11, 1943. The *X-6* was scuttled after it set a two-ton underwater mine next to the *Tirpitz* that exploded, slightly damaging the ship. Cameron was awarded the Victoria Cross for this mission.

X-7

British midget submarine commanded by Godfrey Place that accompanied *X-6* on the September 11, 1943, mission against the *Tirpitz*. It also released a two-ton underwater mine but was sunk when the mine detonated. Place and one crew member were able to escape, only to be captured by the Germans.

X-23

British submarine that was one of two selected to lay markers delineating the sides of the invasion corridor to Normandy in June 1944. It was the first Allied vessel to arrive at Normandy, remaining submerged on the bottom of the English Channel for sixty-four hours because the invasion had been delayed.

X-24

British Navy submarine that along with *X-23* marked the limits of the D-Day invasion for the landing barges in the British zone.

X-Card

U.S. gas rationing card that entitled the holder to unlimited gas supplies and was the highest priority of the U.S. gas rationing system. Over 200 Congressmen received these cards, to the consternation of those who legitimately needed them. Ministers also fell within the category.

X-Craft

British midget submarines measuring fifty-one feet long and weighing thirty-five tons. The three-man subs could travel six and a half knots per hour on the surface, reducing to five knots when submerged. Each submarine carried two underwater mines, which were used in the attempt to sink the *Tirpitz* on September 11, 1943.

X-Day

Designator of the date set by Japanese Admiral Isoruku Yamamoto for the surprise attack on the U.S. Fleet at Pearl Harbor (December 7, 1941).

X-Process

German method of night bombing using high-frequency beams to guide bombers over a target and to signal when to release the bombs. It was used at Coventry and was not effectively jammed by the British until 1941. The British then developed a method of bending the beams so that the bombs fell harmlessly on unpopulated areas.

X Report

Anti-Hitler conspirators' declaration for general peace terms to be established after the assassination of Hitler. It was written by Hans von Dohnanyi, the lawyer of the group.

XX

Designator of the British counterintelligence double-cross system. It was part of MI-5 and was established to control captured German agents in England, through whom it fed false information back to their contacts. It was also called the Twenty Committee.

Y

Yachts

Aldebaran—Kaiser Wilhelm of Germany (owned by actor Sterling Hayden)
Alder—William Boyce Thompson
Alva—William Vanderbilt
Aranir—John Ford
Arethusa—King George VI of England
Aurora—Benito Mussolini
Baldur—Joseph Goebbels
Casiana—Manuel Quezon
Grille—Adolf Hitler
Heimdal—King Haakon of Norway
Mona—William B. Leeds
Pilar—Ernest Hemingway
Potomac—President Franklin Roosevelt
Saca—Errol Flynn
Sluggy—Humphrey Bogart

Yagodnik

Russian airfield built on an island in the Dvina River twenty miles from Archangel. The British Royal Air Force No. 617 Squadron refueled here on a shuttle mission to bomb the German battleship *Tirpitz* in the last days of the war. They flew Lancaster bombers and dropped the 12,000-pound tallboy bomb, but only succeeded in damaging the *Tirpitz*, which was at anchor in Alten Fiord.

Yalta Conference

February 1945 meeting of the Big Three, President Franklin Roosevelt, Prime Minister Winston Churchill, and Premier Joseph

Stalin. Yalta was a Soviet port on the Black Sea that was used as a summer resort. The discussions were held in Livadia, the summer palace of Czar Nicholas II. Stalin brought 14,000 bottles of wine and vodka in order to keep the meetings loose.

Yamamoto, Isoruku (1884–1943)

Japanese admiral and Chief of the Combined Fleet. He advocated carrier warfare and was opposed to a war with the U.S., but he realized that if it came, Japan had to make a decisive first strike to knock out the U.S. Pacific Fleet. Yamamoto planned the attacks of both Pearl Harbor and Midway. He was killed on April 18, 1943, by U.S. Army Air Force P-38's near Bougainville. Yamamoto had served as an ensign on the cruiser *Nishin* during the 1905 Battle of Tsushima Straits, where he lost two fingers of his left hand. He had also been a delegate to the 1934 London Disarmament Conference and was threatened with assassination by radicals in Japan because of his position.

MOVIE PORTRAYALS:
The Gallant Hours (1960), by James T. Goto
I Bombed Pearl Harbor (1961), by Toshiro Mifune
Admiral Tayamoto (1968), by Toshiro Mifune
Tora! Tora! Tora! (1970), by S. Yamamura
Midway (1974), by Toshiro Mifune

Yamashita, Koshiro

Japanese flight officer. He became the first ace in a Zero fighter when he shot down five Chinese aircraft in a single engagement on September 13, 1940. It was also the first battle that a Zero was involved in.

Yamashita, Tomoyuki (1885–1946)

Japanese general who conquered Malaya, Singapore, Bataan, and Corregidor. He was the commander of Japanese forces in the Philippines and became known for his nickname, "the Tiger of Malaya." Yamashita surrendered to U.S. forces in the Philippines on September 2, 1945, after which he was put on trial. As technical commander of an area, he was responsible for the conduct of his men even though he may not have been aware of atrocities committed. Yamashita was held accountable for the atrocities of Japanese naval personnel in Manila whom he never commanded. The trial allowed opinion and hearsay to be admitted as evidence and he was convicted and sentenced to death on the anniversary of Pearl Harbor. It was rumored that General Douglas

MacArthur had a hand in the verdict because Yamashita was the general who defeated him in the Philippines. Three years later, Admiral Soemy Toyoda was tried under the same charges and acquitted when it was proven that he had no knowledge of atrocities.

Yamato

Japanese battleship weighing 72,000 tons, the largest battleship ever built. The Japanese believed her to be "unsinkable" and sent her toward Okinawa on a suicide mission to engage the U.S. invaders. The *Yamato* was only equipped with enough fuel to get to Okinawa, where it was intended that she should beach herself and use the eighteen-inch guns as part of the defending firepowers. However, the *Yamato* was caught and sunk by U.S. carrier aircraft on April 7, 1945. It took over 300 aircraft to finally sink her, thinning out the air cover over the U.S. fleet to such an extent that kamikaze aircraft were able to get through and score hits on almost thirty U.S. ships.

Yank

GI Army newspaper that was first published on June 6, 1942, the same day as the Battle of Midway. It prided itself on being written and published by GI's, and as such expressed the average soldier's feelings toward the Army and the war.

Yankee Doodle

Nickname of Major General Ira C. Eaker's B-17, which he flew as commander of the Eighth Army Air Force in England.

Yankee Doodle

U.S. Army answer to the German V-1 flying bomb. It was launched from a ramp via a rocket-propelled undercarriage that was subsequently jettisoned. It actually flew faster and was more accurate than the V-1.

Yasui, Kenny

Nisei American who was known as the "Baby York," after Sergeant Alvin York's capture of Germans in World War I. While in the India-Burma Theater, Yasui posed as a Japanese colonel and ordered sixteen Japanese soldiers to stack their rifles, after which he marched them off to captivity.

Yawata

Japanese city which was nicknamed the "Pittsburgh of Japan" because one fifth of Japanese steel was produced there. It was the site of the Imperial Iron and Steel Works which was attacked on June 15, 1944, by B-29's from China in the first bombing of

Japan since the Doolittle Raid of April 1942. Not a single bomb struck the target.

Y-Day

Designator for the day of the German attack on Poland. It was originally set for August 26, 1939, but was moved to September 1, 1939.

Y-Day

June 1, 1944. Date established by General Dwight Eisenhower by which all preparations had to be completed for the D-Day invasion.

Yeager, Charles (1923–)

First person to break the sound barrier (1947). During World War II he flew a P-51 named *Glamorous Glennis* and is officially credited with shooting down twelve and one-half German aircraft. Yeager shot down five in a single engagement on October 12, 1944. He is also given credit for downing two ME-109's without firing a shot when the pilots bailed out as he lined up to shoot at them. He was shot down once over France but escaped via the underground to Spain, from which he made it back to the Allies.

Yellow Peril

Phrase used by the Allies throughout World War II to describe the Japanese. It was coined by German Kaiser Wilhelm II in 1895.

Yeo-Thomas, Frederick F. (1902–1974)

British Royal Air Force wing commander. He was head of F Section (France) of the SOE and was known as the "White Rabbit." Yeo-Thomas had fought in World War I while underage and also with the Poles against the Bolsheviks in 1919 and 1920. He was captured by the Russians and escaped the night before he was to be shot. In World War II, he worked with the French underground until he was captured by the Germans in 1944. They tortured him and sent him to Buchenwald concentration camp, where he took on the identity of a dead French Air Force officer, which enabled him to escape. Yeo-Thomas was recaptured and sent to a prisoner-of-war camp from which he again escaped, this time successfully making it back to Allied lines in April 1945.

Yeremenko, Andrey (1892–1970)

Soviet Marshall. He is credited with saving the city of Stalingrad in the initial phases of the battle in 1942.

Y-Gun

Double-barreled gun located at the stern of a ship. It was in the shape of a Y and could throw depth charges to each side of the ship simultaneously to combat submarines.

YK

Letters on the Fiesler Storch reconnaissance plane used by Field Marshall Erwin Rommel in North Africa during World War II.

Yokota, Minoru

Japanese Naval officer. He commanded the submarine *I-26*, which sank the first ship by a Japanese submarine in World War II, the *Cynthia Olson*, 750 miles northwest of Seattle. Yokota put two torpedoes into the carrier U.S.S. *Saratoga* in the Solomons on August 31, 1942, and sank the cruiser *Juneau* off Guadalcanal on November 13, 1942.

York, Alvin C. (1887–1964)

U.S. Army sergeant and Medal of Honor winner in World War I. He attempted to enlist in the U.S. Army for World War II but was too old. He did, however, serve as a member of the local draft board throughout the war. Before he allowed the 1941 film about his life, *Sergeant York*, to be produced, he stipulated that Gary Cooper had to portray him and also that the film had to be accurate.

Yorker

Designator of the beach assaulted ten miles west of Oran in Operation Torch, November 8, 1942.

Yorktown, U.S.S. (CV-5)

U.S. Navy aircraft carrier which was nicknamed the "Fighting Lady." It was damaged in the Battle of Coral Sea and repaired in record time at Pearl Harbor to be able to fight in Midway. The *Yorktown* was bombed by aircraft from the Japanese carrier *Hiryu* on June 4, 1942, and disabled. As the crews struggled to save her, the Japanese submarine *I-168*, torpedoed her on June 6, 1942. Sinking the following day, she became the second U.S. carrier to be lost in the war. When she sank, there were three men trapped below decks bravely playing acey-deucey because they had realized that they could not be rescued. When the new *Yorktown* was commissioned in 1943, many sailors reported mysteriously hearing the sounds of a card game coming from the equivalent room on the new carrier.

Yorktown, U.S.S. (CV-10)

U.S. Navy aircraft carrier. Launched on January 21, 1943, the *Yorktown* began construction just six days prior to the attack on Pearl Harbor. It was to have been christened by First Lady Eleanor Roosevelt, but just as she was to do so, the ship started to slide down the ways by itself. The *Yorktown* is now on display in Charleston, South Carolina.

You Can't Take It With You

Play being performed by Allied prisoners of war at Stalag Luft III near Sagan in January 1945, when the Germans ordered them to evacuate westward to avoid the advancing Russians.

You Can't Take It With You and Going Places

Two 1938 American movies playing at Paris' Champs Elysées on June 27, 1940, the day France surrendered to the Germans. James Stewart and Ronald Reagan, respectively, appeared in the films.

Young, Cassin (1894–1942)

U.S. Navy captain. He was awarded a Congressional Medal of Honor for the Pearl Harbor attack when he was blown off the U.S.S. *Vestal* by the exploding *Arizona* and swam back to the *Vestal* to continue fighting. Young was killed on board the cruiser *San Francisco* along with Admiral Daniel Callaghan when it was hit by fourteen-inch shells from Japanese battleships during the Battle of Guadalcanal on November 13, 1942.

Young, Desmond (1892–1966)

British historian. He served as a general with the 10th Indian Brigade and was captured by a Corporal Bayer of the Afrika Korps in June 1942 in North Africa. After serving as a prisoner throughout the war, Young became the official biographer of Field Marshall Erwin Rommel. In the 1951 movie, *Rommel—The Desert Fox,* he portrayed himself.

Young, Gig (1917–1978)

Hollywood actor. He served in the U.S. Coast Guard for three years in World War II, under his real name, Byron Elsworth Barr.

"You're a Sap, Mr. Jap"

Song copyrighted three hours before Congress declared war on December 8, 1941.

Yoshikawa, Takeo (1912–   )

Name of the lone Japanese spy out of 157,905 Japanese civilians in Hawaii. Prior to the attack on Pearl Harbor he had measured the depth of the channel, passing the information along to his superiors in Japan.

Z

Z

Letter on the yellow badges worn by Jews in Yugoslavia. It stood for Zidow (Jew) and was the equivalent to the *J* worn by German Jews.

Z209

Number of the Catalina flying boat piloted by Leonard B. "Tuck" Smith, an American, who spotted the *Bismarck* on May 26, 1941, resulting in the attack and sinking of the German pocket battleship.

Z Day

German designator for the reoccupation of the Rhineland on March 7, 1936.

Zacharias, Ellis M. (1890–)

U.S. Navy captain who served as Deputy Chief of Naval Intelligence during World War II. His specialty was Japanese intelligence, enabeling him to predict the attack on Pearl Harbor. Zacharias had been commander of the cruiser *Salt Lake City,* which delivered aircraft to Wake Island on December 7, 1941, at the time of the Pearl Harbor attack. He was a graduate of Annapolis, class of 1912, along with Richard Byrd.

Zaitsev, Vassili

Russian sniper at Stalingrad who was officially credited with killing 242 Germans, for which he was made a Hero of the Soviet Union. Zaitsev was seriously wounded in an explosion in the last weeks of the Battle for Stalingrad.

Zanuck, Darryl F. (1902–)

Hollywood producer. He was commissioned a lieutenant colonel in the U.S. Army in 1941 to make training films. Zanuck participated in the North African invasion as a colonel and was discharged in 1943.

MOVIE PORTRAYAL:
Moviola (1980 TV mini series), by Peter Maloney

Zebra
Beach designator for the landing east of Oran in Tripoli on November 8, 1942.

Zeppelin
Code name of the German high command's communications center which was located at Zossen, thirty miles south of Berlin, and connected all of occupied Europe.

Zeppelin Stadium
Name of the massive stadium at Nuremberg designed by Albert Speer and the site of the prewar propaganda rallies of the Nazis.

Zero
World War II Japanese fighter which is alleged to have been copied from Howard Hughes's H-1, which was turned down by the U.S. Army in 1937. It had remarkable range for its day and could stay in the air ten to twelve hours with proper fuel conservation. The Zero first appeared in China in 1940, enabling Claire Chennault to send a report back to Washington that included pictures of the aircraft as well as performance figures acquired through combat reports. The U.S. War Department took the stand that the report was fake because no aircraft could do what Chennault attributed to the Zero, and the report was subsequently thrown away. The Zero received its name because it was designed in the 2,600th year of the Nipponese dynasty (1940).

Zero Hour
Name of Japanese propagandist Tokyo Rose's radio program broadcast to U.S. troops throughout the Pacific during World War II.

Zero Zero
Code used when referring to Admiral Chester Nimitz.

Zhukov, Georgi K. (1896–1974)
Russian Marshall. He was Russia's most powerful and successful commander and was personally involved in nearly every major victory from Moscow to Berlin. He had fought in Spain during the Spanish Civil War and also served as a military adviser to China prior to World War II. At Stalingrad, Zhukov appointed the same commanders to the same sectors as he had previously done in the

Battle of Moscow, and thus unintentionally disclosed the overall plan to the Germans.

Zigzag

Cover name given to Eddie Chapman by British intelligence after he became a double agent.

Zimbalist, Efrem, Jr. (1923–)

Hollywood actor. He enlisted in the U.S. Army on April 2, 1941, serving as a first lieutenant in the infantry. It was in the Army that Zimbalist first met director Joshua Logan, who helped him begin his acting career.

Zip

Code word used by General Sir Harold Alexander to notify Prime Minister Winston Churchill that the German offensive of September 1, 1942, in North Africa had commenced. This developed into the Battle of Alam Halfa, which resulted in the retreat of Field Marshall Erwin Rommel.

Zip

Prime Minister Winston Churchill's nickname for his one-piece jump suit that he wore in the event of an air raid. It was also referred to as a "Siren Suit."

Zippo

Name of the most common cigarette lighter carried by the American GI during World War II. Wartime Zippo's differed from their peacetime counterparts in that they were painted flat black so that they would not reflect light and thus give away a position.

Zombies

Nickname that the Canadians gave to the 70,000 men drafted in World War II solely for home defense.

Zucca, Rita Louise

Italian propaganda broadcaster in World War II who used the title "Axis Sally." She was born in New York City but later renounced her American citizenship. Zucca served nine months in an Italian prison after the war for her activities (see Gillars, Mildred).

Zuider Zee

Dutch coastal area that at present is being slowly drained to create more usable land for Holland. During World War II, it was used as one of the main air routes from England to Germany for both Allied and Axis aircraft and had the heaviest concentration of flak in Europe implanted along the sides. The Dutch estimate that over a thousand aircraft lie on the bottom; as the waters recede, they are making an effort to salvage them. A Gotha bomber from

World War I, that crashed after bombing London in 1915 has even been salvaged.

Zuiho

Japanese aircraft carrier weighing 13,900 tons. It had formerly been a submarine tender before being converted to a carrier. The *Zuiho* participated in the sinking of the U.S. carrier *Hornet* and was in turn damaged by two 500-pound bombs on October 26, 1942, dropped by U.S. Navy Lieutenant Stockton B. Strong and Ensign Charles Irvine during the Battle of Santa Cruz. The *Zuiho* was sunk during the Battle of Leyte Gulf in October 1944 by aircraft from Admiral William Halsey's carriers.

Zuikako

Japanese aircraft carrier weighing 25,675 tons that participated in the December 7, 1941, attack on Pearl Harbor. It was sunk during the Battle of Leyte Gulf in October 1944.

Zumwalt, Elmo, Jr. (1920–)

U.S. Navy officer and later a member of the Joint Chiefs of Staff. (His messages were referred to as Z-grams). During World War II he served as an ensign on the destroyer U.S.S. *Phelps,* where he was seasick most of the time. Later in the war, Zumwalt was assigned to the combat information center on the destroyer U.S.S. *Robinson* and participated in the Battle of Leyte Gulf in October 1944.

Zwaardvisch

Dutch submarine, built by the British, based in Australia, and under American command, that sank a German submarine, *U-168,* on October 6, 1944, while the *U-168* was en route to Japan with technical data. It was one of the best Allied efforts of the war.

Check your answers to the back cover quiz...

1. HMS Audacity—A British ship that could carry six aircraft. Formerly a German merchant ship, it had been captured by the British and was sunk by a German U-boat on December 21, 1941.

2. A German coding machine that looked like a typewriter, it encoded and decoded messages via a series of drums that could be selected for a prescribed pattern. The Germans believed it to be foolproof, but the British were able to obtain a working model before Poland fell and were able to decipher nearly all Enigma messages for the rest of the war. The British intercepts were called Ultra.

3. A German spy who landed in Florida from U-584 on June 17, 1942, as part of Operation Pastorius. He was picked up by the FBI, tried, found guilty of espionage and executed on August 8, 1942. (His birthday was December 7.)

4. The Black fighter pilots of the 99th Pursuit Squadron. Founded at Tuskegee Institute, they fought in Italy in World War II.

5. This air battle on June 19, 1944 was part of the larger Battle of the Philippine Sea. It virtually destroyed Japanese naval power for the rest of the war. US Navy aircraft shot down 480 Japanese planes and lost only 130 of their own.

6. The battleships were Hiei and Kirishima.

7. This was a German attempt to capture Marshal Josef Tito on May 25, 1944. Glider troops were landed near Tito's headquarters at Drvar, but all they brought back was his dress uniform.

8. The code name of Alamagordo, New Mexico where the first atomic bomb was detonated on July 16, 1945.

9. "Ode to Autumn" by the deceased French poet Verlaine was broadcast over the BBC to warn the French resistence of the time of the invasion. The Germans learned of this and received the messages, but could not believe the Allies would actually announce over the BBC such top-secret information. They thought it was a hoax and ignored it.

10. Edward R. Murrow began his broadcasts with, "This is London." Walter Winchell began his with, "Good evening, Mr. and Mrs. America and all the ships at sea, let's go to press."